DATE DUE

AG 5 04			
NO 3 0 06			

DEMCO 38-296

James Madison and the American Nation 1751–1836

AN ENCYCLOPEDIA

Editorial Board

James Madison and the American Nation 1751–1836

AN ENCYCLOPEDIA

Robert A. Rutland

Editor in Chief

CHARLES SCRIBNER'S SONS
Macmillan Library Reference USA
Simon & Schuster Macmillan
NEW YORK

Simon & Schuster and Prentice Hall International
LONDON · MEXICO CITY · NEW DELHI · SINGAPORE · SYDNEY · TORONTO

Charles Scribner's Sons
An Imprint of Simon & Schuster Macmillan
1633 Broadway
New York, NY 10019-6785

Printed in the United States of America

printing number
2 3 4 5 6 7 8 9 10

Library of Congress Cataloging-in-Publication Data

James Madison and the American nation, 1751–1836:
an encyclopedia / edited by Robert A. Rutland.
p.   cm.

Includes bibliographical references and index.

ISBN 0-13-508425-3 (acid-free)
1. Madison, James, 1751–1836—Encyclopedias.
2. United States—History—Colonial period, ca. 1600–1775—Encyclopedias.
3. United States—History—Revolution, 1775–1783—Encyclopedias.
4. United States—History—1783–1865—Encyclopedias.
I. Rutland, Robert Allen, 1922– .
E342.J36 1994
973.4—dc20   94-12322
                                   CIP

The paper in this publication meets the
requirements of ANSI/NISO
Z39.48-1992 (Permanence of Paper).

Editorial and Production Staff

Publisher
Charles E. Smith

Editorial Director
Paul Bernabeo

Senior Project Editor
Stephen Wagley

Manuscript Editor
Jerilyn Seife Famighetti

Proofreaders
Katharyn Dunham
David Shapiro

Executive Assistant
Glady Villegas Delgado

Assistant Project Editors
Stephen Garrett   Sara E. Simon
Sarah Gardner Cunningham

Keyboarder
Innodata Inc.

Designer and Compositor
Robert Engle Design

Indexer
Katharyn Dunham
ParaGraphs

Case Designer
Mike McIver

Production Supervisor
Winston Sukhnanand

Contents

Preface

James Madison's life spanned the experience of the American people from colonial days to the beginning of the sectional conflict that led to the Civil War. Born in the reign of George II, he died during the administration of Andrew Jackson.

His years of service in the Virginia legislature, the Continental Congress during the American Revolution and the Articles of Confederation, the Federal Convention that produced the Constitution of the United States, the House of Representatives, and the cabinet coincided with the emergence of the new nation and the institution of the presidency. Indeed, he filled the office himself and knew the other six men who would fill it to 1837. He was an early adviser of George Washington and was secretary of state under Thomas Jefferson. As chief executive he held an office created by an ever-changing Constitution—and the presidency could change, too, as Madison learned. James Monroe was his secretary of war and secretary of state; John Quincy Adams negotiated the treaty that ended the War of 1812; Andrew Jackson gained glory in the Battle of New Orleans. With John Adams he carried on a brief and cool correspondence, though in 1817 Adams hailed him as a national hero.

There is no need to quarrel over whether the soft-spoken Virginian was destined to become the Father of the Constitution or simply be remembered as a johnny-on-the-spot at Philadelphia in 1787. Madison's intellect was universally respected in his day—even Alexander Hamilton admitted that much—and the dimensions of his mind are still recognized as the Constitution moves into its third century. Madison stood at the forefront of the Founders who invented a form of government that the world admires and tries to imitate with every sunrise.

This man of principle and intellect has long been an object of admiration; now he has his own encyclopedia. Here we have tried to answer most of the questions about Madison's public career, one that linked several generations of Americans. We have sought to make the information available in succinct, well-written, authoritative prose. But we realize that in history and biography the last word can never be said with pompous finality. Matters great and small are dealt with here; people famous and obscure—George Washington and Billey Gardner, Mary House and Napoleon—find their place in this volume. Aaron Burr will never be a national hero, but he deserves some credit for introducing Madison to Dolley Payne, and in these pages he gets it. Madison dealt with the serious issues of war and peace, nationhood, and justice for all. By and large, we give him good marks, but we recognize that he made errors of judgment. Although he decried factionalism as a baneful disease in the body politic, he nevertheless played a major role in founding a political party. Although he was a brilliant political theorist and practitioner, he was a bad war president.

James Madison and the American Nation includes four hundred articles prepared by eighty-eight contributors. Most of them are college professors still teaching their classes, but not a few are professors emeriti retired after distinguished careers. Contributors also include museum directors, curators of important historical collections, and editors of vast, learned projects that will be treasured and consulted by scholars well into the twenty-first century.

In the spirit of the trail-blazing *Encyclopédie*, which appeared in 1751, the year of Madison's birth, we have used a straightforward A-to-Z arrangement. We have researched photographic files from the Library of Congress to remote graphic hideaways for illustrations to give more life to the entries. Each entry is followed by a bibliography and, when appropriate, cross-references. At the end of the encyclopedia are the texts of important documents, a chronology, a synoptic outline, and the index.

Publishers are in business to make money, but some publishers, such as the late Alfred A. Knopf, also seek to bring out books on history that are both attractive and provocative. The concept for this encyclopedia sprang from Charles E. Smith, who fits the Knopf mold, and who is a bookman of long experience in dealing with urgent deadlines and tardy professors. His suggestion fell on fertile ground, for I had made Madison the subject of my research and writing for most of my professional life and I had recently finished my tenure as editor in chief of Madison's presidential papers.

We doff a collegial mortarboard to all the scholars who assisted in the preparation of this work. Most of all we salute Stephen Wagley, senior editor in the Academic Reference Division of Simon & Schuster, for his diligence, patience, and tact as he moved this work forward with all deliberate speed. After four years of anxiety and hard work, *James Madison and the American Nation* stands as a contribution to the understanding of a complex, enduring, and enlightened American patriot, James Madison, and the nation he helped create.

ROBERT ALLEN RUTLAND

Directory of Contributors

A

DONALD R. ADAMS, JR.
Department of Economics
West Virginia University

Dallas, Alexander James
Girard, Stephen
Panic of 1819

WILLIAM R. ALLEN
Department of Economics
University of California, Los Angeles

Smith, Adam

ROBERT S. ALLEY
Department of Humanities
University of Richmond

Anglican Church
Baptists
Bradford, William
Leland, John
Memorial and Remonstrance
War Hawks

RICHARD L. AYNES
School of Law
University of Akron

Twenty-Seventh Amendment

B

JAMES M. BANNER, JR.
James Madison Memorial Fellowship
Foundation Washington, D.C.

Cabot, George
Dwight, Timothy
Hartford Convention

LANCE BANNING
Department of History
University of Kentucky

Federalist, The
Hamilton, Alexander
Kentucky and the Western Country
Republicanism
States' Rights

CHARLENE BANGS BICKFORD
First Federal Congress Project
George Washington University

King, Rufus

GEORGE ATHAN BILLIAS
Department of History, Emeritus
Clark University

Gerry, Elbridge

KENNETH R. BOWLING
First Federal Congress Project
George Washington University

Capital, location of the
Election, Congressional, 1788–1789
Funding Act of 1790
Judiciary Act of 1789
Tariff of 1789

JAMES C. BRADFORD
Department of History
Texas A & M University

Constellation
Constitution
Farragut, David Glasgow
United States Navy

JOSEPH BRADLEY
Department of History
University of Tulsa

Alexander I

CHARLES E. BRODINE, JR.
Naval Historical Center
Washington Navy Yard

Chesapeake-Leopard Affair
Lawrence, James

JEFFREY P. BROWN
College of Arts and Sciences
New Mexico State University

Adams, John Quincy
Ames, Fisher
Gore, Christopher

PAUL BROWN
Department of Philosophy
University of Tulsa

Hume, David

CHARLES E. BROWNELL
Department of Art History
Virginia Commonwealth University

L'Enfant, Pierre-Charles

C

COLIN G. CALLOWAY
Department of History
University of Wyoming

Creek Indians
Hawkins, Benjamin
Prophet, The
Shawnee Indians

FRANK A. CASSELL
Albert A. Robin Campus
Roosevelt University

Smith, Samuel

PHILANDER D. CHASE
The Papers of George Washington
University of Virginia

Craik, James
Washington, George

GERALD CLARFIELD
Department of History
University of Missouri–Columbia

Jay's Treaty
Missouri Compromise

R. T. CORNISH
History Department
Whitman College

George III

NOBLE E. CUNNINGHAM, JR.
Department of History
University of Missouri–Columbia

Election, Presidential, 1800
Republican Party

D

DONALD O. DEWEY
School of Natural and Social Sciences
California State University, Los Angeles

Carrington, Edward
Democratic-Republican Societies
Duvall, Gabriel
Floyd, Catherine (Kitty)
Giles, William Branch
Henry, John
House, Mary
International Law
Monroe, James
Paterson, William
Randolph, John (of Roanoke)
Roane, Spencer
Smith, Margaret Bayard
Smith, Samuel Harrison
Supreme Court
Virginia Statute for Religious Freedom
Wheaton, Henry
Wolcott, Alexander, Jr.
Yazoo Lands Frauds

FREDERICK C. DRAKE
Department of History
Brock University

Argus
Barclay, Robert Heriot
Buffalo, New York
Detroit, Battle of
Dobbins, Daniel
Drummond, Gordon
Fort Dearborn
Fort Erie
Fort Niagara
Lake Erie, Battle of
Royal Navy
Yeo, Sir James Lucas

WILLIAM S. DUDLEY
Naval Historical Center
Washington Navy Yard

Berkeley, George Cranfield
Chesapeake
Guerrière
Jones, William
Little Belt
Macdonough, Thomas
Porter, David
Rodgers, John
Wasp

E

R. DAVID EDMUNDS
Department of History
Indiana University

Indians
Tecumseh

CLIFFORD EGAN
Department of History
University of Houston

Genet, Edmond Charles

DOUGLAS R. EGERTON
Department of History
Le Moyne College

Clinton, De Witt
Coxe, Tench
Freneau, Philip
Rush, Benjamin
Smith, Robert

F

PAUL FINKELMAN
Department of History
Virginia Polytechnic Institute
and State University

Bank of the United States
Federalist Party
New Jersey Plan

WILLIAM M. FOWLER, JR.
New England Quarterly
Boston, Massachusetts

Boston
New England
Strong, Caleb

HARRY W. FRITZ
Department of History
University of Montana

Biddle, Nicholas
Logan, George
Mitchill, Samuel Latham
Tertium Quids

PATRICK J. FURLONG
Department of History
Indiana University, South Bend

Congresses
    Second Congress
    Third Congress
    Fourth Congress
Otis, Harrison Gray
Pickering, Timothy
Sherman, Roger

G

JEROME R. GARITEE
Towson, Maryland

Privateers

NORMAN A. GRAEBNER
Department of History, Emeritus
University of Virginia

Continental System
Foster, Augustus John
Gardoqui, Diego de
Great Britain
Madison, James
    Secretary of State

Neutrality
Orders in Council
Spain
Treaty of Ghent

H

MARY A. HACKETT
The Papers of James Madison
University of Virginia

Barlow, Joel
Cadore, duc de
Daschkoff, Andrei Iakovlevich
Erving, George William
Graham, John
Livingston, Robert R.
Martineau, Harriet
Otto, Louis-Guillaume
Pichon, Louis-André, Baron
Rose, George Henry
Rumiantsev, Count Nikolai
Russell, Jonathan
Russia
Toussaint-Louverture,
    François-Dominique
Turreau, de Garambouville,
    Louis-Marie
Yrujo, Marquis de

JOHN DENIS HAEGER
College of Arts and Sciences
Central Michigan University

Astor, John Jacob

EARL N. HARBERT
Department of English
Northeastern University

Adams, Henry

C. M. HARRIS
Dagsboro, Delaware

Hoban, James
Latrobe, Benjamin Henry
Princeton University
Thornton, William
Todd, John Payne
Trist, Eliza House
White House

RONALD L. HATZENBUEHLER
Department of History
Idaho State University

Embargo Act of 1807
Macon's Bill No. 1 and No. 2
Nonintercourse Acts

MARTIN J. HAVRAN
Department of History
University of Virginia

Baring, Alexander, baron Ashburton
Canning, George
Castlereagh, Viscount
    (Robert Stewart)
Jackson, Francis James
Liverpool, Lord
Pakenham, Edward
Perceval, Spencer

DONALD R. HICKEY
Department of History
Wayne State College

Armistice of 1812
Bladensburg, Battle of
Blockades by France and England
Horseshoe Bend, Battle of
New Orleans, Battle of
Rule of 1756

DON HIGGINBOTHAM
Department of History
University of North Carolina
at Chapel Hill

Hull, William
Madison, James
    American Revolution
United States Military Academy

CHARLES F. HOBSON
The Papers of John Marshall
College of William and Mary

Congresses
    First Congress
Fletcher v. Peck
Marbury v. Madison
Marshall, John
Randolph, Edmund
Veto Power
Virginia Plan

STEVEN H. HOCHMAN
The Carter Center
Emory University

Beckley, John
Ritchie, Thomas
University of Virginia

THOMAS A. HORNE
Department of Political Science
University of Tulsa

Locke, John

CHRISTINE F. HUGHES
Naval Historical Center
Washington Navy Yard

Decatur, Stephen, Jr.
President

I

STANLEY J. IDZERDA
Department of History
College of Saint Benedict

Lafayette, Marquis de

J

ARTHUR M. JOHNSON
Bigelow Laboratory
Boothbay Harbor, Maine

Maine, District of

K

JOHN P. KAMINSKI
Department of History
University of Wisconsin

Antifederalists
Clinton, George

RALPH KETCHAM
Department of History
Syracuse University

Cabinet
Madison, James (1723–1801)

STEPHEN G. KURTZ
New Harbor, Maine

Adams, John

L

JOHN LAURITZ LARSON
Department of History
Purdue University

Bonus Bill

STUART LEIBIGER
Princeton, New Jersey

Cumberland Road
Jones, Joseph
Lincoln, Levi
Mason, John
Ross, Robert

LEONARD W. LEVY
Department of History, Emeritus
Claremont Graduate School

Bill of Rights
Judicial Review
Religion, Establishments of
Virginia Report of 1800

CHARLES D. LOWERY
Department of History
Mississippi State University

Barbour, Thomas, and the Barbour
    Family
Bland, Theodorick
Coles, Isaac
Edwards, Ninian
Eppes, John Wayles
Eve, George
Gaines, Edmund Pendleton
Grundy, Felix
Jackson, John G.
Lee, Henry
Macon, Nathaniel
Nicholas, Wilson Cary
Page, John
Pendleton, Edmund
Tayloe, John II
Taylor, John (of Caroline)

STEPHEN LUCAS
Department of Communication Arts
University of Wisconsin

Henry, Patrick

M

DREW R. McCOY
Department of History
Clark University

Agriculture
American Colonization Society
Biographies of James Madison
Coles, Edward
Jay-Gardoqui Negotiations
Latin America
Madison, James
    Retirement
Mercantilism
Nullification Doctrine
Political Economy
Rives, William Cabell
Sectionalism
Slavery
Tariff of 1816
Trist, Nicholas P.
Virginia Convention of 1829

GARY L. McDOWELL
Institute of United States Studies
University of London

Lee, Richard Henry

JOHN MAHON
Department of History, Emeritus
University of Florida

Brock, Isaac
Chrysler's Farm, Battle of
Florida
Hull, Isaac
Impressment
Thames, Battle of the
War of 1812

THOMAS A. MASON
Indiana Historical Society

Cass, Lewis
Harrison, William Henry
Hornet
Indiana Territory
Tippecanoe, Battle of

DAVID B. MATTERN
The Papers of James Madison
University of Virginia

Anderson, Joseph
Brackenridge, Hugh Henry
Bradley, Stephen
Campbell, George Washington

Claiborne, William C. C.
Crowninshield, Benjamin
Eustis, William
Granger, Gideon
Holmes, David
Ingersoll, Jared
Johnson, Richard Mentor
Leib, Michael
Lewis, Morgan
Morris, Robert
Parish, David
Ripley, Eleazer Wheelock
Tompkins, Daniel
Varnum, Joseph B.
Wagner, Jacob
White, Alexander

FRANK C. MEVERS
New Hampshire State Archives

Louisiana
Meigs, Return Jonathan
Mississippi Territory
Prevost, George
Webster, Daniel

ANN L. MILLER
Montpelier Research Center
Montpelier Station, Virginia

Cutts, Richard and Anna
Hite, Isaac
Maddison, John
Madison, Ambrose
Madison, Dolley
Madison, Nelly Conway
Madison Family
Montpelier
Orange County, Virginia

JAMES L. MOONEY
Naval Historical Center
Washington Navy Yard

Chauncy, Isaac
Cochrane, Alexander
Cockburn, George
Fulton, Robert
Jones, Jacob

GARY E. MOULTON
The Papers of Lewis and Clark
University of Nebraska

Clark, William
Lewis, Meriwether

N

LARRY L. NELSON
Ohio Historical Society

Fort Meigs

O

FRANK LAWRENCE OWSLEY, JR.
Department of History
Auburn University

Blount, Willie
Coffee, John
Crawford, William H.
Jackson, Andrew
Laffite, Jean
Mathews, George
Wirt, William

P

IAN C. B. PEMBERTON
Department of History
University of Windsor

Lake Champlain, Battle of

MERRILL D. PETERSON
Department of History
University of Virginia

Calhoun, John C.
Clay, Henry
Constitution Making
Jefferson, Thomas

G. KURT PIEHLER
The Papers of Albert Gallatin
Baruch College of the City University
of New York

Gallatin, Albert

MARK PITCAVAGE
Department of History
Ohio State University

Dearborn, Henry
Scott, Winfield
Terre aux Boeufs
United States Army

R

BRUCE A. RAGSDALE
Office of the Historian
U.S. House of Representatives

Caucuses of 1808 and 1812
Congresses
Eleventh Congress
Twelfth Congress
Thirteenth Congress
Fourteenth Congress
Gales and Seaton

JACK N. RAKOVE
Department of History
Stanford University

Articles of Confederation

RICHARD RANKIN
Department of History
Queens College, Charlotte

Madison, James (1749–1812)
Witherspoon, John

MALCOLM J. ROHRBOUGH
Department of History
University of Iowa

Public Lands

ROBERT A. RUTLAND
Department of History, Emeritus
University of Virginia

Albemarle County, Virginia
Annapolis Convention of 1786
Bowdoin, James
Burr, Aaron
Coles, Isaac A.
Columbian Centinel
Dawson, John
Dohrman, Arnold
Duane, William
Election, Presidential, 1808
Election, Presidential, 1812
Gardner, William (Billey)
Gelston, David
Goldsborough, Charles W.
Helvidius
Invisibles
Jay, John
Library of Congress
Madison, James
Birth and Childhood
Education
Presidency

Mason, George
Maury, James
Mississippi River
Murray, William Vans
Napoleon I
National Gazette
National Intelligencer
New York State
Nicholas, George
Pinckney, Charles
Pinckney, Charles Cotesworth
Snyder, Simon
Story, Joseph
Tyler, John
Winder, William

S

CHARLES H. SCHOENLEBER
Department of History
University of Wisconsin–Madison

Bayard, James Asheton, Sr.
Bedford, Gunning, Jr.
Dexter, Samuel
Taggart, Samuel

JEFFREY D. SCHULTZ
The Wilson Papers
Washington, D.C.

Wilson, James

TINA H. SHELLER
Department of History
University of Maryland, College Park

Baltimore
Barbary States
Carroll, Daniel
France
Hanson, Alexander Contee
Pinkney, William
Santo Domingo
Washington, D.C.

DAVID CURTIS SKAGGS
Department of History
Bowling Green State University

Elliott, Jesse Duncan
Hamilton, Paul
Lundy's Lane, Battle of
Mackinac Island
Perry, Oliver Hazard
River Raisin, Battles of
Shelby, Isaac
Smyth, Alexander

C. EDWARD SKEEN
Department of History
Memphis State University

Armstrong, John, Jr.
Brown, Jacob Jennings
Clay, Green
Compensation Act of 1816
Hampton, Wade
Van Rensselaer, Stephen
Wilkinson, James
Winchester, James

JAMES MORTON SMITH
Director Emeritus
Henry Francis du Pont Winterthur
Museum and Gardens

Alien and Sedition Acts of 1798
Dickinson, John
Lyon, Matthew
Morris, Gouverneur
Rodney, Caesar A.
Smith, William Loughton
Virginia and Kentucky Resolutions
Yates, Robert

PAUL H. SMITH
Manuscript Division
Library of Congress

Madison, James
Continental Congress

REGINALD C. STUART
Dean of Humanities and Sciences
Mount Saint Vincent University

British North America
Montreal

T

BRENT TARTER
Virginia State Library and Archives

Privy Council of Virginia
Virginia Convention of 1776

HOWARD TEMPERLEY
School of English and American Studies
University of East Anglia

Erskine, David Montagu
Joy, George
Russell, Benjamin

JOAN CARPENTER TROCCOLI
Gilcrease Museum
Tulsa, Oklahoma

Peale, Charles Willson
Stuart, Gilbert

U

MELVIN I. UROFSKY
Department of History and Geography
Virginia Commonwealth University

Constitution of 1787
Federal Convention

V

THEODORE M. VESTAL
Department of Political Science
Oklahoma State University

Montesquieu

Alphabetical List of Entries

Abbreviations Used in This Work

Adm.	Admiral	**Mass.**	Massachusetts
Ala.	Alabama	**Mich.**	Michigan
Ark.	Arkansas	**Miss.**	Mississippi
Art.	Article	**Mo.**	Missouri
b.	born	**n.**	note
c.	*circa*, about, approximately	**N.C.**	North Carolina
cf.	*confer*, compare	**n.d.**	no date
chap.	chapter (pl., chaps.)	**N.H.**	New Hampshire
Cong.	Congress	**N.J.**	New Jersey
Conn.	Connecticut	**no.**	number (pl., nos.)
d.	died	**n.p.**	no place
D.C.	District of Columbia	**n.s.**	new series
Del.	Delaware	**N.Y.**	New York
diss.	dissertation	**o.s.**	old style, according to the Julian calendar
DR	Democratic-Republican	**p.**	page (pl., pp.)
ed.	editor (pl., eds); edition	**Pa.**	Pennsylvania
e.g.	*exempli gratia*, for example	**pt.**	part (pl., pts.)
enl.	enlarged	**R**	Republican
esp.	especially	**Rep.**	Representative
et al.	*et alii*, and others	**rev.**	revised
etc.	*et cetera*, and so forth	**R.I.**	Rhode Island
exp.	expanded	**S.C.**	South Carolina
f.	and following (pl., ff.)	**sec.**	section (pl., secs.)
F	Federalist	**ser.**	series
Fla.	Florida	**ses.**	session
Ga.	Georgia	**Stat.**	Statutes at Large
Gen.	General.	**supp.**	supplement
HMS	His Majesty's Ship	**Tenn.**	Tennessee
ibid.	*ibidem*, in the same place (as the one immediately preceding)	**Tex.**	Texas
		USA	United States Army
i.e.	*id est*, that is	**USN**	United States Navy
Ill.	Illinois	**USS**	United States Ship
Ind.	Indiana	**v.**	versus
Ky.	Kentucky	**Va.**	Virginia
La.	Louisiana	**vol.**	volume (pl., vols.)
Lt. Gen.	Lieutenant General	**Vt.**	Vermont
M.A.	Master of Arts	**W**	Whig
Maj. Gen.	Major General		

James Madison
and the
American Nation
1751–1836

AN ENCYCLOPEDIA

ADAMS, HENRY (1838–1918), American historian, author. In his posthumous classic, *The Education of Henry Adams* (1918), Henry Adams claimed that James Madison, like "all other points" except George Washington, had "shifted their bearings" under close study, until Washington "alone remained steady, in the mind of Henry Adams, to the end." Adams did not specify exactly the shift in Madison's role in history, but he did leave behind the most influential early account of Madison's presidency in his nine-volume *History of the United States during the Administrations of Thomas Jefferson and James Madison* (1889–1891). Today, the *History* remains indispensable in understanding Madison and has influenced generations of American historians.

Even before he began the *History*, Henry Adams had read about Madison in the private papers of Adams's ancestors John and John Quincy Adams. From them, Henry inherited his family's quarrel with "the Virginia school," representing "State-rights republicans," which seemed at first glance to stand for a political position diametrically opposed to that of the Adamses, who were staunch nationalists. Yet, in the long course of writing his *History*, Henry Adams was led to a very different conclusion, both about the character and the ability of James Madison and about the truth-telling possibilities of history itself. For, almost as much as Jefferson, Madison challenged Adams's understanding of human nature, as well as of the role that statesmen played in determining the course of history. Together, the two Virginians provided a problem in historiography that Adams never solved.

As its major thrust, the *History* develops at length the proposition contained in John Quincy Adams's diary entry for 20 October 1821:

> Jefferson and Madison did attain power by organizing and heading a system of attack upon the Washington Administra-

tion, chiefly under the banner of States rights and State sovereignty. They argued and scolded against all implied powers, and pretended that the Government of the Union had no powers but such as were expressly delegated by the Constitution.

Savoring the irony created by events, Henry Adams developed his narrative to emphasize how, first, the Louisiana Purchase of 1803 and then the War of 1812 had contradicted the original positions of both Virginians. In effect, he used the *History* to supply massive documentation for the same conclusion that John Quincy Adams had penned in 1821: "Through the sixteen years of the Jefferson and Madison Administrations not the least regard was paid to the doctrines of rejecting implied powers, upon which those gentlemen had vaulted into the seat of government."

Citing Madison's inconsistencies in thought and action, Henry Adams portrays him as vacillating, sometimes inept, and often lacking in presidential leadership. The *History* presents little of Madison's complexity and instead makes him into a complaisant follower of the more strong-willed Jefferson as a member of "the Virginia school." Yet this exclusion from the *History* of so much of Madison's distinguished public service (particularly before he became president) troubled Adams less than it might have, for two important reasons.

First, as the years passed, Adams found the labor of writing the *History* increasingly difficult, and his personal life was disrupted by his wife's illness and depression, which ended with her suicide in 1885. Adams's Madison volumes (more than those on Jefferson) reflect the author's uneasy mind. Moreover, as he lost his personal confidence, Adams became disenchanted as his research and writing undermined the historiographical faith with which he had begun the *History*. In quiet asides, the historian cautioned his reader: "History is not often able to penetrate the private lives of famous men" and, again, "Some misunderstanding must always take place when the observer is at cross-purpose with the society he describes."

In a private letter of 1883, Adams expressed this historical skepticism directly: Madison and Jefferson become "mere grasshoppers kicking and gesticulating on the middle of the Mississippi River . . . carried along on a stream which floated them . . . without much regard to themselves." Even before he had finished the *History*, Adams was declaring the study of "famous men" such as James Madison a regrettable diversion, insufficient to the purposes of serious history. Meanwhile, with the insight of a popular novelist, Henry Adams knew that the Madison of his *History* would have a future life of his own, one that Adams could not control.

BIBLIOGRAPHY

Adams, Henry. *History of the United States during the Administrations of Thomas Jefferson and James Madison.* Edited by Earl N. Harbert. 1986.
Samuels, Ernest. *Henry Adams.* 1989.

EARL N. HARBERT

ADAMS, JOHN (1735–1826), revolutionary statesman, second president of the United States. No record of a private encounter between James Madison and John Adams has come to light. Sixteen years separated them in age, but fundamental differences over political and constitutional principles separated them and fed their mutual mistrust. The liberties of Americans in Madison's view were based upon citizenship and equality under law, protected by checks against the abuse of authority through the balances and separation of powers in the new Constitution, and protected against the domination of factions or interest groups by the size and complexity of the sprawling nation. Adams, far removed from the events leading to the adoption of the Constitution during his ministry at the Court of St. James's, attempted to influence the outcome of the constitutional debate by publishing in 1786 and 1787 his three-volume *Defence*, a rambling discourse against the dangers of single-assembly government, a structure that he mistakenly believed to be gaining favor at home. Liberties, he insisted, could be preserved only by adapting the British constitution to America and by granting recognition and representation to monarchical, aristocratic, and democratic interests, whatever name they were called. In calling for a powerful executive and a division of the legislature into upper and lower houses, Adams was in step with the majority of the Framers of the Constitution, but by insisting that a free republic required constitutional recognition of social and economic interests or "orders," which he described as "king, lords, and commons," Adams appeared to hold views that were both irrelevant and ridiculous in the eyes of Madison and of many of his contemporaries. When in 1790 Vice President Adams advocated the use of exalted titles in addressing the president, "Highness" and "Excellency" among them, Madison's suspicions about Adams's aristocratic proclivities were confirmed.

For his part, Adams began to mistrust Madison's political integrity when Madison endorsed discrimination between original and present bondholders in funding the Revolutionary War debt, a question that had long been settled in the minds of the advocates of a strong national government. Adams branded Madison as untrustworthy and superficial, and Madison's leadership of the congressional opposition to measures of the Washington administration in the years that followed only confirmed Adams's harsh judgment.

Despite his distrust, Adams recognized Madison's intelligence and abilities. In the face of mounting aggression on the part of revolutionary France, Adams's first decision as president-elect in 1797 was to approach Madison through Jefferson and to ask him to undertake a diplomatic mission to Paris. Adams was now critical of the economic measures backed by Alexander Hamilton and was suspicious of Hamilton's political maneuvering, but Madison was cautious about drawing close to the unpredictable Adams and decided against taking on the mission even as Adams backed down in the face of the strong objections to Madison voiced by members of his cabinet. Within weeks Madison scathingly denounced Adams's belligerence toward France as the president asked Congress to strengthen naval and military forces and roused public indignation against French attacks upon American shipping into war fever. In private life at Montpelier, Madison described Adams's policies as inexplicable in professing to leave the door open to negotiation while rearming aggressively. To Jefferson he wrote that Adams had made "degrading" public manifestos deliberately to inflame public opinion, and he was outraged when Adams signed the Alien and Sedition Acts. In response he drafted the protest against them contained in the Virginia Resolutions and agreed reluctantly to stand for the Virginia House of Delegates. Adams clearly obstructed the military buildup strongly promoted by Hamilton and extreme Federalists and in 1799 shocked friends and foes alike by naming a peace mission to France, but he remained in Madison's judgment "a perfect Quixote as a statesman." Madison expressed contempt for Adams when, after losing his bid for reelection in 1800, the outgoing president flooded the federal judiciary with anti-Jeffersonian appointees.

PRESIDENT JOHN ADAMS.   The portrait of Adams is surrounded by the coats of arms of the states. Amos Doolittle, *A New Display of the United States*, engraving, 1799.   PRINTS AND PHOTOGRAPHS DIVISION, LIBRARY OF CONGRESS.

Madison never understood Jefferson's insistence that, along with his many flaws, Adams had redeeming qualities until Madison's own responsibilities and difficulties multiplied during Jefferson's second term and later during his own presidency. Adams's attitude toward Madison began to change as his son, Sen. John Quincy Adams, came to support the administration. Both men favored the Louisiana Purchase, and both refused to condemn every measure taken by Jefferson and Madison to protect American rights from the harsh policies of Britain as their Federalist colleagues did. John Adams condemned the Embargo and pointed to the Jeffersonian refusal to build a strong American navy as a crucial mistake, but as President Madison stiffened in his resolve to defend American rights Adams began to change. When Madison in December 1811 sought congressional approval of a program of military and naval preparedness and a protective tariff, Adams was won over.

During the War of 1812 Adams scorned the Federalists for their lack of patriotism and openly supported Madison. In letters to Benjamin Rush (that he must have known would be made known to Jefferson and Madison), Adams praised Madison as possessing "genius, talents, learning, industry and more correct ideas than his predecessor." He expressed his support for Madison's reelection and his hopes for the president's recovery from illness, and in a memorable letter to Rush he praised Madison's defense of American rights as "necessary against England, necessary to convince France that we are something, and, above all, necessary to convince ourselves that we are not, Nothing." Later, after Madison's retirement, Adams delivered his final judgment in a letter to Jefferson: "Notwithstanding a thousand faults and blunders, his Administration has acquired more glory and established more Union than all of his three predecessors, Washington, Adams and Jefferson, put together."

Madison's restraint had limits. Writing to Adams directly for the first time, he gratefully acknowledged the reports he had received of Adams's support with the hope that he was worthy of it. He did not, however, encourage Adams's hope that a discussion of their political and constitutional differences would be welcome.

BIBLIOGRAPHY

Adams, Charles F., ed. *The Works of John Adams.* 6 vols. 1870–1875.
Brant, Irving. *The Fourth President: A Life of James Madison.* 1970.
Ketcham, Ralph. *James Madison: A Biography.* 1971.
Rutland, Robert A. *James Madison: The Founding Father.* 1987.
Smith, Page. *John Adams.* 2 vols. 1962.

STEPHEN G. KURTZ

ADAMS, JOHN QUINCY (1767–1848), sixth president of the United States, secretary of state, diplomat, U.S. representative and senator. John Quincy Adams, the son of John and Abigail Adams, was born on 11 July 1767 in Braintree, Massachusetts. He gained exposure to international issues during the Revolutionary War, when he joined his father on diplomatic missions to France. Adams also served during the 1780s as secretary to the American diplomatic mission to Russia. Returning to the United States, he graduated from Harvard College in 1787. Adams subsequently studied law under Theophilus Parsons and was admitted to the bar in 1790.

In the early 1790s Adams wrote a series of political essays, including a sharp critique of Thomas Paine's *Rights of Man* published under the name "Publicola." Thomas Jefferson and James Madison were surprised to learn that this essay was written by the younger Adams. In 1794 President George Washington commissioned Adams as minister to the Netherlands. Adams was later delegated by his father to serve a similar mission in Berlin. He returned in 1801 to Boston and briefly practiced law.

Elected to the Massachusetts legislature in 1802, Adams barely lost an election for a congressional seat late that

JOHN QUINCY ADAMS IN 1811.
PRINTS AND PHOTOGRAPHS DIVISION, LIBRARY OF CONGRESS.

year, but in February 1803 he and Timothy Pickering were selected to fill two seats in the U.S. Senate. (Adams received the longer, six-year term). Although he questioned the constitutionality of the Louisiana Purchase and privately worried that it might incite New England to secede, Adams broke ranks with his fellow Federalists to support the bill funding the Purchase.

During the next several years, he frequently spoke with Secretary of State Madison about Yazoo land sales, the impeachment of Samuel Chase, John Randolph's transparent ambitions, and other issues. Adams was already impressed with what he had heard about Madison's role at the Federal Convention, and the two men grew to respect each other. By 1806 Adams began to attend gatherings at the presidential mansion and at Madison's home. At a time when many Federalists accepted the machinations of the Spanish diplomat the marquis de Casa Yrujo, Adams backed a bill giving presidents the power to expel foreign diplomats. Adams was a Federalist who could work with Jefferson's administration.

Eschewing Federalist leanings, Adams grew increasingly worried when Great Britain seized American ships and sailors, and he deeply regretted the willingness of many Federalists to apologize for the British. After the *Chesapeake-Leopard* affair in 1807, Adams tried in vain to rouse Federalists to resist Great Britain and began to attend Republican town meetings. By the fall, Adams was openly pledged to support any measures that would put pressure on Britain. Adams introduced congressional resolutions condemning British seizures, supported Jefferson's embargo, and tried to win passage of a bill allowing commercial vessels to arm against the British. Federalists were outraged at what they regarded as a betrayal of their party's position, and when Adams attended the national Republican caucus in January 1808 to support George Clinton for president, the Massachusetts legislature elected James Lloyd to succeed Adams in the Senate even before Adams's term had expired. Adams promptly resigned from the Senate and briefly returned to the practice of law.

President Madison quickly turned to this experienced diplomat and new Republican. Early in 1809 Adams came to the capital to argue a case before the Supreme Court. After the Senate unanimously rejected William Short's nomination as minister to Russia, Madison nominated Adams to the post. Senators from both parties combined to defeat Adams's nomination; however, Madison persisted in his support and finally won approval for Adams with a second nomination as minister to Russia.

Adams arrived in Russia in the fall of 1809, shortly before Alexander I decided to reject his Napoleonic alliance and seek the support of neutral nations. This eased Adams's tasks in Russia. He kept Madison well informed about European developments and warned him that British policies relied upon support from disaffected New England Federalists. In 1811, when Adams expressed an interest in returning to the United States, Madison immediately nominated him to the Supreme Court. But Adams decided to remain in Russia, and, during the War of 1812, he was appointed to the team of diplomats who sought to negotiate a peace treaty. Adams defended New England's access to coastal fisheries and, with Albert Gallatin, was perhaps one of the two members most responsible for attaining the Treaty of Ghent. Madison rewarded him with an appointment as minister to Great Britain. This was the nation's most critical overseas mission, and the appointment was yet another indication of Madison's confidence in his Massachusetts supporter.

Adams became secretary of state under President James Monroe, a step that pleased former President Madison. Monroe and Adams continued to consult with Madison about diplomatic issues, especially when those issues involved Russia or revolutionary Latin American nations. Although Madison recommended a joint British-American agreement to protect the independence of the new Latin nations, Monroe and Adams turned in 1823 to the unilateral proclamation that became known as the Monroe Doctrine.

Madison remained politically neutral during the 1824 election that led to Adams's selection as president by the House of Representatives. The former president had previously supported at least some of the measures that John Quincy Adams proposed as president, including the creation of a cabinet-level interior department, but probably regarded other proposals by Adams as giving unwarranted power to the federal government. Both Madison and Monroe quietly ignored appeals by Adams's supporters in Virginia to serve as Adams electors in the 1828 election.

Madison, Adams, and Andrew Jackson all joined in 1834 to support the New York Temperance Society's appeal for national sobriety, and the two former presidents continued to respect each other. After Madison died, Adams, in an 1836 eulogy delivered in Boston, offered strong praise for Madison's numerous activities.

Adams was elected to the U.S. House of Representatives in 1831 and enjoyed a long career there. He repeatedly spoke out against the expansion of slavery and against the restrictions on free speech created by the southern-sponsored Gag Rule. After seventeen years in Congress, Adams died on 23 February 1848.

BIBLIOGRAPHY

Fischer, David H. *The Revolution of American Conservatism.* 1965.
Hargreaves, Mary W. *The Presidency of John Quincy Adams.* 1985.
Livermore, Shaw. *The Twilight of Federalism.* 1962.

Nagel, Paul. *Descent from Glory: Four Generations of the Adams Family.* 1983.

Richards, Leonard. *The Life and Times of Congressman John Quincy Adams.* 1988.

JEFFREY P. BROWN

AGRICULTURE. Agriculture played a significant, even central, role in Madison's life and career in two respects: it was at the core of his vision of a republican political economy for America, and it provided the primary basis for his family's livelihood. Appropriately, he developed a serious, scientific interest in the subject.

Madison's understanding of human nature and social development, rooted in the Scottish Enlightenment, underlined the significance of agriculture to the history of man. His republican dream for the United States was based on the hope that his country might remain, for as long as possible, at a predominantly agricultural stage of development, which represented a middle stage between the undesirable extremes of a rude, primitive, pre-agricultural mode of existence and a highly refined, corrupt, heavily commercialized state of society. According to this vision, Americans would ideally become prosperous and civilized without succumbing to decadence and luxury. Above all, in this predominantly agricultural society, the majority of citizens would remain economically competent, industriously employed in virtue-sustaining occupations, and hence independent, thereby providing the necessary basis for a successful experiment

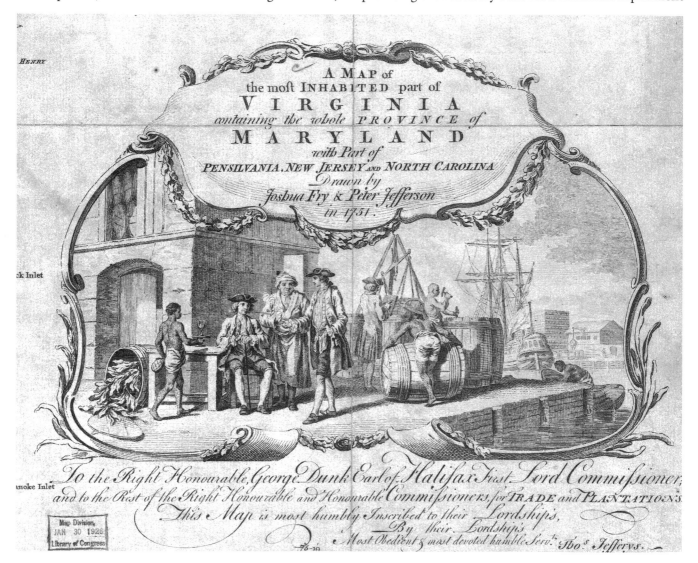

AGRICULTURE IN VIRGINIA.   The products of Virginia agriculture are prepared for shipment. Cartouche from Joshua Fry and Peter Jefferson's *Map of the most inhabited part of Virginia*, published by Thomas Jefferys, 1751. The surveyor Peter Jefferson was the father of Thomas Jefferson.

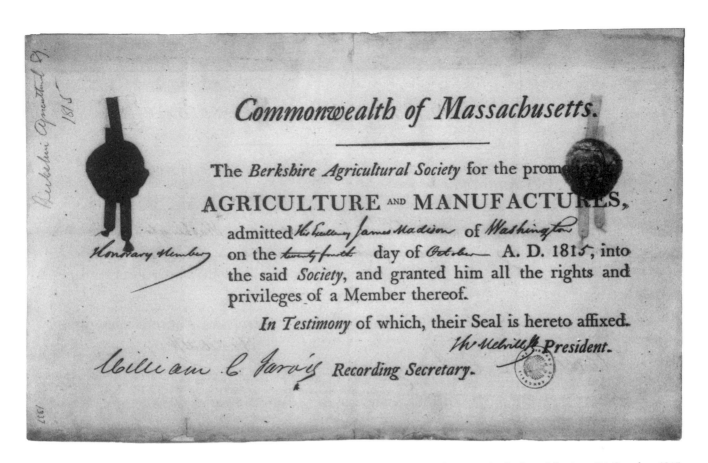

AGRICULTURE.   Madison's certificate of membership in the Berkshire, Massachusetts, Agricultural Society, 24 October 1815.
JAMES MADISON PAPERS, LIBRARY OF CONGRESS.

in self-government. Throughout his long career as a statesman, Madison labored in pursuit of this broad social and political vision grounded in agriculture.

Madison's family estate, Montpelier, was a working plantation that he took considerable pleasure in managing for most of his adult life. During his later years, when agricultural conditions in Virginia were in general decline, he became a disciplined student of scientific farming. In early 1818, as the newly elected president of a local agricultural society, he prepared a learned address in which he analyzed local conditions in the larger context of the role of agriculture in the history of human civilization. In this rich and fascinating document that scholars have often ignored, the mature Madison illuminated virtually every aspect of his thinking about agriculture, from its centrality to his political thought to his specific recommendations on such things as plowing and fertilizing. He explained in detail, for example, how the symmetry and economy of nature placed limits on the extent to which man could exploit natural resources for his support. Madison went on to show how man was uniquely able to adjust that symmetry to his own advantage, resulting in increased population, better standards

of living, and overall greater happiness. Given the primary importance of agriculture, Madison was deeply concerned that his countrymen were neglecting the study of its principles and practices. His fellow Virginians received a strong scolding for their errors in husbandry, as Madison called upon them to adopt new habits in plowing and manuring that might replenish their worn-out soil. He was also critical of his fellow Virginians' reckless destruction of woodlands, urging a new and enlightened policy of conservation more appropriate to a society that had moved beyond its frontier stage of development. Indeed, in a tone that would warm the hearts of modern environmentalists, the normally mild-mannered Madison sternly rebuked his countrymen for their carelessly exploitative relationship with nature.

Two years before he resigned his position as president of the Agricultural Society of Albemarle, Madison again lamented the unyielding habits and irrational practices of so many of his fellow farmers in Virginia. Hoping to see the creation of a professorship in agriculture (the incumbent would work closely with a professor in chemistry) at the newly established University of Virginia, he lamented the deepening crisis in the agriculture of his home state. Madison himself may have experimented with progressive procedures and techniques at Montpelier, but they brought only a modicum of help or relief amid the periodic bad harvests, insect damage, glutted markets, and declining prices of the 1820s and 1830s. Even the best efforts of "the best farmer in the world," as his friend Thomas Jefferson had once called him, could not save Montpelier from the debt and decline that bedeviled Madison during his final years.

BIBLIOGRAPHY

Ketcham, Ralph. *James Madison: A Biography.* 1971.

McCoy, Drew R. *The Elusive Republic: Political Economy in Jeffersonian America.* 1980.

Madison, James. "Address to the Agricultural Society of Albemarle, Virginia," May 1818. In *Letters and Other Writings of James Madison.* Edited by William C. Rives and Philip R. Fendall, vol. 3, pp. 63–95. 1865.

DREW R. MCCOY

ALBEMARLE COUNTY, VIRGINIA. Originally occupied by hunter Indians, Albemarle County, located in the Piedmont in central Virginia, adjoins Orange County and is drained by the Fluvanna, James, and Rivanna rivers. The area was attractive to land-seeking settlers, who came in search of arable land for tobacco crops early in the eighteenth century; the Indians had already moved to the west and south, leaving the frontier region free of fear from hostile attacks.

Named to honor the duke of Albemarle, in 1744 the county was split off Goochland County. The new county comprised all or part of present Albemarle and five other counties lying above the fall line of the James River. Gradually other counties were spun off to meet the exigencies of the time until 1777, when the creation of the county of Fluvanna brought the process to an end and Albemarle reached its present-day size of about 750 square miles, with Charlottesville as the county seat.

By 1762, when Charlottesville was created and named after Charlotte, wife of George III, the county contained farms and plantations where tobacco was the main cash crop. But the Albemarle soil was not salubrious for intensive leaf-culture, so wheat began to replace tobacco as the dominant crop. As in the Tidewater, certain landholding families came to political prominence in the decade preceding the Revolution, and members of these families—bearing such surnames as Fry, Walker, Cabell, Jefferson, Carter, and Ballou—often intermarried. Thomas Jefferson was born at Shadwell, near Charlottesville, and he was elected to the House of Burgesses in December 1768 to begin his public career representing Albemarle in the colonial legislature.

During the Revolution, Jefferson returned to his home, Monticello, when he was serving as governor (1779–1781), and the British cavalry leader Banastre Tarleton pursued him to the outskirts of Charlottesville. Madison was a frequent visitor to the county after his friendship with Jefferson ripened (the distance between Montpelier and Monticello is about thirty miles, or a long day's coach ride), often accompanied by Mrs. Madison. Madison shared Jefferson's interest in the improvement of farming methods, the raising of livestock, and the effort to promote wheat and corn as the principal cash crops for Piedmont farmers.

Upon his retirement from the White House in 1817, Madison resumed his efforts to make Montpelier more profitable, and it was probably at Jefferson's urging that the Albemarle Agricultural Society chose Madison as its president. Madison accepted the honorary post and in May 1818 summarized his views on farming in a speech that was later reprinted as a thirty-one-page pamphlet and widely distributed.

When the Panic of 1819 caused land values to fall drastically, the plunge in acreage prices was notable in Albemarle and other Piedmont farming communities. The ensuing depression forced the breakup of such large Albemarle holdings as Monticello, and by 1833 land values had slumped to half their 1818 value.

Jefferson's influence led to the decision to build a state university in Charlottesville in 1819. The University of Virginia first admitted students in 1825. Madison succeeded Jefferson as its rector, serving from 1826 to 1833.

Albemarle County was a conservative farming area that supported the Confederacy in 1861–1865, lapsed into a secondary role during the southern agricultural depression after the Civil War, and was the site of an important railroad junction early in the twentieth century. As the university grew and textile manufacturing was introduced, the county prospered until the Great Depression, then had a revival of its economy after World War II. Over 500,000 visitors went to Monticello annually during the 1990s, and the joint city-county Jefferson-Madison library was evidence of a strong local interest in learning and history.

BIBLIOGRAPHY

Moore, John Hammond. *Albemarle: Jefferson's County 1727–1976.* 1976.

ROBERT A. RUTLAND

ALEXANDER I (1777–1825), emperor of Russia (1801–1825). Son of the despotic emperor Paul and grandson of Catherine the Great, Alexander was brought up in the opposing worlds of the parade ground and the Enlightenment. Throughout his adult life, Alexander was torn between the ideals of discipline, order, and the exercise of autocratic power and the ideals of law, constitutions, and representative government.

A palace coup and the murder of his father brought Alexander to the throne in 1801. In 1802 he created the ministry system that lasted until 1917. In 1803 Alexander decreed that landlords could free their serfs. His reign also brought the first program of public education, the opening of five universities, the spread of voluntary societies to promote learning and charity, and the "golden age" of Russian literature. However, Alexander I is better known for what he did *not* accomplish. Plans for far-reaching reforms, the last of which would have created a constitutional monarchy based on a federalist system with separation of powers, were drawn up repeatedly but never implemented. This ambitious plan was a casualty of mutiny at home, Metternich's warning against any "concessions to the liberal spirit," and Alexander's own fear of revolution.

Alexander committed much of his energy to foreign policy. Without a doubt, Russia's victory over Napoleon in 1812–1814 was the high point of the period for both monarch and people. Thomas Jefferson believed that Alexander could become the leader of a radical reconstruction of Europe, and indeed Alexander was the first

ALEXANDER I, EMPEROR OF RUSSIA, 1801–1825.
PRINTS AND PHOTOGRAPHS DIVISION, LIBRARY OF CONGRESS.

European monarch to formulate ideals of international policy, such as the rights of nations, a league between great states, a new code of international law, and disarmament. Alexander ordered diplomatic relations to be established with the United States in 1808 and four years later offered to mediate the war between the young republic and Great Britain. (Indifference in London and the distraction of war in Europe prevented Alexander from pursuing this offer successfully.)

Entering Paris in triumph in 1814, Alexander accepted the restoration of the Bourbons but at the same time imposed a constitutional charter on Louis XVIII. Alexander inspired the convening of the Congress of Vienna in 1814, the mystical Holy Alliance of 1815, and the Quadruple Alliance of 1814 agreed to by Russia, Prussia, Austria, and Great Britain.

For a long time, historians sought explanations for Alexander's failed efforts at liberal reform in the "troubled soul" of an "enigmatic tsar." Alexander could condemn the slave trade in 1818 and free the serfs in Russia's Baltic provinces but could not abolish serfdom in Russia; he could promote written constitutions in Finland and Poland but deny them to his own subjects. A constitutional monarchy was feasible when the monarchy supplied the constitution but even then desirable only if it promoted and preserved social order and stability. In Alexander's view, Russia was not ready for a constitution or representative government. Alexander admired the American republic and corresponded with Jefferson but opposed the movement for self-government in Latin America ("Where are the Franklins, the Washingtons, the Jeffersons of South America?" he once remarked.)

Alexander I faced the dilemma of the paternalistic reformer, caught between the high ideals of devolving power and the practical exercise of power. In the estimation of Thomas Jefferson, "A more virtuous man, I believe, does not exist, nor one who is more enthusiastically devoted to better the condition of mankind. He will probably, one day, fall a victim to it, as a monarch of that principle does not suit a Russian noblesse." Indeed, Alexander's premature death precipitated a revolt of young officers in Saint Petersburg (the Decembrist revolt of 1825), aspiring to impose a constitutional monarchy.

BIBLIOGRAPHY

Grimsted, Patricia Kennedy. *The Foreign Ministers of Alexander I: Political Attitudes and the Conduct of Russian Diplomacy, 1801–1825.* 1969.

McConnell, Allen. *Tsar Alexander I: Paternalistic Reformer.* 1970.

Raeff, Marc. *Michael Speransky: Statesman of Imperial Russia.* 1957.

JOSEPH BRADLEY

ALIEN AND SEDITION ACTS OF 1798.

The Alien and Sedition Acts were enacted during the Quasi-War with France as an integral part of a national defense and internal security program. In recommending his preparedness measures to a Federalist-dominated Congress, President John Adams asked for unanimous action, which suggested that any opposition by the Republicans, led by Vice President Thomas Jefferson, would be viewed as disloyal.

Quickly labeling the Jeffersonians as the "internal foe," the Federalists first passed the Naturalization Act of 1798 (1 Stat. 566), which nearly tripled the residence requirement for immigrants (who gravitated to the Republicans) to qualify as citizens. The Alien Enemies Act (1 Stat. 577), which was supported by the Jeffersonians as well as the Federalists, authorized the imprisonment or banishment of the "external foe" (citizens of an enemy nation in time of war) and has remained a part of American wartime policy since 1798. The Act Concerning Aliens (1 Stat. 570) was a temporary measure that allowed the president extraordinary power over aliens, establishing guilt by suspicion for a two-year period and authorizing the chief executive to order the deportation of any foreigner whom he deemed dangerous to the peace and safety of the United States or whom he had reasonable grounds to suspect of being concerned in any treasonable or secret machinations against the government. Although no aliens were deported under the law, several shiploads fled the country while the law was being debated in Congress.

To cap off their internal-security program during the crisis with France, the Federalists passed the Sedition Act (1 Stat. 596) in order to deal with "internal enemies" and "domestic traitors" who published any "false, scandalous and malicious writing" against the president, Congress, or the federal government or attempted to bring them into contempt or disrepute by exciting against them "the hatred of the good people of the United States." By identifying the administration with the government and the government with the Constitution, the Federalists equated criticism of their administration with opposition to the government and subversion of the Constitution. By linking the Republicans with the French, they treated political opposition to administration measures as nearly treasonous.

James Madison called the original version of the Act Concerning Aliens "a monster that must forever disgrace its parents." He quickly discerned the use that the Federalists would make of the foreign crisis in order to strike at political opposition at home. "Perhaps it is a universal truth," he wrote in May 1798, "that the loss of liberty at home is to be charged to provisions against danger, real or pretended, from abroad." He worried about the effect of the proposed Sedition Law even before Congress had enacted it. When he received the Federalist *Gazette of the United States* from Philadelphia but not the Republican *Aurora*, he wrote Jefferson: "I hope the bridle is not yet put on the press." The Kentucky and Virginia Resolutions, written by Jefferson and Madison, were meant to deny the constitutionality of these controversial laws.

The Federalists enforced the Sedition Act exclusively against Republican politicians, printers, and spokesmen, arresting twenty-five, indicting twenty-one, trying twelve, convicting eleven, and acquitting one. Rep. Matthew Lyon of Vermont was the first person convicted under the law; he was reelected while serving his prison sentence. New York Assemblyman Jedidiah Peck was indicted for circulating a petition calling for the repeal of the Alien and Sedition legislation.

The most zealous enforcement came on the eve of the 1800 election, when the editors of eight leading Jeffersonian newspapers were prosecuted. The Sedition Act expired on 3 March 1801, President Adams's last day in office. Following his inauguration the next day, President Thomas Jefferson quickly pardoned prisoners still in jail and dismissed all prosecutions pending under the law.

[See also *Virginia and Kentucky Resolutions.*]

BIBLIOGRAPHY

Smith, James Morton. *Freedom's Fetters: The Alien and Sedition Laws and American Civil Liberties.* 1956.

JAMES MORTON SMITH

AMERICAN COLONIZATION SOCIETY.

Founded in 1817, the American Colonization Society was a philanthropic organization that promoted the resettlement of African Americans on the west coast of Africa. Under its auspices, with the indirect assistance of the United States government, the colony of Liberia was established in the early 1820s. The Society's sponsors were a diverse mix of New England clergymen, other old-line Federalists (especially from the upper South and the border states), and southern Jeffersonians.

Despite its high-sounding statement of goals, the larger purposes of the Society were ambiguous. Liberia's settlers were recruited from among the ranks of free blacks, not of slaves, but most white supporters of the project construed colonization as fundamentally antislavery. Their hope was that if the Society could demonstrate the practicality of relocating substantial numbers of blacks on their native continent, slaveholders would be encouraged to emancipate their slaves. But some southern leaders of the Society, hoping to attract widespread support in their region of the country, explicitly separated the project from any larger emancipation scheme. Indeed, the removal of a reputedly troublesome free black population could and did appeal to slaveholders seeking to protect, not weaken, their "peculiar institution." The Society thus enjoyed little enthusiastic support among free blacks, most of whom preferred to remain where they were and hope for better times in America. And by the early 1830s, with the emergence of a radical abolitionist movement in the northern states, the Society suffered declining support among whites actively committed to ending slavery.

James Madison was an exception to this trend, since he remained a strong supporter of the Society from its founding until his death. For him, there was nothing ambiguous about the larger purpose of the Society, which was to promote an end to slavery in the United States. He was convinced that southern slaveholders, whose prejudice against blacks and hence an integrated society he believed was permanent, would never voluntarily free their slaves unless they were shown that they might do so without creating a racial nightmare for themselves. Because he saw the Society as an essential part of any viable scheme to end American slavery peacefully, he advocated expanding the scope of its activities and also called for extensive support of those activities by the federal government. In truth, Madison had doubts about the practicality of colonization, but he refused to abandon faith in it for fear that any such widespread loss of faith among his fellow southerners would promote an accommodation of slavery as a matter of principle as well as expediency. By early 1833 he could see firm evidence of this kind of accommodation, and he responded by accepting election as president of the American Colonization Society, a largely ceremonial position he held until his death three and a half years later.

Madison's support of the Society extended even beyond the grave. In his will he bequeathed $2,000—twice the sum he left to his alma mater in Princeton, New Jersey—to an organization whose success he had always believed essential to the revolutionary cause of ending slavery.

[See also *Slavery*.]

BIBLIOGRAPHY

Fredrickson, George M. *The Black Image in the White Mind: The Debate on Afro-American Character and Destiny, 1817–1914.* 1971.

McCoy, Drew R. *The Last of the Fathers: James Madison and the Republican Legacy.* 1989.

Staudenraus, P. J. *The African Colonization Movement, 1816–1865.* 1961.

DREW R. MCCOY

AMES, FISHER (1758–1808), Massachusetts Federalist leader. Fisher Ames, the son of a physician and innkeeper, was born on 9 April 1758 in Dedham, Massachusetts. He graduated from Harvard College in

FISHER AMES.   Engraving by J. F. E. Prud'homme after a portrait by Gilbert Stuart.
PRINTS AND PHOTOGRAPHS DIVISION, LIBRARY OF CONGRESS.

1774, briefly served with Massachusetts forces during the revolutionary war, and studied law under William Tudor. He was admitted to the bar in 1781 and became increasingly active in Dedham politics. Ames called for severe repression of Shays's Rebellion and won acclaim for his speeches at the Massachusetts ratifying convention in 1788, where he favored adoption of the federal Constitution.

Ames was elected to Congress late in 1788 and quickly emerged as a leading opponent to Rep. James Madison's coalition. Ames attacked Madison's efforts to discriminate against British trade and opposed the latter's constitutional amendment mandating congressional districts with small populations. Ames believed that Madison feared the political power of ordinary Virginians and was easily duped by French diplomats. However, Ames always regarded Madison as an honest man and gradually came to respect his talents.

Ames strongly supported Alexander Hamilton's program and made a modest profit speculating in government bonds. He led the House coalition that defeated Madison's attempt to compensate the original holders of Revolutionary War bonds and favored the creation of the First Bank of the United States. Ames believed that southerners opposed the bank because they feared that its location in Philadelphia would make that city the permanent national capital. He worked hard to promote such New England interests as a time extension for Ohio Company land payments and the creation of bounties for cod fishermen and overcame Madison's opposition to both of these proposals.

Although Ames became gravely ill in 1795, probably with tuberculosis, he helped defeat Madison's attempt to prevent the implementation of Jay's Treaty. Ames argued that failure to ratify the treaty would produce a horrifying frontier war, and his eloquent speech was well remembered by his colleagues.

Fisher Ames retired from Congress after 1796. Although he approved the Alien and Sedition Acts, Ames never felt that President John Adams was sufficiently concerned about the dangers of either popular democracy or French influence upon the United States. He declined appointment as a diplomat and quietly backed Hamilton's attempt in 1800 to replace Adams with Charles C. Pinckney. Ames grew pessimistic about the nation's future, perhaps as a reflection of his worsening health, and he saw Thomas Jefferson's victory in 1800 as a clear sign of political decay. Ames wrote that even Madison, whom he respected, had "a vein of absurdity" concerning popular democracy.

Ames helped found the *New-England Palladium*, a sober and severe Federalist newspaper, and became an ally of George Cabot, Timothy Pickering, and other members of the Essex Junto. These New England politicians strongly denounced the Jefferson and Madison administrations, and at least some questioned whether New England should remain a part of the United States. Ames condemned the Louisiana Purchase as a "mean and despicable" action designed to help Napoleon. He sympathized with Pickering's New England secession movement but urged Pickering to be cautious and defended the general idea of the American union. His pamphlets, including "The Dangers of American Liberty" (1805), foresaw political chaos, mob looting, and assassinations if democracy and French ideas remained unchecked. He also argued that only the British navy protected the United States against French aggression.

Despite his failing health, Ames prospered as a merchant, lawyer, and turnpike investor. He was chosen president of Harvard in 1805 but declined the appointment. Fisher Ames died on 4 July 1808. His funeral became an occasion for ardent Federalist speeches against the Embargo Act of 1807, and George Cabot published Ames's collected works in order to keep his ideas before the public.

BIBLIOGRAPHY

Bernhard, Winfred E. A. *Fisher Ames: Federalist and Statesman, 1758–1808.* 1965.

Fischer, David H. *The Revolution of American Conservatism.* 1965.

JEFFREY P. BROWN

ANDERSON, JOSEPH (1757–1837), U.S. senator, comptroller of the U.S. Treasury. Born near Philadelphia, Pennsylvania, Anderson was commissioned an ensign in the New Jersey Continental Line in 1776 and served for the duration of the revolutionary war, rising to the rank of major. He practiced law in Delaware until President Washington appointed him a justice for the U.S. territory south of the Ohio River in 1791. His stint as territorial judge in what would become the state of Tennessee opened the way to a political career, and in 1796 he was elected a delegate to the Tennessee constitutional convention.

In 1797 Anderson began an eighteen-year career in the U.S. Senate when he was appointed to fill the term of William Blount, who had been expelled. Anderson became one of the Senate's workhorses, consistently among the top seven senators appointed to committees and often serving as chair. In the Sixth Congress (1799–1801), the Republican Anderson voted often enough with the Federalists to elicit the disgusted comment from Vice President Thomas Jefferson that the Tennessean was "perfectly at market," a remark that indicated Anderson's independence of mind and impatience with party discipline. This posture characterized Anderson's tenure in the Senate, making him a staunch but not uncritical supporter of Jefferson's and Madison's administrations. Henry Adams correctly described him as "an independent much given to opposition at critical moments," as when he voted against Madison's proposal for a mission to Russia (1809), against Albert Gallatin's nomination to the peace mission to Great Britain (1813), and against the embargo of 1813.

The great majority of Anderson's votes, however, supported administration measures, including the impeachment of John Pickering (1803) and the foreign affairs appropriation for the purchase of Florida (1806). He backed the administration in his role as chairman of the Senate select committee on Madison's war message (1812); he also spearheaded passage of the resolution authorizing Madison to seize the Floridas (1813). In 1815 Madison appointed Anderson comptroller of the U.S. Treasury, a position he held until 1836.

BIBLIOGRAPHY

Adams, Henry. *History of the United States of America during the Administrations of Thomas Jefferson and James Madison.* 2 vols. 1986.

Cunningham, Noble E., Jr. *The Process of Government under Jefferson.* 1978.

Stagg, J. C. A. *Mr. Madison's War: Politics, Diplomacy, and Warfare in the Early American Republic, 1783–1830.* 1983.

DAVID B. MATTERN

ANGLICAN CHURCH. The Church of England took root in North America with the settlement of Jamestown by the English in 1607. From that year until 1776, it was the tax-supported established church in Virginia.

The first Virginia Assembly, which met in 1619, decreed that "all ministers shall duely read divine service and exercise their ministerial function according to the Ecclesiastical lawes and orders of the churche of Englande." Throughout the remainder of the century, numerous laws enforcing uniformity of religion were passed. In 1660 the Assembly voted to suppress Quakers; if any Quakers gained entry to the colony, they were to be expelled. In turn, by the close of the century, the Anglican Church was completely subordinate to the state.

After the English Revolution of 1688, the bishop of London, who had responsibility for the Virginia church, appointed James Blair his representative in the colony. Blair did much to revitalize the Anglican establishment and supported the founding of the College of William and Mary for the purpose of educating a native Virginia ministry.

Dissenting Protestants were moving into Virginia in increasing numbers by the middle of the eighteenth century. Presbyterians, led by Samuel Davies, challenged the rigid control exercised by the Anglican establishment, insisting that the Assembly abide by Parliament's Act of Toleration. By 1759 Davies's persuasiveness, a burgeoning Presbyterian population, and a growing spirit of independence among the colony's residents combined to ensure toleration for dissenters.

Tension between Anglican clergy and the colonial government erupted in bitter conflict in 1755. The Assembly, concerned with adverse economic conditions facing the colony, moved to pay clergy in money instead of tobacco. The clergy appealed successfully to the king in council to disallow that action. However, colonial officials refused to abide by the royal decree. In 1763 a suit by Rector James Maury sought damages from his vestry for its refusal to carry out the king's command. The jury awarded Maury one penny in damages, and the court refused a new trial. Maury's action embittered many citizens in a time of rising nationalism.

The arrival of Baptists in the colony occasioned severe persecution. Many Baptists refused to obtain licenses to preach and were often imprisoned as a result. To such punishment Madison reacted in 1774, writing, "That diabolical Hell conceived principle of persecution rages among some and to their eternal Infamy the Clergy can furnish their quota of imps for such business." Although Madison's father

was an Anglican vestryman, there is no evidence that the son ever affiliated with the Anglican Church.

Since 1609 the bishop of London had steadfastly refused to place a bishop in the colonies. This decision complicated the church's problem as the Revolution approached, for it meant that the Anglican establishment in Virginia had to rely directly on ecclesiastical authority in London. The Virginia Convention of 1776, for all practical purposes, ended the Anglican establishment in Virginia. As of 1 January 1777, funding for the church ceased. The Convention suspended "until the end of the next session of the Assembly" authorization for vestries to levy funds to "provide salaries for the ministers." The suspension became permanent when no further action was taken. By 1784 the Anglican Church had been replaced by the Protestant Episcopal Church. Madison, seeking to defeat a general levy for the support of teachers of religion, voted to incorporate the Episcopal Church without funding because, as he wrote to Jefferson, "A negative of the bill too would have doubled the eagerness and the pretexts for a much greater evil, a General Assessment, which, there is good ground to believe was parried by this partial gratification of its warmest votaries." Madison foresaw that a coalition of non-Episcopalians would soon overturn the new establishment. In January 1787 "an act to repeal the act for incorporating the Protestant Episcopal Church" became Virginia law, eliminating the last vestige of the Anglican establishment.

[See also *Establishments of Religion.*]

BIBLIOGRAPHY

Eckenrode, H. J. *Separation of Church and State in Virginia.* 1910.
Hening, William Waller. *The Statutes at Large; A Collection of All the Laws of Virginia.* Vol. 9. 1821.
Hutchinson, William T., et al., eds. *The Papers of James Madison.* Vols. 1, 8, 9, 10. 1962–.

ROBERT S. ALLEY

ANNAPOLIS CONVENTION OF 1786. Generations of historians were led to believe the Annapolis Convention, now regarded as the forerunner of the Federal Convention of 1787, was Madison's unsuccessful brainchild. Nineteenth-century Virginia historians gave Madison credit for conceiving of the interstate gathering as a palliative for the declining health of the loose-jointed new nation. Efforts to amend the Articles of Confederation had been thwarted, several reputable historians observed, and Madison maneuvered the call for a general convention in the Virginia legislature, with the goal of revising the Articles into a more workable scheme of national government.

Earlier in his career, Madison had opposed the idea of

MARYLAND STATEHOUSE AT ANNAPOLIS.   Engraving by John Vallance after Charles Willson Peale, *Columbian Magazine*, Philadelphia, 3 February 1789.   MARYLAND HISTORICAL SOCIETY, BALTIMORE.

a convention aimed at restoring the confederation to its wartime vigor. In 1783, Madison had joined Alexander Hamilton at the Continental Congress in criticizing a proposed rump meeting, "not as absolute violations of the Confederacy, but as ultimately leading to them & in the mean time exciting pernicious jealousies." By 1786, Madison had become somewhat desperate.

Madison's own words indicate that he helped pass John Tyler's resolution in the Virginia House of Delegates calling for the meeting, but was lukewarm about its prospects. An earlier meeting at Mount Vernon had been poorly attended and made only halting steps to resolve interstate jealousies. Indeed, Madison himself had not appeared at Mount Vernon, although he was an official delegate. The evidence shows that Madison favored passage of Tyler's resolution in the spring of 1786, but with many misgivings. In January 1786, Madison told Monroe that Tyler's proposal would "probably miscarry," but added that it was "better than nothing" and "may possibly lead to better consequences than at first occur."

Public men in other states shared Madison's pessimism. A Massachusetts delegate attributed the meeting to "Mr. Maddison" but decided it was a useless exercise and did not attend. Even the Maryland legislature took little notice of the convention and failed to send a delegation. Thus Virginia was the only southern state represented,

joined by delegates from four states north of the Mason-Dixon line. New York sent Alexander Hamilton, however, and he was probably ahead of Madison in his feeling that drastic action was needed to repair the tottering confederation. Cynics suggested that Annapolis was chosen as the site because innkeeper George Mann's hostelry there was probably the best-run inn on the Atlantic seaboard. If the delegates did not make headway in public matters, at least they would have decent bed and board.

Early in September 1786 Madison came to Annapolis, stayed nine days at Mann's tavern, and watched as Hamilton dominated the proceedings. John Dickinson, the chief drafter of the Articles of Confederation, served as the chairman and he was the only signer of Hamilton's final report. As the country reeled under Shays's Rebellion in western Massachusetts, the bitterness engendered by Rhode Island's paper money crisis, and the embarrassment of an empty national treasury, Hamilton surely discussed the proper remedies with Madison, but the final document was Hamilton's work. The New York delegate took note of the poor representation, alluded to "the Situation of the United States [as] delicate and critical," and called for a meeting in May 1787 to remedy "important defects" in the Articles of Confederation.

Edmund Randolph and St. George Tucker, the other members of the Virginia delegation, went along with

Hamilton's proposal but without enthusiasm. The September 1786 report was sent to all the states for their implementation, with an unwritten but understood call for swift action.

For all its shortcomings, the Annapolis Convention became an important step as the young republic stumbled toward nationhood. Madison returned to Virginia and prepared for the legislative session at Richmond in October. His talks with Hamilton and other critics of the confederation reinforced a belief that better days lay ahead. The call for a proposed national convention in Philadelphia left him a glimmer of hope.

On 6 November 1786 Madison introduced legislation providing for a Virginia delegation at the Philadelphia assembly. Two days later, Madison reported to George Washington on the proceedings in Richmond and added "I have some ground for leaning to the side of Hope."

BIBLIOGRAPHY

Little has been written about the Annapolis Convention, perhaps because historians are inclined to overlook stepping-stones for the real bridge in the national crisis of 1786–1787. These works are good for general background:

Brant, Irving. *James Madison: The Nationalist, 1780–1787.* 1948.
Syrett, Harold C., and Jacob Cooke, eds. *The Papers of Alexander Hamilton.* 1961–1987. Vol. 3. Pp. 686–690.

ROBERT A. RUTLAND

ANTIFEDERALISTS.

ANTIFEDERALISTS.   Even before the Federal Convention met, James Madison worried about the influence of antifederal men, soon known as Antifederalists because of their defense of powerful state interests. He believed that two New York delegates, Robert Yates and John Lansing, Jr., leaned "too much towards State considerations to be good members of an Assembly which will only be useful in proportion to its superiority to partial views & interests." As the Convention approached, Madison felt almost overwhelmed. To obtain "the concurrence of the Convention in some system that will answer the purpose, the subsequent approbation of Congress, and the final sanction of the States" presented too many opportunities for antifederal men to sabotage the reform effort. As the Convention ended, Madison felt that most Americans would support the new plan of government, but he "expected that certain characters will wage war against any reform whatever."

Madison encountered Antifederalists in the first test the Constitution faced—the congressional debate over the transmittal of the Constitution to the states. At first he agreed with those delegates who argued that Congress did not have authority to amend the Constitution. He asserted that Antifederalists could not agree on amendments and that a bill of rights was unnecessary "because the [Constitution's] powers are enumerated and only extend to certain cases." When forced to admit that Congress had the power to amend the new Constitution, he suggested the inexpediency of having two constitutions before the states—one directly sent to them by the Convention and an amended congressional version.

While attending Congress in New York City from September 1787 through March 1788, Madison served as a national clearinghouse for Federalist information. He regularly corresponded with friends and political acquaintances throughout the country, relating news and commenting on the strength of Federalists and Antifederalists in different states.

Madison soon realized that Virginia was the key to the entire ratification struggle and that he would be required to play an important role in the fight to obtain his state's ratification. Early in November he indicated his willingness to serve in Virginia's ratifying convention. Madison sensed that Virginia was divided into three groups: those who favored the Constitution without amendments, those who largely supported the Constitution but wanted some amendments, and those who opposed the Constitution. To a great extent, Madison focused his attentions on the second group, because it held the balance of power. Madison showed these middle-of-the-roaders that they could agree among themselves on few amendments and that the Constitution could be amended safely and more easily after the new government went into effect, when experience showed the need for any changes.

The prominence of Virginia Antifederalists concerned Madison. He regretted the refusal of Governor Edmund Randolph and George Mason to sign the Constitution in the Constitutional Convention, the opposition of Richard Henry Lee and William Grayson in Congress, and the ever-threatening presence of Patrick Henry. He worried that Henry and Mason might combine their influence in the legislature either to reject the call of a state convention or to hamstring the operation of such a convention.

By February 1788, he saw a dangerous shift to the Antifederalists in Virginia. "At first there was an enthusiasm for the Constitution. The tide next took a sudden and strong turn in the opposite direction. The influence and exertions of Mr. Henry, and Col. Mason and some others will account for this." Madison tirelessly kept up his effort to convince moderate Antifederalists such as Edmund Pendleton and Randolph (both of whom eventually voted for ratification) that they should follow the model set by the Massachusetts convention by supporting unconditional ratification of the Constitution with only recommendatory amendments.

By March 1788, Madison had come to view Antifederalists with deep suspicion. He saw the ratification struggle as a battle between union and disunion, and he was angered by what he considered Antifederalist lies and misconceptions published in the newspapers; he was saddened by George Mason's bitterness and abandonment of moderation, and he became increasingly alarmed that Patrick Henry favored either a separate existence for Virginia outside the Union or the establishment of a southern confederacy dominated by Virginia. Persuaded by his friends that he could not be elected to the state convention unless he came home and campaigned, Madison returned to Orange County to stand for election. He wrote letters to influential friends and on their advice met with Baptist ministers, including John Leland, to assure them that the Constitution would never be used to restrict religious freedom.

On the eve of the Virginia ratifying convention, no one knew whether Federalists or Antifederalists had a majority of delegates. To some it seemed as if the delegates from Kentucky (then a part of Virginia) might hold the balance. Consequently, Madison contacted John Brown, the lone Virginia delegate to Congress from Kentucky, as well as several Kentucky delegates to the ratifying convention to assure them that the new federal government under the Constitution would protect the interests of the West and would be less likely than the Confederation Congress to surrender the American right to free navigation of the Mississippi River and full use of the port of New Orleans. The weakness of the Articles of Confederation, he told them, endangered all American interests, especially those of westerners.

Madison approached the Virginia convention cautiously. He realized the difficulty facing him from the combined weight of Henry, Mason, William Grayson, John Tyler, and, much to his dismay, his close friend James Monroe. He felt helpless to affect the outcome, because it was unlikely "that many proselytes will be made on either side." Pressure remained, however, because one Federalist blunder might lose votes.

Madison believed that Antifederalists planned to prolong the convention debates, hoping to receive favorable word that New York had voted against ratification. If no assistance arrived from New York, Madison thought that Virginia Antifederalists hoped "to weary the members into an adjournment without taking any decision." Some Antifederalists even thought they had a chance to defeat the Constitution.

Virginia Federalists pursued a conciliatory strategy intended to forestall a secession of the adamantly Antifederalist delegates and to mollify the middle party. Madison hoped to placate these honest Antifederalists by prefacing the form of ratification with "a few obvious truths which can not affect the validity of the act, and to follow it with a recommendation of a few amend- ments to be pursued in the constitutional mode." The strategy worked perfectly as the delegates by a ten-vote margin adopted the Constitution with a preamble and forty recommended amendments.

Madison's suspicion of Antifederalists persisted even after the vote to ratify the Constitution on 25 June. Diehard Antifederalists, in a caucus on 27 June, attempted to gain endorsement of an address exhorting their constituents to continue their opposition to the Constitution. Although the majority of Antifederalists at this caucus rejected the proposed address, Madison felt that Henry would use the state legislature as a forum to encourage Virginia and the other states to petition Congress for a second general convention. Madison's uneasiness heightened when the New York convention unanimously endorsed the idea of a second convention. Something dramatic, Madison believed, had to be done to pacify Antifederalists nationwide and forestall the political chaos that might ensue from a second convention. Madison's proposal of a bill of rights in the First Federal Congress accomplished this goal.

[See also *Bill of Rights; Constitution of 1787; Federal Convention;* and biographies of figures mentioned herein.]

BIBLIOGRAPHY

Kaminski, John P., and Gaspare J. Saladino, eds. *Ratification by the States: Virginia.* Volumes 8–10 of *The Documentary History of the Ratification of the Constitution.* 1988–1993.

Ketcham, Ralph. *James Madison: A Biography.* 1990.

Miller, William Lee. *The Business of May Next: James Madison and the Founding.* 1992.

Rutland, Robert A. *James Madison: The Founding Father.* 1987.

Rutland, Robert A. *The Ordeal of the Constitution: The Antifederalists and the Ratification Struggle of 1787–1788.* 1966.

Rutland, Robert A., et al., eds. *The Papers of James Madison.* Vols. 9–11. 1975–1977.

JOHN P. KAMINSKI

ARGUS. The USS *Argus,* a swift brig built by Edward Hartt at Boston in 1803, left New York in June 1813 with a crew of 140 under Captain William H. Allen to carry William H. Crawford, minister plenipotentiary, to France. The ship arrived at L'Orient on 11 July, was refitted, and, after leaving port, intercepted twenty traders from Bristol, Ireland, and Wales in St. George's Channel over the next thirty-one days. Vice Admiral Sir Edward Thornborough at Cork dispatched the British brig *Pelican* under Captain John F. Maples to search for the raider, and at dawn on 14 August the British sighted the *Argus.*

The *Argus* now had 127 officers and men and was armed with eighteen twenty-four-pound carronades and two long twelve-pounders. The *Pelican* had 118 officers and men and sixteen thirty-two-pound carronades, plus four long six-pounders. The *Argus* had 81.4 percent of the *Pelican*'s broadside and the heavier vessel prevailed. Allen missed attacking from the windward side, and a running-and-raking action ensued in heavy seas at grape shot, then musket shot, distance (100 yards). After four minutes Allen was wounded in the leg and was carried below. The *Argus*'s braces, stays, standing rigging, and preventer braces were shot away, and most of her spars were destroyed. By 6:30 A.M. the *Pelican* lay in raking position for eighteen minutes and then took position on her starboard bow keeping up a heavy cross-fire. The shattered *Argus*, carronades unseated, surrendered at 6:47 A.M. while the *Pelican*'s crew was in the act of boarding. The *Pelican* lost two killed and five wounded; the *Argus* lost six killed outright; five died later of wounds including Allen, and twelve were wounded. An American court of inquiry concluded that the crew was exhausted by the continued fatigue of constant action over the previous month.

BIBLIOGRAPHY

Chapelle, Howard. *The History of the American Sailing Navy: The Ships and Their Development.* 1935.
Chapelle, Howard. "The Ships of the American Navy in the War of 1812." *Mariner's Mirror* 18 (1932): 287–311.
Dudley, William S., ed. *The Naval War of 1812.* Vol. 2. 1992.
James, William. *Naval History of Great Britain from 1793–1820.* Vol 6. 1837.

FREDERICK C. DRAKE

ARMISTICE OF 1812.

The armistice of 1812 was a cease-fire agreed to by British and American military officials on the Canadian-American frontier seven weeks after the beginning of the War of 1812. The truce lasted for only three weeks because it was repudiated by the United States.

The United States had gone to war primarily to secure two objectives: the repeal of the British orders in council and an end to impressment. Almost as soon as the war began, President Madison sent out peace feelers, evidently hoping that the declaration of war itself would shock the British into making concessions. In addition to urging the departing British minister, Augustus J. Foster, to work for peace, the administration authorized Jonathan Russell, the American chargé d'affaires in London, to open negotiations for an armistice. By the time Russell received his instructions, the British had repealed the orders in council, but, because they refused to give up impressment, the negotiations foundered.

The British were confident that the repeal of the orders in council would end the war, and hence they launched their own peace initiative. Foster, who had heard of the repeal of the orders in late July after leaving the United States, sought while in Halifax to arrange a cease-fire. At his suggestion, Sir George Prevost, the governor-general of Canada, asked Gen. Henry Dearborn, commander of American troops in New York and New England, to accede to an armistice.

Dearborn agreed to a mutual suspension of offensive operations as of 9 August, with the agreement subject to approval by the administration in Washington. The armistice applied not only to those troops immediately under Dearborn's command, but to those on the Niagara frontier. The administration, however, refused to sanction any agreement that did not provide for an end to impressment. Hence, in mid August, Secretary of War William Eustis ordered Dearborn to disavow the agreement. In accordance with this order, Dearborn notified Prevost that the truce would end on 30 August.

Though in force for only three weeks, the armistice probably worked to Great Britain's advantage. Prevost claimed that it boosted Canadian morale and enabled him to strengthen his defenses. In addition, Prevost's representative in the negotiations, Col. Edward Baynes, was given a guided tour of American military installations in New York and Vermont and correctly judged that Dearborn's forces were unprepared for offensive operations. The armistice may also have aided Gen. Isaac Brock in his campaign against Detroit because it freed him to concentrate his small British force on the Detroit River without worrying about covering the Niagara front at the other end of Lake Erie.

Ironically, the armistice of 1812 suspended hostilities on the same terms that the United State accepted two years later in the Treaty of Ghent. The peace treaty did not mention impressment or any of the other maritime issues that had caused the war. Instead, it merely provided for returning to the status quo ante bellum.

[See also *Treaty of Ghent; War of 1812.*]

BIBLIOGRAPHY

Brant, Irving. *James Madison.* 1941–1961.
Hickey, Donald R. *The War of 1812: A Forgotten Conflict.* 1989.
Updyke, Frank A. *The Diplomacy of the War of 1812.* 1915.

DONALD R. HICKEY

ARMSTRONG, JOHN, JR.

(1758–1843), soldier, politician, secretary of war. Educated in private schools, Armstrong also attended Princeton for two years but left in 1776 to join the Continental army, serving as aide-de-camp to Brig. Gen. Hugh Mercer and to Maj. Gen. Horatio Gates with the rank of major. He served at the battles fought at Princeton, Trenton, and Saratoga. Near the end of the war, in the final encampment at Newburgh, New York, Armstrong penned anonymously the controversial

"Newburgh Addresses," an appeal intended to pressure Congress into redressing the army's grievances. The onus attached to Armstrong's authorship, once it was revealed, damaged his future prospects.

After the war Armstrong served in various positions in the state of Pennsylvania, including secretary of the Supreme Executive Council and adjutant general of the Pennsylvania militia. He was also a delegate to the Annapolis Convention, where he may have met James Madison for the first time. Armstrong also served as a delegate from Pennsylvania to the Continental Congress under the Articles of Confederation from 1787 until that Congress expired. As a nationalist, Armstrong was welcomed by Madison, but whether the two men worked together, is unknown.

Armstrong married Alida Livingston, sister of Chancellor Robert R. Livingston of New York, in 1789. This marriage made him wealthy, and he settled along the Hudson River to tend his extensive landholdings. The connection with the Livingstons certainly influenced Armstrong's selection as a U.S. senator from New York in 1800. In 1804, when Chancellor Livingston asked to be relieved as minister to France, President Thomas Jefferson chose Armstrong as Livingston's successor. Armstrong's six-year tenure as minister to France was controversial. He was involved in numerous pamphlet wars with American merchants in Paris and their supporters in America who were critical of his handling of claims arising under the Louisiana Purchase treaty. Armstrong also attacked French measures harmful to America's neutral trade, thereby arousing the wrath of Napoleon. To his credit, Armstrong frequently urged his government to take stronger retaliatory measures against the French emperor. Although President Jefferson and Secretary of State Madison may have occasionally winced at the strong language Armstrong directed at Bonaparte's rapacious policy toward the United States, his letters were publicly printed and weakened Federalist charges that the administration had a pro-French bias. Armstrong, for his part, complained of neglect at the hands of Secretary of State Madison and was chagrined by Madison's failure to follow his advice.

Although Armstrong was not treated well by President Madison on his return, he supported the government's movement toward war with Great Britain. He also strongly supported Madison against DeWitt Clinton in the presidential election of 1812. As a reward, Armstrong was appointed brigadier general and assigned the defense of New York harbor. When William Eustis resigned as secretary of war during the War of 1812, Madison reluctantly appointed Armstrong to the post in March 1813, despite opposition within his cabinet. Armstrong's irascible temperament was well known, but Madison recognized Armstrong's talents. Madison later justified Armstrong's appointment by saying it was his hope that "a proper mixture of conciliating confidence and interposing control would render objectionable peculiarities less in practice than in prospect."

Initially, Armstrong infused new energy into the Department of War. He brought new, younger staff officers into the department to cope with the myriad problems of administration, and he presided over the preparation of revised rules and regulations for the army. But Armstrong treated his officers imperiously, and he interfered far too often in matters more properly left to the field commanders. He even went to the northern front in the fall of 1813, but his presence was resented by Maj. Gen. James Wilkinson, and Armstrong only worsened matters.

Perhaps Armstrong's most significant contribution was his advancement of junior officers of merit. As a consequence, by 1814 a new generation of bolder officers, such as Jacob Brown, Andrew Jackson, Winfield Scott, and Edmund P. Gaines, helped to improve the performance of the military. Madison supported Armstrong in these appointments despite efforts by more senior officers to overturn Armstrong's action. This younger generation of officers influenced the American military establishment up to the Civil War.

Ultimately, Armstrong feuded with fellow cabinet officer James Monroe, who resented Armstrong and viewed him as a potential rival for the presidency. By the summer of 1814, Armstrong's relations with President Madison had also deteriorated. Madison now turned from "conciliating confidence" to "interposing control." The debacle at Bladensburg, Maryland, and the subsequent burning of Washington brought the simmering dispute to a head. Armstrong was widely blamed by the people of the district for his seeming indifference to their defense; he regarded the capital city as too insignificant militarily to warrant a British attack. Madison's response to demands for Armstrong's dismissal was equivocal, and Armstrong resigned in September 1814 in disgust. His resignation, however, was seen by many as a tacit admission of failure, and Armstrong's career was ruined. He never again held a political office.

As one of the best writers of his generation, Armstrong employed his talents primarily for polemical purposes. In his later years he wrote several articles critical of his enemies, particularly Wilkinson and Monroe, but he did not count Madison among his enemies. His assessment of Madison, expressed privately a short time after Madison's death, was that "His sin grew out of his terrors, & however an infirmity like this might have lessened my reverence for the man, it had no tendency to destroy my belief in the general purity of his official conduct."

BIBLIOGRAPHY

Armstrong, John. *Notices of the War of 1812.* 2 vols. 1836, 1840.
Pratt, Julius. "John Armstrong, Jr." *Dictionary of American Biography.* Vol. 1. Edited by Dumas Malone. 1928.
Skeen, C. Edward. *John Armstrong, Jr., 1758–1843: A Biography.* 1981.

C. EDWARD SKEEN

ARMY, UNITED STATES. See *United States Army.*

ARTICLES OF CONFEDERATION.

When James Madison first took his seat in the Continental Congress in March 1780, the Articles of Confederation that Congress had proposed to the states in November 1777 still remained a year away from ratification. Much of Madison's political activity and thinking over the next seven years centered on this document, the precursor to the Federal Constitution of 1787 that Madison played so instrumental a role in framing.

As a delegate to Congress from March 1780 until October 1783, Madison was closely involved first in the maneuvers that finally allowed the Confederation to take effect in March 1781, and then in the early efforts to amend the Articles to give Congress a measure of financial independence. As a member of the Virginia House of Delegates from 1784 to 1786, Madison attempted to persuade his fellow legislators to support Congress and to approve the several amendments to the Articles it had submitted to the states. The lessons he drew from these dual experiences as congressional delegate and state legislator finally persuaded Madison that no mere amending of the Articles of Confederation would cure the underlying "vices of the political system of the United States." By winter 1787, he believed that a new federal government had to be constructed along lines entirely different from those sketched by the "compilers" of the Confederation a decade earlier.

Although several drafts of a confederation compact were prepared by individual members of Congress as early as 1775, serious work on a formal union for the thirteen new republics that made up the United States began only in June 1776. Concurrently with its appointment of committees to draft a declaration of independence and a plan for foreign treaties, Congress named a thirteen-member committee, chaired by John Dickinson of Pennsylvania, to prepare articles of confederation. Its report was debated between mid July and 20 August 1776, when impasses over the control of western lands and the apportionment among the states of representation and common expenses, coupled with a series of reverses in the conduct of the war, discouraged Congress from pushing the Articles through to completion. Debate resumed in spring 1777 but quickly bogged down over the same issues. Only in the fall, after the British occupation of Philadelphia forced Congress to retreat to the security of York, did its members muster the will to complete the Confederation. Anxious to capitalize on the victory at Saratoga to conclude an alliance with France, a majority of delegates voted to allow each state to retain a single vote in Congress, to apportion common expenses among the states according to the assessed value of improved lands, and to deny the Union any significant authority to set state boundaries or control the unsettled lands of the interior.

As a compact among semisovereign states, the Articles required ratification by all thirteen legislatures. The principal opposition to the Confederation came from a bloc of "landless" states—notably Maryland, Delaware, Rhode Island, and New Jersey—that argued that title to the vast transappalachian interior should first be transferred from the claiming states (led by Virginia) to the Union. Such a transfer, the landless states insisted, would provide Congress with a substantial resource to defray the costs of the war, thereby reducing the tax burden that they otherwise would have to impose on their own constituents. By 1779, all the landless states but Maryland had acceded, under protest, to the Confederation; but continued opposition from Maryland prevented the Articles from taking effect.

As a theory of federalism, the Articles proposed a simple and pragmatic division of authority between the Union and the states. A unicameral Congress would have responsibility for the general conduct of war and foreign relations, and the states would retain sovereign authority over their "internal police," including all powers of legislation and taxation. In contrast, the states would act as the administrative auxiliaries of Congress, converting general recommendations taken under the authority of the Articles into specific acts of legislation shaped to the peculiar circumstances of each state. As Madison later observed, this reliance on the states was the fatal defect of the federal system—but this weakness accurately reflected the prevailing tendency to keep states strong during the early years of the Revolution, while ignoring bitter lessons learned from the actual conduct of the war.

During his first year in Congress, Madison took an active part in the movement to complete the ratification of the Confederation while combining his duties as a delegate from Virginia with his responsibilities as a member of the national government. Like other state leaders, Madison supported Virginia's yielding its claims to territory above the Ohio River, provided that Congress accept the conditions that the state placed on its cession. In Congress, Madison acted repeatedly to sustain those conditions, but to his constituents he stressed the need to defer to the general good in order to complete the Confederation. In 1780,

20

he took the leading role in the discussions that eventually led to the initial Virginia cession offer. This offer in turn helped to persuade the Maryland assembly to ratify the Articles of Confederation in February 1781.

By that point in the war, however, few delegates believed that the Articles as drafted would provide an adequate framework for national government. Madison had entered Congress at a time when its system for financing the war had collapsed, leading it to give the states greater responsibility for raising supplies. Skeptical of this power shift from the outset, Madison grew more pessimistic as the states encountered problems in fulfilling the quotas assigned by Congress. When ratification of the Confederation became imminent, he accordingly supported the first effort at its amendment—a proposal to grant Congress a 5 percent impost on foreign imports—which was submitted to the states even before the Articles took effect. But Madison's pessimism carried him further still. As a member of a committee created to suggest how to exercise congressional powers under the Articles, Madison apparently proposed a radical amendment authorizing Congress to employ military or naval forces against delinquent states that failed "to fulfill their federal engagements." Though Madison thought this scheme offered "an easy and efficacious mode" to secure state compliance with federal acts, most other delegates dismissed his notion out of hand.

Before suggesting other amendments to the Articles, Congress awaited the fate of its impost (tariff) proposal of 1781. By summer 1782, opposition from Rhode Island, followed by Madison's own state of Virginia, doomed the impost to rejection. Yet by then most delegates realized that any solution to the financial problems of the Union required more comprehensive measures. Amid rumors of unrest emanating from both the public creditors and a potentially mutinous army, Congress launched a protracted set of deliberations that were driven by the ambitious plans of Robert Morris, the superintendent of finance, as well as by congressional awareness of how politically difficult it was to secure unanimous state agreement when particular economic interests were affected directly. Among other provisions, Morris's financial program included the consolidation of a national public debt and the granting to Congress of power to levy land, poll, and excise taxes. But the more Congress debated these measures, and the more troubled some delegates became over Morris's heavy-handed attempts to manipulate their debates, the more problematic his proposals appeared.

At first, Madison supported Morris and the general notion of independent national revenues that lay at the core of his program. But Madison was not a member of the superintendent's inner circle of supporters—a group that included James Wilson and Thomas FitzSimons of Pennsylvania and the newly elected New York delegate, Alexander Hamilton—and when opposition within Congress to the Morris program proved intractable, Madison opted for an independent course. In a crucial meeting at FitzSimons's Philadelphia house on 20 February 1783, Madison led a group of delegates who agreed that the only form of national taxation with any realistic prospects of adoption by the states would be a revised version of a tax on imports. The next day, Madison outlined a compromise that eventually formed the basis of the new revenue plan that Congress proposed to the states on 18 April. Under its terms, Congress would ask authority to collect an impost to be assigned to the union for a period of twenty-five years, while the states would assign additional taxes of their own choosing to meet national obligations. To allow the common expenses to be apportioned more efficiently and equitably than the existing formula, the new plan also proposed to amend the Articles so that expenses would be divided among the states according to population, with slaves being counted (at Madison's suggestion) according to the three-fifths ratio that the Constitution later applied to the issue of representation.

Under Article 5 of the Confederation, no delegate could serve more than three years out of any six. Madison's term of service in Congress accordingly expired with the close of the congressional year in October 1783. Returning to Virginia for the first time since winter 1780, he was briefly at loose ends until he was elected to the Virginia Assembly the following spring. Because his service to the state in Congress had been so distinguished, much was expected of Madison when he entered the legislature—just as he expected much of himself. High on his list of priorities was to inculcate among his colleagues a due sense of the importance of meeting their national responsibilities. At the same time, he remained intensely interested in the course of national politics as Congress wandered from Princeton to Annapolis and Trenton before finally settling in New York. Through his correspondence with James Monroe and annual trips northward, Madison kept abreast of the ongoing discussions within Congress about possible steps to seek further amendments to the Confederation.

Most of these discussions centered on issues of trade. As American merchants met discriminatory treatment from the British government, which denied American ships

WEAKNESSES OF CONFEDERATION *(left).*   The wagon representing Connecticut sinks in the mire as rival factions of the Council of Twelve—"Federals" under a beaming sun, "Antifederals" under storm clouds—pull in opposite directions. *The Looking Glass for 1787,* engraving attributed to Amos Doolittle, 1787.   PRINTS AND PHOTOGRAPHS DIVISION, LIBRARY OF CONGRESS.

access to imperial harbors both in the West Indies and the home islands, and as American artisans faced stiff competition from a flood of British imports dumped on American markets, pressure grew for concerted retaliatory measures. Under the Articles of Confederation, however, Congress lacked authority to regulate foreign commerce, and inconsistent state efforts to remedy these problems only demonstrated why national action was important. In May 1784, Congress proposed two new amendments designed to give it limited authority over foreign commerce. But as with the revenue proposal of April 1783, these amendments never surmounted the obstacle of unanimous state ratification.

Like other critics of the Confederation, Madison hoped that the adoption of discrete and prudently drawn amendments would gradually enlighten ordinary Americans and their legislatures to the benefits of an effective union. But in fall 1785 his failure to persuade the Virginia Assembly to grant adequate commercial powers to Congress left Madison alarmed that the Union itself might dissolve unless dramatic steps were taken to amend the Articles. Recognizing that amendments emanating from Congress were fated for rejection, he supported John Tyler's motion to have Virginia call a special convention to frame a single amendment confined to the subject of commerce. Though uncertain that the convention would succeed, Madison saw that his own election as a commissioner was reason enough to make this strategy of reform his own. When the commissioners met in September 1786, however, only twelve delegates from five states appeared at Annapolis—too few to do anything of consequence. Rather than adjourn empty-handed, however, the commissioners issued a call for a general convention to assemble at Philadelphia the following May. Back home for the fall session of the assembly, Madison made the endorsement of this call the first item of his legislative agenda, while privately he undertook his own preparations for the new convention. Returning to Congress in February 1787, he began to draw his thoughts together in letters to Thomas Jefferson, Edmund Randolph, and George Washington as well as in a memorandum that he entitled "Vices of the Political System of the United States."

In these efforts, Madison drew critical lessons from the record of his own involvement in the various efforts to adopt and revise the Articles of Confederation. At the very center of his constitutional thinking lay a conviction that the fundamental and inherent defect of the Confederation was its reliance upon the state legislatures. States were expected both to implement national measures and to perceive the common interest whenever their internal politics and parochial concerns intervened. However reasonable it seemed in 1777 to believe that the states would

do their duty, the lessons of the past decade convinced him that "a unanimous and punctual obedience of 13 independent bodies, to the acts of the federal Government, ought not to be calculated on." From this observation, Madison proceeded to fashion his powerful critique of the dangers of republican politics within the states, arguing that the demagoguery of the state legislatures and the swirl of interest and passion among their constituents would not only frustrate national measures but also promote the passage of unjust legislation.

This general diagnosis of the problems of state government in turn influenced the program Madison intended to present to the Federal Convention. The approach he had envisioned in 1781, requiring the Union to act through the states by resolutions and recommendations or vesting it with the coercive authority over delinquent states was discarded. Madison now concluded that the national government must be empowered to act directly upon the people of the United States by making, executing, and adjudicating its own laws. This shift meant reconstituting the Union as a normal government with three independent branches, including a bicameral legislature. Such a change in turn enabled the Federal Convention to draw appropriate lessons about the proper design of the national government from the examples of the republican constitutions of the states, rather than the unicameral Continental Congress.

Madison drew two other critical conclusions from his analysis of the defects of the Confederation. First, to convince the large states to delegate the requisite powers to the national government, he believed it was necessary to replace the repugnant principle that gave each state an equal vote in Congress with a system of proportional representation that could be applied to *both* houses of the new legislature. Madison thereby set the stage for the protracted struggle between large and small states that dominated the opening debates of the Convention. Madison also recognized that the procedural requirements for amending the Confederation would have to be abandoned. In part this was because the refusal of Rhode Island even to send a delegation to Philadelphia indicated that unanimous state ratification could not be expected. But equally important, he understood that the new government should rest on a more durable foundation than the assent of the state legislatures. To render a federal constitution legally superior to the state constitutions whose authority it must limit, some expression of popular sovereignty would be required. A constitution designed to alter the existing balance of power between the Union and the states not only had to act directly on the people but to draw its authority from them as well. Neither condition had operated under the Confederation; both were essential to Madison's plans for the new government.

[See also *Constitution Making*; *Constitution of 1787*; *Madison, James*, article on *Continental Congress*; *Public Lands*.]

BIBLIOGRAPHY

Banning, Lance. "James Madison and the Nationalists, 1780–1783." *William and Mary Quarterly*, 3d ser., 40 (1983): 227–255.

Jensen, Merrill. *The New Nation: A History of the United States during the Confederation.* 1950.

McCoy, Drew R. "James Madison and Visions of American Nationality in the Confederation Period: A Regional Perspective." In *Beyond Confederation: Origins of the Constitution and American National Identity.* Edited by Richard Beeman, Stephen Botein, and Edward C. Carter, pp. 226–258. 1987.

Rakove, Jack N. *The Beginnings of National Politics: An Interpretive History of the Continental Congress.* 1979.

Rakove, Jack N. *James Madison and the Creation of the American Republic.* 1990.

JACK N. RAKOVE

ASHBURTON, ALEXANDER BARING, BARON. See *Baring, Alexander, baron Ashburton.*

ASSUMPTION ACT. See *Funding Act.*

ASTOR, JOHN JACOB

ASTOR, JOHN JACOB (1763–1848), fur trader, merchant, financier. John Jacob Astor was the quintessential American capitalist. The founder of an American dynasty of wealth and power, he first came to America in 1783 searching for financial opportunities in the aftermath of the American Revolution.

Astor's primary occupation was fur trading, a business that placed him at the intersection of American economic and political development. Furs were a leading North American export and highly prized in Europe and Asia. Yet the fur business was controlled by British companies headquartered in Montreal. Fur trading thus was linked to American expansion to the West. Because Astor's business interests were so intertwined with America's political future, he developed extensive connections with leading politicians, including Thomas Jefferson, Albert Gallatin, and James Madison.

In the early nineteenth century, Astor expanded his fur trade throughout New York State and the Great Lakes and shipped furs to China and Europe. President Thomas Jefferson and his secretary of state, James Madison, were soon committed to expanding America's western empire beyond the Louisiana Purchase, perhaps to the Pacific Ocean. When Lewis and Clark crossed the

JOHN JACOB ASTOR. Engraving after a painting by Alonzo Chappel.

American continent, they suggested that a fur trade outpost on the Columbia River could be utilized as a crossroads for trade with China.

Throughout the first decade of the nineteenth century, the American and British governments competed for hegemony in the West. By 1807 Jefferson's inner circle had already foreseen the potential for war with Great Britain. In any such conflict, the Americans knew that they must drive the British from Canada and capture control of the fur trade. Given such circumstances, they listened to an amazing proposal from John Jacob Astor in 1808. Essentially, Astor proposed to establish an American fur company that would be transcontinental in scope and that would control all commercial relations with Native Americans from the backcountry of New York State, through the Great Lakes, up the Missouri River, and across the Rocky Mountains to an outpost on the Pacific Coast. Astor went ahead with his plan on the mistaken belief that Jefferson and Madison had promised military and political support.

In 1810, with Madison now president, Astor sent two

expeditions to the Pacific Coast, one by sea and one overland.

The War of 1812, however, changed Astor's plans and his relationship with the American government. He continued to be an important figure because the federal government realized the critical relationship of the fur trade to the control of the Indians. More important, Astor had now become so powerful among American businessmen that he provided access for government officials desperate for loans to finance the war. Astor helped the government float several bond issues that secured needed capital. In return, Astor was a constant presence in Washington during the war years, asking for and receiving permission to continue his fur trade with Canada and to send his ships to trade with Europe. Astor also wanted the American government to send military forces to Astoria on the Pacific Coast to protect the settlement from a British takeover. On several occasions, Madison appeared to promise such aid by authorizing an American naval vessel, only to divert it at the last minute to meet military exigencies elsewhere. Because of American neglect or inaction, Astoria fell to the British in 1814.

At war's end, Astor was thoroughly disappointed with government officials, but he continually sought assurances from President Madison during Madison's last year in office. Astor received a promise that American officials would reassert their claim to Astoria. More important, in 1816 Congress passed a law excluding British citizens from the American fur trade, finally giving Astor the help he required to build the American fur trade. As Madison left office, Astor was reestablishing the American Fur Company with a headquarters on Mackinac Island.

BIBLIOGRAPHY

Haeger, John Denis. *John Jacob Astor.* 1992.
Jackson, Donald. *Thomas Jefferson and the Stony Mountains.* 1981.
Porter, Kenneth Wiggins. *John Jacob Astor: Businessman.* 2 vols. 1931.
Ronda, James. *Astoria and Empire.* 1990.

JOHN DENIS HAEGER

B

BALTIMORE. The leading Chesapeake port, Baltimore was the great boomtown of late-eighteenth-century America. A quiet village of 250 inhabitants at midcentury, it mushroomed into a bustling flour port of 6,000 people during the twenty-five-year period prior to the Declaration of Independence. The Revolutionary War accelerated the town's growth. The only major American port that did not suffer from British occupation or bombardment, Baltimore expanded in size and regional importance as a result of the war. By war's end, Baltimore dominated the commerce of the entire bay.

Virginians, led by James Madison, attempted to create, through federal legislation designed to channel foreign trade to a limited number of ports, a major port in their state to compete with Baltimore. Regional rivalries in Virginia, however, crippled the effectiveness of Madison's Port Bill of 1784 and doomed his effort at state mercantilism. In the same year, George Washington and other private investors sought to improve the navigation of the Potomac River, hoping to siphon off the trade of western Maryland and northern Virginia that went to Baltimore and route it instead to ports at Georgetown and Alexandria.

Despite Baltimore's defeat in Congress over location of the national capital, the town prospered and grew in the 1790s. During this period the Scotch-Irish, German, and French merchants and tradesmen in town found themselves increasingly at odds with the Federalist administrations of Washington and Adams, with their pro-British foreign policy and the harsh Alien and Sedition Acts. By 1798 Baltimore, led by Representative Samuel Smith, was firmly in the ranks of the Republican party, and in 1800 the newly incorporated city of Baltimore helped elect Thomas Jefferson to the presidency.

During the administrations of Jefferson and Madison, Baltimore remained a Republican stronghold. However, its vocal merchant community, partisan newspaper editors, and volatile politicians frequently made the city a greater source of political difficulty for the Republican presidents than did any Federalist enclave.

As British harassment of American shipping increased, Baltimore merchants in January 1806 submitted a forceful petition to Congress, published as *Memorial of the Merchants of Baltimore, on the Violation of Our Neutral Rights*, which protested British attacks on American merchant ships. The Jefferson administration's failure to take effective action against the British angered Baltimore's merchants and their influential political spokesman, Smith. The pent-up frustration of town traders exploded onto the streets of Baltimore in June 1807 when the British warship *Leopard* attacked the American naval frigate *Chesapeake*. Citizens urged the president to make a strong response and pledged support for any action Jefferson might adopt. Jefferson's decision to pursue economic sanctions drew widespread support in Baltimore. In December 1807 Smith helped guide the Embargo legislation through the Senate.

Although Baltimore's commercial economy suffered greatly as a result of the Embargo, city merchants stood firmly behind Jefferson's policy. Continued support for the Embargo led Baltimore's Republican leaders to campaign for James Madison in 1808. Though Federalists made significant gains in Maryland's legislature that year, Baltimore voted solidly Republican. Madison rewarded the city's party faithful by appointing Robert Smith, brother of Samuel Smith, secretary of state.

Disagreements over foreign policy and political tensions between cabinet members quickly destroyed the Republican coalition that had elevated Madison to the presidency. Samuel and Robert Smith, advocating a more forceful response to continued British interference with American shipping, joined other party "invisibles" or "malcontents" to oppose Madison's program of economic coercion.

The Smith brothers were not the only critics of Madisonian policy from Baltimore. Since 1808 the Federalist party had staged a revival in the city, led by a cadre of influential lawyers and by the newspaper editors Jacob Wagner and Alexander Contee Hanson. Shrill rhetoric and vituperative personal attacks made Wagner's and Hanson's *Federal Republican*, one of the leading Federalist papers in the country, a constant source of controversy and discontent among Republicans. When the *Federal Republican* denounced the Madison administration for its decision to declare war in June 1812, furious Republicans destroyed the newspaper office. One month later, a mob attacked Hanson and a group of his Federalist compatriots while they stood defenseless in a Baltimore jail. The brutality of the assault and the apparent indifference of the city's Republican leadership to the violence appalled the nation and led to a political backlash against Republicans in Maryland.

The ignominy that the mob violence of 1812 brought upon Baltimore did not last long. Two years later, city residents redeemed themselves through their valiant defense of Baltimore against a British invasion. In September 1814, fifteen thousand troops under the able leadership of Madison's erstwhile opponent, Gen. Samuel Smith, repelled the advance of British forces fresh from their destructive assault on Washington. The retreat of British troops following the Battle of North Point and the bombardment of Fort McHenry ended the northern march of the enemy and furnished the theme for Francis Scott Key's lyrics for "The Star-spangled Banner."

BIBLIOGRAPHY

Browne, Gary L. *Baltimore in the Nation, 1789–1861.* 1980.

Cassell, Frank A. *Merchant Congressman in the Young Republic: Samuel Smith of Maryland, 1752–1839.* 1971.

Pancake, John S. "Baltimore and the Embargo, 1807–1809." *Maryland Historical Magazine* 47 (1952): 173–187.

Renzulli, L. Marx. *Maryland: The Federalist Years.* 1972.

Sheller, Tina H. "Artisans and the Evolution of Baltimore Town, 1765–1790." Ph.D. dissertation, University of Maryland, 1990.

TINA H. SHELLER

ATTACK ON FORT MCHENRY.   Fort McHenry was the major defense of the city of Baltimore. The British fleet bombarded the fort on 13 September 1814, but failed to capture it or the city. Colored aquatint by John Bower, Philadelphia, c. 1815.

PRINTS AND PHOTOGRAPHS DIVISION, LIBRARY OF CONGRESS.

BANK OF THE UNITED STATES, PHILADELPHIA. Colored line engraving by William Russell Birch, Philadelphia, 1798–1799.

BANK OF THE UNITED STATES. Two generations of Americans debated the constitutionality and the political expediency of the Bank of the United States. In the 1790s these questions split Washington's cabinet; twenty-five years later politicians of all stripes supported the bank. Both James Madison and Thomas Jefferson wavered in their support for the bank; John Marshall wrote his second most important opinion defending it. In the 1820s and 1830s Andrew Jackson and Martin Van Buren built a national political machine by attacking the financial institution they called the "monster bank."

At the Federal Convention, James Madison proposed empowering Congress "to grant charters of incorporation in cases where the Public good may require them." Charles Pinckney made a similar proposal, but neither suggestion drew support. Such a federal power was important, however, because at the time no state had enacted general incorporation laws. Later, Madison amended Benjamin Franklin's motion on canals to give the United States the authority "to grant charters of incorporation," and Edmund Randolph seconded the motion. However, Rufus King feared that Madison's motion would produce interstate conflict and lead to "the establishment of a Bank" in New York or Philadelphia. After a brief debate the convention defeated Franklin's motion, and with it Madison's amendment.

The First Bank. In 1790 Secretary of the Treasury Alexander Hamilton asked Congress to charter the Bank of the United States, to be located in Philadelphia. In his *Report Relative to a Provision for the Support of Public Credit*, Hamilton argued that a national bank was necessary for the nation's prosperity. Hamilton envisioned a government that actively participated in the economy and that created monopolies as it saw fit.

The Senate, including Rufus King, unanimously endorsed Hamilton's proposal.

In the House, Madison vigorously opposed the bank, arguing that, although a bank might be "convenient," it was not a "necessary and proper" function of the government. He concluded that it would be unconstitutional to charter the bank. Madison told the House that "a power to grant charters of incorporation had been proposed in the General [Federal] Convention and rejected." Rep. Elbridge Gerry, also a delegate to the Federal Convention, countered that, because no record of the convention was available, Madison's argument rested on "the memories of different gentlemen" that "would probably vary, as they had already done, with respect to those facts." Gerry noted that "no motion was made in that Convention, and therefore none could be rejected for establishing a National Bank." By a vote of 39 to 20, the House approved the bank.

Before signing the bill, President Washington sought the advice of three of his cabinet officers. Attorney General Edmund Randolph and Secretary of State Thomas Jefferson both opposed the bank. Reflecting Madison's views, Jefferson reminded the president "that the very power now proposed as a means, was rejected as an end, by the Convention which formed the constitution." Jefferson conceded that the bank would be convenient for the collection of taxes, but he argued that "the Constitution allows only the means which are 'necessary,' not those which may be 'convenient,' for effecting the enumerated power." He argued that "a little difference in the degree of convenience, cannot constitute the necessity which the constitution makes the ground for assuming any non-enumerated power."

Hamilton acknowledged that the Federal Convention had rejected a proposal to allow Congress to finance the construction of canals, but he claimed that neither by "authentic document, or even by accurate recollection" could anyone determine whether the convention had considered and rejected empowering Congress to incorporate banks. Hamilton asserted that, "whatever may have been the intentions of the framers of a constitution," it was "incumbent to interpret that Constitution according to the usual & established rules," which meant by a common-law analysis of the text. Hamilton argued that the government possessed "implied as well as express powers" and that the power to collect taxes and regulate trade implied congressional power to create a bank. Hamilton's arguments for a broad interpretation of the "necessary and proper" clause persuaded Washington, who then signed the bill chartering the Bank of the United States for twenty years.

In 1811 the Congress refused to recharter the bank, on public-policy grounds and because many representatives doubted the constitutionality of the bank. Thereafter, the First Bank of the United States continued to operate under a charter granted by the state of Pennsylvania but did not function as a national bank.

The Second Bank. In 1814 Congress passed legislation chartering a new national bank. President Madison vetoed this bill because he felt it inadequate for "reviving the public credit," "providing a national medium of circulation," and "aiding the Treasury" in collecting taxes. Madison explicitly "Waiv[ed] the question of the Constitutional authority of the Legislature to establish an incorporated bank as being precluded . . . by repeated recognitions under varied circumstances of the validity of such an institution in acts of the legislative, executive, and judicial branches of the Government, accompanied by indications, in different modes, of a concurrence of the general will of the nation." This suggests that Madison, the "father of the Constitution," no longer believed the intentions of the Framers could possibly govern the nation more than a quarter of a century later. Madison apparently believed the nation's frame of government was a "living Constitution."

In his annual message of 1815 Madison waved aside the charge of inconsistency and declared that "the probable operation of a national bank will merit consideration." The man who had strenuously argued against the constitutionality of the bank in 1791 and who had vetoed a bank bill in 1814, now asked Congress to create such a bank. Jefferson also retreated from his 1791 position on the bank and endorsed Madison's position.

Rep. John C. Calhoun introduced a new bank bill, and in 1816 Madison signed a bill chartering the Second Bank of the United States. In *McCulloch* v. *Maryland* (1819), Chief Justice John Marshall provided a powerful argument in favor of expansive congressional power and the bank's constitutionality. Marshall explained the meaning of the "necessary and proper clause": "This provision is made in a constitution intended to endure for ages to come, and consequently, to be adapted to the various crises of human affairs. To have prescribed the means by which government should, in all future time, execute its powers, would have been to change, entirely, the character of the instrument, and give it the properties of a legal code. It would have been an unwise attempt to provide, by immutable rules, for exigencies which, if foreseen at all, must have been seen dimly, and which can be best provided for as they occur."

In 1832 Congress passed a bill extending the charter of the bank, but President Andrew Jackson vetoed the bill. Echoing Madison's and Jefferson's 1791 opposition to the bank, Jackson conceded the bank was "in many respects convenient for the Government and useful to the people." But, he argued, convenience did not make the bank constitutional. Jackson believed the 1816 charter had been unconstitutional because the Bank had too many "powers and privileges" and was a monopoly. Jackson vetoed the Bank recharter because it was "unauthorized by the Constitution, subversive of the rights of the States, and dangerous to the liberties of the people." Vice President John C. Calhoun, who had introduced the bill chartering the Second Bank of the United in 1816, now applauded Jackson's veto. Jackson then ordered the removal from the Bank of all funds owned by the United States government. The Bank began to call in loans and restrict credit, thus setting in motion the forces that helped cause the Panic of 1837.

BIBLIOGRAPHY

Clark, M. St. Clair, and D. A. Hall. *Legislative and Documentary History of the Bank of the United States.* 1832.
Finkelman, Paul. "The Constitution and the Intentions of the Framers: The Limits of Historical Analysis." *University of Pittsburgh Law Review* 50 (1989): 349–398.
Hamilton, Alexander. *Report Relative to a Provision for the Support of Public Credit.* 1790.
Hammond, Bray. *Banks and Politics in America from the Revolution to the Civil War.* 1957.
Remini, Robert V. *Andrew Jackson and the Bank War.* 1967.

PAUL FINKELMAN

BAPTISTS. Protestant Baptists have their origins in the English Separatist movement of the early seventeenth century. Members first appeared in America in Rhode Island, where Roger Williams founded a Baptist church in 1639. In 1641 John Clarke started a church in Newport. By midcentury, Baptists had spread throughout the middle colonies. In 1707 the Philadelphia Baptist Association was formed and later founded Rhode Island College (now Brown University) to train ministers. Baptists made their first appearance in Virginia in the eighteenth century.

Both groups established roots in Virginia, but the Separates experienced persecution at the hand of the Virginia government because they would not adhere to demands that their ministers be licensed to preach. By the 1760s many Separates endured much persecution. In 1765 prominent Separate Baptist Samuel Harris preached without license in Culpeper County, where he was molested by a mob. He encountered no trouble, however, in adjoining Orange County. Colonial authorities sought to stifle the new movement by jailing Separate leaders who violated the requirement that they obtain official approval to preach.

There were two types of Baptists in the colonies. Regular Baptists, centered in the Philadelphia Association, accepted the rules of the Act of Toleration (1689), which included a requirement that non-Anglicans seek licenses to preach. Separate Baptists, products of the Great Awakening, refused to conform to traditional behavior. (The Great Awakening created a distinctly American expression of Protestantism characterized by evidences of spiritual "gifts" and enthusiasm in religious experience. This expression was in contrast with the staid, sometimes rigid worship typical of what came to be known as old-light or old-side Presbyterians and Congregationalists. Regular Baptists generally accepted this traditional outlook; the Separate Baptists believed in direct leadership by the Spirit.)

When Madison returned to Virginia from Princeton in 1772, persecution of Baptists was commonplace. Madison referred to the treatment of Baptists in a 1774 letter to William Bradford, in which he described "[t]hat diabolical Hell conceived principle of persecution" that raged nearby. It is clear from the evidence that what Madison saw in Orange and "the adjacent County" affected him for the rest of his life. His insistence upon the inclusion of the phrase "free exercise of religion" in the Virginia Declaration of Rights of 1776 certainly was a direct result of what he had seen two years earlier. Also during 1776, many Baptist petitions were sent to the Virginia Convention asking that they "be allowed to worship God in our own way."

When, in 1784, Madison, as a member of the Virginia General Assembly, led the opposition to the General Assessment Bill, which would have provided state support for teachers of the Christian religion, he was supported by the Baptists, both Regular and Separate, who flooded the legislature with memorials against the bill. One of Madison's strongest Baptist supporters was John Leland, an ardent advocate of religious freedom who served as a minister in Orange County during the decade of the eighties. As Madison moved to the national arena in 1787, his association with Baptists in Virginia remained strong. In 1788, during the debate over ratification of the U.S. Constitution, Baptist support for the proposed document grew as a result of Madison's assurances about a bill of rights.

When Madison convinced the Congress to enact a bill of rights in 1789, he was concerned about whether the states, particularly Virginia, would accept it. In November of that year he wrote to George Washington that "one of the principal leaders [Leland] of the Baptists lately sent me word that the amendments had entirely satisfied the disaffected of his Sect, and that it would appear in their subsequent conduct." In return, Baptist admiration for Madison was always high. In 1810 Baptist historian Robert Semple wrote that, in the struggle for religious freedom, Madison "will ever hold a most distinguished place."

A final chapter in the struggle for religious liberty took place when Baptists successfully urged the repeal of the law incorporating the Episcopal Church in Virginia. In 1787 Regular and Separate Baptists formed the "United

Baptist Churches of Christ, in Virginia." By 1790 the 204 Baptist churches in Virginia had more than 20,000 members, or 5 percent of the white population. Two hundred years later the Baptist Association was the largest religious denomination in the state.

[See also *Establishments of Religion.*]

BIBLIOGRAPHY

Alley, Reuben E. *A History of Baptists in Virginia.* 1973.

Hudson, Winthrop. *Religion in America.* 1987.

Hutchinson, William T., et al., eds. *The Papers of James Madison.* Vols. 1, 12. 1962–.

Semple, Robert B. *A History of the Rise and Progress of the Baptists in Virginia.* 1810.

ROBERT S. ALLEY

BARBARY STATES. Pirates from the North African states of Morocco, Algiers, Tunis, and Tripoli preyed upon American shipping between 1776 and 1816. For centuries, the Barbary pirates, sailing from ports bordering the southern Mediterranean for two thousand miles from Egypt west to the Atlantic, had terrorized European ship captains and their crews. The major European powers escaped the pirates' depredations by paying annual tributes to the rulers of the Barbary states. By the eighteenth century, France and Great Britain began to perceive the North African marauders as useful in limiting commercial access to the lucrative markets of the Mediterranean to merchants of only the wealthiest and most powerful nations. Though possessing the military power to end the piracy, they tolerated the lawlessness of the Barbary states and paid the annual tributes for protection from it.

After the United States declared its independence and was no longer under the protection of Great Britain, American shippers saw their thriving trade in the Mediterranean threatened by the attacks of Barbary pirates. In response to the demands of American merchants for protection, Congress in 1794 authorized the construction of six frigates. Before the ships could be launched, however, the dey of Algiers made a treaty with the United States. Reluctantly, Congress authorized the purchase—in ransom money, presents, large commissions, and annual tribute—of a treaty with Algeria in 1795, as well as treaties with Tripoli (1796) and Tunis (1797).

The purchased peace was short-lived. Only weeks after Jefferson assumed the presidency, the pasha of Tripoli declared war on the United States. In response, the Unit-

THE BARBARY WAR.   Attack on Tripoli in August 1804. Lithograph by Nathaniel Currier, 1846.
PRINTS AND PHOTOGRAPHS DIVISION, LIBRARY OF CONGRESS.

ed States sent a naval squadron, rather than tribute, to Tripolitan waters. For four years, American warships cruised along the Barbary coast. In 1803 Commodore Edward Preble's ships blockaded the harbor of Tripoli and harassed Tripolitan shipping and fortifications. The success of Preble's blockade, together with the threat of invasion by an army led by the American consul in Tunis, William Eaton, induced the pasha to agree to a treaty in June 1805 that abolished all annual payments from the United States, but still allowed for the ransoming of captured Americans. The first Tripolitan war represented only a partial victory for the Jefferson administration. The United States would no longer pay tribute to Tripoli, but Barbary piracy could continue. Nevertheless, the war represented a courageous display of American resolve in a region where the United States had long suffered humiliation, and Jefferson savored the victory.

Immediately after the War of 1812, the United States took decisive military action in the southern Mediterranean. After the dey of Algiers declared war on the United States in early 1815, President Madison ordered two naval squadrons under the commands of Stephen Decatur and William Bainbridge to the Barbary coast. By June 1815 Decatur had secured a treaty with the dey that ended all payment of tribute and provided for the release of all American prisoners. Soon after, Decatur obtained similar agreements with leaders in Tunis and Tripoli. The Senate ratified the Algerine treaty in December 1815. Four months later, Captain Oliver Perry arrived with the ratified treaty in Algiers, where he found the dey already dissatisfied with its provisions. The dey refused to recognize the agreement and instead wrote to Madison, suggesting that the treaty of 1795 be renewed. Madison held firm to the terms obtained by Decatur, informing Secretary of State Monroe that the United States "will make no change in the late treaty, nor concessions of any sort" to avoid war.

American determination to stand up to the duplicity of the dey received a boost in August 1816, when a combined British-Dutch fleet bombarded Algiers and destroyed the pirate vessels. Several months later, in December 1816, American negotiators returned to Algiers and obtained the dey's agreement to a modified treaty. This treaty was sent to the United States Senate in January 1817, although, because of an oversight, it was not ratified until 1822.

BIBLIOGRAPHY

Allen, Gardner W. *Our Navy and the Barbary Corsairs.* 1905.
Irwin, Ray W. *The Diplomatic Relations of the United States with the Barbary Powers, 1776–1816.* 1931.
Wright, Louis B., and Julia H. McLeod. *The First Americans in North Africa: William Eaton's Struggle for a Vigorous Policy against the Barbary Pirates, 1799–1805.* 1945.

TINA H. SHELLER

BARBOUR, THOMAS, AND THE BARBOUR FAMILY.

Thomas Barbour (1735–1825) and the Barbour family were neighbors of the Madisons, as well as their political associates on the local, state, and national levels. Thomas Barbour, a member of Orange County's ruling planter gentry, was associated for many years with James Madison and his father in Virginia politics. From 1769 to 1775 Barbour served in the House of Burgesses, where he stood consistently with other Virginia revolutionary patriots on all matters affecting colonial rights. During the Revolution he and James Madison, Sr., were leaders of the local revolutionary movement and government; as county lieutenant and sheriff, Barbour was responsible for supplying and drilling the Orange militia, collecting taxes, and upholding the law.

For almost forty years, Barbour and the senior Madison were the principal figures on the county court, where they assumed a large part of the administrative burden of running the county. This shared political responsibility, along with common political values based upon the oppositional ideology of the eighteenth-century English "Old Whig" party, promoted a close relationship between the Barbours and the Madisons. A mutual dependence, not only in politics but also in business, social, and religious matters, bound the two families together.

This closeness was strained in 1787 when Thomas Barbour came out against the United States Constitution, which James Madison, Jr., had helped to frame in Philadelphia. Objecting to the Constitution's failure to guarantee religious liberty and to the omission of a bill of rights, Barbour led the Antifederalist opposition in Orange County. He offered himself as a candidate for Virginia's ratifying convention, only to be soundly defeated by Madison. This political difference was the exception, not the rule, in the families' histories; the ties between the Madisons and the Barbours survived the post-Revolution strains and were strengthened in the early 1800s.

In time, a close political relationship developed between James Madison, Jr., and James Barbour (1775–1842), Thomas Barbour's oldest son. James Barbour and his brother Philip Pendleton Barbour (1783–1841) both achieved prominence in national politics during the nineteenth century. Philip Pendleton Barbour was elected to seven terms in Congress, serving with interruptions from 1814 to 1831. He was chosen Speaker of the House in 1821, became a prominent Jacksonian leader in Virginia during the late 1820s, and was appointed to the United States Supreme Court in 1836. James Barbour, in addition to being a powerful political leader at the state level during the presidencies of Thomas Jefferson and Madison, served three terms as governor of Virginia, represented Virginia in the United States Senate from 1814 to 1825, was secretary of war under President John Quincy Adams, and served a short term as minister to England.

James Barbour looked to James Madison as a political mentor and, as a member of the Virginia legislature and, subsequently, of the United States Senate, frequently acted as spokesman for Madison's political programs and policies. Unlike his brother Philip Pendleton, a political ideologue who totally embraced the ultraconservative tenets of Old Republicanism, James Barbour embodied the best of both the spirit and the practice of Jeffersonian democracy. He was a warm advocate of President Madison's nationalist policies after the War of 1812.

BIBLIOGRAPHY

Lowery, Charles D. *James Barbour, A Jeffersonian Republican.* 1984.
McCoy, Drew. *The Last of the Fathers: James Madison and the Republican Legacy.* 1989.

CHARLES D. LOWERY

BARCLAY, ROBERT HERIOT (1786–1837),
British naval officer. Barclay was one of three naval lieutenants appointed by Admiral Sir John Borlase Warren and sent to the Great Lakes station in April 1813. He was superseded when Sir James Lucas Yeo, appointed by the Admiralty, arrived three weeks after him. Yeo offered Barclay command of the Saint Lawrence river gunboats, but Barclay declined and was then appointed to command the Canadian Provincial Marine squadron on Lake Erie.

With Barclay at Amherstburg, on London Peninsula across the river from Detroit, in July 1813 were 7 British seamen, Captain Robert Finnis, 108 members of the Canadian Provincial Marine, 54 members of the Royal Newfoundland Fencibles, and 106 soldiers of the Forty-first Foot. They were joined by an additional 36 sailors. Barclay and the army commander at Fort Malden, General Henry Procter, were informed by Sir George Prevost, commander in chief of British forces in the Canadas, that "the ordnance and the naval stores you require must be taken from the Enemy whose resources on Lake Erie must become yours." Provisions, however, were nearly exhausted, and on 10 September 1813 Barclay sailed to open the blockaded supply route.

Barclay's six-vessel squadron, headed by the newly built *Detroit* and the *Queen Charlotte*, was much inferior to Oliver Hazard Perry's nine vessels, led by the powerful brigs *Lawrence* and *Niagara*. Barclay was outgunned in total firepower (1,536 to 887 pounds, or 57.7 percent) and in broadside (304 to 208 pounds in long guns and 632 to 288 pounds in carronades, for a total of 936 to 496 pounds, or 52.9 percent). The subsequent action was hard-fought but sloppily sailed by both sides. The battle

confirmed the command of the lake gained by Perry in August, opened the way for William Henry Harrison's invasion in October, undermined the British position in Michigan, and raised the possibility of an American expedition to the Upper Lakes in 1814, which had been part of Madison's policy since the loss of Michilimackinac and the defeat at Detroit in August 1812.

BIBLIOGRAPHY

Buckie, Robert. "'His Majesty's Flag Has Not Been Tarnished': The Role of Robert Heriot Barclay." *Journal of Erie Studies* 17, 2 (Fall 1988): 85–102.
Drake, Frederick C. "A Loss of Mastery: The British Squadron on Lake Erie, May–September, 1813." *Journal of Erie Studies* 17, 2 (Fall 1988): 47–75.
Welsh, William J., and David C. Skaggs, eds. *War on the Great Lakes: Essays Commemorating the 175th Anniversary of the Battle of Lake Erie.* 1991. Essays by Gerry Altoff, Alec Douglas, and Frederick C. Drake.

FREDERICK C. DRAKE

BARING, ALEXANDER, BARON ASHBURTON (1774–1848), British banker, financier of American enterprise. The London banking house Baring Brothers, headed from 1810 by Alexander Baring, played a conspicuous role in American public and private finance and in Anglo-American relations during the early decades of the Republic. Baring's served as bankers for the United States abroad and as brokers of investments in American business. The duc de Richelieu, Louis XVIII's minister, in 1818 described the firm as one of the "six great powers of Europe."

Alexander Baring apprenticed mainly in the wealthy Amsterdam banking house of Hope and Company, whose flight from Holland following that country's invasion by France in 1794 brought him to the United States. There he strengthened Baring's mercantile connections, married a daughter of the U.S. senator and entrepreneur William Bingham (whose vast Maine lands Baring marketed), and witnessed the debate in Congress on Jay's Treaty (1794). This experience increased his sensitivity to violations of American neutrality. After his return to England in 1804, he strove both on the board of the Bank of England (from 1805) and in Parliament (1806–1835) to remove barriers to free trade created by the British orders in council and by American reprisals. In 1808 he published a pamphlet in which he argued that the orders damaged Britain's commerce more than America's and that renewed American commercial dependence on Britain would lead to economic recovery in Britain. Baring also helped Secretary of the Treasury Albert Gallatin in negotiations leading to the purchase in 1803 by the

United States of the Louisiana Territory from France for $15 million. Baring and his partners made a fortune by buying and brokering $11.25 million of 6 percent bonds in the sale but repaid the benefaction during the War of 1812. During that conflict, the firm maintained foreign confidence in American credit and used its own funds to make interest payments to holders of U.S. bonds. Baring himself was an intermediary, especially between Gallatin and Viscount Castlereagh, in concluding the Treaty of Ghent (1814). Baring's last visit to America occurred in 1842, when he and Daniel Webster arranged the boundary-setting treaty that bears their names.

BIBLIOGRAPHY

Alberts, Robert C. *The Golden Voyage: The Life and Times of William Bingham 1752–1804*. 1969.
Walters, Raymond, Jr. *Albert Gallatin, Jeffersonian Financier and Diplomat*. 1957.
Ziegler, Philip. *The Sixth Great Power: Barings 1762–1929*. 1988.

MARTIN J. HAVRAN

BARLOW, JOEL (1754–1812), American writer, businessman, diplomat. Barlow was born in Redding, Connecticut, graduated from Yale College in 1778, and served as chaplain during the Revolution. Following a stint at newspaper publishing, he studied law and was admitted to the bar in 1785. A member of the group of political satirists known as the Hartford Wits, Barlow yearned to become a great epic poet and spent years writing *The Vision of Columbus*, which was published to great acclaim in 1787.

Poetry provided no livelihood, however, and that same year Barlow began selling Ohio land shares. In 1788 he sailed for France as sales agent for the Scioto Associates. Although the land-sale venture failed, he remained abroad for the next seventeen years, trading, observing, and supporting the changes in French government and writing on political issues. His essay in response to Edmund Burke's attack on the French Revolution, published in England and America, enhanced his reputation on both continents, while his 1792 *Address to the National Convention*, extolling the republican principles of the French Revolution, led that body to declare him a French citizen in 1793. During the Reign of Terror, Barlow and his wife moved from Paris to Hamburg, where he spent fifteen months brokering imports. He returned to France wealthy and, through the influence of his old friend David Humphreys (now minister to Portugal), was named special agent for negotiations between the United States and Algiers for the release of enslaved American sailors. Although a treaty was signed before his 1796 arrival in Algiers, Barlow stayed on to arrange fulfillment of the terms and to negotiate agreements with Tunis and

JOEL BARLOW.   Engraving by Asher B. Durand after a portrait by Robert Fulton.
PRINTS AND PHOTOGRAPHS DIVISION, LIBRARY OF CONGRESS.

Tripoli. In spite of his considerable diplomatic skills, complications impeded the settlements, and he did not return to France until 1797. He spent the next two years in Paris writing and trying to smooth relations between the United States and France during the Quasi-War.

Napoleon's 1799 coup made France less attractive to the republican expatriate, while Thomas Jefferson's 1800 election promised a more sympathetic American government, and the Barlows began to think of returning home. Although encouraged to return by Jefferson, who urged him to write a republican history of the United States, Barlow lingered in France for several more years promoting Robert Fulton's designs for submarines and steamboats. The poor health of Barlow's wife further delayed their departure, but in the summer of 1805 they returned at last to the United States, where Barlow soon renewed his friendship with Jefferson and met James Madison. He rewrote his epic, which was printed in 1807 as *The Columbiad*, then moved to Washington, where his estate, Kalorama, quickly became a gathering place for members of the administration.

After Madison was elected president, Barlow and Fulton solicited him to appoint Barlow secretary of state, but Madison refused, although he added that he still retained full confidence in Barlow. Early in 1811 Madison named Barlow minister to France to negotiate trade and spoliation differences arising out of the Napoleonic Wars. Arriving in Paris in September, Barlow pressed for the resumption of normal trade relations, restoration of seized ships and cargoes or payment for seizures, proof of revocation of the Berlin and Milan decrees, and a new commercial treaty. The French procrastinated, hoping further deterioration in Anglo-American relations would lead to hostilities between England and the United States. Negotiations dragged on through 1812 while Napoleon and his foreign minister, the duc de Bassano, pursued the Russian campaign. In November Barlow traveled to Vilna, Lithuania, to press Bassano for clearer responses to his demands, arriving just in time to witness the collapse of the French army and Napoleon's retreat from Russia. While pursuing the fleeing emperor westward, Barlow contracted pneumonia and died on 24 December 1812 at Zarnowiec, Poland.

BIBLIOGRAPHY

Brant, Irving. *James Madison.* Vol. 5. 1941.

Egan, Clifford L. *Neither Peace nor War: Franco-American Relations, 1803–1812.* 1983.

Howard, Leon. *The Connecticut Wits.* 1943.

Todd, Charles Burr. *The Life and Letters of Joel Barlow, LL.D., Poet, Statesman, Philosopher.* 1886.

Woodress, James. *A Yankee's Odyssey: The Life of Joel Barlow.* 1958.

MARY A. HACKETT

BAYARD, JAMES ASHETON, SR. (1767–1815), member of Congress. Bayard was born in Philadelphia, graduated from Princeton in 1784, read law, and in 1787 was admitted to the bar in New Castle County, Delaware. He served in the House of Representatives (1797–1803) as a Federalist. In mid February 1801, after thirty-five ballots, he broke party ranks and ended the deadlock in the presidential balloting in the House, which then elected Jefferson president. On 19 February the Senate confirmed John Adams's nomination of Bayard as U.S. minister to France, a post Bayard declined. From 15 January 1805 until 3 March 1813 Bayard represented Delaware in the Senate, first filling an unexpired term and then being elected in 1805 and 1811. Although he seldom engaged in debate, Bayard criticized Republican foreign policy in major speeches on 14 February 1809 and on 16 June 1812. In the latter he defended his motion to postpone a vote on the declaration of war against Great Britain until 31 October, asserting that "neither the Government, nor the people had expected, or were prepared for war." Such a delay would allow American merchantmen time to return safely,

REP. JAMES A. BAYARD.   Spots on the portrait result from discoloration (called foxing) in the original print.
PRINTS AND PHOTOGRAPHS DIVISION, LIBRARY OF CONGRESS.

while winter storms would hinder British naval action against the "defenceless" American coast. Admitting that America had legitimate grievances against British maritime policy, Bayard criticized Republicans for tolerating French depredations. The Senate defeated Bayard's motion. Seeking political balance, in April 1813 Madison appointed Bayard as one of five peace commissioners. Bayard signed the Treaty of Ghent, but declined Madison's appointment as U.S. minister to Russia. His health failed, and Bayard returned to the United States, barely alive, in August 1815.

BIBLIOGRAPHY

Borden, Morton. *The Federalism of James A. Bayard.* 1955.

CHARLES H. SCHOENLEBER

BECKLEY, JOHN (1757–1807), first Librarian of Congress, first clerk of the U.S. House of Representatives, an organizer of the national Republican party. At the age of eleven, John Beckley was brought from England to Virginia to be trained as a scribe in the office of the clerk of Gloucester County. From that time on he was almost constantly employed in public service. As the American Revolution created new institutions and new opportunities, Beckley's zeal for the cause of self-government and his high professional competence brought him numerous appointments, including clerk to the Virginia Senate in 1777 and to the House of Delegates in 1779.

In 1787, he went to Philadelphia hoping to be elected secretary of the Federal Convention. In Philadelphia he stayed at the house of Elizabeth Trist, where James Madison also boarded. He lost this election, but when the new federal government was established in 1789, with Madison's support he won election as clerk of the U.S. House of Representatives.

Along with Madison, Beckley soon became alarmed by the policies of Secretary of the Treasury Alexander Hamilton, and they took the lead in organizing a congressional opposition that became the Republican party. In 1796 Beckley managed the makeshift presidential campaign for Thomas Jefferson, and from then on he developed a network of correspondence with Republican leaders in key states.

In retribution for Beckley's support of Jefferson, the victorious Federalists managed to prevent Beckley's reelection as clerk of the House in March 1797. In that same year, Beckley was responsible for the public exposure of Alexander Hamilton's adulterous affair with a Philadelphia matron. Beckley stayed in Philadelphia, where he continued his partisan activities and played a critical role in organizing Jefferson's victory in the election of 1800.

In December 1801 Beckley was once again elected clerk of the House. In February 1802 Jefferson appointed him the first librarian of Congress. Beckley favored James Monroe, rather than Madison, to succeed Jefferson as president, but his illness and eventual death kept him from playing an active role in the campaign.

BIBLIOGRAPHY

Berkeley, Edmund, and Dorothy Smith Berkeley. *John Beckley: Zealous Partisan in a Nation Divided.* 1973.

Malone, Dumas. *Jefferson and His Time.* Vol. 6. *Jefferson and the Ordeal of Liberty.* 1962.

STEVEN H. HOCHMAN

BEDFORD, GUNNING, JR. (1747–1812), lawyer, federal judge. Bedford was born in Philadelphia and attended Princeton, graduating in 1771 in the same class as James Madison. He read law, was admitted to the bar in 1774, moved to Delaware in 1779, and was that state's attorney general from 1779 to 1789. Elected to the Continental Congress in February 1783, Bedford served on the committee on officers' pay and voted with Madison to commute the half pay for life to full

GUNNING BEDFORD. Portrait by Charles Willson Peale. PRINTS AND PHOTOGRAPHS DIVISION, LIBRARY OF CONGRESS.

pay for five years. Both men voted for the comprehensive revenue package of 1783, although they disagreed over some of its specific elements. On 20 June 1783 Bedford alienated Madison and other Virginia delegates by proposing a qualified acceptance of Virginia's cession of western lands that would have limited the amount of land granted to the Virginia soldiers who had fought with George Rogers Clark.

At the Federal Convention in 1787 Bedford favored a three-year presidential term (with a nine-year limit) and opposed giving Congress the power to nullify state laws, arguing that such power would enable the large states to "crush the small ones." On 30 June, acting under a specific charge in his legislative appointment, he vehemently demanded equal representation for all states in Congress, threatening that the small states might have to seek protection from "some foreign ally" if the large states continued to mistreat the small ones. Madison responded on 5 July by affirming his belief that Delaware would not seek "her fortunes apart from the other States" if the new government was "founded on just principles." Apologizing for his lack of moderation, Bedford qualified his earlier remarks, suggesting that the small states "would not consider the federal compact as dissolved untill it should be so by the acts of the large States," at which time foreign nations having financial demands on the country "would find it their interest to take the small States by the hand, in order to do themselves justice." Bedford signed the Constitution and voted to ratify it in the Delaware convention in December 1787. He served as U.S. district judge for Delaware from 1789 until his death.

BIBLIOGRAPHY

Harrison, Richard A., ed. *Princetonians, 1769–1775: A Biographical Dictionary*. 1980.

CHARLES H. SCHOENLEBER

BERKELEY, GEORGE CRANFIELD

BERKELEY, GEORGE CRANFIELD (1753–1818), British naval officer. George Cranfield, fourth earl of Berkeley, entered the Royal Navy in 1766. In November 1805, Berkeley, by now a vice admiral, took command of the Halifax station, where he was in command during the notorious *Chesapeake-Leopard* incident. Berkeley instructed Captain Salusbury Humphries to search for and take British sailors recruited by the Americans off *Chesapeake*, by force if necessary, for trial and punishment. HMS *Leopard* halted *Chesapeake* just outside the Virginia Capes and demanded to search the vessel, even though she, like *Leopard*, was a public ship of war. When James Barron, commodore of the Mediterranean Squadron, as senior officer, refused this indignity, Humphreys opened fire on the unprepared *Chesapeake*. Barron's ship fired one gun, struck colors, and the British took out four men thought to be British. When Barron attempted to surrender his ship, Humphreys refused his sword and departed for Halifax. President Jefferson could have had war at that moment had he wished to exploit the situation. Instead, a long drawn out negotiation commenced, not resolved until 1811. Berkeley's inflexible orders, obediently carried out by Humphreys, resulted in lingering enmity for the British among many American naval officers. Barron was court martialed and suspended from the Navy, for failing to prepare his ship for battle on the probability of an engagement. Humphreys was disciplined, placed on half-pay, and deprived of further sea commands. Berkeley suffered little for this incident. The *Chesapeake-Leopard* incident is usually considered a major cause of the War of 1812.

Berkeley was recalled from North America and posted to command on the coast of Portugal. In 1810, he was advanced to the rank of admiral and in 1812 returned to England and retired from the service. He died on 25 February 1818.

[See also *Chesapeake-Leopard Affair*.]

BIBLIOGRAPHY

Laughton J. K. "Berkeley, George Cranfield." *Dictionary of National Biography*. 1885.
Perkins, Bradford., *Prologue to War: England and the United States, 1805–1812*. 1961.

WILLIAM S. DUDLEY

BIDDLE, NICHOLAS (1786–1844), litterateur, editor, and public banker. Scion of a prominent Philadelphia Quaker family, Biddle entered the University of Pennsylvania at the age of ten and graduated as covaledictorian from Princeton at fifteen. Although he studied law, his real interests lay in poetry and writing. An avid reader, he joined the Tuesday Club, whose members issued the *Port Folio*, America's first literary magazine. Biddle also prepared for publication the manuscripts of Meriwether Lewis and William Clark; *History of the Expedition* appeared in 1814.

Although from a strong Federalist family, Biddle was secretary to the Republican minister to France, John

NICHOLAS BIDDLE.
PRINTS AND PHOTOGRAPHS DIVISION, LIBRARY OF CONGRESS.

Armstrong (1804–1806), and to James Monroe in London (1806–1807). He supported Monroe against James Madison in 1808. He broke fully with Federalism when, as state senator in 1815, he wrote the Pennsylvania Assembly's refutation of the report of the Hartford Convention. Monroe appointed him a director of the second Bank of the United States in 1819 and he became president of the bank in 1822. Biddle never understood the widespread public and agrarian antipathy toward this giant, urban, semipublic institution. His decision in 1832 to seek recharter, even though the Bank had four years to live, was a mistake. Andrew Jackson's presidential veto launched a monumental bank war, which destroyed the nation's constitutional responsibility to manage its currency and finances. Biddle stayed on as president of a reorganized state bank of the United States until 1839.

BIBLIOGRAPHY

Govan, Thomas Payne. *Nicholas Biddle: Nationalist and Public Banker, 1786–1844.* 1959.
Hammond, Bray. *Banks and Politics in America from the Revolution to the Civil War.* 1957.

HARRY W. FRITZ

BILL OF RIGHTS. At the Federal Convention, Madison voted against a motion to preface the Constitution with a bill of rights. Returning to the Continental Congress in New York, he was dismayed by the effort of Richard Henry Lee to amend the Constitution by adding a bill of rights adapted from Virginia's constitution. Madison led the fight to defeat Lee's amendments, which he saw as a means of sabotaging the Constitution. Any amendments made by Congress would require the unanimous vote of the state legislatures, rather than approval by nine state ratifying conventions. The "inexpediency" and confusion of procedures allowed Madison's views to prevail without consideration of the substantive merits of Lee's proposals. About a month later, Madison wrote a seventeen-page letter to Jefferson in Paris, reporting his views on the Constitution. Much of the letter later was incorporated into Madison's essays in *The Federalist*. At the time the subject of a bill of rights scarcely interested him. His only reference to it was in his comment that George Mason considered the "want of a Bill of Rights as a fatal objection" and that Lee had proposed congressional amendments along lines suggested by Mason.

That Madison had not seriously considered a bill of rights is evident from his contributions to *The Federalist*. In *Federalist* 38, reviewing objections to the Constitution, he asked, "Is a bill of rights essential to liberty?" and summarily answered, "The Confederation has no bill of rights." The answer was deceptive, because the Congress

of the proposed government had greater powers than the Congress of the Confederation and, unlike its predecessor, could act directly on individuals. In *Federalist* 44 he examined state violations of "personal security and private rights" without considering why "additional fences against these dangers" should not be erected against the United States as well as against the states. In *Federalist* 48 he discussed checks on legislative and executive violations of power without even referring to a bill of rights except for an incidental disparagement of "parchment barriers." Clearly, Madison had heavy scales on his eyes, for he could not see that many people feared the new government, not because it would deprive the states of rights, but because it might deprive citizens of theirs.

The Antifederalist Challenge. By the spring of 1788, however, Madison had learned to distinguish between those, like Patrick Henry, who sought to repudiate the Constitution by capitalizing on its lack of a bill of rights and those, like the Baptist preacher Elder John Leland, who favored a stronger union but genuinely feared that a government based on a document that could protect against religious tests without protecting religious liberty was a potential danger. Henry was most effective with the theme, "Don't ratify. They're taking away your liberties!" When George Nicholas advised Madison that the Massachusetts precedent of ratification with recommended subsequent amendments offered the best hope for obtaining Virginia's approval of the Constitution, Madison agreed. A promise of amendments might appease popular fears and stymie an Antifederalist movement for a second constitutional convention, which might prove fatal to a stronger union.

At the Virginia ratifying convention in June 1788, Madison was forced to think about a bill of rights for the first time. Patrick Henry thundered against ratification because freedom of religion would be "prostituted" by the new government. Madison offered several proofs that Henry was wrong. First, he argued, the new government would have no jurisdiction over religion: "There is not the shadow of a right in the general government to intermeddle with religion." Second, a bill of rights was unnecessary to protect freedom of religion because it existed as a result of the multiplicity of sects. Madison maintained that if a majority of the people were of one sect, a bill of rights would not prevent an exclusive establishment of religion. Finally, Madison said, although a bill of rights might enumerate certain rights, such an enumeration might be construed to imply that any rights not enumerated were lost. "If an enumeration be made of our rights," Madison said, "will it not be implied that everything omitted is given to the general government?" He thought that "an imperfect enumeration" was "dangerous."

The Constitution, in fact, contained an imperfect enu-

THE BILL OF RIGHTS.   Twelve articles amending the Constitution were adopted by Congress in September 1789 and submitted to the states for ratification. Article 1 was rejected; article 2 became the Twenty-seventh Amendment in 1992. Articles 3 through 12 became the first ten amendments to the Constitution (the Bill of Rights) in December 1791. [See text of the articles in appendix.]

NATIONAL ARCHIVES AND RECORDS SERVICE.

meration of rights by prohibiting religious tests for office, bills of attainder, and ex post facto laws; providing for trial by jury in criminal cases; forbidding titles of nobility; offering a narrow definition of treason; and protecting the writ of habeas corpus. By Madison's logic, all the omitted rights, including those that he would later call "the great rights of mankind," were by implication lost or subject to the powers of the general government. He believed—and never wavered in the belief—that the rights of the people depended less on parchment provisions than on public opinion, an extended republic, a federal system, a pluralistic society of competing interests, and a national government of limited powers structured to prevent any interest from becoming an overbearing majority. He also believed the Constitution was structured to prevent any branch of government from exercising a power that could jeopardize liberty.

In the closing days of the Virginia convention, Madison argued down Henry's attempt to persuade the state ratifying convention to condition approval of the Constitution on previous crippling amendments. To win wavering votes, Madison successfully urged that the Constitution be ratified with such amendments as might be recommended to the First Federal Congress. A committee then recommended a detailed bill of rights for Congress's consideration.

In mid October 1788 Madison answered a letter from Jefferson, who had criticized the absence of a bill of rights. Madison said he had "always" favored a bill of rights so long as it did not concede to the government powers not included in the enumeration. But, he admitted, he never thought the omission to be "a material defect" and did not view a bill of rights "in an important light." He still believed that the government lacked powers to infringe basic rights and that an imperfect enumeration of rights placed those unenumerated in danger. Moreover, he doubted whether rights could be defined with a "requisite latitude." Finally, experience had shown that in times of crisis majorities repeatedly violated "parchment barriers." Madison believed that the only value of a bill of rights in a popular government was to articulate principles that would serve as political truths and educate the people and inhibit majority impulses by raising standards for self-control.

Within months, Madison realized that statecraft and political expediency both dictated a firmer commitment to a bill of rights. His own political position in Virginia was seriously deteriorating. The Antifederalists, who controlled the state legislature, elected two of their number to the U.S. Senate and then gerrymandered Madison's own congressional district in order to exclude him from the House. When he realized he might lose the election because people believed that he opposed a bill of

rights, Madison advised Baptist leaders that he sincerely believed that the First Federal Congress should submit to the states amendments safeguarding "all essential rights, particularly the rights of Conscience in the fullest latitude, the freedom of the press, trials by jury, security against general warrants &c." With Baptist support Madison narrowly won the election. At last he was committed to a bill of rights.

Four states (including his own) had called for a second constitutional convention, whose purpose Madison feared would be to "mutilate the system." To energize confidence in the government and give it a chance to operate, the new government would have to allay people's anxieties. Madison realized that a bill of rights would win popular support and isolate those Antifederalists whose objective was subversion of the Union. Once a bill of rights was adopted, eliminating popular fears, no chance would remain for divisive subversion. By redeeming his campaign pledge, Madison saw that he would strengthen the Union.

A letter from Jefferson, which arrived in late May 1788, fortified his resolve to win over an uninterested Congress. Many Federalists thought that the House had more important tasks, such as the enactment of tonnage duties and a judiciary bill. The opposition party understood that the adoption of a bill of rights would undermine its chance to obtain amendments that would weaken the powers of the government. Antifederalists did everything possible to obstruct Madison's proposals. They began by stalling, then tried to annex amendments aggrandizing state powers, and finally deprecated the importance of the very safeguards of personal liberty that they had previously demanded. Madison would not be deterred. He was patient, insistent, unyielding, and ultimately triumphant. His accomplishment in the face of militant opposition and apathy entitles him to be remembered as Father of the Bill of Rights.

Madison's Proposal. On 8 June 1789 he spoke in the House, delivering his long, imperishable speech recommending amendments. All government power, he contended, is subject to abuse and should be guarded against by constitutionally securing "the great rights of mankind." Although the government possessed only limited powers, it might, unless prohibited, abuse its discretion by its choice of means under the necessary and proper clause; it might, for example, use general warrants to enforce its revenue laws. The objective was to limit all branches of the government, not just the executive as in Great Britain, thereby preventing tyranny by "the body of the people, operating by the majority against the minority."

Madison responded to the argument that a bill of rights was unnecessary because the states already provided constitutionally protected freedom. Some states, he observed, had no bills of rights, others "very defective ones." Moreover, the states constituted a greater menace to liberty than the national government. Accordingly, he urged an amendment providing that "no State shall violate the equal rights of conscience, or the freedom of the press, or the trial by jury in criminal cases." Although Madison defended this amendment as "the most valuable amendment in the whole list," it was defeated in the Senate.

To the contention that a mention of some rights would endanger those not enumerated, Madison replied that the danger should be guarded against by what became the Ninth Amendment. He also argued that a bill of rights would allow courts to become "the guardians of those rights" because they would be "naturally led to resist every encroachment upon rights expressly stipulated for in the constitution by a declaration of rights." Although Madison regarded his measures as a bill of rights, he recommended that each provision be incorporated at an appropriate point within the original Constitution, rather than being clustered together as an appendage.

Madison's speech stirred little immediate support. Every speaker who followed, regardless of party affiliation, either opposed his recommendations or believed the House should attend to more important matters. Six weeks later Madison "begged" for a consideration of his amendments. Eventually, he won. In the midst of the drafting of the Bill of Rights, Madison explained privately why he was so committed to "the nauseous project of amendments," a reference to the unremitting hostility that he had provoked. Coolly he explained that the amendments were necessary to beat the Antifederalists at their own game. If Federalists did not support the amendments, Antifederalists would claim that they had been right all along and gain support for a second convention. The amendments, Madison wrote, "will kill the opposition everywhere" and allow the government to operate effectively. He had, in fact, upstaged and defeated the Antifederalists. Sen. Richard Henry Lee reported to Patrick Henry that the idea of subsequent amendments in the form of a bill of rights "was little better than putting oneself to death." On the other hand, and ironically, Madison lost his effort to incorporate the rights at various points within the Constitution. Members thought the document should remain as its Framers drafted it and that the matter of form was so "trifling" that the House should not waste its time debating the placement of the various amendments. Thus, because opponents in both parties sought to downgrade the importance of the amendments, they were lumped together and added to the Constitution as separate articles.

Madison's achievement consisted, not only in the adoption of the amendments, but in the way he stamped them with his own creativity. Every state constitution protect-

ing the freedom of the press said it "ought" not be violated; Madison changed that flabby verb to the imperative "shall." No state had a due-process-of-law clause in its constitution, and only one had recommended such a safeguard. Madison did not have to include it. On search and seizure, he might have proposed merely that the United States would not enforce its laws by searches and seizures that violated the laws of the states, most of which still allowed general warrants, or he might have emulated Virginia's provision by saying that general warrants ought not be granted. Facing a variety of minimal options, anyone of which would have been politically adequate, Madison chose the maximum protection conceivable at the time, describing a right of the people to be free from unreasonable searches and seizures, and he virtually invented the "probable cause" provision for the issuance of warrants. Instead of saying that a person could not be compelled to give evidence against himself, the common formulation, he recommended that no person should be compelled to be a witness against himself, a broader phrasing. He enumerated several rights that were uncommon. Only one state provided against double jeopardy, and only two guaranteed compensation for private property taken for a public use. Madison also devised the Ninth Amendment to protect unenumerated rights. His personal touch invested the amendments with a breadth and variety that far transcended the mere necessity to discharge a political pledge. Statecraft as well as politics characterized the work of the Father of the Bill of Rights.

[See also *Antifederalists; Constitution Making; Twenty-seventh Amendment.*]

BIBLIOGRAPHY

Brant, Irving. *The Bill of Rights: Its Origin and Meaning.* 1965.
Levy, Leonard W. *Original Intent and the Framers' Constitution.* 1988.
Rutland, Robert A. *The Birth of the Bill of Rights.* 1991.
Schwartz, Bernard. *The Great Rights of Mankind: A History of the American Bill of Rights.* 1977

LEONARD W. LEVY

BIOGRAPHIES OF JAMES MADISON. Biographers of Madison have generally focused on his public career, rather than on his personality, character, and private life. Such an emphasis is in large part unavoidable. Diminutive in stature and reserved, even self-effacing, in his presentation of himself to others, Madison was anything but colorful, hardly the stuff of folklore or storytelling in his own time. Like so many eighteenth-century figures, he also jealously guarded his privacy from the prying eyes of posterity. He wanted later generations to know what he had said and done as a statesman, not the details of his private experience, and he organized and preserved his papers accordingly. As a recent biographer, Jack N. Rakove, has aptly summarized the point, "it is the public man alone whom we can know with any confidence." The private Madison remains an elusive figure.

Madison's first biographer, and the only one to have known him personally, was his political disciple William Cabell Rives. Rives's partial life of Madison, covering his career through the middle of the 1790s in three volumes, is of little value to modern scholars, in part because it tells readers more about Rives than about Madison. Written during the Civil War era, Rives's biography reeks of bitter nostalgia, offering a protracted lament for Madison's lost eighteenth-century world of neoclassical, hierarchical republicanism allegedly swept away by the tidal waves of Jacksonian democracy. Actually, Rives had a generally sound, if somewhat overdramatized, appreciation of the character and texture of Madison's republicanism; having known the man personally, he was able to understand and suggest that Madison's personal character was a telling manifestation of the political culture he had participated in. For all its faults, including a ponderous and pretentious style, this first biography thus offers a unique and sometimes interesting approach to Madison in spite of its flaws.

Madison has been adequately, if not exceptionally well, served by more scholarly twentieth-century biographers. By far the most thorough is Irving Brant, whose six-volume treatment, published over a twenty-year period in the middle of the century, remains the standard secondary source for anyone interested in the details of Madison's lengthy career. Brant's volumes are written in a lively, engaging style, offering a comprehensive account of Madison's public and private lives. Brant was overly sympathetic to his subject, whom he hoped to rescue from obscurity, and his portrait is therefore uncritical and flattering. Brant also made an extended, and ultimately controversial, interpretive case for the depth and consistency of Madison's nationalism. Although many scholars have dissented from Brant on specific points of interpretation, his prodigious research greatly facilitated, and perhaps made possible, the efforts of subsequent biographers to depict Madison's life on a smaller scale.

Readers can now choose from among a number of solid one-volume biographies, ranging from Ralph Ketcham's relatively long, 671-page treatment to Rakove's leaner, 181-page survey. Two other recent biographers worthy of note have attempted to get to the heart of Madison's career by emphasizing its personal side and by focusing on specific periods of his life. Robert Rutland's biography begins with Madison's immersion in the struggle to ratify the Constitution, while Drew R. McCoy uses Madison's long retirement as a vehicle for exploring the inter-dependence of the public and private dimensions of his republican experience.

[See also *Rives, William Cabell.*]

BIBLIOGRAPHY

Brant, Irving. *James Madison.* 6 vols. 1941–1961.
Ketcham, Ralph. *James Madison: A Biography.* 1971.
McCoy, Drew R. *The Last of the Fathers: James Madison and the Republican Legacy.* 1989.
Rakove, Jack N. *James Madison and the Creation of the American Republic.* 1990.
Rives, William C. *History of the Life and Times of James Madison.* 3 vols. 1859–1868.
Rutland, Robert A. *James Madison: The Founding Father.* 1987.

DREW R. McCOY

BLADENSBURG, BATTLE OF. The Battle of Bladensburg was the most humiliating defeat suffered by the United States during the War of 1812. Fought on 24 August 1814 in the Maryland countryside, the battle was significant because it enabled the British to occupy and burn the nation's capital.

Having been freed from their European commitments by Napoleon's defeat and abdication in the spring of 1814, the British launched an offensive in the Chesapeake the following summer. Commanding the British forces were Gen. Robert Ross and Adm. Alexander Cochrane. Also assisting in the operations was Adm. George Cockburn, who knew the area because he had overseen predatory raids there the previous year.

Although the threat was manifest, American officials did little to prepare the nation's capital for defense. Secretary of War John Armstrong was convinced that Washington would never be attacked, and other officials were also slow to perceive the danger. Not until 1 July did President Madison create a special military district embracing Washington and put Gen. William Winder in charge of its defense. A political general who was overwhelmed by the task before him, Winder frittered his time away traveling through the countryside inspecting the terrain.

After sailing up the Patuxent River, the British landed 4,500 men at Benedict, Maryland, on 19–20 August. The troops reached Upper Marlboro on 22 August. By this time American officials realized the capital's peril and began frantically putting the city in a state of defense. Additional militia were called out, joined by some regulars as well as about five hundred sailors and marines under Commodore Joshua Barney.

The American force—perhaps seven thousand troops in all—was arrayed in three lines facing the eastern branch of the Potomac River. The third line was too far away to support the first two, and Secretary of State James

Monroe (who had no authority in the matter) redeployed the troops so that the second line could not support the first. The president arrived on the scene just before the battle began and very nearly rode into the approaching British columns.

About 1:00 P.M. on 24 August, just as the last militia took their places, Ross appeared with the British army on the opposite side of the Potomac. The defenders had neglected to destroy the bridge (the water was shallow enough to ford anyway), and first one British brigade and then another got across the river. The British outflanked the first American line, forcing it to fall back. Just as the British were attacking the second line, Winder—who appeared to be confused from the outset—ordered it to fall back. The withdrawal turned into a rout—immortalized in song and poetry as "the Bladensburg races."

Only Joshua Barney's sailors, who anchored the third line, held firm, tearing into the advancing British units with grapeshot from their heavy naval guns. The British routed the militia protecting Barney's flank and then took Barney's position by storm. By 4:00 P.M. the battle was over. The United States had suffered only 70 casualties, while the British had sustained 250.

By the time the battle had ended, most people—soldiers, officials, and residents alike—had fled from Washington. The British marched into the capital that night and under Cockburn's direction torched most of the public buildings. The occupation of the American capital was the high-water mark for the British during the War of 1812. For the United States, on the other hand, the defeat at Bladensburg and the destruction of the capital was a humiliating experience. Madison was subjected to much criticism, and Armstrong was compelled to resign from the cabinet.

BIBLIOGRAPHY

Lord, Walter. *The Dawn's Early Light.* 1972.
Mahon, John K. *The War of 1812.* 1972.
Williams, John S. *History of the Invasion and Capture of Washington.* 1857.

DONALD R. HICKEY

BLAND, THEODORICK (1742–1790), physician, delegate to the Second Continental Congress, United States representative. Born in Prince George County, Virginia, the son of Theodorick Bland and Frances Bolling, Bland went as a youth to Great Britain to be educated. Graduating from Edinburgh University in 1763 with the M.D. degree, he returned home the next year and practiced for barely a decade before retiring to his tobacco plantation, Farmingdale.

During the 1770s, Bland ardently defended colonial rights. When Lord Dunmore, the royal governor, seized

REP. THEODORICK BLAND.
PRINTS AND PHOTOGRAPHS DIVISION, LIBRARY OF CONGRESS.

the powder and arms from the public magazine in Williamsburg, Bland was among the small party of patriots who, on 24 June 1775, forcibly removed weapons from the governor's palace. When war began, he was appointed captain of the First Troop of Virginia Cavalry and, after 1778, served as colonel of the First Continental Dragoons, which fought the British forces across New Jersey and Pennsylvania.

In 1781 Bland was elected to the Second Continental Congress, where for three years he was a political thorn in James Madison's flesh. Described by critical contemporaries as a vain and impudent braggart, Bland frequently tried to upstage Madison in Congress and seemed to relish the role of political antagonist. In 1783, following an unsuccessful bid for president of Congress, Bland resigned his seat. He returned to politics in 1786 by serving two terms in the Virginia legislature. At the 1788 Virginia ratifying convention, Bland joined Patrick Henry and other Antifederalists in opposing the Constitution Madison had helped to draft. Elected to the First Congress under the new government, the cross-grained Antifederalist continued his obstructionist ways. To Madison's chagrin, Bland alone among the Virginia delegation supported Alexander Hamilton's plan for the federal government's assumption of state debts. He died on 1 June 1790 during the great influenza epidemic that swept New York City and before the final vote on the plan.

BIBLIOGRAPHY

Bickford, Charlene B., and Kenneth R. Bowling. *Birth of the Nation: The First Federal Congress, 1789–1791.* 1989.
Biographical Directory of American Congresses. 1989.
Campbell, Charles. *The Bland Papers.* 2 vols. 1840.

CHARLES D. LOWERY

BLOCKADES BY FRANCE AND ENGLAND.

During the French revolutionary and Napoleonic wars (1793–1815), Great Britain and France both employed blockades to deprive each other of the benefits of neutral trade. Under international law, it was generally recognized that a belligerent nation had to give neutral powers official notice of a blockade and had to maintain a naval force at the blockaded port that could actually threaten vessels entering or leaving the port. Both Great Britain and France frequently violated these rules, and as a result American merchants suffered extensive losses.

Though there were some violations of the rules of blockade in the 1790s, the most serious occurred after the turn of the century. With Great Britain paramount on the high seas after the Battle of Trafalgar (1804) and France supreme on the European continent after its triumph at Austerlitz (1805), each nation saw economic warfare as a means of striking at the enemy and enriching itself at the expense of neutrals. This species of warfare involved the use of "paper blockades"—blockades that were illegal because they were not adequately enforced and often not adequately publicized.

The first round in the war of the blockades was the Fox Blockade of northern Europe, which was proclaimed by Great Britain in an order in council issued in 1806. France retaliated with the Continental decrees, proclaiming a blockade of the British Isles and threatening to seize any neutral vessel that traded with Britain or even allowed itself to be searched by British officials. The British responded with additional orders in council that established a blockade of all continental ports under French control.

Both powers conceded that they lacked the naval power to enforce such extensive blockades, but each claimed that it was only retaliating for the illegal acts of the other. Both sides also used the trade war as a pretext for looting neutral commerce. The British seized neutral ships on the high seas, while the French (whose navy was bottled up in port) confiscated neutral vessels after they reached the continent.

Although the British and French decrees appeared to render any trade with Europe impossible, there were numerous loopholes that enterprising merchants could exploit. Moreover, New Englanders claimed that the profits were so great that they could make money even if only one ship in three got through. Nevertheless, the losses under the British and French regulations were heavy. Between 1807 and 1812 the two belligerents and their allies seized about nine hundred American vessels.

The repeal of the belligerent decrees became the overriding objective of American foreign policy in the years from 1807 to 1812. The United States sought to achieve this goal by adopting a series of commercial sanctions aimed at Britain and France and their colonies. Known as the restrictive system, these measures were largely the inspiration of Secretary of State James Madison. Although the restrictive system failed to elicit any concessions from the belligerents, in 1810 French officials pretended to repeal the Continental decrees, and thereafter Madison (who was now president) focused the nation's wrath on Great Britain.

The British orders in council generated an enormous amount of criticism in the United States and became the leading cause of the War of 1812. President Madison focused almost exclusively on this issue in November 1811 when he recommended that Congress prepare for war, and in his war message seven months later he again criticized Britain for adopting "pretended blockades," particularly "the sweeping system of blockades, under the name of Orders in Council." Although the British announced the suspension of the orders in council on 16 June 1812—two days before the United States declared war—it took weeks for this news to reach the United States. By then the die was cast, and the United States would not call off the war without further concessions.

[See also *Continental System; Orders in Council.*]

BIBLIOGRAPHY

Perkins, Bradford. *Prologue to War: England and the United States, 1805–1812.* 1961.
Phillips, W. Allison, and Arthur H. Reede. *Neutrality: Its History, Economics, and Law: The Napoleonic Period.* 1936.
Savage, Carlton. *Policy of the United States toward Maritime Commerce in War.* 1934–1936.

DONALD R. HICKEY

BLOUNT, WILLIE

(1768–1835), lawyer, jurist, legislator, governor of Tennessee. Willie (pronounced Wiley) Blount, born in Bertie County, North Carolina, was the son of Jacob Blount and his second wife, Hannah Salter Baker Blount. The half-brother of William Blount, territorial governor of Tennessee, Willie Blount was educated at Princeton and Columbia and then read law with a North Carolina judge. In 1790 he moved to Tennessee to serve as William Blount's private secretary. In 1794 he was licensed to practice law and in 1796 was elected a superior court judge. The next year he was elected to serve in the state legislature. In 1802 Blount married Lucinda Baker, also from Bertie County, and the couple raised their own two daughters as well as William's younger children.

Willie Blount was elected governor of Tennessee in 1809 and reelected in 1811 and again in 1813. Like most frontier governors, he supported internal improvements and development and settlement, and made an effort at Indian removal.

Blount's most significant contribution as governor was his strong support for Andrew Jackson during the Creek Indian War and the War of 1812. He recognized the importance of Jackson's military operation and provided him with all available money and men. He recommended the general highly to the secretary of war in Washington, and, without Blount's support, Jackson might not have enjoyed as much success. One set of events that occurred during Blount's governorship were the 1811 earthquakes that created Reelfoot Lake.

As required by Tennessee's constitution, Blount retired from the governorship after his third consecutive term. He ran again for the office in 1827, only to be defeated by Sam Houston, and in 1834 he was a member of the Tennessee constitutional convention. He spent the years from 1815 until his death in 1835 at his home near Clarksville in Montgomery County, some forty miles north of Nashville.

BIBLIOGRAPHY

Folmsbee, Stanley J., Robert E. Corlew, and Enoch L. Mitchell. *Tennessee: A Short History.* 1969.
Masterson, William H. *William Blount.* 1954.
Phillips, Margaret I. *The Governors of Tennessee.* 1978.

FRANK LAWRENCE OWSLEY, JR.

BONUS BILL. In February 1817, the Fourteenth Congress passed a bill pledging the "bonus" due to the government from the new national bank to a fund for improving the nation's roads and canals. Although it raised a controversial question—could Congress build roads and canals in the states?—the Bonus Bill capped a long effort by Jeffersonian Republicans to address the problem of national internal improvements within the limits of their orthodox principles of strict constitutional construction.

The problem simply was this: some of the new republic's most promising transportation improvements required so much money and interstate cooperation that only Congress seemed competent to sponsor them. Congress enjoyed no explicit power to build public works, and Republicans were loath to assume one under the doctrine of broad constitutional interpretation. Yet extraordinary growth and burgeoning westward migration threatened to tear the Union apart before the development of integrating networks of communication might effectively bind it together. In 1805 Jefferson called for funding of internal improvements (including a constitutional amendment enlarging federal authority). In 1808 Treasury Secretary Albert Gallatin produced a comprehensive plan for a national system of roads and canals, suggesting ways to begin work at once even if an amendment proved necessary (which he doubted). James Madison appeared to share Gallatin's enthusiasm for internal improvements and also his doubts about Jefferson's amendment. Therefore, in 1816, when President Madison accepted Congress's new national bank and protective tariff, observers assumed that internal improvements must naturally follow.

The Bonus Bill proposed no specific improvements but established a fund from which Congress later could appropriate aid to national works. Hostile amendments diverted money to the states (rather than to designated projects) and required state legislative consent (which amounted to local veto power). Thus crippled, the bill was unlikely to accomplish its original objectives, yet its sponsors, Henry Clay and John C. Calhoun, pressed for its adoption. Thinking they had laid at least a cornerstone on which to build Gallatin's system, Clay and Calhoun were stunned on 2 March 1817 when Madison vetoed the Bonus Bill.

In his veto message, Madison explained that existing precedents (however distasteful) sustained the second national bank, but further "latitude of construction" threatened the "definite partitions" between the "General and State Governments." Although construction projects were not among the enumerated powers of Congress, roads and canals clearly were useful, necessary, and popular, and it would be no problem to secure an amendment enlarging federal authority. Certain the work would go forward once the power was obtained, Madison focused on the two-tiered structure of American government. What Madison feared most in the Bonus Bill was the effort by politicians, in the name of popular majorities tempted by national pork-barrel feasts, to stretch the limits of the Constitution through ordinary legislation. Neither the balance of power among federal branches nor the functional limits on national jurisdiction could long withstand the assault of Congresses emboldened by the passions of the people. Faced with democratization in politics, the nation's foremost expert on the dangers of interested majorities threw up the barricades once more to preserve the balance that made the American government "partly federal and partly national."

Madison's veto astonished Republican advocates of internal improvement, who had labored in vain for years to regain the initiative. The veto transferred political advantage to obstructionists in the states who resisted every enlargement of federal power; Madison's scruples destroyed an objective he clearly supported. In the end, his defense of limited national power, intended to prevent congressional majorities from trampling diverse interests within the Union, restored energy to the states rights advocates that his Constitution was designed to restrain.

BIBLIOGRAPHY

Larson, John Lauritz. "'Bind the Republic Together': The National Union and the Struggle for a System of Internal Improvements." *Journal of American History* 74 (1987): 363–387.
McCoy, Drew R. *The Last of the Fathers: James Madison and the Republican Legacy.* 1989.

JOHN LAURITZ LARSON

BOSTON.

Founded in 1630 Boston is one of the oldest towns in America. The economy of the town was tied to overseas and coastwise trade. More than one-third of all American tonnage was owned in Massachusetts. In the revolutionary period, Boston was the economic and political center of New England. By 1800 its population had reached nearly 25,000 people.

Politically, Boston was a Federalist stronghold. Dominated by the Federalist party and the Congregational Church, Boston was a conservative stronghold. Jefferson's embargo of 1807 struck at the heart of the town's economy and Federalist leaders incited the town meeting to declare that those who obeyed the act were "enemies of the people." The replacement of the Embargo with Madison's nonintercourse policy provided only a slight respite to the town and did little to weaken its resentment toward the Republican administration in Washington. Despite political turbulence, however, the town continued to grow. By 1810 the population had risen to 33,000. Although still primarily a trading town by the eve of the War of 1812, the value of manufactured goods in Boston had grown to nearly $10,000,000 annually.

Although it was a seaport, during the war Boston was never threatened by the British navy because local merchants were sympathetic to the British, and in fact, many carried on an illegal trade with the enemy. During the Revolution, Boston had fitted out several hundred privateers, but in the War of 1812 she sent fewer than 100 to sea, a clear indication of the sentiments in the town. Because most trade was closed during the war, a good deal of local capital that otherwise would have been directed toward maritime commerce was turned toward other investments, particularly textiles. On the other hand, Boston financiers all but ignored urgent pleas for government loans in 1812–1813. By 1814 the value of manufactures had risen to nearly $15,000,000, and in that same year Uriah Cotting organized the Roxbury Mill Company to provide water power for the town. After the War of 1812, Boston's economy recovered but her place as a leading port was taken by New York. Boston's population continued to grow, reaching 43,000 in 1820.

[See also *Embargo Act of 1807; New England; Nonintercourse Acts; War of 1812.*]

BIBLIOGRAPHY

Kirker, Harold, and James Kirker. *Bulfinch's Boston, 1787–1817.* 1964.
Whitehill, Walter M. *Boston: A Topographical History.* 1959.
Winsor, Justin, ed. *The Memorial History of Boston, Including Suffolk County, Massachusetts, 1630–1880.* 4 vols. 1880–1881.

WILLIAM M. FOWLER, JR.

BOWDOIN, JAMES

(1752–1811), merchant, diplomat. Born in Boston, the only son of Massachusetts Governor James Bowdoin II, James Bowdoin III graduated from Harvard in 1771, made two trips to England, and briefly attended Christ Church, Oxford. He returned to America in 1775 and found his country at war, but did not serve in the army, probably because of poor health. Untrained in the law and uninterested in the clergy, Bowdoin followed family tradition and joined his father's prospering mercantile firm.

Bowdoin entered public life when he was elected to the Massachusetts legislature in 1786, where he served until 1790. He was also a delegate at the 1788 Massachusetts ratifying convention. The political warfare that erupted over the Jay Treaty probably led to Bowdoin's defection from the Federalists to the Republican party. Bowdoin supported Thomas Jefferson when he sought the presidency in 1800. Perhaps Bowdoin became a Republican because he resented the undue influence of Great Britain in Federalist councils, and tariff laws that favored British goods which at times glutted the American market. In 1804 the president appointed him as the American minister to Spain.

Weakened by illness, possibly tuberculosis, Bowdoin reached Spain to find Spanish-American relations so precarious that he decided not to proceed to Madrid. (Bowdoin had commissioned Gilbert Stuart to paint portraits of Jefferson and Madison. They were most likely intended to be hung in the American ministry in Madrid, but were eventually bequeathed to Bowdoin College.) Instead, he traveled to Paris and met with the American minister to France, John Armstrong, to discuss hopes of a negotiated settlement on the nagging Florida boundary question.

Caught between Armstrong's arrogance and Napoleon's shiftiness, Bowdoin made little headway as a diplomat but did acquire a large collection of books and paintings. His health continued to decline and he returned to America in 1808 with little accomplished for his years spent abroad.

Before his death, Bowdoin gave funds and land holdings for the creation of a college, named in honor of his father, in the Maine district of Massachusetts.

BIBLIOGRAPHY

No full-length biography of Bowdoin exists, perhaps owing to the dispersion of his papers and their paucity. The largest collections are in the Hawthorne-Longfellow Library, Bowdoin College Library, Brunswick, Maine, and the Massachusetts Historical Society, Boston. There is much useful information in Marvin S. Sadik, *Colonial and Federal Portraits at Bowdoin College* (1966), and Richard H. Saunders III, "James Bowdoin III," in *The Legacy of James Bowdoin III* (1994).

ROBERT A. RUTLAND

BRACKENRIDGE, HUGH HENRY (1748–1816), writer, jurist. Transplanted to York County, Pennsylvania, from Scotland at the age of five, Brackenridge quickly showed an aptitude for learning that eventually enabled him to enter the College of New Jersey at Princeton. There he became close friends with Madison, and the two, along with Philip Freneau and William Bradford, in 1769 established the Whig Society, a collegiate club that engaged in a battle of wits with the rival Cliosophic Society. There are indications that, after their graduation in 1771, Madison and Brackenridge continued to correspond while the latter wrote poetry and worked as a schoolmaster and clergyman. During the American Revolution Brackenridge served as a chaplain in the Continental army and employed his pen in the revolutionary cause.

In 1778 Brackenridge began to read law, taking time out the next year to start the *United States Magazine* in Philadelphia, a venture that failed before the year was out. He was more successful as a polemicist and, following in Thomas Paine's footsteps, was employed by the French minister in Philadelphia to write pro-French propaganda. In 1780 he moved to Pittsburgh to practice law and to give scope to his political ambitions, and, within a few years, he became influential in western Pennsylvania politics, serving in the state legislature and helping to establish the first frontier newspaper, *The Pittsburgh Gazette*. He was a strong supporter of the Constitution but later aligned himself with Republicans critical of the Federalist-dominated national government and, like Madison, contributed partisan essays to Freneau's *National Gazette* in 1791 and 1792.

In 1800 Brackenridge's political support for the Republican party was rewarded with his appointment to the Pennsylvania Supreme Court, and his reputation as a judge was enhanced by the publication of his *Law Miscellanies* in 1814. Although he wrote poems, plays, and histories, he is probably best known for his novel *Modern Chivalry*, parts of which first appeared in 1792 but which Brackenridge continued to revise until 1815.

BIBLIOGRAPHY

Harrison, Richard A. *Princetonians, 1769–1775: A Biographical Dictionary.* 1980.
Marder, Daniel. *Hugh Henry Brackenridge.* 1967.

DAVID B. MATTERN

HUGH HENRY BRACKENRIDGE.   Illustration from *Duyckinck's Cyclopedia of American Literature.*
PRINTS AND PHOTOGRAPHS DIVISION, LIBRARY OF CONGRESS.

BRADFORD, WILLIAM (1755–1795), friend of Madison, attorney general of Pennsylvania, attorney general of the United States. Bradford earned his B.A. in 1772 and his M.A. in 1775, both from the College of New Jersey (now Princeton University). He enlisted as a private in the Continental army in 1776 and rose to the rank of colonel before ill health forced him to resign in 1779. He became attorney general of Pennsylvania in 1782. In 1794, by then a staunch Federalist and joined by marriage to the influential Boudinot family, he accepted appointment

WILLIAM BRADFORD.   Stipple engraving by David Edwin.
PRINTS AND PHOTOGRAPHS DIVISION, LIBRARY OF CONGRESS.

as attorney general of the United States from President Washington. He died in office in the summer of 1795.

Bradford and Madison were close friends in their days at Princeton. Upon returning to Virginia in 1772, Madison entered into extended correspondence with his friend; eighteen letters or copies of letters from each man dating from 1772 to 1776 are extant. From 1773 through 1776, Bradford was perhaps Madison's only correspondent. The men shared their hopes and vocational aspirations. In letters of 1773 and 1774 Madison first expressed in writing his thoughts on liberty of conscience and first demonstrated his growing interest in politics. Madison visited his friend in Philadelphia in 1774. Apart from this exchange of ideas and feelings, there exists no first-hand information concerning Madison's thoughts and knowledge relating to the crucial political events that took place prior to 1776.

Few letters between the friends exist from later years. Madison's last known letter to Bradford was written in the fall of 1779; in it, Madison suggested that Bradford visit Virginia as a means of treating the ill health that had forced him to resign his military commission. The friendship appears to have been maintained over the succeeding fifteen years.

BIBLIOGRAPHY

Hutchinson, William T., et al., eds. *The Papers of James Madison.* Vol. 1. 1962.
Ketcham, Ralph. *James Madison.* 1990.

ROBERT S. ALLEY

BRADLEY, STEPHEN ROW (1754–1830), jurist, U.S. senator. Born in Cheshire, Connecticut, Bradley graduated from Yale College in 1775 and served during the Revolution as a captain of volunteers, an aide-de-camp to Gen. Isaac Wooster, and a camp commissary. In 1779, after studying law with Judge Tapping Reeve at Reeve's famous school in Litchfield, Connecticut, Bradley moved to the New Hampshire Grants, which would soon become the state of Vermont. That same year he was chosen one of five agents to present Vermont's case for independence to the Continental Congress, and in 1780 he wrote a manifesto, *Vermont's Appeal to the Candid and Impartial World,* arguing for the district's right to statehood. For seven years he represented the town of Westminster in the Vermont Assembly and then was appointed judge of the Vermont Supreme Court in 1788 and brigadier general of the militia in 1791.

With Vermont's admission to the Union in 1791, Bradley began his career in the U.S. Senate. He served a four-year term, failed to win reelection in 1794, and was again elected in 1801, serving until his retirement in 1813. Bradley was a leading Republican member, chairing the Republican presidential caucuses of 1804 and 1808 and serving as president pro tempore of the Senate in 1802–1803 and 1808. But he was a Republican of independent mind, one of the Republican "malcontents" who opposed Jefferson's and Madison's administrations on several key issues, including the Pickering and Chase impeachments, the appropriation of funds for the purchase of Florida, the nomination of William Short as minister to Russia, and the motion to occupy East Florida. His opposition to the war measures of the Madison administration led to his retirement from the Senate in 1813. He returned to Westminster, Vermont, and then, in 1818, moved to Walpole, New Hampshire, where he lived until his death.

BIBLIOGRAPHY

Adams, Henry. *History of the United States of America during the Administrations of Thomas Jefferson and James Madison.* 2 vols. 1986.
Johnson, Allen, ed. *Dictionary of American Biography.* 1928.
Stagg, J. C. A. *Mr. Madison's War: Politics, Diplomacy, and Warfare in the Early American Republic, 1783–1830.* 1983.

DAVID B. MATTERN

BRITISH NORTH AMERICA. When James Madison became president, British North American comprised six provinces—Upper and Lower Canada, New Brunswick, Prince Edward Island, Nova Scotia, and Newfoundland, with a combined population of approximately 300,000. French and Anglo-Saxons who immigrated to Canada after 1763 (many of the latter loyalists) constituted the principal ethnic groups. The Maritimes most resembled the new nation to the south in character and retained close ties to New England, but British military and civil officials as well as loyalist elites rejected republicanism and feared American influence. Borderland societies knit by localism, kinship, and trade straddled the ill-defined boundary from the Atlantic to the Great Lakes basin.

Contemporary sources reveal considerable ignorance and ambiguity among Americans about the provinces. Americans saw the provinces in many lights over time: as British bases, as sources of competition and opportunity, and as places of refuge and settlement. But throughout the years of the early republic few Americans wanted to incorporate the provinces into the United States, and then only at moments of Anglo-American crisis.

In 1784 James Monroe suggested passive subversion—efforts to make Canadians jealous of American liberties, while avoiding an aggressive policy. In 1811 and 1812 newspapers, among them the *National Intelligencer* and the *New England Palladium*, published articles on the provinces because of the likelihood of war between the United States and Great Britain. The *Military Monitor*, founded to record the war, was another source from which Americans could glean information about their northern neighbors.

Madison had only vague notions about the provinces beyond their obvious status as British possessions and their commercial and strategic resources. He wanted to bar British Indian traders from American territory and for that reason urged a fixed boundary reaching to Lake of the Woods. He also knew that borderland smugglers were subverting his economic policies; in the John Henry affair, Madison falsely believed that documents he had purchased would expose the provinces as a base for subversive activities. Montreal struck him as strategically important, but more as a vital trading center for the fur trade than as a military nexus.

In 1811–1812 military Republicans, such as Henry Clay, argued that the Canadian provinces would easily succumb to an American invasion. Canada did not figure in Madison's war message in June 1812, but New England Federalists and the vocal Tertium Quids, who claimed to embody pure republican values, seized upon any reference to the provinces to denounce Madison's war of conquest. Some within the administration wanted to eject the British from North America, but when Madison told Albert Gallatin that the United States must hold Canada "as a hostage for peace & justice," he implied a willingness to trade captured territory for diplomatic concessions.

Modern historians, despite some Canadian views to the contrary, generally agree that the provinces were a target, a strategic objective only. American borderlanders feared hostilities in 1812, but most southerners saw no value in acquisition of the provinces, while New Englanders refused even to recapture Castine, Maine, from the British. The military stalemate, except in the strategically marginal far west, gave American diplomats in Ghent no leverage, so they followed instructions and accepted a peace on the status quo ante bellum.

Invasion and destruction left strong anti-American feelings in a new generation of Canadian leaders and persuaded British authorities to bolster population and defenses in the provinces. Ordinary Canadians, on the other hand, rebuilt personal and economic links with the northern states. The St. Croix Valley was self-declared neutral ground during the war and thereafter became in effect an American-Canadian economic unit. An interlocked transportation network evolved on the Great Lakes even as surveyors fixed the boundary between the United States and Canada. American consuls established themselves in Canadian ports from 1830 on. The border was never undefended while Madison lived, but most Americans expected their northern neighbors to continue as part of a separate society within the British Empire. Some chauvinistic Americans apparently believed the Canadians would eventually petition for entry into the Union.

BIBLIOGRAPHY

Errington, Jane. *The Lion, the Eagle, and Upper Canada: A Developing Colonial Ideology.* 1987.

Heriot, George. *Travels through the Canadas.* 1971.

Manning, William R., ed. *Diplomatic Correspondence of the United States: Canadian Relations.* Vol. 1. 1940.

Smith, Michael. *Geographical View of the British Possessions in North America.* 1814.

Stagg, J. C. A. "James Madison and the Coercion of Great Britain: Canada, the West Indies, and the War of 1812." *William and Mary Quarterly*, 3d ser., 38 (January 1981): 3–34.

REGINALD C. STUART

BROCK, ISAAC (1769–1812), British general. Brock was born on the Isle of Guernsey on 6 October 1769. At fifteen, he bought a commission as an ensign in the British army, and in 1790 he purchased a lieutenancy and served with distinction in Jamaica and Barbados. At twenty-eight he purchased a lieutenant colonelcy, and he fought with honor in Europe between 1799 and 1801. In

GEN. ISAAC BROCK.
PRINTS AND PHOTOGRAPHS DIVISION, LIBRARY OF CONGRESS.

his case the British system of promotion by purchase advanced an exceptionally competent officer.

In 1802 Brock's regiment, the Fortieth Foot, was sent to Canada, where Brock remained, except for one year, the remainder of his life. He became a major general in 1810 and in October 1811 was named administrator and military commander of Upper Canada. Meeting the legislature and dealing with the people, he came to doubt the loyalty of many citizens of the province.

While dining at Fort George on the Canadian side of the Niagara Pines with American officers on 25 June 1812, he learned that Britain and the United States were at war. Since there were only 1,200 regulars scattered west of the Ottawa River, plus eleven thousand untrained and ill-equipped militia, Brock sought Indian help. He lacked the temperament for passive defense, but his superior, Sir George Prevost, cautioned him against any involvement with Indians that might unite the United States behind the war effort. Movement of the western-most American army released Brock from restraint. He was at York with the legislature when he learned that Brig. Gen. William Hull had marched to Detroit with two thousand men. By capturing the *Cuyahoga*, which was carrying Hull's papers across Lake Erie, he learned the details of Hull's mission. Hull was at the end of a precarious supply line, threatened by Tecumseh's Indians and by

British ships on the lake. Desperately needed supplies were waiting at the River Raisin, thirty miles away, but in two battles the Indians prevented access to them.

Traveling in small boats with three hundred men, Brock reached Amherstburg at midnight on 12 August. American forces dispatched by Hull to try to reach the supplies were on his flanks; Fort Detroit, with forty cannons and a large garrison, was on his front. Earlier, he had told Prevost that the fort was too strong to be taken by assault, so his object was to lure Hull's army into the open to fight. Brock took the initiative. On 14 August, uninterrupted by Hull, he planted five cannons bearing on the fort. The next day he sent a summons to surrender to the American general. "The numerous body of Indians," he wrote, ". . . will be beyond control the moment the contest commences." When Hull refused to surrender, the five cannons began a brisk bombardment. On 16 August Brock crossed the Detroit River with 330 regulars, four hundred militia, and six hundred Indians. The cannonade continued, creating some bloodshed within the fort. To Brock's surprise, a white flag appeared, and, after an hour of negotiation, Hull surrendered, including all forces within the district. Thanks to his own superb daring and to the incompetence of the enemy, Brock had cleared the western theater of American power. His fame rests on this decisive victory.

Returning to the Niagara theater, full of optimism, Brock wrote that, if permitted, he could clear the Americans out of that area. Permission was denied, however, and the initiative shifted to the enemy. Brock was wakened early on 12 October by the roar of battle to the south. He sent eight hundred men under Maj. Gen. Roger Sheaffe toward the action, but he himself galloped off, as well. American forces had scaled the cliff behind Queenston and now occupied the plateau 310 feet above the town. Brock rallied some men by the river and rushed to the plateau. A tall man wearing a red tunic, he led an attack. An American scout, firing from cover, killed him instantly. That afternoon Sheaffe arrived with his eight hundred men and won the battle. Brock, who ought to have marched with the main body, was dead at forty-four.

BIBLIOGRAPHY

Dictionary of National Biography. 22 vols. 1917–.
Hitsman, J. Mackay. *The Incredible War of 1812: A Military History.* 1965.
Stanley, George F. G. *The War of 1812: Land Operations.* 1983.

JOHN MAHON

BROWN, JACOB JENNINGS

BROWN, JACOB JENNINGS (1775–1828), soldier, general in chief of the U.S. Army. Born of Quaker parents in Bucks County, Pennsylvania, Brown was educated in private schools. Entering business, he acquired a large amount of land in western New York on Lake Ontario, where he founded Brownsville. A natural leader, he became a regimental commander of militia in 1809, and in 1811 he was appointed a brigadier general. When the War of 1812 began, he attracted attention by his successful defense of Sackets Harbor in May 1813, where, with a small group of regulars and undisciplined militia, he repelled a superior British force. He was rewarded with a regular commission in July 1813. Whether Secretary of War John Armstrong or President Madison was responsible for the promotion is unclear. Apparently Armstrong deserves credit for first suggesting Brown, but Madison actually placed Brown on the list.

Brown served under Maj. Gen. James Wilkinson in the aborted campaign against Montreal in late 1813. After Wilkinson was dismissed and the other ranking officer on the northern frontier, Maj. Gen. Wade Hampton, resigned, Brown took command of the Niagara frontier. In early July 1814 he aggressively carried the campaign across the Niagara River with about 3,500 regulars trained by Brig. Gen. Winfield Scott. After besieging Fort Erie at the south end of the Niagara peninsula and forcing the British garrison there to surrender, Brown moved north and encountered the main force of the British army at the Chippewa River. In the battle that ensued, American troops, led primarily by Scott and his well-trained regulars, drove the British from the field. Brown was unable to assault Fort George at the north end of the Niagara peninsula because the American fleet operating on Lake Ontario failed to cooperate. Brown fought a major battle in late July against a reinforced British army at Lundy's Lane, near Niagara Falls. After a desperate battle that resulted in high casualties on both sides and after both Brown and Scott were wounded and the command devolved on Brig. Gen. Eleazar Ripley, the Americans were compelled to disengage and withdrew to the safety of Fort Erie.

Brown was able to resume command in September, and he immediately launched an attack on the British forces besieging Fort Erie, driving them away. The campaign ended after the Americans withdrew from Fort Erie late in the fall of 1814. President Madison and Secretary of War James Monroe intended to name Brown as commander of the invading force into Canada in 1815, but the war's end made these plans moot. Nevertheless, American troops had shown that under proper leadership they could stand up to the best regular troops in the British army, and Brown was awarded a medal by Congress for his heroism in the Niagara campaign.

After the war, Brown was called by President Madison to Washington to help supervise the reduction of the army and to set up the peacetime military establishment. Promoted to major general, Brown was appointed to command the Northern Division; Maj. Gen. Andrew Jackson was given command of the Southern Division. When the army was further reduced in 1821 and Jackson resigned, Brown was named general in chief and was assigned to Washington. Despite small budgets and the general hostility toward standing armies that prevailed in Congress, Brown maintained a high level of professionalism in the army until his death in 1828.

BIBLIOGRAPHY

Cruikshank, Ernest, ed. *The Documentary History of the Campaign on the Niagara Peninsula.* Repr. 4 vols. 1971.
Hickey, Donald R. *The War of 1812: A Forgotten Conflict.* 1989.
Hoard, Gerald C. *Major General Jacob Brown.* 1979.
Spaulding, Thomas Marshall. "Jacob Jennings Brown." *Dictionary of American Biography.* Vol. 3. Edited by Allan Johnson. 1929.

C. EDWARD SKEEN

GEN. JACOB JENNINGS BROWN.   Stipple engraving by T. Gimbrede of a portrait by J. Wood.
PRINTS AND PHOTOGRAPHS DIVISION, LIBRARY OF CONGRESS.

BUFFALO, NEW YORK. In 1812 Buffalo was a small port on Lake Erie, the home base of Rep. Peter B. Porter (later a New York militia brigadier general) and of the firm of Porter, Barton and Company, which shipped goods to Detroit, Fort Dearborn, and other lakeshore communities. The town became an army base for Brig. Gen. Alexander Smyth's 1,650 regulars in September 1812 and served as a supply base for the U.S. Lake Erie squadron. Five schooners sailed from Black Rock to join Oliver Hazard Perry at Erie, Pennsylvania, in June 1813.

As a reprisal for New York General George McClure's burning of Newark and much of Queenston on 10 December 1813 before his retreat across the Niagara River, Sir Gordon Drummond mounted a winter campaign with one thousand British regulars and four hundred Indians. Drummond's forces captured Fort Niagara on 18 December and destroyed Lewiston, Youngstown, the Indian village of Tuscarora, Fort Schlosser, and Manchester before stopping at Tonawanda Creek. Eleven days later Sir Phineas Riall and his unit routed Gen. Amos Hall's force of two thousand men, which shrank to 1,200 just before a spirited battle near Black Rock. Hall's depleted force was pushed through Buffalo and on 30 December Black Rock and Buffalo were burned, along with two schooners, a sloop, the public buildings, and massive stores of military supplies. The British suffered 112 casualties, and the American forces, 76. Lewis Cass described Buffalo a week later: "A scene of distress and destruction such as I have never before witnessed."

Buffalo remained undefended until Brig. Gen. Winfield Scott began drilling his division there. After Maj. Gen. Jacob Brown's Niagara campaign (July–September 1814), Maj. Gen. George Izard took command and set up winter quarters in Buffalo after retiring from Fort Erie.

BIBLIOGRAPHY

Cruikshank, Ernest A. *Documentary History of the Campaign upon the Niagara Frontier.* Vol. 9. 1908.

Cruikshank, Ernest A. *Drummond's Winter Campaign, 1813.* 2d ed. 1900.

Graves, Donald E. "Winfield Scott's Camp at Buffalo in 1814." In *War along the Niagara: Essays on the War of 1812 and Its Legacy.* Edited by Arthur Bowler. 1991.

Stanley, George. *The War of 1812: Land Operations.* 1983.

Wood, William, ed. *Select British Documents of the Canadian War of 1812.* Vol. 3, part 1. 1926. Part 2. 1928.

FREDERICK C. DRAKE

BURR, AARON (1756–1836), New York political leader, U.S. senator, vice president of the United States, military adventurer. Burr's parents were Aaron Burr, second president of the College of New Jersey (later Princeton) and Esther Edwards, daughter of the eminent cleric Jonathan Edwards. Orphaned at an early age, Burr was reared by relatives and graduated from Princeton (where he met fellow student Madison) at sixteen. Short of

stature but vivacious and handsome, Burr started toward a ministerial career but switched to the study of law. As a young soldier in the Revolution he served in the Quebec campaign and was on the staffs of Benedict Arnold and Washington. He left the army in 1779, started a law practice in New York, and married a widow ten years his senior, Theodosia Prevost.

Burr took naturally to the polarized political climate in New York and was soon allied with Gov. George Clinton, determined to thwart the plans of Alexander Hamilton and his many family connections. After serving a term as attorney general in New York, Burr was elected as a Republican to the U.S. Senate and served from 1791 to 1797 as a loyal party man but without distinction. During this period Burr befriended Madison and even arranged for his introduction in 1794 to the young widow, Dolley Payne Todd, who soon became Madison's wife.

After he lost his Senate seat, Burr was elected to the state legislature, but public disclosure of his many vested interests in banking and land speculations led to his defeat for reelection.

Burr soon had higher office in mind. When the New York Republican caucus met to choose a candidate for the 1800 presidential election, Jefferson's bid for the top place was recognized, but through clever machinations Burr obtained the party's endorsement for the vice presidency. Much correspondence between the leading Republicans in New York, Pennsylvania, and Virginia followed; Madison joined in the campaign to win southern

AARON BURR.   Engraving by J. A. O'Neill after a portrait by John Vanderlyn.
PRINTS AND PHOTOGRAPHS DIVISION, LIBRARY OF CONGRESS.

support for Burr over John Adams and thus ensure victory for a Jefferson-Burr ticket. But their plans miscarried, with the result that in the electoral college balloting Burr was tied with Jefferson, 73 to 73, and the presidential election was thrown into the House of Representatives.

Although Burr denied that he was interested in the presidency, his subsequent actions were those of an ambitious, if not an ambivalent, man. He never sought to change any votes and thus break the tie created by his henchmen. Jefferson and Madison thought Burr was not candid, and it was only after a single Federalist vote switched on the thirty-sixth ballot that Jefferson was elected.

Under the Constitution, Burr became vice president in 1801, but he never regained Jefferson's confidence, and his national career in the Republican party was ruined. Even before Burr's ruling in the Senate prevented the impeachment conviction of the Federalist judge Samuel Chase, Jefferson had already decided to replace Burr on the ticket in 1804. In February of that year the congressional caucus chose Jefferson for the presidential nomination and named George Clinton as his running mate.

Burr accepted the situation and returned to New York to enter the gubernatorial race; a scurrilous campaign ended in his defeat. Smarting from his long-standing feud with Hamilton, Burr demanded that Hamilton apologize for some campaign insinuations and finally challenged Hamilton to a duel. Hamilton was fatally wounded in the duel, and Burr was indicted for murder in both New York and New Jersey in the summer of 1804, but he returned to Washington and presided over the Senate until his term expired in 1805. His farewell speech deeply affected many senators.

The remainder of Burr's life was hounded by tragedy. His harebrained scheme to create a western empire carved out of Spanish holdings in North America led him into collusion with Gen. James Wilkinson and produced only repeated frustrations. Wilkinson turned on Burr and was arrested, sent to Richmond, and tried there for treason in a court presided over by Chief Justice John Marshall. Marshall's ruling on the constitutional interpretation of treason led to Burr's acquittal, but Burr's triumph was short-lived. In 1808 he moved to Europe in search of financial backing for his western scheme (he even suggested France might regain Canada), but foreign governments were cool to his proposal, and he had trouble obtaining a passport to return home.

In 1812 Burr was back in New York, where he attempted to practice law, but a much-publicized divorce case (he had married a wealthy widow and spent money lavishly) left his reputation in tatters. Meanwhile his beloved daughter, Theodosia, had died in a shipwreck off Cape Hatteras.

Both Madison and Burr died in 1836—one mourned by the nation he had helped shape, and the other, discredited.

BIBLIOGRAPHY

Kline, Mary-Jo, ed. *The Political Correspondence and Public Papers of Aaron Burr*. 2 vols. 1983.
Lomask, Milton. *Aaron Burr*. 1979.
Schachner, Nathan. *Aaron Burr: A Biography*. 1961.

ROBERT A. RUTLAND

C

CABINET. On the whole, President James Madison's cabinets were among the weakest in American history. Although there were some bright spots, and although Madison himself took great pains both in selecting and in working with his cabinet, incompetence, indifference, disloyalty, and misplaced egotism contributed to the uneven picture of the Madison presidency.

Assembling a Cabinet. Madison began by making such use as he could of Jefferson's cabinet, in which he had served for eight years. He retained Jefferson's attorney general, Caesar A. Rodney of Delaware, an able lawyer and a zealous Republican. The post, however, was considered only part-time (the federal government faced few lawsuits then), so Rodney retained his private practice in Wilmington and was away from Washington for weeks and even months at a time. Jefferson's secretary of war, Gen. Henry Dearborn, was eased out and given the important (and lucrative) post of collector of the port of Boston, leaving open his cabinet position. Also open was the post of secretary of state, formerly held by Madison himself. The other two members of Jefferson's cabinet, Secretary of the Treasury Albert Gallatin and Secretary of the Navy Robert Smith, were retained by Madison, but for very different reasons.

The key appointment was that of secretary of state. Gallatin, Madison's able, trusted, and highly valued colleague in republicanism in Congress during the Federalist years and then for eight years in Jefferson's cabinet, was the logical choice. With foreign affairs dominating the scene during the climactic years of the Napoleonic Wars, Madison wanted to have Gallatin at his right hand in the State Department. Factionalism within the Republican party, however, thwarted the plan. A powerful group in the Senate, claiming to be the true Republicans and led by Sen. Samuel Smith of Maryland (brother of Robert Smith), sought to impose its will on the president and

had a particular animosity toward Gallatin. One of the group, Sen. W. B. Giles of Virginia, himself coveted the State Department post, and Sen. Smith wanted the position for his brother. The so-called Invisibles mustered enough support in the Senate to block Gallatin's nomination to the State Department post, so Madison's only recourse was to have Gallatin continue at the Treasury Department (which did not require Senate confirmation). Madison enjoyed the company of the affable, generous Robert Smith, but Smith was widely acknowledged to be lazy and largely ignorant of foreign affairs. Madison nonetheless agreed reluctantly to appoint him to the State Department in hopes of softening the hostility of Senator Smith and his faction in Congress. Madison realized that he would have to be his own secretary of state, down to writing the dispatches that could not be entrusted to the inept Robert Smith.

Political necessity also dictated weak appointments in the War and Navy departments. To replace Dearborn, Madison appointed a congenial New Englander, Dr. William Eustis, who had no apparent qualifications for the post except for being a loyal Republican and the son-in-law of the Republican patriarch of New Hampshire, John Langdon. Madison achieved further obligatory sectional balance by appointing the unobjectionable (but unqualified) former governor of South Carolina, Paul Hamilton, as secretary of the navy. Thus Madison began his administration with four remarkably inept or unavailable cabinet colleagues and one extraordinarily able but politically controversial member in a post neither he nor the president preferred for him.

The situation soon deteriorated, as Gallatin had predicted it would. The Senate Invisibles and their newspaper accomplices kept up a steady attack on the omnicompetent Gallatin and asserted their views directly in the cabinet through Robert Smith. With persistent dis-

Madison's Vice Presidents and Cabinet Officers, 1809–1817

Vice President	State	Treasury	War	Navy	Attorney General	Postmaster General
George Clinton, 1809–1812	Robert Smith, 1809–1811	Albert Gallatin, 1809–1814	William Eustis, 1809–1812	Paul Hamilton, 1809–1812	Caesar A. Rodney, 1809–1811	Gideon Granger, 1809–1814
	James Monroe, 1811–1817				William Pinkney, 1811–1814	
Elbridge Gerry, 1813–1817			John Armstrong, 1813–1814	William Jones, 1813–1814		
		George W. Campbell, 1814	James Monroe, 1814–1815		Richard Rush, 1814–1817	Return J. Meigs, Jr., 1814–1817
		Alexander J. Dallas, 1814–1816				
			William H. Crawford, 1815–1816	Benjamin W. Crowninshield, 1815–1817		
		William H. Crawford, 1816–1817				

loyalty, indiscretion, and incompetence, Smith so disrupted cabinet meetings that Gallatin threatened to resign unless Smith was replaced. At the same time, although Madison's own drafting of diplomatic messages masked Smith's inabilities in that regard, Smith's foolish and disloyal remarks to French and British ministers in Washington repeatedly undermined delicate negotiations. Finally, in April 1811, with a congressional recess allowing him to make lengthy interim appointments, Madison resolved to fire Smith. In painful and hostile meetings the president confronted the secretary, accused him of disloyalty and incompetence, and asked him to resign. Smith bristled and threatened to use his political influence to destroy Madison's presidency. Madison, perhaps hoping to avoid all-out war in the party, offered Smith a face-saving appointment as minister to St. Petersburg. Instead, Smith asked for appointment to the embassy in London, or perhaps to the Supreme Court. Regarding him as utterly unqualified for such important posts, Madison refused. An angry Smith departed.

Actually, Madison had been preparing for the inevitable dismissal of Smith by seeking reconciliation with James Monroe, a longtime friend and valued colleague from whom he had become temporarily estranged because of differences over Monroe's diplomacy in London in 1806–1807 and because of Monroe's hesitant challenge to Madison in the presidential election of 1808. Assured that Monroe would be receptive, Madison offered him the State Department, and Monroe, ambitious and eager to be part of the government again, accepted. Because this shift also mollified Gallatin, Madison found his cabinet strengthened by Monroe's presence, as the crisis of relations with France and Great Britain reached a climax. The replacement in December 1811 of Attorney General Rodney by William Pinkney, a loyal and able Maryland lawyer and diplomat, added further luster to the Madison cabinet.

The War Cabinet. The declaration of war on Great Britain in June 1812, with the consequent heavy demands on the War and Navy departments, required changes in their inept leadership. Military disasters at Detroit and in New York State revealed Secretary Eustis's utter incompetence: he fussed in his Washington office over supplies of shoes and hats for the army while showing no capacity to direct a war effort. After receiving several refusals, Madison finally settled on John Armstrong, an ambitious New Yorker with considerable military and diplomatic experience. But Armstrong was allied with New York Republicans deeply antagonistic to Madison and so egotistical that he had difficulty following orders. Aware of Armstrong's potentially serious flaws, Madison still appointed him, hoping that his experience and energy would provide effective direction to the war effort.

By late 1812 it was clear that Navy Secretary Hamilton was not only incompetent but also an alcoholic; he was often drunk at public occasions and was seldom able to work past noon in his office. He recognized his disability and resigned. Madison soon appointed William Jones, a Philadelphia merchant, sea captain, and loyal Republican, to replace Hamilton. Madison later declared Jones to be "the fittest minister who had ever been charged with the Navy Department." Madison finally had able administrators and vigorous colleagues to guide the war effort, but he would soon suffer grievously from Armstrong's headstrong and disloyal tenure in the War Department.

Gallatin's restlessness in the Treasury Department, and Madison's continuing desire to make use of his diplomatic abilities, finally led to his appointment in April 1813 to head a peace commission in Europe. For Madison, Gallatin's departure ended more than twelve years of almost daily friendship, support, and advice from one of the most able cabinet officers in American history. When the Senate refused to confirm Gallatin's interim appointment, Madison simply continued Gallatin's tenure in the Treasury Department and assigned Navy Secretary Jones to manage its day-to-day administration. Later that year, when brighter diplomatic prospects finally led the Senate to confirm Gallatin's appointment to the peace commission, Madison named Sen. George W. Campbell of Tennessee as secretary of the Treasury. Though an ardent Republican and War Hawk with good connections in Congress, Campbell was in ill health and unacquainted with finance, making him a poor substitute for the departed Gallatin. At the same time, after Pinkney resigned as attorney general to devote himself to his private practice, Madison appointed an able young Philadelphian, Richard Rush, to the post. Although not as distinguished a lawyer as Pinkney, Rush was devoted to the president and became a trusted friend and colleague for as long as Madison lived.

The obvious intention of Great Britain, after its victory over Napoleon, to launch a powerful assault on the United States in the summer of 1814 made the problematic situation in the War Department at first dangerous and finally tragic. Secretary Armstrong, though apparently full of zeal for the war effort, in fact concealed vital information from the president, intrigued with quarreling officers in the field, and failed to carry out mobilization and strategic orders from the cabinet. This deceit and insubordination played a large role in the bungled campaign that resulted in the British capture of Washington in August 1814.

When the cabinet was able to reassemble in the gutted city, Madison and many others placed much of the blame for the destruction on Armstrong. The president confronted Armstrong with his derelictions, sought and received his resignation, and as an interim appointment chose the energetic Monroe to be secretary of war as well as secretary of state.

In the still-ominous and unsettled circumstances of the fall of 1814, Secretary of the Treasury Campbell, ill and without ideas on how the country should face its financial crisis, resigned. Madison fortunately found an able replacement in the Philadelphian Alexander J. Dallas, who promptly brought order and direction to the nation's finances. Worn out from two years of arduous and effective service, Navy Secretary Jones asked to be relieved of his office. To replace him, Madison found a virtually unique specimen—a seafaring Republican merchant from New England, Benjamin Crowninshield, who served ably in the Navy Department until the end of Madison's administration. Unable to find a worthy person to take over the State Department from Monroe (who chose as his first post the War Department), Madison simply continued Monroe in the State Department as well. Thus, as the government waited anxiously through the gloomy winter of 1814–1815 (the good news of peace from Ghent and of victory at New Orleans did not reach Washington until February 1815), Madison at last had a cabinet of loyal and able men.

The Postwar Cabinet. With the war over, Monroe chose to give up the War Department and return full time to the State Department, from which he hoped, as Madison had done, to succeed to the presidency. Secretary Dallas took over as interim secretary of war until the able Republican William H. Crawford of Georgia could return from Europe to lead that department. Sustained by Henry Clay, John C. Calhoun, and others in Congress and supported by Madison's premier diplomats in Europe, Gallatin and John Quincy Adams, Madison's cabinet at the end of his administration—Monroe, Dallas, Crawford, Crowninshield, and Rush—set the direction for the broad assertion of federal power that characterized the National Republicans in the next twelve years.

[See also biographies of cabinet officers mentioned herein.]

BIBLIOGRAPHY

Ammon, Harry. *James Monroe, The Quest for National Identity*. 1991.

Brant, Irving. *James Madison, Commander-in-Chief, 1812–1836*. 1961.

Brant, Irving. *James Madison, the President, 1809–1812*. 1956.

Ketcham, Ralph. *James Madison, A Biography*. 1991.

Rutland, Robert A. *The Presidency of James Madison*. 1990.

Skeen, C. Edward. *John Armstrong, Jr., 1758–1843, A Biography*. 1981.

Stagg, J. C. A. *Mr. Madison's War*. 1983.

Walters, Raymond, Jr. *Albert Gallatin, Jeffersonian Financier and Diplomat*. 1957.

RALPH KETCHAM

CABOT, GEORGE (1752–1823), merchant, senator, Federalist party leader. Born in Salem, Massachusetts, one of eleven children of a merchant and his wife, Cabot entered Harvard in 1766 but was forced to withdraw in 1768 for rebelliousness and neglect of his studies. To set him straight, his older brothers sent him to sea, where shipboard discipline seems to have nourished and structured Cabot's native abilities. By age seventeen, Cabot had become captain of a schooner in the transatlantic trade. Married in 1774, by 1777 he joined his brothers in managing a fleet of privateers, which prospered during the Revolution. By the late 1790s, one of the richest men in New England, he retired from active commerce.

Cabot remained deeply involved in state and national business affairs, helping to establish some of the nation's earliest enterprises. Both before and after his retirement, he was at various times director of a state bank and of two insurance companies, investor in a cotton manufactory, director of the First Bank of the United States, and later president of its Boston branch. By virtue of these positions, as well as of his links through marriage (his own and those of his relatives) to other members of the social and commercial elite of Massachusetts, Cabot was the incarnation of New England maritime Federalism.

In the late 1770s Cabot had plunged into politics. He rose quickly through county and state service to a position of national responsibility. A member of the Massachusetts constitutional convention of 1780, elected to the Annapolis Convention of 1786 (which he declined to attend), and a participant in the state's ratifying convention of 1788 (where he forcefully backed a strong federal government), in 1791 Cabot was a elected a U.S. senator, a post he held until his resignation in 1796. Later he refused John Adams's offer to appoint him as the first secretary of the navy.

From the start, Cabot sought to strengthen public authority and its exercise by men of wealth, civic dedication, and "sound principles"—that is, by men like himself. Desiring the deference of others, scornful of democracy—"government of the worst," he called it, by which he meant efforts to include all adult white males in the active work of electing public officials and evaluating their policies—Cabot, like his Federalist colleagues, was an old-style republican. An advocate of strong commercial relations with Great Britain, he detested the French Revolution and its consequences. Yet, although he was the embodiment of the elite gentry of maritime Massachusetts, ever jealous of the Bay State's place in the nation, Cabot was firm in his commitment to the young American union, as he demonstrated during Republican administrations of Thomas Jefferson and James Madison.

Cabot, like many Americans of the time, observed the rise of popular politics and political parties with dismay. A realist, he recognized the unavoidability of partisan activities in defense of his own Federalist principles. Therefore, although reluctantly, he often interrupted his retirement after 1796 with political work. By 1805 he had become one of the leaders of the Massachusetts Federalist party, thus of the Federalists nationally. After his party failed twice to defeat Jefferson and Madison (in 1804 and 1808), Cabot helped organize a nearly successful campaign in 1812 to replace Madison as president with the New York Republican De Witt Clinton.

Cabot's principal contribution to the nation was his steadfast Federalist unionism, born out of his generation's effort to create a strong national government under the Constitution. Despite his deep differences with the Republicans, he condemned and fought against the disunionist schemes of some fellow New England Federalists in 1808 and 1812. In 1814 Cabot was elected president of the Hartford Convention, convened in protest against Madison's administration of the War of 1812; he deftly led the gathering to legal protests and away from secessionist inclinations, his aim being to keep the "young hot-heads from getting into mischief." Nonetheless, Cabot's name has ever since been indissolubly, if unfairly, linked with disunion, if only because this partisan gathering became a symbol in later years of the regional tensions that tore at the Union until the Civil War.

BIBLIOGRAPHY

Banner, James M., Jr. *To the Hartford Convention: The Federalists and the Origins of Party Politics in Massachusetts, 1789–1815.* 1969.
Lodge, Henry Cabot. *Life and Letters of George Cabot.* 1878.

JAMES M. BANNER, JR.

CADORE, DUC DE (1756–1834), French statesman, diplomat. Jean-Baptiste Nompère de Champagny, duc de Cadore attended military school in Paris, entered the navy in 1774, and fought in the American Revolution. One of the first nobles to go over to the Third Estate in 1789, he was later secretary of the Assembly and member of the Committee of Marine. In 1801 Napoleon, whom he greatly admired, named him ambassador to Vienna, where his gentlemanly demeanor facilitated Franco-Austrian relations. Appointed interior minister in 1804, he replaced Talleyrand in 1807 as minister of foreign relations, implementing Napoleon's policies in the commercial war that complemented the military war with England. In 1808 Cadore notified the U.S. minister to France, John Armstrong, that Napoleon considered British actions as creating a state of war between England and the United States and would regard Americans as allies provided they cooperated with his trade restrictions, but Madison rejected this attempt to draft the United States to the French side. The 1807 Embargo Act and the 1809 Nonintercourse Act, which had failed to impress the belligerents with the importance of American trade, were succeeded in 1810 by Macon's Bill No. 2, which reopened trade with Europe and authorized Madison to reimpose nonintercourse with one belligerent if the other removed its restrictions. In August Cadore wrote Armstrong that the Berlin and Milan decrees would be rescinded provided Great Britain repealed its orders in council or the United States defended its rights against British aggression. Political controversy in the United States raged over the proper response to the "Cadore Letter," since Napoleon seemingly had declared a change in policy but French actions continued unchanged. On 2 November Madison's proclamation imposing nonintercourse on England if the orders in council were not repealed was issued, but by the time the series of events that followed Cadore's letter had culminated in the American declaration of war against England in 1812, Cadore, disagreeing with Napoleon's Russian policy, had left the foreign ministry.

BIBLIOGRAPHY

Brant, Irving. *James Madison*. Vols. 4, 5. 1941.
Egan, Clifford L. *Neither Peace nor War: Franco-American Relations, 1803–1812*. 1983.
Stagg, J. C. A. *Mr. Madison's War: Politics, Diplomacy, and Warfare in the Early American Republic, 1783–1830*. 1983.

MARY A. HACKETT

CALHOUN, JOHN C. (1782–1850) representative, senator, secretary of war, secretary of state, vice president of the United States. A political theorist and an ardent defender of the slaveholding South, Calhoun was born in the South Carolina upcountry and educated at Yale College and the Litchfield Law School. He moved effortlessly from the bar to politics and was elected from his district to the "War Hawk" Congress, where his vigorous support of nationalist policies won him celebrity as "the young Hercules who carried the war on his shoulders." He wrote the strident report of the House committee on foreign relations that backed Madison's call for a declaration of war against Britain. Perhaps his youthful brush with Connecticut Federalism contributed to his hostility to the whole system of "peaceable coercion" practiced by Jefferson and Madison. In any event, he advocated in its place a more forceful stance that would unite the country in ardent patriotism. After the war Calhoun joined with Henry Clay and other Republicans who favored a strong nationalist policy to push for a greater role for the federal government in the development of the country. He pursued this vision as secretary of war in President Monroe's administration.

Then in the 1820s Calhoun drastically modified his system of politics. Disappointed in his hope of succeeding Monroe as president, he found himself elected vice president, while John Quincy Adams emerged victorious in the bitterly contested presidential election. Calhoun soon

REP. JOHN C. CALHOUN.   Calhoun was first elected to Congress from South Carolina in 1810.
PRINTS AND PHOTOGRAPHS DIVISION, LIBRARY OF CONGRESS.

fell out with the Adams administration and allied himself with the increasing popular Andrew Jackson and his party. This move would prove disastrous for Calhoun's presidential ambitions. Meanwhile, a political earthquake rocked his home state of South Carolina. Faced with a deteriorating local economy, leading South Carolina politicians blamed their troubles on the protective tariff and on national consolidation. Calhoun's political friends joined the states' rights revival and called for "nullification" of the tariff. In 1828, at the instigation of the state legislature, Calhoun secretly drafted the South Carolina Exposition. Although its constitutional theory was grounded in the Virginia and Kentucky Resolutions of 1798, which had become the sacred texts of states' rights advocates, the Exposition departed from the historic resolutions in two crucial respects. First, it transformed a theory devised to secure majority rule into a theory intended to protect an aggrieved minority interest. Second, it proposed a remedy more precise and far-reaching than any Jefferson and Madison had offered, one that required the constitution-making authority of three-fourths of the states to authorize a power disputed and "nullified" by a single state.

Although Madison was implicated in this development, the Nullifiers made Jefferson the author and hero of their doctrine. Madison, in taking up his pen to refute it, was especially attentive to lifting the incubus of nullification from his old friend. In 1830 he wrote a four-thousand-word essay, published in the *North American Review*, that demolished nullification as theory and may have contributed to its defeat in 1833. Madison recognized the dangers of majority rule and had been careful in the Constitution to provide safeguards against them. But this "preposterous and anarchical pretension"—nullification—struck at the root of popular government itself.

Calhoun's political course was not determined by nullification, but the concept remained an important element in his thinking. The theory finally evolved into the theory of the "concurrent majority," which Calhoun described in two works, *A Disquisition on Government* and *A Discourse on the Constitution*, both published the year after his death in 1850. The theory, of course, had been shaped by the need to defend the South in the great sectional conflict over slavery.

BIBLIOGRAPHY

Niven, John. *John C. Calhoun and the Price of Union*. 1988.
Wiltse, Charles M. *John C. Calhoun*. 3 vols. 1944–1951.

MERRILL D. PETERSON

CAMPBELL, GEORGE WASHINGTON

(1769–1848), lawyer, representative, senator, secretary of the Treasury, diplomat. Born in Scotland but resettled in Mecklenburg County, North Carolina, at the age of three, Campbell later farmed and taught school there until his entrance into the senior class of the College of New Jersey at Princeton in 1793. He graduated a year later near the top of his class and began reading law, eventually moving to Knoxville, Tennessee, where he passed the bar in 1798 and soon built a successful practice. In 1803 he won a seat in the U.S. House of Representatives as a Republican and served there until 1809.

A dependable supporter of the Jefferson administration, Campbell was one of the House managers in the Senate impeachment trials of John Pickering and Samuel Chase, and he replaced John Randolph of Roanoke as chairman of the House Ways and Means Committee in the 1807–1809 sessions. His staunch support of the trade embargo against Great Britain led to a duel he fought in 1808 with Rep. Barent Gardenier of New York, who had accused the Republican majority of acting more in the interest of France than of the United States. Campbell retired from Congress and was appointed a judge of the Tennessee Supreme Court but left this post in 1811 when

he was elected to the U.S. Senate. There he quickly became one of the Madison administration's most vocal supporters, backing all military measures and serving as chairman of the Committee on Military Affairs from 1812 to 1814. In February 1814 Madison chose Campbell to replace Albert Gallatin as secretary of the Treasury, an appointment that was politically sound but unfortunate for the financial well-being of the United States. Campbell lacked the financial background to deal with the many problems involved in financing the war. Baffled, he resigned eight months later after reporting a large deficit and offering no suggestions for meeting the crisis. After retiring to private life, he was again elected to the Senate in October 1815. There, as chairman of the Finance Committee, he reported the bill creating the Second Bank of the United States. President Monroe appointed him minister to Russia in 1818, a post that he held until 1820. Returning to Tennessee, he resumed his law practice, served on the boards of various banks, including the Nashville branch of the Bank of the United States, and was a friend and supporter of Andrew Jackson. His last public post was a seat on the French Spoliation Claims Commission, which sat in Washington, D.C., from 1832 to 1835.

GEORGE W. CAMPBELL.   In February 1814 Madison appointed Campbell to succeed Albert Gallatin as secretary of the Treasury.

PRINTS AND PHOTOGRAPHS DIVISION, LIBRARY OF CONGRESS.

BIBLIOGRAPHY

Adams, Henry. *History of the United States of America during the Administrations of Thomas Jefferson and James Madison*. 2 vols. 1986.

Looney, J. Jefferson, and Ruth L. Woodward. *Princetonians, 1791–1794: A Biographical Dictionary*. 1991.

Stagg, J. C. A. *Mr. Madison's War: Politics, Diplomacy, and Warfare in the Early American Republic, 1783–1830*. 1983.

DAVID B. MATTERN

CANADA. See *British North America*.

CANNING, GEORGE (1770–1827), British secretary of state for foreign affairs. Canning rose from a modest gentry family of Anglo-Irish stock to become one of Georgian England's premier statesmen. His enemies rarely let him forget his widowed mother's affair with an actor or his own brief flirtation at Oxford with antiaristocratic republicanism. His bitter personal rivalry with Viscount Castlereagh interrupted, and nearly ruined, his career. His personality was a bundle of seeming contradictions; he could be witty or sarcastic, feisty or gentle, gracious or asocial. Americans had little good to say about him. The diplomats William Pinkney and John Quincy Adams, exasperated by Canning's cunning, accused him of wantonly discarding precepts of international law; Madison distrusted him, and James Monroe considered him devious. Despite his limitations, however, Canning promoted worthy enterprises out of principle: Catholic emancipation at home and abolition of slavery and the slave trade abroad. In 1824 he nearly persuaded the United States Senate to ratify a bilateral convention suppressing the slave trade.

Canning served twice as foreign secretary. In 1807–1809, during the Napoleonic Wars, he planned the reduction of Denmark and Holland and pressed to a crisis Britain's commercial and maritime undeclared war with the United States. Returning to Whitehall in 1822, Canning discovered that the world had changed since his earlier years at the Foreign Office. Repressive regimes associated with the Holy Alliance were violating national sovereignty in Europe, while former Spanish colonies in South America had won both independence and diplomatic recognition by the United States.

During his first term as foreign secretary, Canning appeared utterly unwilling to resolve grievances with the United States, in some cases dating to the 1790s, except on British terms. The British orders in council, coupled with Napoleon's Continental System, led Madison to interdict trade with both France and Britain. By spring 1809, because of the faltering British economy, Canning pro-

GEORGE CANNING. Canning was British foreign secretary from 1807 to 1809 and again in 1822.
PRINTS AND PHOTOGRAPHS DIVISION, LIBRARY OF CONGRESS.

posed that the orders might be lifted if the United States agreed to stiff terms, which Canning instructed David Erskine, the British minister in Washington, to present to Madison. Canning demanded that the United States resume commerce with Britain while continuing to interdict French trade, affirm the Rule of 1756, and permit the Royal Navy to enforce these provisions. When Erskine concluded that Madison would not accept the last two provisions, he and the president arranged a pact confirming only the first two. Madison lifted British interdiction in June, but Canning disavowed the pact and recalled Erskine in disgrace. Madison at once reinstituted the Nonintercourse Act. By the time Erskine's successor, Francis James Jackson, informed Madison that the British government would accept nothing less than American compliance with Canning's original terms, Lord Bathurst had replaced Canning at the Foreign Office.

Thirteen years later, in 1822, Canning returned to the Foreign Office. One of the critical issues facing him then was the threat to the newly independent republics in South America posed by Prince Metternich's European alliance, which opposed liberalism and reform everywhere it could. Particularly worrisome was France, which entertained territorial ambitions both in Europe and in Latin America at the expense of the much-weakened Spanish monarchy. The United States was also deeply concerned about the prospects for the survival of the infant republics in South America. Canning proposed that Britain and the United States make a joint declaration against European adventurism in the New World. Madison, in retirement at Montpelier, thought the plan worth considering, but President Monroe instead followed the counsel of Secretary of State John Quincy Adams. He argued that by agreeing to Canning's proposition, the United States might preclude its own possible expansion, especially in Cuba, and open lucrative markets to British commerce to the detriment of American interests. Hence, he promulgated the Monroe Doctrine unilaterally in December 1823, much to Canning's consternation.

BIBLIOGRAPHY

Brant, Irving. *James Madison: Secretary of State 1800–1809.* 1953.
Clarke, John. *British Diplomacy and Foreign Policy 1782–1865: The National Interest.* 1989.
Hinde, Wendy. *George Canning.* 1973.
Walters, Raymond, Jr. *Albert Gallatin, Jeffersonian Financier and Diplomat.* 1957.

MARTIN J. HAVRAN

CAPITAL, LOCATION OF THE. In the years immediately following the Revolutionary War, the location of the federal seat of government was among the top three or four issues to which Madison, often in conjunction with Thomas Jefferson, devoted his energies. While he emphasized the importance of the site to the survival of the Union, he also recognized the potential impact of the choice on the local economy, claiming the value in 1789 to be about $500,000.

In the spring of 1783, Madison and Jefferson proposed to the Maryland delegates in the Continental Congress that Maryland and Virginia make a joint offer of a site focused on Georgetown, Maryland. Leery of the influence that such a location would give Virginia, Maryland refused. Madison was pleased with the result of the October 1783 congressional debate on the location, for the compromise between the North and the South—to build two federal towns—bought time for a single Potomac site. Madison, who had remained in Congress specifically to participate in the residence debate, was not a member when the issue came up again in 1784 and 1785.

Madison again became directly involved in the issue as a member of the Federal Convention. He introduced the language for Congress's exclusive jurisdiction over its capital, a concept proposed unsuccessfully by a congressional committee on which he served in 1783. He defended exclusive jurisdiction against a strong attack from Antifederalists during debate over ratification of the Constitution.

Madison was wedded to the idea that political necessity required locating the temporary seat of government at Philadelphia before the government went to the Potomac. Consequently he worked hard to return Congress to that city after it left in 1783 and again in 1788 during the bitter congressional debate over where the First Federal Congress should convene. Nevertheless, Madison would not allow his support for a Potomac capital to interfere with his commitment to a stronger federal government. Thus, when Congress threatened to return to Philadelphia in 1787, he opposed the idea because it might inhibit the freedom of the Federal Convention. Again, when the Pennsylvanians planned to move in March 1789 that the First Federal Congress adjourn to Philadelphia, Madison opposed the plan, knowing that the divisive issue would again tear Congress apart and cripple the new government at its birth. He promised support if the issue was postponed until the end of the session.

By August 1789 it was apparent to the Pennsylvanians that there could be no short-term adjournment to Philadelphia without a prior agreement on a permanent seat of federal government. After several weeks of complex bartering, they sided with New Englanders who wished to keep Congress at New York but were willing to locate the permanent capital on the Susquehanna River. Southerners saw the Susquehanna location as adding to an existing imbalance in the Union that favored the North. Madison's passionate language in the ensuing debate marked a fundamental shift in his political stance from architect of a strong federal government to defender of states' rights and from leader of the Federalists to spokesman for an opposition party built on a foundation of decentralization. He urged the importance of a centrally located capital in a large republic, conceding some validity to the thesis he had so decisively argued against in *Federalist* 10.

Despite Madison's efforts, the House bill retained the Susquehanna location. The Senate struck that site out and agreed to one at Germantown, near Philadelphia. In a brilliant political move, Madison proposed an amendment, knowing that if the bill were returned to the Senate it would die as a result of his lobbying efforts.

By mid June 1790, after five months of debate and politicking, Congress had accomplished nothing in regard to the location of the capital or to Secretary of the Treasury Alexander Hamilton's proposal that the federal government assume the Revolutionary War debts of the states. The situation had become so intolerable by the end of May that Madison reportedly considered forcing an adjournment of Congress. Instead, encouraged by Jef-

RELOCATING THE CAPITAL. The government leaves New York by ship as a devil lures "Bobby" (Pennsylvania Senator Robert Morris) and his colleagues over falls to Philadelphia and beyond to Conogocheque creek on the Potowmack River in Maryland; a smooth route leads directly to the same site (at upper left) if only Congress had been willing to stay in New York temporarily. The cartoon attributes President Washington's signature on the residence bill to "self gratification." Etching, probably done at New York, 1790. PRINTS AND PHOTOGRAPHS DIVISION, LIBRARY OF CONGRESS.

ferson and perhaps by George Washington, he negotiated a compromise by which he promised to secure for Hamilton the necessary votes to assume the state debts provided a bill locating the capital on the Potomac River passed Congress. Madison did not need any votes for such a bill, only Hamilton's control of the New Englanders to prevent them from undercutting a deal between Pennsylvania and the South. The compromise he negotiated resolved sectional tension and brought the capital to the Potomac River. President Washington signed the Residence Act (S-12) on 16 July 1790.

Throughout the 1790s, as representative and as private citizen, Madison continued to support the development of the capital city and to protect it against its political enemies. On several occasions in 1790–1791 President Washington turned to Madison for advice on implementing the Residence Act, and the two worked closely together in February 1791 when they perceived a major threat from the bill to create the First Bank of the United States. Once his relationship with Washington became strained, Madison worked with the federal city commissioners, two of whom, Daniel Carroll and Alexander White, were House members whom he had persuaded to vote for the assumption of state debts in 1790.

As secretary of state after 1801, Madison saw his role in the development of the city overshadowed by that of President Jefferson, who personally supervised public efforts on the capital's behalf. It was as president that Madison made his final and one of his most important contributions to Washington, D.C. The burning by the British of the Capitol and the presidential mansion in 1814 offered a great opportunity to those who had been attempting to move the capital away from the Potomac almost since the day Congress arrived there in 1800. While the Democratic-Republican press reminded readers that Madison had played a prominent role in the compromise that brought the capital to the Potomac and that to go elsewhere would be a breach of public faith equivalent to a repudiation of the public debt, Madison exerted pressure on party members in Congress. A motion to relocate failed by five votes.

[See also *Funding Act of 1790*; *Washington, D.C.*]

BIBLIOGRAPHY

Bowling, Kenneth R. *The Creation of Washington, D.C.: The Idea and Location of the American Capital.* 1991.

KENNETH R. BOWLING

CARRINGTON, EDWARD (1749–1810), Virginia military officer and Federalist officeholder. Edward Carrington served on the Cumberland, Virginia, county committee of safety in 1775 and became a lieutenant colonel in the Continental army in November 1776. He continued in military service until the fighting ceased, by which time he had become deputy quartermaster general. He hoped to continue his military career, but in 1782 Congress rejected his request to command a regiment of Pennsylvania artillery. Madison chaired a committee that toned down Congress's brusque rejection and explained that individual states were authorized to appoint officers for their own troops. Thus began a friendship that endured despite the men's widely differing political philosophies, for Carrington became a leading supporter of Hamilton in Virginia.

Carrington served with Madison in Congress in 1786–1787 after serving in the Virginia Assembly but was an unsuccessful candidate for the Virginia convention to ratify the Constitution in 1788. When Madison went to Congress in 1789, Carrington sought his assistance in securing a Federal appointment "which may be tolerably respectable and permanent." When offered the position of U.S. marshal for the Virginia district court, Carrington asked Madison to decide if the appointment was "eligible & not derogatory in its Nature." He took the job. In 1791, when Carrington became federal supervisor for collection of the liquor tax in Virginia, he asked Madison to be his "lawful Agent" in settling his accounts as marshal.

By then, Carrington was already beginning to part from Madison politically. He wrote to Madison of his support for Hamilton on the issue of federal assumption of state debts, the first real issue that found Madison and Hamilton in open conflict. Carrington declined to serve as secretary of war when offered the cabinet post in 1795. He was foreman of the jury in the treason trial of Aaron Burr in 1807 and served twice as mayor of Richmond (in 1806 and 1809.)

BIBLIOGRAPHY

Brant, Irving. *James Madison: Father of the Constitution, 1787–1800.* Vol. 4. 1950.

Hutchinson, William T., et al., eds. *The Papers of James Madison: Congressional Series.* 1964

DONALD O. DEWEY

EDWARD CARRINGTON.
PRINTS AND PHOTOGRAPHS DIVISION, LIBRARY OF CONGRESS.

CARROLL, DANIEL (1730–1796), planter, delegate to the Federal Convention, commissioner of the District of Columbia. Carroll was a brother of John Carroll, first archbishop of Baltimore, and a cousin of Charles Carroll of Carrollton, a signer of the Declaration of Independence.

The proximity of Carroll's Montgomery County, Maryland, property to the Potomac River made him for years an active proponent of river navigational improvements. In state as well as national politics, Carroll was a leader of the "Potomac faction," which represented the southern, plantation-dominated portion of the state against the interests of the "Chesapeake faction," which represented the wheat farms and the urban regions of northern and western Maryland.

Carroll began his public career during the Revolution as a member of the Maryland State Council (1777–1781) and the Maryland Senate (1781–1791). Carroll served as a delegate to the Continental Congress (1781–1783) and to the Federal Convention of 1787. During the debates over the Constitution, Carroll was an ally of Madison, consistently advocating a strong nationalist position.

Carroll collaborated with Madison to secure ratification of the Constitution in Maryland and Virginia. Through frequent correspondence, Carroll provided

DANIEL CARROLL.   Portrait by John Wollaston.
MARYLAND HISTORICAL SOCIETY, BALTIMORE.

Madison with details of Antifederalist machinations in Maryland and warned him of similar efforts in Virginia. Carroll served with Madison in the First Congress as a member of the House of Representatives. In the famous Compromise of 1790, Madison persuaded Carroll to provide a key vote in favor of Hamilton's funding (assumption) bill in order to gain the support of the secretary of the Treasury for bringing the national capital to the banks of the Potomac. In 1791 Washington rewarded Carroll for his vote by appointing him one of the first three commissioners of the District of Columbia. After a stormy tenure in office, marked by frequent conflicts with proprietors of land in the District and disputes with the French architect and engineer Pierre-Charles L'Enfant, Carroll, exhausted and "enfeebled by age," resigned his position in 1795. He died the following year.

BIBLIOGRAPHY

Geiger, Mary Virginia. *Daniel Carroll: A Framer of the Constitution.* 1943.
Hutchinson, William T., et al., eds. *The Papers of James Madison: Congressional Series.* Vols. 10–14. 1962–.
Papenfuse, Edward C., et al., eds. *A Biographical Dictionary of the Maryland Legislature, 1635–1789.* 2 vols. 1979–1985.

TINA H. SHELLER

CASS, LEWIS (1782–1866), soldier, statesman. Born in Exeter, New Hampshire, Cass was educated at Phillips Exeter Academy and taught school for a year in Wilmington, Delaware. In 1799 he moved with his family to Marietta, Ohio, where he studied law with Return Jonathan Meigs, Jr., and in 1803 was admitted to the bar. In 1806 he won election without opposition as the youngest member of the Ohio House of Representatives, where he opposed Aaron Burr's conspiracy and drafted resolutions supporting President Thomas Jefferson. The following year, Jefferson appointed Cass the U.S. marshal for Ohio, and Madison reappointed him to a second four-year term in 1811. As colonel of the Third Ohio Infantry Regiment and later as a brigadier general commanding part of the Army of the Northwest, Cass took part in Brig. Gen. William Hull's unsuccessful invasion of Canada. While leading an expedition to the River Raisin, he was included against his will in Hull's surrender of Detroit and paroled. After the British released Cass, Madison appointed him a colonel in the regular army and a major general of volunteers. Cass supported Maj. Gen. William Henry Harrison at the battle of the Thames on 5 October 1813.

On 29 October 1813 Madison appointed Cass as Hull's successor as governor of the Michigan Territory. Cass served in that office for eighteen years, longer than any other territorial governor in American history. Several territorial secretaries served as acting governor in his absences during his long tenure. From Zanesville, Ohio, he wrote Madison in May 1814 to urge the removal of Reuben Atwater, the incumbent secretary and Hull's cousin. As the governor recommended, in October Madison appointed Cass's friend William Woodbridge. Cass also made recommendations to Madison on judicial appointments in the territory. Early in Cass's governorship, French Canadians were the most numerous settlers in the Michigan Territory, and Cass worked to co-opt them into the new American regime. He also urged that the federal government adopt a program of internal improvements, notably roads to connect Michigan with more developed regions.

Cass concluded numerous land-cession treaties with the Indians and in 1820 led a five-thousand-mile exploration through the Great Lakes to the headwaters of the Mississippi River. He wrote numerous published essays on Indians and on the American West. As secretary of war from 1831 to 1836, Cass implemented President Andrew Jackson's Indian removal policy and directed the Black Hawk and Seminole wars. He served as minister to France from 1836 to 1842. As U.S. senator from Michigan from 1845 to 1848 and again from 1849 to 1857, he advocated popular sovereignty as a means of dealing with the question of expansion of slavery in the territories.

LEWIS CASS.   Line-and-stipple engraving by T. B. Welch from a drawing by James Barton Longacre.
PRINTS AND PHOTOGRAPHS DIVISION, LIBRARY OF CONGRESS.

The Whig nominee Zachary Taylor defeated Cass, the Democratic candidate, in the 1848 presidential election, when New York and Pennsylvania antislavery Democrats defected to the Free-Soil party candidate, Martin Van Buren. Cass concluded his long public career by serving as secretary of state from 1857 to 1860. He resigned in protest against President James Buchanan's decision not to reinforce the forts at Charleston, South Carolina, during the deepening crisis over secession. During his last years, Cass lived in Detroit and read widely in the fields of politics and history.

BIBLIOGRAPHY

Gilpin, Alec R. *The Territory of Michigan, 1805–1837.* 1970.
McCarty, Dwight G. *The Territorial Governors of the Old Northwest: A Study in Territorial Administration.* 1910.
Prucha, Francis P. *Lewis Cass and American Indian Policy.* 1967.
The Territorial Papers of the United States: The Territory of Michigan. Edited by Clarence Edwin Carter. Vols. 10–12. 1942–1945.
Woodford, Frank B. *Lewis Cass: The Last Jeffersonian.* 1950.

THOMAS A. MASON

CASTLEREAGH, VISCOUNT (ROBERT STEWART) (1769–1822), British secretary of state for foreign affairs.

Castlereagh's career coincided with flashpoints in the international relations of Great Britain during the years from the Irish rebellion in 1798 to Castlereagh's suicide in 1822. He discharged massive responsibilities while serving as secretary for war and the colonies and later as foreign secretary (for the decade beginning in 1812). His reputation stands squarely on his gifts as a diplomat and an administrator: prosecuting the war in Spain, arranging and sustaining the Grand Alliance against Napoleon, and restructuring the European state system at the Congress of Vienna.

Anglo-American affairs during Madison's presidency must be considered against the backdrop of the wider world in which Castlereagh moved with assurance. Longstanding grievances against the British understandably preoccupied Americans, and Castlereagh realized this when he carefully studied British-American relations upon entering the Foreign Office. He considered war with the United States as mutually unwelcome, costly, and distracting, of only secondary importance to Britain compared with the overarching struggle with Napoleonic France. Castlereagh has often been characterized as a stiff, repressively conservative imperialist. In fact, he behaved forthrightly toward the United States, even during the War of 1812, recognized the finality of the American Revolution, treated the young republic with respect, and laid a foundation for the cordial relations that prevailed between the United States and Britain until the American Civil War.

American associates of Castlereagh generally thought well of him. Richard Rush, the American minister to London, called him fair and honest. A decade later, John Quincy Adams praised his integrity. They, and others, realized that, for all his aloofness and his stubborn defense of British policy, Castlereagh looked for practical solutions to vexing issues that seemed irreconcilable on principle.

When Castlereagh became foreign secretary in 1812, the pan-European war, an economic depression at home, and the American Nonintercourse Act left him uncertain what to do to alleviate the tension and distrust that had driven Britain and America to the brink of war. Madison's distrust of him was confirmed when the president read Castlereagh's letter to the British minister in Washington in April 1812. In the letter, the foreign secretary stated flatly that Britain would not relent on the orders in council. Madison and Congress responded with a declaration of war. What Madison may not have perceived, however, is that Castlereagh had necessarily followed the anti-American policy of Prime Minister Spencer Perceval, rather than his own inclinations. Castlereagh defended the orders as both justified and effective, but he also urged Parliament to suspend them temporarily in hope of averting the war. But by then it was too late. Castlereagh never took his eyes off the larger European theater for long, and he encouraged strenuous prosecution of the North American war because of his conviction, born out of his experience as a diplomat, that military victory usually brought a favorable peace treaty. Nevertheless, he sought peace from the outset. When, in 1813, Tsar Alexander I of Russia offered to mediate the dispute, Castlereagh appeared receptive. Madison dispatched a delegation, headed by Albert Gallatin, to Europe. Although nothing came of this initiative, it led after a few months to bilateral negotiations at Ghent. When both sides became mired in an impasse over a host of issues, ranging from Britain's demands for a buffer state for American Indians and a clearer definition of the U.S.-Canada boundary to America's concern over impressment and naval disarmament on the Great Lakes, Castlereagh ordered the British commissioners to come to generous, if ambiguous, terms speedily. The subsequent rapprochement between Adams and Castlereagh in London and the mission of Sir Charles Bagot in Washington eventually cleared up leftover business.

With his life's great work behind him, and oppressed by years of unrelenting criticism by his enemies, Castlereagh fell into a deep depression and finally took his life in 1822.

BIBLIOGRAPHY

Derry, John W. *Castlereagh*. 1976.
Perkins, Bradford. *Castlereagh and Adams: England and the United States, 1812–1823*. 1964.
Rutland, Robert A. *The Presidency of James Madison*. 1990.
Stagg, J. C. A. *Mr. Madison's War: Politics, Diplomacy, and Warfare in the Early American Republic, 1783–1830*. 1983.
Webster, Charles K. *The Foreign Policy of Castlereagh*. 2 vols. 1925–1931.

MARTIN J. HAVRAN

CAUCUSES OF 1808 AND 1812.

Republicans in Congress had used a nominating caucus to select a vice presidential candidate in 1800 and the presidential ticket in 1804. On the evening of 23 January 1808, eighty-nine Republican representatives and senators gathered in the Senate chamber and voted on nominations for president and vice president. Perhaps at President Jefferson's prompting, Sen. Stephen R. Bradley of Vermont, the president pro tempore of the Senate, announced the caucus meeting in a printed circular distributed two days earlier to 149 members of Congress. The assembled group appointed Bradley as president of the meeting and Richard Mentor Johnson as secretary. Eighty-three of those assembled voted for James Madison for president, three voted for George Clinton, and three for James Monroe. In the tally for the vice-presidential nomina-tion, seventy-nine supported George Clinton, five backed John Langdon, three voted for Henry Dearborn, and one voted for John Quincy Adams. In a resolution introduced by Sen. William Branch Giles, the participants in the caucus declared that they "acted only in their individual characters as citizens" and "from a deep conviction of the importance of union to the Republicans throughout all parts of the United States."

The defensive resolution and the concern for union indicated the open dissension among congressional Republicans. Soon after the caucus meeting, John Randolph and sixteen other members of the House, most of whom now supported James Monroe for president, released a public letter denying the legitimacy of the nominating caucus. Randolph charged that the organizers of the caucus extended only selective notice of the meeting and orchestrated the nomination so as to exclude any opposing views. Earlier nominating caucuses had consolidated party consensus, according to Randolph, but that of 1808 was designed to exclude those Republicans who opposed Madison's candidacy. An opponent of Jefferson, Randolph also suggested that any nominating caucus might interfere with the people's "right of election without undue bias."

In 1812 Republicans in Congress again used a caucus to renominate Madison as president. At a meeting in the Senate chamber on the evening of 18 May, eighty-two senators and representatives "in pursuance of a notice given to the Republican Members of Congress generally," elected Joseph Varnum as chairman and Richard Mentor Johnson as secretary. In a unanimous vote, the assembled members resolved that "James Madison of the state of Virginia, be recommended to the people of the U.S. as the proper person to fill the office of President." Again they declared that each acted only as individuals. The caucus appointed a committee of correspondence consisting of a single member from each state except Connecticut and Delaware. The consensus of the meeting scarcely concealed the division among congressional Republicans, many of whom, including the New York delegation, chose not to attend.

The caucus also recommended John Langdon of New Hampshire as vice presidential candidate on the Republican ticket but he declined. The caucus met again on 8 June and by a vote of seventy-four to three selected Elbridge Gerry of Massachusetts to run on the ticket with Madison. At this second meeting, Henry Clay offered a motion to reopen voting for the presidential nomination so that those who had not attended the caucus of 18 May might add their voices. An additional ten members of Congress endorsed Madison's presidential nomination. With the endorsement of ninety-two members of Congress, Madison's presidential candidacy, according to the *National Intelligencer*, enjoyed "a larger number of voices . . . than has ever been united in the recommendation of a candidate for the Presidency."

BIBLIOGRAPHY

Brant, Irving. "The Election of 1808." In *History of American Presidential Elections, 1789–1968*. Edited by Arthur M. Schlesinger, Jr., and Fred L. Israel. 1971.

National Intelligencer.

Risjord, Norman. "The Election of 1812." In *History of American Presidential Elections, 1789–1968*. Edited by Arthur M. Schlesinger, Jr., and Fred L. Israel. 1971.

BRUCE A. RAGSDALE

CHAUNCEY, ISAAC (1772–1840), naval officer. Born in Fairfield County, Connecticut, Chauncey went to sea as a boy, commanded a merchant ship at nineteen, and was appointed a lieutenant in the navy in 1799.

Chauncey began his naval career supervising work on the frigate *President*, then being built in New York's East River. Through this assignment, he gained invaluable experience in ship construction. After patrolling the Caribbean during the waning Quasi-War with France, he sailed for the Mediterranean to protect American merchantmen from predatory Barbary corsairs. During subsequent operations along the North African coast, he also served on the *Chesapeake* and the *New York*. In 1803, when powder detonated near the main magazine of the *New York*, he and David Porter bravely led fire-fighting parties that extinguished the flames.

Promoted to master commandant in 1804, Chauncey commanded the *John Adams* when that ship sailed to the Mediterranean that summer with supplies and then soon headed home with the superseded Commodore Preble embarked. He next commanded the brig *Hornet*. Chauncey received a captain's commission in 1806, and then undertook a voyage to the Orient for John Jacob Astor.

Chauncey took command of the New York Navy Yard in 1807 and still held that post when Congress declared war on England in June 1812. On 31 August, Secretary of the Navy Paul Hamilton placed him in command of naval forces on Lakes Ontario and Erie. The newly appointed commodore spent several weeks in New York, feverishly creating a logistics system while assigning officers, recruiting men, and hiring shipwrights, smiths, riggers, and various other craftsmen to work at the Sackets Harbor base on Lake Ontario. He picked the shipbuilder Henry Eckford to oversee construction of American warships on Lake Ontario, a fortunate decision because the ensuing naval struggle turned out to be more a contest between rival shipyards than a conflict between fighting fleets.

Winter ice was about to shut down navigation on the lakes when Chauncey himself reached Sackets Harbor.

COMMODORE ISAAC CHAUNCY.   Stipple engraving by David Edwin after a portrait by J. Wood.
PRINTS AND PHOTOGRAPHS DIVISION, LIBRARY OF CONGRESS.

His fourteen-gun brig *Oneida* and a handful of feebly armed schooners then faced a Canadian flotilla of six vessels, led by Sir James Yeo, a naval officer schooled in the deep-draft ships of the Royal Navy.

Both commanders suffered from a common naval malady, fearing defeat more than they desired victory. Therefore, each adopted a strategy of avoiding a decisive fleet action unless he enjoyed overwhelming superiority; when either commodore found that his were the weaker forces afloat, he kept his own ships safely in port and built a man-of-war more powerful than the largest enemy ship. Upon the completion of the new champion, his squadron would sally forth on the lake to support its army's operations with impunity during a brief reign, while his rival retired to his base to construct a still more powerful "dreadnought."

This cyclical exchange of roles continued for more than two years. Ultimately, Chauncey lost the confidence of President Madison, who finally picked the aggressive Stephen Decatur to take command on the lakes. However, before this change occurred, the Treaty of Ghent brought down the curtain on this relatively bloodless mode of warfare.

In the summer of 1816 Chauncey sailed for Naples in the new ship of the line *Washington* to command the American

Mediterranean squadron. He held that post into 1818 and, except for another stint as commander of the New York Navy Yard from 1825 to 1832, served thereafter on the Board of Navy Commissioners, a post he held to his death.

BIBLIOGRAPHY

Dudley, William S. *The Naval War of 1812: A Documentary History.* 2 vols. 1985, 1992.
Elting, John R. *Amateurs, To Arms! A Military History of the War of 1812.* 1991.
Haller, Willis, C. Gerard Hoard, and Robert Marshall. *The Building of Chauncey's Fleet.* 1983.
Roosevelt, Theodore. *The Naval War of 1812.* 1897.

JAMES L. MOONEY

CHESAPEAKE. A 38-gun frigate, the USS *Chesapeake* was launched at Norfolk in 1799. She sortied from Norfolk in June 1800 to join the other American ships on patrol against French navy cruisers and privateers, capturing the privateer *La Jeune Créole* in 1801, and was one of the few vessels kept on active service at the end of the Quasi-War with France. In 1802, she departed for the Mediterranean, blockading Tripoli and escorting American merchant ships until departing for home in 1803.

In 1807, she sailed again for the Mediterranean with Commodore James Barron. Unfortunately, the ship's recruiting officer in Norfolk, Virginia, had signed some British seamen who had deserted from a Royal Navy squadron. As *Chesapeake* departed the Chesapeake Capes on 22 June 1807, HMS *Leopard* intercepted her and demanded that Barron permit the British to muster his crew. When Barron refused, *Leopard* attacked. The British boarded and took off four men suspected of being deserters. President Jefferson could have turned the incident into a cause of war, but he preferred economic and diplomatic pressure to obtain British apologies and a change in the British policy of impressment and seizure of American ships.

U.S. naval officers considered the incident an insult that they longed to avenge. Thus, the *Chesapeake-Leopard* affair was one factor that pushed the United States into the War of 1812. The Madison administration worked to obtain the return of two American seamen taken from *Chesapeake.* By an agreement signed on 12 November 1811 the British government agreed to pay an indemnity to the families. The seamen were returned to the *Chesapeake* in Boston on 11 July 1812.

After the war commenced on 18 June, *Chesapeake* cruised for merchant prizes under the command of Capt. Samuel Evans and returned to Boston, where Capt. James Lawrence assumed command. On 1 June 1813, Lawrence sortied from Boston to meet HMS *Shannon* in a ship-to-ship engagement. *Shannon* defeated her in a brief but bloody fight and took her as a prize to Nova Scotia. *Chesapeake* eventually sailed to England where in 1822 she was sold at auction and broken up. A miller near Portsmouth purchased the timbers and constructed the Chesapeake Mill, which still stands as a popular attraction for American tourists in Hampshire, England.

[See also *Chesapeake-Leopard Affair.*]

BIBLIOGRAPHY

Emmerson, John C., ed. *The Chesapeake Affair of 1807.* 1954.

WILLIAM S. DUDLEY

CHESAPEAKE-LEOPARD AFFAIR. On 22 June 1807 the U.S. frigate *Chesapeake*, under the command of Master Commandant Charles Gordon, set sail from Hampton Roads, Virginia, for the Mediterranean, with Capt. James Barron, the newly appointed commodore of the American squadron there, aboard. After clearing Cape Henry, the *Chesapeake* was hailed by the British ship *Leopard*, whose captain had orders to intercept the American frigate and to search it for British deserters. When Barron refused to permit such a search, the English warship ranged alongside and opened fire. Unable to return fire because of its unprepared state, the *Chesapeake* lay helpless as the *Leopard* fired broadside after broadside. After thirty minutes of cannonading, Barron ordered the *Chesapeake*'s colors struck. A British boarding party then removed four men from the American ship. The *Chesapeake* returned to Hampton Roads, severely damaged in hull and rigging, with three crew members dead and eighteen wounded, including Barron.

The news of the *Leopard*'s attack on an American vessel enraged the country and prompted calls for a declaration of war against Great Britain. On 2 July, President Jefferson responded by expelling all British warships from American waters, but he resisted calling Congress into special session to consider military measures. Instead, he gave the British government an opportunity to disavow the incident. But because the administration linked a settlement of the *Chesapeake-Leopard* affair with a resolution of the impressment issue, negotiations faltered. The British government not only refused to disavow the attack on the *Chesapeake* but reaffirmed the Royal Navy's right to impress British nationals. By the time this news arrived in Washington, public support for war had evaporated. Unable to use force to compel a change in British policies, Jefferson turned to economic coercion. In December, following the president's recommendations, Congress passed the Embargo Act.

A final diplomatic settlement of the *Chesapeake-Leopard*

affair came in November 1811 when Great Britain agreed to return the surviving men taken off the *Chesapeake* and to pay reparations to the families of the killed and wounded.

BIBLIOGRAPHY

Perkins, Bradford. *Prologue to War: England and the United States, 1805–1812.* 1970.
Spivak, Burton. *Jefferson's English Crisis: Commerce, Embargo, and the Republican Revolution.* 1979.
Stevens, William O. *An Affair of Honor: The Biography of Commodore James Barron, U.S.N.* 1969.

CHARLES E. BRODINE, JR.

CHILDHOOD OF JAMES MADISON. See *Madison, James*, article on *Birth and Childhood*.

CHRYSLER'S FARM, BATTLE OF (11 November 1813). Maj. Gen. James Wilkinson took command of American forces in the third week of August 1813 to conduct an offensive thrust from Sackets Harbor, New York. Because Wilkinson had delayed the offensive, the campaigning season was virtually spent. John Armstrong, the secretary of war, had arrived with Wilkinson and had designated two objectives for the offensive: Kingston, Montreal, or both.

Because of the severe winterlike storms, bad management, and the general's poor health, the flotilla of three hundred boats and the land force of seven thousand men did not enter the Saint Lawrence until 5 November, headed for Montreal. Armstrong placed Maj. Gen. Wade Hampton, who had four thousand men at Plattsburg, under Wilkinson's command, although the two generals detested one another. Wilkinson ordered Hampton to rendezvous with him at Saint Regis, 120 miles downstream, from Sackets Harbor.

Commodore Isaac Chauncey, the American commander on Lake Ontario, failed to prevent British gunboats from following Wilkinson into the river and harassing the rear of the flotilla. A land force under Lt. Col. Joseph W. Morrison shadowed the American expedition and skirmished with troops led by Winfield Scott, Alexander Macomb, and Maj. Gen. Jacob Brown. On 10 November the flotilla reached the head of Long Saute, a rapids eight miles long, and tied up opposite John Chrysler's farm. While a detachment led by Brown cleared away opposition along the rapids, two thousand men under Brig. Gen. John P. Boyd camped at the farm.

Brown sent word for Boyd to advance on 11 November, but the British under Morrison attacked Boyd's column. Boyd's troops returned fire, but the attackers had withdrawn behind a strong defensive line, anchored on

WILLIAM C. C. CLAIBORNE.   Engraving by James Barton Longacre after a miniature by A. Duval.
PRINTS AND PHOTOGRAPHS DIVISION, LIBRARY OF CONGRESS.

the right by the river with the gunboats and on the left by dense woods. Morrison's force, eight hundred strong, came from the Forty-ninth and Eighty-ninth Foot Regiments with a few volunteers and Indians. Sleet and snow fell, and, although the ground was muddy, heavy fighting continued for more than two hours. With darkness coming on and ammunition running low, Boyd led his force toward the flotilla. Morrison's men left their defense line and pressed the retiring force hard. The eight hundred British had held off two thousand Americans, 1,800 of whom Boyd had sent into the action in successive groups. Losses were heavy: the British lost 22 killed, 148 wounded, 9 missing, while the United States had 102 killed, 237 wounded, and 100 taken prisoner.

Thus ended the Battle of Chrysler's Farm, an action without important consequences but still the major combat in Wilkinson's failed campaign.

BIBLIOGRAPHY

Lossing, Benson J. *The Pictorial Field Book of the War of 1812.* 1867.
Stanley, George F. G. *The War of 1812: Land Operations.* 1983.

JOHN MAHON

CHURCH OF ENGLAND. See *Anglican Church*.

CLAIBORNE, WILLIAM CHARLES COLES

(1775–1817), representative, governor of the Mississippi Territory, governor of Louisiana. Born into an old but impoverished Virginia family, Claiborne was educated at the Richmond Academy and briefly attended the College of William and Mary before striking out on his own at the age of fifteen. He worked for John Beckley, the clerk of Congress, who would become a major organizer and publicist of the Republican party. John Sevier, a North Carolina representative and soon to be the first governor of Tennessee, advised him to study law and to seek his fortune in the western territories south of the Ohio River. After a few months of study in Richmond, Claiborne passed the bar and moved to Tennessee, where he was licensed to practice law in 1794. He was member of the Tennessee constitutional convention of 1796 and was appointed a judge of the state supreme court.

In 1797 Claiborne filled the seat in the House of Representatives left vacant by the resignation of Andrew Jackson. After serving a second term, he was appointed governor of the Mississippi Territory by President Jefferson. This post led to extensive correspondence with Madison, who as secretary of state was ultimately responsible for territorial matters. Despite the closing of the New Orleans deposit in October 1802, bitter factional politics, and conflicts between Native Americans and white settlers, the governor held the confidence of the Jefferson administration to such a degree that after the purchase of Louisiana in 1803, he was made governor of the new territory. Claiborne's tenure as governor was a rocky one, as a contentious mix of French and Spanish settlers, free blacks, slaves, Native Americans, and immigrant Americans thwarted his efforts to establish U.S. rule over the fractious territory. His administration was hampered by the hostility of the French and Spanish settlers, whose dislike was exacerbated by Claiborne's inability to speak either language. In addition, Claiborne was opposed by ambitious Americans, one of whom, Daniel Clark, severely wounded him in a duel in 1807.

Claiborne was ignorant of the machinations of Aaron Burr and James Wilkinson in 1806 but was powerless when Wilkinson ordered arbitrary arrests and other violations of legal rights. After Madison annexed West Florida in 1810, Claiborne took possession of the Baton Rouge district and incorporated it into the new state of Louisiana, and he became the state's first governor in 1812. His last great service was to aid in the defense of New Orleans against the British in 1815. Elected to the U.S. Senate in 1817, he died before taking his seat.

BIBLIOGRAPHY

Adams, Henry. *History of the United States of America during the Administrations of Thomas Jefferson and James Madison.* 2 vols. 1986.

Hatfield, Joseph T. *William Claiborne: Jeffersonian Centurion in the American Southwest.* 1976.

DAVID B. MATTERN

CLARK, WILLIAM

(1770–1838), commander (with Meriwether Lewis) of the first United States exploration of the Louisiana Territory and the Pacific Coast, superintendent of Indian affairs in Saint Louis.

Clark was born in Caroline County, Virginia. While in the army in the 1790s he first met Lewis. Clark resigned his commission in 1796 and returned home to Kentucky. The men's friendship was renewed in 1803 when Lewis asked Clark to serve as cocommander on a planned transcontinental exploration.

Clark joined the expedition near Louisville as Lewis came down the Ohio River. From a wintering camp near Saint Louis the men moved up the Missouri River in May 1804. Over the next two and a half years they crossed the Great Plains, the Rocky Mountains, and the Great Columbian Plain to reach the Pacific Coast, then largely retraced their steps to return to Saint Louis in September 1806.

WILLIAM CLARK.
PRINTS AND PHOTOGRAPHS DIVISION, LIBRARY OF CONGRESS.

On the expedition Clark's principal responsibility was making maps of the party's route. From these detailed sheets he later prepared a grand map of the West. After Lewis's death Clark also helped publish the expedition's records. In later years he served in various public capacities in Saint Louis, where he made his home, most notably as superintendent of Indian affairs under Madison.

[See also *Lewis, Meriwether.*]

BIBLIOGRAPHY

Bakeless, John. *Lewis and Clark, Partners in Discovery.* 1947.
Lavender, David. *The Way to the Western Sea: Lewis and Clark across the Continent.* 1988.
Moulton, Gary E., ed. *Journals of the Lewis and Clark Expedition.* 11 vols. 1983–.

GARY E. MOULTON

CLAY, GREEN (1757–1828), businessman, soldier. Born in Powhatan County, Virginia, Clay received little formal education. He moved to Kentucky in 1780, worked as a surveyor, and eventually acquired a large amount of land, which became the basis for substantial and diverse business interests. Clay served in the Virginia ratifying convention in 1788, where he resisted the arguments of Madison and other supporters of the Constitution and voted against ratification. The following year, 1789, he was elected to represent the Kentucky district in the Virginia legislature. Clay served in the Kentucky constitutional convention in 1799 and, at various times, in both houses of the Kentucky legislature. He was also a major general of the Kentucky militia.

Clay's most renowned exploit came during the War of 1812, when he led an expedition sent early in 1813 to relieve Maj. Gen. William Henry Harrison, who was being besieged at Fort Meigs by British and Indians. Clay reached his destination, but one detachment of his force overzealously pursued Indians, fell into a trap, and was defeated. Since the pursuers acted contrary to Clay's orders, Clay bore no blame for the disaster. Clay was in command at Fort Meigs later that summer when the British and Indians again besieged the fort. Clay was well prepared and refused to be drawn out of the fort, and the siege was eventually lifted. Clay was with the American force that recaptured Detroit, but he did not accompany the army that pursued and defeated the British at the Battle of the Thames.

Clay returned to his business interests and did not serve during the remainder of the war. One of Kentucky's founders, Clay was a cousin of Henry Clay; he was also the father of Cassius Marcellus Clay, who had a distinguished career in Kentucky and national politics.

BIBLIOGRAPHY

Clay, Cassius Marcellus. *The Life of Cassius Marcellus Clay: Memoirs, Writings, and Speeches.* Repr. 1971.
Collins, Lewis. *Historical Sketches of Kentucky.* Repr. 1971.
Coulter, E. Merton. "Green Clay." *Dictionary of American Biography.* Vol. 4. Edited by Allan Johnson and Dumas Malone. 1930.

C. EDWARD SKEEN

CLAY, HENRY (1777–1852), representative, senator, secretary of state, and three-time candidate for president. Clay was a native of Virginia who read and studied law with George Wythe, the chancellor of the Commonwealth of Virginia, and Attorney General Robert Brooke. In 1797 he immigrated to Kentucky and started his illustrious career. In Lexington Clay quickly established himself as a leader of the Jeffersonian lawyer aristocracy of the bluegrass country. In 1798 he made his maiden political speech—a fiery attack on the Alien and Sedition Laws—and fully supported the protest resolutions of Virginia and Kentucky. Indeed, Clay always insisted that he subscribed to the constitutional principles of Madison's Virginia Report of 1800. Rapidly adapting to Kentucky's rough-and-tumble politics, Clay entered the state legislature in 1804, but he was destined for a larger stage and after two brief stints in the House of Representatives won election as a War Hawk to the crucial Twelfth Congress, where he was at once propelled into the Speaker's chair. From that post the flamboyant Kentuckian organized committees and inspired Congress for war against Great Britain. "What are we to gain by war?" Clay asked, answering, "What are we to lose by peace? Commerce, character, a nation's best treasure, honor!"

Madison welcomed the militant spirit that the War Hawks brought into Congress and depended on their support after war was declared in 1812. When things went badly, both in the cabinet and on the battlefield, Clay expressed disappointment in the president. "It is vain to conceal the fact . . . ," he wrote to a friend, "Mr. Madison is wholly unfit for the storms of War. Nature has cast him in too benevolent a mould. Admirably adapted to the tranquil scenes of peace—blending all the mild and amicable virtues, he is not fit for the rough blasts which the conflict of Nations generate." Nevertheless, Clay dutifully defended Madison against all attacks and championed every measure to prosecute the war. He ingratiated himself with both the president and Mrs. Madison and enlivened the capital's social scene by his charm and gaiety.

In January 1814, Madison nominated Clay to a five-member commission to negotiate peace with Great Britain. Federalists were appalled by the appointment; to them, Clay was as diplomatic as a gamecock. By his appointment,

REP. HENRY CLAY.   Clay was speaker of the House of Representatives and a leading War Hawk when war was declared on Great Britain in 1812. In 1814 he served as one of the American peace commissioners at Ghent. Engraving by G. Parker after a bust by E. Brackett.   PRINTS AND PHOTOGRAPHS DIVISION, LIBRARY OF CONGRESS.

however, Madison signified his own courage and at the same time secured Clay's influence with Congress.

Whatever the disappointments of the Treaty of Ghent, Clay put upon it the face of victory and returned home in triumph. Back in the Speaker's chair in the Fourteenth Congress, he rallied behind the ambitious program of national improvement and consolidation presented by Madison in his seventh annual message. Its principal measures—a protective tariff, internal improvements, a national bank—formed the basis of Clay's "American System," and in this sense Madison's platform became Clay's. With regard to a national bank, this required an abrupt change of position—the only one Clay ever acknowledged—but a change Madison, too, had undergone.

Clay was shocked by the president's veto—the last act of his administration—of the Bonus Bill, which would have used the money from the bank charter to support internal improvements. Forewarned of the veto, and the constitutional grounds for it, Clay pleaded with Madison to leave the bill on his desk for Monroe to consider, but Madison was adamant. Speaking in the House just over a year later, Clay said, "Of all the acts of that pure, virtuous, and illustrious statesman, whose administration has so powerfully tended to advance the glory, honor, and prosperity of the country, he [Clay] most regretted, for his sake and the sake of the country, the rejection of the bill of the last session. He thought it irreconcilable with Mr. Madison's own principles—those great, broad, liberal principles on which he so ably administered the government." It was a rejection of Madison's own bill, and, Clay concluded, "not even an earthquake that . . . swallowed up half this city could have excited more surprise."

Clay admired Madison above any other American statesman save George Washington, and Madison admired Clay. After his retirement from the presidency, Madison followed the westerner's career with interest. Had he chosen to endorse presidential candidates, he would surely have endorsed Clay. He admired Clay's genius for compromise. In 1833 he tendered the senator his thanks and appreciation for the way Clay resolved the nullification crisis and compromised the divisive issue of the tariff. According to George Tucker, his close friend, Madison spoke anxiously of the rampant slavery agitation not long before his death and remarked, "Clay has been so successful in compromising other disputes, I wish he could fall upon some plan to compromise this—and then all parties . . . might unite to make him President." Clay tried, but, alas, it was not to be. With regard to slavery, he also took his opinions from Jefferson and Madison. He succeeded the latter as president of the American Colonization Society. In 1850, when he put together his last great compromise, Clay received from Edward Coles a copy of Madison's "Advice to My Country," a heretofore unpublished document, in which he declared, "The advice nearest my heart and deepest in my convictions is that the Union of the States be cherished and perpetuated." In that view Clay gloriously concurred.

BIBLIOGRAPHY

Eaton, Clement. *Henry Clay and the Art of American Politics.* 1957.
Peterson, Merrill D. *The Great Triumvirate: Webster, Clay, and Calhoun.* 1987.
Remini, Robert V. *Henry Clay: Statesman of the Union.* 1991.

MERRILL D. PETERSON

CLINTON, DE WITT (1769–1828), New York politician. Born in Orange County, New York, the nephew of George Clinton, the first governor of New York state, De Witt graduated from Columbia College at the head of his class in 1786. His family connections earned him an appointment to the board of fortifications, a position of considerable influence and patronage, and in 1797 he was elected to the state assembly, where he established himself as a staunch Republican, a bellicose critic of President John Adams, and an opponent of Gov. John Jay.

Appointed to the U.S. Senate in 1802, Clinton resigned the following year to run for mayor of New York, believing that the post would allow him to advance his uncle's career—George Clinton would soon replace Aaron Burr

DE WITT CLINTON.   Engraving by Delaplaine, 1813.
PRINTS AND PHOTOGRAPHS DIVISION, LIBRARY OF CONGRESS.

as vice president—and replenish his own depleted fortunes. De Witt's new role and his drive to remain solvent led him into an alliance with the city's merchant elite, whose wealth and counsel served to seduce him away from the mainstream of his agrarian-dominated party. In 1807 Clinton broke with the administration over the Embargo Act. Thomas Jefferson's self-imposed blockade bore heavily on Clinton's own grain-producing state and, more important, on the Manhattan merchant princes. Clinton's stand won him support from the embattled Federalist party and brought him the enmity of Jefferson and the secretary of state, James Madison.

Rumors that Clinton was openly courting the Federalists grew louder as the presidential election of 1812 approached. Despite the bad war news from the Canadian front, the Republican congressional caucus renominated Madison in May. Many New York party members, however, were determined to replace Madison with the tall, charismatic Clinton. The mayor's supporters, with his consent, advanced his candidacy in a lengthy pamphlet crafted to appeal to militant Republicans and antiwar Federalists alike.

Many Federalists were pragmatic enough to accept Clinton's overtures, and when the party held its first-ever convention in New York City in September 1812, all but a handful of the seventy delegates reluctantly agreed to support the renegade mayor. Most shared the view of the Massachusetts Federalist Timothy Pickering, who was far "from desiring Clinton for President" yet would "vote for any man in preference to Madison."

The fusion strategy almost proved successful. Clinton carried all of New England except Vermont, swept his home state and New Jersey, and won half of Maryland's electoral vote, giving him a total of 89 electoral votes. The race in Pennsylvania was close, but the state's economy, which was booming thanks to military spending, tipped the state into Madison's column; had Pennsylvania voted with its northern neighbors, Clinton would have won the election.

Although the election was the closest presidential race in twelve years, the contest damaged Clinton's political career. His flirtation with the Federalists ruined him with his own party, while the collapse of the Federalists after the Hartford Convention eliminated the possibility of another campaign under their standard. In 1815 the Republican "war-party" faction removed him from his office of mayor.

BIBLIOGRAPHY

Bobbe, Dorothie. *De Witt Clinton*. 1933.
Hanyan, Craig. *De Witt Clinton: Years of Molding, 1769–1807*. 1988.
Siry, Steven E. *De Witt Clinton and the American Political Economy: Sectionalism, Politics, and Republican Ideology, 1787–1828*. 1990.

DOUGLAS R. EGERTON

CLINTON, GEORGE (1739–1812), governor of New York, vice president. The son of well-to-do Irish Presbyterian immigrants, Clinton served in the provincial assembly and the second Continental Congress. He fought in the War of the Revolution and in June 1777 was elected the first governor of the State of New York, serving six consecutive three-year terms and another term beginning in 1801.

Soon after peace, Clinton abandoned his wartime support for a stronger Congress and sought to make New York a self-sufficient state able to withstand the perceived incursions of Congress and neighboring states. Madison supported Clinton's obstinate refusal to grant independence to Vermont and praised the governor's handling of New York's cession of its far western lands to Congress and his assistance in suppressing Shays's Rebellion. But by 1787 Madison agreed with most other observers that Clinton had become "unfederal," advancing the interests of his state over those of the country. During the ratification debate over the new Constitution, Clinton refused to take a public stance, although he was thought to be the author of a series of six Antifederal essays signed Cato. Elected to the state ratifying convention, where he served as president, he led the large Antifederalist majority in advocating amendments before adopting the Constitution. When New Yorkers received news of Virginia's ratification (the tenth state to ratify), Clinton sanctioned the crossover of enough Antifederalists to guarantee New

VICE PRESIDENT GEORGE CLINTON.
PRINTS AND PHOTOGRAPHS DIVISION, LIBRARY OF CONGRESS.

York's ratification by a vote of thirty to twenty-seven. Clinton himself, however, voted against ratification and signed a circular letter from the convention recommending to the states the calling of a second constitutional convention to propose amendments.

Clinton became the Antifederalist candidate for vice president in the first federal elections, but was defeated through the efforts of Alexander Hamilton. Narrowly reelected governor in 1789, Clinton formed a new coalition with Robert R. Livingston and the rising Aaron Burr that put Burr into the U.S. Senate in 1791.

Madison supported Clinton after the disputed gubernatorial election of 1792, and convinced Jefferson that Clinton should remain the Republican challenger to Vice President John Adams. Madison and James Monroe strongly objected to replacing Clinton with Burr. Clinton remained the unofficial Republican candidate, but lost the vice presidency by a vote of seventy-seven to fifty.

With Federalism dominant in both the country and in New York, Clinton refused to stand for reelection in 1795. For the next five years, he concentrated on his land investments, which had already made him a wealthy man. In April 1800 he was coaxed out of retirement to run for the state assembly from New York City in a campaign orchestrated by Burr, with an eye on the presidential election later in the year. Whichever party won the New York City election would control the state legislature, and the legislature in New York elected presidential electors. Clinton's position on the ballot with several other wartime heros produced a Republican victory.

Jefferson considered only Clinton and Burr as vice presidential candidates in 1800. Clinton made himself available in a lukewarm fashion, while Burr avidly sought and won Jefferson's endorsement. In 1801 Clinton was easily elected governor, but throughout this last term, he was a figurehead for the strong Republican leadership headed by his nephew De Witt Clinton.

With the political demise of Burr, Jefferson selected Clinton to be his vice president in 1804, thus maintaining the important New York–Virginia alliance. At the time it was rumored that Jefferson had selected Clinton as vice president because he would be too old to mount an effective campaign against Madison for the presidency in 1808. Clinton received sixty-seven electoral votes while his nearest challenger received twenty. An increasingly wide gulf grew between Jefferson and Clinton as Madison's role in the administration expanded and as Clinton perceived himself as a competitor for the presidency in 1808.

In January 1808 the Republican congressional caucus nominated Madison for president and Clinton for vice president. Clinton refused to accept or reject the nomination, while he left the door open for a run at the presidency. Federalist leaders meeting in New York City in August 1808 considered, but then rejected, an endorsement of Clinton as their candidate for president. Clinton received 113 electoral votes for vice president, more than double his nearest competitor.

Old, hard of hearing, and in poor health, Clinton was ill-suited to be vice president, whose primary role was to preside over the Senate. His most significant act as vice president was to cast the tie-breaking vote defeating the bill for rechartering the Bank of the United States. He died in office in Washington, D.C., in April 1812.

BIBLIOGRAPHY

Kaminski, John P. *George Clinton: Yeoman Politician of the New Republic.* 1993.
Smelser, Marshall. *The Democratic Republic, 1801–1815.* 1968.
Spaulding, E. Wilder. *His Excellency George Clinton: Critic of the Constitution.* 1938.

JOHN P. KAMINSKI

COCHRANE, ALEXANDER FORRESTER INGLIS (1758–1832), British admiral.

Cochrane's success in the war with France in the 1790s won him increasingly important assignments. Following long service in the Atlantic theater of war, Cochrane was able to make a foray into politics after the signing of the Treaty of Amiens. In Parliament he made powerful friends who advanced his naval career. He was promoted to rear admiral in the spring of 1804 and given command of British blockading operations off the Spanish naval base at El Ferrol. In 1805 pursuit of a French squadron took Cochrane to the Caribbean.

Early in 1814, the British government selected Cochrane to relieve Adm. John B. Warren in command of the North American station and promised him an army of battle-tested veterans recently made available by Napoleon's defeat. In addition to bringing Americans to their knees, Cochrane hoped to gain prize money that would improve his personal financial situation. As he awaited the arrival of troops, Cochrane wavered between various targets for his first attack until advice from Rear Adm. George Cockburn (his second-in-command, who was already anathema to Americans as the commander of the smaller fleet that had burned and terrorized Chesapeake settlements) persuaded him to attack Washington.

The British troops, commanded by Maj. Gen. Robert Ross, finally reached Bermuda on 24 July and, a week later, sailed for the Chesapeake. The *Tonnant*, Cochrane's flagship, passed between the Virginia capes on 11 August and headed up the bay to join Cockburn. The combined task force ascended the Patuxent, landed troops at Benedict, and easily brushed aside an American defense force at Bladensburg, allowing them to push on to the American capital. After putting the torch to most of Washington's public buildings, they returned to their ships to prepare for a thrust at Baltimore.

However, the burning of Washington rekindled American patriotism and, for the first time since the outbreak of war, united the country. The people of Baltimore worked feverishly as they prepared to repel the invaders, and they were ready when the British transports landed their troops at North Point. That afternoon, as his men marched toward the bristling city, Ross was killed by a sniper's bullet. Thereafter, the British soldiers faced stiffening resistance, prompting Colonel Brook, their new commander, to ask Cochrane to attack Baltimore from the rear as a diversion. Troops at Fort McHenry blocked such a movement, and the failure of the ensuing British naval bombardment to reduce that stronghold doomed the whole expedition, forcing Cochrane to withdraw from the Chesapeake.

Gen. Andrew Jackson deftly parried Cochrane's subsequent drive up the Mississippi. The American victory in the battle of New Orleans was probably the most one-sided defeat in the history of British arms. After learning of the signing of the Treaty of Ghent, Cochrane returned to England. Despite seeing little subsequent active service, he was promoted to admiral in 1819. He died in Paris.

BIBLIOGRAPHY

Carter, Samuel, III. *Blaze of Glory; The Fight for New Orleans, 1814–1815.* 1971.
Elting, John R. *Amateurs, to Arms! A Military History of the War of 1812.* 1991.
Lord, Walter. *The Dawn's Early Light.* 1972.

JAMES L. MOONEY

COCKBURN, GEORGE

COCKBURN, GEORGE (1772–1853), British admiral. Cockburn entered the Royal Navy at the age of nine and rose steadily in rank and renown while serving in the turbulent years after the French Revolution and during the ascendancy of Napoleon.

Frustration during the first months of its war with the United States prompted the British government to launch a series of punitive raids along the Atlantic coast to draw American forces away from the Canadian frontier. In November 1812 Cockburn reported to Adm. John B. Warren, the overall commander of the operations. Cockburn's squadron entered the Chesapeake on 3 March 1813 and, throughout the summer, carried out a campaign of pillage and arson, destroying Havre de Grace, Maryland; Hampton, Virginia; and many other coastal settlements while enriching officers and crews with prize money before retiring to Bermuda.

Meanwhile, determined to crush American resistance during 1814, the British sent Vice Adm. Alexander Cochrane, an even more forceful and ruthless leader than

Warren, to oversee future operations along the Atlantic coast. At Cockburn's urging, the new commander in chief pointed his first thrust at Washington. Cockburn accompanied Maj. Gen. Robert Ross overland and persuaded the wavering army commander to continue his drive to the capital. Once in Washington, he sanctioned the general's burning of the Capitol, the White House, and other public buildings.

Cockburn then accompanied Ross in the attack on Baltimore. After Ross was felled by a sniper's bullet, everything went wrong for the British. Their naval bombardment of Fort McHenry and their ground attacks were not synchronized and failed. The British soon withdrew from the Chesapeake.

Thereafter, Cockburn's squadron conducted hit-and-run raids along the southern coast of the United States. After the war the admiral continued his steady rise in the Royal Navy through almost four decades of peace, becoming admiral of the fleet in 1851. His last noteworthy mission came in the autumn of 1815 when he carried Napoleon to Saint Helena.

BIBLIOGRAPHY

Elting, John R. *Amateurs, to Arms! A Military History of the War of 1812.* 1991.
Lord, Walter. *The Dawn's Early Light.* 1972.
Roosevelt, Theodore. *The Naval War of 1812.* 1897.

JAMES L. MOONEY

COFFEE, JOHN

COFFEE, JOHN (1772–1833), soldier, surveyor, merchant, land speculator. John Coffee, son of Joshua and Elizabeth Coffee, was born in Virginia, but his family moved to North Carolina when he was two. In 1798 Coffee and his mother moved to Haysborough, Tennessee, on the Cumberland River near Nashville. He soon entered the mercantile business as a partner of Andrew Jackson and later became a land surveyor and a land speculator. In 1809 he strengthened his ties to the Jacksons when he married Mary Donelson, niece of Rachel Jackson, Andrew's wife.

When the War of 1812 began, Coffee offered his services to the government (he had long been active in the Tennessee militia). He was in the service of the United States from 10 December 1812 to 20 June 1815, serving under Jackson in the inconclusive Natchez campaign in 1813, the Creek campaign in 1813–1814, and the Pensacola–New Orleans campaign in 1814–1815. He fought in all of Jackson's major battles, including Horseshoe Bend, Talladega, and Pensacola, and at New Orleans in both the night battle of 23 December 1814 and the major battle of 8 January 1815.

76

During the Creek War, Coffee and his volunteer regiment made two successful forays as independent units—a raid on the Creek settlements on the Black Warrior River and an attack on the Creek village at Tallushatchee. In the Creek and other campaigns of the War of 1812, Coffee served ably as Jackson's second in command.

After the war, Coffee moved to Florence, Alabama, where he was a farmer and a land speculator. His last official position was that of surveyor general of the northern district of the Mississippi Territory. Coffee died on 7 July 1833 and was buried on his plantation near Florence.

BIBLIOGRAPHY

Boom, Aaron. "John Coffee Citizen Soldier." *Tennessee Historical Quarterly* 22 (September 1963): 223–237.
Owsley, Frank L., Jr. *Struggle for the Gulf Borderlands: The Creek War and the Battle of New Orleans, 1812–1815*. 1981.
Remini, Robert V. *Andrew Jackson*. 3 vols. 1977, 1981, 1984.

FRANK LAWRENCE OWSLEY, JR.

COLES, EDWARD

COLES, EDWARD (1786–1868), private secretary to President Madison, governor of Illinois. Edward Coles earned some measure of public recognition during his lifetime as an opponent of slavery and as a disciple of Madison and Thomas Jefferson. Born and raised in Albemarle County, not far from Jefferson's Monticello, Coles self-consciously rejected his inheritance as a Virginia planter because of his opposition to slavery. In 1819 he migrated to the new state of Illinois after granting freedom to the slaves his father had bequeathed to him. Several years later, as governor of Illinois, he was instrumental in preventing the legalization of slavery in his adopted state. Although Coles's political career proved short-lived, he remained publicly committed to the antislavery cause and to the principles of the revolutionary generation as he interpreted them, especially during the crisis of the Union in the 1850s.

Coles developed a close personal relationship with Madison, whose wife, Dolley, was Coles's cousin. For six years of Madison's presidency, between 1809 and 1815, Coles served as his private secretary and regular companion. Impressed by President Madison's even-tempered, stoical self-control during the taxing ordeal of the War of 1812, Coles later attempted to convey to posterity a sense of Madison's exemplary temperament and character. During Madison's presidency Coles, grappling with his personal

ADM. GEORGE COCKBURN (*left*). The British admiral stands before the burning city of Washington; the Capitol is at the right. Engraved by C. Turner after a painting by I. J. Halle.
PRINTS AND PHOTOGRAPHS DIVISION, LIBRARY OF CONGRESS.

aversion to slavery, engaged both Madison and Jefferson on that vexing issue, in the latter case in a correspondence that twentieth-century scholars have frequently cited and analyzed. After returning to Illinois and then moving to Philadelphia, Coles remained in close touch with the elderly Madison through both correspondence and visits. Their personal relationship became the basis for Coles's adoption of the role of Madison's disciple or legatee.

This relationship was generally cordial, if not intimate, and certainly not without misunderstanding, tension, and disagreement. Coles became a highly partisan opponent of Andrew Jackson, and his efforts to recruit Madison to the anti-Jackson cause in the early 1830s greatly annoyed the older man. And they never saw exactly eye to eye on slavery, especially with regard to the planned disposition of Madison's own slaves. Coles believed he had convinced Madison that he should emancipate them in his will; when Madison did not, Coles desperately looked for ways to explain, to himself and to others, why his hero had failed to act magnanimously. This incident became part of an enduring pattern in Coles's behavior for the rest of his life. Convinced that he knew what Madison's legacy should be, Coles often failed to grasp the subtlety and complexity of his mentor's words and deeds; hence, Coles unwittingly misrepresented them to the next generation. Moreover, Coles hoped to convince his compatriots that the Republican party's position on the expansion of slavery into the territories—an issue that had special personal meaning for the Virginian who had fled to the sanctuary of free soil in Illinois—had a pure Jeffersonian pedigree. Later, Madison's legatee was a fervent supporter of Lincoln and the Union during the Civil War. He suffered a tragic—and ironic—personal loss when his youngest and favorite son affirmed familial loyalty to Madison's Virginia and died fighting for the Confederacy.

BIBLIOGRAPHY

Alvord, Clarence Walworth, ed. *Governor Edward Coles*. 1920.
McCoy, Drew R. *The Last of the Fathers: James Madison and the Republican Legacy*. 1989.

DREW R. MCCOY

COLES, ISAAC

COLES, ISAAC (1747–1813), Virginia Antifederalist representative, maternal uncle of Dolley Madison. Born 2 March 1747 in Richmond, where his father, John Coles, was a prosperous merchant, he was educated at the College of William and Mary. Settling in Halifax County, he represented his county in the House of Burgesses of the Virginia Assembly from 1772 to 1774. He joined the group of burgesses who signed the nonimportation association in May 1774. During the Revolutionary War he served as a militia officer and was again active in the Assembly during the 1780s. He also participated in the Virginia convention of 1788, where he joined his first cousin Patrick Henry in opposing the proposed Constitution.

Elected from his district as an Antifederalist to the First Federal Congress, he carried his objections to the Constitution to New York, the nation's capital. Once the Constitution was amended to incorporate a bill of rights, Coles became a political supporter of both Madison and Jefferson. He did not serve in the Second Federal Congress but was elected to the Third and was reelected as a Republican to the Fourth, serving continuously from 4 March 1793 to 3 March 1797. Overshadowed by such fellow Virginia representatives as Madison, John Page, and William Branch Giles, he was a minor figure in the House. In 1798 he retired from politics and moved to Pittsylvania County, Virginia, where he devoted himself to farming and occasionally engaged in some political activity, including campaigning for Jefferson's election as president in 1800. Coles was not a close political associate of Madison. However, Madison acknowledged that he was "indebted for his matrimonial success to the friendly aid" of Coles. Coles's nephew, also named Isaac Coles, served at different times as private secretary to both Jefferson and Madison.

BIBLIOGRAPHY

Biographical Directory of the United States Congress, 1774–1989. 1989.

CHARLES D. LOWERY

COLES, ISAAC A. (1780–1841), relative of Dolley Madison, secretary to President Madison. Born in Albemarle County, Virginia, Coles was the nephew of former congressman Isaac Coles of Halifax County, with whom he is sometimes confused. Coles was a distant kinsman of Dolley Madison and a frequent visitor at Montpelier. Coles served briefly as a diplomatic courier while Madison was secretary of state, and when the Madisons moved into the White House, Coles became an official member of the presidential family with a room of his own since he served as the president's secretary.

One of Coles's chief duties as Madison's secretary was to carry official papers from the executive mansion to the Congress. On 29 November 1809, as Coles was delivering Madison's message to Congress, he encountered Rep. Roger Nelson of Maryland in the lobby of the Senate chamber. Eyewitnesses said Nelson tried to extend his hand in greeting but Coles hit Nelson and said, "I am willing for this matter to end here; you attacked my character, and I have taken this method to take satisfaction or to chastise you." Nelson denied that he had slurred Coles, but the matter did not end there.

Two days later, Coles sent an apology to the Speaker of the House, but a committee was appointed to investigate the incident. In its report the committee deemed the assault on Nelson a breach of privilege. No punishment for Coles was recommended, but he soon resigned, and was succeeded by his brother, Edward Coles.

BIBLIOGRAPHY

Coles, William B. *The Coles Family of Virginia.* 1931.
Rutland, Robert A., et al., eds. *The Papers of James Madison:* Presidential Series. Vols. 1 and 2. 1984, 1992.

ROBERT A. RUTLAND

COLLEGE OF NEW JERSEY. See *Princeton University.*

COLUMBIAN CENTINEL. Originally the *Massachusetts Centinel*, this influential Federalist newspaper was published by Benjamin Russell, a leading figure in eighteenth-century American journalism. A capable writer and businessman, Russell took charge of the *Centinel* in 1784 and on the masthead proclaimed, "Uninfluenced by party, we aim only to be just." Russell had no intention, however, of helping those who opposed the political forces that coalesced into the Federalist party as they came to be a dominant force in New England politics.

Operating in a regional center of shipping, commerce, and manufacturing, Russell aimed for a readership that included working men and farmers, as well as the substantial Boston business community that supported the *Centinel* through advertisements and a healthy circulation. The conservative bent of the newspaper's editor was evident in Russell's condemnation of Shays's Rebellion in 1786, when the debt-ridden farmers in western Massachusetts were condemned for their rough treatment of authorities sent to foreclose on delinquent mortgages.

Russell's newspaper became the bellwether journal in New England during the 1787–1788 ratification of the Constitution. Using a cartoon, Russell hailed each state's ratification as adding "another pillar" to the "federal edifice," and other newspapers adopted the illustrated device to dramatize the political process. Thereafter, the *Centinel* was a vital source of information in New England, as political reports and foreign news (including the latest dispatches on the Napoleonic Wars) that first appeared there were reprinted with a credit line that lent authenticity to the story.

After the rise of the Republican party, Russell made the *Centinel* the organ voice of Federalists as he denounced the opposition as pro-French and untrustworthy. When Jefferson ran for the presidency in 1800, the *Centinel* warned readers that the Virginian was a dangerous radical capable of bringing New England to its knees. The *Centinel* editorials depicted Madison as a Jeffersonian puppet, and in 1812 Russell's lukewarm support for De Witt Clinton revealed the fissure in Federalist ranks.

As the Federalist party declined, so did the *Centinel*'s influence, and Russell's greeting of President Monroe with editorial remarks that "an era of good feeling" had descended upon the nation was resented by hardline Federalists. The *Centinel* prospered, but its political power in national elections was, like the Federalist party itself, moribund. In 1840 the *Centinel* merged with the Boston *Daily Advertiser.*

BIBLIOGRAPHY

Brigham, Clarence. *American Newspapers 1690–1820.* 2 vols. 1947.
Lee, James M. *History of American Journalism.* 1923.
Rutland, Robert A. *The Newsmongers: Journalism in the Life of the Nation 1690–1972.* 1973.

ROBERT A. RUTLAND

COMPENSATION ACT OF 1816. This controversial law changed the method of paying members of Congress and raised their pay. For years representatives and senators had complained that their pay, set in 1789 at $6 per diem, was inadequate. The inflation associated with the War of 1812 and the fact that Congress was paid in depreciated currency worth only 75 percent of par made their complaints seem valid. The popular representative and War of 1812 hero Richard M. Johnson of Kentucky agreed to move the first resolution, and he later chaired the committee that brought in the bill to raise congressional pay. In lieu of per diem payments, the bill proposed an annual salary of $1,500, which critics later argued almost doubled the pay of members of Congress. In defense of the bill, Johnson argued that the salary was less than the pay received by twenty-eight government clerks. Despite some opposition, most notably from Benjamin Huger, a wealthy Federalist from South Carolina, the bill received strong support, and it passed the House easily (the entire process took only four days). The Sen-

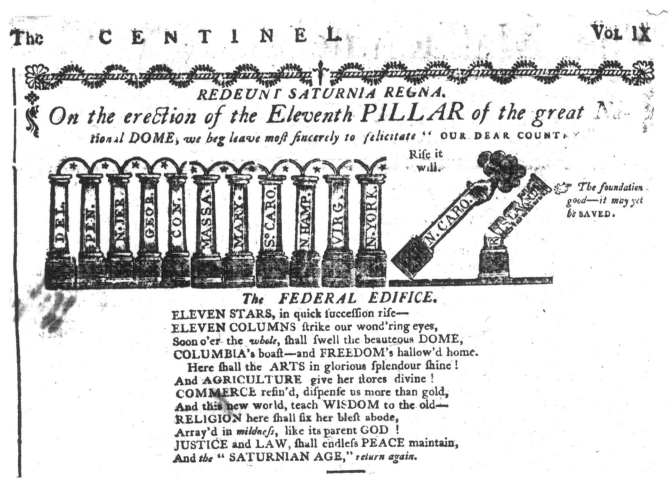

THE FEDERAL EDIFICE.   This cartoon appeared in Benjamin Russell's *Massachusetts* (later *Columbian*) *Centinel* after New York became the eleventh state to ratify the Constitution. Woodcut, Boston, 1788.
PRINTS AND PHOTOGRAPHS DIVISION, LIBRARY OF CONGRESS.

ate also speeded the bill to passage, and it was signed into law on 19 March by President Madison, who was privately reported to have favored the bill.

William Coleman, the Federalist editor of the New York *Evening Post*, first aroused public outrage against the salary law. Coleman hoped to attach the odium for passage of the law to the Republican party, ignoring the fact that two-thirds of the Federalists also voted for the law. All around the country public indignation, fanned by the press, rose to heights unprecedented in the country's history. Mass protest meetings adopted resolutions denouncing the law. Speakers alleged that high pay for representatives was contrary to republican simplicity and that a desire for money would crowd the government with venal, corrupt, and mercenary individuals. Complaints were also heard about "hard times" and "Madison's tax gatherers." Some members of Congress were burned in effigy, and several state legislatures adopted resolutions instructing their representatives to work to repeal the law.

The breadth of the reaction shocked veteran politicians and inspired to action citizens heretofore uninvolved in politics. Many members of Congress, sensing the new political situation, sought to assuage public opinion by pledging to vote to repeal the law in the next session of Congress. Others, reading their chances for reelection as nil, simply declined to run again. In the fall elections, more than two-thirds of Congress, including many such as Huger who had voted against the law, were defeated or had declined to run for reelection. The wrath of the people fell on Federalists and Republicans alike, regardless of how they voted, on the supposition that "the receiver is as bad as the thief."

In the lame-duck session of the Fourteenth Congress, a chastened Congress assembled to comply with the public demand for repeal, although some members grumbled that the people had no right to instruct their representatives how to vote. After a long and intense debate, the law was repealed by large margins in both houses of Congress—a sacrifice to the awakening power of the people at the end of Madison's presidency.

The Compensation Act of 1816 was an important milestone as the country shifted from the deferential quality of the first party system to the popular politics that characterized the second party system. The successful politicians of the new era were those who adapted to the egalitarian doctrines and the broader participatory politics foreshadowed by the public response to the Compensation Act of 1816.

BIBLIOGRAPHY

Adams, Henry. *History of the United States of America during the Administrations of Thomas Jefferson and James Madison.* Vol. 9. 1891.

Skeen, C. Edward. "*Vox Populi, Vox Dei:* The Compensation Act of 1816 and the Rise of Popular Politics." *Journal of the Early Republic* 6 (1986): 253–274.

C. EDWARD SKEEN

CONGRESS. [This entry consists of eight articles. Four concern the congresses in which James Madison served as a representative:

First Congress
Second Congress
Third Congress
Fourth Congress

Four concern the congresses that sat during his two terms as president:

Eleventh Congress
Twelfth Congress
Thirteenth Congress
Fourteenth Congress

For discussion of the election for the First Congress, see *Election, Congressional, 1788–1790.*]

First Congress (1789–1791)

The First Congress ranks almost as high in historical importance as the Federal Convention that framed the new charter of government. Because the Framers left much to the discretion of the first legislature, constitutional interpretation was involved in the very act of putting the government into operation.

First Session (4 March 1789–29 September 1789). During its first session, Congress was in fact the government, and the initiative lay with the House of Representatives. The principal accomplishments of this session were the enactment of tariff and tonnage bills, the organization of the executive and judiciary departments, and the approval of proposed amendments to the Constitution. By common consent the "first man" in the House was Madison, who characteristically made himself the best informed person on legislative business. No member exercised greater influence in the debates or did more to shape legislation than Madison.

On the tariff question, for example, Madison's research convinced him that Congress could levy moderately high duties without impairing the government's effectiveness in collecting them. Although he successfully resisted pressure to accept lower duties, Madison was unable to gain Senate approval of discriminatory duties, whereby nations in treaty with the United States would pay smaller tariff and tonnage duties than those not in treaty—notably, Great Britain. In the bills organizing the executive departments, Madison was largely responsible for placing the power to remove executive officers in the president alone. Later an opponent of executive aggrandizement, Madison in 1789 was predisposed to interpret the Constitution to enlarge the president's prerogative, believing that an overbearing Congress was the greater danger to liberty.

Madison's most impressive demonstration of leadership at the first session was in securing congressional approval of constitutional amendments. Without his patronage, his continual prodding of legislators who from inertia or outright opposition were disinclined to act, this subject would never have gained a hearing. Knowledgeable in the ways of legislative bodies, Madison assumed the difficult labor of digesting a plan, consisting mainly of a bill of rights, and shepherding it through the various stages of debate and amendment. After undergoing several modifications,

SPEAKER OF THE HOUSE FREDERICK A. C. MUHLENBERG. A Pennsylvania Federalist, Muhlenberg was Speaker of the first House of Representatives (1789–1791) and the third House of Representatives (1793–1795). Detail of a portrait by Samuel B. Waugh.
PRINTS AND PHOTOGRAPHS DIVISION, LIBRARY OF CONGRESS.

Madison's amendments were substantially incorporated in a series of twelve articles that Congress sent out to the states for ratification in September 1789. [See Appendix for text of the proposed amendments.]

Second Session (4 January 1790–12 August 1790). During the second session, the legislative initiative passed to Secretary of the Treasury Alexander Hamilton, who submitted his first report on public credit to the House in January 1790. This report set forth a scheme for funding the public debt—providing for the regular and punctual payment of interest on public securities—and for assuming the state debts contracted during the Revolution. In complete sympathy with the goal of restoring public credit, Madison nevertheless took a leading role in opposing major parts of Hamilton's financial program. He proposed, for example, to discriminate between present and original holders of public securities, paying to the former the highest market rate and paying the balance to the original creditors. His motive was to render some measure of justice to a class of creditors, mainly soldiers, who through hardship or ignorance had parted with their certificates for a paltry sum. The House, however, rejected discrimination by a wide margin. Madison also objected to federal assumption of state war debts, mainly out of his desire to protect the interests of his state. Ultimately, assumption was tied to the location of the national capital, a hotly debated issue in both the first and the second sessions. The upshot was the so-called Compromise of 1790: a modified assumption more favorable to Virginia and an agreement that the permanent capital would be located on the banks of the Potomac after a ten-year residency in Philadelphia.

Third Session (6 December 1790–3 March 1791). Hamilton's program also monopolized the brief third session. In a further report on public credit, the Treasury secretary called upon Congress to charter a national bank. No part of Hamilton's proposals aroused more intense opposition from Madison than did the bank scheme. His objections to funding and assumption had been tactical and limited, but the bank in his view represented a fundamental departure from the proper course to be followed by a federal government of limited powers. When the bank bill came before the House in February 1791, Madison twice spoke against it, but to no avail. While challenging the bill on its merits, he concentrated his attack on its unconstitutionality. Madison insisted that the Constitution did not, either in express terms or by implication, authorize Congress to charter a bank. Madison adduced all the arguments of strict construction of the Constitution that soon received classic formulation in Jefferson's opinion advising President Washington to veto the bank bill.

The undisputed leader of the House during the first session, Madison more often than not found himself in the minority on major questions of financial policy that arose in the second and third sessions. Enactment of the bank bill particularly alarmed him and seemed to cast the funding and assumption measures in a more ominous light. And given the inevitable tendency of Hamilton's program to consolidate financial (and hence political) power in the Northeast, even the prospect of a Potomac capital appeared to be in jeopardy. Despite these setbacks (including another defeat of his proposal to levy discriminating duties against Great Britain), Madison at the close of the First Congress was not yet convinced that an organized opposition to the leadership of the secretary of the Treasury was needed.

[See also *Bill of Rights; Capital, Location of; Funding Act.*]

BIBLIOGRAPHY

Bickford, Charlene Bangs, and Kenneth R. Bowling. *Birth of the Nation: The First Federal Congress, 1789–1791.* 1989.

Bowling, Kenneth R. *Politics in the First Congress, 1789–1791.* 1990.

Hutchinson, William T., et al., eds. *The Papers of James Madison: Congressional Series.* 1962–.

CHARLES F. HOBSON

Second Congress (1791–1793)

Although he spoke less often than in the First Congress, Madison remained one of the most prominent representatives in the Second. Madison was pained by the hostility he encountered, but he was nevertheless described by newspapers as a chief opponent of Alexander Hamilton's financial program.

First Session (24 October 1791–8 May 1792). The session started slowly, and Madison had time to write eighteen essays on political and economic topics that were published anonymously in Philip Freneau's new newspaper, the *National Gazette.*

As before, President Washington asked Madison's advice in preparing his opening address, and Hamilton believed that Madison took advantage of the opportunity to intrigue against his recommendations. Madison also again chaired the committee that prepared the House response to the president's address. Defense of the western frontiers, apportionment of representation according to the first census, and improvement of the postal service were the leading subjects for debate, but Madison was strangely silent. He spoke briefly on apportionment,

THE SEAT OF CONGRESS.   Congress moved from New York to Philadelphia in 1790 as a result of the passage of the Funding Act. Sessions were held in the State House, also called Independence Hall, which had served as the seat of both the congress that produced the Declaration of Independence in 1776 and the Federal Convention that produced the Constitution in 1787. This view shows the front of the building on Chestnut Street. Engraving by E. C. Childs after a drawing by George Strickland, 1828.
MAP DIVISION, LIBRARY OF CONGRESS.

appealing for harmony, and then at length on the bill to encourage the New England cod fisheries.

Although there was little financial business before the House during this session, Madison's unsigned essays in the *National Gazette* were a clear challenge to Hamilton's entire financial program and its underlying philosophy of an ordered society firmly governed by its well-born leaders. Hamilton responded with an angry letter to Edward Carrington a few weeks after Congress adjourned, a revealing letter that Carrington was surely expected to show to his friends in Virginia and use to stir opposition to Madison on his home ground. "Mr. Madison," Hamilton wrote, "cooperating with Mr. Jefferson, is at the head of a faction decidedly hostile to me and my administration. . . ." Once his friend, but now inspired by "personal and political animosity," Madison had worked behind the scenes to undermine Hamilton through "his votes and a variety of little movements and appearances."

Madison's correspondence reveals this hardening of political feelings, but in public he said little. Hamilton surely suspected that Madison was the author of the essay entitled "Parties" in the *National Gazette* and that Hamilton was the intended target when Madison wrote: "In every political society, parties are unavoidable. A difference of interest, real or supposed, is the most natural and fruitful source of them. The great object should be to combat the evil." When Madison denounced "an unmerited accumulation of riches" and praised the idea of political equality, he was directly challenging the foundations of the Hamiltonian system. Against an elite of wealth and position, Madison advocated "making one party a check on the other" in a political system where parties were a legitimate element of republican government. From early 1792 on, the conflict between Madison and Hamilton was direct and fundamental but not yet visible to the public.

Despite the growing political antagonism, Madison remained on excellent terms with the president. In April 1792, when he was considering the congressional apportionment bill, Washington asked Madison's assistance in preparing his veto message, and in June he sought advice about a farewell message in the event he declined reelection.

Second Session (5 November 1792–3 March 1793). Hamilton's opponents expected to gain strength from the congressional elections, and they hoped that the short second session would be a quiet one. John Beckley, the clerk of the House, told Madison in September 1792 that the struggle was between the Treasury and "the republican interest." Hamilton's friends, beginning to be called Federalists, agreed that the spirit of party was growing so strong that little business could be settled before the next Congress. A few weeks before Congress convened, William Smith of South Carolina published a vicious pamphlet, *The Politicks and Views of a Certain Party, Displayed*, attacking Thomas Jefferson and Madison for organizing the opposition to Hamilton's financial program. Madison prepared a detailed response but then decided not to publish it.

Madison again chaired the committee preparing the response to the president's opening address, but instead of the customary unanimous approval there was a sharp debate. Madison spoke briefly in firm opposition to allowing Hamilton to propose tax legislation because, Madison believed, this would be an unconstitutional delegation of the legislative authority of the House. By January, Fisher Ames of Massachusetts characterized Madison as the "desperate party leader" of a disciplined opposition, but the speeches attacking Hamilton were made by others.

The last six weeks of the session were consumed by a bitter partisan debate on two series of anti-Hamilton resolutions prepared by William Branch Giles of Virginia. Those of 23 January requesting detailed information from the secretary of the Treasury were accepted without a vote. Hamilton responded quickly and in great detail, but on 27 February, only four days before the session expired, Giles introduced eight resolutions directly accusing Hamilton of violating specific laws, exceeding his instructions from the president, and neglecting his duties. In his ninth resolution Giles indirectly but unmistakably called upon the president to remove Hamilton from office. Supporters of the Treasury secretary believed that Madison had prompted Giles on both occasions, but there is no evidence that he did so. Madison spoke only once, in favor of the later accusations, but in more moderate terms than were typical of Giles's fiery oratory. On each of six roll call votes, however, Madison joined with Giles as part of congressional minorities that included from seven to fifteen members. When Congress adjourned in great bitterness on 3 March, the partisan struggle over financial policy and executive influence was clear to every newspaper reader. Madison was undoubtedly the most distinguished of the Republican representatives, although others might have led the congressional assault against Hamilton.

BIBLIOGRAPHY

Annals of Congress. 1849.

Bell, Rudolph M. *Party and Faction in American Politics: The House of Representatives, 1789–1801.* 1973.

Cunningham, Noble E., Jr. *The Jeffersonian Republicans: The Formation of Party Organization, 1789–1801.* 1957.

Hoadley, John F. *Origins of American Political Parties, 1789–1803.* 1986.

The Papers of Alexander Hamilton. Edited by Harold C. Syrett. Vols. 9–14. 1965–1969.

Rutland, Robert A., et al., eds. *The Papers of James Madison:* Presidential Series. Vol. 14. 1983.

Ryan, Mary P. "Party Formation in the United States Congress, 1789 to 1796: A Quantitative Analysis." *William and Mary Quarterly* 3d ser., 28 (October 1971): 524–542.

PATRICK J. FURLONG

Third Congress (1793–1795)

James Madison and Thomas Jefferson both looked forward to greater strength in the Third Congress for what they described privately as the "republican party," although they did not yet use the term publicly. Before Congress convened they considered what policies the Republicans should follow, particularly on the troublesome question of neutrality now that Great Britain was at war with Revolutionary France. In his Helvidius essays, written to counter Hamilton's Pacificus essays, Madison argued learnedly that Congress was the constitutional authority for shaping foreign policy, not the president.

The immediate problem was a meeting place for Congress, as Philadelphia was stricken with a deadly yellow fever epidemic. When President Washington asked for his advice, Madison replied that the president should suggest that the members meet "voluntarily" at nearby Germantown and quickly enact a law to meet the emergency, as he had no constitutional or statutory authority to alter the place where Congress should convene. By November, however, cold weather ended the epidemic and Congress met on schedule in Philadelphia.

First Session (2 December 1793–9 June 1794). Although party feelings were strong, the session began quietly, as most of the representatives heartily wished to avoid American involvement in the spreading European war. Madison, as usual, chaired the committee to prepare the House response to the president's opening address, but there was also strong Federalist representation. The result was a bland statement that was adopted without opposition.

Just before his retirement from the State Department at the end of the year, Jefferson submitted a lengthy report on foreign restrictions against American commerce. Madison opened the House discussion of the report on 3 January 1794 and introduced seven resolutions calling for higher duties and various restrictions on trade with nations not having a commercial treaty with the United States. Everyone understood clearly that Madison's target was Britain, while Hamilton and his friends wished a close commercial and political relationship with the British. On both sides of the issue meetings were held in several states, rousing public opinion and sending resolutions to Congress.

Madison's commercial resolutions were debated almost daily for more than a month, to the virtual exclusion of other business, until reports of the British seizure of more than two hundred American vessels turned the attention of Congress to the possibility of war. In the turmoil, Madison's resolutions were never brought to a vote, but they were part of a determined effort to rally the Republican interest and alter the foreign and commercial policies established by Hamilton and his congressional supporters. Theodore Sedgwick, a Massachusetts Federalist, privately accused Madison of backing away from his own resolutions rather than face the foreign-policy consequences of their approval.

On 25 March the House passed without debate a temporary embargo designed to protect American shipping while diplomatic efforts were made to persuade the British to alter their policies. Madison did not speak on Jonathan Dayton's proposal to sequester debts owed by American citizens to British creditors, nor did he speak on the bill to suspend all commercial intercourse with Britain. Madison favored more drastic economic measures instead of larger armed forces, and argued against the new taxes needed to pay for them, particularly a tobacco excise that would strike directly at his Virginia constituents. In a skillful maneuver, Madison undermined

ABIGAIL ADAMS.   The First Lady referred to her husband's opponents in Congress as "the Madisonian party." Engraving after a portrait by Gilbert Stuart.
NEW YORK PUBLIC LIBRARY PICTURE COLLECTION.

the Federalist effort to pass a stamp tax by adding a provision taxing transfers of government bonds.

The session adjourned in general frustration, for neither party was sufficiently organized to prevail in a closely divided House. Madison was regularly criticized in the opposition newspapers and the letters of Federalist members for his leading role in blocking all Federalist proposals.

Second Session (3 November 1794–3 March 1795). The president's opening address for the second session condemned "certain self-created societies" for opposing the government's efforts to enforce the whiskey excise in western Pennsylvania. Washington clearly meant the Democratic-Republican clubs composed of Republican supporters, and there was a heated debate as Republicans defended the rights of free speech and petition and Federalists accused the clubs of encouraging the Whiskey Rebellion. Madison tried to avoid the issue by drafting a mildly phrased response to the president's address, but a Pennsylvania Federalist (prompted by Hamilton) proposed an amendment that the Republicans strongly opposed. Refusal to pay taxes was criminal, Madison agreed, but political opinions were constitutionally protected. After bitter debate, the House accepted a compromise response without a recorded vote, but earlier amendments showed a very close balance of party strength.

Surprisingly, the debate seemed to ease party feelings, for the remainder of the session passed quietly as Congress waited for the result of John Jay's mission to London. One Federalist suspected that Madison's recent marriage had calmed his political feelings and made him more agreeable in conversation, while Federalists generally sensed an absence of systematic Republican opposition. For his part, Madison greatly feared the Federalist effort to use Washington's immense prestige to condemn the Republicans along with the "self-created" political clubs.

In mid December Madison reported a naturalization bill from committee and spoke several times in support of it, but naturalization was not a party question and the bill passed easily. Madison said little during the long debates on taxes and the national debt, yet he was consistently viewed as the leader of the Republican party in Congress. His leadership was quiet and virtually invisible to the public, but Federalist leaders such as Theodore Sedgwick understood his position clearly, while Zephaniah Swift of Connecticut explained privately that despite his lack of oratorical spirit, Madison "has unquestionably the most personal influence of any man in the House of Representatives." In a family letter of early 1795, Abigail Adams referred to the anti-administration forces as "the Madisonian party," an accurate assessment of Madison's role in the Third Congress. As the session ended Madison published anonymously a twenty-four page pamphlet, *Political Observations*, defending the Republican position on commercial policy.

BIBLIOGRAPHY

Annals of Congress. 1849.

Bell, Rudolph M. *Party and Faction in American Politics: The House of Representatives, 1789–1801.* 1973.

Cunningham, Noble E., Jr. *The Jeffersonian Republicans: The Formation of Party Organization, 1789–1801.* 1957.

Hoadley, John F. *Origins of American Political Parties, 1789–1803.* 1986.

Hutchinson, William T., et al., eds. *The Papers of James Madison: Congressional Series.* Vol. 15. 1962–. Edited by Thomas A. Mason, Robert A. Rutland, and Jeanne K. Sisson. 1985.

Ryan, Mary P. "Party Formation in the United States Congress, 1789 to 1796: A Quantitative Analysis." *William and Mary Quarterly* 3d ser., 28 (1971): 524–542.

PATRICK J. FURLONG

Fourth Congress (1795–1797)

The Senate approved Jay's Treaty by the narrowest possible majority in June 1795, but President Washington did not immediately ratify the unpopular treaty with Great Britain. The president and the Federalists in Congress intended for the details of the treaty to remain secret until after ratification, but a Republican senator leaked the full text to a friendly newspaper, stirring strong criticism of the treaty at public meetings. Madison secretly drafted a richly detailed antitreaty petition that was published in Virginia in October, but in public he remained silent.

First Session (7 December 1795–1 June 1796). Madison and the Republican representatives faced a predicament, for they despised the treaty but the House had no constitutional role in its becoming the supreme law of the land. Jay's Treaty, however, established three joint commissions to consider complex details of ship seizures, colonial debts, and boundary surveys, and these commissions required operating funds that required approval by the House.

Madison believed that Jay's Treaty was a betrayal of American commercial interests as well as a Federalist effort to aid the British in their struggle against Revolutionary France. His dilemma was when and how to attack the treaty, already constitutionally approved and ratified. As Congress convened the Federalists caucused to select their candidate for Speaker and settle party policy in support of the treaty, but the Republicans did not meet as a group. In private Madison worried about Republican firmness and feared that the antitreaty forces might not prevail. As usual, he chaired the committee that drafted the House response to the president, but he was outvoted by its two Federalist members.

Not until 1 March did the president formally promulgate the treaty, and even then he did not request appropriations for the three joint commissions. On 2 March Edward Livingston, a young and impatient Republican from New York, introduced a resolution calling upon the president for copies of Jay's instructions and correspondence, touching off two months of intense debate that virtually defined the two political parties. Madison was taken entirely by surprise, and to a great degree lost control of Republican actions. He spoke in favor of Livingston's proposal in an unsuccessful effort to soften the New Yorker's challenge to the president. His one long speech was a calm constitutional lecture on the treaty-making power. Albert Gallatin of Pennsylvania emerged as the leading spokesman for the Republicans, attracting fierce Federalist criticism of the kind previously aimed at Madison.

The call for Jay's papers passed easily, but Madison and the Republicans were shocked when Washington withheld the documents on the grounds the House had no constitutional role in the making of treaties. It was only after the president's refusal that the Republican members of the House caucused to consider the party's response. Madison introduced two resolutions challenging the president for refusing the documents, but they were merely a political gesture. The Republican majority melted away during the long and bitter debates on appropriating the $90,000 required to carry the treaty into effect, despite Madison's best efforts in debate and behind the scenes. Both parties made unprecedented use of petitions from meetings throughout the country, and Madison believed that the influence of powerful merchants together with an unreasonable fear of war overwhelmed the voice of the people and undermined the resolve of several Republican representatives. The Federalists prevailed by a single vote.

Madison's displeasure was clearly visible. John Adams described him as "worried to death," while Theodore Sedgwick, one of the leading Federalists in the House, called Madison "of all men the most miserable." William Cobbett, an acerbic journalist writing as "Peter Porcupine," observed that the Republicans seemed at a loss for leadership: "Citizen Madison was formerly reckoned as a sort of chief; but he has . . . sunk out of sight." The treaty business, Madison told Thomas Jefferson, "has to me been the most worrying & vexatious that I ever encountered." The remainder of the session passed quietly, as the disheartened Republicans offered little opposition. Their high hopes of rejecting Jay's Treaty were shattered, and the defeat left the party "in a very crippled condition," as Madison explained to Jefferson. To James Monroe in Paris he wrote of an initial Republican majority that melted away because some men were not "firm enough for the crisis." The president seemed not to resent Madison's outspoken criticism of the treaty, for two weeks after the end of the debate he invited Madison to dinner. Like Washington, Madison had now decided to retire from political life.

Second Session (5 December 1796–3 March 1797). At the second session there was a virtual stalemate and little was accomplished. For the first time Madison was not named as chairman of the committee to prepare the answer to the president's opening address, although he was included as a member. He declined to join a small group of Republicans who opposed the final version of the response. He did not speak at length on any issue during the session and made no effort to exercise leadership. He did favor a national university in the city of Washington, as long as no federal funding was involved. Madison's brilliant career in Congress was coming to an end, and he was happy to leave the political struggle and return to his family and farm in Virginia.

[See also *Jay's Treaty.*]

BIBLIOGRAPHY

Annals of Congress. 1849–1855.

Bell, Rudolph M. *Party and Faction in American Politics: The House of Representatives, 1789–1801.* 1973.

Combs, Jerald A. *The Jay Treaty: Political Battleground of the Founding Fathers.* 1970.

Cunningham, Noble E., Jr. *The Jeffersonian Republicans: The Formation of Party Organization, 1789–1801.* 1957.

Hoadley, John F. *Origins of American Political Parties, 1789–1803.* 1986.

Hutchinson, William T., et al., eds. *The Papers of James Madison:* Congressional Series. Vol. 16. 1962–. Edited by J. C. A. Stagg, Thomas A. Mason, and Jeanne K. Sisson. 1989.

Ryan, Mary P. "Party Formation in the United States Congress, 1789 to 1796: A Quantitative Analysis." *William and Mary Quarterly* 3d ser., 28 (1971): 524–542.

PATRICK J. FURLONG

Eleventh Congress (1809–1811)

The Eleventh Congress included 142 members and 3 territorial delegates in the House of Representatives and 34 seats in the Senate. According to the apportionment that followed the census of 1800, Virginia remained the largest House delegation with 22 seats, followed by Pennsylvania with 18 and New York and Massachusetts with 17 each. At the session of May 1809, the House reelected Joseph Varnum of Massachusetts as Speaker and the Senate selected Andrew Gregg of Pennsylvania as president pro tem. He was succeeded by John Gaillard of South Carolina on 10 February 1810 and John Pope of Kentucky on 23 February 1811. Following approval of the rules, the House reestablished nine standing committees. Among the most important appointments were John Wayles Eppes as chairman of Ways and Means and Thomas Newton, Jr., as chairman of Commerce and Manufactures. During the Eleventh Congress, the Senate had four standing committees, three of which were joint administrative committees.

According to an act passed by the preceding Congress on 30 January 1809, the Eleventh Congress convened on 22 May 1809, rather than the usual meeting in December. A special session of the Senate, called by President Jefferson in December 1808, met from 4 March to 7 March without substantive action. The session of May was called in expectation of a possible foreign crisis that would require a declaration of war or military appropriation.

First Session (22 May 1809–28 June 1809). In fact Madison's message of 23 May reported an expected improvement in relations with Great Britain as a result of his recent negotiations with the British minister David Erskine. Madison presented the new Congress with his proclamation of 19 April, which reopened American trade with Great Britain as of 10 June 1809. The apparent relaxation of tensions in foreign affairs also eased partisan conflict in Congress and Madison's relations with members of his own party in Congress, some of whom had already effectively challenged his planned nomination of Albert Gallatin as secretary of state. Madison suggested that the Congress consider revising the navigation laws in accordance with the renewed commerce and he left for the legislature any decision on defense spending. "Aware of the inconveniences of a protracted Session, at the present season," Madison withheld any further recommendations for legislation. Congress responded with an act opening commerce to the British and with little other substantive legislation before adjourning on 28 June.

Second Session (27 November 1809–1 May 1810). When Congress reconvened for its second session on 27 November 1809, the Erskine agreement had collapsed and once again the government faced the need to establish some policy to defend American shipping rights. Nathaniel Macon of North Carolina introduced for the administration a bill that would have permitted American ships to trade with European ports while closing American ports to the ships of France and Great Britain as long as those nations imposed restrictions on American commerce. After the House approved the measure, Federalists and anti-administration Republicans in the Senate defeated the bill. A subsequent bill opened American trade and granted the president authority to reimpose nonintercourse on either France or Great Britain if the other lifted restrictions on American shipping. The so-called Macon's Bill No. 2 was approved by Congress on 1 May 1810, the final day of the second session.

Third Session (1 May 1810–3 December 1810). Two days after the final session of the Eleventh Congress opened President Madison presented a message proposing a wide range of legislation, including navigation laws, to protect American commerce, the creation of a national university, and the suppression of the illegal slave trade. In the closing days of the session, the Congress reimposed nonintercourse with Great Britain.

The limited accomplishments of the Eleventh Congress included approval of the bill authorizing the citizens of Orleans Territory to organize a government as the state of Louisiana, an act providing for the census of 1810, further appropriations for the Cumberland Road, and, in a secret session in January 1811, authorization for the president to extend United States jurisdiction over East Florida.

Henry Adams concluded that "seldom if ever was a Congress overwhelmed by contempt so deep and general as that which withered the Eleventh in the midst of its career." Conspicuous among its many failures was the inability to resolve the question of the recharter of the Bank of the United States. As secretary of the Treasury, Gallatin was eager to extend the life of the bank and reported to Congress the usefulness of the institution, particularly with the impending need for the government to borrow money in the face of reduced revenues from commerce. In the second session the House considered a bill to recharter but failed to act before adjourning. In the final session, the bank faced determined opposition from representatives who hoped to gain greater influence for state banks. After recharter failed in that body, Gallatin called on Sen. William Crawford to introduce the measure in the Senate, where it faced opposition from William Branch Giles and Henry Clay. In the closing weeks of the Congress, the Bank of the United States suffered defeat when Vice President George Clinton cast a tie-breaking vote against rechartering.

In the final session of the Eleventh Congress, the debate on reimposing nonintercourse precipitated a notable change in the rules of procedure for the House of Representatives. Following an extended speech by Barent Gardenier of New York in the early hours of the morning of 28 February 1811, five members called for a vote on the previous question. In conformity with the standing practice of the House, the Speaker ruled that a favorable vote on the previous question permitted discussion of the main question, and Gardenier attempted to resume his speech. An appeal by Thomas Gholson of Virginia led to a vote of the membership which overruled the Speaker and ended all further debate. Despite vociferous protests, notably from John Randolph of Roanoke, the rules change stood and became the principal means of closing off debate in the House of Representatives.

BIBLIOGRAPHY

Adams, Henry. *History of the United States of America during the Administrations of Thomas Jefferson and James Madison.* 1986.

Journal of the House of Representatives. Eleventh Congress. 1826.

Rutland, Robert A., et al., eds. *The Papers of James Madison: Presidential Series.* 1984.

BRUCE A. RAGSDALE

Twelfth Congress (1811–1813)

Public dissatisfaction with the indecision of the Eleventh Congress produced a high turnover in congressional elections for the Twelfth Congress. The House gained more than seventy new members. Since the Eleventh Congress failed to approve reapportionment legislation following the census of 1810, seats in the Twelfth Congress continued to be distributed according to the law of 1802. With the admission of Louisiana as a state on 30 April 1812 and the creation of the territories of Illinois and Missouri, the House of Representatives in the Twelfth Congress eventually contained 143 members and 4 territorial delegates. The admission of Louisiana increased the size of the Senate to 36 seats.

Among the new members of Congress were those whom John Randolph dubbed the War Hawks for their aggressive stance against British encroachments on neutral shipping rights and American territory. Most notable of the new members was Henry Clay, who entered the House of Representatives for the first time after serving two short terms in the Senate. Clay later said he preferred the "turbulence of the House" to the proceedings of the Senate. Although members of Congress were far more likely to move from the House to the Senate than the reverse, Clay's change of seats was due in part to a recognition that the House played a larger role in the initiation of legislation and received more public attention. Among the newcomers joining Clay in the House were Felix Grundy of Tennessee, and John C. Calhoun, William Lowndes, and Langdon Cheves, all from South Carolina. On his first day in the House, Clay was elected Speaker. The Senate elected as its president pro tem William H. Crawford of Georgia. Both houses retained the same committee structure as in the previous Congress.

First Session (4 November 1811–6 July 1812). On 24 July 1811, Madison issued a proclamation convening the Congress on 4 November, a month earlier than the constitutionally mandated meeting. In his message to Congress 5 November, Madison reported on the failure of diplomatic efforts to redress American grievances against both Great Britain and France. He urged Congress to establish "an armor and attitude demanded by the crisis" and offered general recommendations for defense measures and commercial regulations. In the following months Madison and his cabinet presented the Congress with further specific measures to prepare the nation for war. In the House, Clay appointed committee members and chairmen who promised support for the president's program, but dissension within the Republican party delayed action or prevented agreement on many defense measures. In the Senate, William Branch Giles, as chairman of the select committee on Foreign Relations, insisted on raising an army of an additional twenty-five thousand troops rather than the ten thousand requested by the president. The House committee tried to reduce the number, but Clay went along with Giles and both houses approved the larger army. While waiting for further word on diplomatic negotiations in Europe but in expectation of war, Madison on 1 April asked Congress to approve an embargo for sixty days. Clay won approval in the House for what he defined as a war act. The Senate agreed after extending the duration of the embargo to ninety days.

In his report to Congress in November 1811, Secretary of the Treasury Albert Gallatin described the decline in revenues that followed the interruption of commerce and made clear the need to increase duties and approve new loans if direct taxes were to be avoided. A report to the House Committee on Ways and Means offered specific suggestions for loans and new sources of revenue. Although Congress in March granted Gallatin the authority to prepare for an $11 million loan, it failed to enact other budget proposals designed to prepare the nation's treasury for war.

On 1 June Madison delivered his message advising a declaration of war against Great Britain. The House met in secret session and referred the war message to the select Committee on Foreign Relations. Two days later Calhoun reported from the committee with a recommendation for war. After rejecting a motion from Josiah Quincy of Massachusetts to debate the war motion in open session, the House on 4 June voted 79 to 49 in favor of the declaration. After two weeks of debate, the Senate voted on 18 June for the House bill with amendments, and the president signed the bill that day. The vote for war was exclusively Republican in both houses. Of the twenty-two Republicans in the House who broke with their party and president, eighteen represented districts in the northeast. Despite the influence of the freshmen congressmen known as the War Hawks, particularly in committee business, the majority of votes for war came from members who had served at least two terms. After passing essential legislation for the prosecution of the war but postponing action on Gallatin's recommendation for war taxes, the first session of the Twelfth Congress adjourned on 6 July 1812.

Second Session (2 November 1812–3 March 1813). Two days after Congress reconvened for its second session Madison delivered a message describing the progress of the war and calling for further defense measures. Congress responded with legislation increasing the pay of soldiers, expanding the size of the army, and appropriating money for the construction of new war ships. In order to fund the government and its military efforts, Congress approved additional loans and the issuance of treasury notes. The Twelfth Congress adjourned on 3 March 1813, the final day of Madison's first administration.

In legislation unrelated to the war, the Twelfth Congress approved an increase in the size of the House of Representatives and the reapportionment of seats in response to the census of 1810. The Congress approved two acts respectively expanding the size of the state of Louisiana and the territory of Mississippi to include parts of West Florida.

BIBLIOGRAPHY

Brown, Roger. *The Republic in Peril: 1812.* 1964.
Journal of the United States House of Representatives. Eleventh Congress. 1826.
Stagg, J. C. A. "James Madison and the 'Malcontents': The Political Origins of the War of 1812." *William and Mary Quarterly* 3d ser., 33 (1976): 557–585.
Walters, Raymond, Jr. *Albert Gallatin, Jeffersonian Financier and Diplomat.* 1957.

BRUCE A. RAGSDALE

Thirteenth Congress (1813–1815)

According to the apportionment act drafted in response to the census of 1810 and approved by Congress in December 1811, the House of Representatives contained 182 members and 4 territorial delegates. For the first time, the Virginia delegation lost its primacy in the House to New York with 27 members. Virginia and Pennsylvania followed with 23 seats each. Among the newly elected members of the House was New Hampshire's Daniel Webster, who for the first time served in Congress alongside Henry Clay and John C. Calhoun. The Senate contained 36 seats.

The House of Representatives created three new standing committees during the Thirteenth Congress. In June 1813, the House approved the establishment of a Committee on the Judiciary with jurisdiction over "all such petitions and matters or things touching judicial proceedings." A Committee on Pensions and Revolutionary Claims, approved by the House on 22 December 1813, relieved the Committee on Claims of consideration of all petitions and appeals regarding military pensions and claims relating to the Revolutionary War. On 26 February 1814, the House established the Committee on Public Expenditures with authority, formerly exercised by the Committee on Ways and Means, to oversee the disbursement of public appropriations and also to report on "such provisions and arrangements as may be necessary to add to the economy of the Departments and the accountability of their officers." The Senate continued to operate with only four standing committees with administrative responsibilities.

First Session (24 May 1813–2 August 1813). By authority of an act passed 27 February 1813, in the closing days of the previous Congress, the Thirteenth Congress first met on 24 May 1813. Clay won reelection as Speaker of the House and William Crawford was again the president pro tempore of the Senate. The Senate elected Joseph Varnum as president pro tem in the second session and John Gaillard in the third session. Within a month the House Ways and Means Committee reported tax bills based on the recommendations of Gallatin. By the close of the first session on 2 August 1813, Congress had approved new taxes on salt and a variety of goods and authorized a loan of more than $7 million. Although the House proved more cooperative with the administration than had the preceding Congress, members of the Senate managed to obstruct key aspects of the president's program. That body refused to confirm Gallatin as an envoy while he retained his position as secretary of the Treasury. The Senate also defeated the House bill to lay an embargo on American trade with British possessions. The approach of British ships on the Potomac threatened the safety of Washington and the Congress during this first session. With few military defenses around the city, the House went into secret session and considered a resolution to distribute government arms among the citizens of the District of Columbia. The British soon turned away from Washington and postponed the threat to the government.

Second Session (6 December 1813–18 April 1814). The second session convened on 6 December 1813, the date appointed by the Constitution for the normal opening session. On the following day Congress received Madison's annual message, reporting on diplomatic efforts and the progress of the war. On 9 December the president delivered a secret message calling for an embargo on American exports in order to keep American goods from falling into the hands of the British. Within a week both houses approved the new embargo. By spring, however, the administration proposed lifting the embargo, which was in turn repealed by Congress in April. In January the Senate confirmed Madison's appointment of a diplomatic mission to be sent in response to Castlereagh's offer of negotiation. The appointment of Henry Clay to the mission necessitated his resignation from the speakership and his congressional seat on 19 January. The House of Representatives on the same day elected Langdon Cheves of South Carolina to serve as Speaker for the remainder of the Congress. Before the second session adjourned on 18 April, the Congress raised the bounty offered for enlistment in the army and appropriated almost $32 million for the military and navy.

Third Session (19 September 1814–3 March 1815). When members of the Thirteenth Congress, called to a third session by presidential proclamation on 8 August, convened in Washington on 19 September 1814, they faced the recent destruction of nearly every public building in the capital at the hands of British forces. With the Capitol building in ruins, the House and Senate convened in cramped quarters at the Patent Office, formerly Blodgett's Hotel and the one government building to escape the British torches. Within the first month of the session, the House of Representatives rejected a proposal to relocate the seat of government.

In the second session of the Thirteenth Congress, John Taylor of the House Committee on Ways and Means reported a bill to establish a new national bank, but the House failed to act upon it before adjournment. During the third session, Secretary of the Treasury Alexander Dallas proposed a new bank similar to the original Bank of the United States. Opposition from Ways and Means chairman John Wayles Eppes and dissension among Republican ranks blocked congressional approval for Dallas's plan. After debating several alternative bills, the Congress finally approved a bank plan supported by an anti-administration coalition. On 30 January, Madison vetoed the bill for a bank that would have provided few valuable services for the government or the financing of the war.

After the loss of the congressional library in the Capitol fire, Thomas Jefferson asked the newspaper editor Samuel Harrison Smith to negotiate the sale of his personal library to the Congress. Despite the opposition of some New England Federalists, Congress in January 1815 approved the purchase of the former president's books at a cost of nearly $24,000.

After the text of the Treaty of Ghent reached Washington on 13 February 1815, the president delivered the treaty to the Senate on 15 February and that body unanimously ratified it the following day. With the demands of war lifted, Congress in the closing days of the session voted to establish a standing army of ten thousand troops and reduced the size of the navy. On 3 March 1813, before adjourning for the last time, the Thirteenth Congress authorized the president to use armed vessels of the United States to protect commerce against the "predatory warfare" of the dey (Turkish title for a local ruler in North Africa) of Algiers.

BIBLIOGRAPHY

Adams, Henry. *History of the United States of America during the Administrations of Thomas Jefferson and James Madison.* 1986.
Journal of the United States House of Representatives. Thirteenth Congress. 1826.
Peterson, Merrill D. *The Great Triumvirate: Webster, Clay, and Calhoun.* 1987.
Stagg, J. C. A. *Mr. Madison's War: Politics, Diplomacy, and Warfare in the Early American Republic, 1783–1830.* 1985.

BRUCE A. RAGSDALE

Fourteenth Congress (1815–1817)

The Fourteenth Congress convened 4 December 1815 in the "Brick Capitol," which was constructed as the temporary meeting place of the national legislature while the burned Capitol was reconstructed. At first appear-

RUINS OF THE CAPITOL.   Washingtonians inspect the Capitol after its destruction by the British on 24 August 1814. The Fourteenth Congress was forced to sit in a nearby building called the Brick Capitol.

PRINTS AND PHOTOGRAPHS DIVISION, LIBRARY OF CONGRESS.

REBUILDING THE CAPITOL.   View of the Capitol in 1819. The ruins of the central portion have been removed and the wing at the right reconstructed.   PRINTS AND PHOTOGRAPHS DIVISION, LIBRARY OF CONGRESS.

ance the new Congress looked much like its predecessors. The House continued with 182 members and 4 territorial delegates while the Senate still had 36 members. Clay, returned from his diplomatic mission, won reelection to his House seat and again served as Speaker. In the Senate, John Gaillard was reelected president pro tem and served in that position throughout the Congress. In the character of its membership and in its record of legislative accomplishments, however, the Fourteenth Congress stood in sharp contrast to the three other congresses that met during Madison's presidency. The first Congress to convene following the ratification of the treaty of peace and the end of the Napoleonic Wars was perhaps the most productive legislative assembly since the First Congress met in 1789.

One measure of the legislative responsibilities of the Congress was the increased number of standing committees. The House on 30 March 1816 established five committees to oversee respectively the accounts and expenditures of the departments of State, Treasury, War, Navy, and the Post Office, and a committee on public buildings. On 29 April of the same year, the House approved the appointment of a standing Committee on Private Land Claims. After many years of relying on a handful of standing committees for internal administration and select committees for consideration of legislation, the Senate, on the motion of James Barbour of Virginia, established committees on Foreign Relations, Finance, Commerce and Manufactures, Military Affairs, Militia, Naval Affairs, Public Lands, Claims, Judiciary, Post Office and Post Roads, and Pensions on 10 December 1815.

First Session (4 December 1815–30 April 1816). On 5 December 1815, Madison's seventh annual message announced the conclusion of hostilities with Algiers and outlined an ambitious legislative agenda for the peacetime Congress. The president proposed a permanent military establishment for the defense of the nation, federal funding of public works that would enhance defense and promote internal development, a system of protective duties, internal improvements, a national bank and uniform currency, and a national university. In a report to Congress submitted soon thereafter, Secretary of the Treasury Alexander J. Dallas provided the outline of a national bank and a new tariff schedule.

The Senate quickly ratified the treaty with Algiers. In the House, Clay helped to promote the nationalist legislation outlined by Madison with his appointment of William Lowndes as chairman of Ways and Means and John C. Calhoun as chairman of the select committee on National Currency. Lowndes's committee reported the bill, which eventually won approval as the most clearly protective tariff yet enacted by the Congress. The Tariff of 1816, approved on 27 April, established duties of 25 percent on woolens and cotton goods and 30 percent on iron. Calhoun's committee reported a bill to establish a national bank along the lines proposed by Dallas and largely based on the structure of the first bank. Clay, who as a senator in 1811 opposed recharter of the Bank of the United States, spoke on the floor of the House to declare his support for the new bank. The bill for the Second Bank of the United States passed both houses easily and was approved by President Madison on 10 April. In other legislation passed before the close of the busy first session on 30 April 1816, the Fourteenth Congress provided funds for the organization of a peacetime army and appropriated money for the construction of fortifications and new armed vessels.

Among the accomplishments of the first session of the Fourteenth Congress, none drew so much popular attention as the Compensation Act, which altered congressional pay for the first time since the 1790s. Members of the House and Senate were still paid $6 for each day in session and in transit to and from the capital. Citing the prolonged sessions of Congress, Rep. Richard M. Johnson of Kentucky moved to establish a salary for representatives and senators. As chairman of the select committee appointed by the House, Johnson reported a compensation bill that provided for an annual salary of $1,500, a sum, according to the committee, less than that paid nearly thirty government clerks. The committee reckoned that the per diem rate would amount to between $9 and $10. With only slight opposition and following the rejection of John Randolph's motion to delay implementation of the salary until after the next election, the bill passed both the House and Senate within ten days.

Second Session (2 December 1816–3 March 1817). The public protest against the Compensation Act was great. So many incumbents were defeated that when the second session of the Fourteenth Congress met, the House soon appointed another select committee on compensation. The committee, again chaired by Richard M. Johnson, defended the act but recommended repeal. By the end of January 1817, the House and Senate approved a return to per diem compensation but left for the following Congress to fix the precise amount.

Madison's final annual message to Congress, delivered on 3 December 1816, called for reciprocal tariff restrictions against foreign nations that continued to discriminate against American vessels. The president also called on Congress to create an executive department under the attorney general and reorganize the federal judiciary. Congress responded with approval of a Navigation Act on 1 March. The second session also approved the so-called Bonus Bill. Drawing from the $1.5 million bonus paid to the federal government by the Bank of the United States and the promise of future bank dividends, Calhoun reported a bill to establish a permanent fund for financing the construction of roads and canals. After passage by both houses, the bill fell to Madison's final veto on 3 March 1817, the last day of the Fourteenth Congress.

BIBLIOGRAPHY

Adams, Henry. *The History of the United States of America during the Administrations of Thomas Jefferson and James Madison.* 1986.
Peterson, Merrill D. *The Great Triumvirate: Webster, Clay, and Calhoun.* 1987.
Remini, Robert V. *Henry Clay, Statesman for the Union.* 1991.
Skeen, C. Edward. "*Vox Populi, Vox Dei:* The Compensation Act of 1816 and the Rise of Popular Politics." *Journal of the Early Republic* 6 (1986): 253–274.

BRUCE A. RAGSDALE

CONGRESSIONAL ELECTION OF 1788–1789. See *Election, Congressional, 1788–1789.*

CONSTELLATION. In the 1794 act founding the U.S. Navy, Congress authorized the construction or purchase of six frigates, three of forty-four guns and three of thirty-six. Joshua Humphreys was engaged to design the new ships and, in collaboration with William Doughty and Josiah Fox, drew the plans for the two classes of vessels. Work began on the *Constellation* in the Sterett shipyard in Baltimore under the supervision of David Stodder, serving as naval constructor, and Thomas Truxton, the vessel's first commanding officer. Construction of the ship was suspended when peace was reached with Algiers but resumed when war threatened with France.

The *Constellation* was launched on 7 September 1797. During its first cruise (June to August 1798), she escorted merchant ships to sea. Dubbed the Yankee Race Horse for her speed, the new ship served in the Caribbean during the Quasi-War with France. Between December 1798 and April 1801 the *Constellation* captured the frigate *L'Insurgente* in the first American victory over a French warship; captured the privateers *Diligent* and *Union;* fought with the *Vengeance,* which twice struck her colors but escaped during the night when the *Constellation*'s loss of her mainmast prevented her following; and recovered three American merchantmen from their French captors. The *Constellation* served with the Mediterranean squadron during the Barbary Wars, blockading Tripoli and assisting in the evacuation of Derna.

From 1805 to 1812 the *Constellation* was in ordinary (i.e., mothballed) at the Washington Navy Yard. With the outbreak of the War of 1812 the ship was readied for sea, but she never escaped the British blockade of the Chesapeake Bay. In 1815 Madison sent two squadrons to the Mediterranean to deal with the Barbary corsairs, who had taken advantage of the War of 1812 to seize American merchantmen. The *Constellation* was one of three frigates and seven smaller ships that set sail in May 1815 under the command of Stephen Decatur. After capturing the Algerine flagship *Mashauda,* Decatur visited Algiers, Tunis, and Tripoli, where he extracted indemnities and promises of safe passage for American shipping. Throughout the 1820s and 1830s the *Constellation* served as flagship on the Brazil station and in the Pacific, Mediterranean, and West Indies. During the 1840s she circumnavigated the globe before being nearly rebuilt from the hull up in Norfolk between 1845 and 1853. Recommissioned in 1855, the "new" *Constellation* was a twenty-two-gun sloop of war and served for three years as the flagship of the Mediterranean squadron, then briefly in Cuban waters defending American ships against search and seizure and as flagship of the African squadron.

The *Constellation* spent the Civil War in the Mediterranean protecting American commerce from Confederate raiders. From 1865 to 1933 the ship served as a receiving or training ship at Norfolk, Philadelphia, Annapolis, and Newport. She was laid up from 1933 to 1940, when President Franklin Roosevelt had her recommissioned to serve as a symbol of America's naval heritage. In 1955 ownership of the *Constellation* was transferred to a group of Maryland citizens, who restored the ship and maintain her as a museum in Baltimore's inner harbor.

BIBLIOGRAPHY

Brady, Cyrus T. "Constellation in the War with France." *McClure's Magazine* 14 (January 1900): 272–281.

Calderhead, William L. "U.S.F. *Constellation* in the War of 1812—An Accidental Fleet-in-Being." *Military Affairs* 40 (April 1976): 79–83.

Chapelle, Howard I. *The History of the American Sailing Navy: The Ships and Their Development.* 1949.

Ferguson, Eugene S. *Truxton of the Constellation: The Life of Commodore Thomas Truxton, U.S. Navy, 1755–1822.* 1956.

JAMES C. BRADFORD

CONSTITUTION. One of six frigates authorized by Congress when it established the U.S. Navy on 27 March 1794, the *Constitution* was designed by Joshua Humphreys in collaboration with William Doughty and Josiah Fox. The forty-four-gun *Constitution* was built at the Hartt shipyard in Boston under the supervision of naval constructor George Clagborne (or Claigborne), launched on 21 October 1797, and put to sea for the first time on 23 July 1798. After cruises along the Atlantic coast to protect American shipping from the French, the *Constitution* was sent to the Caribbean. Its Quasi-War captures included the *Niger*, the *Spencer*, and the *Sandwich*. Laid up after the war, it was recommissioned in 1803, becoming Edward Preble's flagship in the war against Tripoli. For four years the squadron led by the *Constitution* blockaded the Barbary coast and seized enemy ships. After a peace treaty was signed in 1805, the *Constitution* remained on station for two more years to monitor compliance.

Upon its arrival in Boston in November 1807, the ship underwent two years of repair before joining the North Atlantic squadron. Following the outbreak of the War of 1812, the *Constitution* put to sea under the command of

USS *CONSTITUTION*.   In July 1812, the *Constitution*, under the command of William Hull, was chased by a British fleet for two days before she outran her pursuers and put into Boston harbor. At the left on the horizon is HMS *Africa*. The *Constitution* is in the left foreground. At the right are (left to right) HMS *Shannon*, HMS *Aeolus*, HMS *Guerrière*, and HMS *Belvidera*. Engraving by W. Hoagland after a painting by M. Corné, 1815.   PRINTS AND PHOTOGRAPHS DIVISION, LIBRARY OF CONGRESS.

Isaac Hull with orders to participate in a raid against British commerce. On 17 July, Hull met with seven British ships off the coast of New Jersey. A sixty-six-hour chase ensued during which Hull outdistanced the British and returned to Boston. On 2 August Hull sortied through the British blockade and cruised along Nova Scotia, capturing two British merchantmen before encountering the frigate HMS *Guerrière*. The *Guerrière* fired first; when the shot failed to penetrate the *Constitution*, the ship received the nickname "Old Ironsides." After each combatant fired several broadsides, the foremast and mainmast of the *Guerrière* toppled, giving the Americans their first naval victory of the war.

After being repaired, the *Constitution* put to sea again on 26 October with William Bainbridge in command. A month later the frigate defeated HMS *Java* off the coast of Brazil. After further repairs, the *Constitution* set sail under the command of Charles Stewart. Cruising in the Windward Islands, the *Constitution* took four merchantmen captive before returning to port, where it remained under tight blockade for nine months. Running the blockade for the fifth time during the war, the *Constitution*, still under Stewart's command, got to sea on 31 December 1814. In January and February she took two merchantmen captive and, 180 miles east of Madeira, gave chase to the British frigate *Cyane* and the sloop *Levant*, both of which were forced to surrender. En route home in company with his prizes, Stewart learned that the war had ended.

The *Constitution* spent the next six years undergoing repairs and for most of the 1820s served as flagship of the Mediterranean squadron. An 1830 survey judged her to be in need of such extensive repairs that Congress scheduled her for sale or scrapping. Oliver Wendell Holmes composed a poem that aroused public sentiment to such a degree that Congress reversed itself and appropriated funds to rebuild the ship. From 1835 to 1844 the *Constitution* served in the Mediterranean squadron and on the South Pacific and home stations before circumnavigating the globe between 1844 and 1846 and patrolling the coast of Africa from 1852 to 1855. Five years of decommissioned status were followed by two decades of service as a training ship and thirteen years as a receiving ship. In 1897 the *Constitution* was towed to Boston for restoration and became a museum ship. On 1 July 1931 "Old Ironsides" was recommissioned and toured ninety U.S. ports along the Atlantic and Pacific oceans before returning to Boston where she remains today, the oldest ship on the Navy List.

BIBLIOGRAPHY

Grant, Bruce. *Isaac Hull, Captain of Old Ironsides: The Life and Fighting Times of Isaac Hull and the U.S. Frigate* Constitution. 1947.
Hollis, Ira N. *The Frigate* Constitution: *The Central Figure of the Navy under Sail.* 1900.
Jennings, John. *Tattered Ensign: The Story of America's Most Famous Fighting Frigate, U.S.S.* Constitution. 1966.
Knipe, Emillie, and Alden Knipe. *The Story of Old Ironsides, the Cradle of the United States Navy.* 1928.
Martin, Tyrone G. *A Most Fortunate Ship: A Narrative History of "Old Ironsides."* 1980.

JAMES C. BRADFORD

CONSTITUTIONAL CONVENTION. See *Federal Convention*.

CONSTITUTION MAKING. James Madison lived in an age of constitution making and is remembered in history as the Father of the Constitution. Before he sat in the Federal Convention and helped to frame the U.S. Constitution, however, he had participated in the making of state constitutions and become a notable political theorist.

State Constitutions. In June 1776 Madison was a twenty-five-year-old freshman representative from Orange County at the Virginia Convention that adopted a constitution for the new commonwealth. Young and shy, he rarely spoke at sessions of the convention but performed an important service in connection with George Mason's Declaration of Rights, specifically Article 16 on religion. Madison substituted language affirming the equal and absolute right of "free exercise" in place of Mason's expression of traditional "toleration" for dissenting religious beliefs. To what extent Madison then shared Thomas Jefferson's critical views of the Virginia constitution is unknown, but its revision became a recurring theme in their relationship.

In 1783 Jefferson sent to Madison the draft of a proposed new state constitution and sought his support for it in the General Assembly. The following year Madison backed petitions from reform-minded western counties and made the cause of a constitutional convention his own. The movement met defeat, however, and Madison lost interest. At the same time Virginians who had migrated to Kentucky began to think about a constitution as a step toward statehood and sought Madison's counsel. By 1788, Jefferson's plan was known to them from its publication in his *Notes on the State of Virginia*. Madison's observations on Jefferson's plan are interesting because they depart from Jefferson's more democratic ideas. Madison held that there were "two classes of rights" in a republic, those of persons and those of property, both of which should be represented in the legislature. He therefore proposed a dual suffrage and a dual electorate as a way to represent people in the lower house and property in the senate. This formulation was a vestige of traditional balanced-government theory, which persisted in Madison's constitutional thought to the end. Madison agreed with Jefferson on the need to invigorate the executive branch. The Virginia governorship was a weak post, subject to annual election, controlled by the legislature, and hampered by a council also answerable to that body. Jefferson and Madison both proposed a "council of revision," an idea probably borrowed from the New York constitution, that could revise bills passed by the General Assembly. Madison was so enamored of this device that he incorporated it in his model for the federal constitution. But he went further than Jefferson in strengthening the executive against the "elective despotism" of the legislature by calling for popular election of the governor. Madison also argued against Jefferson's provision for periodic revision of the constitution through new conventions elected by the people. In a new state like Kentucky, prudence dictated some means of improving upon the first attempt to draft a constitution, but periodic revision such as Jefferson proposed and such as the Pennsylvania constitution provided through its council of censors meeting every seven years was, in his view, a mistake.

When in 1829 Virginians finally came to revise the state constitution, Madison—the lone survivor of the convention of 1776—found himself a delegate to the convention that met in Richmond. He had not changed his mind on the wisdom of constituting government on the dual basis of persons and property. "It would be happy if a state of society could be found and framed," he declared in typically tough-minded fashion, "in which an equal voice in making the laws could be allowed to every individual bound to obey them. But this is theory only, which like most theories, confessedly requires limitations and modifications." He was still consumed by fears of a democratic majority riding roughshod over the rights of property owners. Indeed, Madison believed the danger had increased and was destined to increase still further as the number of propertyless people grew. The most sensitive problem facing the convention was the protection of one class of property—slaves—from a popular majority of nonslaveholders given power by equalization of suffrage and representation. On this issue Madison stood with the conservative majority from east of the Blue Ridge in support of a plan to incorporate the interest in slaves into the rule of representation. This could readily be done by means of the three-fifths clause (allowing a slave to be counted as three-fifths of a person) of the U.S. Constitution—a rule that Madison understood because he had helped to create it.

The Federal Constitution. Madison's model for a strengthened federal constitution was contained in the Virginia Plan presented to the Federal Convention by the head of Virginia's delegation, Gov. Edmund Randolph, and adopted as the basis of discussion. In the end many of its best features were, in Madison's opinion, lost, particularly the power of Congress to nullify state laws deemed incompatible with the federal compact. Madison set forth his argument on this point in a long and brilliant letter to Jefferson dated 24 October 1787, in which he gave his friend a glimpse of the interest-centered political philosophy he had expounded in the convention and would further polish in *The Federalist*, especially Numbers 10 and 51. "*Divide et impera*, the reprobated axiom of tryanny," he wrote, "is under certain qualifications the only policy, by which a republic can be administered on just principles." The doctrine cannot hold, however, in governments of too small a sphere, since there are insufficient interests to check "oppressive combinations." It is necessary to expand the sphere. "The great desideratum in Government is," he continued, "so to modify the sovereignty as that it may be sufficiently neutral between different parts of the Society to controul one part from invading the rights of another, and at the same time sufficiently controuled itself, from setting up an interest adverse to that of the entire Society." This should be possible, Madison thought, within the extended American republic under a government of checks and balances.

In *Federalist* 49 Madison went out of his way to criticize the provision for periodic change of constitutions advocated by Jefferson in *Notes on Virginia*. Again he brought into bold relief the contrast between his constitutional theory and Jefferson's. Too frequent appeals to the people to "new model" government, he maintained, would dangerously excite "the public passions" and disturb the public peace. Such calls must of necessity "deprive the government of that veneration which time bestows on everything, and without which perhaps the wisest and freest government would not possess the requisite stability." The reason of the people and the sovereign will might be sufficient reliance for government in "a nation of philosophers," Madison averred. "But a nation of philosophers is as little to be expected as a philosophical race of kings wished for by Plato."

Madison preferred to run the risk of ongoing interpretation of written constitutions rather than the risk of instability associated with frequent change. It was Madison, in fact, who precipitated the first congressional debate over interpretation of the Constitution when in 1789 he wrote into a bill creating the Department of State a provision empowering the president to remove the incumbent head. No such authority was contained in the Constitution itself, and logic seemed to dictate that removal should follow the same course as appointment, that is, require the advice and consent of the Senate. But Madison prevailed by making a case for executive responsibility. Thus in the first year of the government an unwritten constitution unknown to the Framers grew up alongside the written frame of government. In 1791 Madison opposed Alexander Hamilton's doctrine of implied powers; when Hamilton resorted to the "general welfare" clause to support government aid to manufactures, Madison insisted that the clause was never meant to sanction a power of government and quipped that, if the objects as well as the means of government are unlimited, "the parchment had better be thrown into the fire at once." In his later executive offices, as secretary of state and as president, Madison proved receptive to broad construction of the Constitution in order to accomplish worthy national objectives. Yet in his last official act—his veto of the Bonus Bill in the absence of explicit authority for internal improvements—he retreated to the safety of strict construction.

[See also *Federal Convention; Virginia Convention of 1776; Virginia Convention of 1829.*]

BIBLIOGRAPHY

Adams, Willi Paul. *The First American Constitutions: Republican Ideology and the Making of the State Constitutions in the Revolutionary Era.* 1979.
Barlow, J. Jackson, Leonard W. Levy, and Ken Masugi, eds. *The American Founding: Essays on the Formation of the Constitution.* 1988.
Rutland, Robert A. *James Madison, The Founding Father.* 1987.

MERRILL D. PETERSON

CONSTITUTION OF 1787. Often called the Father of the Constitution, James Madison nonetheless denigrated his brain child only two weeks before the Federal Convention ended. After nearly all the major points in the new scheme of government had been agreed upon, Madison wrote to his friend and mentor, Thomas Jefferson (then the American minister to France), that the new constitution "will neither effectually answer its national object nor prevent the local mischiefs which everywhere excite disgusts ag[ain]st the state governments."

Making the Constitution. The reasons for Madison's unlikely outburst can be found by comparing the Virginia Plan—the outline of government presented by Gov. John Randolph to the convention on 29 May, which Madison had helped to devise—to the final document. The Virginia Plan called for a bicameral legislature, with the lower house to be elected by the people of the various states and the upper house to be chosen by the lower. The legislature would choose the executive, who, along with part of the new national judiciary, would have an absolute veto over acts of the legislature. The power of the executive was undefined, but the judiciary would have definite and extensive powers, as would the Congress. Under this plan, the legislature would have all of the powers Congress had enjoyed under the Articles of Confederation, as well as the power "to legislate in all cases in which the separate States

are incompetent." Finally, acts of state legislatures would be subject to nullification by the national government.

The Virginia Plan spoke to the weaknesses that Madison and others perceived in the Articles of Confederation and offered a strong, centralist solution to those problems. It also eliminated any question about where the power resided, since the national Congress would have a veto over state legislation. To implement this power, Congress would have the authority to use force against any state opposing the national authority.

The delegates to the Federal Convention would not accept the strong government embodied in the Virginia Plan, and, it often appeared to Madison, they whittled away one feature after another during that long, hot summer, leading Madison to write in despair to Jefferson on 24 October 1787. Soon after writing that letter, however, Madison changed his mind, at least in part because of the opposition he saw gathering against the new Constitution. He came to believe that with all its faults, the proposed Constitution provided a stronger frame of government than any other option then available.

And in fact, the Constitution of 1787 would become the basis for the powerful and effective government that Madison believed the new country needed. Years later, William Gladstone would describe the document as "the most wonderful work ever struck off at a given time by the brain and purpose of man." Madison later came to see the Constitution in that light and took pardonable pride in his role in its creation.

Only five thousand words long, the Constitution of 1787 has provided an effective framework for governing the United States for more than two centuries. There have been only twenty-seven amendments, and of these none have made any significant change in the structure of government. The various clauses and articles have, of course, been open to interpretation and reinterpretation to meet the changing needs of a developing society.

Although it differed significantly from the Articles of Confederation, the Constitution, like the Articles, provided for a federal system. The Framers believed that power had to be distributed between the national and the state governments and that this division would balance the two and serve to protect individual liberties. As Madison wrote in *Federalist* 51 and in many letters between 1787 and 1791, the national government was the protector of a citizen's rights and a buffer against the whims of public opinion.

The federalism embodied in the Constitution is uniquely American, and, although over the past two hundred years, power has tended to gravitate toward the national government, the idea of a partnership remains a central tenet of constitutional thought. Chief Justice Salmon P. Chase caught this sense in the post-Civil War era when he spoke of "an indestructible Union of indestructible States." The men at Philadelphia saw both the state and the national governments as joint participants in the political process.

While the state and federal governments shared powers, the Constitution clearly gave the national government sovereignty over the states, although it took a civil war ultimately to confirm this view. The first words of the preamble to the Constitution—"We the People of the United States"—indicated that the Constitution and the government it created derive authority and legitimacy directly from the people and not, as under the Articles, from the states. Article VI reinforced this point, declaring the Constitution and the laws and treaties made by the national government to be the supreme law of the land, with the judges in every state bound by them and with state constitutions and laws giving way to those of the United States.

A Structure of Government. The wording of the Constitution also reveals some of the theories of government held by the Framers. In the preamble, they set out not only the source of governmental authority but also the purposes of that government—forming a more perfect union, establishing justice, ensuring domestic tranquility, providing for the defense of the nation, promoting its welfare, and securing the blessings of liberty for all time.

Article I, dealing with the legislative power, is the longest of all seven articles. Clearly, the Framers intended the legislature to be the most powerful of the three branches of government. The lower house, as the Virginia Plan had originally suggested, was to be chosen directly by the people, but the upper house was to consist of two senators from each state; until the twentieth century senators were chosen by the state legislatures.

The governing powers of the nation were to reside in the Congress, and many of the sections of Article I address directly the perceived weaknesses of the Articles of Confederation. Congress now had the power to raise revenue independently, regulate the currency, oversee interstate and foreign commerce, and raise an army. Moreover, the so-called elastic clause gave Congress a broad range of authority in choosing what means it would select to implement its delegated powers. Article I also placed limits on the states, which could no longer issue money, abrogate contracts, make treaties with foreign countries, or levy tariffs or export duties. Simple majority votes in both houses prevented any one state from obstructing the will of the majority.

The second article of the Constitution provides for an executive, the absence of which Madison and others considered a major weakness of the Articles. But whereas Article I is specific in its enumeration of powers, Article II is much vaguer. A good part of this section deals with how the president shall be elected (indirectly, through an electoral college), rather than with the president's powers and duties.

The actual specific grants of power are few: the president shall be commander in chief; may establish departments and require written reports from their operating heads; shall appoint various officers, such as judges or consuls, with the advice and consent of the Senate; may issue pardons and reprieves; and may convene or adjourn Congress.

In fact, the real powers of the presidency are not spelled out. The Constitution implies that the president, who exercises "the executive power," should interpret that power broadly. The chief magistrate is to be in charge of foreign affairs and the military and may recommend specific legislation to Congress. Such powers, in the hands of timid men, make for a weak presidency; the full range of power inherent in the office can be seen only when exercised by a Jefferson, a Lincoln, or a Roosevelt. One reason the Framers may have left the role of the president less well defined than that of the Congress is that most Americans expected George Washington to be the first occupant of that office. They not only trusted him but expected him to define the powers and the style of the chief executive and did not want to tie his hands in that matter.

Although the Constitution sets up three branches of government, which practice has made co-equal, a reader of the document may wonder just how much power the Framers intended to give to the judiciary. Article III is half the size of Article II and, even more than with the executive, ascribes the powers of the courts implicitly rather than explicitly: "The judicial Power of the United States shall be vested in one supreme Court and such inferior Courts as Congress may from time to time ordain and establish." To insulate the judges from political pressure, the Framers gave them life tenure; judges could be removed by impeachment only, for violating the general rubric of "good behavior." The Constitution assigned jurisdiction for suits between citizens of different states to the federal courts and granted original jurisdiction in a few specific situations to the Supreme Court, but for the most part it left the matter of defining the federal judiciary and its jurisdiction to Congress. Included in Article III is the provision defining treason, requiring the testimony of two witnesses in open court to such conduct.

Clearly missing from Article III is a specific provision granting the courts judicial review, that is, the power to declare acts of Congress or of the states unconstitutional. There has been an ongoing debate among scholars and politicians as to whether the Framers actually intended the courts to have this power or whether judges have usurped it. But the question is moot, for John Marshall established that power for the Supreme Court in the landmark case *Marbury* v. *Madison* (1803), in which he claimed for the Court the power to overturn legislation as the ultimate interpreter of the Constitution. However, an argument can be made that in using the phrase "the

WE, the People of the United States, in order to form

a more perfect union, to establish justice, insure domestic tranquility, provide for the common defence, promote the general welfare, and secure the blessings of liberty to ourselves and our posterity, do ordain and establish this Constitution for the United States of America.

ARTICLE I.

Sect. 1. ALL legislative powers herein granted shall be vested in a Congress of the United States, which shall consist of a Senate and House of Representatives.

Sect. 2. The House of Representatives shall be composed of members chosen every second year by the people of the several states, and the electors in each state shall have the qualifications requisite for electors of the most numerous branch of the state legislature.

(a) No person shall be a representative who shall not have attained to the age of twenty-five years, and been seven years a citizen of the United States, and who shall not, when elected, be an inhabitant of that state in which he shall be chosen.

(b) Representatives and direct taxes shall be apportioned among the several states which may be included within this Union, according to their respective numbers, which shall be determined by adding to the whole number of free persons, including those bound to servitude for a term of years, and excluding Indians not taxed, three-fifths of all other persons. The actual enumeration shall be made within three years after the first meeting of the Congress of the United States, and within every subsequent term of ten years, in such manner as they shall by law direct. The number of representatives shall not exceed one for every forty thousand, but each state shall have at least one representative: and until such enumeration shall be made, the state of New-Hampshire shall be entitled to chuse three, Massachusetts eight, Rhode-Island and Providence Plantations one, Connecticut five, New-York six, New-Jersey four, Pennsylvania eight, Delaware one, Maryland six, Virginia ten, North-Carolina five, South-Carolina five, and Georgia three.

(c) When vacancies happen in the representation from any state, the Executive authority thereof shall issue writs of election to fill such vacancies.

(d) The House of Representatives shall choose their Speaker and other officers; and they shall have the sole power of impeachment.

Sect. 3. The Senate of the United States shall be composed of two senators from each state, chosen by the legislature thereof, for six years: and each senator shall have one vote.

(a) Immediately after they shall be assembled in consequence of the first election, they shall be divided as equally as may be into three classes. The seats of the senators of the first class shall be vacated at the expiration of the second year, of the second class at the expiration of the fourth year, and of the third class at the expiration of the sixth year, so that one-third may be chosen every second year: and if vacancies happen by resignation, or otherwise, during the recess of the Legislature of any state, the Executive thereof may make temporary appointments until the next meeting of the Legislature.

(b) No person shall be a senator who shall not have attained to the age of thirty years, and been nine years a citizen of the United States, and who shall not, when elected, be an inhabitant of that state for which he shall be chosen.

(c) The Vice-President of the United States shall be, ~~ex officio~~, President of the senate, but shall have no vote, unless they be equally divided.

(d) The Senate shall choose their other officers, and also a President pro tempore, in the absence of the Vice-President, or when he shall exercise the office of President of the United States.

(e) The Senate shall have the sole power to try all impeachments. When sitting for that purpose, they shall be on oath. When the President of the United States is tried, the Chief Justice shall preside: And no person shall be convicted without the concurrence of two-thirds of the members present.

(f) Judgment in cases of impeachment shall not extend further than to removal from office, and disqualification to hold and enjoy any office of honor, trust or profit under the United States: but the party convicted shall nevertheless be liable and subject to indictment, trial, judgment and punishment, according to law.

Sect. 4. The times, places and manner of holding elections for senators and representatives, shall be prescribed in each state by the legislature thereof: but the Congress may at any time by law make or alter such regulations.

(a) The Congress shall assemble at least once in every year, and such meeting shall be on the first Monday in December, unless they shall by law appoint a different day.

Sect. 5. Each house shall be the judge of the elections, returns and qualifications of its own members, and a majority of each shall constitute a quorum to do business: but a smaller number may adjourn from day to day, and may be authorised to compel the attendance of absent members, in such manner, and under such penalties as each house may provide.

(a) Each house may determine the rules of its proceedings; punish its members for disorderly behaviour, and, with the concurrence of two-thirds, expel a member.

(b) Each house shall keep a journal of its proceedings, and from time to time publish the same, excepting such parts as may in their judgment require secrecy; and the yeas and nays of the members of either house on any question shall, at the desire of one-fifth of those present, be entered on the journal.

(c) Neither house, during the session of Congress, shall, without the consent of the other, adjourn for more than three days, nor to any other place than that in which the two houses shall be sitting.

Sect. 6. The senators and representatives shall receive a compensation for their services, to be ascertained by law, and paid out of the treasury of the United States. They shall in all cases, except treason, felony and breach of the peace, be privileged from arrest during their attendance at the session of their respective houses, and in going to and returning from the same; and for any speech or debate in either house, they shall not be questioned in any other place. No senator or representative shall, during the time for which he was elected, be appointed to any civil office under the authority of the United States, which shall have been created, or the emoluments

MAKING THE CONSTITUTION. The Committee on Style had a broadside of the draft printed on 12 September 1787. Madison added the words "by lot" to Article I, section 3, paragraph a (with an explanation at the lower left) and crossed out the words "ex officio" in paragraph c. The final version was signed on 17 September.

JAMES MADISON PAPERS, LIBRARY OF CONGRESS.

THE CONSTITUTION OF THE UNITED STATES.   The first page of the document signed at Philadelphia
NATIONAL ARCHIVES AND RECORDS SERVICE.

judicial power" the Framers intended the courts to have this power, reflecting existing jurisprudential theory as well as some limited practice. Furthermore, the supremacy clause would seem to require some agency to determine when in fact an act of Congress or of the states comes into conflict with the Constitution.

Article IV includes provisions that regulate conduct among the states as well as conduct between the states and the federal government. As part of the federal philosophy of comity among the states, each state is required to give full faith and credit to the acts of other states, and the citizens of each state enjoy all the privileges and immunities of residents of other states when they travel to other states. This article also provides for the admission of new states to the Union, the governing of territories, and the guarantee to the states of "a Republican Form of Government." Article IV also calls upon states to return runaway slaves to their rightful owners.

Slavery, although never mentioned in the Constitution, figured in other parts of the final document. After debating how slaves would be counted for purposes of representation in the Congress and for taxation, the delegates arrived at a compromise. Five slaves would be counted as equal to three free persons for purposes of both representation and taxation, a proposition Madison supported. Congress could not abolish the importation of slaves for twenty years, although it could place a head tax on such imports. When the drive to do away with slavery picked up momentum in the 1840s, abolitionists such as William Lloyd Garrison denounced the Constitution as "a covenant with death and an agreement with hell" because it recognized and supported slavery. But in the debates at the Federal Convention, as in the document itself, slavery played a minor role. Although some of the writers personally opposed slavery, the Constitution was not the document they chose to express that feeling.

Article V addresses one of the most glaring defects of the Articles of Confederation—the requirement for unanimity in amending the agreement. Under the Constitution, an amendment can be proposed to the states either by passage by a two-thirds vote of both houses of Congress or by a convention called upon application by two-thirds of the state legislatures; an amendment goes into effect if ratified by three-fourths of the states, either in their legislatures or by special ratifying conventions. Indeed, the Framers did not intend to make the ratifying process easy; thousands of proposals have been made in the past two centuries, but only twenty-seven have gained the necessary approval.

Article VI deals with the supremacy of the national government and also defines the new government to be established under the Constitution as the legitimate successor to the old government under the Articles. All officers of both the state and the federal governments were bound by oath (but not by religious test) to uphold the Constitution, which was declared the supreme law of the land.

Finally, to evade the unanimity provision of the Articles of Confederation, Article VII states simply that the Constitution will go into effect upon ratification by nine states.

Separation of Powers. Taking the Constitution as a whole, perhaps its most striking feature is how extensively it implemented the prevailing ideas (Montesquieu had a wide American audience) on separation of powers. Unlike the Articles and most of the existing state constitutions, clear lines divided the legislative, executive, and judicial functions. In a sharp departure from recent experience, the Framers placed great—if not well-defined—powers in the hands of the president. Madison, Hamilton, and others wanted to make the presidency even more independent by instituting direct election by the people, but in the end they settled for indirect selection through the electoral college. The convention did, however, leave the method of selecting electors to the states, and in time nearly all states decided to choose their electors through popular vote.

The Articles attempted to forestall tyranny by creating a weak government; the delegates to the Federal Convention also feared tyranny but recognized the need for strong and effective government. To escape this dilemma, the Constitution provides a series of checks to prevent any one branch of government from dominating the others. Although some parallels may be found in the Whig ideas of British government (strong Parliament, weak monarchy), the Senate did not correspond to the House of Lords, nor the president to the king. Representatives, directly elected from specific districts, had only two-year terms, giving the people frequent opportunities to pass on their conduct in office. The indirectly elected senators held six-year terms, for the Framers believed that insulating them from biennial elections would make them more deliberative. The president could veto bills, but Congress could override the veto. Judges received life tenure but could be removed for improper behavior. The extensive powers of president and Congress often had to be exercised cooperatively.

The chief defect of the Constitution of 1787, at least in the eyes of many contemporaries, was the absence of a bill of rights. George Mason of Virginia, who attended all the Philadelphia convention, refused to put his name to the Constitution, in part because it lacked specific guarantees of individual liberties. When Madison sent a copy of the Constitution to Jefferson in Paris, Jefferson approved of the scheme in general, but, he declared, "A bill of rights is what the people are entitled to against every government on earth . . . and what no just government should refuse." Madison believed such an explicit list unnecessary, and, as Hamilton wrote in *Federalist* 84, "the constitution is itself . . . A BILL OF RIGHTS." Public opinion ruled otherwise. As the price for ratification in several states, the backers of the Constitution agreed to add a bill of rights when the first Congress convened. By then James Madison had come around to the view that, if not absolutely necessary, written protections of basic liberties were still of value, and he took on the task of shepherding those amendments through the Congress.

In fact, comparing the Constitution of 1787 to the Constitution as it stands today, we see that the framework is still the same. Although relations between the states and the federal government have changed considerably, we still operate under a federal system. The national government has three branches, and if the Congress is not as powerful in relation to the other branches as the Framers had intended, it is still a potent institution, well able to hold its own against even the strongest presidents. Aside from a few minor technical changes, additions have involved the expansion of our liberties, a trend most of the delegates to Philadelphia probably would have approved.

[See also *Articles of Confederation; Bill of Rights; Constitution Making; Federal Convention; New Jersey Plan; Virginia Plan;* and appendix for text of the Constitution.]

BIBLIOGRAPHY

Diamond, Martin. "The Declaration and the Constitution: Liberty, Democracy, and the Founders." *The Public Interest* 41 (1975): 39–55.

Jillson, Calvin C. *Constitution Making: Conflict and Consensus in the Federal Convention of 1787.* 1988.

McDonald, Forrest. *Novo Ordo Seclorum: The Intellectual Origins of the Constitution.* 1985.

Miller, William Lee. *The Business of May Next: James Madison and the Founding.* 1992.

Wood, Gordon S. *The Creation of the American Republic, 1776–1787.* 1969.

MELVIN I. UROFSKY

CONTINENTAL CONGRESS. See *Madison, James,* article on *Continental Congress.*

CONTINENTAL SYSTEM. Napoleon's Continental System was created to thwart Britain's control of the oceans by making the European continent one large French bastion. Napoleon's smashing victory over Austria and Russia at Austerlitz in December 1805 rendered his armies seemingly invincible in Europe, even as Lord Nelson's destruction of the French fleet at Trafalgar in October symbolized Britain's command of the oceans. By 1806 Britain faced the problem not only of France's growing dominance on the continent but also of neutral vessels serving France's commercial interests by operating freely in the coastal trade of Napoleon's continental empire. Napoleonic France and Britain both understood that their respective positions in world politics could be sustained only through the downfall of the other. In May 1806 the British government acknowledged France's exploitation of neutral trade by declaring a blockade of the European coast from Brest to the Elbe, to be enforced only between the Seine and Ostend. Outside those limits, the British would permit neutrals to carry noncontraband goods, provided that the ships avoided enemy ports. The prohibition did not extend to neutral vessels carrying France's colonial trade through American ports. For the United States, this omission seemed to resolve the pressing questions of continuous voyage and the Rule of 1756, which maintained that trade prohibited in time of peace could not be pursued during wartime.

Without the sea power to reach Britain, Napoleon could strike British commerce only from his continental fortress. During October 1806 the French armies routed Prussian forces at Jena and Halle, permitting Napoleon to enter Berlin. There, on 21 November, he issued his Berlin Decree, which proclaimed a paper blockade of Great Britain and closed the continent to British trade. Napoleon had no navy to prevent goods from entering British ports; he intended only to keep ships from leaving Britain by threatening to confiscate any vessel that had entered a British port. Assuming that maintaining Britain's current levels of production required access to the European market, Napoleon believed that his power on land was sufficient to injure British manufacturing and commerce and thereby undermine that country's war-making capacity. Aware of the danger, Britain responded on 7 January 1807 with an order in council prohibiting neutral trade between ports under French control. Secretary of State James Madison complained that the new imposition would ruin American trade by denying neutral vessels the right to visit successive ports along the European coast. For neutral American shippers, profitability depended on the right to drop cargo at a series of ports and to acquire goods for export along the way.

Napoleon's victory over Russia's forces at Friedland on 4 June 1807 convinced him that he had at last gained mastery over Europe, especially when, in the Treaties of Tilsit of July, he persuaded Tsar Alexander I to extend the Continental System to Russian ports while Prussia was to close all its harbors to British trade. Napoleon now began to enforce his Berlin Decree through numerous seizures. For a time, insurance for British shipments to the continent became unobtainable. London countered Napoleon's renewed war on British trade with its order in council of 11 November, which declared a blockade of all countries in the Napoleonic system, as well as of their colonies, and condemned their products as lawful prizes. By 1812, this British document had become the American rationale for war.

Before that crisis, however, the British, having no desire to eliminate all trade with Europe, had agreed to permit ships to pass through the blockade if they were leaving or bound for a British port. When Portugal refused to enter the Continental System, Napoleon occupied that country. Then, on 17 December, his Milan Decree completed his Continental System by closing the entire European coastline to British trade. Thereafter, any neutral vessel that sailed from a British port or submitted to British search ceased to be neutral and became subject to seizure. The United States soon responded to the Anglo-French commercial restrictions with policies of nonimportation and embargo that ultimately led to war.

[See also *Blockades by England and France; Orders in Council.*]

BIBLIOGRAPHY

Brant, Irving. *James Madison: Secretary of State, 1800–1809.* 1953.

Burt, A. L. *The United States, Great Britain, and British North America from the Revolution to the Establishment of Peace after the War of 1812.* 1940.

Spivak, Burton. *Jefferson's English Crisis: Commerce, Embargo, and the Republican Revolution.* 1979.

NORMAN A. GRAEBNER

COXE, TENCH (1755–1824), political economist, propagandist. Born and educated in Philadelphia, a man of consistent if pragmatic economic views, Coxe spent his life shifting from one political alliance to another in search of a government that would benefit his fledgling nation and also advance his career and pocketbook. As an economic nationalist who believed in central planning, the young merchant exhibited Tory sympathies during the early days of the Revolution and enriched his purse by supplying woolen goods to the British army. When General Howe retreated from Philadelphia, Coxe abandoned his loyalist contacts and opened a correspondence with a French trading company, an opportunity made possible by the 1778 alliance between France and the United States. But Coxe's efforts to rebuild his damaged business were hampered by the ineffective Confederation of 1783–1789.

Coxe's belief that only a stronger political union would cure the lingering depression of the 1780s won him appointment as a Pennsylvania delegate to the Annapolis Convention. After long conversations with James Madison, a Virginia delegate, Coxe returned to Philadelphia an ardent advocate of a remodeled government. He enthusiastically endorsed the newly proposed Constitution in 1787–1788 and wrote nearly thirty essays in favor of ratification. Madison circulated one of the longer pamphlets, *Address to the Convention of Virginia*, in "the man-

ner most likely to be of service" and republished four more. Although none of Coxe's essays were as elegant as Madison's celebrated articles (in *The Federalist*), they were perhaps more influential. Designed to reassure Virginia planters that agriculture was "the great leading interest" of the North as well as the South, Coxe's essays were easier for most unlettered agrarians to understand.

Coxe and his Virginia ally parted ways, however, on the question of Secretary of the Treasury Alexander Hamilton's fiscal plans. Coxe emphatically approved of the funding and assumption acts, which he had first recommended in his *Enquiry into a Commercial System* of 1787. Never shy about advancing his opinions or career, Coxe tendered an "offer of service" to Hamilton in early 1790, when Assistant Secretary William Duer's forced resignation created a vacancy at the Treasury. Madison, who well knew of Coxe's support for manufactures and tariffs, was disappointed but hardly surprised.

Despite his ready support for Hamilton's programs, as well as his frequent willingness to take up his pen as propagandist, Coxe was overlooked for promotion when Hamilton retired in late 1794. Thereafter, Coxe, who had always maintained friendly personal relations with Madison, drifted toward the Republicans. Soon after assuming the presidency, John Adams, on the

TENCH COXE. Engraving by F. T. Stuart.
PRINTS AND PHOTOGRAPHS DIVISION, LIBRARY OF CONGRESS.

advice of Oliver Wolcott, removed Coxe from office.

The Republican victory in 1800 breathed new life into Coxe's career. In the spring of 1801 he approached Madison in search of a job. Although President Jefferson showed little enthusiasm for Coxe's theories, he reluctantly appointed him purveyor of public supplies. In 1808 Coxe repaid Madison for his efforts by writing dozens of articles on his behalf in the Philadelphia *Democratic Press.* Madison was grateful, but he recognized that the political turncoat had few supporters in Congress. When Coxe's position was abolished in 1812 because of the reorganization of the Quartermaster corps, Madison declined to name him to another post. Coxe retired to live with his daughter and died in 1828.

BIBLIOGRAPHY

Cooke, Jacob E. *Tench Coxe and the Early Republic.* 1978.
Du Bin, Alexander. *Coxe Family.* 1936.
Hutcheson, Harold. *Tench Coxe: A Study in American Economic Development.* 1938.

DOUGLAS R. EGERTON

CRAIK, JAMES

CRAIK, JAMES (c. 1730–1814), chief physician and surgeon of the Continental army. Craik, whom James Madison helped to obtain a high office in the reorganized Continental medical department during the fall of 1780, was an experienced military surgeon and an intimate friend of George Washington. Born near Dumfries, Scotland, Craik studied medicine at the University of Edinburgh and began his medical career in 1751 as an army surgeon in the West Indies. Three years later Craik was in Virginia, where he became surgeon of the newly authorized provincial regiment of which Washington soon took command. During the disastrous Fort Necessity and Braddock campaigns of 1754 and 1755 and the hard frontier duty that followed, the two men came to know and trust one another. At the end of the war, Craik settled on a plantation near Port Tobacco, Maryland, about half a day's ride from Mount Vernon, where he was a frequent visitor.

Washington did not forget his old comrade in arms at the beginning of the Revolutionary War, but, wishing to avoid any imputations of partiality as commander in chief, he avoided openly favoring friends and relatives over other candidates for offices. Not until the spring of 1777 did Washington find a suitable opportunity to bring Craik into the medical department as deputy director general of the hospital in the middle states. During the Philadelphia campaign later that year and at Valley Forge the following winter, Craik proved his worth by seeing that Washington's beleaguered army received adequate medical care, and in June 1780 he organized a hospital in Rhode Island for arriving French troops. Washington was disturbed to

hear in September 1780 that Congress's new arrangement of the medical department "might possibly be influenced by a spirit of party out of Doors," and he promptly wrote delegates James Duane, John Mathews, and Joseph Jones, asking that Craik and Dr. John Cochran of New Jersey be retained "among the first Officers in the Establishment." Jones, who was on leave in Virginia, referred the matter to his colleague Madison at Philadelphia.

Madison's precise role in this affair is not known, but he and Craik apparently became fairly well acquainted during the fall of 1780. On 5 October Congress appointed Cochran chief physician and surgeon of the army, second only to the director general, and Craik became one of three chief hospital surgeons under Cochran. When Congress promoted Cochran to director general on 3 March 1781, Craik was named chief physician and surgeon of the army in his place. Craik served in that capacity until the end of the war, further distinguishing himself by his capable management of the hospitals at the siege of Yorktown in the fall of 1781. Craik's only subsequent contact with Madison occurred in February 1787 when Craik presumed on their "former acquaintance" to ask for Madison's assistance in settling his wartime accounts.

BIBLIOGRAPHY

Blanton, Wyndham B. *Medicine in Virginia in the Eighteenth Century.* 1931.
Fitzpatrick, John C., ed. *The Writings of George Washington from the Original Manuscript Sources, 1745–1799.* 39 vols. 1931–1944.
Hutchinson, William T., et al., eds. *The Papers of James Madison: Congressional Series.* 17 vols. 1962–1991.

PHILANDER D. CHASE

CRAWFORD, WILLIAM HARRIS

CRAWFORD, WILLIAM HARRIS (1772–1834). Georgia political leader, U.S. senator, cabinet member, presidential candidate. William H. Crawford, one of eleven children born to Joel Crawford and Fannie Harris Crawford, came from the Piedmont of Virginia. The Crawford family moved, first to South Carolina and eventually to Columbia County, Georgia. There Crawford completed his education and taught school for several years. Soon after being admitted to the bar, he married Susanna Giradin.

Crawford was elected to the Georgia legislature in 1803 and soon allied himself with James Jackson and George Troup. After an active and sometimes violent political career in Georgia, during which he fought two duels, he was elected to the U.S. Senate in 1807. He proved to be an active and often outspoken senator and, although a Republican, chastised President James Madison in 1810 for failing to advocate a stronger military force. Crawford became president pro tempore of

WILLIAM H. CRAWFORD.   Madison appointed Crawford secretary of war in 1815 and secretary of the Treasury in 1816. Engraving by Asher B. Durand after portrait by John Wesley Jarvis.

PRINTS AND PHOTOGRAPHS DIVISION, LIBRARY OF CONGRESS.

the Senate when Vice President George Clinton died.

In 1813 President Madison appointed Crawford the U.S. minister to France, a post he retained until August 1815. During his service in France, Crawford was not officially a member of the team that negotiated the Treaty of Ghent, but he served as an adviser and undoubtedly played a role in the negotiations. In April 1815, even before Crawford returned home, Madison appointed him secretary of war. In this capacity he clashed with Andrew Jackson over the issue of how harshly to treat the Indians. Crawford was known to be more humane than most of those charged with dealing with the Indians. In August 1816 President Madison appointed him secretary of the Treasury, a position he continued to fill until the end of the Monroe presidency.

Many of Crawford's friends in the Republican party tried to persuade him to run for the presidency against James Monroe in 1816. He absolutely refused to run, however, and eventually continued on as Monroe's secretary of the Treasury. In 1824 Crawford did run for president with the full support of Madison, Monroe, Martin Van Buren, and Nathaniel Macon. As the "insider's" choice, he was the target of attacks by the other candi-

dates. Because of its support of states' rights and the national bank, Crawford's group became known as the radical faction of the Republican party.

Attacks on Crawford as the presidential front-runner had dogged him throughout Monroe's second administration. Although Crawford was supported by both Madison and Monroe in the 1824 election, he had three strong opponents—John Quincy Adams, Henry Clay, and Andrew Jackson. Crawford remained the favorite candidate until the fall of 1823, when he suffered a serious and crippling stroke. An attack on the caucus system, as well as Crawford's illness, caused him to achieve only third place in the November election. The election was thrown into the House of Representatives, where Adams was elected.

Crawford recovered from his ailments sufficiently to become a judge in 1827. Although he hoped to run for the presidency, he never again had the opportunity. He died on 15 September 1834 and was buried at his home at Lexington, Georgia.

BIBLIOGRAPHY

Green, Philip J. *The Life of William Harris Crawford.* 1965.
Grice, Warren. *The Georgia Bench and Bar.* 1931.
Mooney, Chase C. *William H. Crawford 1772–1834.* 1974.
Shipp, J. E. D. *Giant Days or the Life and Times of William H. Crawford.* 1909.

FRANK LAWRENCE OWSLEY, JR

CREEK INDIANS.   The Creek Indians, often called Muskogees because most spoke Muskhogean dialects, inhabited much of the area that is now Alabama and Georgia. The Creeks were a loose confederacy of some sixty or more autonomous towns. In time, the Creek towns were classified as either Upper or Lower towns, according to geographic location. Clan ties and annual meetings of the national council, composed of town civil and war leaders, held the confederacy together, while each town's governmental and ceremonial activities centered on a town square.

Creeks suffered heavily in the sixteenth century from Spanish contact, which exposed them to devastating European diseases. Early in the eighteenth century, they became involved in the English colonial deerskin trade. The Creeks attempted to steer a neutral course in the colonial wars but gave the British qualified assistance in the American Revolution. After the Revolution, they came under great pressure from the United States, particularly the state of Georgia. In response, the Creek chief Alexander McGillivray, son of a Scottish father and a member of the influential Wind clan, attempted to centralize Creek government and ably courted Spain in an effort to build a network of protective alliances against

American expansion, but town headmen opposed to McGillivray signed treaties ceding land to Georgia.

Benjamin Hawkins, appointed as the federal tribal agent in 1796, worked hard to introduce American ways of life among the Creeks, adding to the divisions in Creek society. Upper Creeks listened attentively to the Shawnee chief Tecumseh's message of pan-Indian resistance in 1811, and religious leaders like Hillis Hadjo urged the Creeks to resist American expansion and influences. The Creek War of 1813–1814 was also a civil war, as Creek warriors (called Red Sticks by their enemies) fought against Americans and their Indian supporters. Andrew Jackson inflicted a string of defeats on the Creeks, culminating in the slaughter of some eight hundred warriors at the Battle of Horseshoe Bend. After negotiating the Treaty of Fort Jackson in 1814, Jackson confiscated huge areas of the Creek homeland. Military defeat and continuing divisions among the Creeks kept them from mounting serious resistance to American removal policies that forced them west of the Mississippi in the 1830s.

BIBLIOGRAPHY

Green, Michael D. *The Politics of Indian Removal: Creek Government and Society in Crisis.* 1982.

Martin, Joel W. *Sacred Revolt: The Muskogees' Struggle for a New World.* 1991.

Wright, J. Leitch. *Creeks and Seminoles: Destruction and Regeneration of the Muscogulge People.* 1986.

COLIN G. CALLOWAY

CROWNINSHIELD, BENJAMIN W. (1772–1851),
merchant, representative, secretary of the navy. One of five sons born to a Salem merchant family, he was, like his brothers, educated at sea aboard his father's ships. After some experience in commanding vessels, Crowninshield joined the family enterprise as a partner and helped advance its position among the dynamic mercantile houses of Salem. Crucial to the Crowninshields' financial success were their close trading ties with France and its possessions; in the 1790s, this alliance led the family to move into the Republican ranks, where it proved to be a powerful counterforce to Federalists in Essex County.

After the election of Jefferson to the presidency in 1801, his administration turned to the family for advice on political appointments in Massachusetts, and Benjamin's brother Jacob defeated Timothy Pickering for a seat in the U.S. House of Representatives in 1802. Upon Jacob's death in 1809, Benjamin assumed the family's political mantle, serving in the Massachusetts state legislature in 1811 and 1812. In 1814 Madison, casting about for a replacement for William Jones as secretary of the navy, nominated Crowninshield for the post. Years later, Madison wrote that he had chosen Crowninshield not only because he was from New England but because he "added to a stock of practical good sense a useful stock of nautical experience and information, and an accommodating disposition," attributes that would be essential to iron out difficulties with the newly created board of naval commissioners. Confirmed by the Senate, Crowninshield at first declined, then accepted the position, but he did not take up his duties until late January 1815. From that time until his resignation in October 1818, Crowninshield served as a competent administrator of the Navy Department, but without leaving any permanent mark on the conduct of the office. He was a presidential elector for the Republican ticket in 1820 and returned to national politics after his election to the U.S. House of Representatives in 1823. He served four terms as a representative but was defeated in his bid for a fifth term in 1830.

BIBLIOGRAPHY

Goodman, Paul. *The Democratic-Republicans of Massachusetts: Politics in a Young Republic.* 1964.

Paullin, Charles Oscar. *Paullin's History of Naval Administration, 1775–1911.* 1968.

Whitney, William T. "The Crowninshields of Salem, 1800–1808." Parts 1 and 2. *Essex Institute Historical Collections* 94 (1958): 1–36, 79–118.

DAVID B. MATTERN

CRYSLER'S FARM, BATTLE OF. See *Chrysler's Farm, Battle of.*

CUMBERLAND ROAD. After its approval by President Thomas Jefferson in 1806, the Cumberland Road, connecting Cumberland, Maryland, on the Potomac River with Wheeling, West Virginia, on the Ohio River, was built between 1811 and 1818. Between 1825 and 1838, the route was extended to Vandalia, Illinois. Also known as the United States Road, the National Turnpike, and the National Road, it played an indispensable role in the settling of the Ohio and upper Mississippi valleys. U.S. Route 40 currently follows the path of the Cumberland Road.

Despite his belief that federal funding of internal improvements was unconstitutional, Madison signed bills extending construction of the Cumberland Road during his presidency. After leaving the White House, Madison noted that Jefferson had "doubtingly or hastily" given his assent to the project, without carefully examining its constitutionality. Madison, in turn, had supported the road "with less of critical investigation perhaps than was due in the case." Nevertheless, he upheld the authority of the federal government to fund the Cumberland Road because it traversed U.S. territories, where Congress had full power. Only within states was Congress unable to sponsor improvements, Madison believed.

By opening a trade route from the Chesapeake region to the Ohio River, the Cumberland Road fulfilled a goal that Madison had pursued as early as 1785. In that year he secured from the Virginia General Assembly a charter for the Potomac Company, a private corporation authorized to open the Potomac River as far as Cumberland and to connect it to the Ohio by means of portage roads and additional river improvements. Although the company never succeeded in linking the Potomac to the Ohio, the Cumberland Road did achieve that objective.

BIBLIOGRAPHY

Hunt, Gaillard, ed. *The Writings of James Madison*. 9 vols. 1908.
McCoy, Drew R. *The Last of the Fathers: James Madison and the Republican Legacy*. 1989.
Young, Jeremiah Simeon. *A Political and Constitutional Study of the Cumberland Road*. 1902.

STUART LEIBIGER

CUTTS, RICHARD, AND ANNA (PAYNE) CUTTS, brother-in-law and sister of Dolley Madison.

Anna Payne (1779–1832) was born 11 November 1779 in Hanover County, Virginia. She was sixth of the eight children of John and Mary (Coles) Payne and was eleven years younger than her sister Dolley, the future Dolley Madison. From childhood until her death in 1832, Anna Payne was the member of the Payne family to whom Dolley Madison was closest and most devoted.

In 1783 Anna Payne moved with her parents and siblings to Philadelphia. Following her sister Dolley's marriage to the Philadelphia attorney John Todd, Jr., in 1790, Anna became a member of their household. For the next fourteen years—a period that included the death of John Todd, Jr., in 1793 and Dolley Todd's subsequent remarriage to James Madison in 1794—the sisters continued to live together and were virtually inseparable. Anna Payne served her eldest sister as companion, confidante, and, to some extent, surrogate daughter—Dolley Madison called her "my sister-child." Anna moved with the Madisons to Montpelier following James Madison's retirement from Congress in 1797, then accompanied them to Washington, D.C., when Madison was appointed secretary of state in the administration of Thomas Jefferson.

Anna Payne married Rep. Richard Cutts (1771–1845) on 31 March 1804. Cutts, born 28 June 1771 on Cutts Island, Saco, Massachusetts (now Maine), was the son of Thomas and Elizabeth (Scammon) Cutts. After attending private schools, Richard Cutts graduated from Harvard University in 1790. He subsequently pursued further education in Europe, studied law, and participated in his family's mercantile shipping and commercial pursuits.

In 1799 and 1800, Cutts was a member of the Massachusetts House of Representatives. From 1801 to 1813 he was a U.S. representative from the District of Maine (then a part of Massachusetts), serving in the Seventh through Twelfth Congresses. In Congress Cutts was a firm supporter of Jefferson and Madison. In addition, he became an important adviser and confidant during Madison's terms as secretary of state and as president and kept Madison abreast of the political climate in Congress and in Washington.

After failing to win reelection to the Thirteenth Congress, Cutts served as superintendant general of military supplies from 1813 to 1817. He was appointed second comptroller of the U.S. Treasury by Madison in 1817 and held this post until he was discharged by President Andrew Jackson in 1829.

Richard and Anna (Payne) Cutts had seven children: James Madison Cutts (1805–1863); Thomas Cutts (1806–1838); Walter Coles Cutts (b. 1808; lost at sea, date unknown); Richard Cutts (1810–1815); Dolley Payne Cutts, called Dolché (1811–1838); Mary Estelle Elizabeth Cutts (1814–1856); and Richard Dominicus Cutts (1817–1883). The Cutts family, especially Anna and the children, frequently made lengthy visits to the Madisons at Montpelier, and the Cutts children included some of the Madisons' most cherished nieces and nephews.

From the middle of his life, Richard Cutts was dogged by various financial problems. A number of his ships and much of the family mercantile property were lost in the War of 1812. Efforts to revive his fortunes failed; in the 1820s he was forced to declare bankruptcy and spent a term in debtors' prison.

The Madisons, along with Dolley's and Anna's sister Lucy (Payne) Todd "and other of her kindred and friends," joined in setting up a trust fund for Anna. In order to provide a home for Anna and her family, James Madison assumed ownership and debt of the Cutts house on Lafayette Square in Washington. (This residence later became Dolley Madison's home when she returned to Washington after her husband's death.)

Anna Cutts remained in Washington, D.C., until her death from chronic heart failure (then called "dropsy of the heart") on 4 August 1832. Richard Cutts later moved to a house on Fourteenth Street, dying there on 7 April 1845.

BIBLIOGRAPHY

Arnett, Ethel Stevens. *Mrs. James Madison: The Incomparable Dolley*. 1972.
Biographical Dictionary of the American Congress. 1928.
Clark, Allen C. *Life and Letters of Dolley Madison*. 1914.

ANN L. MILLER

D

DALLAS, ALEXANDER JAMES (1759–1817), lawyer, Pennsylvania political leader, secretary of the Treasury. Born in Jamaica and educated in England, Dallas migrated to the United States in 1783. Early success as a member of the Philadelphia bar, coupled with his Antifederalist political activities, led to Dallas's appointment as secretary of the commonwealth under Governor Thomas Mifflin in 1791. Dallas held that position through Mifflin's administration and was reappointed by Mifflin's successor, Thomas McKean. During his ten-year tenure as secretary, Dallas used his position to strengthen the organization of the burgeoning Democratic-Republican party in Pennsylvania and was one of the founders of the Democratic Society of Philadelphia in 1793.

These political activities, as well as his close friendship with Albert Gallatin, a member of President Jefferson's cabinet, resulted in Dallas's appointment as United States attorney for eastern Pennsylvania in 1801. Dallas served in this capacity during both of Jefferson's administrations and was reappointed by President Madison.

By 1813 Dallas was poised to enter the national scene. In the spring of 1813 the United States had been at war with England for nearly a year, and its lack of military success was matched by serious financial difficulties. Moreover, the demise of the First Bank of the United States in 1811 left the federal government bereft of its principal connection with the nation's banking community. Gallatin, as secretary of the Treasury, was forced to appeal directly to bankers and business leaders in his attempt to float government loans, while Dallas acted as a valuable connection between the Treasury and the Philadelphia financial establishment.

In March 1813 Dallas discussed the fate of a $16 million loan, of which Gallatin had placed less than $6 million, with David Parish, a financial soldier of fortune with strong European commercial ties. With Dallas acting as liaison, Parish, Stephen Girard, and John Jacob Astor formed a syndicate to purchase the remainder of the loan and save the Treasury from virtual bankruptcy.

To add to the administration's difficulties, Gallatin was appointed to the peace commission dispatched by Madison to Europe in May 1813, leaving the Treasury in the hands of the acting secretary, William Jones, who proved unequal to the task. In October 1814 Madison offered the Treasury to Dallas, and, after both the candidate's initial reluctance and some objections by Pennsylvania's senators were overcome, Dallas was confirmed as secretary.

Despite his lack of formal financial training and experience, Dallas's two years at the Treasury were characterized by competency and success. The nation's finances were reordered by debt refunding and the restoration of specie payments in February 1817. Dallas was the principal figure in the drafting and passage of legislation establishing the Second Bank of the United States. Federal revenues were enhanced by a Dallas-inspired tariff act in 1816—the first protective tariff act in the nation's history.

Dallas returned to Philadelphia and his private law practice in the spring of 1816, but his return to private life was short. In early January 1817 he was stricken by a chronic illness and died on the morning of 16 January 1817.

BIBLIOGRAPHY

Walters, Raymond J., Jr. *Alexander James Dallas*. 1943.

DONALD R. ADAMS, JR.

DASCHKOFF, ANDREI IAKOVLEVICH (1776–1831), Russian diplomat. Daschkoff, an official in the department of commerce, was appointed Russian representative to the United States at the opening of diplomatic relations between the two countries in 1808.

He was named consul general, chargé d'affaires, and special representative of the Russian American Company, a fur-trading company on the Pacific coast, and was appointed minister plenipotentiary in 1811. His initial mission was defined as commercial rather than diplomatic, and he was particularly instructed to encourage trade development. His attempts to arrange a commercial treaty prohibiting Americans from selling arms to natives near the Russian fur colonies were rejected by Madison after Daschkoff admitted he had no powers to negotiate territorial limits.

Daschkoff's initial offer of Russian mediation after the outbreak of war in 1812 was indifferently received, but Madison quickly accepted the formal offer Daschkoff relayed from his government early in 1813, an offer that the British, mistrusting Russia's position on neutrality, rejected. Daschkoff eventually accepted the Federalist argument that "nothing concerns the President more than his reelection." He criticized Madison's management of the war, which he suggested was initiated to ensure party unity, and reported that Madison's lack of foreign experience left him incapable of understanding Europe or appreciating Russian power. He regarded American relations with France as a betrayal. Daschkoff's smoldering sense of administration neglect came to a head when Vice Consul Nikolai Kozlov was jailed at Philadelphia after being accused of raping a twelve-year-old servant girl. The case was transferred to the federal courts and dismissed, but Russian authorities accepted Daschkoff's definition of the incident as a breach of diplomatic immunity and demanded an apology. When the administration responded that consuls did not enjoy immunity, Daschkoff independently suspended relations for a year in 1816. His objectionable behavior led to a request for his recall, and he took his formal leave in March 1819.

BIBLIOGRAPHY

Bashkina, Nina N., et al., eds. *The United States and Russia: The Beginning of Relations, 1765–1815.* 1980.
Bolkhovitinov, Nikolai N. *The Beginnings of Russian-American Relations, 1775–1815.* 1975.
Hildt, John C. *Early Diplomatic Negotiations of the United States with Russia.* 1906.

MARY A. HACKETT

DAWSON, JOHN (1762–1814), Virginia legislator, U.S. representative. Probably born in Spotsylvania County, Virginia, Dawson graduated from Harvard University in 1782. He practiced law in Fredericksburg and was distantly related to the influential Dr. Joseph Jones. Dawson represented Spotsylvania County in the Virginia House of Delegates, served briefly in the last Continental Congress,

and was a delegate to the Virginia Convention of 1788, where he voted against ratification of the Constitution.

Dawson soon started what became a lifelong, if not intimate, correspondence with Madison. He was placed on the Virginia Privy Council in 1789 and thus kept his hand in state politics. In 1794 he was nominated for the U.S. Senate but was easily defeated in the state senate balloting. He maintained his ties with Republican leaders in Madison's congressional district, and, when Madison announced his decision not to seek reelection to the House of Representatives, Dawson became a candidate to succeed him. Vigorously opposed by Thomas Posey, Dawson proved to be an adept campaigner on the hustings and emerged as a victor in the March 1797 balloting.

Dawson continued to keep Madison informed of political affairs in what may have been a one-sided correspondence, although Dawson was a loyal Republican. President Adams sent him to Paris on a diplomatic mission in 1801, with the amended documents to end the Quasi-War with France. Dawson voted for the compromise resolution in 1805 that favored a settlement of the Yazoo land claims by a commission, a vote that offended fellow Virginian John Randolph of Roanoke. Dawson took leave from his House seat to serve as an aide to Generals Jacob Brown and Andrew Jackson during the War of 1812. He died on 31 March 1814, before the war ended.

BIBLIOGRAPHY

Hutchinson, William T., et al., eds. *Papers of James Madison: Congressional Series.* Vol. 7. 1971.
Jordan, Daniel P. *Political Leadership in Jefferson's Virginia.* 1983.
Risjord, Norman. *The Old Republicans: Southern Conservatives in the Age of Jefferson.* 1965.

ROBERT A. RUTLAND

DEARBORN, HENRY (1751–1829), cabinet officer, army general. Dearborn emerged in the 1790s as a prominent Jeffersonian Republican, serving in Congress (1793–1797) and helping to build the Republican party in the District of Maine. Because of his status as a New England Republican, Dearborn was appointed secretary of war by Thomas Jefferson in 1801, a post he held for eight years. Dearborn did not have the close relationship that Secretary of State James Madison and Secretary of the Treasury Albert Gallatin had with Jefferson, but he was a competent administrator, and his opinion was relied on for military affairs. As secretary of war, Dearborn oversaw the reduction in the army from an authorized strength of 5,438 in 1801 to 3,312 1802 and then, following the *Chesapeake* incident in 1807, its expansion to 10,000.

As war with Great Britain neared, Dearborn was appointed a major general on the basis of his service in the

GEN. HENRY DEARBORN.   Portrait by Charles Willson Peale.
INDEPENDENCE NATIONAL HISTORICAL PARK, PHILADELPHIA.

Revolution and as secretary of war. In early 1812 he served as military consultant to President James Madison, who preferred his advice to that of Gen. James Wilkinson or of Secretary of War William Eustis. Dearborn spent the last months before war was declared trying to organize a seaboard defense in New England. Here the Madison administration received a serious rebuff when the governors of Rhode Island, Connecticut, and Massachusetts refused to provide militia.

Once the war began, Dearborn tried to raise an army that had the general goal of capturing Montreal and loosely coordinated military efforts along the Niagara frontier. Dearborn consistently overestimated the number of British troops and by October had given up the idea of taking Montreal. Instead, he hoped for victory at Niagara, but the American commanders there, Stephen Van Rensselaer and Alexander Smyth, met defeat in an inept campaign culminating at the Battle of Queenston Heights (13 October 1812). Following this loss, Dearborn once more turned his thoughts toward Montreal and took command of American forces in the Northeast to lead them to Canada. Dearborn encountered a 5,000-strong enemy force on 18 November just south of the

Canadian border. The next day, militia officers informed Dearborn that much of the American militia would not cross into Canada. Because of the militia's defiance and his inflated estimate of enemy strength, Dearborn called off his offensive on 22 November to go into winter quarters, ending an ignominious campaign. Dearborn offered to resign but Madison kept him on.

For 1813, Dearborn originally planned to take Kingston, York, and major British posts along the Niagara—Forts George and Erie—but dropped Kingston from his goals because of his old fear—exaggerated estimates of British strength. In April American troops traveled across Lake Ontario to take York (now Toronto), which fell on 27 April. American casualties were high, and the British forces retreated in good order. After York's capture, American forces were transported to the Niagara River, to take Forts George and Erie, which fell by the end of May. Once again, however, the British forces retreated unmolested. In early June Dearborn sent part of his army west into Upper Canada under Gen. William Winder, but Winder was defeated in a surprise attack and taken prisoner. This defeat, coupled with Dearborn's collapsing health—the sixty-two-year-old general could barely stand—meant the end both of the campaign and of Dearborn's position. Dearborn turned over his command in July and spent the rest of the war in Massachusetts.

Following the War of 1812, Dearborn remained politically active. In 1817 he was an unsuccessful candidate for governor of Massachusetts, and from 1822 to 1824 he served as U.S. minister to Portugal.

BIBLIOGRAPHY

Erney, Richard Alton. *The Public Life of Henry Dearborn.* 1979.
Horsman, Reginald. *The War of 1812.* 1972.

MARK PITCAVAGE

DECATUR, STEPHEN, JR. (1779–1820), naval officer. As James Madison's political career spanned the first critical decades of the nation's federal government, Decatur's naval career paralleled the development of a strong navy. Both men played key roles in strengthening their respective institutions.

Decatur joined the navy as a midshipman in 1798. He was promoted to lieutenant within a year and survived the reduction-in-force cuts required by the Peace Establishment Act of 1801. Decatur became a naval hero for his service during the first Barbary Wars (1801–1805), during which he engineered a perfectly executed expedition to destroy the captured U.S. frigate *Philadelphia*. Congress promoted him in 1804 to captain for this exploit. He was twenty-five.

STEPHEN DECATUR.   Engraving after the portrait by Alonzo Chappel.

After returning to the United States in 1805, Decatur superintended the construction of gunboats—the backbone of the Jeffersonian naval defense program. He cruised the coasts of the southern states in the frigates *Chesapeake* and *United States* in the years before the War of 1812.

Decatur's capture of the British frigate *Macedonian* in October 1812 was the highlight of his wartime efforts. British warships thwarted his escape from New York in the *United States* in 1813 and in the frigate *President* in 1814. He surrendered the *President* in January 1815.

Shortly after the War of 1812 ended, the Navy Department ordered Decatur to avenge the depredations of the Barbary states against American commerce. After capturing the Algerine fleet's flagship and brig, Decatur dictated peace terms to the three powers, only seventy-one days after sailing from New York.

Decatur was greeted as a conquering hero when he returned to the United States, and President Madison, in his 5 December 1815 message to Congress, praised Decatur's "skill and prowess" in bringing the Barbary states to terms. Madison recognized Decatur's feats by appointing him to the Board of Naval Commissioners. As a commissioner, Decatur opposed Capt. James Barron's efforts to be reinstated in the navy. Barron challenged Decatur to a duel and, to uphold the respectability of the navy, Decatur accepted. Decatur died on 22 March 1820 from the wound he received at Barron's hand.

BIBLIOGRAPHY

Dunne, W. M. P. "'The Inglorious First of June': Commodore Stephen Decatur on Long Island Sound, 1813." *Long Island Historical Journal* 2 (1990): 201–220.

Dunne, W. M. P. *Stephen Decatur.* 1994.

Mackenzie, Alexander Slidell. *Life of Stephen Decatur, A Commodore in the Navy of the United States.* 1846.

Roosevelt, Theodore. *The Naval War of 1812.* 1882. Repr. 1987.

CHRISTINE F. HUGHES

DEMOCRATIC-REPUBLICAN PARTY. See
Republican Party.

DEMOCRATIC-REPUBLICAN SOCIETIES.
The Democratic-Republican Societies were political pressure groups that flourished 1793–1794 as a response to the Washington administration's attempts to keep the United States aloof from the conflicts between Great Britain and revolutionary France. In response to the invitation from the Democratic Society of Pennsylvania, in summer 1793, to the other states to establish associations in support of the French cause, against British interests, and to restrict federal power, societies were eventually formed in every state but New Hampshire and Georgia. By the end of 1794 there were thirty-five societies from South Carolina to Maine. Most of the societies disappeared in the winter of 1794–1795 almost as rapidly as they had sprung up, after Federalists, including Washington, attempted to blame them for the unrest in western Pennsylvania that they called the Whiskey Rebellion.

Although they were called Democratic-Republican societies by many contemporaries and by nearly all historians, only the societies from Dumfries, Virginia, and Washington, North Carolina, actually used both adjectives in their title. Other societies divided almost evenly with fifteen using Republican and seventeen Democratic. Eleven of the Democratic societies were established in 1794, whereas the Republican name was chosen regularly from 1793 to 1798. Other societies used titles associating themselves with admired patriotic themes, including the Constitution, patriotism, the Committees of Correspondence, and Madison. The Madisonian Society of Greenville, South Carolina, and the Franklin or Republican Society of Pendleton, South Carolina, were the only societies to honor statesmen. In 1794 the Republican Society of South Carolina praised "Citizen James Madison" for helping the United States to "preserve faith in her allies" through his criticism of Washington's Proclamation of Neutrality.

The societies that called themselves Committees of Correspondence chose wisely, for the drafting of letters, resolutions, and declarations occupied much of their time. Although they agreed on many of the issues that would become basic to the Republican party, the societies stopped well short of becoming actual political parties. Neither Madison nor Jefferson was directly associated with any of the societies, although neither man hesitated to defend them against Federalist attacks.

In his draft of the formal response by the House of Representatives to Washington's annual message of November 1794, Madison attempted to ignore the president's attempt to associate the Whiskey Rebellion with "certain self created societies." When Federalists in Congress insisted on responding to Washington's charge, Madison battled for the societies' freedom of political expression. The House finally settled on a compromise, referring instead to "combinations of men" rather than "societies." Madison's correspondence in the winter of 1794–1795 contains frequent references to this debate. In a letter to Monroe, Madison described the president's attack on the societies as "perhaps the greatest error of [Washington's] political life. . . . The game was, to connect the Republicans in Congs. with those Societies—to put the P[resident] ostensibly at the head of the other party." The House was so evenly divided over this issue that, as Madison wrote, even a motion "to limit the censure to the Societies within the scene of insurrection . . . was carried [only] by the casting vote of the Speaker."

Although the national party leaders did not affiliate with the Democratic-Republican societies, the societies were training grounds for practitioners of partisan politics. Three of Madison's eventual cabinet members—Albert Gallatin, Alexander J. Dallas, and Caesar A. Rodney—were active participants.

[See also *Republican party*.]

BIBLIOGRAPHY

Hutchinson, William T., et al., eds. *The Papers of James Madison: Congressional Series*. 15 vols. 1962– . Vol. 15. 1985.
Link, Eugene Perry. *Democratic-Republican Societies, 1790–1800*. 1965.

DONALD O. DEWEY

DETROIT, BATTLE OF.

In 1812 the town of Detroit, whose population included about half the forty-eight hundred residents of the Michigan Territory, sprawled along the Detroit River. In July, some four thousand regulars and militia led by Brig. Gen. William Hull, the governor of the territory, arrived at Detroit intending to invade Upper Canada via Sandwich. Hull's force crossed the river to move toward Fort Malden at Amherstburg, but, after a skirmish at the Canard River and upon learning of the loss of Michilimackinac, Hull recrossed on 8 August and on 11 August vacated Sandwich.

During the night of 15–16 August, six hundred Indians, allies of the British, crossed the river. On the next morning three tiny units, each containing slightly more than two hundred British regulars and militia and led by Maj. Gen. Isaac Brock, the governor of Upper Canada, crossed unopposed at Spring Wells. Brock ordered an immediate advance led by Col. Henry Proctor. An artillery bombardment followed, and Hull was faced with the desertion of the Michigan militia. After an eighteen-pound shell landed in his officers' mess, killing four, Hull requested a flag of truce and a one-hour cessation of hostilities. Brock accepted but implied he might not be able to restrain his Indian allies. Surrender terms were quickly arranged that, to their dismay and anger, included the Ohio colonels Lewis Cass and Duncan McArthur and their volunteers. A force of sixteen hundred Ohio volunteers was paroled, but the terms of capitulation included thirty-three cannon, twenty-five hundred muskets, military stores, and the army brig *Adams*. General Hull and 582 regulars were sent to Quebec City as prisoners of war. The British suffered no casualties.

The capitulation was a severe blow to Madison's strategic objective of invading Upper Canada and meant a war of recovery, rather than a war of conquest, in the West. Hull was paroled, court-martialed, and sentenced to death, but the sentence was commuted by Madison.

BIBLIOGRAPHY

Gilpin, Alex. *The War of 1812 in the Old North West*. 1958.
Hickey, Don. *The War of 1812: A Forgotten Contest*. 1989.
Hitsman, J. Mackay. *The Incredible War of 1812*. 1965.
Stanley, George. *The War of 1812: Land Operations*. 1983.

FREDERICK C. DRAKE

DEXTER, SAMUEL

(1761–1816), lawyer, member of Congress, member of the cabinet. Born in Boston and graduated from Harvard in 1781, Dexter read law with Levi Lincoln, began practice in 1786, and served in the Massachusetts Senate (1792–1793). He was a Federalist representative in the Third Congress (1793–1795). On 23 January 1794 Dexter opposed Madison's resolutions on commercial discrimination, claiming that British restrictions had not harmed American trade and that passage of the resolutions would lead to British retaliation and possible war. Madison denied that his resolution would put *"war on the table."* Dexter also argued that discrimination would not encourage the growth of domestic manufacturing, an assertion likewise denied by Madison. On 27 November

SAMUEL DEXTER.   Etching by H. B. Hall.
PRINTS AND PHOTOGRAPHS DIVISION, LIBRARY OF CONGRESS.

1794 Madison opposed condemning the democratic societies; Dexter immediately refuted Madison's arguments point by point. In early February 1795 Dexter asked Madison to meet and discuss their political differences. Madison invited Dexter to "dinner on Sunday, en famille," after which they could talk "alone & free from interruption."

Dexter was elected to the Senate, serving from 4 March 1799 until 30 May 1800, when he resigned to become secretary of war. On 1 January 1801 he became secretary of the Treasury, serving briefly in Jefferson's holdover cabinet until 6 May 1801 (when Albert Gallatin received a recess appointment). Dexter then returned to Boston to practice law. On 30 August 1809 he congratulated Madison on his election to the presidency but reiterated his opposition to the Embargo and to the Nonintercourse Act.

Even though he was active in Federalist organizational efforts in Massachusetts, Dexter won the support of Republicans in his unsuccessful bids for governor in 1814, 1815, and 1816 because he opposed extreme Federalist opposition to the War of 1812 and the separatist drift within Federalist ranks. He declined Madison's offer of appointment as envoy to Spain in 1815. Throughout his political career he opposed Madison on numerous issues but insisted that their disagreement was over principle and not the result of "party politics & person rancour."

BIBLIOGRAPHY

"Sigma" (Manlius Lucius Sargent). *Reminiscences of Samuel Dexter, Originally Written for the Boston Evening Transcript.* 1857.

CHARLES H. SCHOENLEBER

JOHN DICKINSON.   Dickinson, the "Penman of the Revolution," holds his *Letters from a Farmer in Pennsylvania to the Inhabitants of the British Colonies*, published in 1768.
PRINTS AND PHOTOGRAPHS DIVISION, LIBRARY OF CONGRESS.

DICKINSON, JOHN (1732–1808), "Penman of the Revolution," political leader in Pennsylvania and Delaware. Dickinson attended the Stamp Act Congress, where he wrote the Declaration of Rights and Grievances (1765); the First Continental Congress, where he drew up the petition to the king and the address to the inhabitants of Canada (1774); and the Second Continental Congress, where he teamed with Thomas Jefferson to write the Declaration of the Causes and Necessity of Taking Up Arms (1775). In 1767 Dickinson's *Letters from a Farmer in Pennsylvania* made him the leading colonial spokesman for American protests against parliamentary taxation.

In 1776 Dickinson disagreed with the timing of the Declaration of Independence and refused to sign it, even though he was the principal author of the first draft of the Articles of Confederation reported to Congress on 12 July. Despite his Quaker background, he was one of only two members of Congress to take up arms against the British during the Revolution.

In 1779 Dickinson was elected to Congress from Delaware and signed the final draft of the Articles of Confederation on behalf of Delaware's ratification. From 1781 until 1782 he served as president of the Supreme Executive Council of Delaware, and from 1782 until 1785 he held a similar position in Pennsylvania. In 1783 a group of mutinous Continental troops marched on Philadelphia to demand that Congress settle their claims for wartime pay. Congress asked Dickinson and the Executive Council of Pennsylvania to call out the state militia to maintain order and to prevent a "wound to the dignity of the Federal Government." When Dickinson refused, Congress moved from Philadelphia to Princeton, New Jersey. No delegate was more critical of Dickinson's unyielding position than James Madison, who referred to "the mutinous insult" and regretted that Dickinson had not taken effective measures "for suppressing the mutiny and supporting the public authority" of Congress.

In 1786 Dickinson represented Delaware at the Annapolis Convention, where he presided and cooperated with James Madison and Alexander Hamilton in issuing the call for a federal constitutional convention in Philadelphia the next year. Dickinson also represented Delaware at the resulting Federal Convention in 1787. Although he had been an advocate of a strong central government, he opposed Madison's uncompromising nationalism and pushed hard for a bicameral congress in which the states would be represented equally in one house and the people represented in the other; this proposal became the basis for the Great Compromise. The Senate, Dickinson argued, should be modeled as near "to the British House of Lords as possible," but he joined Madison in supporting a federal veto of state legislation.

Dickinson opposed the slave trade but agreed to the compromise that barred Congress from banning it before 1808. Illness forced him to leave the Federal Convention three days before it closed, but he wanted to make sure that his name was on the document, so he asked George Read to sign his name to the engrossed document. He vigorously supported ratification of the Constitution in a series of newspaper essays and was pleased when Delaware became the first state to ratify it.

Dickinson retired from politics after 1787 and declined appointment as a U.S. senator from Delaware, but he remained sympathetic to the Republican party and spoke eloquently against Jay's Treaty at a public meeting in Wilmington in 1795. In 1800 he wrote Madison to praise his report on the Alien and Sedition Acts as "an inestimable contribution to the cause of liberty." In 1801 he published *The Political Writings of John Dickinson, Esq., Late President of the State of Delaware and of the Commonwealth of Pennsylvania.*

BIBLIOGRAPHY

Flower, Milton E. *John Dickinson, Conservative Revolutionary.* 1983.
Jacobson, David L. *John Dickinson and the Revolution in Pennsylvania.* 1965.

JAMES MORTON SMITH

DOBBINS, DANIEL

DOBBINS, DANIEL (1776–1856), sailing master in the War of 1812, builder of the first vessels of the Lake Erie squadron. When Jay's Treaty (1794) opened the Great Lakes to American commerce, nineteen-year-old Daniel Dobbins, born in Mifflin County, Pennsylvania, realized the need for increased American shipping activity to move supplies across the lakes. At Erie, he learned to sail the coastline to Black Rock, near Buffalo. In December 1796, the dying "Mad" Anthony Wayne urged Dobbins to pilot lake ships. Between 1800 and 1809 Dobbins commanded the sloop *Good Intent* (1801–1804), the *Ranger* (1805–1807), the *General Wilkinson* (1808), and the schooner *Salina.* After 1809 he worked with Ramsey Crooks, a fur buyer for John Jacob Astor's American Fur Company.

On 17 July 1812, Dobbins, the *Salina*, and the schooner *Mary* were captured when Michilimackinac fell. Both vessels were recaptured at Detroit by Gen. William Hull's forces, only to be retaken by Gen. Isaac Brock's when Hull capitulated on 17 August. Dobbins escaped and proceeded via Cleveland and Erie to Washington, D.C., the first participant in the losses in the West to inform Secretary of War William Eustis and President Madison directly. Dobbins was questioned closely at an emergency cabinet meeting about the efficacy of building a war fleet on the Upper Lakes. On 11 and 16 September 1812, Secretary of the Navy Paul Hamilton instructed Dobbins to commence building a war fleet for Lake Erie, authorized $2,000 in expenditures, and appointed Dobbins a sailing master in the U.S. Navy. At Erie, Dobbins cut the first tree for the keel of the brig *Niagara* and engaged Ebenezer Crosby as master builder for four new gunboats. The designs of two of the gunboats were altered by Isaac Chauncey in December 1812. Ironically, Dobbins was in Buffalo procuring supplies for Oliver H. Perry during the commodore's victorious action of 10 September 1813. Dobbins served as a sailing master in the Navy until 1826, then entered the Revenue Marine Service until he retired.

BIBLIOGRAPHY

Dobbins, William W. *History of the Battle of Lake Erie and Reminiscences of the Flagships Lawrence and Niagara.* 1913.
Metcalf, Clarence S. "Daniel Dobbins, Sailing Master, U. S. N., Commodore Perry's Right Hand Man." *Inland Seas* 14 (1958): 88–96, 181–191.
Severance, Frank H., ed. "The Dobbins Papers." *Publications of the Buffalo and Erie County Historical Society* 8 (1905): 257–379.

FREDERICK C. DRAKE

DOHRMAN, ARNOLD

DOHRMAN, ARNOLD (1749–1813), Portuguese merchant, U.S. commercial agent in Lisbon. Dohrman was a Portuguese merchant who befriended American captives from his offices in Lisbon during the revolutionary war. In addition to aiding American seamen, Dohrman outfitted a privateer to prey on British ships moving in the sea lanes off Lisbon. When British crews sent captured American seamen ashore on the Portuguese coast, Dohrman aided the stranded sailors and also sent cargoes of supplies to the United States for consignment to the American army.

Dohrman's eagerness to aid Americans came to the attention of Madison when Patrick Henry wrote to the Virginia delegation in the Continental Congress on Dohrman's behalf. Henry noted Dohrman's "generous Interposition . . . in relieving & emancipating our distressed Countrymen." Henry sought an appointment for Dohrman as the U.S. commercial agent, a post that paid no salary and was mainly honorific. Henry's request was granted by Congress on 21 June 1780.

After the signing of the Treaty of Paris, Dohrman's financial situation deteriorated, and he fell behind in payments to the military contractor Philip Mazzei and others, finally seeking help from friends in Congress. Eventually, with the aid of Madison, Jefferson, and Rep. Nathaniel Macon, Dohrman was awarded a grant of cash and a township in the public domain located in Ohio. Dohrman moved his family, "thirteen in number," to the vicinity of Steubenville, Ohio, in 1809 and wrote to the president acknowledging Madison's role in his successful emigration to America.

BIBLIOGRAPHY

Hutchinson, William T., et al., eds. *Papers of James Madison: Congressional Series.* Vol. 2. 1962.

ROBERT A. RUTLAND

DRUMMOND, SIR GORDON (1772–1854),

British general and colonial administrator. Gordon Drummond was the senior British commanding officer in Upper Canada in 1814. Born in Quebec, the son of a Scottish agent for a London merchant firm who served as the deputy paymaster general for British forces in Quebec, Drummond was educated in England after his father died. He entered the British Army as ensign of the First Foot in 1789 and served in the Netherlands campaign at the siege of Nijmegen (1794–1795), in Egypt (in 1801), in Jamaica (1805–1807), and in Quebec (1808–October 1811). He was promoted to lieutenant general on 4 June 1811. From October 1811 to the summer of 1813, he commanded the military district of Northern Ireland. Possibly because of his previous service in the Canadas, he was sent to North America in August 1813, ranking second in seniority to the commander in chief in the Canadas, Sir George Prevost. After briefly commanding the troops at Chateauguay, Drummond succeeded Sir Roger Hale Sheaffe as commander of the forces in Upper Canada.

Drummond first planned a winter campaign to recapture Detroit and to destroy American vessels at Put-in-Bay, but his plan was foiled by mild weather that prevented a movement across the lake over the ice. When Drummond arrived on the Niagara frontier on 16 December 1813, his forces quickly attacked and captured Fort Niagara, New York, which dominated the Niagara River debouchment and naval anchorages at the western end of Lake Ontario. His forces then destroyed Lewiston, Black Rock, and Buffalo to avenge the burning of Newark (an act Madison later disavowed) after American forces had withdrawn on 10 December. Drummond thus restored British military control of the Niagara peninsula. In late July 1814, as commander of the British Army of the Center opposing the attacking American Left Division under Maj. Gen. Jacob J. Brown, Drummond arrived from York as the British general, Phineas Riall, ordered a withdrawal. Countermanding the order, Drummond rushed reinforcements forward. The resultant battle of Lundy's Lane (25 July) was the hardest fought of the war on the Niagara frontier. All four senior commanders—Drummond, Riall, Winfield Scott, and Brown—were wounded. Battle casualties for the British were 876; American casualties totaled 861 killed, wounded, or missing.

Brown's forces retired to Fort Erie the next day. In a subsequent bombardment on 13 August and an attack on 15 August, Drummond's two columns were beaten back by Brown's army, commanded by Eleazor W. Ripley after Brown was injured. The second column, although penetrating the fort, was not reinforced, and an ammunition explosion killed many of the attackers, including Drummond's brother William. Drummond admitted to Prevost that the assault was a disaster. A subsequent sortie ordered on 17 September by Brown when he resumed command led to the capture of two batteries and the destruction of three siege guns before Drummond's reinforcements drove the attackers back to the fort. British casualties on this outing were 609; American losses were 511. Drummond abandoned the siege on 21 September and recrossed the Chippewa River. Brown's army returned to the New York shore on 5 November after blowing up Fort Erie.

Drummond's civil administration was characterized by severe discipline, martial law, suspension of habeas corpus, and confiscation of traitors' property. In May and June 1814 Drummond remanded defendants to trial in the assize court at Ancaster, where twenty were tried for treason and eight were hanged, with others sentenced to deportation.

In April 1815 Drummond became commander in chief when Prevost was recalled to England to explain his conduct of the war. Drummond supervised the restoration of the captured territory according to the terms of the Peace of Ghent (24 December 1814). He was awarded a K.C.B. (knight commander of the Order of the Bath) on 2 January 1815 and a G.C.B. (knight grand cross of the Order of the Bath) on 11 March 1817. At his death in 1854 he was the senior general in the British Army.

BIBLIOGRAPHY

Cruikshank, Ernest A. *Documentary History of the Campaign upon the Niagara Frontier.* Vol. 8. 1907. Vol. 9. 1908.

Cruikshank, Ernest A. *Drummond's Winter Campaign, 1813.* 2d ed. 1900.

Cruikshank, Ernest A. *The Siege of Fort Erie, August 1–September 23, 1814.* 1905.

Cruikshank, Ernest A. "Sir Gordon Drummond, K.C.B." *Ontario History Papers and Records* 29 (1933): 8–13.

Stanley, George. *The War of 1812: Land Operations.* 1983.

Weekes, W. M. "The War of 1812: Civil Authority and Martial Law in Upper Canada." *Ontario History* 48 (1956): 147–161.

FREDERICK C. DRAKE

DUANE, WILLIAM

DUANE, WILLIAM (1760–1835), printer, newspaper publisher, Republican leader. Born in New York of emigrant Irish parents, Duane was returned to Ireland by his widowed mother and there learned the printing trade. He traveled to India in 1787, started a profitable newspaper, and had accumulated considerable property when he offended the powerful East India Company authorities and was banished following the seizure of his holdings. He sought to retrieve his seized Indian property through the English courts but had no success. He departed for America with a bitter feeling toward English justice.

Duane arrived in Philadelphia and soon became associated with Benjamin Franklin Bache, who published the *Aurora* and carried on a verbal war with the Federalists. Bache was one of the intended targets of the Sedition Act passed in 1798, but he died in a yellow fever epidemic, and control of the *Aurora* fell to Duane (who married Bache's widow). Duane resumed the attacks on Federalist officials and policies and was arrested in 1799 on charges that he had caused a riot by circulating a petition calling for repeal of the Alien Act. A state court refused to convict Duane, but a band of Federalists attacked him for an exposé he had printed, and only the timely arrival of a group of Republicans prevented the mob from harming Duane.

Duane was indicted in the fall of 1799 for violating the Sedition Act, but his case was never brought to trial, and eventually he was given a full pardon by President Jefferson. Duane had published a copy of a Federalist proposal (the Ross election bill) that would have thwarted a popular election victory for Jefferson in 1800; the resulting public furor was the death knell for the Federalist plan.

During the Quasi-War with France, Duane kept up his attacks on the Federalists, whom he accused of pro-British conspiracies. Duane's publication of Federalist war plans discredited the Federalists as they attempted to exploit the XYZ Affair. The *Aurora* was steadfastly in Jefferson's camp during the 1800 election campaign and helped carry the mid-Atlantic states for him.

When the nation's capital was moved from Philadelphia to Washington, Duane attempted to move along with it, but his plans to obtain government printing contracts miscarried. Angry and suspicious, Duane broke with Albert Gallatin, a key Jefferson supporter, and quarreled with Gov. Thomas McKean. Even his loyalty to Madison wavered.

In the Olmstead case fiasco, which involved Gov. Simon Snyder of Pennsylvania and President Madison, Duane criticized Snyder for interfering in a federal judicial matter. Duane sympathized with the state militiamen who were arrested and asked Madison to intercede by pardoning the "Militia men who under a blind opinion of obedience to their superiors . . . are now imprisoned." Madison soon signed their pardon.

During the 1812 election, Duane gave Madison important support as he ridiculed New York Republicans for their makeshift alliance to promote De Witt Clinton's presidential hopes. Duane charged Clinton with a hypocritical flirtation with the Federalists and damaged Clinton's prospects in essays that praised Madison's firmness against Great Britain.

Duane had been critical of Madison's administration, but when the War of 1812 started he was made an adjutant-general and served until the Treaty of Ghent was signed. He resumed editorship of the *Aurora* and remained a force in Republican political circles until he retired in 1822. He accepted a minor judicial post in 1823 and performed his duties until 1835. A short-lived attempt to revive the *Aurora* in order to fight the power of the Bank of the United States was not successful.

BIBLIOGRAPHY

Cunningham, Noble E., Jr. *The Jeffersonian Republicans in Power.* 1963.

Higginbotham, Sanford W. *The Keystone of the Democratic Arch: Pennsylvania Politics, 1800–1816.* 1952.

ROBERT A. RUTLAND

DUVALL, GABRIEL

DUVALL, GABRIEL (1752–1844), comptroller of the Treasury, associate justice of the U.S. Supreme Court. Duvall was a leader of the Republican party in Maryland. He served in the Maryland House of Delegates and was a member of the U.S. House of Representatives from 1794 to 1796. Madison expedited Duvall's admission to Congress in November 1794 when Duvall's seating was delayed by technicalities. Duvall vigorously opposed the Sedition Act in 1798 and was a Maryland elector for Jefferson in the election of 1800. In that contest, he would have had dramatic impact on American political and constitutional history if he had followed his own instincts, rather than Madison's advice, and had not cast an electoral vote for Aaron Burr; had he done so, he would have averted the tie between Burr and Jefferson that threw the election into the House of Representatives. Duvall was appointed comptroller of the Treasury in 1802, a position that he held through both Jefferson administrations and most of Madison's first term, until Duvall was appointed to the U.S. Supreme Court.

President Madison appointed Duvall, a close political and personal friend, to the Supreme Court on 15 November 1811, the same day that he appointed Joseph Story. Both were confirmed by the Senate two days later. Membership on the Court then remained unchanged for twelve years, through John Marshall's dominant years as chief justice. Duvall retired from the bench in 1835, only a few months before Marshall's death.

Because Duvall was twenty-seven years older than Story, he technically outranked him, but age was the only way in which he outranked or brooked comparison with Madison's second and last Supreme Court appointment. Duvall has been aptly described as a competent associate justice who left only a modest mark on the literature and jurisprudence of the Court. He dissented from Marshall's *Dartmouth College* v. *Woodward* decision (1819) but did not explain his vote. He persuaded Madison in April 1812 to veto legislation that would have authorized the president to assign district court duties to Supreme Court justices "in case of the absence or the disability" of the district judges. Madison regarded this as an improper executive intrusion into the judiciary, as well as intrinsically unjust to Supreme Court justices.

BIBLIOGRAPHY

Brant, Irving. *James Madison: The President, 1809–1812.* 1956.
Haskins, George Lee, and Herbert A. Johnson. *History of the Supreme Court of the United States.* Vol. 2: *Foundations of Power: John Marshall, 1801–1815.* 1981.

DONALD O. DEWEY

DWIGHT, TIMOTHY (1752–1817), Congregational churchman and theologian, educator, poet. Born in Northampton, Massachusetts, Dwight was the grandson of Jonathan Edwards, the great eighteenth-century American Calvinist theologian. After his graduation from Yale in 1769, Dwight served briefly in the revolutionary army at West Point before returning home after his father's death to care for his mother and twelve siblings, as well as for his wife and young son. Licensed as a preacher in 1777, he served from 1783 to 1795 as pastor of the Congregational Church in Greenfield, Connecticut, where he also ran a celebrated school. In 1795 he succeeded Ezra Stiles as president of his alma mater, a post he held until his death. Inaugurating chairs in law, languages, medicine, and chemistry, Dwight set Yale on its modern course as a world-renowned seat of learning.

Dwight's theology stressed democratized Calvinism, and his importance as a theologian lay in his belief that conversion was open to everyone by striving for grace. Religion, Dwight preached, should appeal mainly to the affections. As a leader of the "Second Great Awakening,"

a series of religious revivals that commenced early in the nineteenth century, Dwight is credited with inaugurating a major revival at Yale in 1802, which led that institution's students away from secularism and back to religious piety. Dwight also advocated interdenominational cooperation against such evils as alcohol and slavery—endeavors that were precursors of later national benevolent and humanitarian societies.

Dwight was associated with the "Connecticut Wits," a group of poets and writers who sought to create an American literature. His "Conquest of Canaan" (1785), a derivative allegory, was the first American epic. In his long poem "The Triumph of Infidelity" (1788), he scornfully satirized liberal theology and religious skepticism. "Greenfield Hill" (1794) was a lengthy pastoral poem unprecedented in its limning of American scenes in an American idiom for an American audience. His final works, *Remarks on the Review of Inchiquin's Letters* (1815) and *Travels; in New-England and New York* (1821–1822), were intended to counteract British depreciation of American life and to focus upon New England's republican, moral ways.

A champion of his region, Dwight was the scourge of other sections, other people, other faiths, and, in particular, the Democratic-Republican party of Jefferson and Madison. In 1798 he helped lead an attack against a purported conspiracy of rationalist, "Jacobinical" deists, the so-called Bavarian Illuminati, who, it was said, were linked to the "godless" French Revolution and who wanted to subvert American liberties. In 1801 he cofounded the short-lived *New England Palladium*, a periodical of Federalist ideology. Like many other clerics, he preached politics from the pulpit (becoming known as the pope of Federalism) and sought thereby both to enlarge the influence of the clergy in political and national affairs and to instill in his congregation the tenets of bedrock Federalism. In this, he was successful, helping to keep Connecticut in the Federalist column and in the control of a small political elite. Yet Dwight's Federalist views—however typical of New England Federalism in their antidemocratic, antisouthern, anti-immigrant, anti-French, anti-Jeffersonian themes—were always tethered to a firm nationalism, albeit a nationalism that saw the United States as provincial Connecticut writ large. For example, although he supported the Hartford Convention of 1814 as the proper forum to express New England's grievances against the Madison administration, he did not join other New Englanders' extremist calls for disunion during the War of 1812. Although the politics to which he gave voice had lost their appeal at the time of his death, Dwight's nationalistic regionalism endured in New England's reformist impulse and the antislavery campaign. His theology and his example as a pulpit orator also lived on in the optimistic, communitarian, perfectibilian, evangelical revivalism that swept the nation soon after; that thrust, along with the voluntary associations founded in revivalism's wake, became a permanent dimension of American culture.

BIBLIOGRAPHY

Berk, Stephen E. *Calvinism versus Democracy: Timothy Dwight and the Origins of American Evangelical Orthodoxy.* 1974.
Silverman, Kenneth. *Timothy Dwight.* 1969.

JAMES M. BANNER, JR.

E

EDUCATION OF JAMES MADISON. See *Madison, James*, article on *Education; Princeton University*.

EDWARDS, NINIAN (1775–1833), Kentucky jurist, governor of Illinois, senator. Born in Montgomery County, Maryland, on 17 March 1775, he was the son of a merchant-planter and representative, Benjamin Edwards, and Margaret Beall Edwards. Educated at Dickinson College in Pennsylvania, he established a law practice in Kentucky. His election to the Kentucky legislature in 1796 led to a succession of judicial appointments that culminated in his 1808 selection as chief justice of the Kentucky supreme court. A staunch Jeffersonian, he was a Republican presidential elector in 1804 and later strongly supported President Madison.

In 1809 Edwards was appointed by Madison to be territorial governor of Illinois, a post he held until 1818. His tenure as the only territorial governor of Illinois, while not without controversy, was successful. During the War of 1812 he commanded the territorial militia and supervised the construction of a defensive chain of seventeen forts linking the Kaskaskia and Mississippi rivers. At the conclusion of the war Edwards was one of the American peace commissioners who acquired major land cessions from the Indians in the West.

When Illinois gained statehood in 1818, Edwards was elected to the U.S. Senate. His support of James Monroe's administration gained him an appointment in 1824 as minister to Mexico, a post he would never assume. During the presidential campaign of 1824 Edwards published several anonymous letters in the *Washington Republican*, charging Secretary of the Treasury William H. Crawford with malfeasance. Unable to substantiate the charge when his authorship of the letters was discovered, Edwards resigned his diplomatic appointment in disgrace. He spent his remaining years in Illinois practicing law, dabbling in various business ventures, and working to rebuild his political reputation. He regained the governorship in 1826 and, after a four-year term, ran unsuccessfully for Congress. He died of cholera on 20 July 1833.

BIBLIOGRAPHY

Biographical Directory of the Governors of the United States, 1789–1978. 1978.
Edwards, Ninian W. *History of Illinois from 1778 to 1833; and Life and Times of Ninian Edwards.* 1870.

CHARLES D. LOWERY

ELECTION, CONGRESSIONAL, 1788–1790. The Confederation Congress adopted an ordinance on 13 September 1788 calling for the First Federal Congress to convene on 4 March 1789. In response, the eleven states that had ratified the Constitution elected their senators and representatives. The election began on 30 September 1788, when Pennsylvania chose its senators, and ended on 16 July 1789, when New York did so. North Carolina elected its senators on 9 December 1789 and its representatives on 4 and 5 February 1790; Rhode Island chose its senators on 12 June 1790 and its representative on 31 August 1790.

At full complement the Senate consisted of twenty-six members, and the House, sixty-five. Local political issues and alliances played an important role in the elections; the only issue of national importance was whether to amend the Constitution. Of the fifty-five men who attended the Federal Convention, twenty-seven sought election to the First Federal Congress; of these, twelve were elected to the Senate, and nine to the House. Despite Federalist fears, only a handful of Antifederalists were elected. Virginia chose two Antifederal senators, and Rhode Island chose one. Massachusetts elected two Antifederal representatives; New York, two; Virginia, three; North Carolina, two; and South Carolina, three.

By far the most important contest in terms of national interest was the one that took place in the Fifth Congressional District of Virginia between Federalist James Madison and moderate Antifederalist James Monroe. Madison was nationally recognized as an important American political leader, and the press gave considerable attention to this local contest.

The Virginia legislature was controlled by Antifederalists, led by Patrick Henry. In the fall of 1788, it elected Madison to serve in the last session of the Confederation Congress. Federalists viewed this decision as an attempt to ensure that Madison would be out of the state during the first congressional election. Despite Madison's preference for a seat in the House, his friends attempted to elect him as one of Virginia's first senators. However, on 8 November 1788, the legislature, by joint ballot, elected as Virginia's senators the Antifederalists Richard Henry Lee and William Grayson, with 98 and 86 votes, respectively; Madison received 77. Patrick Henry gave an impassioned speech against Madison in the House of Delegates, attacking him as an opponent of constitutional amendments and reportedly asserting that if he were elected there would be "rivulets of blood throughout the land." Off the floor it was rumored that Madison advocated surrendering to Spain American rights to navigate the Mississippi River.

To keep Madison out of the House of Representatives, Henry and the Antifederalists imposed a novel requirement that candidates for the House had to have resided in the district in which they were running for at least a year. This meant that Madison could not run in one of several decidedly Federalist districts in which he did not reside. While the legislature established congressional districts based on geography, politics played a role in establishing certain boundaries, particularly in the case of the Fifth District, which included Federalist Orange County, Madison's home. Federalists and Antifederalists sparred over which Piedmont counties to include in the Fifth District. Madison's supporters gained little consolation from the fact that most of the possible choices were Antifederal and sought unsuccessfully to include Federalist Fauquier County to the north, but his opponents, led by Henry, managed to include Antifederal Amherst County to the south. The final district consisted of Antifederalist Amherst, Culpeper, Spotsylvania, Goochland, and Fluvanna counties; Federalist Orange and Albemarle counties; and Louisa County, whose delegates at the Virginia Ratification Convention had split their votes.

By the end of November it had become clear that Madison's opponent in the congressional race would be his friend James Monroe. Worried supporters pressed Madison to return home to campaign. He was reluctant to do so because he wished to spend the winter in Philadelphia engaged in research and recovering from a serious case of hemorrhoids. Despite the difficulty of travel, Madison left for Orange County in mid December. En route, he spent a week at Mount Vernon with George Washington, engaged in serious discussions about the new government.

As the underdog, Madison campaigned vigorously during January 1789, concentrating particularly on critical Culpeper County. On 19 January, Madison and Monroe debated at the Culpeper courthouse; during the next two weeks, they held several other debates. During one of these debates, Madison's nose was frostbitten, and the candidate carried the scar for the rest of his life.

The major issue of the campaign was whether Madison was "dogmatically attached to the Constitution in every clause, syllable & letter" or whether he would support amendments to it. The other important issue related to religion. The influential Baptists in the district feared that religious freedom had no safeguards under the Constitution, and many apparently accepted the rumor that Madison, despite his legislative record, no longer supported religious liberty. With the able support of the Reverend George Eve and other Baptist leaders, Madison was able to retain his longstanding support from the Baptists.

On the issue of amending the Constitution, Madison promised to work actively for amendments. At public gatherings throughout the district, his supporters read copies of published letters he had written to influential local residents, stating this sentiment in writing. Specifically, Madison came out in favor of amendments that would safeguard all "essential rights," provide for periodic increases in the membership of the House of Representatives, and protect the people against nuisance appeals by wealthy citizens to a distant United States Supreme Court. "In a number of other particulars," Madison declared, "alterations are eligible either on their own account or on account of those who wish for them."

On 2 February 1789 Madison defeated Monroe by a vote of 1,308 to 972.

Election Results, Fifth District, Virginia, 1789

COUNTY	MADISON	MONROE
Albemarle	174	105
Amherst	145	246
Culpeper	256	103
Fluvanna	42	63
Goochland	132	133
Louisa	228	124
Orange	216	9
Spotsylvania	115	189

BIBLIOGRAPHY

DenBoer, Gordon, Lucy Trumbull Brown, and Charles D. Hagermann, eds. *The Documentary History of the First Federal Elections.* Vol. 2. 1984.

KENNETH R. BOWLING

ELECTION, PRESIDENTIAL, 1800.

The election of 1800 was the first contest for the presidency that resulted in the transfer of political power in the national government from one political party to another. Thomas Jefferson later called the change "as real a revolution in the principles of our government as that of 1776 was in its form." It was a change produced by a party that employed innovative methods of party organization and campaigning and by a candidate who clearly defined his position on the issues.

Jefferson affirmed his belief in limited national government, "preserving to the states the powers not yielded by them to the Union." He promised reductions in government expenditures, including spending for the army and the navy, which had been greatly expanded under President John Adams, a Federalist. "I am for a government rigorously frugal and simple, applying all the possible savings of public revenue to the discharge of the national debt," Jefferson declared. He also stressed his commitment to the protection of civil liberties, promising an end to the alien and sedition laws passed by a Federalist Congress and enforced by the Adams administration. "I am for freedom of religion . . . for freedom of the press, and against all violations of the constitution to silence by force and not by reason the complaints or criticisms, just or unjust, of our citizens against the conduct of their agents."

Adams, as an incumbent president, had to run on his record, which included a military buildup in anticipation of war with France, increased taxes, and the alien and sedition laws to curb internal dissent. Neither party, however, limited its electioneering to the issues. Republicans charged Adams with being a monarchist, while Federalists pictured Jefferson as a deist who would "destroy religion, introduce immorality, and loosen all the bonds of society."

In 1800 no uniform method of choosing presidential electors prevailed. In only five of the sixteen states were electors directly elected by the people. Because most electors were chosen by state legislatures, elections to select members of those assemblies became the key contests in many states, and these elections came at different times during the year. An early major contest came in the spring elections in New York, where Aaron Burr managed the Republican campaign in New York City and Alexander Hamilton directed the Federalist effort. After the Republican victory in the city gave that party a majority in the New York legislature that would choose the state's presidential electors, the Republican congressional nominating caucus rewarded Burr with the vice presidential nomination. Hamilton, who opposed the reelection of Adams and sought the election of another Federalist, Charles Cotesworth Pinckney, instead, now concentrated his efforts on maneuvering to persuade the Federalists to support Adams and Pinckney equally as the best hope of keeping Jefferson from becoming president.

The election of 1800 was so closely contested that the outcome could not be predicted until the result of the last state to cast its electoral vote was known. In Pennsylvania the two houses of the state legislature deadlocked over the method to be employed in choosing presidential electors, and as late as November 1800 it appeared that the state would not cast a vote. At the beginning of December Jefferson concluded that the outcome of the election would depend on South Carolina, where the legislature was then meeting. Because Pinckney was a native son of the state, Federalists who supported Hamilton's scheme hoped that South Carolina would vote for Pinckney and Jefferson and make Pinckney president. In a close contest, the South Carolina legislature chose eight electors, all of whom cast their electoral votes for Jefferson and Burr. Meanwhile, in Pennsylvania, the Republican House and the Federalist Senate reached a compromise to divide the state's electoral vote, eight for Jefferson and seven for Adams.

Jefferson's expectation that the South Carolina vote would decide the election, however, was not fulfilled. When all the returns were known, the electoral vote stood at Jefferson 73, Burr 73, Adams 65, Pinckney 64, John Jay 1. Republican party loyalty had been greater than expected, and no arrangements had been made to withhold a vote from Burr to ensure a plurality for Jefferson. Under the constitutional provisions then prevailing, each elector cast two votes without distinguishing between president and vice president. The candidate with the largest number of electors' votes became president; the candidate who received the second highest total became vice president. Jefferson, who had come in second in 1796, had been vice president under Adams, though never a part of Adams's administration.

Thus, after over a year of widespread campaigning, the election was to be decided by the House of Representatives—not by the newly elected Republican-controlled Congress, but by the Federalist Congress elected in 1798. Balloting began in the House on 11 February 1801. On the first ballot, Jefferson received the votes of eight states, Burr had six, and the divided delegations of Maryland and Vermont did not vote. With sixteen states in the Union, the vote of nine states was required for election.

Before balloting began, the House agreed to remain in continuous session until a president was chosen. By midnight, nineteen ballots had been taken, each with the same result. By the next morning, twenty-seven ballots had failed to produce a winner. With some suspensions of balloting without adjourning, balloting continued for nearly a week. From the outset, Hamilton pleaded with Federalist members to vote for Jefferson rather than Burr, but no member followed his advice, expecting some Republicans to switch to Burr in order to decide the election before 4 March, when Adams's term ended. As Republican ranks held firm, Federalists on 17 February finally capitulated by not voting, or casting blank votes. On the thirty-sixth ballot, Jefferson received the votes of ten states and was elected president. Burr received the votes of four New England states; Delaware and South Carolina, both Federalist-controlled, cast blank ballots. Despite Hamilton's appeals, no Federalist-controlled state voted for Jefferson.

In the election of 1800, not only did the Republican Thomas Jefferson succeed the Federalist John Adams as president, but a Republican majority in the new Congress in 1801 replaced a Federalist majority. That this transfer of power was peacefully accomplished demonstrated the maturity of the young American political system.

BIBLIOGRAPHY

Appleby, Joyce. *Capitalism and a New Social Order: The Republican Vision of the 1790s.* 1984.
Cunningham, Noble E., Jr. *In Pursuit of Reason: The Life of Thomas Jefferson.* 1987.
Cunningham, Noble E., Jr. *The Jeffersonian Republicans: The Formation of Party Organization, 1789–1801.* 1957.

NOBLE E. CUNNINGHAM, JR.

ELECTION, PRESIDENTIAL, 1808. Following a party caucus in Congress called by Sen. Stephen Bradley (probably the result of a conference at the White House, although there is no evidence that Jefferson urged Bradley's action), Republicans chose Madison as their presidential candidate on 23 January 1808. A small group of representatives, led by the feisty John Randolph, ignored the meeting and became active on behalf of James Monroe, who was temporarily at odds with Madison and refused to repudiate backers of his candidacy.

Madison's position as President Jefferson's chief confidant and cabinet workhorse for eight years gave him the party support required, for electoral votes were controlled in most states by the legislatures, which outside of New England were dominated by Republicans. In 1804 the Federalists had furnished halfhearted opposition to Jefferson, but in 1808 they showed more concern over

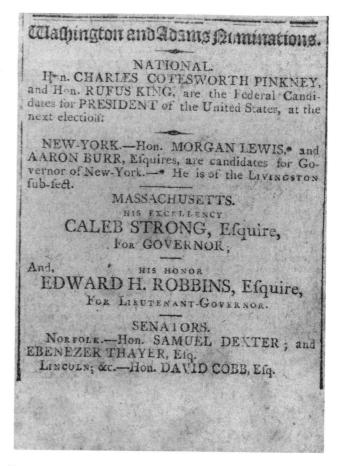

FEDERALIST CANDIDATES IN 1808.   A newspaper notice endorses Charles Cotesworth Pinckney (misspelling his name in the process) and Rufus King as running mates for president and vice president. Morgan Lewis and Aaron Burr are mentioned as candidates in the New York gubernatorial election. Caleb Strong, the former governor of Massachusetts, was a candidate for his old office.

COURTESY OF THE DAVID J. AND JANICE L. FRENT
POLITICAL AMERICANA COLLECTION.

the Embargo Act than the presidency, since they believed that the closing of American ports would destroy the New England economy.

Although custom required Madison to remain silent, he was aware of dissension in the New York Republican ranks, where De Witt Clinton's friends hoped to replace Vice President George Clinton on the ticket with his nephew. Partisan newspapers such as the New York *American Citizen* attacked Madison as a southern slaveholder, while the Boston *Columbian Centinel* denounced the caucus system and its candidate. The Philadelphia *Aurora* and the Washington *National Intelligencer* assured Republicans that Madison was the qualified successor to Jefferson, and the editor of the Richmond *Enquirer*

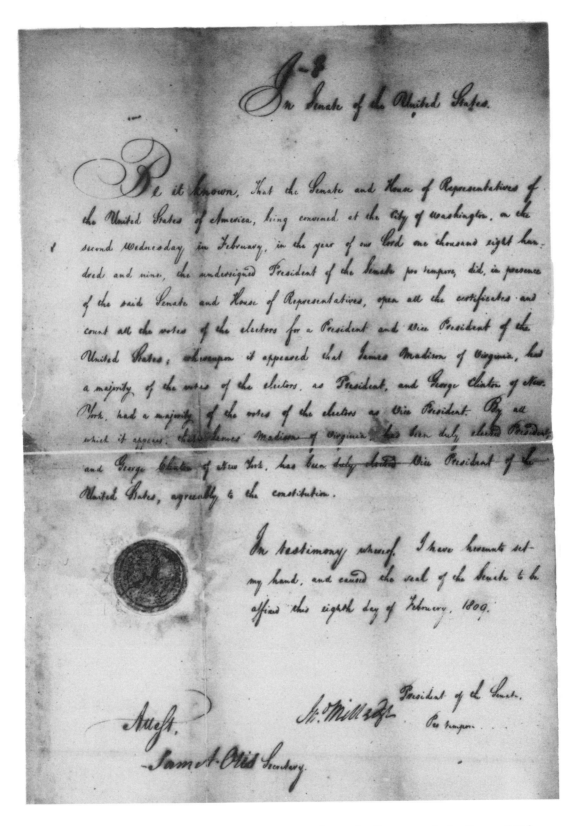

ELECTION OF 1808   Report of the counting of the electoral college votes in the Senate, 8 February 1809. The document was signed by Senator John Milledge of Georgia, president pro tem of the Senate.   JAMES MADISON PAPERS, LIBRARY OF CONGRESS.

admitted the caucus system had flaws but asked: "Where is there a *better* plan?"

Disillusioned Federalists were determined to offer a candidate but balked at a New York proposal to back George Clinton as the lesser of two evils and finally nominated Charles Cotesworth Pinckney for president and Rufus King for vice president. Pinckney was respectable but had lost badly as the 1804 Federalist standard-bearer, and his prospects were no better in 1808.

Once the states began choosing electors, it was apparent that Madison would carry the vital states and win handily, and by early December Madison's election was certain. New York electors gave Madison a thirteen-to-six majority; Pennsylvania, Virginia, and the South went for Madison. Only in New England did the Federalists reject Madison. Monroe made a pitiful showing in Virginia, and in the final tally Madison had 122 electoral votes to 47 for Pinckney. Monroe received no electoral votes for president but had three cast for him as vice president. George Clinton was reelected as vice president.

Madison had made no speeches, issued no promises, and spent no money on the campaign. He would become the fourth president with all but one section of the nation, and both houses of Congress, ready to continue the policies of the Jefferson administration.

BIBLIOGRAPHY

Brant, Irving. *James Madison: Secretary of State 1800–1809.* 1953.

Rutland, Robert A. *James Madison: The Founding Father.* 1987.

Rutland, Robert A. *The Presidency of James Madison.* 1990.

Schlesinger, Arthur M., Jr., and Fred Israel, eds. *The History of American Presidential Elections, 1789–1968.* 3 vols. 1971.

ROBERT A. RUTLAND

ELECTION, PRESIDENTIAL, 1812.

The United States was still at peace in May 1812, but war seemed increasingly likely to a nation that was unprepared to fight but not afraid of a second war with Great Britain. When the congressional caucus chose Madison to run for a second term as president, much war talk resounded in the Capitol corridors. Hoping to give the Republican ticket sectional balance, the caucus picked John Langdon of New Hampshire as Madison's running mate but had to settle for Elbridge Gerry of Massachusetts when Langdon declined. Having a New England man on the ticket was deemed prudent, for the region had been damaged economically by the Embargo Act, and the gesture of nominating Gerry was a bid for party peace.

Within weeks of the May caucus, the country was aroused by the news that the British would not back off from their naval blockade of continental Europe or the Royal Navy's impressment policy. Madison sent a war message to Congress, and by June the nation was at war, thus ensuring the first wartime election in the young republic's history.

Unity in the Republican party's ranks was shaken when DeWitt Clinton of New York, now free to act on his own beliefs after the death of his uncle, George Clinton, began soliciting support for a presidential bid. Clinton's friends held a special convention that challenged the caucus system of selecting a party nominee. Clinton accepted the rump meeting's nomination and tried to form a coalition with dispirited Federalists who thought Clinton might be a preferable alternative to four more years of a Madison administration.

Still, the idea of supporting Clinton was too much for some mainstream Federalists to swallow. Chief Justice John Marshall was suggested as their best prospect, but Marshall did not encourage the promotion of a mock candidacy; Rufus King, a former senator and still an influential Federalist, told his friends that a hopeless Federalist candidacy was preferable to giving Madison the election by default. Let Madison be reelected, King advised, and then when the Republicans brought on a national debacle, Federalists could return to power as the country's saviors. A confused Federalist gathering in New York adjourned without a nominee or an endorsed candidate.

Madison, busy managing a war that was supposed to bring the easy conquest of Canada, was bound by tradition from any kind of campaign gesture and depended on Republican newspapers to promote his candidacy. Only through messages sent to various state Republican committees, duly published in friendly newspapers, did Madison promise to carry on a relentless war against England and then press for an honorable peace. Clinton forces had no newspapers behind them with the circulation of the Philadelphia *Aurora* or the Washington *National Intelligencer* through which to counterattack when the loyal Republican journals claimed Clinton was a hypocrite who talked of peace in New England and shouted for war in the western areas. Desperate southern Federalists, unhappy with the Clinton compromise, nominated King in a gesture of futility, for his nomination was ignored everywhere except in Virginia. In New York, regular Republicans used Tammany societies to promote Madison over Clinton. Clinton retaliated by insisting that the war was a disaster because of Madison's lack of leadership and concentrated on winning Pennsylvania's crucial twenty-five electoral votes.

Returns from New England encouraged Madison's opponents, but votes in Pennsylvania, the Northwest, and the South gave Madison a solid edge. In the Electoral College, Madison had 128 votes to Clinton's 89 (Clinton carried New York and New Jersey, as well as most of New England). The election results in 1812 were closer than those in 1804 or 1808, but the wartime president believed he had all but one section of the nation behind his administration. The loyalty of New England would soon be tested, but, for the moment, Madison thought he was vindicated.

BIBLIOGRAPHY

Roseboom, Eugene H. *A History of Presidential Elections: From George Washington to Richard M. Nixon.* 1970.

Rutland, Robert A. *The Presidency of James Madison.* 1990.

Schlesinger, Arthur M., Jr., and Fred Israel, eds. *The History of American Presidential Elections, 1789–1968.* 3 vols. 1971.

ROBERT A. RUTLAND

ELLIOTT, JESSE DUNCAN (1782–1845), United States naval officer. One of the most controversial officers of the fledgling U.S. Navy, Elliott was born in Maryland to Scotch-Irish parents who had immigrated to Pennsylvania. One of three brothers who served as naval officers, Elliott was the only one who had a successful career. He may have falsified his birth records in order to enter the navy as midshipman in 1804. Elliott's

CAPT. JESSE DUNCAN ELLIOTT   Stipple engraving by David Edwin.
PRINTS AND PHOTOGRAPHS DIVISION, LIBRARY OF CONGRESS.

appointment was aided by family connections with Henry Clay, Albert Gallatin, and the Smith brothers of Maryland; as a consequence Elliott became a devoted partisan of the Jeffersonian Republicans.

While a midshipman Elliott served under the ill-fated Commodore James Barron aboard the *Chesapeake* and was one of the few officers who testified in Barron's behalf during his court-martial. In fact, Elliott may have perjured himself while testifying. A lieutenant at the outbreak of the War of 1812, Elliott distinguished himself by leading a joint army-navy attack on British vessels in the Niagara River and capturing the *Detroit* and the *Caledonia*. For this he received the thanks of Congress and in 1813 was awarded a sword from that body and promotion over thirty others to the rank of master commandant. Briefly in command of the Lake Erie squadron, Elliott started construction of a fleet at Black Rock in the Niagara River. In early 1813 he was succeeded in command by Oliver Hazard Perry, who changed the location of the construction site to Presque Isle (now Erie), Pennsylvania. While Perry supervised construction, Elliott served on Lake Ontario.

In August 1813 Elliott returned to Lake Erie as Perry's second in command, even though he was older, had a better combat record, and was junior in rank by only a few months. During the Battle of Lake Erie (10 September 1813) Elliott kept his brig, the *Niagara*, in the line of battle behind the slow-sailing *Caledonia*, which occupied the place between the *Niagara* and Perry's identical brig, the *Lawrence*. Perry's flagship fought off three British vessels for more than two hours with little assistance from the *Niagara* or from the smaller trailing vessels. Elliott finally broke the line and was moving into the fight when Perry transferred his flag from the severely damaged *Lawrence* to the *Niagara* and sent Elliott to bring up the trailing vessels.

Many of the *Lawrence*'s officers blamed Elliott's tardiness upon either cowardice or envy. But Perry sought to protect his second with a mildly complimentary after-action report. Elliott was dissatisfied and began a thirty-year quarrel with Perry and his partisans, eventually enlisting the novelist and historian James Fenimore Cooper on his side. Elliott's political connections were reflected in a decision by Congress to award him the unusual honor of having a separate gold medal struck (in addition to Perry's), commending his conduct on Lake Erie with a Latin inscription that, translated, reads: "Who thinks nothing done while anything remains to be done."

Elliott became a captain in 1818 and continued his controversial career. He seconded Commodore James Barron in the latter's duel with Perry's friend Commodore Stephen Decatur in 1820. Thereafter, Decatur's widow published Perry's charges against Elliott, bringing before the public the intraservice controversy. No amount of protestation by Elliott could win public support for him in the dispute.

Querulous, vindictive, and feisty, Elliott distinguished himself as head of the naval forces in Charleston harbor during the nullification crisis of 1833 and engaged in a bitter controversy with Boston Whigs when, as commandant of the Boston navy yard (1833–1835), he had the figurehead of President Andrew Jackson put on the *Constitution*. As commodore of the Mediterranean squadron (1835–1838), Elliott returned to face thirteen charges of misconduct that resulted in a court-martial conviction. Unable to utilize his political connections in President Van Buren's administration, he was relieved of active duty until President John Tyler suspended his punishment in 1843.

BIBLIOGRAPHY

Cooper, James Fenimore. *The Battle of Lake Erie.* 1843.

Friedman, Lawrence J., and David Curtis Skaggs. "Jesse Duncan Elliott and the Battle of Lake Erie: The Issue of Mental Stability." *Journal of the Early Republic* 10 (1990): 493–516.

Long, David F. "William Bainbridge and the Barron-Decatur Duel: Mere Participant or Active Plotter?" *Pennsylvania Magazine of History and Biography* 103 (1979): 34–52.

Palmer, Michael A. "A Failure of Command, Control, and Communications: Oliver Hazard Perry and the Battle of Lake Erie." *Journal of Erie Studies* 17 (1988): 7–26.

Westcott, Allan. "Commodore Jesse D. Elliott: A Stormy Petrel of the Navy." *U.S. Naval Institute Proceedings* 54 (1928): 773–781.

DAVID CURTIS SKAGGS

EMBARGO ACT OF 1807. Following the British ship *Leopard*'s attack on the American vessel *Chesapeake* in the summer of 1807, President Thomas Jefferson was in a mood for war. Writing to Secretary of the Navy Robert Smith on 8 October, he said, "Everything we see and hear leads in my opinion to war." Congress was not in session, but the president worked through the fall to unite his administration behind a plan for action. When Congress reconvened, he expected its members to "bring their minds to the same state of things with ours."

In fact, the unanimity the president sought never materialized. Factionalism in the cabinet and divisions in Congress led to a watered-down annual message and paralysis. The speeches made by members of Congress in late 1807 reveal the wide diversity of opinion about the best strategy to be pursued and the multiplicity of options available. Some, like the South Carolinian David R. Williams, believed the nation had only two alternatives: "assertion of rights or submission to aggression." Others, however, expressed doubts that the nation was ready for war and sought an intermediate solution.

As approved by Congress on 22 December 1807 (and amended on 9 January 1808), the Embargo Act prevented "all ships and vessels in the ports and places within the limits or jurisdiction of the United States" from sailing to any "foreign port or place." Foreign ships already in the United States were permitted to leave, but no other ships were to be allowed to enter for the purpose of trade. Further, owners of ships bound for a U.S. port or of fishing vessels were required, prior to sailing, to post a bond equal to twice to four times the value of the vessel and its cargo.

As written, the Embargo appeared to treat Great Britain, France, and other nations equally, but the specific intent of the act was to deny American goods to the British and thus force British recognition of American neutral rights. "It cannot be doubted," wrote the Virginian Burwell Bassett to one of his constituents, "that a judicious use of this power will bring England to her senses & convince her of the futility of attempting to appropriate . . . the common highway to her own use."

During its fifteen-month existence, the Embargo divided the nation. Farmers in the South and the West found few markets for their produce; many merchants in the middle states and in New England evaded the enforcement procedures or openly smuggled goods in and out of the country. By early 1809, Republican representatives from Massachusetts and New York were seeking repeal of the act, which was accomplished in March.

Given more time, greater public support, and stronger enforcement procedures, perhaps the Embargo might have produced its intended results, including repeal of the British orders in council. But many students of the period question the purposes of the act and the means chosen to accomplish its goals. Given the major schisms within the Republican party and the inability of the Embargo to win popular support at home, an exclusive reliance on commercial coercion was ineffective in changing British policy.

Madison's role as secretary of state in planning and implementing the Embargo remains obscure. Long a believer in the power of commercial restriction to force a change in British behavior, he may have been instrumental in shaping the initial act, but attempts at enforcement fell mainly to Treasury Secretary Albert Gallatin. With the Embargo's repeal, neither Madison nor Gallatin seemed inclined to chart a vigorous new course. As he assumed the presidency, Madison inherited the same divided party and the lack of policy options that had frustrated Jefferson after the attack on the *Chesapeake*.

BIBLIOGRAPHY

Mannix, Richard. "Gallatin, Jefferson, and the Embargo of 1808." *Diplomatic History* 3 (1979): 151–172.

Sears, Louis M. *Jefferson and the Embargo.* 1927.

Spivak, Burton. *Jefferson's English Crisis: Commerce, Embargo, and the Republican Revolution.* 1979.

RONALD L. HATZENBUEHLER

DEATH OF THE EMBARGO, WITH ALL ITS " RESTRICTIVE ENERGIES."

A wit first celebrated this great event in the FEDERAL REPUBLICAN, in the manner to be seen below ; but he has had the politeness to revise and correct the article for the Evening Post, with additions : in this improved state it is now presented to our readers, aided by an appropriate engraving devised by the author and admirably executed by one of our fellow-citizens. Here it comes—

" TO THE GRAVE GO SHAM PROTECTORS OF " FREE TRADE AND SAILORS' RIGHTS"—AND ALL THE PEOPLE SAY AMEN !"

TERRAPIN'S ADDRESS.

Reflect, my friend, as you pass by :
As *you are, now,* so, once, was *I* ;
As *I* am *now,* so *you* may be :—
Laid on your back to die like me !
I was, indeed, true Sailor born ;
To quit my friend, in death, I scorn.
Once Jemmy *seem'd* to be my friend,
But, basely, brought me to my end !
Of head bereft, and light, and breath,
I hold *Fidelity,* in death :—
For " *Sailor's Rights*" I still will tug :
And, Madison to death I'll hug,
For his perfidious zeal display'd,
For " *Sailor's Rights and for Free Trade.*"
This small atonement I will have—
I'll lug down Jemmy to the grave.
Then Trade and Commerce shall be free
And Sailors have their liberty—
Of head bereft, and light, and breath,
The *Terrapin,* still true in death,
Will punish Jemmy's perfidy :
Leave *Trade,* and *brother Sailors Free !*

PASSENGERS REPLY.

Yes Terrapin, bereft of breath,
We see thee faithful still, in death :
Stick to't—" *Free Trade and Sailor's Right :*
Hug Jemmy—press him—hold him—bite—
Ne'er mind thy head—thou'lt live without it,
Spunk will preserve thy life—don't doubt it—
Down to the grave t'atone for sin,
Jemmy must go, with Terrapin.
Bear *him* but off, and we shall see
Commerce restor'd and Sailors Free !
Hug, Terrapin, with all thy might,
Now for " *Free Trade* and *Sailor's Right :*"
Stick to him, Terrapin, to thee the nation
Now eager looks :—then die for her salvation.
FLOREAT RESPUBLICA.
Banks of Goose Creek,
City of Washington,
15th April 1814.

EMBARGO OF 1807   The Embargo, represented by a giant turtle, turns on its creator, Secretary of State Jemmy Madison. Although the Embargo had been repealed in 1809, a woodcut by Alexander Anderson after John Wesley Jarvis was published in the *New-York Evening Post* in 1814 to embarrass President James Madison.

PRINTS AND PHOTOGRAPHS DIVISION, LIBRARY OF CONGRESS.

127

EPISCOPAL CHURCH. See *Anglican Church.*

EPPES, JOHN WAYLES (1773–1823), United States representative and senator, nephew and son-in-law of Thomas Jefferson. Born in Chesterfield County, Virginia, on 7 April 1773, John Eppes was the son of Francis and Elizabeth Wayles Eppes. After completing his education in Philadelphia under Jefferson's guidance, he was admitted to the bar in 1794 and established a successful practice in Richmond. In 1797 he married his cousin, Maria Jefferson, whose untimely death at Monticello in 1804 left him a widower. He remained close to Jefferson and was a loyal supporter of Jefferson's Republican policies.

After a two-year term in the Virginia legislature (1801–1803), Eppes was elected to Congress for four consecutive terms (1803–1811). A strong defender of Jefferson and Madison, he quickly clashed with John Randolph and narrowly avoided a duel with the acerbic Old Republican leader in 1804. With Jefferson's encouragement, he moved into Randolph's district and challenged him unsuccessfully in the 1811 congressional election. Two years later, when Randolph's adamant opposition to the War of 1812 had alienated many of his constituents, Eppes again ran against Randolph and this time defeated him.

With the United States facing bankruptcy, Eppes, who chaired the House Ways and Means Committee during the Thirteenth Congress (1813–1815), offered a plan to finance the war by issuing Treasury notes which, though they would not be legal tender, would be receivable in all payments owed the government. He opposed a national bank as unconstitutional but, out of loyalty to Madison, dutifully reported an administration resolution declaring it expedient to establish a bank. In 1815 Randolph won back his congressional seat from Eppes, but the Virginia legislature sent Eppes to the U.S. Senate the next year. He served in the Senate only two years, retiring in 1819 because of poor health. Eppes spent his last years supervising his profitable Buckingham County plantation, Millbrook, where he died on 15 September 1823.

BIBLIOGRAPHY

Biographical Directory of American Congresses. 1989.
Dictionary of American Biography. Vol. 6. 1931.

CHARLES D. LOWERY

ERSKINE, DAVID MONTAGU (1776–1855), British diplomat. In July 1806 Erskine was appointed minister plenipotentiary to the United States, a post for which, despite his youth and lack of experience, he was thought to be well qualified because he had an American wife. Early on he worked hard to improve relations between the two countries, already strained by Britain's blockade of the European mainland and its practice of impressing American nationals into service in the Royal Navy. In June 1807 matters deteriorated further when the British ship *Leopard* attacked the U.S. frigate *Chesapeake* off Hampton Roads. For a while it seemed as if war would break out, but to Erskine's relief Congress was persuaded instead to impose an embargo cutting off trade with both Great Britain and France.

After Madison's inauguration in March 1809 Erskine approached him with a proposition, the idea of the British foreign secretary, George Canning, that the United States drop restrictions on trade with Britain in return for the removal of the orders in council that authorized the Royal Navy to search and seize American vessels. Close scrutiny reveals that Canning's proposal was hedged around with restrictions that both Erskine and Madison, in their eagerness to improve relations between the two countries, chose to ignore. What Britain was proposing, in fact, was simply that the Embargo Act be amended to allow trade with Britain but not France; otherwise, the Royal Navy would continue interfering with American shipping precisely as before. In short, the Royal Navy would be allowed to enforce the American prohibition on French trade, a humiliating condition that Madison rejected and Erskine did not press. For a moment, it seemed as if one of the two principal impediments to an Anglo-American rapprochement (the other being impressment) had been removed, and Madison even went so far as to issue a proclamation lifting the ban on trade with Britain.

The euphoria proved short-lived. The British cabinet rejected the Erskine-Madison accord since Madison had dropped Canning's key provision. Erskine was recalled to England, and replaced by Francis James Jackson, a bullying diplomat with hard-line views whom Madison eventually declared persona non grata. Erskine remained unemployed until 1824, when he was appointed to a diplomatic post in Germany, where he remained until his retirement in 1843.

BIBLIOGRAPHY

Adams, Henry. *History of the Administrations of Thomas Jefferson and James Madison.* 1986.

Perkins, Bradford. *Prologue to War: England and the United States, 1805–1812.* 1961.

HOWARD TEMPERLEY

ERVING, GEORGE WILLIAM (1769–1850), American diplomat. The son of a Loyalist who left Boston with Howe in 1776, Erving was reared in England and educated at Oriel College, Oxford. His father came to regret his expatriation and encouraged Erving to return to the United States when he came of age. Erving plunged into politics and, as an ardent Jeffersonian, visited Madison at Montpelier in 1800 to discuss measures to prevent Burr from attaining the presidency.

Monroe, who had introduced Erving to Madison, suggested the young man for a diplomatic position, and in 1801 Erving was named claims agent for spoliation cases at London. His long and detailed letters to Madison were filled with pointed comments on European politics and criticisms of the American minister, Rufus King, and the American claims commissioners. Madison's letter granting Erving permission to charge a commission on claims he handled figured in Robert Smith's 1811 attack on the president. In 1804 Erving became legation secretary and chargé d'affaires at Madrid. He remained in Spain during the Peninsular War, returning to the United States in 1810 after deciding that conditions had deteriorated to the point where his presence was no longer useful. From 1811 to 1813 he was minister at Copenhagen for the negotiation of spoliation claims against Denmark.

In 1814 Erving was appointed minister to Spain, but difficulties connected with Madison's refusal to recognize the Spanish minister, Luis de Onís, delayed Erving's acceptance until 1816. Erving spent several years negotiating the spoliation claims treaty and resented what he considered John Quincy Adams's mishandling of the questions of royal land grants in Florida and of the western boundary of Louisiana when negotiations were transferred to Washington. After his repeated requests for a leave of absence for health reasons were ignored, Erving tendered his resignation, leaving Madrid in 1819. Madison reportedly kept a bust of Erving at Montpelier and once said he "had never had a more capable and faithful minister in his service."

BIBLIOGRAPHY

Ammon, Harry. *James Monroe: The Quest for National Identity.* 1971.

Brugger, Robert J., et al., eds. *The Papers of James Madison: Secretary of State Series.* Vol. 2. 1986.

Curry, J. L. M. "Diplomatic Services of George William Erving." *Proceedings of the Massachusetts Historical Society,* 2d ser., 5 (1889–1890): 6–33.

MARY A. HACKETT

EUSTIS, WILLIAM (1753–1825), doctor, representative, secretary of war, governor of Massachusetts. Born in Cambridge, Massachusetts, Eustis graduated from Harvard College in 1772 and studied medicine with Joseph Warren. He served as a surgeon in the Continental army from 1775 to 1783, then retired to private practice. Despite his officer background, his membership in the Society of the Cincinnati, and his service under Benjamin Lincoln during Shays's Rebellion, Eustis became an Antifederalist voice in the Massachusetts legislature from 1788 to 1794. At odds with the dominant Federalists, Eustis was part of Jefferson's "Revolution of 1800," and he ran successfully for Congress on the Republican ticket. He served two terms in the House of Representatives, defeating Federalist stalwarts Josiah Quincy in 1800 and John Quincy Adams in 1802 before losing his bid for reelection to Adams in 1804. His support of the Jefferson administration in the House was rewarded in 1807 when Jefferson appointed him secretary of war to replace Henry Dearborn. Madison continued him in the post after Madison's election in 1808. Eustis was a moderate Republican with social ties to prominent Federalists and a man who possessed, in Madison's words, "an accomplished mind, a useful knowledge of military subjects . . . and a vigilant superintendance of subordinate agents."

It was Eustis's misfortune to hold a cabinet post at a time when extraordinary pressures were placed upon the War Department. The imminent war with Great Britain drove Eustis to attempt a reorganization and expansion of the U.S. army in early 1812, a task for which he proved to be unequal. To make matters worse, Congress refused to authorize two undersecretaries of war to ease Eustis's burden. The workload was crushing, and even though Eustis did his best, it was clear he was unable or incompetent to discharge his assignments. Prominent Republicans, such as William Crawford and Albert Gallatin, called for Eustis's dismissal, but Madison refused to ask for his resignation until after Madison's reelection in November 1812. Eustis resigned one month later. In 1814 Madison appointed Eustis U.S. minister to Holland, a position he held until 1818. He returned to the House in 1820 and kept his seat for three years, while he ran three times (1820, 1821, and 1822) for governor of Massachusetts. Defeated in his three earliest attempts, Eustis was elected governor twice, in 1823 and 1824, and died while in office.

BIBLIOGRAPHY

Goodman, Paul. *The Democratic-Republicans of Massachusetts.* 1964.

Hunt, Gaillard. *The Writings of James Madison.* Vol. 9. 1910.

Stagg, J. C. A. *Mr. Madison's War: Politics, Diplomacy, and Warfare in the Early American Republic, 1783–1830.* 1983.

DAVID B. MATTERN

EVE, GEORGE (1748–c. 1818), influential Baptist minister of Orange County, Virginia. At a religious revival in 1772 in his native Culpeper County, Eve had a conversion experience that led to his ordination in 1778. For twelve years he served the Blue Run Baptist Church, located near Montpelier, and preached at churches and gatherings throughout the county. He was instrumental in initiating a religious awakening in Orange and neighboring counties that began about 1778 and that continued for nearly a decade. In 1790 he moved to Kentucky, where he was involved in the great revival that swept the backcountry beginning about 1800. In 1803 he returned to Orange County for a short time to lead a revival at Barboursville, located a few miles from Montpelier, that won almost one hundred converts.

Though Madison was technically a communicant of the Episcopal Church, he was on good terms with Eve, whom he sometimes favored with books and biblical commentaries from New York or Philadelphia bookstores. In 1788 Madison called on Eve to assist him in his campaign for election to the First Congress under the new Constitution. Baptists throughout the district had been told by Antifederalists that Madison was unequivocally "attached to the Constitution in every clause, syllable, & letter" and that he would oppose all amendments, including one to protect the liberty of conscience, which Baptists held dear. Convinced of Madison's good faith, Eve persuaded a large Baptist gathering that Madison could be trusted to support amendments guaranteeing religious freedom. Eve's influence with the Baptists, whose vote was important in the outcome of the election, helped secure Madison's election to Congress in 1789.

BIBLIOGRAPHY

Rakove, Jack N. *James Madison.* 1990.
Semple, Robert B. *A History of the Rise and Progress of the Baptists in Virginia.* 1894.

CHARLES D. LOWERY

F

FARRAGUT, DAVID GLASGOW (1801–1870), naval officer. The son of George Farragut (1755–1817), a naval and military officer, the future admiral was christened James Farragut at Campbell's Station, Tennessee. By 1807 the family lived in New Orleans, where George Farragut commanded a gunboat. The Farraguts became close friends with the Porter family, and David Porter informally adopted young James after the Farraguts cared for Porter's ill father. Porter arranged for Farragut's education and for his appointment as a midshipman in 1810. In August 1811 Farragut joined Porter in the *Essex* for a three-year cruise to the Pacific. At age twelve Farragut took command of a captured whaling ship, the *Alexander Barclay*, and, during the voyage from Tumbes, Peru, to Valparaiso, Chile, put down an attempt by its former captain to seize control of the ship. After returning to the *Essex*, Farragut performed so well in the battle against the *Phoebe* and the *Cherub* that Porter said, but for Farragut's age, he would have recommended the boy for promotion. Captured by the British, Farragut remained a prisoner until November 1814. Navy records of that year show that he changed his first name from James to David to honor David Porter.

For the next forty-five years Farragut served in a variety of billets at sea and ashore and progressed through the ranks; he was a captain when the Civil War broke out.

MIDSHIPMAN FARRAGUT REPORTS FOR DUTY. James Farragut was appointed a midshipman in 1810 with the help of David Porter; Farragut later changed his given name to David in Porter's honor.

His southern background rendered his loyalty suspect, and Farragut was not given an important post until his January 1862 appointment to command of the West Gulf blockading squadron. His capture of New Orleans brought promotion to rear admiral, the first use of that rank in the U.S. Navy, and his defeat of Confederate forces defending Mobile Bay in 1864 brought promotions that made him the first vice admiral (December 1864) and admiral (July 1866) in the U.S. Navy.

BIBLIOGRAPHY

Farragut, Loyall. *Life of David Glasgow Farragut, the First Admiral of the United States Navy, Embodying His Journal and Letters.* 1879.

Lewis, Charles Lee. *David Glasgow Farragut.* 2 vols. 1941–1943.

Mahan, Alfred Thayer. *Admiral Farragut.* 1892.

JAMES C. BRADFORD

FEDERAL CONGRESS, FIRST. See *Congresses,* article on *First Congress.*

FEDERAL CONVENTION. On Sunday, 13 May 1787, George Washington arrived in Philadelphia "amidst the acclamation of the people," as James Madison observed, "as well as more sober marks of the affection and veneration which continue to be felt for his character." And, Madison might have added, the hopes that people attached to the forthcoming convention, ostensibly called to revise the Articles of Confederation.

Not everyone believed as strongly as did Washington and his young colleague Madison that the new republic would be endangered unless the Articles were replaced with a stronger form of government. But the disenchantment with the Articles had been sufficient to move the Continental Congress, following the Annapolis Convention and resolutions by several state legislatures, to agree halfheartedly on 21 February 1787 to call a convention to meet in Philadelphia on the "second Monday in May next." Twelve of the thirteen states— all but obstinate Rhode Island—named delegates; the news that Washington would attend changed the minds of skeptical delegates. New Hampshire, while in favor of the gathering,

delayed naming its representatives; however, they arrived in time to participate in some of the more important decisions of the meeting.

An Assembly of Demigods. Historians still debate the impact of Charles Beard's *An Economic Interpretation of the Constitution* (1913), which began a lively but not always fruitful debate over the fifty-five men who attended the Federal Convention and their interests. Beard claimed that because the delegates represented personal property interests and stood to benefit from a stable government, they created a conservative government to protect their type of property. The thesis was immediately challenged and to some degree shunted aside. Since then, historians have characterized the Framers as nationalists, cosmopolitans, and "young men of the Revolution."

When Thomas Jefferson, then serving as American minister to France, first saw the list of delegates to the Philadelphia convention, he wrote to his friend John Adams, "It really is an assembly of demigods." With the exception of Jefferson and Adams (then minister to Great Britain), nearly all of the important political figures in the country attended. Even George Mason conceded to his son that "America has certainly, upon this occasion, drawn forth her first characters."

From New England came Elbridge Gerry and Rufus King of Massachusetts, along with Connecticut's William Samuel Johnson, Roger Sherman, and Oliver Ellsworth. The New York legislature, under prodding by Gov. George Clinton, sent along two clearly antifederalist lawyers, Robert Yates and John Lansing, Jr., to check the brilliant and quite nationalistic federalist delegate Alexander Hamilton. New Jersey sent a distinguished delegation consisting of William Livingston, William Paterson, and the convention's youngest member, twenty-six-year-old Jonathan Dayton. Neighboring Pennsylvania sent the oldest delegate, the venerable eighty-one-year-old Benjamin Franklin, who had been advocating some form of union ever since the Albany Plan of 1754. Franklin's colleagues included Gouverneur Morris, who had recently moved from New York, and Robert Morris, who almost singlehandedly had staved off bankruptcy for the Confederation.

From the South came John Rutledge of South Carolina, recognized as one of the finest legal minds in the country, along with Charles Cotesworth Pinckney and his young cousin Charles. Perhaps most important was the Virginia delegation, headed by George Washington

and also including the young governor of the commonwealth, Edmund J. Randolph; George Mason, author of the state's bill of rights; and James Madison, then only thirty-six years old, who had been one of the leading figures in securing the convention (and whose detailed notes provided insights into the framing of the Constitution for later generations).

It is easier to describe the characteristics of this group than to identify particular ideological biases. Although relatively young (the average age was just over forty-three), the delegates had extensive experience in government; forty-two had served in the Continental Congress, and many more had also participated in state assemblies. Three had been at the Stamp Act Congress in 1765, seven had attended the First Continental Congress, and eight had signed the Declaration of Independence. While conversant with the political theories of the Enlightenment, they knew from their own experience in government that theory by itself would be of little help in their task. John Dickinson of Pennsylvania, who had relied on theory in drafting the Articles of Confederation, declared that "*Experience* must be our only guide; *reason* may mislead us."

Thirty-one delegates were college graduates, a percentage far above the popular norm; two, in fact, were college presidents, three others had taught college, and one out of five had taught school at some point in his life. Most of these men were, in fact, well-to-do or comfortably off; only three, Roger Sherman, William Few, and William Pierce, could be considered of modest means. Although only a dozen were practicing lawyers, two-thirds of the delegates had studied law. Most held property, some of them a great deal of it, and many of the southerners owned plantations and slaves. That they were an elite group in a nation of equals is indisputable, but the Framers felt no sense of alienation from the people whom they represented in Philadelphia. They may have been more nationalistic than the norm, more concerned with creating a stable and strong government than some, but this was no cabal out to inflict an antidemocratic regime on the country.

The Virginia Plan. On 14 May, the appointed day for the opening, only two delegations—those of Virginia and Pennsylvania—had reached the city; there would be no quorum until the 25th. Those eleven days, however, did not go to waste, as Madison and the other Virginia delegates discussed the critical question of whether the

THE STATE HOUSE, PHILADELPHIA *(left)*.   Now called Independence Hall, the state house was the site of the signing of the Declaration of Independence in 1776 and the meetingplace of the Federal Convention in the spring and summer of 1787. By 1787, the tower (a reconstruction is familiar to visitors to the building in the late twentieth century) had been replaced by a simple steeple. Colored line engraving by William Russell Birch, Philadelphia, 1798–1799.

PRINTS AND PHOTOGRAPHS DIVISION, LIBRARY OF CONGRESS.

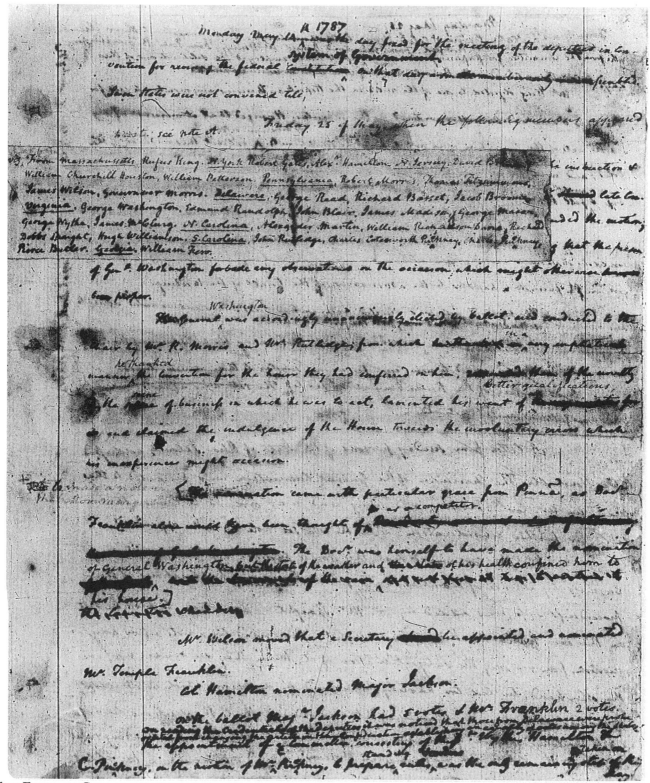

THE FEDERAL CONVENTION BEGINS. The first page of Madison's notes reflects the slow beginning of the Federal Convention. Since a quorum of states was not represented on 14 May (entry at the top of the page), the opening of the convention was delayed until 25 May. Madison listed the names of the delegates on a strip of paper pasted onto the margin and covering the notes for 25 May.

JAMES MADISON PAPERS, LIBRARY OF CONGRESS.

convention could disregard the instructions of the Congress and, instead of revising the Articles of Confederation, propose a wholly new structure of government.

The question could not be answered until the convention opened, but Madison had already been at work on a frame of government, which he had outlined in letters to Jefferson, Randolph, and Washington. Thus, the report issued by the Virginia delegation was Madison's idea. Madison understood that a gathering of such men could not be allowed to waste its time debating vague ideas; rather, it should be confronted by a specific proposal. While it might eventually reject that plan, the idea would nonetheless form the basis of the debate and help to shape the final version of the new constitution.

Madison's Virginia Plan, as it came to be called, proposed separate executive, legislative, and judicial branches within a strong national government that could enact laws binding on the states, as well as on individual citizens. The legislative power would be lodged in a bicameral congress, with a lower house chosen by popular vote and an upper chamber elected by the lower house from nominees submitted by the state assemblies. The Congress would have all the powers granted under the Articles of Confederation, as well as the authority "to legislate in all cases in which the separate States are incompetent." In addition, it would have the power to nullify state laws, and it could define the limits of the national government's authority, as well as that of the states. The executive would be chosen by the Congress for an unspecified term and would be ineligible for reelection. The executive, together with part of the judiciary, would constitute a Council of Revision, with an absolute veto over acts of the Congress. The Virginia Plan offered a frankly nationalistic and centrist alternative to the federal system under the Articles, with the national government clearly superior to those of the states. While the convention did not adopt all the parts of the Virginia Plan, Madison's strategy did prove effective, for his plan became the basis for deliberation and defined the contours of the debates.

The Delegates Begin Their Work. By 25 May twenty-nine delegates had arrived from seven states, and the convention formally opened in the East Room of the State House, the same place where the Declaration of Independence had been signed and where the old Congress had met. The Pennsylvania delegation had planned to have Benjamin Franklin make the opening motion, but he was indisposed that day, so Robert Morris moved that General Washington be elected presiding officer. The assembly unanimously ratified the motion, and Washington took the chair. In a brief speech, he asked the delegates for their indulgence in any errors he might make as presiding officer. Washington, in fact, often let others

preside and spoke hardly at all during the next three and a half months, but he exercised a calming and stabilizing effect on the delegates. And the news that he was the president had a soothing effect throughout the country; this was the only news that reached citizens from New England to Georgia until September.

Although the delegates chose William Jackson of Philadelphia as the official clerk, Madison more or less nominated himself to be unofficial secretary. With his keen sense of history, Madison suspected that Jackson would do little more than keep a tally of motions and votes, and he believed that posterity deserved a more "exact account of what might pass." Years later he wrote:

> I chose a seat in front of the presiding officer, with the other members on my right and left hand. In this favorable position for hearing all that passed, I noted . . . what was read from the chair or spoken by the members; and losing not a moment unnecessarily between the adjournment and reassembling of the Convention, I was enabled to write out my daily notes during the session or within a few finishing days after its close. . . . It happened also that I was not absent a single day, nor more than a casual fraction of an hour in any day, so that I could not have lost a single speech, unless a very short one.

Although a few others in attendance kept notes from time to time, Madison's record is the principal source of our knowledge of what occurred at the convention from May through September 1787.

After electing Washington and Jackson, the delegates discussed the rules that would govern their deliberations; these rules were adopted at the meeting on 29 May. Because the Delaware delegation had been given strict rules about certain procedures, the other states agreed to follow the voting rules of the Continental Congress, in which each state had an equal vote, and agreed that decisions would be made by a simple majority of the states present.

The convention also adopted two other rules designed to facilitate debate and decision making. First, it adopted a rule of secrecy so that it could debate matters openly and freely without having to worry about newspaper reports or reaction back home; also, without public notice of their original stance, the delegates could change their minds and accept compromises more easily. The wide windows of the room were nailed shut and guards posted outside. While some information inevitably leaked out— old Dr. Franklin was an inveterate anecdotalist—for the most part the convention operated outside the glare of public disclosure. Madison later noted that "no Constitution would have ever been adopted by the convention if the debates had been public."

The second rule was that of mutability, also intended to make it possible for the delegates to think and rethink

As the weakness and wants of man naturally lead to an association of individuals, under a common authority, whereby each may have the protection of the whole against danger from without, and enjoy in safety within, the advantages of social intercourse, and an exchange of the necessaries & comforts of life; in like manner feeble communities, independent of each other, have resorted to a Union, less intimate, but with common Councils, for the common safety agst powerful neighbors, and for the preservation of justice and peace among themselves. Ancient history furnishes examples of their confederacies, tho' with a very imperfect account, of their structure, and of the attributes and functions of the presiding authority. There are examples of modern date also, some of them still existing, the modification and transactions of which are sufficiently known.

It remained for the British Colonies, now United States, of North America, to add to those examples, one of a more interesting character than any of them: and leading to another, without a precedent a system founded on popular rights, and combining a federal form with the forms of internal Republics, as may resemble each other. Whilst the Colonies enjoyed the protection of the parent country as it was called, against foreign danger, and were secured by its superintending controul, against conflicts among themselves, they continued independent of each other, under a common, tho' limited dependence, on the parental authority. When however the growth of the offspring in strength and in wealth, awakened the jealousy and tempted the avidity of the parent, into schemes of usurpation & exaction, the obligation was felt by the former of uniting their counsels and efforts to avert the impending calamity.

MADISON'S PREFACE.   Madison revised his notes in the 1820s and prepared this "sketch never finished nor applied" for a preface. It was not used when the notes were published.

JAMES MADISON PAPERS, LIBRARY OF CONGRESS.

their positions. Under this rule, the convention could reconsider votes already taken by the majority so that a position arrived at early in the deliberations could, should circumstances warrant, be changed to take into account later developments.

Following the adoption of the rules, Governor Randolph, as head of the Virginia delegation, asked for the floor. In a mild and conciliatory fashion meant to avoid alarming delegates still committed to the Articles, Randolph reviewed what he and others perceived as the chief defects of that document. He then proposed fifteen resolutions, the first of which seemed to follow the directions given by the Congress:

> Resolved that the Articles of Confederation ought to be so corrected and enlarged as to accomplish the objects proposed by their institution, namely "common defense, security of liberty, and general welfare."

The fourteen resolutions that followed, however, embodied the Virginia Plan and were meant to demolish the Articles and replace them with something else, a purpose clear to all those assembled.

The Great Compromise. On the morning of 30 May the convention adopted a procedure it would follow throughout, resolving itself into a committee of the whole; Washington then left the chair, and various other delegates served as chair pro tem. Randolph moved adoption of his first resolution, and when Gouverneur Morris noted that the resolution was inconsistent with the other fourteen, the delegates agreed to put it aside and discuss the next three, of which the most important was "that a *national* government ought to be established consisting of a *supreme* legislative, executive, and judiciary." Here was the heart of the Virginia Plan, and, although not explicitly acknowledging what they were doing, the delegates, by a vote of six states to one (Connecticut, with New York split), had in effect agreed to scrap the Articles and start from scratch.

Had the other five state delegations been present, it is likely there would have been more debate on this issue, but the resolution still would have passed, although by a narrower margin. Emboldened by the vote, the Virginia and Pennsylvania delegations, led by Madison and James Wilson, pushed forward almost heedlessly, practically ignoring some of the doubts raised by representatives of the smaller states. By 13 June the committee of the whole reported nineteen resolutions, all elaborations upon the Virginia Plan, although with some significant differences.

The delegates had dropped several suggestions, including the council of revision and the power to use force against recalcitrant states. They adopted a three-year term for members of the lower house and a seven-year term for members of the upper; members of Congress would be paid out of the national Treasury, not by the states, and the upper house, or Senate, would be elected by the state legislatures. The delegates also agreed that there would be a single executive, chosen by the Congress for a seven-year term and ineligible for reelection; the executive would have a veto over legislation but could be overridden by a two-thirds vote of both houses. Finally, there would be a "supreme tribunal" chosen by the upper house.

Over the next few days, every one of the resolutions was adopted, usually by no less than a 7–4 vote, and the delegates voted unanimously to seek approval of the new document in the state legislatures, rather than in the Continental Congress. It seemed as if the nationalists would soon have their new, centrist, and quite powerful government.

But delegates from the smaller states had grown restive. They were not opposed to a stronger national government; even the most ardent supporter of the Articles among them recognized their weaknesses and the need, at the very least, to correct those defects. But the new government seemed more and more to them one that would be dominated by the larger states and in which small states would have little power or participation in decision making.

Thus on 15 June William Paterson of New Jersey proposed nine resolutions that he hoped to substitute for those already adopted in the committee of the whole. Although the proposal became known as the New Jersey Plan, its parentage derived from several of the smaller state delegates. In essence, the plan took the delegates back to the initial question; it proposed, not a new constitution, but amendments to the Articles of Confederation. Recognizing the weaknesses of the document, the New Jersey Plan proposed giving Congress additional powers, including the power to regulate commerce and to raise revenue through import duties and a stamp tax; the small-state plan also provided for a plural executive and a supreme court and gave the national government power to call forth state militias in order to enforce the laws and treaties of the United States.

In addition, although it was admittedly federal rather than national, the New Jersey Plan declared that all laws and treaties made by the Congress "shall be the supreme law of the respective states . . . and that the judiciary of the several states shall be bound thereby in their decisions, anything in the respective laws of the individual states to the contrary notwithstanding."

The New Jersey Plan was, in effect, a nationalist plan. What Paterson and the others worried about, and what Madison initially refused to consider, was the role the states would play in this new scheme. The Virginia Plan saw the Congress reflecting the population patterns of

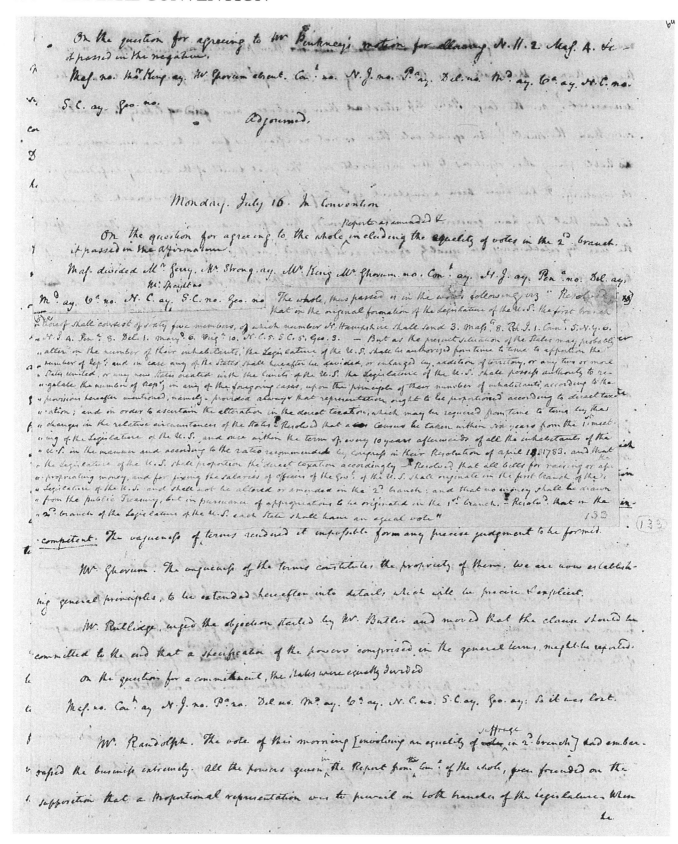

THE GREAT COMPROMISE. Madison's notes for 16 July summarize the comments of the delegates in debate. The smaller handwriting appears on a slip of paper attached to the large sheet at the margin; it contains the texts of resolutions and details the number of representatives each state would have in the House.

the nation; the New Jersey Plan saw the states as the building blocks of a new government.

The momentum of the convention had, however, already gone too far for Paterson's proposals to make any headway, insofar as he wanted to cancel out those provisions of the Virginia Plan that had been adopted. A number of delegates recognized, however, that unless some agreement could be reached between the larger and smaller states, the whole enterprise might founder. On 18 June John Dickinson moved postponement of Paterson's proposals, at which point Alexander Hamilton of New York, who up to this point had been silent, took the floor and for the next six hours dumbfounded the delegates as he proposed what he called a "sketch" of government that would have reduced the states to little more than minor administrative units, with a chief executive chosen for life by electors themselves chosen by the populace, a Senate with members chosen for life, and an absolute veto power in the president. He attacked both the Virginia and the New Jersey plans as being too democratic, and when he finished the delegates were perplexed.

Whether Hamilton expected his radical plan to receive serious consideration is uncertain. Perhaps he deliberately went so far in order to make the Virginia Plan appear more palatable. The next day the delegates defeated the New Jersey Plan, seven states to three, but the issues it had raised would not go away, and Madison himself promised an adjustment in the "affair of representation."

But that adjustment did not materialize, nor did Madison seem in any hurry. While the delegates discussed other aspects of the proposed scheme of government, the advocates of the Virginia and the New Jersey plans seemed to harden in their positions so that by early July it appeared to some that the convention and its work might collapse on the point of representation. There were by then several ideas circulating among the delegates, however, and gradually, step by step, they reached consensus on 16 July, when the convention adopted the so-called Great Compromise.

Also known as the Connecticut Plan after its chief sponsors, Roger Sherman, Oliver Ellsworth, and William Samuel Johnson, the compromise had a simplicity that makes one wonder why the delegates failed to reach it sooner. Everyone by then had agreed that representation in the lower house of the Congress should be proportionate to population. Sherman suggested that in the upper house every state should have an equal vote, thus satisfying the small states. Behind the debate, of course, was not geography but power. The Virginia Plan, with both houses reflective of population, would have made the larger states the dominant force in the new union. Given the choice, however, between the Connecticut Plan or no plan, the larger states reluctantly fell into line. With the issue of representation resolved, the convention moved to fill in the other features of the new government.

The Issue of Slavery. Even before the vote on the Connecticut Plan, Madison warned that he saw "the great danger to our general government" coming from the opposing interests of North and South, with those states having slaves opposed to those without slaves. The first issue of this expected confrontation had already, in fact, been resolved when the delegates agreed that the census would be the basis not just for determining representation in Congress but also for taxation; the southern states wanted their slaves counted for representation but not for taxation, the opposite of what the northern states wanted. A compromise put forward by James Wilson had proposed counting slaves (called "all other persons") as three-fifths of free people for both purposes.

Although slavery would, in fact, ultimately threaten the Union, it does not appear to have been a critical issue at the Federal Convention. Southerners, of course, wanted protection of what would later be called their "peculiar institution," but the northern states seemed almost indifferent to the issue. At one point Roger Sherman asked why the delegates should quibble over the matter, when "the abolition of slavery seemed to be proceeding throughout the United States." Indeed, many southerners at the time believed that slavery would soon wither away. In the meantime, however, they wanted to make sure the new federal government would not interfere with their "property." The northern delegates, in turn, had come to Philadelphia not as abolitionists but as politicians seeking to create a stronger national union. For them slavery was at most a minor consideration, and, as in the representation/taxation issue, something on which a commonsense compromise would eventually be reached.

As a result, the delegates easily handled the few items in the Constitution dealing with slavery, although they never used that obnoxious term. In 1789 state laws governed slavery, and the Framers left it that way. They did pass several provisions on slaves and slavery: that Congress could enact a fugitive slave law; that states would be bound to help return runaways; that exports, including slaves, could not be taxed; and that the importation of slaves could be taxed but could not be prohibited for twenty years, a provision that seemed to anticipate an end, rather than a continuation, of the slave trade. Little time was spent on any of these provisions, and the delegates, even those personally opposed to slavery, would surely have been confused had they known that two generations later their work would be condemned by abolitionists as "a covenant with death and an agreement with hell."

Fleshing Out the Constitution. While one could identify groups that were associated with certain controversies (such as large states and small states on representation and

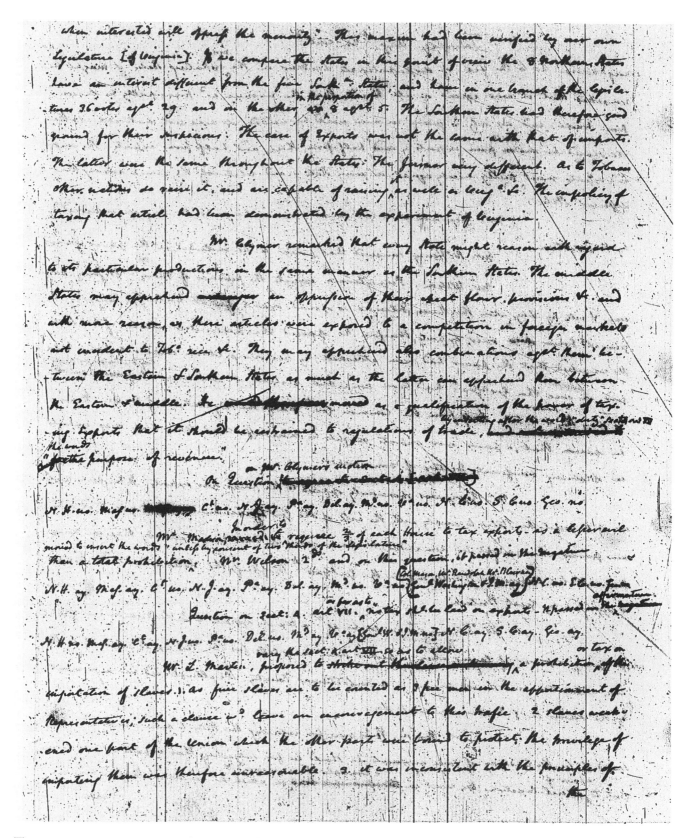

northern and southern states on slavery), the Convention never split into permanent factions. Rather, as the delegates discussed the various powers of and the limitations on the various branches of the government, different coalitions formed and disappeared, reflecting the various attitudes of the delegates. Once the two great decisions had been made—that there should be a new constitution and that it would create a strong central government—the basic skeleton of the new government had been erected; the summer of 1787 was spent fleshing out that skeleton.

A Committee on Detail, headed by John Rutledge, was appointed on 23 July, and it turned out a proposed draft that included, according to Edmund Randolph, "essential principles only" in order to make it possible to accommodate the document "to times and events" and that used "simple and precise language and general propositions." The delegates debated the draft, clause by clause, from 6 August to 10 September, when they approved it and sent the much-amended document to a Committee on Style to be revised into suitable form. The Committee on Style included some of the best writers at the Convention. William Samuel Johnson chaired the group, which also included Gouverneur Morris, James Madison, Rufus King, and Alexander Hamilton. Madison later credited Morris with much of the Constitution's final wording; Morris produced a revised draft for the committee's consideration in just two days and also came up with the inspired wording of the preamble, designating the people as the source of government's authority and legitimacy.

Adopting the Constitution. On 17 September 1787 a clerk read the version of the Constitution submitted by the Committee on Style to the forty-two delegates still present. Then Benjamin Franklin rose to speak. He had written out his comments, which he asked James Wilson to read for him. Franklin admitted that there were several parts of the new document that he did not approve, but he was not sure he would "never" approve them, for the older he grew, the less sure he was of his own infallibility. He called for unanimous approval and offered the formula that would make it possible: "Done in Convention, by the unanimous consent of *the States* present . . . In Witness whereof we have hereunto subscribed our names." Moments before the final vote, Nathaniel Gorham of Massachusetts proposed, in order to "lessen the objections to the Constitution," that the number of representatives be changed from one for every forty thousand to one for every thirty thousand. After Rufus King and Daniel Carroll of Maryland seconded the motion, George Washington, in one of the rare occasions when he formally addressed the Convention, endorsed the proposed change, which was then adopted without opposition.

The dissenters to the Constitution then spoke. Edmund Randolph, the proposer of the Virginia Plan,

apologized for declining to sign but said he wanted to maintain "freedom of action." Elbridge Gerry warned that the document might precipitate a civil war, and George Mason, who approved of much of the Constitution, refused his signature because (among other things) it contained no bill of rights.

After Hamilton urged approval, the Convention adopted the Constitution by a vote of ten states to none, with South Carolina divided and New York not voting. Thirty-nine delegates then signed their names to what the British statesman William Gladstone would later describe as "the most wonderful work ever struck off at a given time by the brain and purpose of man."

Then, according to Madison's notes, "the Convention dissolved itself by an Adjournment sine die."

[See also *Constitution Making; Constitution of 1787.*]

BIBLIOGRAPHY

Collier, Christopher, and James L. Collier. *Decision in Philadelphia: The Constitutional Convention of 1787.* 1986.

Farrand, Max, ed. *The Framing of the Constitution of the United States.* 1913.

Hunt, Gaillard, and James Brown Scott, eds. *The Debates in the Federal Convention of 1787 . . . Reported by James Madison.* 1970.

Jillson, Calvin C. *Constitution Making: Conflict and Consensus in the Federal Convention of 1787.* 1988.

Miller, William Lee. *The Business of May Next: James Madison and the Founding.* 1992.

Rossiter, Clinton. *1787: The Grand Convention.* 1966.

Warren, Charles. *The Making of the Constitution.* 1928.

MELVIN I. UROFSKY

FEDERALIST, THE. *The Federalist* was Alexander Hamilton's idea, conceived, begun, and almost certainly continued through its first few weeks with no intention of enlisting Madison's participation. Although the two great continentalists had worked together intermittently for years, their common dedication to a stronger union flowed from quite contrasting visions of the future, and their close political relationship had never warmed into a friendship. Thus, when Hamilton decided that a major newspaper project would be necessary to combat the opposition to the Constitution in New York—a larger enterprise than even he could handle while he carried on his busy practice of the law—he first sought assistance from local allies whose political ideas were more consistent with his own. Madison was drawn into the project only after other options failed and very nearly at the final moment for securing his assistance.

Authorship and Publication. The first installment of the series signed by Publius—a pseudonym selected by Hamilton to remind readers of the hero who had given

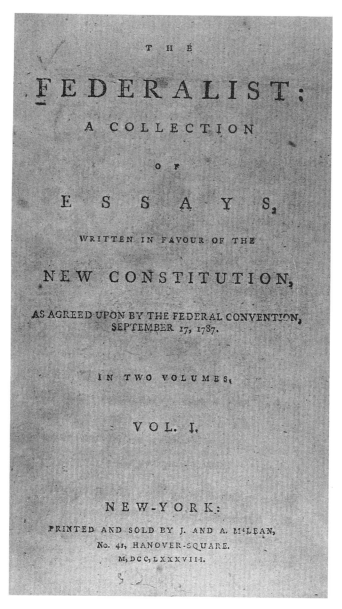

THE FEDERALIST. The title page of a 1788 edition published in New York. The essays—by Madison, Hamilton, and Jay—had appeared in New York newspapers during the debate over the Constitution.

RARE BOOK AND MANUSCRIPTS DIVISION,
NEW YORK PUBLIC LIBRARY.

Rome a stable, republican constitution—was published in the New York *Independent Journal* on 27 October 1787. Tradition says that it was written on the sloop on which the author was returning to the city from Albany, where he had traveled for the fall session of the state's supreme court. By the time the article appeared, John Jay had been enlisted in the project. The noted diplomat and author of the New York constitution wrote the next four numbers, which were published on 31 October, 3 November, 7

November, and 10 November. Sometime after Jay wrote number 5, however, his ability to carry on was threatened by an illness, and Hamilton's appeals to other allies were not successful. Madison was in New York, where he had resumed his seat in the Continental Congress shortly after the adjournment of the Federal Convention. He may well have been informed about the series, but it was not until about 8 November—sometime just before or even after the Virginian left for Philadelphia with no expressed intention of returning to New York—that Hamilton appealed for his cooperation. Six days after his arrival in Philadelphia, Madison abruptly returned to New York and quickly agreed to contribute. Initially, he may have planned to fill a gap until a fourth collaborator could be found. But failure to find an additional contributor, combined with Jay's continuing debility, proved fateful for the series and the country. With Madison's assumption of a larger role, *The Federalist* took the shape responsible for its enduring reputation.

Seventy-seven of the eighty-five essays that make up *The Federalist* appeared originally as letters to *The Independent Journal* and other weekly and semiweekly newspapers in New York. (The final eight were added by Hamilton to a two-volume collection of the papers published in the final days of March 1788.) Most of the essays were written with astounding speed. In the beginning, Madison remembered, he and Hamilton had shown their essays to one other before the articles went to press. Haste obliged them to dispense with such a close collaboration. In the struggle to produce one thousand words per day, it sometimes happened that an author was composing the conclusion of an essay while the printer put its early pages into type. Neither Hamilton nor Madison was conscious of participating in the writing of a classic. Probably the original copies were handed to the printer, set in type, and then discarded. Neither saved his drafts.

These circumstances help explain a century of disagreement over which collaborator wrote a few contested numbers. Authorship of the majority of essays has never been in dispute. Jay wrote numbers 2–5 and 64. Hamilton wrote numbers 1, 6–9, 11–13, 15–17, 21–36, 59–61, and 65–85, or fifty-one of the eighty-five letters. Madison wrote numbers 10, 14, and 37–48. But early in the nineteenth century, Madison and Hamilton advanced competing claims to authorship of numbers 18–20, 49–58, and 62–63. Neither man was trying to mislead posterity or to enlarge his reputation with a lie, but memories and records had become imperfect by this time. Carelessness and a mistake with Roman numerals complicated the confusion. Stylistic similarities between the major authors, who were never in such close agreement as they were when were urging the adoption of the Constitution, made the puzzle difficult to solve. Not until the 1960s did computerized comparisons of styles, reinforced by more conventional analysis of the competing claims, produce a general agreement that Madison was probably responsible for all the contested numbers. Letters 18–20, as Madison explained, were written after Hamilton had given him some notes, but Hamilton's materials do not appear to have exerted a substantial influence. Counting these three essays as essentially his own, Madison was probably responsible for twenty-nine of the eighty-five essays: 10, 14, 18–20, 37–58, and 62–63.

Madison's Contribution. Apparently, the three collaborators never made a single, firm decision on how to divide their labors. Essay No. 1 sketched a basic structure for the series. After Jay became disabled, the younger men divided the responsibilities according to their expertise and interests. When Madison enlisted in the project, Hamilton was well along with section one of his original prospectus: an examination of the benefits of union, including the necessity of union for preventing interstate disputes. Madison's initial and most famous contribution, No. 10, proceeded logically from No. 9's contention that the union operated as a check on local factions. Here, the Virginian made his celebrated argument that private rights and public good might both be safest in a well-constructed, large republic, challenging the widely held assumption that a people's government was fitted only for a polity of limited extent. In an enlarged republic, Madison maintained, a multiplicity of interests would impede formation of majorities that might pursue their special interests to the detriment of other people's rights or of long-term public needs.

Madison reemphasized the value of extending the republic in *Federalist* 14, which completes section one of the original design. In essays 18–20, which drew upon his preconvention notes on ancient and modern confederations, he bolstered Hamilton's analysis of the debilities of the existing system and reinforced the argument that these could not be overcome unless the central government was freed from its dependence on the states. Hamilton wrote most of sections 1–3, examining the benefits of union, the failure of the old Confederation, and the principal requirements of a more effective constitution, and placing special emphasis on the military needs and the commercial and financial benefits of an invigorated union. Then, with essay 37, the collaborators prepared to open their defense of the proposed reform. At this point, Madison wrote an unbroken stream of twenty-two essays (Nos. 37–58), which were published between 11 January and 20 February 1788. Before Madison could complete articles, he was forced to cope with mounting pressure to return to Orange County for the elections to the Virginia ratifying convention. Nevertheless, he stayed until the final moment to prepare two essays on the Senate (62–63). Only then, Madison evidently believed, could he pass the

point-by-point discussion back to Hamilton, who was well equipped to defend the executive and judicial powers.

As the central subject for the body of his essays, Madison selected the fundamental principles of the reform and the arrangement and extent of the legislative powers: Article I of the new Constitution. More sympathetic than Hamilton to the residual powers of the states, he undertook a rigorous definition of the federal principle in No. 39 and in related essays. More theoretically inclined than Hamilton, Madison offered an extended explanation of the principle of checks and balances in essays 47–51. Numbers 62–63, on the theoretical advantages of a Senate, completed his defense of the organization of Congress and the division of legislative powers.

As overarching, organizing themes for all his contributions, Madison developed three essential points: first, in the words of No. 10, that the proposed reform was perfectly consistent with the "spirit" as well as with the form of "popular government" (37, 39, 51, 55, 57); second, that the Constitution's scrupulous division of the three great powers would make the reconstructed central government the best constructed representative republic that humanity had yet devised (47–48, 51, 55–58, 62–63); and, finally, that in the partly national but also partly federal structure of the system, together with the constitutional enumeration of specific federal powers, patriots would find as many new securities for liberty as reason could demand (14, 39, 41–46, 62). When he had finished, Madison believed that he had shown that private rights and popular self-governance would both be safer under the Constitution than in any other government yet devised. Not only was the Constitution faithful to the fundamental precepts of the republican Revolution, it was probably the only means by which the Revolution could be saved.

The Federalist did not accomplish Hamilton's immediate objective, for the voters of New York elected a convention of nineteen supporters and forty-six opponents of the Constitution. That convention nonetheless ratified the Constitution, principally because the prior decisions of ten states had made it clear that the new government might go into effect, whatever they decided. Nevertheless, *The Federalist* circulated widely in the narrowly divided states that made decisions after the beginning of 1788, and they were widely read or widely drawn upon by the informed elite who filled the state conventions. From his Paris post, Thomas Jefferson described them as the greatest work on government that he had ever read. Within the lifetimes of the authors, the collected essays were accepted as the classic commentary on the Constitution. To this day, with the exception of the records of the Federal Convention, no document has exercised a more important influence on interpretations of the Constitution. Numerous authorities have judged these graceful essays, created in the highly charged atmosphere of a political contest, the supreme achievement of American political thought.

[See also *Constitution Making; Constitution of 1787; Republicanism.*]

BIBLIOGRAPHY

Carey, George W. *The Federalist: Design for a Constitutional Republic.* 1989.
Cooke, Jacob E., ed. *The Federalist.* 1961.
Dietze, Gottfried. *The Federalist: A Classic on Federalism and Free Government.* 1960.
Engeman, Thomas S. *The Federalist Concordance.* 1980.
Epstein, David F. *The Political Theory of "The Federalist."* 1984.
Mosteller, Frederick, and David L. Wallace. *Inference and Disputed Authorship: The Federalist.* 1964.
Rossiter, Clinton, ed. *The Federalist Papers.* 1961.

LANCE BANNING

FEDERALIST PARTY. The Framers who created the Constitution of 1787 thought parties—or factions, as they usually called them—were pernicious entities organized for narrow, venal, and self-serving reasons. They used phrases like "cabal, faction, & violence" to describe the dangers of parties. "All those factions which are perpetually dividing the Nation" concerned Benjamin Franklin. James Wilson feared "every gust of faction" would lead to unwarranted impeachments of judges; Charles Pinckney feared the "influence of heat and faction" would lead to presidential impeachments for trivial reasons. Madison concluded that "one of the greatest evils incident to Republican Govt. was the spirit of contention & faction."

Ironically, in the 1790s those same founders created political parties. The policies and personnel of the Federalist party were evident in 1790, and by 1794 two distinct parties had emerged: the Republicans (also called Democrats), led by Madison and Jefferson, and the Federalists, led by John Adams and Alexander Hamilton. In this new context, Federalists generally stood for a strong national government and a diminution of state authority. The party had aristocratic tendencies—John Adams wanted to call the president of the United States "His Highness"; Alexander Hamilton praised the British monarchy. There was no exact correlation between wealth and party affiliation (Adams and Hamilton were not rich, whereas Jefferson was), but most of America's rich elite, North and South, were Federalists. The party favored centralized economic policy, assumption and full funding of all remaining state and national revolutionary war debts, and aggressive enforcement of tariff and tax laws. In foreign policy Federalists favored stronger relations with England and opposed close ties to revolu-

tionary France. Ideologically, the party stressed order over liberty and showed little toleration for dissent.

A keystone of the Federalist policy was the Bank of the United States, the brainchild of Alexander Hamilton. Although the First Bank of the United States was chartered before the two parties crystallized, the fight over its existence can be seen as a prelude to the formation of parties. Madison in Congress and Jefferson in the cabinet argued that, according to a strict construction of the Constitution, the Bank was unconstitutional. They also opposed the centralization of economic power in such an elitist monopoly. Hamilton, setting the tone for Federalist constitutional theory, argued for broad national powers under the necessary and proper clause. Through the Bank Hamilton created a system of national currency and laid the groundwork for an expanding economy. Hamilton also wanted national support and subsidies for the nation's nascent manufacturing sector. This was the one aspect of Federalist economic policies that Congress, even with a Federalist majority, refused to adopt.

Federalists appealed to America's small urban population, to the wealthy, to those involved in shipping and commerce, and generally to the elite. In the South most Federalists lived in cities or towns or were wealthy planters. The Society of the Cincinnati, an organization of former army officers, was overwhelmingly Federalist.

While not militarists, Federalists believed in a strong professional army and the judicious use of force. In 1794 the Federalists sent fifteen thousand troops to Pennsylvania, not only to put down the tiny Whiskey Rebellion, but also to underscore the power of the new national government. Federalists also used the new standing army to crush Indians in the Old Northwest. In 1798, when war with France seemed likely, the Federalist majority in Congress favored a large standing army.

In the 1790s Federalists successfully maneuvered British troops out of frontier and border areas and convinced Spain to guarantee American access to the Mississippi River. In 1793 Washington proclaimed American neutrality in the European conflicts. However, Jeffersonians continued to agitate for greater connections with France. Revolutionary France symbolized the anarchy and chaos that Federalists feared was the result of too much democracy. Complicating this situation were religious differences; most of America's small Catholic population was aligned with Jefferson (as were the rising evangelical Christian sects) while the Federalist party was strongest in those places (like Connecticut and Massachusetts) where Protestant churches were still officially established. By 1798 the nation was involved in the undeclared Quasi-War with France. Republicans, led by Jefferson, still wanted the nation to tilt toward France and believed that Jay's Treaty, ratified in 1795, favored England.

Federalist xenophobia, clumsy attempts by the French to interfere with American politics through the efforts of Edmond Genet, the pressures of the Quasi-War, and the upcoming election of 1800 led to the Federalists' greatest political error: the adoption of the Alien and Sedition Acts in 1798. The Alien Acts were designed to slow the naturalization of immigrants (who usually voted Republican) while implying that Jefferson and his followers were corrupted by foreign influence. These laws raised passions throughout the nation. More damaging still was the Sedition Act, which allowed for prosecutions of anyone who defamed the president, the Congress, or the United States. (Significantly, it did not prohibit defamation of the vice president, who at the time was Adams's rival, Thomas Jefferson.) This blatantly political act was set to expire on 3 March 1801, the day before the new president would take office.

Events soon revealed the partisanal effect of the laws. The first person convicted under the Sedition Act was Matthew Lyon, a Jeffersonian representative from Vermont who had written that President Adams was "pompous." Federalist judges, particularly Supreme Court Justice Samuel Chase, abandoned all semblance of impartiality as they presided over trials of Jeffersonians under the act. The Alien and Sedition Acts ultimately discredited the Adams administration and helped cause Adams's defeat in 1800.

Both the Federalists and the Republicans were active in the North and the South. But, with the exception of a few Virginia Federalists, led by George Washington and John Marshall, and a few South Carolinians, most of the Federalist leadership, including John Adams, Alexander Hamilton, James Wilson, and John Jay, was from the North. All Federalist Speakers of the House, most of the Federalist presidents pro tempore of the Senate, and most of the Federalist presidential candidates were northerners. Most of the Republican presidents pro tempore and House Speakers were southerners. For twenty-four years three southern Republicans— Jefferson, Madison, and Monroe—held the presidency.

While insensitive to civil liberties, Federalists were more supportive of the rights of blacks than were Republicans. A number of leading Federalists, including John Jay and Alexander Hamilton, were members of early antislavery societies and helped end slavery in the North. In the 1790s Philadelphia's Republican newspapers published advertisements for the sale of slaves, while Federalist newspapers refused to accept them. The first Federalist president, George Washington, freed his own slaves in his will, and Adams never owned slaves. By contrast, Jefferson, Madison, and Monroe never disassociated themselves from slavery on either a personal or a political level. In the North, where they could vote under the same rules as whites, it is believed that free blacks usually supported the Federalist party.

The Federalist party successfully governed the United States from the ratification of the Constitution until Jefferson took office in 1801. Jefferson's victory over Adams in 1801 was extraordinarily narrow; in fact, Adams may have actually won more popular votes. Had the Constitution's three-fifths clause not increased the number of southern electoral votes by counting slaves, Adams would have been reelected. As he left office, President Adams and a compliant lame-duck Congress created numerous judicial offices for Federalists, setting the stage for the Supreme Court's decision in *Marbury* v. *Madison* (1803). After 1801 Federalists continued to hold office in Congress and at the state level, but only in 1812 did they come close to taking the presidency again. The Federalist Hartford Convention marked the sectional appeal of the declining party, and by 1820 the party had ceased to exist. However, while the party was out of power in the executive and legislative branch, a Federalist, Chief Justice John Marshall, continued to implement Federalist constitutional theory until the 1830s.

BIBLIOGRAPHY

Borden, Morton. *Parties and Politics in the Early Republic, 1789–1815.* 1967.
Broussard, James. *The Southern Federalists, 1800–1816.* 1978.
Cooke, Jacob E. *Alexander Hamilton.* 1982.
Cunningham, Noble E., Jr. *The Jeffersonian Republicans: The Formation of Party Organization, 1789–1801.* 1957.
Hofstadter, Richard. *The Idea of a Party System: The Rise of the Legitimate Opposition in the United States, 1780–1840.* 1969.
Kerber, Linda K. *Federalists in Dissent.* 1970.
Livermore, Shaw. *The Twilight of Federalism: The Disintegration of the Federalist Party, 1815–1830.* 1962.
Miller, John C. *The Federalist Era.* 1960.
Mitchell, Broadus. *Alexander Hamilton.* 2 vols. 1957, 1962.
Smith, James Morton. *Freedom's Fetters: The Alien and Sedition Laws and American Civil Liberties.* 1956.

PAUL FINKELMAN

FIRST FEDERAL CONGRESS. See *Congresses,* article on *First Congress.*

FLETCHER V. PECK. *Fletcher* v. *Peck* was the first case in which the Marshall Court invalidated a state law as repugnant to the Constitution. The Court also for the first time interpreted the clause of the Constitution that prohibited the states from enacting laws "impairing the Obligation of Contracts." In *Fletcher,* as well as in subsequent cases, the contract clause supplied the Marshall Court with its principal weapon in restricting state legislative powers and in effect served as a general restraint against interference with property rights.

The case arose out of the notorious Yazoo land sales of the 1790s. In 1795 the state of Georgia passed an act selling 35 million acres of its western lands (most of what is now Alabama and Mississippi) to four land companies at a price of less than two cents an acre. A year later a newly elected legislature repealed the 1795 act amid popular denunciation of the Yazoo sale as a corrupt bargain. The 1796 repeal act declared the sale act and subsequent sales made under it to be null and void. Inquiry revealed that all but one of the legislators who had voted for the 1795 sale act held shares in the land companies and thus had personal interests in the purchase.

Before the repeal went into effect, the original Yazoo purchasers hastily sold the lands to third parties throughout the country. A large number of these subsequent purchasers were in New England, organized as the New England Mississippi Land Company. Claiming ignorance both of the fraud attending the original sale and of Georgia's intention to revoke the sale, the New England speculators tried to recoup their investments by petitioning Congress. The Yazoo claimants grounded their petitions on the invalidity of Georgia's rescinding act, which they insisted could not take away rights acquired by innocent purchasers. *Fletcher* v. *Peck* was the legal offshoot of their campaign to obtain compensation from the federal government.

This campaign began in earnest after Georgia ceded its western lands to the United States in 1802. The next year Madison and two other commissioners who negotiated the cession proposed a compromise whereby 5 million acres of the ceded lands would be reserved for satisfying claimants under the Georgia sale act of 1795. Attempts to incorporate this compromise into public law were repeatedly frustrated, however, largely because of the bitter opposition of Rep. John Randolph of Virginia, who made a career of denouncing the Yazoo speculators.

In the meantime, Robert Fletcher, then a New Hampshire resident, sued John Peck of Boston in the federal court at Boston. Fletcher, to whom Peck had sold a Yazoo tract whose title derived from the Georgia act of 1795, asserted several grounds on which Peck's title was defective, contrary to the assurances contained in the deed. After Judge William Cushing gave judgment for Peck on circuit in 1807, the case was appealed to the U.S. Supreme Court, where it was argued at the 1809 and 1810 terms. Although circumstances indicated that Fletcher's suit against Peck was an arranged case between friendly parties, the justices overcame their initial reluctance and agreed to decide the case on its merits.

In his opinion for the Court, Marshall refused as a matter beyond judicial competence to inquire into the corruption of the legislature in passing the 1795 act. Instead, he declared that act to be a valid public grant and also a contract protected by the Constitution. He then voided the 1796 rescinding act as an unconstitutional impairment of the obligation of contract. He denied that the contract clause was intended to embrace private contracts only and argued that the general language of that clause signified an intention to bring public contracts such as legislative grants within its operation as well. The Court's expansive reading of the contract clause eventually brought corporate charters within the protection of the Constitution (as decided in the 1819 case of *Dartmouth College* v. *Woodward*).

In a letter to Madison, Jefferson referred to *Fletcher* as another of Marshall's "twistifications of the law." Madison left no record of his own reaction to the case, though as a commissioner some years earlier he had expressed an opinion that the Yazoo titles had no legal validity. Whatever he thought of the particular holding in this case, Madison clearly sympathized with the larger goal of preventing state legislative interferences with private rights. The Marshall Court's interpretation of the contract clause in many ways answered the purposes of Madison's proposed federal veto of state laws. In adopting the contract clause, Marshall noted in *Fletcher*, the American people "have manifested a determination to shield themselves and their property from the effects of those sudden and strong passions to which men are exposed. The restrictions on the legislative power of the states are obviously founded in this sentiment; and the constitution of the United States contains what may be deemed a bill of rights for the people of each state." Madison had no quarrel with this statement.

Fletcher had no immediate impact on efforts to settle the question of the Yazoo titles, though it did provide claimants additional ammunition in their continuing campaign for reimbursement from the federal government. Finally, in 1814, Congress enacted legislation setting aside up to $5 million to indemnify Yazoo claims.

[See also *Yazoo Lands Frauds.*]

BIBLIOGRAPHY

Haines, Charles Grove. *The Role of the Supreme Court in American Government and Politics, 1789–1835.* 1944. Repr. 1973.

Haskins, George Lee, and Herbert A. Johnson. *Foundations of Power: John Marshall, 1801–15.* 1981.

Magrath, C. Peter. *Yazoo: Law and Politics in the New Republic: The Case of Fletcher v. Peck.* 1966.

Warren, Charles. *The Supreme Court in United States History.* 2 vols. Rev. ed. 1926.

CHARLES F. HOBSON

FLORIDA. During James Madison's terms as president, the two Floridas, East and West, belonged to Spain, a nation that was powerless to control more than the area around Pensacola and St. Augustine. There was scant wealth in Florida, and its population comprised no more than 12,300 blacks and whites and about 5,000 Indians. Nevertheless, Madison was eager to acquire Florida, Spain wanted to retain it, Great Britain did not want the United States to have it, and the Indians considered it theirs. The struggle among these contenders kept Florida in constant turmoil.

Madison acquired a strip of West Florida below the thirty-first parallel from the Mississippi to the Perdido River by proclaiming it (on 27 October 1810) a part of the United States, under the terms of the Louisiana Purchase. Spain and Britain both denounced this seizure, but neither interfered.

Congress on 15 January 1811 secretly authorized the president to annex the rest of Florida provided it could be done peaceably but authorized the use of force if a foreign power threatened. The justification was that East Florida was collateral to be held until Spain paid several million dollars owed the United States as compensation for property destroyed during the Quasi-War with France in 1798.

Madison verbally instructed Gen. George Mathews, a distinguished Georgian, to carry out Congress's mandate. Mathews decided that the only way to achieve the transfer was to foment a revolution among United States citizens living in Florida with the aim of overthrowing the Spanish government's rule. At first he involved a small group of prominent citizens of Spanish Florida, who were expected to repudiate the Spanish regime, secure control, and offer the province to the United States. Mathews was so certain that the administration meant for him to have military support that he convinced Capt. Hugh Cunningham to enter Florida waters without orders from the Navy Department. The so-called Patriots, backed by two of Cunningham's gunboats (acting not for the United States but for the revolutionaries, according to the rationale), occupied Fernandina on Amelia Island in March 1812. On 13 March ten of the Americans declared East Florida independent of Spain and offered it to the United States.

But to achieve the revolution, the Patriots had to capture St. Augustine, an impossibility without clandestine military aid from the United States. Captain Cunningham, unsure and constantly asking for orders, remained in Spanish waters. Lt. Col. Thomas Adam Smith, commanding the American army troops in Point Petre in the United States, sent fifty soldiers to within two and one half miles of St. Augustine. Capt. John Williams reinforced these troops with Marines

from Cumberland Island. Ninety Patriots joined the military detachment.

The Americans elected John Houstoun McIntosh, a wealthy American who had become a Spanish citizen, to be their director. On 26 March 1812 McIntosh summoned the Spanish governor to surrender St. Augustine but received no reply. British warships hovering off St. Augustine made American occupation of Spanish land increasingly awkward, so awkward indeed that Secretary of State James Monroe revoked the powers that Madison had verbally given to General Mathews. In a letter on 4 April he wrote, "The measures you have adopted to get Amelia Island and parts of East Florida are not authorized by the laws." Thus the administration saved face and made General Mathews a scapegoat. The president made David Mitchell, governor of Georgia, his emissary for East Florida.

Congress declared war against Great Britain on 18 June 1812. The next day the House of Representatives passed a bill to annex Florida, but on 3 July the Senate defeated it by a vote of 16 to 14, to the chagrin of the administration. Monroe at once wrote Mitchell that the president thought it advisable to remove the military forces, but his letter was ambiguous. Mitchell replied on 17 July, "I have carefully avoided making any proposition for withdrawing the troops under the fullest conviction that such a step was not intended."

Meanwhile, the Spanish governor, Sebastian Kindelan, encouraged the Indians and one hundred black soldiers to attack the revolutionaries. The blacks knew well that transfer of Florida to the United States would result in their becoming slaves, and their presence as a military force aroused great concern in neighboring Georgia, which feared attacks by blacks on white citizens. Col. Daniel Newnan led 250 Georgia militia into Florida, promising them large tracts of land as a reward for victory. But from 24 September to 11 October 1812, the Indians pressed Newnan so hard that he retreated to Georgia, with a loss of eight killed, nine wounded, and nine missing. Though Georgia celebrated Newnan's battle as a great victory, the state legislature refused to vote to invade Florida again without additional support.

After Madison was reelected, he sought to persuade Congress to authorize the occupation of East Florida. The War Department replaced Governor Mitchell with a military person, Maj. Gen. Thomas Pinckney, and placed the navy in Florida waters under Pinckney's orders. Pinckney concentrated all available troops south of Virginia at Point Petre, just north of the Spanish border, and was promised adequate power to take St. Augustine if Congress authorized it.

Eastern Tennesseans, although five hundred miles from Spanish Florida, feared Indians enough to involve themselves in Florida. Col. John Williams raised an elite troop of volunteers, all mounted on strong horses and all well armed. This troop headed from Knoxville for Florida without an official call from the U.S. government, simply notifying the president on 4 December of their destination.

The Alachua Indians sued for peace, but the administration made no effort to halt the 250 troops that crossed the St. Mary's River on 3 February 1813 and headed for the Alachua Indian towns. Colonel Smith joined them with 220 U.S. soldiers, and the hybrid army charged into Payne's town (the home of the Alachua Indians and their chief, Payne), only to find it deserted. They proceeded to ravage the Indian country, and after killing twenty Indians and capturing nine blacks, they marched out of Florida. Meanwhile, their invasion elicited a vigorous protest from Georgia, for it seemed to suggest that Georgia could not handle its own border problems.

In the meantime, Monroe was negotiating with Governor Kindelan. If the governor would grant amnesty to the American insurgents, the United States would withdraw its military forces from Florida. Kindelan agreed, and on 18 March 1813 General Pinckney received the order to evacuate East Florida. McIntosh and his associates pleaded with Pinckney to delay removal of the troops, but Pinckney followed his orders. By 6 May 1813 all United States forces were out of Spanish Florida. They had been there, without official sanction, for a year and fifty days.

Anarchy soon erupted in East Florida. Because the Spanish government was too weak to keep the peace, lawless bands looted and burned without restraint. One of these, headed by Buckner Harris, a sometime Patriot revolutionary, led seventy men across the St. Mary's intent on establishing a colony on the land of the Alachua Indians. His followers built a blockhouse where Payne's town had been, and on 25 January 1814 they assembled as the legislature for the District of Elotcheway of the Republic of East Florida. They maintained their position for four months, but on 5 May 1814 the Indians and blacks wiped out the settlement and killed Harris.

By this time the European coalition had defeated Napoleon, leaving Britain free to concentrate on its conflict with the United States. In May 1814 British warships appeared off the mouth of the St. Mary's, occupied Amelia Island, and launched a naval strike against West Florida. A man-of-war appeared off the Apalachicola River under instruction from Adm. Alexander Cochrane to draw Indians and blacks into British service. Every Indian and black who joined the British service would be clothed, fed, and paid. The admiral himself moved on west toward New Orleans in response to orders giving him permission to attack the city. He left behind one important installation—a fort on the Apalachicola, sixty miles inside Spanish Florida—that was well stocked with weapons and ammunition and garrisoned by blacks and Indians. The war ended in 1815 with the situation in Florida unchanged.

In 1816 the United States built Fort Scott on the Flint River, north of the Spanish border. The only practicable way to provision it was via the Apalachicola in Spanish territory. Accordingly, a supply convoy started up the river without receiving permission from Spain. Spain was powerless to stop the convoy, but the black troops at the fort had no intention of letting it pass. However, a lucky shot from one of the ships blew up the British powder magazine, killing three hundred of the Indians and blacks and destroying irreplaceable supplies.

When James Madison's second term ended in 1817, the United States was poised to send an army into West Florida under Andrew Jackson to subdue the Indians and stop the escape of fugitive slaves into Florida. Florida had been in turmoil when Madison took office and remained a diplomatic sore spot until the Adams-Onís Treaty of 1819 provided for the cession of Florida. In return, the United States assumed some $5 million in claims by American citizens against Spain.

BIBLIOGRAPHY

Mahon, John K. *The War of 1812.* 1972.
Owsley, Frank L., Jr. *Struggle for the Gulf Borderlands.* 1981.
Patrick, Rembert W. *Florida Fiasco.* 1954.
Pratt, Julius W. *The Expansionists of 1812.* 1925.
Tebeau, Charleton W. *A History of Florida.* 1976.

JOHN MAHON

FLOYD, CATHERINE (KITTY)

FLOYD, CATHERINE (KITTY) (1767–1832), James Madison's first known romantic attachment and fiancée. Rep. William Floyd of New York and his family were living at the Philadelphia boarding house of Mrs. Mary House when Madison first moved there in 1780. The youngest of Floyd's three children was thirteen-year-old Catherine. When Floyd returned to Congress in November 1782, Kitty Floyd was fifteen. Soon she and the thirty-one-year-old Madison were a principal topic of good-natured whispering among the other boarders, Thomas Jefferson foremost among them. We know of the romance largely through the correspondence (most of it in a numerical cipher-code) between Jefferson and Madison.

Jefferson hinted in an April 1783 letter that he hoped that Kitty and Madison might someday be his neighbors near Monticello. Madison confirmed Jefferson's assumptions in a coded letter that he inked out when he reclaimed his correspondence after Jefferson's death in 1826. (This letter was dated 22 April 1783, two days

CATHERINE FLOYD.   Kitty Floyd and James Madison exchanged miniatures. Miniature by Charles Willson Peale, Philadelphia, 1783. [For the miniature of Madison, see *Madison, James*, article on *Continental Congress*.]
RARE BOOK AND SPECIAL COLLECTIONS DIVISION, LIBRARY OF CONGRESS.

before Kitty's sixteenth birthday and a week before she left Philadelphia and Madison's life.) More than a century later the original ciphered words in these letters showed through to reveal Madison's youthful romance. In August Madison wrote Jefferson in language so deceptive that no one could imagine that he was discussing a failed romance, if the previous letters had not already revealed his painful secret. During her absence in New York, Kitty had found that she yearned for William Clarkson, a nineteen-year-old Philadelphia medical student, much more than for Madison. She married Clarkson in 1785. Clarkson practiced medicine for nine years before becoming a Presbyterian minister. He died midway through Madison's presidency.

BIBLIOGRAPHY

Brant, Irving. *James Madison: The Nationalist, 1780–1787.* 1948.
Ketcham, Ralph. *James Madison: A Biography.* 1971.

DONALD O. DEWEY

FORT DEARBORN. Situated on the Chicago River, Fort Dearborn was a weakly garrisoned and almost indefensible structure, with two blockhouses and a stockade, resembling a trading post more than a military outpost. It was normally supplied by merchant schooners sailing from Buffalo through Detroit, then across Lakes Huron and Michigan. After the fall of Michilimackinac in July 1812, Brig. Gen. William Hull, whose army was at Detroit, ordered Capt. Nathan Heald, the American commander of Fort Dearborn, to evacuate its fifty-four regulars, twelve militia, and twenty-seven women and children. Heald poured the fort's liquor into the river, destroyed the surplus arms and ammunition, and abandoned the fort on 15 August 1812. The Potawatomi and Winnebago Indians had learned from Tecumseh of the British victory at Michilimackinac. Soon four hundred Indians attacked the retreating column and killed twenty-six regulars, all the militia, and some of the women and children. The remainder were taken prisoner by the Potawatomi chief, Blackbird. The fort was burned.

The fall of Michilimackinac on 25 July and the Fort Dearborn massacre convinced the western Indians to join their fortunes to the British war effort. Fort Wayne on the Maumee River, the only remaining American post in the old Northwest, was soon under siege. The string of military defeats, including the surrender of Hull's army at Detroit on 17 August and the defeat of Van Rensselaer's army at Queenston on 13 October, thwarted the Madison administration's efforts to conquer Upper Canada and fueled the American determination to reverse these early disasters. They also led Madison to replace his secretary of war, William Eustis.

BIBLIOGRAPHY

Gilpin, Alex. *The War of 1812 in the Old North West.* 1958.
Hickey, Don. *The War of 1812: A Forgotten Contest.* 1989.
Hitsman, J. Mackay. *The Incredible War of 1812.* 1965.
Stanley, George. *The War of 1812: Land Operations.* 1983.

FREDERICK C. DRAKE

FORT ERIE. At the opening of hostilities in the War of 1812, Fort Erie, a stone and palisade fort commanding Lake Erie's debouchment into the upper Niagara River, was held by a small British detachment. On 28 November 1812, the defenders successfully repelled Brig. Gen. Alexander Smyth's weak attack across the Niagara but abandoned the fort when Maj. Gen. Henry Dearborn and Commodore Isaac Chauncey captured Fort George on the lower Niagara River on 27 May 1813. The American victory released five schooners from Black Rock, almost opposite Fort Erie, to join Oliver H. Perry's small squadron at Erie, Pennsylvania.

Then, after a British victory at Stoney Creek on 6 June 1813, American forces burned Fort Erie and concentrated on holding Fort George. Lt. Gen. Gordon Drummond's British forces repossessed both forts and captured Fort Niagara in December 1813.

On 3 July 1814, Fort Erie's two companies capitulated to Maj. Gen. Jacob Brown's Left Division. After Brown's campaign—the battle of Chippewa on 5 July and the battle of Lundy's Lane on 25 July—his army, occupying Fort Erie, was besieged by Drummond's regulars. The bastions were rebuilt, a wide ditch constructed, and seven-foot-high earthworks extended to the shore and westward. The siege lasted seven weeks (3 August–21 September). Drummond's attack on 15 August was repulsed with heavy losses (57 killed, 309 wounded, and 538 missing or prisoners). A sortie by sixteen hundred American regulars and militia on 17 September captured two siege batteries but failed to take the dominating main battery before being driven back. The American losses were 79 killed and 432 wounded or missing, while British casualties included 115 killed, 176 wounded, and 315 missing. Drummond raised the siege on 21 September. The Americans, under the command of Maj. Gen. George Izard, who replaced Brown, blew up the fort and retired across the river on 5 November, returning the strong point to British possession.

BIBLIOGRAPHY

Cruikshank, Ernest A. *Documentary History of the Campaign upon the Niagara Frontier.* 9 vols. Vol. 8. 1907. Vol. 9. 1908.

Cruikshank, Ernest A. *Drummond's Winter Campaign, 1813.* 2d ed. 1900.

Cruikshank, Ernest A. *The Siege of Fort Erie, August 1st–September 23rd, 1814.* 1905.

Hitsman, J. Mackay. *The Incredible War of 1812.* 1965.

Stanley, George. *The War of 1812: Land Operations.* 1983.

FREDERICK C. DRAKE

FORT MEIGS. Located at the foot of the Maumee River rapids near present-day Perrysburg, Ohio, the post was built by troops commanded by William Henry Harrison. The fort served as a temporary supply depot and staging area after Harrison's plans for a winter offensive against British-occupied Detroit collapsed in the wake of James Winchester's defeat at Frenchtown (Monroe, Michigan) on the River Raisin.

The earth-and-wood palisaded camp enclosed nearly ten acres and included seven two-story log blockhouses, five artillery batteries, two underground powder magazines, and various work and storage buildings. A boat harbor, artificer yards, and a bakehouse located outside the stockade completed the complex. Ranging in size from approximately nine hundred to two thousand men, the garrison comprised U.S. regulars, enrolled Ohio, Kentucky, Pennsylvania, and Virginia militia, and several companies of independent volunteers.

The British directed two invasions against Fort Meigs. In April 1813, 2,400 British regulars, Canadian militia, and native allies led by Henry Procter and the Shawnee chief Tecumseh invested the outpost. Beginning 1 May, the fort was subjected to five days of heavy artillery bombardment, but the British inflicted only light casualties on the American defenders. However, Procter's forces routed a 1,200-man column of reinforcements commanded by Green Clay, capturing or killing more than 650 members of the expedition. Unable to subdue the fort, the British lifted the siege, withdrawing on 9 May. Returning in July, more than three thousand Indians and 350 regulars staged a mock battle, unsuccessfully attempting to lure the Americans from the fort. When the ruse failed, the army retreated on 24 July. Substantially reduced in strength in September 1813, the fortification continued to be held by the Ohio militia until it was abandoned by the military in May 1815.

BIBLIOGRAPHY

Boehm, Robert B., and Randall L. Buchman, eds. *Journal of the Northwestern Campaign of 1812–1813 under Major-General Wm. H. Harrison by Bvt. Lieut.-Colonel Eleazer D. Wood, Captain Corps of Engineers, U.S. Army.* 1975.

Lindley, Harlow, ed. *Fort Meigs and the War of 1812; Orderly Book of Cushing's Company 2nd U.S. Artillery April, 1813–February, 1814, and Personal Diary of Captain Daniel Cushing October, 1812–July, 1813.* 1975.

Nelson, Larry L. *Men of Patriotism, Courage, and Enterprise; Fort Meigs in the War of 1812.* 1985.

LARRY L. NELSON

FORT NIAGARA. A western post commanding the mouth of the Niagara River, Fort Niagara was turned over to the United States by Jay's Treaty and occupied in 1796. Garrisoned by American forces, whose officers were dining with their British counterparts in Fort George across the river when news of the declaration of the War of 1812 arrived, Fort Niagara served as the staging area for Gen. Henry Dearborn's and Commodore Isaac Chauncey's 27 May 1813 attack on Fort George, which was then abandoned by Gen. John Vincent. U.S. forces were pinned inside the fort, an American base for invasion of the Niagara peninsula, after the British victory of 6 June at Stoney Creek.

After the burning of Newark in December 1813 by Gen. George McClure, Fort Niagara fell, in a surprise bayonet attack and without a shot fired, to a British force of 550 regulars in the early hours of 19 December 1813. The

Americans had left the gates open for the changing of the guard, and the garrison was asleep in its tents. The Americans lost 65 killed and 14 wounded, and 344 were taken prisoner, while the British lost 6 killed and 5 wounded. From Fort Niagara, British troops razed the settlements at Lewiston, Black Rock, and Buffalo on the Niagara frontier. Holding the fort was deemed important by Lt. Gen. Gordon Drummond, who commanded British forces on the Niagara peninsula in 1813–1814, for the guns of Forts George and Niagara dominated the Niagara River mouth and ensured a secure anchorage for Sir James Lucas Yeo's British squadron on Lake Ontario (while, conversely, denying it to Commodore Isaac Chauncey's American squadron). The fort remained in British hands until the signing of the Treaty of Ghent, which returned it to the United States.

BIBLIOGRAPHY

Babcock, Louis L. *The War of 1812 on the Niagara Frontier.* 1927.
Cruikshank, Ernest A. *Documentary History of the Campaign upon the Niagara Frontier.* 9 vols. Vol. 9. 1908.
Cruikshank, Ernest A. *Drummond's Winter Campaign, 1813.* 2d ed. 1900.
Hitsman, J. Mackay. *The Incredible War of 1812.* 1965.
Stanley, George. *The War of 1812: Land Operations.* 1983.
Wood, William, ed. *Select British Documents of the Canadian War of 1812.* Vol. 2. 1923.

FREDERICK C. DRAKE

FOSTER, AUGUSTUS JOHN (1780–1848), English diplomat. Augustus Foster landed at Annapolis on 29 June 1811 to assume his duties as British minister to the United States. Having served earlier as secretary of the British legation, he was well known in Washington. Unfortunately, Foster's personal popularity among American officials contrasted sharply with the unfortunate state of British-American relations.

Congress's adoption of Macon's Bill No. 2 in May 1810 created a potential dilemma for Britain. To find an effective substitute for the Nonimportation Act, Congress opened trade with Britain and France but added that if

DEFENSE OF FORT NIAGARA, 19 DECEMBER 1813. A Soldier's Wife. Colored engraving by T. Walker, 1860.
PRINTS AND PHOTOGRAPHS DIVISION, LIBRARY OF CONGRESS.

either country repealed its edicts against neutral commerce before 3 March 1811 and the other did not follow, the United States would reassert its nonimportation regulations against the country imposing restrictions. On 5 August the French foreign minister, the duc de Cadore, announced that on 1 November 1810 France would revoke its Berlin and Milan decrees. Madison accepted the French declaration at face value and on 2 November announced that, unless Britain revoked or modified its edicts within three months, the United States would terminate all commerce between the two countries.

In London the American minister, William Pinkney, confronted the British government with the Cadore letter, only to face demands that the United States prove that France had actually revoked its decrees. In the absence of proof, the British government remained obdurate, and in February 1811 Madison terminated all commerce with Britain.

Foster's initial instructions restated the British position. The orders in council would continue until France demonstrated that it had repealed the decrees and municipal regulations that had closed continental ports to British goods. Secretary of State James Monroe reminded Foster that the United States expected no less than the elimination of all British restrictions on American commerce. Through subsequent months Foster reminded Monroe that Napoleon, not Britain, was responsible for the war being waged in Europe. Britain's protection of its commerce and its distrust of France's ambiguous declarations, he argued, were reasonable. "Americans, as not being at war," Foster admonished Monroe in October, " . . . may be less scrupulous as to the evidence necessary to prove the fact; but, sir, it surely cannot be expected that Great Britain, who is contending for every thing dear to her, should not require more proof."

Monroe rejected Foster's appeal outright. Privately, however, American officials were deeply troubled by France's behavior. The success of French policy required a British rejection of Napoleon's overtures. French ambiguity would triumph if the United States alone gave France the benefit of the doubt. From Saint Petersburg, John Quincy Adams warned the administration that France sought to trap the country in war against England.

When the Twelfth Congress convened on 11 November 1811, Madison gave notice that Britain's refusal to follow France in revoking its decrees was evidence of that country's inflexible hostility toward the United States. Facing powerful anti-British sentiment in both Congress and the administration, Foster reported to London that only the absence of American military preparedness prevented an immediate conflict. Throughout the spring of 1812, Foster pressed the administration for proof of France's revocation of its decrees against

neutral commerce. On 1 April he recorded Monroe's response to his most recent requests: "He told me . . . that the President . . . could not now entertain the question as to whether the French decrees were repealed, having already . . . declared that they were so."

French ambiguity had triumphed. Foster's offers of late May did not include British revocation of its orders in council. A disappointed Madison, convinced that Britain would never recede, accepted the necessity of war. On 17 June, by a vote of 19 to 13, the Senate adopted the war resolution. That evening Foster visited the Madisons, finding the president remarkably civil. His mission to preserve peace had failed, but Madison did not hold him accountable.

BIBLIOGRAPHY

Brant, Irving. *James Madison: The President, 1809–1812.* 1956.
Burt, A. L. *The United States, Great Britain, and British North America from the Revolution to the Establishment of Peace after the War of 1812.* 1940.
Graebner, Norman A. *Foundations of American Foreign Policy: A Realist Appraisal from Franklin to McKinley.* 1985.

NORMAN A. GRAEBNER

FRANCE. In one of the great ironies of history, eighteenth-century France, a Catholic monarchy, assisted in the birth of one of the first Protestant republics, the United States. Seeking to weaken Great Britain and avenge its humiliating loss in the Seven Years' War, France provided aid to the American revolutionaries from the very start of their armed conflict with England. In 1776 Louis XVI authorized the expenditure of 1 million livres in secret aid to the American colonists, and two years later France and the United States entered into a formal alliance. It was this alliance that proved the decisive factor in the War for Independence.

From the outset of the Revolution, American opinion about France was divided. A fundamental distrust of French motives and ultimate intentions led the American peace commissioners to conduct unauthorized separate peace negotiations with Great Britain. American views of France became sharply defined against the backdrop of revolution beginning in 1789. Most Americans greeted the first news of the French Revolution with sympathy and even enthusiasm. As the Revolution progressed, however, skeptics such as George Washington, Alexander Hamilton, John Adams, and Gouverneur Morris found their worst suspicions confirmed in the seemingly dangerous democratic principles advanced by French leaders and in the growing anarchy evident in the streets. Gradually the split in American perceptions of the French Revolution acted to highlight and crystallize major divisions in domestic politics. The Federalists, who hoped to build a strong national economy based on a close relationship with British financial interests and who feared the growth of democratic tendencies in American society, united around Alexander Hamilton in opposing American support of revolutionary France. Those Americans who believed the United States owed France a large debt of gratitude for its assistance during the American Revolution, who were more at ease with French culture, who were more concerned with the agricultural markets of continental Europe than with the financial markets of London, and who were deeply concerned with the seemingly dangerous drift away from republicanism evident in Hamiltonian policies, organized around Thomas Jefferson in favor of a pro-French foreign policy. The Republican leaders, Jefferson and Madison, strongly supported the Revolution out of a deeply held conviction that the French were fighting for republicans everywhere.

During the 1790s the opposing Federalist and Republican perspectives on foreign policy became sharper as Americans sought to clarify the status of the French alliance. When news of the execution of Louis XVI reached the United States in March 1793, Hamilton and his Federalist followers urged Washington to renounce the French treaties of 1778. Jefferson countered Hamilton's contentions by claiming that treaties bound nations, not governments, and Washington heeded the advice of his secretary of state. Following France's declaration of war on Great Britain in 1793, however, Washington issued a proclamation of neutrality declaring that the United States would be "friendly and impartial" toward both belligerents. Republicans opposed the proclamation, believing that under the terms of the alliance, America owed more to France than a passive neutrality.

Despite Washington's proclamation, France still considered the alliance in effect. Its first minister to the United States, Edmond Genet, cultivated support for France and sought direct assistance for French forces in flagrant violation of American neutrality. With both Federalist and Republican approval, Washington asked for Genet's recall in the summer of 1793.

The French viewed Jay's Treaty (1794) as a violation of the alliance of 1778 and angrily denounced the pact, severed diplomatic relations, and attempted to influence the course of American politics, hoping the election of Jeffersonian Republicans would improve Franco-American relations. French interference in domestic politics and vigorous protests throughout the country against Jay's Treaty deeply alarmed Washington. He used the occasion of his Farewell Address to attack the French alliance, advising his countrymen against "a passionate attachment of one Nation for another," and urging them "to steer clear of permanent alliances with any portion of the foreign world."

France's relationship with the United States deteriorated further in 1797, as French vessels seized American ships and all Americans found serving the British. As American maritime losses mounted, President Adams sent a special mission to Paris to negotiate an end to French hostilities. When that mission ended in the humiliation of the American commissioners (the XYZ Affair), the Adams administration prepared the nation for war. For the next three years (1797–1800), the United States and France clashed in an undeclared Quasi-War, fought mainly at sea. The Treaty of Mortefontaine (Convention of 1800) terminated the fighting and formally ended the Franco-American Alliance of 1778.

With the Republicans in power beginning in 1801, American foreign policy shifted away from the Federalist pro-British orientation to a diplomacy more favorable to France. Neither Jefferson nor Madison held any illusions about the progress of French liberty and republicanism under Napoleon. Yet both Republican leaders looked to Bonaparte as the only European leader capable of holding in check the dominant military power of Great Britain.

In the early years of the Jefferson administration, it was, ironically, France rather than Great Britain that first threatened American interests. In 1802 Jefferson learned that France had reacquired Louisiana from Spain in 1800 under the secret Treaty of San Ildefonso. The retrocession of Louisiana, together with the French army's invasion of Santo Domingo early in 1802, made clear to Jefferson and Madison Napoleon's imperial ambitions in North America. Jefferson advised Napoleon to cede the American territory France had gained from Spain to the United States or face the prospect of an Anglo-American alliance.

Military setbacks rather than implied American threats determined Napoleon's actions in Louisiana. The destruction of the French army on Santo Domingo by the end of 1802, the failure of a French naval fleet harbored near Rotterdam to sail to Louisiana during the winter of 1803, and the prospect of renewed fighting in Europe led Napoleon to offer the territory to the United States. On 30 April 1803, the United States purchased Louisiana from France for $15 million in cash and claims.

The American deal fit into Napoleon's plans, for soon France and Great Britain were again at war, and the United States was again treated as a pawn in the larger struggle between the two world powers. Both Great Britain and France attempted to control American oceanic trade through a series of orders in council and Napoleonic decrees that subjected neutral American shipping to illegal searches and seizures. Jefferson and Madison responded to this commercial warfare with the

Embargo of 1807–1809, followed by the Nonintercourse Act of 1809. The president and his secretary of state believed that halting the flow of American products to the belligerents would force them to acknowledge America's maritime rights as a neutral country.

Both the Embargo and the Nonintercourse acts failed to achieve American objectives and proved more injurious to American interests than to those of Great Britain and France. In May 1810 Congress made a third attempt at economic coercion with Macon's Bill No. 2. Napoleon gladly seized the opportunity offered by the bill to gain an advantage over his English adversaries. On 5 August 1810 the French foreign minister, the duc de Cadore, wrote to the American minister in Paris informing him that the Berlin Decree of 1806 and the Milan Decree of 1807 were now revoked. Though he had no proof of France's intention to eliminate these trade restrictions, Madison quickly accepted the Cadore letter as a genuine statement of French intentions. He instituted a policy of nonintercourse against Great Britain beginning on 11 February 1811. Madison's easy acceptance of the unsubstantiated pledges of the Cadore letter was guided by the conviction that French deception could be tolerated to the extent that it could be employed against America's most fearsome enemy, Great Britain.

Sixteen months after the proclamation of nonintercourse against Great Britain, the United States and its former mother country were at war. In his calculations, Madison believed Napoleon's army would continue to act as a drain on British military strength. He also thought that Napoleon would be grateful to the United States for engaging France's enemy in war and would therefore attempt to improve Franco-American relations through a commercial treaty. In these expectations Madison miscalculated badly. French depradations on American commerce continued as Napoleon showed little regard, much less gratitude, for America's martial efforts. Furthermore, France's role as a co-belligerent collapsed in early 1814 with Napoleon's defeat and abdication. In the spring of 1814 the United States stood alone and extremely vulnerable in the war against Great Britain, aware that the French power that Republicans had long considered a shield against British military and naval might had been destroyed.

[See also Blockades by England and France; Neutrality.]

BIBLIOGRAPHY

DeConde, Alexander. *Entangling Alliance: Politics and Diplomacy under George Washington.* 1958.

DeConde, Alexander. *The Quasi-War: The Politics and Diplomacy of the Undeclared War with France, 1797–1801.* 1966.

Egan, Clifford. *Neither Peace nor War: Franco-American Relations, 1803–1812.* 1983.

Hoffman, Ronald, and Peter Albert, eds. *Diplomacy and Revolution: The Franco-American Alliance of 1778.* 1981.

Kaplan, Lawrence S. *Entangling Alliances with None: American Foreign Policy in the Age of Jefferson.* 1987.

TINA H. SHELLER

FRENEAU, PHILIP M. (1752–1832), poet, polemicist. Following a private education, Freneau entered the sophomore class at the College of New Jersey (later Princeton) in 1768. The next year James Madison joined Freneau as both classmate and—according to popular tradition— roommate.

In 1791 Freneau edited the New York *Daily Advertiser,* an underfinanced newspaper dedicated to upholding the ideals of the French Revolution and to criticizing the fiscal policies of Treasury Secretary Alexander Hamilton. When the federal government moved to Philadelphia later that year, Madison, now serving in the House of Representatives, sought an editor able to counter the labors of John Fenno, whose Federalist-leaning *Gazette of the United States* supported Hamilton's programs. After Secretary of State Thomas Jefferson agreed to pay him an annual salary of $250 to translate documents, Freneau agreed to edit a new publication, called the *National Gazette,* whose first edition, spewing invective at the "stock-jobbers and monarchy-jobbers," appeared on 31 October 1791.

Although Freneau's pen required little assistance, the anonymous writings of both Jefferson and Madison found their way into the Republican-sponsored journal. Madison's essay "Property," published 27 March 1792, broadened the definition of ownership to include not only land and objects but "every thing to which a man may attach a value and have a right," including civil and religious liberties. A just government, Madison concluded, gave special preference to no particular economic endeavor but recognized that each individual valued property in a different manner. Hamilton's policies, which Madison believed favored the rising business class in the urban North, were consequently unjust.

Freneau's rigid dedication to principle, as well as his staunch support of the French minister Edmond Genet, occasionally caused Madison political embarrassment. Hard-pressed financially, Freneau suspended publication after the devastation caused by the 1793 yellow fever epidemic. He briefly edited the *Time-Piece,* a New York literary journal, and then retired to a farm in northern New Jersey. He perished in a blizzard in December 1832.

BIBLIOGRAPHY

Axelrad, Jacob. *Philip Freneau: Champion of Democracy.* 1967.

Leary, Lewis. *That Rascal Freneau: A Study in Literary Failure.* 1941.

Marsh, Philip M. "Madison's Defense of Freneau." *William and Mary Quarterly*, 3d ser., 3 (1946): 269–274.

DOUGLAS R. EGERTON

FULTON, ROBERT (1765–1815), artist, engineer, inventor, entrepreneur. Born in Lancaster County, Pennsylvania, Fulton early displayed great artistic and mechanical ability. Following a brief apprenticeship with a silversmith in Philadelphia, he supported himself by painting portraits and miniatures until he sailed for London in 1786 to polish his skills under the tutelage of the American expatriate painter Benjamin West. When several years of intense artistic effort failed to win him a standard of living that he deemed acceptable, he turned to mechanical work.

The ambitious young man soon introduced many widely varied inventions, including machines to cut and polish marble, to spin flax, and to make rope. However, he directed most of his thought to improving canal transportation.

Fulton also recommended several innovations in naval warfare to both the British and the French, including submarines, torpedoes, harpoon guns, cable cutters,

ROBERT FULTON.   Painting by Charles Willson Peale.
INDEPENDENCE NATIONAL HISTORICAL PARK, PHILADELPHIA.

guns that could be fired under water, and steam-powered boats. Both governments showed interest in his ideas, but neither gave Fulton lasting support.

Late in 1806 he returned to America to build a steamboat and to offer his naval inventions to the United States. He arranged for a demonstration of his torpedoes, which was held on land in January 1807 before Secretary of State Madison and Secretary of the Navy Smith. The weapon's success won Fulton permission to conduct experiments in New York harbor, but before the tests could take place, the British ship *Leopard*'s attack on the U.S. frigate *Chesapeake* on 22 June 1807 so outraged Americans that President Jefferson considered having Fulton sink some of the Royal Navy's warships that were lurking outside the Virginia capes. However, the offending British vessels withdrew from American waters, obviating such operations.

When the United States finally declared war on England in 1812, Fulton devoted most of his energy to advocating the use of his novel weapons and tactics in operations against British naval forces. Early in the conflict, he stressed using torpedoes, but, after the Royal Navy blockaded American ports and began preying on shipping and settlements along the Atlantic coast and in the Chesapeake, he concentrated on problems of harbor defense. During the last year of the war, he built the world's first steam warship, the *Demologos*, to protect New York from English warships. The *Demologos* was being outfitted when news of the Treaty of Ghent reached New York. It fired a salute during its builder's funeral after Fulton died in February 1815.

BIBLIOGRAPHY

Dickinson, H. W. *Robert Fulton, Engineer And Artist: His Life And Works.* 1913.

Hutcheon, Wallace. *Robert Fulton: Pioneer of Undersea Warfare.* 1981.

Philip, Cynthia Owen. *Robert Fulton: A Biography.* 1985.

JAMES L. MOONEY

FUNDING ACT OF 1790. The Constitution of 1787 provided that all debts contracted before its adoption remained valid against the United States. At the end of 1790 the federal debt, principal and interest due, was estimated to be $54,124,464. Of that amount $11,710,378 was foreign debt owed in France, Holland, and Spain. The remainder was domestic debt amassed by Congress through various forms of deficit financing: bills of credit, also known as continental currency; interest-bearing loan office certificates sold to anyone willing to invest in the revolutionary cause; non–interest-bearing certificates, or promissory notes, given for the purchase or impressment of supplies; and indents of interest, promissory notes offered by Congress after 1784, when it stopped paying domestic interest.

How to handle that debt and establish a good public credit rating for the United States was the most difficult and complex issue faced by the First Federal Congress. Politically the issue was intimately related to the question of federalism: whichever level of government paid the debt would likely also possess the major taxing power and the allegiance of the people. Americans supported payment of the foreign debt, but many had different opinions about the federal domestic debt. Some proposed scaling it down or repudiating it, while others believed it should be assumed by the states. A more divisive question was whether to pay it off as quickly as possible through the sale of western lands or by adopting a long-term funding system.

Secretary of the Treasury Alexander Hamilton proposed a funding system in his report on public credit on 14 January 1790. Funding meant payment of the interest, not the principal; indeed, Hamilton asked for a cap of 2 percent on the amount of principal that could be paid yearly. Funding meant creating from federal revenues a fund to pay an estimated annual interest of $2,239,163. In addition, Hamilton called for assumption of most of the estimated remaining $25,000,000 in state debt.

Hamilton's plan committed the United States to fiscal capitalism. The secretary argued that a funded debt would be a national political and economic blessing rather than an evil as popularly believed. It would establish and maintain public credit, thereby reviving confidence in the United States government both at home and abroad, tie the commercial interests as well as the state creditors to the success of the federal government, and better cement the Union. It would allow the federal government to borrow money on its good credit in order to support itself and stimulate economic growth.

Congress began debate on the report in the House on 8 February. Most members quickly endorsed its proposals in general. Madison led the opposition to two. On both he had changed his position from 1783, when Congress considered a similar funding plan. First, Madison favored discriminating between the original holders of the debt certificates, or public securities (for example, soldiers and those who had loaned Congress material or money), and holders who had purchased them at far less than face value. The certificate market had become a growing business in the 1780s as speculators bought and sold for short-term as well as long-term gains. By 1790 most of the debt certificates were no longer in the hands of those Americans who had actually loaned money or provided services. Madison believed strongly that justice required that the original creditor

receive something. He proposed on 11 February that holders of public securities originally issued to someone else receive the highest market value of such securities and that the balance of the sum due from the public be paid to the original holder. His opponents considered his plan as an unconstitutional violation of contracts and it met defeat on 22 February, 36 to 13.

The focus of the debate then turned to the assumption of state debts, the second important part of Hamilton's plan that Madison opposed. The political implications of assumption stirred up the debate over federalism and exacerbated sectional tensions left by the 1789 debate over the location of the capital. Most congressmen from the North and from South Carolina welcomed the proposal as a means of escaping their state debt and as a force for political stability. Southerners saw assumption as an unconstitutional seizure of state authority that might lead to the abolition of the states. Madison's leadership of the anti-assumptionists publicly confirmed the change of mind that he had first intimated during the location debate in September: he would act more consciously as a defender of states' rights, as a southerner, and as a Virginian. Representative Theodore Sedgwick of Massachusetts spoke for many New Englanders when he called Madison an apostate preparing to assume leadership of a political party in opposition to the Federalists. Week after week, Madison prevented the House from including assumption in the funding bill. The critical vote came on 12 April, when it lost 31 to 29. On 2 June the House sent the funding bill, without provision for assumption, to the Senate, where a motion to add assumption to the bill was tabled.

After five months of debate and politicking, Congress had accomplished nothing in regard to two paramount issues: assumption and the location of the capital. Congress had reached its first impasse under the new Constitution. The situation had become so intolerable by the end of May that Madison reportedly considered forcing Congress to adjourn, a solution Sedgwick thought wise under the circumstances. With talk of disunion and even civil war on the rise, particularly in Massachusetts and Virginia, with the South and Pennsylvania fuming over the continued residence of Congress so far north (it sat in New York City), and with the North angry over the refusal of Congress to assume the state debts, a fundamental compromise of almost constitutional magnitude appeared the only solution.

On 21 July, by one vote—that of Charles Carroll of Maryland—the Senate agreed to the funding bill to which it had attached assumption. With Madison still in opposition, the House concurred on 29 July, and the president signed the Funding Act on 4 August 1790.

Passage of the act, with its provision for an assumption

of the state debts, resulted from the Compromise of 1790, the first of three pre–Civil War compromises between the North and the South. At a dinner in mid June, hosted by Jefferson, Madison and Hamilton arranged a trade off. Madison played his role in it by convincing Senator Carroll and four Maryland and Virginia representatives to throw their support behind assumption and later to support the Excise Act of 1791, which raised the funds needed to pay the additional interest. In return, Hamilton assisted Madison in securing the passage of an act locating the federal capital on the Potomac River, and agreed to certain concessions in regard to the amount of southern debt to be assumed and the rules for settling Revolutionary War accounts among the states.

[See also *Capital, Location of the.*]

BIBLIOGRAPHY

Anderson, William G. *The Price of Liberty: The Public Debt of the American Revolution.* 1983.

Bickford, Charlene, and Kenneth R. Bowling. *Birth of the Nation: The First Federal Congress, 1789–1791.* 1989.

Ferguson, E. James. *The Power of the Purse: A History of American Public Finance, 1776–1790.* 1961.

KENNETH R. BOWLING

G

GAINES, EDMUND PENDLETON (1777–1849), frontier soldier, War of 1812 hero. Born 20 March 1777, in Culpeper County, Virginia, Gaines was the son of James Gaines and Elizabeth Strother. Raised on the North Carolina and Tennessee frontiers, he entered the army as an ensign in 1797. His military career spanned half a century and involved service on almost every prong of the expanding frontier—the old Northwest, the Southwest, and the trans-Mississippi West.

He spent his early career in the Mississippi Territory surveying the Natchez Trace and serving as military collector at Mobile and commandant at Fort Stoddert. During the War of 1812 he served as major in the Niagara theater. For his bravery at Chrysler's Farm, where his regiment courageously covered the American retreat, and at Fort Erie, where his command repulsed Wellington's regulars, he was awarded a gold medal by Congress. President James Madison, a distant relative, praised Gaines for his role in "the splendid victories" at Niagara and rewarded him with a permanent commission as brigadier general.

Subsequently, Gaines fought in the two Seminole Indian wars, the Black Hawk War, and the Mexican War. His fiery temper and disputatious nature involved him in many wrangles with administrative superiors, including a bitter thirty-year feud with Gen. Winfield Scott. During the Mexican War he became embroiled in a controversy with the War Department that resulted in his court martial. Acquitted of the charges, he nevertheless was removed from his command of the western department and placed in a command where there was less potential for conflict.

During his years of frontier command, Gaines steadfastly opposed the efforts of whites to destroy the Indians. He argued forcefully for assimilation, not removal. He was also a strong voice for internal improvements, which he deemed essential to the development and prosperity of the West. He died of cholera in New Orleans on 5 June 1849.

BIBLIOGRAPHY

Silver, James W. *Edmund Pendleton Gaines, Frontier General.* 1949.

CHARLES D. LOWERY

MAJ. EDMUND PENDLETON GAINES.
PRINTS AND PHOTOGRAPHS DIVISION, LIBRARY OF CONGRESS.

GALES AND SEATON. Joseph Gales, Jr. (1786–1860) and William Winston Seaton (1785–1866) worked together for almost fifty years as prominent publishers and printers in Washington, D.C. Gales was born in 1786 in Eckington, England, the son of a printer and reformer who emigrated to the United States in 1795 in an effort to escape political persecution. In 1807 the younger Gales arrived in Washington, where he worked as a reporter of congressional debates for the *National Intelligencer.* Gales assumed the editorial direction of the paper from Samuel Harrison Smith in 1810. When the paper became a daily in 1812, Gales invited his brother-in-law, William Seaton, to become his partner. A native of King William County, Virginia, where he was born in 1785, Seaton worked as a young man for several newspapers, including one owned by Joseph Gales, Sr. The brothers-in-law continued to publish the *National Intelligencer* until Gales's death in 1860 and Seaton's retirement four years later.

Gales and Seaton personally recorded much of the congressional debate published in their newspaper, with Gales working in the Senate and Seaton in the House. As Republicans they enjoyed a close relationship with the Madison administration and the majority party in Congress and were dependent on the government for much of their work. Following the British attack on Washington, Congress compensated the publishers for the loss of their office. Gales and Seaton were elected printers for the House and Senate from 1819 to 1827. They soon operated the largest print shop in the capital.

In addition to their newspaper reports on Congress, Gales and Seaton began publication in 1824 of the *Register of Debates,* the first publication dedicated to the record of congressional proceedings. They suspended publication in 1837, after facing competition from the *Congressional Globe,* published by Francis Blair and John Rives, who had succeeded Gales and Seaton as congressional printers. In 1834, Gales and Seaton produced the first two volumes of the *Annals of Congress.* After receiving a congressional subscription in 1849, they resumed preparation of the *Annals,* which drew from various sources to reconstruct congressional debate between 1789 and 1824.

BIBLIOGRAPHY

McPherson, Elizabeth Gregory. "The History of Reporting the Debates and Proceedings of Congress." Ph.D. diss., University of North Carolina, 1940.

Ritchie, Donald A. *Press Gallery. Congress and the Washington Correspondents.* 1991.

Smith, W. E. "Gales, Joseph." *Dictionary of American Biography,* vol. 4, pp. 100–101.

Smith, W. E. "Seaton, William." *Dictionary of American Biography,* vol. 8, pp. 541–542.

BRUCE A. RAGSDALE

GALLATIN, ALBERT (1761–1849) representative, financier, diplomat, secretary of the Treasury. The Geneva-born Gallatin immigrated to Massachusetts in 1780 and served for a time as a resident tutor at Harvard College. In 1784 Gallatin took up permanent residence in western Pennsylvania and engaged in a series of agricultural and commercial enterprises. In 1789 he married Sophia Allegre, who lived for only a few months after their marriage. Four years later Gallatin married Hannah Nicholson, the daughter of John Nicholson, a prominent Jeffersonian Republican leader.

Gallatin's political career began in 1788, when he served at the Antifederalist Harrisburg convention that proposed a series of amendments to the U.S. Constitution. Two years later Gallatin was elected as a delegate to the Pennsylvania state constitutional convention of 1789 and 1790 that overturned Pennsylvania's more radical constitution of 1776. In late 1790 Gallatin entered the Pennsylvania Assembly and quickly gained a reputation as an expert in the area of public finance and taxation. During the Whiskey Rebellion, Gallatin sought to moderate the more radical opposition in western Pennsylvania to the federal excise taxes levied by Congress as part of Alexander Hamilton's fiscal program.

In 1793 the Pennsylvania legislature elected Gallatin to the U.S. Senate, but the Senate, in a narrow vote that reflected the increasing partisan divisions in Congress, expelled him in 1794 on the grounds that he failed to meet the citizenship requirements set by the Constitution for this office. In 1794 Gallatin won election to the House of Representatives and quickly emerged as a leader, along with James Madison, of the emerging Republican party. On the floor of the House, Gallatin opposed the Jay Treaty, excessive military expenditures, especially for the navy, and internal taxes. In his *Sketch of the Finances of the United States* (1796) and *Views of the Public Debt, Receipts, and Expenditures* (1800), Gallatin challenged Hamilton's fiscal policies and offered a detailed and clear analysis of the burden of a growing national debt, fueled in part, Gallatin insisted, by wasteful military expenditures.

Appointed secretary of the Treasury in 1801, Gallatin became one of the most influential figures in both Jefferson's and Madison's cabinets. Both Gallatin's contemporaries and later historians have applauded Gallatin for his personal rectitude, perspicacity, and skill as a conscientious administrator. During the early years of the Jefferson administration, Gallatin implemented financial policies that led to the elimination of internal duties, the reduction of public expenditures, and a reduction in the public debt. Never doctrinaire, Gallatin supported and secured the necessary financing for the Louisiana Purchase, and in his *Report on Roads and Canals* (1808) he called for limited federal support for internal improvements

SECRETARY OF THE TREASURY ALBERT GALLATIN.   Gallatin was secretary of the Treasury in the Jefferson administration. Madison retained him in the post until 1813, when he appointed Gallatin one of the peace commissioners to Saint Petersburg. In 1814 he was one of the American diplomats who negotiated the Treaty of Ghent. Etching by H. B. Hall, 1870, after the portrait in Independence Hall, Philadelphia.
PRINTS AND PHOTOGRAPHS DIVISION, LIBRARY OF CONGRESS.

designed to improve access to western lands and markets.

Gallatin's policies of fiscal stringency were jeopardized by the resumption of the Napoleonic Wars in Europe. After the *Chesapeake* incident in 1807, Jefferson's decision to support an embargo on all overseas trade was unpopular, even disruptive in New England, and proved nearly impossible to enforce, particularly along the Canadian border. In contrast to Jefferson and Madison, Gallatin had been skeptical of the value of economic coercion against European belligerents; nonetheless, as Treasury secretary he valiantly tried to press customs collectors, together with state authorities, into enforcing the Embargo.

In part because of his foreign birth, Gallatin emerged

as a lightning rod for critics of the Jefferson and later of the Madison administrations. After Madison's election to the presidency, Gallatin expressed a strong interest in moving to the State Department. Madison, fearing that Gallatin's nomination would be rejected by the Senate, decided to retain him at the Treasury and instead appointed Robert Smith as secretary of state. Gallatin and Smith remained bitter opponents, and in 1810 Gallatin demanded that Madison choose between the two. Although Smith was forced to resign from the cabinet, his removal further worsened Gallatin's and Madison's standing with Robert Smith's powerful brother, Sen. Samuel Smith of Maryland, as well as with a faction of Pennsylvania Republicans influenced by the newspaper publisher William Duane.

Despite the failure of the Embargo, Congress to the dismay of Madison and Gallatin enacted the Nonintercourse Act, which barred trade with Great Britain and France until they accepted American neutral rights. In April 1809, Madison reached an agreement with David M. Erskine, the British minister to the United States, on many of the outstanding differences between the two nations. But the British government repudiated the Erskine agreement negotiated in the opening months of Madison's first term and replaced Erskine with a new minister. Gallatin supported Madison's decision to reimpose economic sanctions against Britain in 1809 in order to avoid national humiliation. The following year Gallatin argued for the resumption of trade with Britain in order to bring in sorely needed revenues from customs duties, and to that end he wrote and played a key role in winning congressional passage of Macon's Bill No. 2. This law permitted American merchant vessels to resume trade with European belligerents but granted the president discretionary power to ban belligerent vessels from entering American ports until they respected neutral rights.

Although Gallatin wanted to avoid hostilities with Great Britain, he increasingly viewed war as inevitable and therefore proposed a series of measures to strengthen the nation's financial position. Gallatin broke with orthodox Republicans and argued for the renewal of the charter for the Bank of the United States, believing that such an institution remained essential to financing the credit of the United States. Madison offered only lukewarm support for the bank, and in the end the renewal lost in a close vote in the Senate in 1811. In 1812 Gallatin embraced measures that earlier in his career he had criticized, urging Congress to finance the impending war through loans, the doubling of customs duties, and the adoption of internal taxes. Congress proved willing to raise customs duties and permitted Gallatin to float additional loans but throughout the War of 1812 balked at enacting taxes.

Even after Congress declared war in 1812, Gallatin insisted that the weak financial position of the United States limited the strategic options available to the Madison administration. During the war, Gallatin offered proposals for the reorganization of the army and advocated a series of coordinated military moves against Canada, but he doubted the popular view that the United States could easily conquer Canada. Moreover, Gallatin adamantly believed that the United States could not afford a large navy and that the inadequate number of trained officers limited the possible expansion of the army. The unpopularity of the war in New England and the lack of the Bank of the United States made it difficult to raise the necessary loans needed to prosecute the war. In early 1813 the reluctance of investors to subscribe to a new set of war loans forced Gallatin to raise interest rates to 7.5 percent.

In 1813 Gallatin sought relief from the burdens of the Treasury and accepted appointment by Madison as one of three peace commissioners charged with arranging the neutral mediation offered by the Russian tsar, Alexander I. While Gallatin was en route to Saint Petersburg, the Senate narrowly rejected Gallatin's nomination to show its displeasure with Madison and because of Gallatin's initial reluctance to resign as Treasury secretary. The British government rejected the proposed mediation but in 1814 agreed to open direct negotiations with the United States.

Madison nominated Gallatin, the most senior official in age and experience, as the fifth peace commissioner to negotiate a treaty of peace to end the War of 1812. John Quincy Adams served as official head of the American delegation at Ghent, but Gallatin's leadership proved vital in reconciling the differences within the American delegation. For instance, Gallatin successfully pressured both Henry Clay and Adams to drop their respective demands that the British recognize the American right to use the fishing grounds off Newfoundland and end their claims to navigation rights on the Mississippi River. The Treaty of Ghent, signed on Christmas Eve, 1814, declared that the outstanding issues regarding trade, impressment, and territorial claims would be the subject of future negotiations.

After serving as peace commissioner, Gallatin in 1815 assisted John Quincy Adams and Henry Clay in negotiating a new commercial agreement with Great Britain. As in Ghent, the American delegation found that the British government still refused to renounce the right of impressment or to lift trade restrictions on American trade with the British West Indies. Gallatin pressed for the only major concession offered to the United States in the convention: American merchants gained expanded rights to trade directly with the British East Indies.

Upon his return to the United States in 1816, Gallatin rejected Madison's offer to return to the cabinet as Treasury secretary. After expressing reluctance, he accepted an appointment as minister to France, where he worked to resolve outstanding spoliation claims from the Napoleonic years. Gallatin returned home in 1823 and settled briefly in western Pennsylvania and later in Baltimore, but his abilities kept him in demand, and in 1826 he accepted an appointment as minister to Great Britain. Upon his return from Great Britain in 1827, Gallatin took permanent residence in New York City and assumed the presidency of the National Bank of New York City in 1831.

Although he never again held public office, Gallatin remained active in the civic and cultural life of New York and the nation. He opposed the annexation of Texas and shortly before his death published a pamphlet, *Peace with Mexico* (1847), that denounced the Mexican War as a war of aggression on the part of the United States.

BIBLIOGRAPHY

Adams, Henry. *Life of Albert Gallatin.* 1879.
Balinky, Alexander. *Albert Gallatin: Fiscal Theories and Policies.* 1958.
Oberg, Barbara. *A Microfilm Supplement to the Papers of Albert Gallatin.* 1985.
Prince, Carl E., and Helene E. Fineman. *The Papers of Albert Gallatin.* 1969.
Rutland, Robert A. *The Presidency of James Madison.* 1990.
Stagg, J. C. A. *Mr. Madison's War: Politics, Diplomacy, and Warfare in the Early Republic, 1783–1830.* 1983.
Walters, Raymond, Jr. *Albert Gallatin: Jeffersonian Financier and Diplomat.* 1957.

G. KURT PIEHLER

GARDNER, WILLIAM (BILLEY) (1759–1795), slave, household servant from Montpelier plantation. In September 1783 Madison was planning to return to Virginia after his term in the Continental Congress came to a close. Billey Gardner, a slave from Montpelier who probably was Madison's servant during his stay in Philadelphia, appears to have discussed the prospects of Madison's allowing him to remain in Pennsylvania and become a freeman. On 8 September 1783 Madison wrote his father, who held the title to Gardner in trust for his son (Madison had inherited the slave from his grandmother's estate while Madison was still a minor).

Madison explained to his father the reasons for disposing of Gardner in Philadelphia, even though local laws in 1783 forbade the selling of the slave "for more than 7 years." Apparently Madison's conscience was touched by the animosity toward slavery he sensed in Philadelphia, and Madison was sympathetic toward Gardner's desire to stay in the North. Madison told his father, "I have judged it most prudent not to force Billey back to Va.

even if it could be done." Gardner, he said, had breathed the air of a free man and thus was "too tainted to be a fit companion for fellow slaves in Va."

Although Madison told his father the seven-year contract for Gardner's sale would not fetch "near the worth of him" in Virginia, Madison said he could not think "of punishing him by transportation merely for coveting that liberty for which we have paid the price of so much blood, and have proclaimed so often to be right, & worthy the pursuit, of every human being." The senior Madison seems to have agreed, for in his will, made out in 1787, the father mentioned the transfer of Gardner's title to his son, who "has since sold" the slave. Thereafter, Gardner engaged in various business dealings on the Philadelphia waterfront and eventually became a sailor. He drowned while on a voyage to New Orleans in 1795.

BIBLIOGRAPHY

Brant, Irving. *James Madison: The Nationalist 1780–1787.* 1948.
Hutchinson, William T., et al., eds. *The Papers of James Madison: Congressional Series.* Vols. 7, 15, 16. 1971–1989.
Rutland, Robert A. *James Madison: The Founding Father.* 1987.

ROBERT A. RUTLAND

GARDOQUI, DIEGO DE (fl. 1781–1789), Spanish diplomat. Born in the northern Spanish city of Bilboa, Diego de Gardoqui was the son of Joseph Gardoqui, a powerful Spanish merchant with a well-established mercantile trade with Great Britain. Diego Gardoqui studied in England and spoke English fluently. During the early months of the American Revolution, acting in behalf of the Spanish government as well as his family's mercantile business, he offered a plan to supply the American Congress with shipments of Spanish supplies and munitions. During 1777 the cargoes of Gardoqui and Sons moved through New Orleans to Fort Pitt on the upper Ohio; thereafter they arrived at Philadelphia where the Spanish agent, Juan de Miralles, supervised their transfer to the Americans.

John Jay, in Madrid during 1781 to gain Spanish recognition of the United States, conferred unsuccessfully with Gardoqui on matters affecting both countries. Spain, although at war with Britain, refused to enter into a formal alliance with the United States. The Madrid government, moreover, denied Americans commercial rights on the Mississippi. That river, declared the Spanish minister, Count Floridablanca, "was an object that the king had so much on his heart that he would never relinquish it." When the British, in the Treaty of Paris, which ended the War of Independence, granted the United States free navigation of the Mississippi to the Gulf, the Spanish government, still in possession of the lower Mississippi, denied the validity of the British decision and, on 29 July 1784, closed the river to all but Spanish vessels. James Madison condemned the Spanish decree. It seemed inconceivable to him that Spain could maintain a narrow policy against the interests of thousands of settlers who required and would demand access to markets.

In 1784 the Madrid government appointed Gardoqui the first Spanish chargé d'affaires to the United States. Gardoqui reached Philadelphia in May 1785 and soon opened negotiations with Jay, now Congress's secretary for foreign affairs, to resolve the unsettled issues in U.S.-Spanish relations. Jay's commission to negotiate with Gardoqui included the provision that he enter into no treaty that did not stipulate an American right to navigation on the Mississippi to its mouth. After eight months of futile negotiations during which Gardoqui refused to budge on the Mississippi question, Jay asked Congress to establish a committee with full power to instruct him in his negotiations. Because his initial instructions on Mississippi navigation had become an insurmountable barrier to any treaty with Spain, Jay asked Congress to rescind those instructions. Jay proposed instead a treaty of commerce with trading provisions favorable to the United States; in exchange Americans would forego navigation of the Mississippi for twenty-five to thirty years. Jay argued that cordial relations with Spain remain the primary consideration. Because congressional instructions alone could establish the foundation of any treaty, James Monroe, with Madison's approval, argued that new instructions required the votes of nine states. Jay's opponents in Congress did not deny the importance of good relations with Spain; they insisted only that those relations rest on the basis of equality, and not on a barter arrangement unacceptable to the southern states.

After a long and tedious debate, seven commercial states voted for repeal of the ultimatum in Jay's original instructions and claimed majority rights to determine national policy; the five southern states, whose populations were moving rapidly into the lands bordering the Ohio and the Mississippi rivers, objected. Madison, having returned to Congress, took the lead in opposing Jay's recommendation. In the interest of national unity, Congress indefinitely postponed making a decision in April 1787. Finally in October 1788 Jay informed Gardoqui that Congress deemed it expedient that they cease their negotiations until March 1789, when the new federal government would assemble. Gardoqui informed President George Washington in July 1789 that he had received permission to return to Spain and resume his career as a prosperous merchant. The Mississippi question remained dormant until the Treaty of San Lorenzo (Pinckney's Treaty) of 1795 opened the river to American commerce.

BIBLIOGRAPHY

Whitaker, Arthur P. *The Mississippi Question, 1795–1803: A Study in Trade, Politics, and Diplomacy.* 1934.
Whitaker, Arthur P. *The Spanish-American Frontier, 1783–1795.* 1927.

NORMAN A. GRAEBNER

GELSTON, DAVID (1744–1828), collector for the port of New York. Active in politics in New York both during the period of resistance and after independence, Gelston was identified with the political fortunes of Aaron Burr during the turbulent 1790s. He served in the provincial congress in 1775–1777 and was a leader in the state legislature (1773–1785), serving as speaker in 1783–1784. As a member of the New York delegation to the last Continental Congress, Gelston witnessed the expiration of the old Confederation in 1789. From 1791 until 1798 he held a variety of posts in state government, including several terms as a member of the New York Senate.

When Burr made his bid for national office in 1800, Gelston worked on the alliance welded between Republicans in New York and in Virginia, with the ostensible purpose of making Jefferson president and casting Burr as his running mate. The tie vote in the Electoral College and the outcome of the election as determined in the House of Representatives eventually led to a rupture between Jefferson and Burr, but not before Burr made a strong recommendation to Jefferson that Gelston be appointed the customs collector for the port of New York. This lucrative position was one of the chief patronage plums available to the Republicans, because the collector received a percentage of the customs collected in his jurisdiction. The busy New York harbor customs receipts probably provided a stipend of more than $7,000 annually, making it one of the highest paying federal jobs in the nation. Jefferson accepted Burr's recommendation, and Gelston was appointed. To keep his position secure, Gelston performed a number of favors for President Madison, including the procurement of brandy and cigars for the Madison household, and Madison in return retained Gelston at the New York post.

BIBLIOGRAPHY

Biographical Directory of the United States Congress 1774–1989. 1989.
Rutland, Robert A., et al., eds. *The Papers of James Madison:* Presidential Series. Vols. 1, 2. 1984, 1992.

ROBERT A. RUTLAND

GENET, EDMOND CHARLES (1763–1834), first minister of the new French Republic to the United States.

Born into a middle-class family headed by a civil servant of the ancien régime, Genet followed his father in the service of the monarchy. With the advent of the French Revolution in 1789, Genet switched his allegiance to the new order.

Chosen for the American mission in November, 1792, Genet's qualifications included a winning personality, considerable diplomatic experience, linguistic skill, revolutionary zeal, and knowledge of the country gleaned through contact with American emissaries in Paris. Arriving in South Carolina in April 1793, Genet was greeted by enthusiastic pro-French crowds as he traveled overland to Philadelphia. He was received by President George Washington early in May, more than two weeks after the President's Proclamation of Neutrality defined America's position in the unfolding wars of the French Revolution. Following his unduly optimistic instructions, Genet sanctioned filibustering expeditions against British and Spanish possessions and, in a celebrated case, approved the outfitting and sailing of a prize ship (the *Little Sarah*, renamed *La Petite Démocrate*).

Perceiving Washington to be unfriendly to the French cause, Genet tried to capitalize on his own imagined popularity and foolishly challenged the president's authority in the court of public opinion. House Republican leader James Madison and Secretary of State Thomas Jefferson realized the significance of Genet's actions on their political followers in the developing struggle between Republicans and Federalists (with whom Washington identified) and successfully distanced themselves from the young Frenchman. Indeed, it was Jefferson who composed the letter requesting Genet's recall in August.

Having fallen in love with Cornelia Tappan Clinton, daughter of the New York political leader George Clinton, and observing the fall of his allies in France, Genet married Cornelia, became an American citizen in 1804 and busied himself with agricultural pursuits, speculative investments, and, occasionally, political skirmishes. He allied himself with Clintonian critics of Madison from 1808 to 1810, lashing out against the continued domination of the national government by the allegedly anti-commercial slave states. He was active in the 1812 presidential campaign, hoping to discredit Madison, but his newspaper articles failed to help De Witt Clinton.

While Genet's mission is considered by historians as a failure, he represented a pariah nation before a government controlled by men skeptical of (if not hostile to) revolutionary France. Genet's presumably more mature and skillful successors were equally unsuccessful during their American tenures.

BIBLIOGRAPHY

Ammon, Harry. *The Genet Mission.* 1973.

Minnigerode, Meade. *Jefferson, Friend of France, 1793: The Career of Edmond Charles Genet, Minister Plenipotentiary, from the French Republic to the United States, as Revealed by his Private Papers, 1763–1834.* 1928.
Woodfin, Maude H. "Genet, Edmond Charles." In *Dictionary of American Biography.* 1931–1934. Vol. 7, pp. 207–209.

CLIFFORD EGAN

GEORGE III (1738–1820), king of Great Britain and Ireland (1760–1820), elector (1760–1814) and later king of Hanover (1814–1820). The long reign of George III (George William Frederick) witnessed the breakup

GEORGE III, KING OF THE UNITED KINGDOM OF GREAT BRITAIN AND IRELAND, 1760–1820.
Engraving, after a portrait by James Northcote, published at Philadelphia, 1822.
PRINTS AND PHOTOGRAPHS DIVISION, LIBRARY OF CONGRESS.

of the British empire in North America and the resumption of war between Britain and the new American republic during the administration of Madison. The accession of George III in 1760 had been welcomed by his subjects in the North American colonies, but by July 1776 he was seen as a tyrant, a monarch unfit to be the ruler of a free people. In short, as Jefferson noted, his reign had been a "history of repeated injuries and usurpations."

Contrary to popular American mythology, George III was a constitutional monarch, who though broadly agreeing with his ministers, had little to do with determining actual policies. When Parliament shifted the focus of its taxation, George III was a witness, not the innovator. Thus between 1763 to 1765 he approved of the Grenville program, which attempted to regulate colonial trade, prohibit colonial expansion west of the Appalachian Mountains, and raise a revenue to support the standing army in America by means of a Stamp Act, the first attempt to directly tax the colonials. George III only reluctantly agreed to the repeal of the act in 1766, and he readily assented to the Townshend Duties of 1767, which attempted to also raise a revenue in America, this time by an indirect tax on colonial trade. His correspondence, however, indicates that he rarely considered America in the years from 1768 to 1774 and seemed to be more concerned with domestic politics and family matters.

Following the Boston Tea Party (1773), he concluded that American disobedience threatened to destroy the whole empire, thus reducing Britain to a second-rate European power, so he strongly supported the coercive policies proposed by Lord North. He remained a forceful advocate for the continued prosecution of the war against the rebellious colonies and may well have prolonged it unnecessarily for two years. Faced with peace, he threatened to abdicate, and, although he witnessed the recovery of Britain after 1783, he remained hostile to the United States.

If he or his ministers did little to reduce the American antagonism aroused by a continued postwar British presence on United States soil and by Britain's crippling trade restrictions, he carried little blame for the final crisis that resulted in the outbreak of war in June 1812. After 1804 he was constantly incapacitated by an illness that baffled contemporary physicians, became blind, and was officially recognized to be insane by January 1811. His last years were spent in mental and visual darkness.

BIBLIOGRAPHY

Brooke, John. *King George III.* 1972.
Butterfield, Herbert. *George III and the Historians.* 1957.
Thomas, P. D. G. *Tea Party to Independence: The Third Phase of the American Revolution, 1773–1776.* 1991.

R. T. CORNISH

GERRY, ELBRIDGE (1744–1814), revolutionary statesman, signer of the Declaration of Independence, vice president of the United States. The careers of Elbridge Gerry and James Madison often merged. Both worked hard as early advocates of American independence, both served in the Continental Congress, and both attended the Federal Convention, and Gerry became Madison's vice president in 1813–1814. Yet the Massachusetts merchant did not always see eye to eye with his Virginia planter compatriot. Their differences reflected perhaps the contrasting styles of the ruling elite in New England, with its town meeting form of government, and the customs of the aristocratic South.

Both men did some of their greatest work at the Federal Convention, where their differences became obvious. Although both advocated a strong central government, Gerry proved to be a more moderate nationalist. His fears of monarchy, militarism, and despotism by a powerful central government that might diminish states' rights and individual rights led him to oppose Madison consistently. Gerry inevitably took a stand as an Antifederalist, and he refused to sign the Constitution.

One major issue on which they disagreed was a federal bill of rights. Initially, Madison did not think one neces-

VICE PRESIDENT ELBRIDGE GERRY.
PRINTS AND PHOTOGRAPHS DIVISION, LIBRARY OF CONGRESS.

sary and opposed any move to create one. Gerry predicted the Constitution would not be ratified without one. He proved right: the document was ratified only after Madison and other leading nationalists gave assurances that a bill of rights would be added to the Constitution.

The views of the two men grew closer over time. Both became Republicans, backed Congress's coercive measures against Britain, and advocated the War of 1812. As governor of Massachusetts, Gerry strongly supported President Madison in Madison's first term and was selected as his running mate for the second. While serving as vice president, Gerry died in office in 1814.

BIBLIOGRAPHY

Austin, James T. *Life of Elbridge Gerry*. 2 vols. 1827–1828.
Billias, George A. *Elbridge Gerry: Founding Father and Republican Statesman*. 1976.
Morison, Samuel E. "Elbridge Gerry, Gentleman-Democrat." *New England Quarterly* 2(1929): 6–33.

GEORGE ATHAN BILLIAS

GHENT, TREATY OF. See *Treaty of Ghent*.

GILES, WILLIAM BRANCH (1762–1830), Virginia Republican representative, senator, governor. William Branch Giles's relationship with Madison was divided dramatically into two phases: the early years, in which he was a consistent follower of Madison in Congress, and the years of Madison's presidency and after, when Giles was equally consistently a political antagonist, despite the fact that they were in the same political party. Giles graduated from the College of New Jersey (later Princeton) in 1781, ten years after Madison. He joined Madison in Congress in December 1790 and roomed with him at the Philadelphia home of Mary House. Giles was a skilled but reckless debater in Congress; adjectives associated with him include "bombastic," "ambitious," "boastful," and even "useless."

Giles never turned against his Republican colleagues while Alexander Hamilton survived (Hamilton described Madison as "the prompter of Mr. Giles and others"). Giles supported Madison's trade policies and opposed a national bank. In January 1793 he proposed nine resolutions censuring Hamilton and argued forcefully against Jay's Treaty. Giles played a key role in compelling President Adams to publish documents on the XYZ Affair. Giles was a strong supporter of Madison's Virginia Resolutions and his Report of 1798–1799. Giles hinted at the turn his political career would later take when he declared in 1799 that he favored disunion. He was administration leader in the House of Repre-

sentatives from 1801 until his service in the Senate from 1804 to 1815.

Giles was a key supporter of Madison's election to the presidency, making the motion for his nomination in the 1808 congressional caucus and then managing the campaign. But his personal animosities and frustrated ambitions soon caused him to break with the president whose campaign he had just directed. He plotted to keep his bitter enemy Albert Gallatin from becoming secretary of state. He warned Madison that if he antagonized Madison's "friends" in the Senate by supporting Gallatin, as Jefferson had done, they would turn against Madison. Perhaps Giles yearned for the position himself. John Randolph quipped that even the inept Robert Smith should be preferred to Giles, for Smith "at least could spell."

Throughout Madison's administrations, the Senate Invisibles, a faction led by Senators Giles, Samuel Smith, and James Leib, who were unified primarily by their hatred for Gallatin, used their balance of power in the Senate to hamstring administration policies. They helped to emasculate the Macon Act and opposed renewal of the charter for the First Bank of the United States. Although he is often included among the War Hawks, Giles mocked the commander in chief while pretending to support him, as when he proposed enlisting 25,000 men rather than the 10,000 requested by Madison and when he proposed naval warfare against both France and England.

Giles remained out of politics from 1815 until 1824, when he began publishing personal newspaper assaults on most leading statesmen. He returned to the Virginia legislature in 1826, where his resolutions declaring protective tariffs unconstitutional helped to make him governor from 1827 to 1830. Giles's venomous articles, published anonymously in 1828, branding Madison as a political apostate forced Madison publicly to disassociate himself and Jefferson from Giles's advocacy of nullification. Madison soon was obliged to repudiate a *Lynchburg Virginian* article in which he was made to appear to have called Giles a "dog in the manger" who was "hurrying Virginia to ruin and contempt." Giles countered with contempt for "Mr. Madison's opinions at seventy-nine years of age," preferring Giles's own conception of Madison's "opinions of fifty." Their last encounter was at the Virginia Constitutional Convention of 1829–1830. In his defense of the overrepresentation of the Tidewater region in the Virginia legislature and, therefore, automatically in the U.S. Congress, Giles finally turned against even Jefferson, the one Republican leader whom he had not yet sullied.

BIBLIOGRAPHY

Brant, Irving. *James Madison: Commander in Chief, 1812–1836*. 1961.

Brant, Irving. *James Madison: The President, 1809–1812.* 1956.
Rutland, Robert A. *The Presidency of James Madison.* 1990.

DONALD O. DEWEY

GIRARD, STEPHEN (1750–1831), merchant, banker. Born in the French maritime center of Bordeaux, the young Étienne Girard hardly seemed destined for the success he would ultimately achieve. Diminutive in stature, withdrawn by nature, and blind in one eye, he nonetheless chose the physically demanding career of a seagoing merchant.

Having risen quickly to the rank of master, Girard was engaged in trade between New York and the West Indies when a combination of inclement weather and the British fleet forced the young mariner into the port of Philadelphia in 1776. The British occupation of Philadelphia induced Girard to open a small store in Mount

STEPHEN GIRARD.   Girard, here caricatured as "Stephen Graspall, banker and shaver," has a vision of a Spanish dollar (the image on the coin is of King Carlos IV). Etching by William Charles, Philadelphia, c. 1808.
PRINTS AND PHOTOGRAPHS DIVISION, LIBRARY OF CONGRESS.

Holly, New Jersey. After the British evacuation, Girard returned to Philadelphia, became a citizen of Pennsylvania, and opened a new business on the banks of the Delaware River.

Abandoning a seafaring career for that of a sedentary merchant, Girard engaged in a number of West Indian commercial ventures, often in league with his brother Jean, who resided in Santo Domingo. At first Girard purchased shares in foreign commercial ventures, but he was successful enough eventually to acquire his own vessels. Continued commercial success, partly fueled by the prosperity generated by American neutrality during the early Napoleonic Wars, helped Girard's commercial fleet grow into one of the largest in the new nation. As the number of his ships grew, so too did the scope of his activities. By the first decade of the nineteenth century, Girard had commercial agents in Europe, the Far East, and South America, as well as the West Indies.

Girard's success was based on his almost single-minded attention to commercial affairs. Following an early and childless marriage, which ended in his wife's insanity and subsequent hospitalization until her death, Girard made his work his sole interest.

Already one of the nation's richest men by 1807, Girard foresaw that the European combatants would soon cease to credit U.S. neutrality. Eager to repatriate his fortune, a large part of which was in European accounts, Girard purchased U.S. Treasury obligations and acquired stock in the Bank of the United States in London, Amsterdam, and other European financial centers. As a result, when Congress failed to recharter the bank in 1811, Girard found himself the major owner of its stock. In an attempt to diversify his holdings in a period of declining international trade, Girard purchased the former bank headquarters, hired its cashier, George Simpson, and proceeded to operate a private banking institution, starting in May 1812. Despite legal difficulties and a cool reception by Philadelphia's chartered banking institutions, Girard's bank prospered.

Within weeks of the opening of Girard's bank, the United States went to war with England, and the federal government entered a period of extreme financial difficulties. While Girard had close financial ties to London, he was philosophically a product of the French Enlightenment. Above all, he was devoted to the Republican cause and assisted the Madison administration whenever possible.

In an attempt to ease the Treasury's embarrassment, in 1813 Girard participated in a syndicate with John Jacob Astor, David Parish, and other wealthy business leaders to help complete a faltering $16 million bond issue. Moreover, Girard, along with Astor and other leading members of the business community, urged the reestablishment of a national bank.

These efforts bore fruit when Girard's friend and legal adviser Alexander J. Dallas accepted Madison's offer to become secretary of the Treasury in the fall of 1814. When the Second Bank of the United States began operation on 1 January 1817, Girard was a major stockholder.

After the war, Girard's activity reflected the growing interest of Americans in domestic economic growth. His bank's portfolio included stock in a number of internal improvement companies. He also made a major personal investment in northeastern Pennsylvania coal lands.

Girard epitomized the merchant adventurer of his era. In amassing his sizable fortune, however, he was alert and responsive to the currents of change in both the international and the domestic economies. He continued to direct his own commercial affairs and those of his bank until his death on 26 December 1831. His estate, totaling nearly $7 million, included bequests to the city of Philadelphia, the state of Pennsylvania, and the U.S. government, but the lion's share went to the endowment of Girard College in Philadelphia.

BIBLIOGRAPHY

Adams, Donald R., Jr. *Finance and Enterprise in Early America: A Study of Stephen Girard's Bank, 1812–1831.* 1978.
McMaster, John B. *The Life and Times of Stephen Girard.* 2 vols. 1918.
Wildes, Harry Emerson. *Lonely Midas.* 1943.

DONALD R. ADAMS, JR.

GOLDSBOROUGH, CHARLES W. (1779–1843),
Navy Department clerk, acting secretary of the navy. A Maryland native, Goldsborough was appointed clerk in the Navy Department in 1798, when the Federalists were still in control. In the interim before Paul Hamilton could take office in 1801, Goldsborough served as acting secretary and was chief clerk from April 1802 until March 1813. Robert Smith, navy secretary under Jefferson, thought Goldsborough a competent civil servant and once praised him as "preeminently qualified for the station" he held.

While still acting secretary, Goldsborough, on Albert Gallatin's recommendation, had issued orders to naval agents requesting that public funds in their jurisdiction be deposited in designated banks, an order that Sen. Samuel Smith resented and that provoked his protest to President Madison. Smith denounced the withdrawal of funds from the Bank of Baltimore, the "One Bank alone [which] has a Republican President." Goldsborough survived the angry blast, and, as chief clerk, he made periodic reports to Madison concerning naval business whenever the president was in residence at Montpelier.

When William Jones succeeded Hamilton as navy secretary in 1813, he believed the Navy Department was "excessively disordered." Jones's memorandum on his dismissal of Goldsborough indicated that "every Branch of the Department of which he has been the principal Director for twelve years" was in a "confused state." Jones gave the chief clerk ten days' grace so that he could submit his resignation without the stigma of being fired. Goldsborough was replaced by Benjamin Homans of Massachusetts, who had been nominated for the post by Vice President-elect Elbridge Gerry. Goldsborough told Jones the ouster would leave him "absolutely poor," and he sought appointment as a naval storekeeper, but nothing seems to have come of his pleas.

BIBLIOGRAPHY

Cunningham, Noble E., Jr. *The Process of Government under Jefferson.* 1978.
Dudley, William S., ed. *The Naval War of 1812: A Documentary History.* 2 vols. 1985–1992.
Rutland, Robert A., et al., eds. *Papers of James Madison:* Presidential Series. Vol. 1. 1984.

ROBERT A. RUTLAND

GORE, CHRISTOPHER (1758–1827), governor
of Massachusetts, senator. Christopher Gore, the son of a prosperous skilled workman, was born in Boston on 21 September 1758. He graduated from Harvard in 1776, studied law under John Lowell, Sr., and became a successful attorney in Boston. Like his father, a revolutionary war Tory exile, Gore was a social conservative. He maintained an elegant estate in Waltham, Massachusetts, and was an active High Federalist. Daniel Webster studied law under Gore.

Gore became a friend of Fisher Ames, Rufus King, and others who would become leading Federalists. In 1788 he urged King to run for representative from Boston in the new national House of Representatives. Gore frequently wrote to Fisher Ames after Ames won the seat and celebrated Ames's reelections as signs of popular approval for the central government. Gore supported Alexander Hamilton's program and in fact made substantial profits through his own speculations in government bonds.

During the 1790s Gore regretted that able young men preferred private careers and the "vulgar pursuit" of success to public service. Fearing that the decline of self-sacrifice would destroy the nation, Gore himself served from 1789 to 1796 as the first U.S. attorney for the district of Massachusetts and won praise for his energy and determination in this position.

In 1796 Gore, along with William Pinkney, was sent to England as a commissioner to settle American spoliation claims and again won praise for his dedication. He served

CHRISTOPHER GORE.   Line-and-stipple engraving by D. Kimberly after a portrait by John Trumbull.
PRINTS AND PHOTOGRAPHS DIVISION, LIBRARY OF CONGRESS.

as chargé d'affaires in England in 1803–1804. Along with other Federalists, Gore advocated support for the Venezuelan revolutionary Francisco Miranda, a step opposed by Secretary of State James Madison.

Gore became active in Massachusetts politics when he returned in 1804. He joined George Cabot and Harrison Gray Otis in 1808 in a committee of correspondence that rallied opposition against the Embargo. He was also a delegate at the national Federalist meeting in 1808 that endorsed Charles C. Pinckney for the presidency.

In 1809 Gore was narrowly elected governor of Massachusetts. As governor, he continued to denounce the Embargo and supported a General Court bill advocating continued good relations with Great Britain. Early in 1810 Gore invited the British minister Francis James Jackson to speak in Boston. This jab at the Republicans, taken during a foreign policy crisis, might have created great problems for the Madison administration. However, in April 1810 Elbridge Gerry ran against Gore for governor and defeated him by a modest margin.

Gore remained politically active, and in 1813 the General Court sent him to the U. S. Senate. There, he con-

sistently opposed the Madison administration's war and diplomatic policies and in 1814 condemned a bill to augment the army as a threat to liberty that the states must resist. As pessimistic as many New England Federalists, Gore believed that the United States would soon dissolve, and he supported the Hartford Convention movement. When Congress passed a bill to use federal taxes to pay for the state militias, Gore described the event as "the spasms of a dying government."

Gore was disappointed both at the post-1815 Republican revival and at the willingness of leading Bostonians to court President James Monroe. After 1816 he left politics to concentrate on his law practice. Gore served as an overseer and fellow of Harvard College and left most of his estate to the institution, which named its library Gore Hall in his honor. He died on 1 March 1827.

BIBLIOGRAPHY

Fischer, David H. *The Revolution of American Conservatism.* 1965.
Pinkney, Helen R. "Christopher Gore, A Federalist of Massachusetts." Unpublished dissertation, Radcliffe College, 1942.

JEFFREY P. BROWN

GRAHAM, JOHN (1774–1820), Republican politician, diplomat. A Virginia native who was educated at Columbia College, Graham served a year in the Kentucky legislature before Madison named him secretary to the American legation at Madrid in 1801. Graham's letters to Madison sharply criticized the performance of the American minister, Charles Pinckney, in whose absences Graham served as chargé d'affaires. Graham returned to the United States in 1803 and in 1804 was named secretary of the Orleans Territory under Gov. William C. C. Claiborne.

While Graham was visiting Washington in late 1806, Madison asked him to be the administration's confidential agent in the investigation of former Vice President Aaron Burr's scheme to attack New Orleans and Mexico. Graham was empowered to confer with local civil and military officials, to arrest and punish the perpetrators, and to raise whatever forces were required to forestall the plan. He tracked Burr through Kentucky and Ohio, gathering information and warning the governors of those states, who then seized the boats and supplies of the conspirators. Graham testified at Burr's 1807 trial in Richmond, Virginia, and at the 1808 court-martial of Burr's coconspirator, Gen. James Wilkinson.

In 1807 Madison named Graham chief clerk at the State Department, where he remained until 1817. When Madison left the presidency he recommended Graham to James Monroe as being "among the most worthy of men," with "a sound and discriminating judgement" and "a purity of character, a delicacy of sentiment, and an amenity of temper and manners" not to be exceeded. That same year Monroe appointed Graham a member of the commission to report on the situation in the rebellious Spanish colonies, and Graham authored the extensive commission report. In January 1819 he was named minister plenipotentiary to the government of Portugal, resident at Rio de Janeiro, and served for a year before returning home, where he soon died.

BIBLIOGRAPHY

Abernethy, Thomas Perkins. *The Burr Conspiracy.* 1954.
American State Papers: Documents, Legislative and Executive, of the Congress of the United States. . . , Miscellaneous. Vol. 1. 1832–1861.
The National Intelligencer. 29 August 1820.

MARY A. HACKETT

GRANGER, GIDEON (1767–1822), lawyer, postmaster general. Born in Suffield, Connecticut, Granger graduated from Yale College in 1787 and passed the bar in 1789, settling down to practice law in his hometown. His politics were acceptably Federalist, and in 1792 he was elected to the state legislature, where he served a total of seven terms. But in 1798 he switched parties and challenged the Federalist candidate for the House of Representatives. This unsuccessful effort, and his support of Jefferson and Burr in the election of 1800, brought him to the attention of national Republicans. After Jefferson's accession to office, Granger was named postmaster general. Granger's tenure in office (1801–1814) was marked by the removal of the most flagrantly Federalist postmasters and their replacement by Republicans sympathetic to the administration. He also oversaw the dynamic expansion of post roads and a dramatic increase in the number of post offices throughout the republic. Granger played an important, and independent, political role in the Jefferson and Madison administrations as a dispenser of patronage, and it was this aspect of duty that led to his downfall in 1814. Granger had never been as friendly to Madison as he had been to Jefferson, and in the years after Madison's election to the presidency, Granger sided with the anti-Madison Republican "malcontents." Granger's disloyalty was most obvious after 1811, when Madison appointed Joseph Story to a seat on the Supreme Court, a seat for which Granger thought himself eminently qualified and for which he had lobbied strongly. While admitting Granger's talents, Madison objected to his connection with the Yazoo Lands frauds controversy and to the uncertainty of his physical and mental health.

In the election of 1812, Madison suspected that Granger had supported DeWitt Clinton's presidential aspirations to the detriment of Madison's. Nonetheless, Madison continued Granger in office until 1814, when Granger insisted on the appointment of Michael Leib, a bitterly Invisible Republican senator from Pennsylvania, as postmaster of Philadelphia. His ire aroused, Madison forced Granger to resign in March 1814. Granger retired to upstate New York and eventually settled in Canandaigua, where he practiced law and was elected to the New York legislature. As Clinton's disciple, he supported the construction of the Erie Canal.

BIBLIOGRAPHY

Cunningham, Noble E., Jr. *The Process of Government under Jefferson.* 1978.
Hamlin, Arthur S. *Gideon Granger.* 1982.

DAVID B. MATTERN

GREAT BRITAIN. James Madison's entrance into public life during the American Revolution inaugurated a personal forty-year effort to advance American economic and security interests in the face of British antagonism and commercial power. Madison discovered as early as 1783 that Great Britain had no intention of dealing fairly with the United States on matters of commerce. Following established mercantile practice, British postwar policy permitted American raw materials and foodstuffs, but not manufactured goods, to enter British ports in American vessels. But an order in council of 2 July 1783 closed the British West Indies to American ships and all goods except for those on a short enumerated list. On 13 September Madison argued for retaliatory power to meet the British challenge. The proclamation of 2 July, he wrote, was proof that Britain was testing the sovereignty of the United States.

The Articles of Confederation had granted Congress the power to enter into treaties, but not the power to enforce them. Congress could neither control the commerce of the states nor impose taxes on them. For Madison the salvation of the country's commerce, security, and welfare lay in strengthening the Articles. Late in 1783 the Virginia legislature, under Madison's prodding, voted to empower Congress to counteract the British regulation. In April 1784 Congress responded by requesting the states to grant Congress the authority to prohibit, for fifteen years, imports and exports on vessels or by the subjects of countries with whom the United States had no commercial treaty, and in May the Virginia legislature voted to grant Congress's request. During 1785 Madison agreed with John Adams and Jefferson, then ministers in London and Paris, respectively, that Congress required the power to coerce Britain through effective retaliation. Madison's views elicited enormous opposition in Virginia from those who feared a New England monopoly of the carrying trade.

Madison's war on British commercial policy elevated him to the forefront of the movement for a stronger government. He took the lead in calling the Annapolis Convention of September 1786 to consider a uniform system of commercial regulations. At the Federal Convention Madison argued effectively for a new constitution that would assign to the federal government the power to regulate commerce, impose taxes, and enforce state compliance with foreign treaties. As a member of the House of Representatives in the new government, Madison, supported by Secretary of State Jefferson, sought tariffs and tonnage dues that would discriminate against Britain. Under Hamilton's powerful influence as secretary of the Treasury, Congress imposed tariffs and tonnage dues but refused to single out Britain for special retribution.

Finally, in late 1793, the great war in Europe, as well as Britain's costly wartime infringements on U.S. commerce, gave Madison the occasion to retaliate against Britain's commercial policy. In December Jefferson submitted to Congress his long report delineating the "Privileges and Restrictions on the Commerce of the United States in Foreign Countries." Jefferson criticized Europeans generally for their mercantilist policies but reserved his strongest condemnation for Britain. In January 1794 Madison, with majority support in the House, offered resolutions advocating additional charges on the goods and tonnage of countries that had no commercial treaties with the United States. The Washington administration, in control of the Senate as well as of the executive branch, determined to counter Madison's anti-British resolutions by defining U.S.-British relations in a treaty. John Jay, Washington's special envoy, reached London in June and proceeded to negotiate a treaty that embodied few British concessions but promised continued peace. Hamilton's brilliant defense of Jay's Treaty put the British-American conflict over commerce and other issues to rest but stimulated Madison and Jefferson to broaden their efforts to create a national party in opposition to the pro-British Federalists.

During Jefferson's presidency (1801–1809), Madison as secretary of state faced British encroachments on American commerce. With the return of war in Europe in 1803, the contest between Britain and France again expanded onto the Atlantic. Britain's complete command of the seas after the Battle of Trafalgar in 1805 mattered little if France succeeded in consigning its imperial commerce, particularly with the West Indies, to neutral carriers. To deny France its colonial trade, the British insisted that Americans obey the principle of the broken voyage by unloading, storing, and paying duties on all goods imported from the French colonies before reshipment. When it became obvious that American officials were clearing untouched cargoes for the ports of continental Europe, the British, in the *Essex* prize case of 1805, not only declared such voyages continuous but also asserted that a cargo's ultimate destination determined its nationality. Jefferson preferred to counter the *Essex* decision with argument rather than force. Madison, in a long pamphlet titled *An Examination of the British Doctrine*, published in January 1806, attempted to refute the British ruling. In April 1806 Congress passed the Nonimportation Act as a mild attempt at coercion but postponed implementation of the act until December. Also in 1806 the British government declared a blockade of much of the European coast, a blockade rendered legitimate in British eyes by the power and reach of the British navy.

During 1807 American commerce became trapped in a gigantic commercial war between Britain and France. Napoleon opened the war in November 1806, responding to the British blockade with his Berlin Decree proclaiming a "paper blockade" of the British Isles and challenging all neutral commerce with Britain by threatening to seize any vessels that stopped at a British port. Great Britain retaliated with its order in council of 7 January 1807, which outlawed all commerce between ports under French control. Madison condemned the British action and reminded the British minister, David M. Erskine, in March that the British order would interfere with the customary practice of American sea captains of disposing of or acquiring cargo at a series of continental ports. By compelling ships to stop at only one port, the British would effectively destroy American commerce with Europe. Both the British and the French committed acts of war against American commerce, but the French seized ships in ports under their direct control, whereas the British captured vessels on the high seas in defiance of neutral rights. Jefferson and Madison recognized no justice in British behavior yet hoped to avoid trouble. The *Chesapeake* affair of June 1807, in which the British stopped an American war vessel in American waters and removed four sailors, merely exacerbated the tension created by the burgeoning conflict of interest on the high seas. Madison complained of continued British insolence in detaining American merchant vessels in American waters.

For Madison the worst was still to come. Following his great victory at Jena over Russian forces and his success in extending his Continental System to Russian ports, Napoleon began to enforce his Berlin Decree with numerous seizures. The British order in council of 11 November 1807 declared a blockade of all countries in the Napoleonic System. Napoleon responded with his Milan Decree of 17 December, which condemned to seizure any neutral ship sailing from a British port or subjected to British search. These profound pressures on American neutral rights compelled the president to act. Even before learning of the Milan Decree he implemented the Nonimportation Act and, on 22 December, recommended to Congress an embargo on American shipping to foreign ports. Congressional majorities committed the country to Jefferson's program. The Embargo effectively shut off the nation's commerce with Britain, but it produced no relaxation in Britain's commitment to its orders in council. During 1808 Jefferson and Madison moved to transform the Embargo from a defense of American vessels and cargoes to a weapon of coercion. The administration informed Britain and France that the Embargo would end by December 1808; thereafter, the United States would resume trade with the nation that removed its restrictions and declared war on the other. Both Britain and France rejected the American offer. The Nonintercourse Act of March 1809 terminated all commerce with Britain and France but promised to restore trade with the belligerent that recognized American neutral rights. Madison assured both European powers that a favorable action by either would provoke American retaliation against the other.

Under Madison's presidency the British-American commercial clash in the Atlantic led inevitably to war. Congress trapped the United States in a growing crisis when, in April 1810, it adopted Macon's Bill No. 2, which reopened trade with Britain and France. This measure provided that if either country revoked its edicts before 3 March 1811, and if within three months thereafter the other nation did not repeal its decrees, the United States would terminate all trade with that country. For members of Congress the refusal of either government to accept the American offer of mutually beneficial commercial relations would be a demonstration of determined hostility. France responded on 5 August 1810 by announcing that it would revoke its Berlin and Milan decrees. On 2 November Madison recognized France's decision and warned the British that they had three months to follow the French lead. When in late February 1811 Madison terminated all commerce with Britain, the British government still refused to respond. In Washington the British minister, Augustus J. Foster, pressed American officials to provide proof that the French had actually repealed their decrees. France's less than forthright behavior troubled American officials as well. Pressed by the War Hawks in Congress, Madison overcame his doubts and, in June 1812, accepted the inevitability of war against Great Britain. With the Treaty of Ghent in December 1814,

Madison's long and often bitter struggle for American rights and independence from British maritime domination had finally come to an end.

[See also *Blockades by England and France; Continental System; Mercantilism; Neutrality; Orders in Council; War of 1812.*]

BIBLIOGRAPHY

Brant, Irving. *James Madison: Father of the Constitution, 1787–1800.* 1950.

Brant, Irving. *James Madison: The Nationalist, 1780–1787.* 1948.

Brant, Irving. *James Madison: Secretary of State, 1800–1809.* 1953.

Ketcham, Ralph. *James Madison: A Biography.* 1971.

Peterson, Merrill D. *James Madison: A Biography in His Own Words.* 1974.

NORMAN A. GRAEBNER

GRUNDY, FELIX (1777–1840), jurist, criminal lawyer, United States representative and senator. Born in Berkeley County, Virginia, the youngest of seven sons of Elizabeth Beckham and George Grundy, Felix Grundy

FELIX GRUNDY.   Engraving by T. B. Welch after portrait by W. B. Cooper.
PRINTS AND PHOTOGRAPHS DIVISION, LIBRARY OF CONGRESS.

grew up on the Allegheny frontiers of Virginia, Pennsylvania, and Kentucky, where three of his older brothers were killed in Indian raids during and following the Revolution. The family settled in Kentucky in 1780, and Grundy enrolled in Bardstown Academy before studying law under the noted Kentucky lawyer George Nicholas. Admitted to the bar in 1795, Grundy established a practice in Bardstown. He served in the state constitutional convention in 1795 and in the state legislature from 1800 to 1805, when he was elected to the state supreme court. After a year he became chief justice of that court.

Unable to support his growing family on his jurist's salary, Grundy moved in 1807 to Nashville, where he and his wife, Ann Rodgers, raised twelve children. In Tennessee he established a successful practice and was known as the ablest criminal lawyer in the Old Southwest. In 1810 he was elected to Congress and soon was identified as a War Hawk. When the war between Great Britain and France intensified, Grundy grew impatient with the Jefferson administration's weak attempts to assert America's rights as a neutral commercial power. Grundy soon joined with other recently elected representatives, including Henry Clay and John C. Calhoun, to push for war with England. It was while he served in the Twelfth and Thirteenth Congresses (1811–1814) that Grundy was most closely associated with Madison. He was at first critical of the president for not assuming a more belligerent, warlike stance toward England. But once Madison decided on war, Grundy became a close ally and a strong supporter who defended Madison against his congressional critics. An ardent expansionist, he unabashedly called for the quick conquest of Florida and Canada. When the nation confronted bankruptcy in 1814, he again rallied to the support of the government by urging the establishment of a national bank. Like Madison, he believed the country's urgent needs obviated any constitutional objections to a bank.

Resigning from Congress in mid 1814, Grundy spent the next fifteen years in Tennessee, pursuing his law practice, serving in the state legislature, and caring for his family and his invalid wife. After a time he became impatient with local politics. In 1827 he ran for Congress in Andrew Jackson's district. He lost, but two years later he was chosen to replace John H. Eaton in the Senate. A loyal Jacksonian, Grundy supported Jackson in his stands on the tariff, nullification, and the national bank. Although he had favored a national bank in 1814, Grundy shifted ground and backed the president in his veto of the bank recharter bill in 1832. Jackson never conferred office upon Grundy, who was his strongest and most loyal Senate supporter, but Martin Van Buren rewarded him in 1838 with a cabinet appointment as attorney general. He served in that capacity for less than two years before resigning to return to his old Senate seat. Grundy died in Nashville on 19 December 1840.

BIBLIOGRAPHY

Parks, Joseph Howard. *Felix Grundy, Champion of Democracy.* 1940.

CHARLES D. LOWERY

GUERRIÈRE. The 38-gun British frigate Guerrière, commanded by Capt. James Richard Dacres, reportedly harassed American merchantmen off the port of New York in 1811. Commodore John Rodgers went in search of her but instead, chased and fired on HMS Little Belt.

In early 1812, *Guerrière* was assigned to Commodore Philip Vere Broke's squadron to blockade New York. She was just arriving to become one of the squadron when Capt. Isaac Hull's *Constitution* hove into sight on the evening of 16 July 1812. Hull closed but became suspicious when Dacres did not answer the American's private signal and *Constitution* stood away to the southeast. *Guerrière*, in company with Commodore Broke's squadron of *Africa, Shannon, Belvidera,* and *Aeolus,* participated in the famous sixty-one-hour chase of *Constitution* that ended in Hull's escape.

For the next month, the British squadron cruised in the hope of meeting Commodore John Rodgers's squadron of *President, Congress, United States, Hornet,* and *Argus,* but Rodgers had sailed far to the east in pursuit of a British merchant convoy. At last, the British squadron split up and *Guerrière* headed for the waters south of Nova Scotia, where Dacres intended to put into Halifax for repairs to his foremast. On his way, according to legend, Dacres broke out a sail emblazoned with the message "Not the Little Belt" referring caustically to the ship Rodgers mistakenly attacked in 1811. Meanwhile, Hull had chosen to search for British targets on the Grand Banks and had learned of the presence of a British frigate, though not of her identity.

Constitution finally caught up with her quarry on the afternoon of 19 August and commenced the approach for battle in a blustery wind with high seas. After two hours of maneuvering for the weather gauge, Dacres attempted to fight at long range. *Guerrière* loosed a broadside that did little damage, while Hull maneuvered for battle at close quarters where his guns would have a more deadly effect. In fifteen minutes, *Guerrière* had lost her mizzenmast, and Dacres knew that he was at a big disadvantage, having lost maneuverability and speed.

On both ships, boarders were called, and Hull suffered the loss of his captain of marines and the wounding of his first lieutenant. Dacres suffered a wound in his back and the loss of his second lieutenant. As the

THE *CONSTITUTION* AND THE *GUERRIERE*.   On 19 August 1812, the *Constitution*, commanded by Isaac Hull, captured HMS *Guerrière*. Engraving by G. Tiebout after a painting by T. Birch. Published by James Webster, 1813.

PRINTS AND PHOTOGRAPHS DIVISION, LIBRARY OF CONGRESS.

two ships struggled to gain maneuvering room, *Guerrière*'s bowsprit was ensnared in *Constitution*'s rigging, and as the American ship moved ahead *Guerrière*'s bowsprit snapped upward, slackening her foremast rigging. *Guerrière*'s foremast, already weakened by cannon fire, went by the board, taking down the mainmast. Hull then stood off to renew his ship's rigging while Dacres's crew struggled to get control of the rolling, mastless hulk. There was nothing Dacres could do, and as soon as *Constitution* returned to a raking position, he surrendered, two hours after the combat had commenced. Captain Hull removed all men and their property from *Guerrière* and set her afire. *Guerrière* lost twenty-three killed and fatally wounded and fifty-six slightly or seriously wounded. Dacres and his crew had fought gallantly, having fewer men and guns than their American opponent. In addition, Dacres should be given credit for having allowed fifteen Americans in his crew to go below before the fight so they would not be obliged to fight against a U.S. ship.

BIBLIOGRAPHY

Maloney, Linda M. *Captain from Connecticut: The Life and Naval Times of Captain Isaac Hull.* 1986.
Roosevelt, Theodore. *The Naval War of 1812.* 1882.

WILLIAM S. DUDLEY

H

HAMILTON, ALEXANDER (1755[?]–1804), early advocate of constitutional reform, coauthor of *The Federalist*, Madison's principal opponent in the party battles of the 1790s. Hamilton was born on the island of Nevis in the British West Indies in 1755 or 1757, the out-of-wedlock child of Rachel Lavien and a Scottish trader who deserted the family when Hamilton was a youngster. Hamilton came to the North American mainland in 1772, sponsored by the New York merchants who had hired him as a clerk. Enrolling at King's College (now Columbia) in 1773, Hamilton soon hurled himself into the resistance movement, writing two important pamphlets during the winter of 1774–1775. At the outset of the war, he organized a company of artillery, led it through the fighting in New York, and won Washington's praise for his conduct at Trenton and Princeton. Promoted to lieutenant colonel, he served as Washington's aide from February 1777 to February 1781, when he resigned after receiving a mild rebuke. Despite the disagreement, Washington appointed him to a field command and let him lead the final charge at Yorktown.

In December 1780, Hamilton had married Elizabeth Schuyler, daughter of Gen. Philip Schuyler, one of the largest landowners and most important politicians in New York. After Yorktown, Schuyler's influence boosted Hamilton's ascent. Within a year, the young lawyer was selected as a delegate to the Continental Congress, where his acquaintance with Madison began.

The Constitution. Hamilton and Madison were allies, for the most part, during the New Yorker's eighteen months in the Continental Congress. Hamilton was seated on 25 November 1782, not long before a deputation from the army arrived in Philadelphia and demanded that Congress resolve outstanding grievances over soldiers' pay and other issues. Through the early months of 1783, against a background of increasing grumblings in the winter camp at Newburgh, New York, Hamilton and other officers pressed for the enactment of Robert Morris's proposal for amendments to the Articles of Confederation that would permit independent federal taxes. Madison was the leader of the congressional proponents of this program, but he was not involved in contacts with the army and was not among the strongest supporters of Morris. As mutinous anonymous addresses circulated at the camp, the young Virginian separated from his allies and proposed the compromise that would become the basis for the congressional recommendations of 18 April 1783: a renewed request for congressional power to impose an impost, combined with an appeal for new taxation by the states. Hamilton was one of only five in Congress who voted against this plan.

Hamilton and Madison shared a commitment to reform, but they held different views of the Union's current situation. In 1783 the dashing, arrogant New Yorker already favored a convention to reorganize the federal system. Madison was not prepared for a solution so extreme. Hamilton's continuing support for Morris's proposals, which incorporated most of the essential elements of the financial program of the 1790s, followed from their mutual desire to look beyond the reestablishment of public credit toward a funding system and a national bank that would speed the nation's economic growth and foster political centralization. As Morris put it, if the discharged soldiers, the civilian public creditors, and the officers appointed to collect the federal taxes could all be made to look to Congress for their pensions, salaries, and other claims, they would cooperate with merchants doing business with the bank to "unite the several states more closely together in one general money connection," to "give stability to government by combining in its support."

Hamilton, like Morris, had long been thinking in these

ALEXANDER HAMILTON.   Engraving by W. G. Jackman after a painting by L. W. Gilbs.
PRINTS AND PHOTOGRAPHS DIVISION, LIBRARY OF CONGRESS.

terms. His private correspondence and his anonymous newspaper series, "The Continentalist," had repeatedly insisted on the need to link the central government with influential men capable of counterbalancing the groups whose interests tied them to the states. A more effective central government, he argued, would require creation of a monied, officeholding class that would depend on that government for the promotion of its interests. Madison was never comfortable with many of the broader implications of Hamilton's elitist program.

As the crisis of the Union deepened in 1785–1786, Madison as well as Hamilton became convinced that underlying difficulties were insoluble within the loose framework of the existing federal system. When they came together next, at the Annapolis Convention in September 1786, the two reformers joined in calling for a constitutional convention. Hamilton contributed in important ways to the convention, although he candidly confessed that no one's notions of a proper constitution differed more from the completed document than his. He also took a major role in the struggle over ratification. He and Madison combined to write nearly all *The Federalist* and stayed in close communication while they led the battles for adoption in Virginia and New York. Then Madison approved of Hamilton's appointment to a key position in Washington's administration. Although Secretary of the Treasury Hamilton expected Madison's support, fundamental differences between the two collaborators were soon reflected in a vicious party war.

Hamilton's Vision of America. Hamilton's design for national greatness was complete in its essentials when he wrote his first report (14 January 1790). Each of his proposals built upon or was intended to facilitate the other aspects of an integrated program. The secretary faced toward the Atlantic and envisioned an arena of competing empires into which America must enter much like any other state. In time, as he conceived it, the United States could play a brilliant part in this arena, and he meant to earn immortal fame as founder of the nation's greatness. First, however, he intended to create the economic and financial underpinnings for successful competition: institutions similar to those that had permitted tiny England to attain the pinnacle of international prestige. And while he did so, he believed, it would be necessary, too, for the United States to avoid a confrontation with Great Britain, the single nation that could threaten it in war or, through investments, assist it most impressively in its striving for greatness. Taking British institutions as a model, Hamilton proposed to build a modern state, a nation able to compete with European empires on the Europeans' terms.

With proper management, Hamilton thought, the heavy burden of the debt from the Revolutionary War could be transformed into an advantage for the country. Federal funding of state as well as national obligations could accomplish more than the establishment of public credit; it could tie the economic interests of a critical proportion of America's elite to the success of national institutions. Moreover, even as it bound the monied interests to the government's success, the funding program would erect a framework for the nation's future role in global competition, transforming governmental obligations into a currency supply that could be multiplied by using the certificates of debt to back creation of a national bank (the Bank of England was Hamilton's model). The bonds and banknotes would foster manufacturing and commerce, whose rapid growth would pave the way for economic independence, and the loose construction of the Constitution necessary to legitimate these measures would help shift power to the federal level and to the executive administration.

Taken as a whole, Hamilton's scheme was brilliant. When implemented, it accomplished much of what he had in mind. But it was incompatible, at almost every point, with Madison's and Jefferson's conceptions of a viable republic.

By 1792, when Hamilton attacked Jefferson's connection with the *National Gazette*, the breach within the government was public and complete. By 1795, when Hamilton resigned his place (but retained his influence over other members of the Federalist administrations), the configurations of the first great party battle were defined. Throughout the decade, it was Hamilton's design to which the Jeffersonians responded, and Hamilton (for whom John Adams's cabinet had more respect than for the president himself) saw himself as a president-maker. Hamilton's position after 1798 as ranking general of the army lay behind the breach between the Hamiltonians and Adams.

Hamilton expended much of his remaining influence in the country and his party to attack President Adams during the campaign of 1800. While Hamilton continued to oppose the Jeffersonians in New York politics and in the press, his prospects for returning to political or military office had diminished drastically by 1804, when he accepted what proved to be a fatal challenge from Aaron Burr. Ever the seeker of fame, Hamilton secured a lasting place among the greatest of the Founders, but his personal life marred his image as an honorable figure in the nation's formative years.

BIBLIOGRAPHY

Banning, Lance. "James Madison and the Nationalists, 1780–1783." *William and Mary Quarterly*, 3d ser., 40 (1983): 227–255.

Ferguson, E. James. *The Power of the Purse: A History of American Public Finance, 1776–1790.* 1961.

Kohn, Richard H. *Eagle and Sword: The Federalists and the Creation of the Military Establishment in America, 1783–1802.* 1975.

McCoy, Drew R. *The Elusive Republic: Political Economy in Jeffersonian America.* 1980.

McDonald, Forrest. *Alexander Hamilton: A Biography.* 1979.

Miller, John C. *Alexander Hamilton: Portrait in Paradox.* 1959.

Stourzh, Gerald. *Alexander Hamilton and the Idea of Republican Government.* 1970.

Syrett, Harold C., and Jacob E. Cooke, eds. *The Papers of Alexander Hamilton.* 26 vols. 1960–1979.

LANCE BANNING

HAMILTON, PAUL (1762–1816), secretary of the navy. Madison's appointment of the South Carolina planter and former governor Paul Hamilton as secretary of the navy provided regional balance to his cabinet but added little administrative and no maritime experience. Hamilton fell under the spell of senior naval officers and came to advocate the revival of the frigate navy of the Federalist era instead of supporting the coastal defense gunboat policy favored by the Jefferson administration. Hamilton was able to secure congressional authority to reactivate the frigates, but with the restriction that the ships be used only for patrolling American waters as adjuncts to the gunboats and harbor fortifications. Hamilton also sought permission to protect American shipping by sending a squadron to the Mediterranean, to increase the number of frigates, and to construct the country's first seventy-four-gun ships of the line but did not received the requested permission before 1812. Moreover, the proposals angered both the Old Republican faction in Congress and the economy-minded secretary of the Treasury, Albert Gallatin.

Once the War of 1812 began, Hamilton had six frigates, nine brigs, and 165 gunboats with which to counter Britain's one thousand ships. The British North American squadron was larger than the entire U.S. Navy. In May 1812 Hamilton consulted with three senior captains, John Rodgers, Stephen Decatur, and William Bainbridge, and received three conflicting and self-serving recommendations on wartime deployment. Initially he followed Rodgers's advice of sailing in squadron, but that strategy failed to produce significant results; when Rodgers cruised far from the American coast, the British squadron was able to capture many American merchantmen. Isaac Hull's victory over the British ship *Guerrière* indicated that single cruising was the better policy, and Hamilton changed his policy. For the remainder of the war, single cruising and commerce raiding dominated American oceanic strategy and tactics. However, none of these actions thwarted the British blockade of American ports or diminished the threat of invasion along the coast. Ironically, the war's only significant fleet actions came in the one area largely neglected by Hamilton and the senior naval officers—the Great Lakes. Only toward the end of 1812, after a series of army disasters, did Hamilton begin to send forces to the lake regions.

By this time it was obvious that the amiable Hamilton was incompetent. Many of his difficulties stemmed from inadequate administrative support in Washington, but Hamilton compounded the problem by excessive drinking that impaired his ability to function. Rep. Nathaniel Macon claimed Hamilton was "about as fit for his place, as the Indian prophet [Tecumseh's brother Tenskwatawa] would be for the Emperor of Europe." Replacement of Hamilton became a political necessity, and on 31 December 1812, he resigned and was succeeded by William Jones.

BIBLIOGRAPHY

Dudley, William S., ed. *The Naval War of 1812: A Documentary History*. Vol. 1. 1985.
Eckert, Edward K. *The Navy Department in the War of 1812.* 1973.
McKee, Christopher. *A Gentlemanly and Honorable Profession: The Creation of the U.S. Naval Officer Corps, 1794–1815.* 1991.
Sharrer, G. Terry. "The Search for a Naval Policy, 1783–1812." In *In Peace and War: Interpretations of American Naval History, 1775–1978*. Edited by Kenneth J. Hagan. 1978.
Stagg, J. C. A. *Mr. Madison's War: Politics, Diplomacy, and Warfare in the Early American Republic.* 1983.

DAVID CURTIS SKAGGS

HAMPTON, WADE (1751/1752–1835), soldier, planter. Born in Halifax County, Virginia, Hampton spent most of his life in South Carolina. He served in the Revolutionary War under the generals Thomas Sumter and Francis Marion, distinguishing himself in the Battle of Eutaw Springs in September 1781. Later he served in the state legislature at various times between 1782 and 1795. He was in the minority that opposed the Constitution at the South Carolina ratification convention in 1788. He served two terms in Congress (1795–1797 and 1803–1805).

MAJ. GEN. WADE HAMPTON.
PRINTS AND PHOTOGRAPHS DIVISION, LIBRARY OF CONGRESS.

Hampton's regular army career began in 1808 when he was appointed a colonel; the following year he was promoted to brigadier general and given command of New Orleans. Placed in charge of the fortifications at Norfolk in 1812, Hampton appealed directly to President Madison in 1813 for an active command in the north. Madison made Hampton a major general and sent him to the Lake Champlain region. This proved an unfortunate move, however, for Gen. James Wilkinson, Hampton's bitter enemy, was soon assigned to the northern frontier to replace Gen. Henry Dearborn. Secretary of War John Armstrong, who visited the front, offered to mediate when the two rivals were called upon to cooperate in a military maneuver.

Trouble ensued when Wilkinson approached Montreal from the Saint Lawrence River in November 1813 and ordered Hampton to join his force for the final assault. Hampton declined, citing depleted supplies and the dispirited condition of his men. To avoid arrest and court-martial at the hands of Wilkinson, Hampton fled to Washington where his wealth and political connections helped him avert a court of inquiry at the hands of Armstrong. Madison accepted Hampton's resignation. For the remainder of his life, Hampton tended his many plantations and his hundreds of slaves. When he died in 1835, he was considered one of the wealthiest men in America.

BIBLIOGRAPHY

Easterby, J. Harold. "Wade Hampton." *Dictionary of American Biography*. Vol. 8. Edited by Dumas Malone. 1932.
Everest, Allan S. *The War of 1812 in the Champlain Valley*. 1981.

C. EDWARD SKEEN

HANSON, ALEXANDER CONTEE (1786–1819),
Federalist editor, representative and senator from Maryland. Hanson was born in Annapolis, Maryland, into a family of distinguished American patriots. An extremist temperament propelled the talented editor from the center to the fringe of American politics by the end of his short life.

Hanson grew up in Annapolis and graduated from St. John's College in 1802. He practiced law in his native city for a brief period. By 1808, he had moved to Baltimore where he and former State Department clerk Jacob Wagner began publication of the *Federal Republican & Commercial Gazette* as a mouthpiece for Federalist opposition to the Jefferson and Madison administrations.

Hanson's wartime opposition to the Madison administration was not well tolerated by the Republican patriots of Baltimore. Two days after Hanson published an editorial censuring the war, Baltimore Republicans destroyed the office of the *Federal Republican*. Hanson and Wagner continued to publish their newspaper in Georgetown. They quietly returned to Baltimore on 26 July 1812, where they quickly fortified a house aided by other Maryland Federalists and began to distribute their newspaper. On the evening of 27 July a crowd attacked Hanson's fortress; by morning, the Federalists had surrendered to the protective custody of town officials. A mob easily gained access to the jail and brutally beat the entrapped Federalists, killing one and severely injuring many others, including Hanson.

The attack on Hanson and his compatriots raised the spectre of French revolutionary terror on the Chesapeake. In Maryland, the Federalists gained control of the state legislature in the fall of 1812. Hanson emerged from his ordeal a hero. He won election to the Thirteenth Congress, where he continued to attack the Madison administration. But his unyielding opposition to Madison cost him the support of Maryland's more moderate Federalists and the leadership of the state party. He resigned from the House of Representatives in 1816. In 1817 he was appointed to the U.S. Senate to fill the unexpired term of Robert Goodloe Harper, a post he held until his death in 1819.

BIBLIOGRAPHY

Cassell, Frank A. "The Great Baltimore Riot of 1812." *Maryland Historical Magazine* 70 (1975): 241–259.
Renzulli, L. Marx. *Maryland: The Federalist Years*. 1972.
Schauinger, Joseph H. "Alexander Contee Hanson, Federalist Partisan." *Maryland Historical Magazine* 35 (1940): 354–364.

TINA H. SHELLER

HARRISON, WILLIAM HENRY (1773–1841),
soldier, statesman, ninth president of the United States. A scion of distinguished Virginia families, Harrison was born at Berkeley, the Charles City County plantation of his parents, Benjamin Harrison, a signer of the Declaration of Independence, and Elizabeth Bassett Harrison. He attended Hampden-Sydney College and studied medicine under Benjamin Rush in Philadelphia.

Harrison entered the army as an ensign in the First Infantry Regiment in 1791, took part in the campaigns against the Indians in the Northwest Territory, and served as Maj. Gen. Anthony Wayne's aide-de-camp. Resigning from the army in 1798, he accepted appointment as secretary of the Northwest Territory and the following year defeated Gov. Arthur St. Clair's son by one vote in an election to become the first territorial delegate to Congress.

In the House of Representatives Harrison chaired the Committee on Public Lands, which reported the Land Act of 1800. He also worked to secure the act that created the Indiana Territory out of the Northwest Territory. In May 1800 President John Adams appointed Harrison governor of the Indiana Territory, comprising present-

HARRISON AT TIPPECANOE.   Gen. William Henry Harrison's officers try to restrain him from riding into the heat of battle. Lithograph by Nathaniel Currier, 1840.

day Indiana, Illinois, Wisconsin, western Michigan, and eastern Minnesota. After Madison became secretary of state in 1801, Harrison sporadically corresponded with him concerning such matters as disputed land claims and the printing of territorial and federal laws.

Between 1802 and 1804 Harrison built a Federal-style house which he named Grouseland, at Vincennes, the territorial capital. He used his appointive power to strengthen the proslavery faction within the territory and initially favored a ten-year suspension of the Northwest Ordinance's ban on slavery in the territories, but when Congress ignored that provision, territorial officials allowed lifetime contracts between masters and servants.

Harrison implemented the Jefferson administration's ambivalent policies toward the Indians. He sought to reduce the causes of conflict between settlers and Indians by regulating traders and by restricting liquor. He concluded a series of treaties by which some Indian tribes (notably the Delawares, Miamis, and Potawatomis) ceded large tracts of land in Indiana and Illinois to the United States. Two Shawnee brothers, Tecumseh and Tenskwatawa (known as the Prophet), had united hostile Indians throughout the transappalachian frontier to oppose the land cessions. Harrison led a combined force of regular troops, militia, and volunteers against the Indian confederacy at the battle of Tippecanoe on 7 November 1811. Both sides suffered comparable losses, but Harrison's force held the field. He advocated a general war against the Indians of the Northwest, but President Madison and Congress ultimately declared war against Great Britain in June 1812.

As a brevet major general in the Kentucky militia, Harrison led a force to relieve Fort Wayne. Madison appointed him brigadier general (and later promoted him to major general) in the regular army and named him commander of the Army of the Northwest. Harrison seized Fort Malden in Upper Canada, reoccupied Detroit, and pursued Maj. Gen. Henry Proctor, defeating Procter's army on 5 October 1813 at the battle of the Thames, where Tecumseh was killed. However, a dispute with Secretary of War John Armstrong caused Harrison to resign his commission in May 1814 while at the same time declaring to Madison "that the war in which we are engaged is just, and necessary." He served as a representative from 1816 to 1819, as a state senator from 1819 to 1821, and as a U.S. senator from Ohio from 1825 to 1828. He was U.S. minister to Colombia from 1828 to 1829 and the foremost of three Whig presidential candidates in the 1836 election, won by the Democrat Martin Van Buren. In 1840 Harrison defeated Van Buren for president as a result of the boisterous "Log Cabin and Hard Cider" campaign, but he died of pneumonia after one month in office.

BIBLIOGRAPHY

Cleaves, Freeman. *Old Tippecanoe: William Henry Harrison and His Time.* 1939.
Goebel, Dorothy Burne. *William Henry Harrison: A Political Biography.* 1926.
McCarty, Dwight G. *The Territorial Governors of the Old Northwest: A Study in Territorial Administration.* 1910.
Governors' Messages and Letters: Messages and Letters of William Henry Harrison. Edited by Logan Esarey. 2 vols. 1922.
The Territorial Papers of the United States: The Territory of Indiana. Edited by Clarence Edwin Carter. Vols. 7–8. 1939.

THOMAS A. MASON

HARTFORD CONVENTION.

HARTFORD CONVENTION. The Hartford Convention was a meeting of delegates, all members of the Federalist party, from five New England states, held in Hartford, Connecticut, from 15 December 1814 to 5 January 1815. Delegates convened to express grievances against the policies of the Democratic-Republican administrations of Thomas Jefferson and James Madison, particularly against the conduct of the War of 1812, and to propose changes in the national government that would address those grievances.

Roots of the Convention. The immediate roots of the convention were in the first decade of government under the Constitution. Since its origin in the 1790s as the party of George Washington, John Adams, and Alexander Hamilton, the Federalist party had espoused an active role for government in national life, spoken up for commercial, manufacturing, and banking interests, and favored a "realistic" policy in foreign affairs—in effect conceding military and commercial ascendancy to Great Britain in the western Atlantic and along the borders of the young nation. Its opposition, the Democratic-Republican party of Jefferson and Madison, represented the interests of the nation's predominantly agrarian economy, championed limited government, sought to open all foreign markets to American goods, and favored a neutral stance regarding the conflicts of other nations. These parties, the world's first political parties in the modern sense of the word, also fought over freedom of speech, immigration, banking policy, and the courts. The Federalists' center of gravity was in New York and New England; that of the Democratic-Republicans was in the middle and southern states.

During the presidencies of Washington and Adams, the Federalists secured a ten-year commercial peace with Britain and fought an undeclared war with France, thus coming to be seen as the pro-British party in American politics. Upon Jefferson's inauguration in 1801 and the resumption of the Napoleonic Wars in Europe, American relations with Britain soured. British and American ships fought at sea. In actions that crippled New England's trading economy, Jefferson, hoping to force Britain to lift restrictions on American trade, attempted unsuccessfully between 1807 and 1809 to embargo all trade with foreign nations. After Madison assumed the presidency in 1809, Anglo-American relations deteriorated further. When the Democratic-Republicans led the nation into war in 1812, Federalist opposition turned bitter and more unified.

Much of the New England Federalists' posture of opposition, however, was rooted further in the past. It arose from a historic sense of regional and cultural superiority, from fears of the North's disadvantage in the face of southern political power, and from concern about the fragility of the nation's republican experiment. Moreover, the Federalists feared that slavery, western migration, foreign immigration, and the rise of partisan politics all represented a threat to the integrity of national life.

A minority party fueled by a regionalist worldview, the Federalist party also faced the problems of a young political institution that, like its Democratic-Republican counterpart, had not yet gained full acceptance in a nation fearful of "factions" and "parties." Principal among these problems was an internal conflict—in no place more intense than in Massachusetts, home of both the most powerful Federalist party and the largest Federalist constituency in the country—over party leadership and the wisdom of various accommodations to a rapidly expanding electorate within a democratizing political culture. One group of Federalists was composed of experienced political figures—in Massachusetts, Harrison Gray Otis, William Sullivan, and Thomas Handasyd Perkins—for whom the adoption of such "modern" political practices as nominating caucuses, partisan rallies, and open electioneering seemed justified by the need to win elections. Another group was made up of traditionalist party figures, such as Timothy Pickering and Congregational minister Jedidiah Morse, who scorned what they saw as the popularity-seeking ways of the more pragmatic party members and who clamored

HARTFORD CONVENTION.   King George III encourages Massachusetts, Connecticut, and Rhode Island to leave the Union, as Rep. Timothy Pickering prays. Etching by William Charles, Philadelphia, 1814.

PRINTS AND PHOTOGRAPHS DIVISION, LIBRARY OF CONGRESS.

for "principled" action against the opposition.

This internal party schism intensified after the United States declared war against Great Britain in 1812. In both 1804 and 1808 a few Federalists, stung by losses to the "southern party" in successive presidential elections, had unsuccessfully advocated the nullification of national laws and even the secession from the Union of the northern states, including New York. Nothing came of these ill-considered plots, but now such efforts were renewed under conditions of war and reached their peak in the summer of 1814, a low point in the war's prosecution. After defeating Napoleon, Britain began to concentrate its forces in North America, and the Royal Navy placed the entire east coast under blockade. In August the British burned Washington and forced Madison to flee. By September they had invaded New York at Lake Champlain and occupied Maine as far south as the Penobscot. Making matters worse, the nation seemed on the edge of bankruptcy, Congress had legislated an embargo on coastal trade to forestall smuggling, and the federal government was threatening to force state militias, including those of New England, into national service. To New England Federalists, a resounding protest against government policies that threatened their region's security seemed essential. In Massachusetts Federalists led the way.

The Convention's Proceedings. In early September 1814, Gov. Caleb Strong ordered the Massachusetts legislature (the General Court) into special session to debate and adopt measures that "the present dangerous state of public affairs may render expedient." Beating back calls for extreme actions, such as cutting off federal customs collections (an act tantamount to nullification), the party's moderates succeeded in passing resolutions that called for a meeting of regional delegates to prepare for New England's defense, promote a "radical reform" in the Constitution, and take such other measures "not repugnant to their obligations as members of the union." Thus the party's most active figures—Otis, Sullivan, and Perkins—sought to take "constitutional and peaceable" steps that would still the clamor for more extreme measures. As reported by George Cabot, who as the party's elder statesman would become president of the Hartford Convention, they were trying to prevent the "young hotheads from getting into mischief."

When the Convention, an extralegal gathering similar to the earlier Continental Congress, opened in Hartford on 15 December 1814, twenty-six delegates were present. Those from Massachusetts, Connecticut, and Rhode Island, official representatives of their state governments, had long been active in party affairs and were sensitive to the party's well-being. They were not inclined to radical measures. Only three delegates, selected by Federalist meetings in Vermont and New Hampshire counties, had been elected directly by the people.

The Convention's sessions were held in secret to encourage free discussion, a circumstance that engendered future recrimination. Thus, the Hartford Convention was long charged with treasonable acts. But its proceedings apparently were tranquil, and the final Convention report, written by Otis, was moderate and temperate. The report attacked the conditions that, Federalists argued, had reduced New England's influence in the nation's councils and had left the region defenseless: the admissions of western states, the three-fifths clause of the Constitution, the too-easy naturalization of immigrants, patronage policies that favored the South and the West, and efforts to conscript state militias for the war. Yet, in recommending that Congress authorize each state to defend itself and rebate taxes for that purpose, the report drew back from endorsing nullification, arguing that such an extreme step, "especially in time of war," could be justified only by "absolute necessity."

The Convention report, reflecting the institutional, party thinking of its author, also proposed seven constitutional amendments to assuage New England's grievances. The first, to end the South's advantage in congressional seats, would have apportioned congressional representation and direct taxation on the basis of the free white population alone, thus excluding enumeration of the three-fifths of the South's slaves who were then counted in the census. A second would have required a two-thirds vote in Congress to admit new states. Two others would have limited embargoes to sixty days and required a two-thirds majority for their passage. A fifth would have mandated two-thirds votes for declarations of war; a sixth would have barred from Congress and other national offices all naturalized citizens; and a seventh, aimed at the "Virginia dynasty" of presidents, would have outlawed the successive election of presidents from the same state.

Although disappointing to the party's "warm bloods," the Convention report was well received in Federalist circles. The governments of Massachusetts, Connecticut, and Rhode Island quickly adopted it and named delegates to convey it to Washington.

But intervening events made the report at once irrelevant. Even as the Convention was meeting, a treaty of peace with Britain was being concluded at Ghent, and in early January 1815, shortly after the delegates adjourned their proceedings, Andrew Jackson's troops routed British regulars at New Orleans. When Americans learned of both developments by mid February, they dismissed the Convention report with ridicule.

While hastening the demise of the party for which it spoke, the Hartford Convention was not without significance as an institutionalized partisan response to the grievances of an aroused populace. The delegates steered near-open rebellion through constitutional channels, abetting the continuing maturation of the American political system. In addition, the Convention raised some enduring questions about the conduct of republican government, both in and out of war, and about its responsibilities to citizens of all regions, parties, and interests. Finally, it gave fresh currency to notions of interposition and nullification that would haunt the nation from 1832, gaining enough acceptance by 1861 to bring on southern secession. The seeds of disunion were the Convention's most fateful legacy.

[See also *Federalist Party; New England; Nullification Doctrine.*]

BIBLIOGRAPHY

Banner, James M., Jr. *To the Hartford Convention: The Federalists and the Origins of Party Politics in Massachusetts, 1789–1815.* 1970.

Stagg, J. C. A. *Mr. Madison's War: Politics, Diplomacy, and Warfare in the Early American Republic, 1783–1830.* 1983.

JAMES M. BANNER, JR.

HAWKINS, BENJAMIN (1754–1816), senator and Indian agent. Writing to the Marquis de Lafayette in 1788, George Washington described Benjamin Hawkins as "that ingenious gentleman." Hawkins's career as senator and Indian agent brought him into close contact with other ingenious gentlemen like Washington, Jefferson, and Madison (he named his only son after Madison) and placed him in the forefront of efforts to impose on Indian tribes programs of "civilization" that these leaders believed to be vital.

Born in North Carolina, Hawkins served as a staff officer to George Washington in the Revolution. He was a member of the Continental Congress from 1781 to 1784 and from 1786 to 1787. In 1785, Congress named Hawkins to serve as commissioner to treat with the southern Indians, and he signed the treaties of Hopewell with the Cherokees in November 1785 and with the Choctaws and Chickasaws early the following year.

After the ratification of the Constitution, Hawkins was elected one of the first senators from North Carolina, serving from 1789 to 1795. In 1796 he negotiated the Treaty of Coleraine with the Creeks and that same year was appointed principal temporary agent for Indian affairs south of the Ohio, replacing James Seagrove, the first federal agent among the Creeks. He spent the rest of his life working in Indian country, acting as superintendent for all southern tribes until 1802 and as agent for the Creeks from then until his death. Well-educated,

BENJAMIN HAWKINS.
PRINTS AND PHOTOGRAPHS DIVISION, LIBRARY OF CONGRESS.

he demonstrated a real interest in Indian history, language, and culture even as he worked to undermine the Indians' traditional way of life. Despite poor health, for twenty years he was the most influential non-Indian in the Creek Nation and largely filled a vacuum left by the death of chief Alexander McGillivray in 1793.

Hawkins devoted himself to promoting the Anglo-American version of "civilization" among the Creeks, which translated into a systematic attempt to produce political, economic, and social revolution in Creek country. He introduced cotton culture, spinning wheels and modern looms, iron ploughs and hoes, new strains of seeds, and domesticated cattle, and established a model farm. He pressured the Creeks to abandon communal land use and hunting for a life based on individual landholding and intensive husbandry. Such a transformation would not only make them into yeoman farmers but would also free "surplus" land for sale to the United States. One of his duties as Indian agent, in addition to maintaining peace between the Creeks and the state of Georgia, was to promote the acquisition of Indian land, and during his tenure the Creek land base shrank considerably as a result of a series of treaties. He also established schools for Creek children.

In addition to implementing social and economic reform, Hawkins imposed far-reaching political and legal changes in the Creek Nation. He tried to centralize

Creek government, so that the important business of the nation would be carried out under his supervision, and even lectured the Creeks on their progress at meetings of the Creek national council. He also attempted to substitute an Anglo-American criminal justice system for the traditional system of clan vengeance, placing crime control in the hands of the national council and delivering a significant blow to the ancient clan systems.

Hawkins centered his operations among the Lower Creeks, who were most vulnerable to pressure from Georgia, and his reforms aggravated divisions between Upper and Lower Creeks. Hawkins's imposition of Anglo-American "civilization," coupled with the fact that the Creeks had lost millions of acres of land by 1811, left many Creeks receptive to Tecumseh's message of united Indian resistance and paved the way for the emergence of militant Creek prophets preaching a return to traditional ways. The divisions in Creek society ultimately exploded in civil war in the so-called Creek War of 1813–1814, which Andrew Jackson suppressed with bloody efficiency and then used as justification for the confiscation of some two-thirds of the remaining Creek territory at the Treaty of Fort Jackson in 1814.

The war broke Creek power forever and disrupted Hawkins's work. Hawkins died at the Indian agency on the Flint River in June 1816. He seems to have devoted himself zealously and selflessly to the transformation of Indian life, a vision he shared with Jefferson and Madison.

BIBLIOGRAPHY

Hawkins, Benjamin. "Letters of Benjamin Hawkins." *Collections of the Georgia Historical Society.* Vol. 9. 1916.
Hawkins, Benjamin. "A Sketch of the Creek Country in the Years 1798 and 1799." *Collections of the Georgia Historical Society.* Vol. 1, part 1. 1848.
Henri, Florette. *The Southern Indians and Benjamin Hawkins 1796–1816.* 1986.
Martin, Joel W. *Sacred Revolt: The Muskogees' Struggle for a New World.* 1991.
Pound, Merritt B. *Benjamin Hawkins, Indian Agent.* 1951.

COLIN G. CALLOWAY

HELVIDIUS. The "Helvidius" essays were written by Madison in response to a series written by Alexander Hamilton under the pseudonym Pacificus. A political storm brewing in the summer of 1793 had laid the groundwork for a two-party system of the kind that the Founding Fathers in 1787 believed ruinous to liberty. The French Revolution led to a crisis within President Washington's cabinet that was solved by his Proclamation of Neutrality, but in its wake came Jefferson's resignation as secretary of state and the alienation of republican-

minded citizens who believed neutrality was dishonorable. Jefferson believed the real reason for the Neutrality Proclamation, which Treasury Secretary Hamilton favored, was the Federalists' desire to curry favor with Great Britain and to keep the commercial and mercantile lines with British firms open for a lucrative trade.

The crisis became full-blown when Edmond Genet, the newly appointed French minister to the United States, defied Washington's proclamation by issuing military commissions and giving out letters of marque to Americans. Using the pseudonym Pacificus, Hamilton charged that pro-French Americans (otherwise known as Democratic-Republicans or Jacobins) were undermining American foreign policy as French sycophants. The 1778 Franco-American treaty could be disregarded, Pacificus said, since no stable French government existed; this claim hit at Jefferson's insistence that the treaty was valid and obligated the United States to defend the French West Indies. Genet's heavy-handed actions shocked Madison and Jefferson, but they thought the Neutrality Proclamation threw away a chance to bring about a favorable trade treaty with the British through negotiations.

Angered by Hamilton's newspaper salvos, Jefferson beseeched Madison to write a series of replies. "For god's sake, my dear Sir, take up your pen, select the most striking heresies, and cut him to peices [sic] in the face of the public. There is nobody else who can & will enter the lists with him," Jefferson wrote Madison in June 1793. Madison was less than eager to engage in a journalistic debate, but he could not resist Jefferson's entreaties. Even as Jefferson wrote, Genet's excessive behavior had made him a cross the Republicans no longer wished to bear. Madison's task was to repudiate Genet but support the French Revolution and to praise Washington but question the declaration of neutrality by an executive proclamation as perhaps an unconstitutional remedy.

Madison approached his chore without relish. As an honorary French citizen (he had accepted the proferred honor from the National Assembly in April 1793), Madison told Jefferson his authorship of the Helvidius papers was "the most grating one I ever experienced." But he set out to persuade readers of *The Gazette of the United States* that the chief issue was executive control, as opposed to legislative control, of American foreign policy. The pseudonym he chose came from Tacitus's description of Helvidius Priscus, a first-century Roman leader who had resisted imperial decrees. Between 24 August and 18 September 1793, Madison's five essays appeared in the Federalist newspaper that had been the original vehicle for Pacificus, and thus the debate was conducted in what might be called a hostile but fair-minded medium. Madison began by asserting that Pacificus gave to the executive powers that were "of a legislative, not an executive nature," and he said that to argue otherwise was to compare the president's constitutional powers to *"royal prerogatives in the British government."* Madison never conceded the presidential claim to broad powers in the field of foreign affairs, as Pacificus implied.

In order to preserve his anonymity, Madison had his essays copied at Montpelier and dispatched to Jefferson in Philaldelphia. Jefferson was authorized to make changes but seemed so delighted he hardly tinkered with the essays before he had them delivered to *The Gazette of the United States.* Madison's strict construction of executive powers became a tenet in the emerging Republican party philosophy, and political writers have since noted Madison's departure in 1793 from the position in favor of a strong central government that he had taken in his *Federalist* essays in 1787–1788.

[See also *Congress,* article on *Third Congress.*]

BIBLIOGRAPHY

Brant, Irving. *James Madison: The Nationalist 1780–1787.* 1948.
Ketcham, Ralph. *James Madison: A Biography.* 1971.
Loss, Richard, ed. *The Letters of Pacificus and Helvidius.* Repr. 1976.
Stewart, Donald H. *The Opposition Press of the Federalist Period.* 1969.

ROBERT A. RUTLAND

HENRY, JOHN (1777–1853), adventurer, British undercover agent, U.S. Army captain. Born in Ireland, John Henry emigrated to New York in 1798 and later lived in Vermont and Massachusetts. He was known to Madison as "Captain Henry" based on two years of U.S. Army service in 1798–1800. While a law student in Montreal in 1807, Henry provided Canadian officials with information on American politics. As Anglo-American tensions increased, he was asked in 1809 by the governor of Lower Canada to determine if New Englanders would "look up to England for assistance" in separating from the United States. Henry spent four months in New England and then passed most of the next two years trying unsuccessfully to collect his salary from his British employers.

Henry returned to the United States late in 1811 in the company of another adventurer, Paul Emile Soubiran, who passed himself off as the count de Crillon. Madison learned of this pair in January 1812 and soon authorized the purchase, sight unseen, of correspondence on Henry's mission for $50,000 from the State Department's secret-service funds. On 9 March he sent the Henry correspondence to Congress with a letter describing an alleged plot for "destroying the Union and forming the eastern part thereof into a political connection with Great Britain." The letters were printed the next day in the *National Intelligencer.* They identified none of the Federalists with

whom Henry had talked, nor did they reveal anything that could not be gleaned from New England newspapers. Rep. John Randolph called the correspondence "a poor shabby shallow dirty electioneering trick." When the House Foreign Affairs Committee attempted to question Henry, it learned that the papers had not been submitted to Congress until after Henry had sailed for France. Napoleon lessened the impact of any anti-British sentiment the correspondence might have aroused by resuming his depredations on American commerce.

Henry lost most of his $50,000 to Crillon, who sold him an imaginary chateau as well as fraudulent bills of exchange. Henry was in Italy in 1820, when he was hired to dredge up information against Queen Caroline of Great Britain for a divorce action. His activities after that are unknown, though his granddaughter stated that he lived until 1853.

BIBLIOGRAPHY

Brant, Irving. *James Madison the President, 1809–1812.* 1956.
Lowrie, Walter, and Matthew S. Clarke, eds. *American State Papers: Foreign Affairs,* 3:545–557. 1832.
Morison, Samuel E. *By Land and by Sea* ("The Henry-Crillon Affair of 1812"). 1953.

DONALD O. DEWEY

HENRY, PATRICK (1736–1799), orator, revolutionary leader, five-time governor of Virginia. Deemed by Thomas Jefferson to be "the greatest orator that ever lived," Patrick Henry achieved his most enduring fame as the popular leader of the revolutionary movement in colonial Virginia. The second child of John Henry and Sarah Winston Syme, he grew up in the Old Dominion's sparsely settled Piedmont region. Like most young men of the backcountry, he received little formal schooling, although he did have the advantage of being tutored by his father, who had attended King's College in Aberdeen, Scotland. After unsuccessful ventures in shopkeeping and in farming, he resolved to become a lawyer and qualified for admission to the bar in April 1760 at the age of twenty-four.

Henry vaulted to public attention three years later as a result of his brilliant closing speech for the defense in the Parson's Cause case. In 1765 he was elected to the House of Burgesses, where he quickly grasped leadership of the nascent Whig protest movement with a defiant speech opposing the Stamp Act and implying that George III might merit the fate of tyrants such as Caesar and Charles I. Thereafter, his matchless oratory, his keen sense of political timing, and his ability to focus and express public resentment over British policy made him, in Spencer Roane's words, "the organ of the great body of the peo-

PATRICK HENRY.

ple." As independence approached, his legendary "Liberty or Death" oration of March 1775 helped fuel the growing martial fever in Virginia, as did his bold action later that spring in forcing payment for the gunpowder that had been removed from the public magazine in Williamsburg by order of Governor Dunmore.

Henry's stature as the foremost champion of the Revolution in Virginia was confirmed with his election as the newly independent state's first governor in June 1776. For the next fifteen years he bestrode Virginia politics like a colossus. Five times he accepted office as the state's chief executive. When not serving as governor, he sat in the assembly, which he dominated so completely that, as George Washington remarked, he had "only to say, let this be law, and it is law." In 1787 Henry led the battle in Virginia against the federal Constitution. Although he was unable to prevent ratification, his insistence on amendments protecting the rights of the people contributed to the eventual creation of the Bill of Rights. After retiring from public life in 1791, he devoted himself to the practice of law and to building up his estate until his death on 6 June 1799.

The paths of Patrick Henry and James Madison first crossed in May 1775, when the twenty-four-year-old Madison presented Henry an address of thanks from the citizens of Orange County for his stalwart defense of American liberty in the gunpowder affair. The next year Henry supported Madison's free exercise of religion clause, which was adopted by the Virginia convention as part of its Declaration of Rights. As a member of Virginia's Council of State in 1778–1779, Madison continued to work on amiable terms with Henry, who was serving his third term as governor.

By the end of the war, however, Madison had become convinced that the Virginia constitution needed revision to reduce the power of the legislature, to improve the court system, and to protect personal liberties. As a member of the state assembly in 1784–1785 he promoted the cause of reform, only to find it blocked at every turn by what he called Henry's "violent opposition." He also clashed with Henry over the latter's proposal to assign a portion of Virginia tax revenues for the support of all Christian ministers in the state. This time Madison emerged victorious. Never again would he and Henry stand on the same side of a major political issue.

When the Virginia ratifying convention met in Richmond in June 1788 to debate the proposed federal Constitution, the stage was set for one of the great forensic battles in American history. Notwithstanding the presence of a star-studded cast of Federalists and Antifederalists alike, Henry and Madison dominated the proceedings. Excoriating the Constitution as "the most fatal plan that could possibly be conceived to enslave a free people," Henry spoke on eighteen of the convention's twenty-three days, and his speeches amounted to one-fourth of all those presented. Summoning the full range of his oratorical powers, he portrayed the dangers to liberty posed by the Constitution so convincingly that one spectator "involuntarily felt his wrists to assure himself that the fetters were not already pressing his flesh."

Slight in stature and weak in voice, Madison could not begin to match Henry's oratorical pyrotechnics. But he was not without rhetorical resources. If eloquence included "persuasion by convincing," John Marshall later stated, "Mr. Madison was the most eloquent man I ever heard." Where Henry was dramatic, Madison was calm and logical; where Henry was sweeping, Madison was precise and detailed; where Henry hypothesized about the dangers of the Constitution, Madison demonstrated its necessity and its efficacy. He was the perfect foil to Henry. Over the course of three weeks of debate, his consummate knowledge of the Constitution, his steady appeal to reason, and his point-by-point refutation of Antifederalist claims ultimately proved more persuasive to the delegates than did Henry's impassioned and turbulent discourse.

In retrospect, the breach between Henry and Madison seems all but inevitable. They were men of different generations, different backgrounds, different temperaments, and different objectives. The scion of a prosperous family, college-educated, broad-minded and nationalistic in outlook, Madison was in many ways the antithesis of Henry, who was devoted above all to the interests of Virginia, regarded Madison as overly bookish and theoretical, and could not forget the personal sting of losing two major contests to his younger rival. Madison, after his period of youthful admiration, came to see Henry as provincial, avaricious, narrowly partisan, and excessively fond of public popularity. In 1791 he rejected Henry's offer to correspond, and the two men remained estranged thereafter. Madison, the Father of the Constitution, never forgave Henry for his opposition to ratification, while Henry, the Trumpet of the Revolution, went to his grave believing that Madison had betrayed the true principles of the Whig cause.

BIBLIOGRAPHY

Brant, Irving. *James Madison*. 6 vols. 1941–1961.

Henry, William Wirt. *Patrick Henry: Life, Correspondence, and Speeches*. 3 vols. 1891.

Kaminski, John P., and Gaspare J. Saladino, eds. *Documentary History of the Ratification of the Constitution*. Vols. 8–10. 1988–1993.

McCants, David A. *Patrick Henry: The Orator*. 1990.

Mayer, Henry. *A Son of Thunder: Patrick Henry and the American Revolution*. 1986.

Meade, Robert Douthat. *Patrick Henry*. 2 vols. 1957–1969.

Peterson, Merrill D., ed. *James Madison: A Biography in His Own Words*. 2 vols. 1974.

STEPHEN E. LUCAS

HITE, ISAAC, JR.

HITE, ISAAC, JR. (1758–1836), brother-in-law of James Madison. Isaac Hite, Jr., was born in Frederick County, Virginia, on 7 February 1758. He attended the College of William and Mary and was the first student elected to the Phi Beta Kappa Society there, but he left in 1780, prior to graduation, to join the Continental Army. Hite served as an aide to Gen. Peter Muhlenberg during the siege of Yorktown and later was one of the charter members of the Society of the Cincinnati.

On 2 January 1783, Hite married Nelly Conway Madison, sister of James Madison. The couple lived at one of the Hite plantations, Old Hall, near what is now Middletown in Frederick County. James and Dolley Madison visited the Hites there while on their honeymoon in September–October 1794; learning of the Hites' plans to build a new house, Madison gave their builder a letter of introduction to Thomas Jefferson and suggested that he take note of some of the features of Jefferson's Monticello. Hite's dwelling, named Belle Grove, was completed in 1797 and still stands.

Isaac and Nelly Hite had three children James Madison Hite (born 1788; died at age three); Nelly Conway Hite (born 1789); and a second James Madison Hite, named after the deceased firstborn (born 1793). After Nelly Hite's death in 1802, Isaac Hite married Anne Tunstall Maury, daughter of the Reverend Walker Maury and Mary Grymes. This second marriage produced ten children.

Hite held a number of civic posts, notably justice of the Frederick County court. Like his brother-in-law President Madison, he was a successful farmer and a proponent of progressive agricultural techniques, and the two men carried on a steady correspondence concerning farming, as well as business and political concerns. Hite eventually owned more than seven thousand acres in the Shenandoah Valley and coupled his farming activities with other business interests such as a mill and general store. He died on 24 November 1836.

BIBLIOGRAPHY

Cartmell, T. K. *Shenandoah Valley Pioneers and Their Descendants: A History of Frederick County, Virginia*. 1909. Repr. 1989.
Nichols, Frederick D., et al. *Belle Grove*. 1969.

ANN L. MILLER

HOBAN, JAMES

HOBAN, JAMES (c. 1758–1831), architect of the White House. Hoban, a "practical architect," as George Washington described him, was born in County Kilkenny, Ireland. He studied architectural drawing in the school of the Royal Dublin Society and gained experience there before coming to America about 1785. He soon set up as a "house carpenter" in Charleston, South Carolina.

Hoban met Washington during the president's visit to Charleston in May 1791. All but summoned to the Federal District the following year to prepare an entry in the architectural competition for the President's House, he submitted drawings that won that competition on 17 July 1792; Hoban then modified his design according to Washington's instructions. He was engaged by the board of commissioners of the Federal District to supervise construction of the public buildings, directing work at the President's House and, from time to time, at the Capitol until Benjamin Latrobe was given that responsibility in 1803.

In 1815, after Congress had appropriated $500,000 to "rebuild" the public buildings destroyed by the British invasion of August 1814, the revived board of commissioners of the District of Columbia assigned Hoban the restoration of the White House and its flanking executive offices. Their choice reflected President Madison's instructions that the work "not deviate from the models destroyed." Hoban largely kept to this directive but made changes with the approval of Col. Samuel Lane, whom Madison appointed the single commissioner of the city in 1816 after the three-member board of commissioners was abolished (for a second time) by Congress. During the Monroe administration, Hoban completed two additional executive offices, which stood to the north of the first two flankers, all based on, but deviating from, the original model for these buildings by George Hadfield. Hoban added the south portico of the White House in 1824; the north portico was completed in 1829–1830. He died the following year a wealthy man, having performed all manner of work related to building and carpentry and having successfully invested in real estate during his long career in the capital.

BIBLIOGRAPHY

Seale, William. *The President's House*. 2 vols. 1986.

C. M. HARRIS

HOLMES, DAVID

HOLMES, DAVID (1770–1832), representative, governor of the Mississippi Territory, governor of Mississippi. Holmes grew up in Frederick County, Virginia, where he assisted his merchant father before moving to Williamsburg in 1790 to read law. After he passed the bar, Holmes practiced law in Harrisonburg, becoming commonwealth's attorney in 1793. Four years later he was elected to the House of Representatives as a Republican. He served there until 1809, when Madison appointed him governor of the Mississippi Territory. Holmes's tenure in the House was characterized by "affable manners, his mild Temper and conciliating Character," and those who supported his appointment indicated that he had the probity, "understanding & Firmness" to hold an executive position.

As governor, Holmes proved to be a capable administrator, and his personal qualities helped smooth the roiled waters of Mississippi politics. He faced, nonetheless, several contentious interest groups, including the hosts of squatters on public lands and the leaders of the powerful Choctaw, Creek, Chickasaw, and Cherokee nations, who resented white encroachment on their lands.

Holmes also dealt with the irritation arising from the proximity of Spanish West Florida and from Spain's control of trading posts along the Gulf of Mexico. The Spanish did little to ease the growing tension, intriguing with the Indians to limit American settlement and raising customs duties to discourage American trade. With the impending collapse of the Spanish empire in the Americas in 1810, Madison sought to exploit the resentment among Mississippians to help the United States gain possession of the Floridas. Holmes was designated the administration's man on the spot, to report on the actions of Americans in West Florida and to prepare to defend them against the Spanish if necessary. His reports to Madison contributed to the president's decision to annex the district of Baton Rouge, and Holmes later cooperated with Louisiana governor W. C. C. Claiborne in occupying the area. During the War of 1812, Holmes mobilized the territory to meet the threat from the Creek Indians. The defeat of the Creeks opened immense tracts of land to white settlement. In 1816 two other great regions were ceded by the Choctaw and Chickasaw Indians.

In 1817 Holmes served as delegate to and president of the constitutional convention preparing Mississippi for statehood. He was elected governor of the new state that year and served until 1820. Appointed to the U.S. Senate in 1820 and elected in his own right thereafter, he resigned in 1825. Elected once again to the governorship of Mississippi in 1825, he was inaugurated but resigned soon after for reasons of health.

BIBLIOGRAPHY

McCain, William D. "The Administrations of David Holmes, Governor of the Mississippi Territory, 1809–1817." *Journal of Mississippi History* 29 (1967): 328–347.
McLemore, Richard Aubrey, ed. *A History of Mississippi.* 1973.
Rutland, Robert A., et al, eds. *The Papers of James Madison:* Presidential Series. 1962–1992.

DAVID B. MATTERN

DAVID HOLMES.   Engraving by C. B.-J. Fevret de Saint-Mémin, 1799.
PRINTS AND PHOTOGRAPHS DIVISION, LIBRARY OF CONGRESS.

HORNET. Originally constructed as a sixteen-gun brig in 1805, the *Hornet* was the third vessel of that name to sail in the United States Navy since 1775. It sailed for the Mediterranean in 1806 and by 1810 was carrying diplomatic dispatches between the United States and Europe. The *Hornet* was refitted as an eighteen-gun sloop of war at the Washington Navy Yard in 1811, although it actually carried twenty guns. Early in 1812 the American minister to France, Joel Barlow, delayed the *Hornet*'s passage for four months in the hope of sending a commercial treaty back to the United States. Amid much anxiety and publicity, President Madison and congressional leaders awaited the *Hornet*'s return as tensions between France, Great Britain, and the United States mounted. Master Commandant James Lawrence sailed from Cherbourg to New York in twenty-one days, arriving on 19 May 1812, but without news of any concessions from Great Britain or France on long-standing wartime restrictions on American shipping. On 1 June a disappointed Madison sent his war message to Congress, which soon declared war against Great Britain.

On 24 February 1813 Lawrence, still commanding the *Hornet*, encountered the British brig *Peacock* off Georgetown, British Guiana (now Guyana). After a cannonade lasting fifteen minutes, the *Peacock* was dismasted and surrendered and sank despite efforts to save it. In January 1815 the *Hornet* departed from New York under the command of Capt. James Biddle. Off Tristan da Cunha, an island in the South Atlantic, sailors aboard the British brig *Penguin* challenged and attempted to board the *Hornet* but were repulsed by a broadside and surrendered after a twenty-minute battle on 23 March. Biddle scuttled the *Penguin* and the following month continued his voyage. On 27 April he pursued a British warship but withdrew when it turned out to be the seventy-four-gun ship of the line *Cornwallis*, commanded by Rear Adm. Sir George Burleton. By dawn on 29 April the *Cornwallis* was within range of the *Hornet*. Biddle managed to extricate the *Hornet* and return it to New York only by jettisoning the ship's boats, anchors, ammunition, and all weapons except one gun. In 1829 the *Hornet* sank in a gale off Tampico, Mexico, with the loss of all hands.

BIBLIOGRAPHY

Dictionary of American Naval Fighting Ships. 8 vols. 1959–1981.
The Naval War of 1812: A Documentary History. Edited by William S. Dudley and Michael J. Crawford. 1985.

THOMAS A. MASON

HORSESHOE BEND, BATTLE OF.

The Battle of Horseshoe Bend was the last battle in the Creek War of 1813–1814. The war pitted the Red Sticks, a group of militant Creeks who deeply resented white encroachments on their lands, against the United States and other Creeks who sided with the whites. At stake was the future of the Creeks' territory, which included most of what is today Alabama.

In response to several Red Stick raids in 1813, Andrew Jackson, a major general in the Tennessee militia, organized a punitive expedition into Creek country. After winning several battles in the winter of 1813–1814, Jackson learned from friendly Indians that about one thousand hostile Creeks had established a village on a wooded peninsula called Horseshoe Bend on the Tallapoosa River. The Creeks had fortified the land approach to their village with a stout breastwork of logs and brush and had placed their canoes on the river so that they could escape if necessary.

Jackson arrived at the Indian camp with about three thousand men at 10:30 A.M. on 27 March 1814. Shortly thereafter he began to bombard the Creeks' breastworks with two small fieldpieces. About the same time, friendly Indians on the other side of the river swam across and made off with the Creeks' canoes. Next, a detachment of Indians and whites used the canoes to cross the river and attack the Creeks from the rear.

At 12:30 P.M., as the battle in the rear was raging, Jackson ordered his men to storm the breastworks. His troops gradually breached the Creeks' defenses, catching the Indians in a fierce crossfire. The fierce and disorganized battle raged into the night and resumed the next morning as Jackson's men searched the peninsula for Indians who had taken refuge in the brush. Most of the Creeks preferred death to surrender, and those who tried to escape were shot down. Even Jackson admitted that the *"carnage was dreadfull."* Close to eight hundred hostile Indians perished in the battle, while Jackson's own force sustained only two hundred casualties.

Although some Creeks escaped to Spanish Florida to continue the resistance, the Battle of Horseshoe Bend shattered the power of the Red Sticks and effectively brought the Creek War to an end. Even though many Creeks had fought on Jackson's side, the Tennessee general insisted that the tribe had forfeited all territorial rights. On 9 August 1814 Jackson forced Creek leaders to sign the Treaty of Fort Jackson, which stripped the Indians of more than 20 million acres of land—more than half of their territory.

The Battle of Horseshoe Bend opened the door to further American expansion into the Old Southwest. It also established Jackson's reputation as an exceptional military leader who could forge undisciplined militia into an effective fighting force and prosecute a difficult wilderness campaign despite myriad logistical problems. Although Jackson had never been popular with Madison and his Virginia friends, in the wake of his success in the Creek War he was offered a major generalship in the regular army by Secretary of War John Armstrong. Madison was annoyed by Armstrong's failure to consult him on the appointment, but he let it stand.

BIBLIOGRAPHY

Cotterill, Robert S. *The Southern Indians: The Story of the Civilized Tribes before Removal*. 1954.
Holland, James W. "Andrew Jackson and the Creek War: Victory at the Horseshoe." *Alabama Review* 21 (1968): 243–275.
Owsley, Frank L., Jr. *Struggle for the Gulf Borderlands: The Creek War and the Battle of New Orleans, 1812–1815*. 1981.

DONALD R. HICKEY

HOUSE, MARY

(1729–1793), Philadelphia landlady patronized by Virginia representatives. Until after her death, Mrs. House's boardinghouse, one block from Independence Hall, was Madison's home and social center whenever he was in Philadelphia. After staying only two days at an inn, Madison moved to her Fifth and Market Streets home, where he resided as a young member of the Confederation Congress from 1780 to 1783. He persuaded the majority of Virginia delegates to the Federal Convention to join him there in 1787, and when the United States Congress returned to Philadelphia he again roomed there from 1790 until the establishment was closed after Mrs. House's death. He also stopped there whenever journeys took him through Philadelphia.

The center of activity was Mrs. House's daughter Eliza Trist. A family friendship began then that outlived Madison himself, for Eliza's grandson Nicholas P. Trist was a political disciple of Madison so long as Madison lived. Madison's lifelong friendship with Thomas Jefferson blossomed at Mrs. House's table; other significant members of "the family" included James Duane, John Dickinson, Robert R. Livingston, and Joseph Jones. It was here that Madison met his first love, Kitty Floyd, the daughter of Rep. William Floyd.

Mrs. House was identified as "the old Lady" when she first appeared in Madison's correspondence, even though she was only fifty-one at the time. She became the center of one of the first congressional immunity cases. Duane asserted to the president of Congress, while defending Mrs. House from a fraudulent lawsuit, that she could not be sued because the many "publick Characters" who roomed with her justly claimed "Privileges and exclusive Right to occupy that House." Between five and ten members of Congress, mostly Virginians or New Yorkers, generally lodged there.

BIBLIOGRAPHY

Brant, Irving. *James Madison: The Nationalist, 1780–1787*. 1948.
Hutchinson, William T., et al., eds. *The Papers of James Madison: Congressional Series*. Vol. 2. 1962–.
Ketcham, Ralph. *James Madison: A Biography*. 1971.

DONALD O. DEWEY

HOUSE OF DELEGATES, VIRGINIA. For discussion of Madison's service in the Virginia House of Delegates in 1784 to 1786, see *Madison, James*, article on *American Revolution*.

HULL, ISAAC (1773–1843), American naval officer, captain of the *Constitution*. Hull was born 9 March 1773 at Newton, Massachusetts. Lacking formal education, he learned seafaring starting as a cabin boy at fourteen and was master of a merchant ship at twenty. Through the influence of his uncle, William Hull, and thanks to his own experience, he received a commission as lieutenant in the U.S. Navy on his twenty-fifth birthday. Aboard the U.S. frigate *Constitution*, he served under Capt. Silas Talbot, who taught him the details of ship handling and how to control a crew with a minimum of corporal punishment.

In 1803 Hull took command of the schooner *Enterprise*. He then spent 1804 and part of 1805 supervising the building of gunboats. In 1805 he joined the squadron commanded by Edward Preble in the war against Tripoli. Cooperating with William Eaton's land campaign, his brig, the *Argus*, and another ship bombarded Derna and ensured its capture on 26 April 1805.

In 1810 Hull took command of the *Constitution*. Just as he finished making needed repairs to the vessel, the United States declared war on 18 June 1812 on Great Britain. Hull received orders to join a squadron at New York commanded by John Rodgers. On his way from Annapolis, at daylight on 18 July, he found himself in the midst of an enemy fleet: four frigates, one ship-of-the-line, and two lesser war vessels. For two days the *Constitution* eluded and outsailed the British, until the pursuers, out-distanced, gave up the chase. Hull made for Boston, where he and his crew received a hero's welcome.

Lacking orders at Boston, Hull had to decide his next move. He decided to try to join Rodgers's squadron; failing that he would cruise in the Gulf of St. Lawrence. By incessant work, he readied the *Constitution* to leave Boston harbor on 2 August, hurrying to avoid a possible British blockade. During the next two weeks the *Constitution* captured three merchantmen. Then on 19 August a war vessel came into view, heading toward the

ISAAC HULL.   Stipple engraving by David Edwin after a portrait by Gilbert Stuart.
PRINTS AND PHOTOGRAPHS DIVISION, LIBRARY OF CONGRESS.

Constitution. Hull managed to prepare the ship for action just as the stranger hoisted British colors and began to maneuver for advantageous position. Hull brought his ship into close range, and after two hours the *Constitution* had wrecked the British frigate *Guerrière.* The odds favored the British vessel, with its fifty-six guns to the American's forty-nine. But Hull had outmaneuvered and outshot the enemy; the *Guerrière's* hull was riddled, the *Constitution's* only lightly damaged. The loss was a severe shock for the Royal Navy. Thereafter, the Admiralty ordered frigate captains never to engage U.S. frigates one-on-one. Hull's success lifted American spirits, which had been depressed by a string of defeats. Only four days before, William Hull, Isaac's uncle, had needlessly surrendered the western American army at Detroit.

The remarkable July escape and the defeat of the *Guerrière* in August 1812 established Hull as a hero, yet during the rest of the War of 1812 he served ashore. Indeed, two-thirds of his last thirty years in the navy were spent in shore duty. From 1823 to 1827, flying his first commodore's pennant, he commanded the Pacific Squadron. From 1829 to 1835 he ran the Washington Navy Yard. In 1838 he applied for active duty and received the choicest command, the Mediterranean Squadron. Hull returned from the Mediterranean in 1841, took extended leave, and died in February 1843.

BIBLIOGRAPHY

Dictionary of American Biography. 1928–. Vol. 5, pt. 1, pp. 360–362.
Maloney, Linda M. "Isaac Hull: Commander in Transition." In *Command Under Sail.* Edited by James C. Bradford. 1985.
The Naval War of 1812: A Documentary History. Edited by William S. Dudley and Michael J. Crawford. 1985.

JOHN MAHON

BRIG. GEN. WILLIAM HULL.   Engraving by F. T. Stuart after the portrait by Gilbert Stuart.
PRINTS AND PHOTOGRAPHS DIVISION, LIBRARY OF CONGRESS.

HULL, WILLIAM (1753–1825), politician, soldier. A graduate of Yale University, Hull was an active participant in most of the major northern campaigns of the Revolutionary War, and he won praise from Washington and from Congress for his contributions. A prominent Massachusetts Republican, Hull in 1805 was appointed governor of the Michigan Territory, where he pressed so vigorously for land cessions that he aroused much Indian resentment.

In the spring of 1812 Hull frustrated the Madison administration by his ambivalence about accepting the rank of brigadier general and commanding officer in the Northwest, as well as by his uncertainty about whether to conduct an offensive or a defensive strategy against the British in Upper Canada (now Ontario). Eventually he accepted the military appointment and decided on an invasion, moving from his Detroit headquarters against British Fort Malden (Amherstburg) at the western end of Lake Erie.

An amiable man, able to inspire his troops by his oratory, Hull remained hesitant when vigorous actions might have succeeded against Upper Canada. He retreated to Detroit, mistakenly believing his troops to be greatly outnumbered by British-Canadian forces under Gen. Isaac Brock. On 16 August 1812 he surrendered the city and his 2,500-man army to an inferior force without firing a shot. Hull's failure, along with setbacks suffered that year by the two other American commanders operating in the Canadian theater, William Henry Harrison and Henry Dearborn, eliminated any hope of realizing Madison's scheme to seize much of Canada as a bargaining chip in peace negotiations with Britain. Hull himself received a court-martial sentence of death by hanging for cowardice, but Madison remitted his sentence because of Hull's record in the American Revolution. Hull spent the rest of his life seeking vindication.

BIBLIOGRAPHY

Gilpin, Alec R. *The War of 1812 in the Old Northwest.* 1958.
Quaife, Milo M. "General Hull and His Critics." *Ohio State Archeological and Historical Quarterly* 47 (1938): 168–182.

DON HIGGINBOTHAM

HUME, DAVID (1711–1776), philosopher and historian. Hume was a central figure in the Scottish Enlightenment, the eighteenth-century intellectual movement in Britain that quickly spread to colonial America. Adam Ferguson (1723–1816), Francis Hutcheson (1694–1746), Thomas Reid (1710–1796), and Adam Smith (1723–1790) were with Hume the central figures in this ferment in moral philosophy, which today would be broken into studies in economics, history, philosophy, political theory, psychology, and sociology. Hume, immersed in Roman Stoic rhetoric and political thought, reevaluated the rational and theological bases of moral philosophy and attempted "to introduce the experimental Method of Reasoning into Moral Subjects."

As a young man Hume lived in France, where he composed his three-volume *Treatise of Human Nature* (1739–1740), published anonymously. The work applied the experimental method to human understanding, passions, and morals. Most of his philosophical, political, and economic works, including *Essays Moral and Political* (1741–1742), *Philosophical Essays concerning Human Understanding* (1748), *An Enquiry concerning the Principles of Morals* (1751), and *Political Discourses* (1752), were written before he was forty. Appointed Keeper of Advocates' Library in Edinburgh in 1752, he turned to writing his six-volume *History of Great Britain* (1754–1762), which became a standard history of Britain in the eighteenth and early nineteenth centuries. Hume became known as a skeptic, and his position on miracles, natural religion, and morals made him a highly controversial figure. In British North America, Hume's essays and history contributed to eighteenth-century intellectual thought and, indirectly, to the Revolution and the founding of a new nation under the Constitution. Nowhere is his influence more evident than in the thought and works of Alexander Hamilton and James Madison.

To the colonies came not only works of the Scottish writers, but men and teachers who were participants in the Scottish Enlightenment. Madison's early teachers in Virginia, the Scot Donald Robertson and Thomas Martin, a graduate of the College of New Jersey (later Princeton), came from that tradition. When Madison went to Princeton, John Witherspoon had recently arrived from Edinburgh to be its president. At Nassau Hall, Princeton, particularly in the moral philosophy course taught by Witherspoon, Madison was immersed in the ideas of the Scottish Enlightenment. In spite of Witherspoon's vigorous presentation of "approved" Scottish thinkers and strong disapproval of the "infidel writer" David Hume, Madison was soon reading Hume.

Attacks on Hume's skepticism, religious views, and moral position led many to question his experimental and naturalistic approach to human nature, government, and morals. Madison, however, applied Hume's experimental methods to human nature and politics. Thus, politics, for Madison, became an exact science that, properly established, would allow for reform and the creation of a new social order. Preparing for the Continental Congress and for the writing of his 1780 essay "Money," Madison drew on Hume's writings. Some scholars even suggest that the language of *Federalist* 10 indicates that Madison had Hume's "Of Parties in General" before him at the time. While not acknowledging his debt to Hume (perhaps even being careful to hide his source because of the antipathy of Witherspoon and Jefferson), Madison committed himself to Hume's application of the science of humanity to government, economics, and human nature.

Under the influence of Hume, Madison looked for the "constant and universal principles of human nature" found in experience and exemplified throughout history; he

DAVID HUME.   Engraving by G. Phillips.
PRINTS AND PHOTOGRAPHS DIVISION, LIBRARY OF CONGRESS.

accepted the preeminence of passion in motivation and action, at the same time acknowledging the fallibility of reason. After 1789, confronted by political factions, the growth of the new government, and troublesome monetary issues, Madison found Hume's essays "Of Parties in General," "Of Money," "Of Commerce," "Idea of a Perfect Commonwealth," "Of the First Principles of Government," and "Of the Balance of Trade" of particular merit. From those essays, Madison extracted ideas that he developed within a dynamic and changing political scene. The extent of Madison's conscious borrowings from Hume is still a matter of conjecture, but the commonality of orientation reflects his great debt to the Scottish philosopher.

BIBLIOGRAPHY

Adair, Douglas. *Fame and the Founding Fathers*. Edited by Trevor Colbourn. 1974.

Capaldi, Nicholas. *Hume's Place in Moral Philosophy*. 1989.

Green, T. H., and T. H. Grose, eds. *The Philosophical Works of David Hume*. 4 vols. 1886. Repr. 1964.

Hume, David. *History of Great Britain from the Invasion of Julius Caesar to the Revolution of 1688*. 6 vols. 1778. Repr. 1983.

Mossner, E. C. *The Life of David Hume*. 1954.

PAUL L. BROWN

I

IMPRESSMENT. From the beginning of modern times, Great Britain had in wartime forcibly removed seamen who it claimed were British subjects from the ships of other nations. The argument advanced in defense of this policy was that the sovereign had a right to the services of his subjects, especially in crises. After the United States became a maritime power, desertions from the British navy averaged 2,500 a year, while the needs for manpower soared because of the war with France in the 1790s. As a result, impressments greatly increased and included the removal of men from American merchant ships. The increase caused the United States in 1796 to appoint two agents, one in England, the other in the West Indies, to protect American seamen. In addition, Congress passed a law requiring sailors to carry certificates of citizenship. Because these papers were often fraudulently obtained, British officers frequently ignored them.

When the Peace of Amiens ended in 1802, British impressments further increased, and the United States sought new ways to stop them. For example, in 1803 Congress passed an act requiring shipmasters, before clearing an American port, to present a list of the crew, noting each man's birthplace and current place of residence. Impressment reached a climax on 22 June 1807 when the British warship *Leopard*, armed with fifty guns, demanded four deserters from the American frigate *Chesapeake*. When the Americans refused, sailors aboard the *Leopard* opened fire, killing three men and wounding eighteen, then removed the four as British deserters. President Jefferson barely averted a declaration of war.

The positions of the two nations on impressment were irreconcilable. Britain claimed that it could not survive if it surrendered the abstract right to impress. The oceans were international highways, and ships plying them were not extensions of national territory. Britain further contended that all seamen born in the British Isles were forever citizens of Britain. The United States, in contrast, considered a ship at sea to be a piece of sovereign territory. Secretary of State James Monroe wrote, "This dastardly practice must cease, our flag must protect the crew or the United States cannot consider themselves an independent nation." As to citizenship, the United States naturalized applicants after five years.

From 1807 to the outbreak of the War of 1812, impressment of American sailors accelerated; the number of men impressed up to 1812 was nearly ten thousand. To keep American ships out of the way, Congress enacted a ninety-day trade embargo in April 1812. Federalists played down the importance of impressment, but to some Republicans, impressing officers were no better than pirates.

The war in Europe was profitable to American shippers, whose ocean-going trade tripled while Britain and France fought. This increase posed a threat to Britain's domination of sea trade. The United States argued that, as citizens of a neutral power, its shippers had a right to trade with belligerents in all goods except the contraband of war. But the British orders in council after 1793 attempted to exclude the United States from any trade with France and its allies. They in effect denied freedom of the seas.

The British government, two days before the United States declared war, repealed the orders in council, expecting that this would prevent the war. News of the repeal came after Congress had declared war, however. The British refused to relinquish their treasured "right," and so Madison continued the war.

On 9 May 1813, the United States sent peace delegates to Europe with instructions, as in all previous negotiations, to insist that Great Britain abandon the principle of impressment. Without this concession, there could be no negotiation. But finally, in June 1814, the United

AMERICAN RESISTANCE TO IMPRESSMENT.   Columbia attempts to teach John Bull to respect American freedom on the seas while Napoleon chortles. Etching by William Charles after a drawing by Samuel Kennedy, Philadelphia, c. 1813.
PRINTS AND PHOTOGRAPHS DIVISION, LIBRARY OF CONGRESS.

States dropped its insistence on this point, and, in consequence, the Treaty of Ghent, signed on Christmas Eve, 1814, did not even mention it. Diplomatic discussions on impressment occurred off and on until 1842, but incidents involving impressment of Americans by the Royal Navy never occurred after the War of 1812.

BIBLIOGRAPHY

Hickey, Donald R. *The War of 1812: A Forgotten War.* 1989.
Tucker, Glenn. *Poltroons and Patriots.* 2 vols. 1954.
Zimmerman, James F. *Impressment of American Seamen.* 1925.

JOHN MAHON

INDIANA TERRITORY.   President John Adams signed the act of Congress creating the new territory on 7 May 1800 and appointed William Henry Harrison as governor on 13 May. Carved out of the Northwest Ter-

ritory, the Indiana Territory included present-day Indiana, Illinois, Wisconsin, western Michigan, and eastern Minnesota. Harrison took up residence at Vincennes, the territorial capital on the Wabash River. He was reluctant to allow Indiana to proceed to the second stage of territorial government, arguing that if land speculators promoted settlement too rapidly, conflict between whites and Indians would worsen. He nevertheless authorized a legislature that convened for the first time in 1805. The later creation of the Michigan Territory in 1805 and the Illinois Territory in 1809 reduced the area of the Indiana Territory nearly to the size of the present state.

Harrison negotiated numerous land-cession treaties with the Indians. The Shawnee brothers Tecumseh and Tenskwatawa (known as the Prophet) led Indian resistance to further land cessions, but at the battle of Tippecanoe in 1811, Harrison dealt a major blow to the movement. Preoccupied with the escalating war against

Great Britain and criticized for holding civil and military appointments simultaneously, Harrison resigned the governorship in December 1812. In his absence, the territorial secretary, John Gibson, served as acting governor until President Madison appointed Thomas Posey as the new territorial governor. Posey, who had unsuccessfully run for election to Madison's old seat in the House of Representatives in 1797, arrived to take up his duties as governor in May 1813. Since his health was poor, Posey chose to live in Jeffersonville, where he could be close to medical treatment, even though the legislature had recently moved the capital from Vincennes to Corydon. In 1816 he negotiated a treaty with the Wea and Kickapoo Indians for the cession of Wabash River valley lands, which expedited Indiana's movement toward statehood. In accordance with an enabling act passed by Congress, a convention met at Corydon 10–29 June and drafted a constitution. In the election for governor of the new state, Posey was defeated by Jonathan Jennings, an antislavery politician. On 11 December 1816 Madison signed the resolution admitting Indiana into the Union.

BIBLIOGRAPHY

Barnhart, John D., and Dorothy L. Riker. *Indiana to 1816: The Colonial Period.* 1971.

THOMAS A. MASON

INDIANS. Based upon the prevailing assumption that the Native American population would be assimilated into the general population of the United States, the Indian policy of the Republican period (1800–1828) was designed to acculturate and "civilize" Indian people, transforming them, it was hoped, into yeomen farmers. To facilitate such assimilation, federal officials implemented a policy, established through the Indian Intercourse Acts, that provided the tribespeople with "agricultural and domestic implements" designed to foster their acculturation. The Indian Intercourse Act of 1802 also restated the government's commitment to regulate trade between the tribes and white merchants and to protect the tribes from unlawful acts by frontier whites. To implement these policies, both Indian agents and missionaries were authorized to initiate "agricultural stations" that might serve as models for the Indians' acculturation.

These Jeffersonian programs encountered difficulties, although officials in Washington may have been motivated by an honest, if misguided, altruism. Most frontier settlers were not, however, and they readily trespassed upon Indian lands, slaughtered game, established illegal homesteads, and even murdered Native Americans. In response, religious revitalization movements emerged

among the Shawnees and Creeks, and when these movements assumed political and military dimensions, federal officials falsely charged that they had been instigated by the British. The Treaty of Fort Wayne (1809) strengthened Tecumseh's efforts to build an Indian confederacy in Ohio and Indiana, and, with the outbreak of the War of 1812, many of the tribes, particularly those north of the Ohio River, supported the British. During the war federal officials sought to ensure the support, or at least the neutrality, of tribal leaders, and they achieved some success in the South, where many friendly Creeks, Cherokees, and Choctaws supported the American military campaign against the hostile Creeks, or Red Sticks.

In the decade following the War of 1812, the federal government utilized the Indians' association with the British during the war to force a series of negotiated land cessions on both sides of the Ohio River. Federal officials took advantage of the Northwest tribes' economic dependence on a declining fur trade to purchase large tracts of land in Ohio, Michigan, Illinois, and Indiana. Indian agents also obtained land cessions from the Creeks, Choctaws, and Cherokees, but the emergence of an acculturated leadership among the southern tribes, and their expanded economic base, made them initially less vulnerable to federal land purchases. Meanwhile, Indian agents and missionaries remained unable to halt the advance of illegal white settlement on the remaining Indian land base, and officials in Washington failed to formulate a policy to accommodate those Indians who still resided east of the Mississippi.

Attempting to centralize federal policies toward the tribes, in 1824 Secretary of War John C. Calhoun arbitrarily created a separate Office of Indian Affairs within the War Department, headed by Thomas L. McKenney. After two tours of the west (1826 and 1827) McKenney became convinced that the federal government's "civilization program" generally had failed and instead advocated a policy of western removal. Meanwhile, federal agents both north and south of the Ohio negotiated another series of treaties with the tribes, purchasing large tracts of Ohio, Indiana, Michigan, Illinois, Georgia, Alabama, and Mississippi. Particularly significant was the Treaty of Indian Springs, negotiated with the Creeks under questionable circumstances and ratified by the Senate in 1825. It was abrogated by the government one year later when President John Quincy Adams learned of the fraudulent nature of the agreement. Tragically, however, much of the Creek land already had been settled by white Georgians, and the tribe still was forced to cede a large portion of its territory in the subsequent Treaty of Washington (1826).

In retrospect, if measured against its professed goals, the Indian policy of the early republic generally was a failure. Most of the tribes north of the Ohio River did not accept the government's model of yeomen farmers (although some adopted cultural patterns markedly similar to those of the Creole French). In the South, where considerable acculturation took place among some mixed-blood Cherokees, Chickasaws, Choctaws, and Creeks, the federal government still failed to protect these tribal elites. Consequently, those of mixed blood and their more traditional kinsmen were overrun by white settlers, and federal officials initiated a policy of Indian removal that later was enlarged under the Jackson administration. The failure of Indian policy during the Republican era and the subsequent removal of the eastern tribes only rationalized a long-standing pattern of Anglo-American aggrandizement.

[See also *Creek Indians; Shawnee Indians.*]

BIBLIOGRAPHY

Horsman, Reginald. *Expansion and American Indian Policy, 1783–1812.* 1967.

Prucha, Francis Paul. *American Indian Policy in the Formative Years: The Indian Trade and Intercourse Acts, 1790–1834.* 1962.

Prucha, Francis Paul. *The Great Father: The United States Government and the American Indian.* Vol. 1. 1984.

Sheehan, Bernard W. *Seeds of Extinction: Jeffersonian Philanthropy and the American Indian.* 1973.

Viola, Herman J. *Thomas L. McKenney: Architect of American Indian Policy, 1816–1830.* 1974.

R. DAVID EDMUNDS

JARED INGERSOLL.   Etching by Albert Rosenthal after a portrait by Charles Willson Peale.
PRINTS AND PHOTOGRAPHS DIVISION, LIBRARY OF CONGRESS.

INGERSOLL, JARED (1749–1822), lawyer, politician. Born in New Haven, Connecticut, Jared Ingersoll was the son of a prominent lawyer of the same name who served as Connecticut's agent to Great Britain. The elder Ingersoll was forced to resign his commission as stamp distributor in 1765 and remained a loyalist throughout the Revolutionary War. The younger Ingersoll graduated from Yale College in 1766 and then read law in Philadelphia. In 1773, at his father's urging, he went to London to continue his studies at the Middle Temple. There he became a confirmed Whig. In 1776 he left for France. Two years later he sailed for Philadelphia, where he came under the wing of Joseph Reed, the president of Pennsylvania's supreme executive council. With the patronage of this powerful man and his own acknowledged legal talents, Ingersoll thrived.

In addition to pursuing important and lucrative legal work, Ingersoll was one of Madison's colleagues in the Continental Congress in 1780–1781, and he served at the Federal Convention in 1787. He held a host of local political offices during his career: member of the Philadelphia Common Council (1789); city solicitor (1798–1801); and attorney general of Pennsylvania (1790–1799, 1811–1817). Ingersoll made a brief foray into national politics when he served as De Witt Clinton's running mate in the presidential election of 1812, which was won by Madison. (One of Ingersoll's sons, Charles Jared Ingersoll, was a strong supporter of Madison and a U.S. representative from Pennsylvania from 1813 to 1815).

Ingersoll is chiefly remembered for his work in the law, including a number of cases he argued before the U.S. Supreme Court. One of the most important was *Hylton* v. *United States* (1796), in which Ingersoll unsuccessfully argued, opposite Alexander Hamilton, the unconstitutionality of the carriage tax. Madison was heavily involved in Ingersoll's preparation of the case and provided him with arguments and sources against the tax. Madison reported that Ingersoll "appeared to advantage" even though his arguments were ultimately ineffective. Ingersoll argued another celebrated case, this one before the U.S. Senate, in 1797, when he, along with Alexander James Dallas, defended the impeached senator from Tennessee, William Blount. In 1821 he was appointed judge of the district court of the city and county of Philadelphia, a post he held until his death the following year.

BIBLIOGRAPHY

Binney, Horace. "The Leaders of the Old Bar of Philadelphia." *Pennsylvania Magazine of History and Biography* 14 (1890): 223–252.

Dexter, Franklin B. *Biographical Sketches of the Graduates of Yale College.* Vol. 3. 1903.

Hutchinson, William T., et al., eds. *The Papers of James Madison: Congressional Series.* 1962–.

DAVID B. MATTERN

INTERNATIONAL LAW. James Madison was one of those rare students of international law—the rules by which most nations generally agree to abide in their relations with other nations—who could turn theory into practice. He began reading the works of leading commentators on the law of nations, such as Grotius, Vattel, Pufendorf, and Montesquieu, at the College of New Jersey (later Princeton), and for years he continued to add their books to his library. His 1793 list for a proposed Library of Congress included forty-nine listings under the heading "Law of Nature and of Nations."

Madison first utilized his studies in 1780, during his first year in Congress. He wrote the instructions to Ambassador John Jay regarding negotiations with Spain over navigation rights on the Mississippi. He insisted that Americans had the right to navigate the river and that Spain's control of the mouth of the river entitled it, at most, to a "moderate toll." He quoted Vattel in justifying "innocent passage" through Spanish territory. Then, in 1793, Hamilton and Madison hurled quotations from the writings of international lawyers back and forth in their newspaper debates over America's abandonment of its treaty with France. Madison grumbled that the attempt to "shuffle off the Treaty altogether by quibbling on Vattel" was contemptible. He remained on the attack until Citizen Genet made friendship with France an embarrassment for Republicans.

British seizure of American ships began when the British renewed the Rule of 1756, which denied neutral shipping the right to enter ports in wartime unless those ports had also been open during peacetime. Resolutions sponsored by Madison in January 1794 called for "reciprocal favors and retaliations" to reward friendly nations and punish others. He wanted to "make the British Nation sensible that we can, by just and pacific means, inflict consequences which will make it her interest, to pay a just attention to our rights and interests." Madison's resolutions died when John Jay was sent to negotiate a treaty with England, but the philosophy behind them reappeared in the Nonintercourse Act of 1809, which authorized President Madison to resume trade with England or France whenever either one stopped preying on American commerce, as both had resumed doing in 1804.

Madison consistently argued that neutral ships must be permitted to trade and carry neutral goods. In 1806 his 204-page pamphlet refuted the Rule of 1756. At the time he thought *An Examination of the British Doctrine which Subjects to Capture a Neutral Trade Not Open in Time of Peace* was a "pretty thorough investigation" of the topic, and each member of Congress received a copy. Its reception cooled his ardor, for he soon recalled it and urged James Monroe to "consider the whole cancelled, and not to appear in your archives" (Madison usually excluded it from listings of his writings). *An Examination* appealed to John Quincy Adams, but William Plumer confessed that "I never read a book that fatigued me more than this pamphlet." John Randolph threw it on the floor of the House, describing it as a "shilling pamphlet hurled against eight hundred ships of war." Madison continued to challenge British practices throughout the ensuing war, arguing that Britain's blockade of the entire American coast violated international law, since warships were not at each port to enforce it. Only when the Napoleonic Wars ended did Madison's emphasis on international law lessen.

The great American commentator on international law Henry Wheaton attributed his definition of the subject to Madison: "International Law, as understood among civilized nations, may be defined as consisting of those rules of conduct which reason deduced, as consonant to justice, from the nature of the society, existing among independent nations, with such definitions and modifications as may be established by general consent."

[See also *Blockades by England and France; Great Britain; Impressment.*]

BIBLIOGRAPHY

Brant, Irving. *James Madison: Secretary of State, 1800–1809.* 1953.

Stagg, J. C. A. *Mr. Madison's War: Politics, Diplomacy, and Warfare in the Early Republic.* 1983.

DONALD O. DEWEY

INVISIBLES. Even before Madison became president, he was warned by Sen. William Branch Giles of Virginia that a clique of senators (later known as the Invisibles) would oppose the nomination of Albert Gallatin as secretary of state in the new administration. Less than candid about his own position, Giles was speaking for himself, Samuel Smith of Maryland, and Michael Leib of Pennsylvania—all determined opponents of Gallatin despite the Swiss-born Republican's success as secretary of the Treasury during Jefferson's presidency.

Madison chose not to defy the trio of miscreants and

seemed to acknowledge its power by naming Smith's brother, Robert Smith, as secretary of state. The choice was unfortunate, for it made the so-called Invisibles (whose name came from remarks made by John Randolph and William Macon, both Republican representatives) feel their strength and at the same time placed Robert Smith in an office he was not competent to hold (Smith had been secretary of the navy in Jefferson's cabinet). "This dreaded cabal drew life only from the President himself," historian Henry Adams noted, "in any other sense it was a creature of the imagination." No friend of Madison's, Randolph nevertheless thought the Invisibles were influential out of all proportion to their real strength in the Senate, but in fact a handful of dissident Federalist senators joined the trio on crucial votes that thwarted some of Madison's plans; for example, Macon's legislation dealing with wartime seaborne commerce was emasculated by the cabal, after Madison had indicated he approved of the original measure.

By 1811 Robert Smith's ineptness, not to mention his disloyalty, forced Madison to oust him. Gallatin also offered his resignation from the Treasury Department and told Madison, "New subdivisions and personal factions, equally hostile to yourself and the general welfare, daily acquire additional strength." Madison rejected Gallatin's resignation and chose James Monroe as Smith's replacement. Madison offered Smith a face-saving diplomatic post, but Smith rejected the gesture and unleashed a vitriolic attack on Madison, which backfired. Thereafter, Madison seemed to discount the effectiveness of the cabal, which disbanded when Leib resigned from the Senate in 1814.

BIBLIOGRAPHY

Adams, Henry. *History of the United States during the Administrations of Thomas Jefferson and James Madison.* 1986.
Smelser, Marshall. *The Democratic Republic 1801–1815.* 1968.

ROBERT A. RUTLAND

J

JACKSON, ANDREW (1767–1845), lawyer, general, political leader, seventh president of the United States. Andrew Jackson, born in 1767 in Waxhaw Settlement, South Carolina, was the son of Andrew Jackson, who died before his son's birth, and Elizabeth Hutchinson Jackson. Early in 1781 Jackson, as a fourteen-year-old, saw service in the American Revolution. By the year's end, he had fought in a war, been wounded, captured, and exchanged, and suffered the loss of his mother and two brothers. In 1784 he moved to North Carolina, where he read law with Spruce Macay.

Jackson's long political career began in 1787 when he received a commission as public prosecutor in the western district of North Carolina. Settling in Nashville, Tennessee, he established a close relationship with the influential Donelson family, and in 1791 he married Rachel Donelson Robards, the former wife of Lewis Robards. Unfortunately, Rachel's first marriage came to haunt Jackson for many years because of questions about the legality of her divorce. Jackson eventually fought several duels defending his wife's honor and killed one of her detractors. A successful merchant, lawyer, and land speculator, Jackson was elected to the U.S. House of Representatives in 1796 and to the U.S. Senate in 1797.

Long active in the West Tennessee Militia, Jackson led three major expeditions against the Creek Indians in 1813 and 1814, culminating in his decisive victory at Horseshoe Bend. The Creek War, which became part of the larger War of 1812 and broke the power of the southern Indians, gave Jackson considerable national recognition.

As a result of his success, Jackson became a major general in the regular army in May 1814 and was given command of the seventh military district, an area that included Louisiana. This appointment resulted in his command at the Battle of New Orleans in January 1815, where he won a resounding victory over the British. Jackson probably saved Louisiana for the United States, since the British did not recognize the Louisiana Purchase and Louisiana was, therefore, not covered by the Treaty of Ghent. Jackson remained in the regular army until 1821; the invasion of Florida in 1818 was his most significant action during this period. He claimed that President James Monroe authorized this invasion with a letter from Rep. John Rhea.

In 1821 Jackson resigned from the army and resumed his political career. Elected again to the Senate in 1823, he became a candidate for the presidency in 1824. In the election, Jackson won a plurality of the vote but not a majority. As a result, the election was sent to the House of Representatives, where John Quincy Adams emerged as president. An angered Jackson accused Henry Clay and Adams of making a "corrupt bargain." Using this phrase as a slogan, Jackson was elected in 1828. Any joy Jackson felt over his election was cut short, however, by the death of Rachel Jackson in December 1828.

Jackson served two terms as president. His administration was characterized by a successful effort to bring about a broader participation in government, encouraging ordinary people to involve themselves in the process. Jackson also perfected the so-called spoils system, replacing political opponents with loyal Democrats. This concept came to be known as Jacksonian democracy. Jackson also alienated proper Washington society by his loyalty to a cabinet officer's wife, which in time led to the creation of a "kitchen cabinet" to handle administrative affairs and left his regular cabinet members with lesser roles.

During his administration, Jackson presided over a massive program of Indian removal, moving most eastern Indian tribes to areas west of the Mississippi. His western frontier ideas also led him to veto renewal of the charter of the Bank of the United States. Jackson was a strong nationalist, as demonstrated by his proposal to use force

GEN. ANDREW JACKSON.   Lithograph published by D. W. Kellogg.

to prevent South Carolina from nullifying federal law. He supported the Texas Revolution but left the vexing problem of annexation to his successors.

Jackson retired to the Hermitage, his home near Nashville, in 1836, remaining there until his death in 1845.

BIBLIOGRAPHY

Bassett, John S. *The Life of Andrew Jackson.* 2 vols. 1911.
James, Marquis. *Andrew Jackson.* 1922.
Owsley, Frank L., Jr. *Struggle for the Gulf Borderlands: The Creek War and the Battle of New Orleans, 1812–1815.* 1981.
Remini, Robert V. *Andrew Jackson.* 3 vols. 1977, 1981, 1984.

FRANK LAWRENCE OWSLEY, JR.

JACKSON, FRANCIS JAMES (1770–1814), diplomat, British minister to the United States. Jackson was the eldest son of Thomas Jackson, George III's chaplain. He enjoyed a privileged diplomatic career starting at age sixteen, when family connections with the peerage brought him a succession of preferments in the Foreign Office: postings to Constantinople, Paris, and Berlin, where he married a Prussian baroness said to be as haughty as Jackson himself. Republicans generally loathed him as the trickster "Copenhagen" Jackson who in 1807 had delivered an ultimatum to Denmark (without giving the Danes adequate time to respond) shortly before the Royal Navy pounded the Danish capital to rubble.

Madison's administration was displeased with Jackson's appointment to Washington as successor to the affable Scot David Montagu Erskine, whose American wife predisposed him to compromise. Foreign Secretary George Canning had recalled Erskine in disgrace after he violated instructions by failing to negotiate the absolute terms under which Britain was prepared to lift the orders in council. Madison and Erskine believed they had found a way to resolve differences between their nations following the imposition of the Nonintercourse Act (1809), the last in a series of events and incidents originating with the still-unresolved *Chesapeake-Leopard* affair (1807). Canning instructed Erskine to stipulate that Britain would exempt the United States from the orders, provided that Madison lifted the American embargo against Britain, sustained the embargo against France, affirmed the Rule of 1756, and recognized the Royal Navy's right to enforce the agreement. Erskine and Madison had agreed only that the orders would be rescinded provided the president restored British trade and continued to bar trade with France. Madison had complied in June, but Canning quickly disavowed the pact, leaving Madison no real option but to reimpose the interdiction.

Nothing that Jackson said or did early in his mission eased the mounting tension. He insisted that only full compliance with the original terms would satisfy his government, alienated Madison by his manner and his peremptory diplomatic notes, ignored strong anti-British sentiment among Republicans while echoing Federalist opinion to the Foreign Office, and lived ostentatiously as Americans struggled with an economic crisis.

Madison finally refused to meet with Jackson again and considered him persona non grata. In response Jackson moved his embassy to New York, made a triumphal but insulting tour of New England, and remained obdurate until his recall in 1811, when yet another diplomatic rupture brought Britain and the United States closer to war.

BIBLIOGRAPHY

Jackson, Lady, ed. *The Bath Archives: The Diaries and Letters of Sir George Jackson.* 2 vols. 1873.
Perkins, Bradford. *Prologue to War: England and the United States, 1805–1812.* 1963.
Rutland, Robert A. *The Presidency of James Madison.* 1990.

MARTIN J. HAVRAN

JACKSON, JOHN G. (1777–1825), United States representative, frontier industrial entrepreneur, brother-in-law of James Madison. Born in trans-Allegheny Virginia (now West Virginia), Jackson epitomized the energy, restlessness, and democratic spirit of the frontier. During his twenty-five years of public life, he was a strong voice for the New West. As state legislator, United States representative, and federal judge, he anticipated Jacksonian democracy by championing many democratic reforms—extension of the franchise, legislative reapportionment, and popular election of state officials—designed to give the underrepresented West a larger voice in state and national affairs.

Jackson began his political career in 1798 as a strict-constructionist, states' rights Republican delegate to the Virginia General Assembly. An outspoken opponent of the Alien and Sedition Acts, he supported the Virginia Resolutions and the follow-up *Report of 1800*, both drafted by his future brother-in-law, James Madison. It was while the *Report* was being debated that Jackson married Mary Payne, a younger sister of Dolley Madison. This marriage, which probably took place at Montpelier, made Jackson a firm ally of Madison and also of Thomas Jefferson.

As a member of the U.S. House of Representatives from 1803 to 1810 and from 1813 to 1817, Jackson did more than support the legislative programs of Jefferson and Madison. He defended the presidents against their Federalist and Old Republican critics and sometimes acted as congressional spokesman for them, especially for Madison. In Congress, influenced as much by his brother-in-law as by his western origins, Jackson abandoned his Old Republicanism and embraced nationalism as articulated by Madison after the War of 1812, the nationalism that subsequently became Henry Clay's American System.

In addition to being an able politician and an effective spokesman for western interests, Jackson was an experimental farmer whose agricultural innovations and industrial and business entrepreneurship made him a pioneer in the economic development of western Virginia.

BIBLIOGRAPHY

Brown, Stephen W. *Voice of the New West: John G. Jackson, His Life and Times.* 1985.
Davis, Dorothy. *John George Jackson.* 1976.

CHARLES D. LOWERY

JAY, JOHN (1745–1829), diplomat, Supreme Court justice. Born to a wealthy New York mercantile family, Jay graduated from King's College in 1764 and read law until he was admitted to the bar in 1768. In 1774 he married into the powerful Livingston family, and with the coming of war he entered public life by serving in the New York provincial congress and was a delegate to the Continental Congress.

Jay took a forthright stand when independence was declared and worked on the committee that drafted the New York state constitution of 1777. He became chief justice of the New York high court, but continued to serve in the Congress and in December 1778 was elected president of the wartime republic's governing body.

Appointed by Congress in 1779 to represent the United States at the Spanish court and seek concessions from the reluctant Spaniards, Jay arrived in Madrid in 1780 on what proved to be a hopeless mission. The Spanish monarchy had no intention of recognizing the United States, but only wanted to see its ancient enemy, Great Britain, humbled by the upstart rebels.

Seeing his presence in Madrid as useless, Jay went to Paris and with John Adams and Benjamin Franklin worked on the preliminary draft of a peace treaty with Great Britain that was negotiated without assistance from French allies. He returned to America in 1784 and was soon pressed into service as the foreign secretary of the newly recognized republic, but the treaty he negotiated with Spain that traded American use of the Mississippi for concessions on American foodstuffs in Spanish markets was criticized by Madison and other southerners in Congress and had no chance of passage on a floor vote. Madison's researches to fortify his position on international navigation made him an expert in the field, but he held no grudge against Jay because of the New Yorker's position (which appeared to sacrifice western interests for eastern trading rights).

CHIEF JUSTICE JOHN JAY.
PRINTS AND PHOTOGRAPHS DIVISION, LIBRARY OF CONGRESS.

Jay was to be one of the authors of the "Publius" papers, intended to influence voters in the 1788 struggle for ratification of the Constitution, but ill health forced him to retire from the endeavor, and he wrote five essays. Thus Madison and Hamilton wrote the remaining eighty articles of what became *The Federalist*, but once ratification was a fact, Jay was destined for a key role in Washington's administration. Washington appointed him as chief justice of the newly formed Supreme Court, and there he made several landmark decisions that established national interest over state concerns. In *Chisholm v. Georgia* (1793) Jay's majority opinion so distressed state political leaders that the Eleventh Amendment was soon enacted to prevent individual citizens from filing suits against any state government.

Jay's diplomatic skills were tested in 1794 when Washington sent him to England to negotiate for the abandonment by the British army of posts in American territory and to solve other festering problems unresolved since the peace of 1783. Jay's concessions angered the southern and western interests and before the treaty he negotiated was finally ratified, opposition by Madison and Jefferson had crystalized in the formation of a political party dedicated to ousting the "pro-British, monarchical" Federalists.

Jay retired from the bench in 1795, only to learn he had been nominated as a Federalist candidate for governor in his home state. Elected in the face of fierce opposition from the Clinton faction in the New York legislature, Jay served six years as governor of New York. He retired in 1800 and rejected Alexander Hamilton's overtures for a spurious plan to deny Jefferson the presidency in 1800 by political trickery. Jay spent the last twenty-eight years of his life as a spectator but not a participant in the demise of the Federalist party, content to be a farmer who was occasionally hailed for his service as one of the nation's founders.

BIBLIOGRAPHY

Morris, Richard B. *John Jay, the Nation, and the Constitution*. 1967.
Morris, Richard B. *Witnesses at the Creation: Hamilton, Madison, Jay, and the Constitution*. 1985.

ROBERT A. RUTLAND

JAY-GARDOQUI NEGOTIATIONS.

The diplomatic negotiations between the American secretary of foreign affairs, John Jay, and the Spanish envoy to the United States, Don Diego de Gardoqui, formed one of the pivotal diplomatic episodes of the Confederation period. After lengthy discussions, the two diplomats agreed in 1786 on a draft treaty that looked toward some resolution of the tension and conflicts that had beset the two countries since the end of the American war for independence. In return for gaining valuable trading privileges for American merchants in the Spanish empire, the United States agreed to relinquish navigation rights on the Mississippi River for a period of twenty-five years. This draft treaty ignited fierce regional conflict in Congress among the American states, pitting New Englanders (who stood to benefit most) against those southerners interested in defending American rights on the Mississippi.

The treaty was never ratified, but the negotiations that produced it were significant. The sectional distrust and polarization they produced brought the Confederation to the brink of collapse, prompting serious talk by early 1787 of a separation into regional confederacies. Staunchly opposed to the treaty, Madison was instrumental both in preventing its ratification and in defusing some of the outrage and hysteria it aroused among southerners. At the Federal Convention in the summer of 1787 he worked to devise a political system that would mute sectional discord and promote regional accommodation and integration. The lingering influence of the Jay-Gardoqui negotiations was evident throughout the debates over ratification, most notably when Madison endeavored to convince his fellow Virginians that the Constitution would not serve as a vehicle for renewed northern aggression against the South.

BIBLIOGRAPHY

David, Joseph L. *Sectionalism in American Politics, 1774–1787*. 1977.
Henderson, H. James. *Party Politics in the Continental Congress*. 1974.
McCoy, Drew R. "James Madison and Visions of American Nationality in the Confederation Period: A Regional Perspective." In *Beyond Confederation: Origins of the Constitution and American National Identity*, edited by Richard Beeman, Stephen Botein, and Edward C. Carter II. 1987.
Smith, Paul H., ed. *Letters of Delegates to Congress, 1774–1789*. Vols. 13, 14. 1986, 1987.

DREW R. MCCOY

JAY'S TREATY.

Even after the Treaty of Paris of 1783 ended the American Revolution, Anglo-American relations remained in disarray. Great Britain's discriminatory trade practices, its retention of seven trading posts in the American Northwest, and the support it provided certain western Indian tribes in their war against the United States formed the crux of the problem. Still, it was not until Britain went to war with France in 1793 that the situation took on the proportions of a crisis. By early 1794, as a result of the Royal Navy's seizure of hundreds of American merchant ships involved in trade with France and its colonies and of Britain's increased machinations among the western Indians, conflict seemed unavoidable.

In a last-ditch effort to avoid war, President Washington sent John Jay to London to negotiate a settlement. Washington wanted the British to evacuate the Northwest posts as well as a favorable commercial treaty and compensation for the recent losses suffered by American merchants at the hands of the British.

Jay won some concessions in his London negotiations. The British agreed to surrender the Northwest posts and to arbitrate both the claims of American merchants and a dispute over the boundary that separated Maine from New Brunswick. But he sacrificed much more, accepting a completely unsatisfactory commercial agreement and abandoning the long-held principle of freedom of the seas that was central to the American position on neutral rights. After a furious partisan debate in a secret session, the Senate dropped the offensive commercial article from the treaty and approved the amended agreement without a vote to spare.

Claiming that the treaty would have the effect of transforming the United States into the nonbelligerent ally of Britain in the war against revolutionary France, Republican leaders organized mass meetings at which resolutions urging the president not to ratify the agreement were passed. But to no avail. After much soul-searching,

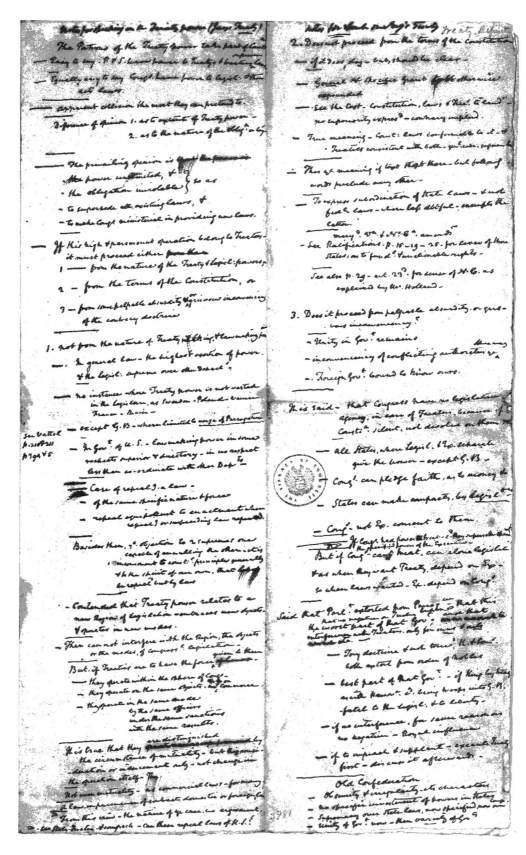

MADISON ON JAY'S TREATY.   The first page of Representative Madison's "notes for speaking on the Treaty power (Jay Treaty)" in the House, 1796.

JAMES MADISON PAPERS, LIBRARY OF CONGRESS.

Washington decided that, in order to avoid war, he would pay the price demanded by the British.

Early in 1796, treaty opponents in the House of Representatives made one last effort to kill the treaty. The president needed $80,000 to implement the agreement. But the House majority, led by Madison, refused to enact the necessary appropriations bill. Claiming the right to vote on the treaty itself, they asked the president to transmit to the House all papers relating to the negotiations. The president refused, and a months-long deadlock ensued.

The Madison-led opposition lost this fight for three reasons. First, many western Republicans, eager for an end to the frontier wars, supported Jay's Treaty because it would eliminate the British from the Northwest posts and deny the western tribes an important source of support. Second, these same westerners were also concerned because Senate Federalists threatened to disapprove the 1795 treaty with Spain, which opened the Mississippi River to American trade, unless Jay's Treaty was implemented. Finally, the threat of war with England, which was the obvious alternative to a ratified treaty, resulted in an economic crisis along the seaboard. Maritime insurance companies refused to cover shippers against capture at sea, the number of sailings dropped off, commodity prices tumbled as markets became glutted, and seamen as well as dockworkers were thrown out of employment. As a result of these considerations, opposition to the treaty dwindled until, on 30 April 1796, the House surrendered its claim to judge the treaty and passed the appropriations bill needed for its implementation.

The fight over Jay's Treaty had two important long-term implications. First, it settled the constitutional question of whether the House had a role to play in the treaty-making function. Second, the political passions it unleashed played a vital part in the subsequent development of political parties, the Federalists and the Republicans.

BIBLIOGRAPHY

Bemis, Samuel Flagg. *Jay's Treaty: A Study in Commerce and Diplomacy.* 1923.

Burt, Alfred L. *The United States, Great Britain, and British North America, 1783–1812.* 1940.

Combs, Jerald A. *The Jay Treaty: Political Battleground of the Founding Fathers.* 1970.

GERARD CLARFIELD

JEFFERSON, THOMAS

JEFFERSON, THOMAS (1743–1826), statesman, philosopher, architect, author of the Declaration of Independence, secretary of state, vice president, third president of the United States. Jefferson first encountered his Orange County neighbor Madison at the fall session of the Virginia General Assembly in 1776. Years later Jefferson remembered Madison (eight years his junior) as a shy and silent member of the House of Delegates. They became better acquainted in 1779 when Madison served on the Council of State and Jefferson was the newly elected governor of the commonwealth. The developing friendship was consolidated in 1783.

Friendship with Madison. Madison, in his fourth year of service in the Continental Congress, had played a part in drawing Jefferson back into public service after the shock of censure for his leadership during the British invasion of Virginia and the grief occasioned by the death of his wife. The latter event temporarily severed Jefferson's emotional ties to Monticello, the hilltop home he had only recently completed, and made him change his mind and accept a congressional commission as minister plenipotentiary to negotiate peace in Europe. Peace came before he could sail, however. Living in Philadelphia under the same roof, the two Virginians became close friends. Jefferson aroused Madison's interest in the reform of the Virginia constitution and, in turn, lent his support to Madison's efforts to strengthen the infant confederation. Jefferson was then preparing a catalog of his personal library. This catalog was Madison's principal source for a

THOMAS JEFFERSON.   Engraving after a drawing by Tadeusz Kosciuszko.

list of some three hundred titles that he included in a report calling for the establishment of a congressional library. Defeat of this recommendation only added to the disillusionment Madison carried into retirement in 1783. In effect, the Virginia friends changed places, for as one went home the other took a seat in Congress.

The friendship endured with scarcely a ripple between them for as long as they lived. They had unlimited confidence in each other; each in his own station was the eyes and ears of the other. They came from the same part of the country—Monticello and Montpelier were separated by only thirty miles—belonged to the same class, responded to the same intellectual currents, and shared the same republican principles. Yet they were men of fundamentally different personal styles and temperaments, and from this, rather than from their similarities, stemmed the creative genius of their partnership.

Jefferson was the bolder thinker, easily caught up in philosophical speculation, taking his cues from nature rather than from history. Madison's was the tougher, more probing, more persistent, and more sagacious mind. He helped to keep Jefferson's feet on the ground even when his head was in the clouds. Jefferson had the gift of brilliant rhetoric, Madison the unadorned power of reasoned persuasion. Both men were reticent in public; some observers thought them stiff and aloof. Jefferson nevertheless radiated political magnetism; Madison, while lacking Jefferson's charisma, excelled in caucuses and committees. He genuinely liked politics and thought it a worthy vocation, whereas Jefferson constantly resisted it. Whatever may have been the secret of their "great collaboration," none can gainsay the truth of John Quincy Adams's penetrating insight: "Mr. Madison was the intimate, confidential, and devoted friend of Mr. Jefferson, and the mutual influence of these two mighty minds upon each other, is a phenomenon, like the invisible and mysterious movements of the magnet in the physical world, and in which the sagacity of the future historian may discover the solution of much of our national history not otherwise easily accountable."

Constitutional Theorists. In 1784 Congress sent Jefferson to France to negotiate treaties of amity and commerce. The following year he was named minister to France to succeed Benjamin Franklin. From this distance Jefferson's correspondence with Madison, already begun, flourished. Seized with "bibliomania" in Paris, adding some two thousand titles to his library, Jefferson also served as a buyer for friends at home, especially Madison. No money changed hands in this fortunate commerce; the balance was struck, imperfectly, by Madison's care of Jefferson's nephews, the Carrs. He performed a greater service for his friend in the House of Delegates, to which Madison had returned as the member from his county in 1784. There he saw to the printing of the *Report of the Committee of Revisors*, largely Jefferson's work, which had languished since its submission five years earlier. Madison systematically called up the bills proposed in this "mine of legislative wealth" for action by the General Assembly. Some of the most important, such as an enlightened code of criminal justice and a comprehensive plan of public education, were defeated. But Madison scored a triumph with the enactment in 1786 of Jefferson's Statute for Religious Freedom. He fully shared its author's commitment to the twin principles of religious freedom and separation of church and state. In Paris Jefferson exulted that "the standard of reason" had at last been raised after so many ages of vassalage to priests, kings, and nobles, and that Virginia had the honor of declaring to the world that "the reason of man may be trusted with the formation of his own opinions."

From his European perch, Jefferson had a different perspective from Madison on the framing of the federal Constitution. European governments faced the problem of too much order and too little liberty, but to Madison and the Framers at Philadelphia the imbalance facing the United States was the opposite. Thus, Jefferson was startled when he first saw the proposed Constitution. "Our convention has been too much impressed by the insurrection [Shays's Rebellion] in Massachusetts; and in the spur of the moment they are setting up a kite to keep the hen yard in order." On reflection, however, he heartily approved the Constitution and recommended but two amendments: a term limitation on the chief executive and the addition of a bill of rights. He quickly withdrew the first suggestion because of the certainty George Washington would be the first president and concentrated on the second. Unconvinced, Madison opposed the addition of a bill of rights, and Jefferson, in his letters, sought to convert him to it. Contrasting the "inconveniencies" of a bill of rights with those attending the want of one, Jefferson wrote, "The inconveniencies . . . are that it may cramp the government in its useful exertions. But the evil of this is shortlived, moderate, and reparable. The inconveniencies of the want of a Declaration are permanent, afflicting and irreparable: they are in constant progression from bad to worse." In time Madison supported a bill of rights, although the pressures exerted by the Antifederalists may have been more persuasive in altering his course than Jefferson's rhetoric.

In 1789, at the dawn of the French Revolution, Jeffer-

PRESIDENT THOMAS JEFFERSON (*right*). Jefferson points to the Declaration of Independence. A bust of Benjamin Franklin sits on the table; scientific instruments are to the right.

PRINTS AND PHOTOGRAPHS DIVISION, LIBRARY OF CONGRESS.

son wrote to his friend about the idea of "the sovereignty of the living generation." Each generation, the life of which he calculated at nineteen years, ought to be free of the debts of its predecessors, free to make its own laws of property, and free to frame its own government. "The earth belongs . . . to the living," Jefferson insisted. This radical extension of natural rights doctrine was too much for Madison, who wrote a cogent refutation of the theory, showing its impracticability (generations are like flowing waves, not fixed mathematical points) and even its elements of injustice. But it was the spirit of the doctrine, rather than its literal application, that most interested Jefferson, and he adhered to it throughout his life.

Secretary of State and Vice President. In 1790, partly at Madison's urging, Jefferson accepted the office of secretary of state in Washington's administration. The opposition Republican party was born out of the collaboration between Jefferson in the cabinet and Madison in Congress. The financial measures of the secretary of the Treasury, Alexander Hamilton, together with the high-toned opinions that accompanied them, were at the root of the problem. At first the Virginians had been cooperative, as exemplified in the political bargain—a bad one, Jefferson later thought—that traded passage of Hamilton's crucial bill on the assumption of state debts for an agreement to locate the permanent capital of the United States along the Potomac. Other aspects of the secretary's financial system, such as the incorporation of a national bank, aroused further distrust. The cooperation between the Virginians was shown by the resemblance between Jefferson's opinion on the constitutionality of the bank, written for the president, and the argument Madison made against the bill's passage in the House of Representatives. The two allies also helped launch an opposition newspaper, the *National Gazette*, in Philadelphia, leading Hamilton to suspect that Jefferson, the revolutionary zealot and Francophile, had "seduced" Madison. Issues in foreign affairs further widened the gulf between the parties. In 1793 Jefferson supported the president's Proclamation of Neutrality yet sought to uphold the country's alliance with France. At Jefferson's behest Madison undertook to answer Hamilton's "Pacificus" papers. Jefferson retired from his office in 1793 but left behind a bombshell in his "Report on Commerce," which recommended a national policy of tariff discrimination against countries that imposed unfair burdens on American trade and navigation. His target was British commercial domination of the new nation. On 3 January 1794 Madison introduced in the House a series of resolutions to implement the policy, but they were swept aside by the events that led to Jay's Treaty at year's end.

One of the treaty's results was the Quasi-War with France in 1798. Amid the hysteria that accompanied it, the Federalists enacted the Alien and Sedition Acts. Jefferson, now vice president, reluctantly agreed to be the Republican presidential candidate against John Adams in 1800. As runner-up in the electoral vote in 1796, he had come into an office that, although of no importance in itself, kept him in the public eye as the leader of his party. Viewing the Alien and Sedition Acts as an attack on the Republican party, he secretly drafted a series of resolutions that were adopted by the Kentucky legislature and also prevailed upon Madison to draft similar resolutions for the Virginia assembly. The Virginia and Kentucky Resolutions of 1798, although conceived in a struggle for political survival, addressed the fundamental issue of freedom and self-government and were the first authoritative expositions of states' rights doctrine under the Constitution. Jefferson's resolutions, by employing the language of nullification, were bolder and more far-reaching than Madison's. In the drafting of the second set of resolutions the following year, Madison's cooler judgment intervened to pull his friend back from dangerous extremes. Madison later had occasion to remark on "a habit in Mr. Jefferson as in others of great genius of expressing in strong and round terms, impressions of the moment."

The Virginia Dynasty. Elected the third president of the United States in 1800, Jefferson appointed his good friend Madison to be secretary of state. The political harmony of the administration during eight years was without parallel. Madison never found occasion to oppose the president, for Jefferson's major policy goals were also his. The Louisiana Purchase doubled Jefferson's "empire of liberty" and underwrote its agricultural expansion, with foreign commerce as its "handmaid" for a century to come. Such was Madison's vision as well. The most important measure of Jefferson's second term, the Embargo of 1807, meant to keep the country out of war and by "peaceable coercion" to obtain justice from Europe's marauding powers, was the culmination of a long sequence of peace-seeking initiatives by Jefferson and Madison. It failed, and Madison, who succeeded to the presidency simultaneous with its repeal in 1809, had to pick up the pieces.

Ultimately, President Madison accepted war as unavoidable. Through all this, Jefferson, in retirement at Monticello, was solid in his support. In 1811 he intervened to end the quarrel between Madison and James Monroe, a younger friend and protégé, and rejoiced upon the latter's appointment as secretary of state. This, in turn, secured the presidential succession and the twenty-four-year reign of the Virginia Dynasty. The notion common among Federalists that Madison (and Monroe, too) was only a puppet on Jefferson's strings was absurd; unfortunately, it kept the Virginians' political opponents from recognizing that the partnership was one between peers.

No sooner had Madison retired to Montpelier than Jefferson enlisted him in his crusade for public education in Virginia. Madison was a member of the commission that met at Rockfish Gap under Jefferson's chairmanship in 1818 and supported Jefferson's plan for the establishment of a state university in Charlottesville. Jefferson planned the university, chartered in 1819, in every detail: the architecture of the buildings and grounds, the faculty and curriculum, the care and feeding of the students. Madison served with him as a member of the Board of Visitors. As Jefferson struggled to cope with impending death and bankruptcy in 1826, he addressed a moving farewell to his friend of fifty years. "To myself," he wrote, "you have been a pillar of support through life. Take care of me when dead, and be assured that I shall leave you my last affections."

And take care of him Madison did. He succeeded Jefferson as rector of the University. He supported the movement for reform of the Virginia constitution, which became possible now that Jefferson was in his grave, and even attended the 1829 convention as a delegate. In 1830 he publicly defended Jefferson and his Resolutions of 1798 against the heresy of nullification as expounded by some South Carolinians. Madison never doubted that the cause of the Union and the Constitution, which lay so heavily on his mind during his last years, was also the cause of his great friend, Jefferson.

BIBLIOGRAPHY

Cunningham, Noble E., Jr. *The Pursuit of Reason: The Life of Thomas Jefferson.* 1987.

Koch, Adrienne. *Jefferson and Madison: The Great Collaboration.* 1950.

Malone, Dumas. *Jefferson and His Time.* 6 vols. 1948–1981.

Peterson, Merrill D. *Thomas Jefferson and the New Nation: A Biography.* 1970.

Peterson, Merrill D., ed. *Thomas Jefferson: A Reference Biography.* 1986.

Peterson, Merrill D., ed. *Thomas Jefferson: Writings.* 1984.

MERRILL D. PETERSON

JOHNSON, RICHARD MENTOR (1780–1850), soldier, United States representative and senator, vice president of the United States. Born and raised in frontier Kentucky, Johnson was the son of Robert Johnson, an active local politician who had a long legislative career but was defeated several times for higher office. Richard M. Johnson studied law, passed the bar in 1802, and two years later launched his political career with his election to the Kentucky legislature. In 1806 he was elected to the

RICHARD MENTOR JOHNSON.
Lithograph by A. A. Hoffay.
PRINTS AND PHOTOGRAPHS DIVISION, LIBRARY OF CONGRESS.

U.S. House of Representatives, where he served until 1819. From the outset Johnson was a solid supporter of the Jefferson and Madison administrations, defending the Embargo and backing Madison for the presidency in 1808. His republicanism was orthodox, encompassing commercial restrictions and reciprocity, economy in spending, reductions in army and naval forces, opposition to the Bank of the United States, and promotion of domestic manufacturers. As a so-called War Hawk, Johnson was in the forefront of those clamoring for a war with Great Britain and voted for war in June 1812. Without resigning his seat in Congress, Johnson left Washington to become an aide to Gen. William Henry Harrison and later commanded a mounted infantry unit in the defense of the northwestern frontier. The unit was discharged in time for the December 1812 session of Congress. The next spring Johnson raised a regiment of mounted volunteers and rode north to join Harrison in the attack on Upper Canada. The regiment played a significant role in the American victory at the Battle of the Thames, as did Johnson, who, it was reported, killed the famous Tecumseh and was himself severely wounded. Johnson and his troops were thanked by Madison in his annual message to Congress in December 1813 for the "decisive blow" they had given to the "ranks of the enemy." By March 1814 Johnson had recovered enough to resume his seat in Congress. As chairman of the standing committee on military affairs, Johnson sponsored bills for invalids' pensions, compensation for war losses, and aid to widows and orphans. He resigned his seat in 1819, but Kentucky almost immediately elected him to the U.S. Senate, where he served from 1819 to 1829. A supporter of Henry Clay, he shifted his loyalties to Andrew Jackson after the election of 1824, submerging some of his private beliefs in public accord with Jackson. When a Sabbatarian movement demanded that the post office cease all Sunday operations, Johnson, as head of the responsible Senate committee, rejected the idea with a reminder that religion should not be a factor in determining government policy. "Our government is a civil, and not a religious institution," his report declared. Johnson also supported American workers when he denounced laws that permitted the imprisonment of debtors. Defeated for reelection to the Senate in 1829, he returned to the House of Representatives, where he served until 1837.

As the champion of working men at a time when voting qualifications were changing to give the vote to laborers who did not own real property, Johnson was suggested in 1833 as a proper successor for Andrew Jackson. Johnson encouraged those who promoted his candidacy in the North, but his popularity in the South was dimmed by his liaison with a mulatto housekeeper, Julia Chinn, who bore Johnson's two children. After Chinn's death, Johnson had a relationship with another mulatto. Johnson did nothing to conceal his private life, and at the 1836 Democratic convention, after he was nominated for the vice presidency, with Martin Van Buren at the head of the ticket, many southern delegates jeered and threatened to bolt.

Despite some apostasy, the Democratic ticket triumphed, but Johnson's tenure as vice president did little for his reputation. In 1840 the Democrats renominated Van Buren but chose no running mate for him (state favorites were to be encouraged). Johnson conducted an independent campaign, but in the election the Democrats were overwhelmed by the Whigs. Johnson dreamed of heading a revived Democratic party in 1844, but party leaders were mortified by his "disgusting popularity" with the common man. Even so, Johnson's name was placed in nomination at the Baltimore presidential convention; when he withdrew, Johnson asked delegates who had voted for him to switch to Lewis Cass. The gesture meant little, and the convention went on to nominate James K.

Polk for president and Silas Wright for vice president. Thus Johnson's political hopes finally came to an end. [See also *Thames, Battle of the*.]

BIBLIOGRAPHY

Meyer, Leland W. *The Life and Times of Colonel Richard M. Johnson of Kentucky.* 1932.
Schlesinger, Arthur M., Jr. *The Age of Jackson.* 1945.

DAVID B. MATTERN

JONES, JACOB (1768–1848), United States naval officer. Born near Smyrna, Delaware, Jones practiced medicine and served as clerk of Delaware's supreme court before being appointed a midshipman in the navy in 1799. While cruising in the frigate *United States* and in the converted merchantmen *Delaware* and *Ganges* he quickly learned the art of leadership at sea, and he won promotion to lieutenant in 1801. Duty in the Mediterranean followed in the *Constellation* and the *Philadelphia*, deployed there for action against Barbary pirates. Imprisoned in Tripoli for almost twenty months after the *Philadelphia* had run aground there on Halloween 1803, he returned home in 1805 and sailed U.S. waters in the frigate *Adams*.

CAPT. JACOB JONES.   Stipple engraving by David Edwin after a portrait by Rembrandt Peale.
PRINTS AND PHOTOGRAPHS DIVISION, LIBRARY OF CONGRESS.

After shore duty at New Orleans, Jones commanded the brig *Argus* in operations along the east coast, winning promotion to master commandant in 1810.

In command of the *Wasp* at the outbreak of war with England in 1812, Jones set sail from Delaware on 13 October 1812 and, five days later, captured the Royal Navy's *Frolic* in a fierce and bloody engagement. However, while the Americans were repairing damages, the British ship of the line *Poictiers* liberated its compatriot and captured the American ship.

Despite the *Wasp*'s surrender to overwhelming strength, its earlier victory boosted American morale. Quickly exchanged, Jones was lionized when he reached New York City in November. Promoted to captain on 3 March 1813, he commanded the *Macedonian*, but British blockaders penned up that prize frigate in port. In the spring of 1814, Jones took the *Macedonian*'s crew to Sackets Harbor, New York, to man the new frigate *Mohawk*, which sortied with Chauncey's squadron late in July to establish control of Lake Ontario. The American vessels found that the British ships had sought haven at Kingston and blockaded that port until retiring to Sackets Harbor for the winter.

After the Treaty of Ghent obviated the resumption of operations against the British, Jones took the *Macedonian* to the Barbary Coast in Decatur's squadron to compel Algiers to respect American rights. In addition to a stint as a navy commissioner, his later assignments included command of the *Guerrière*, the *Constitution*, the Mediterranean Squadron, and the Pacific Squadron.

BIBLIOGRAPHY

Cleaver, Mark M. *The Life, Character, and Public Services of Commodore Jacob Jones.* 1906.

Dudley, William S., ed. *The Naval War of 1812: A Documentary History.* 2 vols. 1985 and 1992.

Etling, John R. *Amateurs, To Arms! A Military History of the War of 1812.* 1991.

JAMES L. MOONEY

JONES, JOSEPH (1727–1805), judge, revolutionary politician. In 1776 Madison and Jones attended the Virginia Convention and served on the committee that drafted a state constitution and a declaration of rights. The two men accepted appointment to the Continental Congress in December 1779, after General Washington pleaded with Virginia to send representatives of the highest caliber to that body. The election of these two nationalists was also a response to military and financial crises that threatened to sink the cause of American independence and coincided with the selection of like-minded delegates by the other states.

From 1780 to 1783, Jones and Madison supported the cession of Virginia's western lands, the ratification of the Articles of Confederation, and other nationalistic measures. They defended the right of Americans to navigate the Mississippi River and tried to provide the Confederation with a reliable income. The two men resided at Mary House's famous boardinghouse in Philadelphia; when Congress moved to Princeton for the summer and fall of 1783, that town's inadequate accommodations forced them to share "one bed in a room not more than 10 feet square." Jones, who was as well acquainted with Washington as he was with Madison, probably deserves credit for initiating an important friendship between the two men during these years.

After retiring from Congress, Jones and Madison entered the Virginia House of Delegates, where they helped charter companies to improve the Potomac and James rivers. A lukewarm supporter of the Constitution of 1787, Jones remained neutral when his Antifederalist nephew, James Monroe, ran against Madison for election to the First Federal Congress and lost. Jones firmly supported Madison and the Republicans when political factions emerged during Washington's presidency.

On his travels between Montpelier and Congress, Madison often visited Jones, who resided in Fredericksburg. Although all but three of Madison's post-1780 letters to Jones are lost, the portion of their correspondence that remains illustrates the two men's warm friendship and provides valuable insight into Madison's life and the political events of the 1780s and 1790s. Jones is often confused with Joseph Jones of Dinwiddie County, who was a contemporary.

BIBLIOGRAPHY

Ford, Worthington Chauncey, ed. *Letters of Joseph Jones of Virginia, 1777–1787.* 1889.

Hutchinson, William T., et al., eds. *The Papers of James Madison: Congressional Series.* 1962–1991.

Malone, Dumas, ed. *Dictionary of American Biography.* 1927–1936.

STUART LEIBIGER

JONES, WILLIAM (1760–1831), secretary of the navy. Jones was born in Philadelphia and served in the Revolutionary War. During the 1790s, he was a successful merchant in Charleston, South Carolina, and Philadelphia. He served one term as a Republican in the House of Representatives from 1801 to 1803. Friends in Washington and in the Navy helped persuade him in late 1812 to accept President Madison's request that he replace Paul Hamilton as secretary of the Navy. The diminutive U.S. Navy had performed well during the

WILLIAM JONES.   Etching by Albert Rosenthal.
PRINTS AND PHOTOGRAPHS DIVISION, LIBRARY OF CONGRESS.

early months of the War of 1812, but the administrative requirements of war had produced chaos in Hamilton's understaffed secretariat.

Many naval officers had rejoiced when Jones, a seagoing man with a good practical sense of what an efficient navy required, became secretary. Among Jones's first acts were the dismissal of Chief Clerk Charles Goldsborough, who had been in the office since it was created in 1798, and his call for a reform in the ways the secretariat did its business. The new chief clerk, Benjamin Homans, had been a trusted associate of Madison's vice president, Elbridge Gerry. He improved the navy's methods of ordering supplies and presided over a rapid expansion of the navy. The long-sought building of seventy-four-gun ships of the line finally became a reality in 1813.

Secretary Jones corresponded with his commodores and commanding officers, framing their orders, discussing their cruising grounds, and instructing them on ship repairs. During 1813, when Albert Gallatin resigned as secretary of the Treasury Jones added the post of Treasury to his navy duties.

As time passed, Jones spent more and more of his time and funds supporting the naval war on the Great Lakes. He understood that the navy's actions on the Canadian border were more significant than single-ship actions on the high seas. Ultimately, Jones's work paid off in victories on Lake Erie (1813) and Lake Champlain (1814) and a stalemate on Lake Ontario, which was dominated by

ship-building contests rather than major sea battles. A heavy price was paid, however, as the Atlantic cruisers were drawn down to supply the lakes flotillas with men and matériel. Jones also supported experimentation in naval technology—such as the development of floating contact mines and the construction of a steam-powered frigate at New York—to seek new ways of defeating the numerically superior British naval forces.

Jones left office in early December 1814, about a month before the war's end. His onerous duties had exhausted and impoverished him. By the end of Jones's tenure, the navy had changed entirely. It had grown in number of ships and sailors, and its officers had become experienced professionals. His reforms were forward looking and long lasting. The navy had achieved popularity and permanence as an American institution, to a great extent because of William Jones's patient exertions and sacrifice of time, money, and energy.

BIBLIOGRAPHY

Eckert, Edward K. *The Navy Department in the War of 1812.* 1973.

McKee, Christopher. *A Gentlemanly and Honorable Profession: The Creation of the U.S. Naval Officer Corps, 1794–1815.* 1991.

Owsley, Frank L., Jr. "William Jones." In *American Secretaries of the Navy.* Edited by Paolo E. Coletta. 2 vols. 1980. Vol. 1, pp. 101–110.

WILLIAM S. DUDLEY

JOY, GEORGE

JOY, GEORGE (c. 1760–c. 1847), American propagandist in England. Joy was the son of John Joy, a prosperous Massachusetts merchant. The Loyalist Joy family fled America in 1776 and took up residence in London. His Loyalist origins notwithstanding, George Joy found much to deplore in Britain's postwar policies toward America and argued forthrightly in defense of American foreign policy positions. At times it was suspected that his family's involvement in transatlantic trade colored his views but the range of his activities indicates that Joy's concerns extended far beyond that. In approaches to both sides he sought to remove misunderstandings, explaining to British ministers that Jefferson and Madison were neither Jacobins nor supporters of French imperialism and to their American counterparts the dire situation in which Britain found itself because of the war with France. He deplored the effects of the orders in council, imposed by Britain in an attempt to monopolize American trade, and he worked actively for their repeal.

Many regarded Joy as a political gadfly; nevertheless, in 1808, Jefferson appointed him American consul at Rotterdam, although for most of the time he continued to live in London, writing letters to the press and a number of pamphlets while at the same time lobbying ministers. Joy took pains to combat the general assumption that American policies were anti-British, pointing out that Americans were no less vociferous in their condemnation of French policies. How his correspondence with Madison began is not clear, but over the years he kept Madison well briefed on British developments. The repeal of the orders in council came too late to stop the war Joy had tried to prevent. For the next two years he continued to defend the American cause, but once hostilities had commenced, few in Britain were prepared to listen. With the signing of the Treaty of Ghent (1814), Joy disappeared from political life, although he was still apparently alive as late as 1847.

BIBLIOGRAPHY

Perkins, Bradford. "George Joy, American Propagandist at London, 1805–1815." *New England Quarterly* 34 (1961): 191–210.
Rutland, Robert A., et al., eds. *The Papers of James Madison: Presidential Series*. Vol. 1. 1984.

HOWARD TEMPERLEY

JUDICIAL REVIEW. Madison did not have a clear and consistent position on judicial review. He tended to support judicial review of state acts, but not of acts of Congress. In 1787 he declared, "A law violating a constitution established by the people themselves, would be considered by the Judges as null and void," but he was referring to the possibility of state judges holding unconstitutional a state act of secession in violation of the U.S. Constitution. His proposed council of revision had nothing to do with judicial review; it joined federal judges with the executive in exercising a veto power over acts of Congress. When the Federal Convention considered extending the Supreme Court's jurisdiction to cases arising under the Constitution, Madison thought that was "going too far" and advocated that jurisdiction in such cases should be "limited to cases of a Judiciary Nature," presumably those involving the special province of the Supreme Court. Yet he informed the convention that the Court would hold unconstitutional state acts violating the ban on ex post facto law. He made no comparable statement respecting congressional acts.

In 1788 Madison declared that no constitution provided a means for settling a case of disagreement in expounding the law. The courts might stamp a law with its final character by refusing to execute it, but "this makes the Judiciary Department paramount in fact to the Legislature, which was never intended and can never be proper." Nevertheless, when he advocated a bill of rights in the First Federal Congress in 1789, he expressly declared himself in favor of judicial review of acts of Congress for the purpose of preventing encroachment on constitutionally protected rights. Eight days later, however, in a debate on the removal power, after conceding the obligation of the judiciary to expound the laws and the Constitution, he again rejected judicial review, claiming that one department of the government had no greater power than another "in marking out the limits of the powers of the several departments."

Later Madison clearly supported judicial interpretation of the Constitution. He became willing to accept Supreme Court decisions as the "final resort" in matters involving constitutional interpretation. He preferred judicial to legislative interpretations, especially in matters concerning the differentiation between national and state powers. When Congress enacted an excise on carriages, he opposed the tax as unconstitutional, yet when the Court sustained its constitutionality, he changed his mind. He would have welcomed judicial review over Hamilton's financial policies and over the Alien and Sedition Acts, for such measures convinced him that Congress was more likely to encroach on state powers than the Court.

Madison believed that Congress might control the Court but that nothing could control congressional excesses. When Spencer Roane and Jefferson repudiated judicial review, Madison disagreed, informing Roane that the judicial power of the United States "must be admitted to be a vital part of the System," especially in cases arising under the Constitution. The need for uniform interpretation of the Constitution guided his thinking. He consistently argued that "an appellate supremacy is vested in the Judicial power of the U.S." And he told Jefferson that the Framers "intended the Authority vested in the Judicial Department as a final resort in relation to the states," especially in constitutional cases. Unlike Jefferson and Roane, Madison supported the results in *McCulloch* v. *Maryland*, although he believed that the Court's opinion so broadly supported congressional powers that the Court could no longer assign legislative limits as was its proper role.

[See also *Fletcher* v. *Peck*; *Marbury* v. *Madison*.]

BIBLIOGRAPHY

Levy, Leonard W. *Original Intent and the Framers' Constitution.* 1988.

LEONARD W. LEVY

JUDICIARY ACT OF 1789. Madison had supported a strong judiciary in the Federal Convention, and, since he was the leader of the Federalists in the House of Representatives in 1789, it might be assumed that he played a key role in the House's consideration of the Senate bill creating the federal judiciary. In fact, he did not. Indeed, in the adoption of this, one of the most important bills taken up by the First Federal Congress, Madison played almost no role.

Madison received comment on the Senate bill from several Virginia political associates but carefully avoided commenting on the specific aspects of the bill he disliked. To Edmund Pendleton he noted only that "defects and inaccuracies were striking." His most revealing letter went to Gov. Samuel Johnston of North Carolina, to whom he mentioned his concern about the cost of the proposed judicial system and the apparent irreconcilable conflict between it and vicinage jury trials.

At Congress, Madison's support for the measure was uncertain. Late in July, Rep. Jeremiah Wadsworth expected that Madison would champion the bill. At the same time, Rep. Fisher Ames expected Madison would lead a moderate Federalist defection against it. However, he did not assume leadership of the opposition for a variety of reasons. His belief that it was essential to have a federal judiciary in place to enforce federal revenue laws underlay his stance.

The Senate bill was too complicated and the opposition too diverse for a viable alternative to be offered in the House so close to the end of the session, and New Englanders were committed to the bill as it stood. Other considerations also played a role. Since the House had postponed consideration of the bill in order to consider the constitutional amendments proposed by Madison, he could not comfortably attack and perhaps derail the bill. Furthermore, at the time that the House was considering the bill, Madison was directing his energies toward securing a location on the Potomac River to serve as the permanent capital of the United States.

For whatever reason, Madison made no motions to amend the bill and gave only one substantive speech. That speech supported concurrent jurisdiction and the establishment of a lower court system independent from the state courts. Madison argued that state judges were not independent enough in their tenure and their salaries to be entrusted with the execution of federal laws; relying on the state courts, he maintained, would return the federal government to the situation that existed under the Articles of Confederation when it was dependent on the states.

As the House completed debate on the bill, Madison told Pendleton that he found the legislation defective in structure and in specific regulations. He also predicted that time would make possible the correction of some violations of southern jurisprudence and that such a reconsideration of the system would take place not far in the future.

Immediately before the final vote, Madison gave a short, lukewarm statement of support (as reported in a contemporary newspaper): "though it was not in all its parts agreeable to his mind, it was as perfect as could be formed at this time, or until experience had discovered its positive defects. Had it been enacted in the form, in which it came from the senate . . . he should have been bound to vote against it. But the amendments made by the house had . . . removed the principal objections to it." Madison was presumably referring to the House amendment that provided for vicinage requirements for juries, for the other House amendments were minor. Madison joined the majority when the landmark legislation passed the House on 22 September 1789.

BIBLIOGRAPHY

Bickford, Charlene B., and Kenneth R. Bowling. *Birth of the Nation: The First Federal Congress, 1789–1791.* 1989.

Bowling, Kenneth R. *Politics in the First Congress, 1789–1791.* 1990.

Holt, Wythe. " 'To Establish Justice': Politics, the Judiciary Act of 1789, and the Invention of the Federal Courts." *Duke Law Journal* 1989: 1421–1431.

KENNETH R. BOWLING

K

KENTUCKY AND THE WESTERN COUNTRY. Kentucky and the western country held a special place in Madison's attention and convictions. Terrifying tales of warfare with Native Americans stood out vividly among his boyhood recollections. Montpelier faced the Blue Ridge Mountains, sheltered refugees from fighting in the Shenandoah Valley, and, after the conclusion of the war with France in 1763, became a stopping place for friends and neighbors moving to Kentucky, at that time the western district of Virginia. During the late 1770s, as a member of the Virginia Council of State, Madison participated in the planning of military expeditions in the West. Then, as a delegate to the Continental Congress in the early 1780s, he helped arrange Virginia's cession of the territory north of the Ohio to the Confederation.

After 1783, the transmontane region was ripe for statehood. Virginians moving to Kentucky included some of Madison's relatives and personal friends, who looked to him to manage the district's legal separation from Virginia and its admission to the Union as a state. Both in Congress and in the Virginia General Assembly, Madison was happy to oblige, for a permanent connection with the lands beyond the mountains was essential to his revolutionary vision for the nation. An effort to guarantee this future played a major part in his decision to support sweeping constitutional reform, and a commitment to the westward movement shaped his policies throughout his career.

In 1784 the Spanish in Louisiana closed the Mississippi River to American shipping, threatening the economic viability of western settlements and the allegiance of Kentucky. The Union was already troubled by its inability to force the European powers to relax restrictions on the nation's oceanic trade. In 1786, as Madison was packing for his trip to the Annapolis Convention, this double-barreled difficulty ushered in the most ferocious sectional dispute of the Confederation years. In order to secure an opening of Spanish markets, seven states in Congress—every state from Pennsylvania north—were willing accept the closure of the Mississippi for a generation. Every southern state—enough to block conclusion of a treaty—was immovably opposed. The bitter deadlock led to serious discussion of a speedy dissolution of the Union and created the distressing context in which Madison called for an urgent meeting of a constitutional convention.

Madison was more disturbed than most. Beyond the mountains, he believed, immigrants from all the Atlantic states could meet and mingle and become a single people, forming new communities to which the older ones would each be bound more tightly than any were to one another. "On the branches of the Mississippi," he explained to Lafayette, there should develop, not "distinct societies but only an expansion of the same one," not "a hostile or a foreign people" but a people who should more and more be seen as "bone of our bones and flesh of our flesh," a people whose essential interests merited the same protection as those of any other portion of the Union. The blocking of the Mississippi at New Orleans could destroy the hope of continental brotherhood and union. Short of that, it could compel the West as well as the Atlantic states to turn increasingly to manufacturing and commerce. The bitterness between New England and the South, the outrage of Kentucky, and the advent of intensive economic change could all combine to reproduce the fractured politics and social miseries of Europe. Continental union and expansion to the west on the other hand, in Madison's view, could perpetuate the mostly agricultural societies that were the best foundation for republics. Fragmentation of the Union and an inability to trade American commodities for European manufactures could endanger everything that Madison held dear. Thus, conditions in the western country deeply influenced Madison's commitment to a stronger constitution, and an image of the westward movement as a guarantee of freedom shaped his course from the Annapolis Convention through the War of 1812.

After the adoption of the Constitution in 1788, Madison's commitment to Kentucky and the West and to national expansion took a high priority. Madison realized that ensuring markets for the nation's agricultural producers involved a range of major policy decisions. His determination to secure a national capital on the Potomac flowed as clearly from a wish to make the federal government accessible to westerners as from the interests of Virginia. In 1789, in 1790, and again in 1794, he argued fiercely for commercial policies that would retaliate against the Europeans' mercantilist regulations and secure the freer trade that would permit continued concentration, by the West and East alike, on agricultural production for world markets. His anger over Jay's Treaty with the British was directed most intensely toward the clause that prohibited retaliation of this sort against the principal offender.

After 1801, as secretary of state and as president, Madison continued to pursue the same goals. Madison enthusiastically supported the purchase of Louisiana, a natural outgrowth of his old commitments to an open Mississippi and to the expansion of farming in the western reaches of the republic. The Embargo and the long experiment in economic confrontation with the British were revivals of his old conviction that the Europeans could be forced into acceptance of the sort of world in which America would not be forced toward intensive economic change. The War of 1812 resulted partly from the president's continuing commitment to the vision he had first articulated in the middle 1780s.

Still, Madison's ideas on aid to the West had limits. His final act in office was his veto of a measure—the Bonus Bill of 1816—that would have permitted massive federal support of internal improvements linking the East and the West, but at the cost of a transgression of the Constitution. Madison had at one time recommended such a program, for the failure of his effort to compel the British to accept free trade had taught him that America would have to turn increasingly toward manufactures and internal trade, which made the western reservoir of untapped lands a more important safety valve than ever. First, however, he insisted on a clear authority to act.

BIBLIOGRAPHY

Harrison, Lowell H. *Kentucky's Road to Statehood.* 1992.
McCoy, Drew R. *The Elusive Republic: Political Economy in Jeffersonian America.* 1980.
McCoy, Drew R. "James Madison and Visions of American Nationality in the Confederation Period: A Regional Perspective." In *Beyond Confederation: Origins of the Constitution and American National Identity.* Edited by Richard Beeman et al. 1987.
Stagg, J. C. A. "James Madison and the Coercion of Great Britain: Canada, the West Indies, and the War of 1812." *William and Mary Quarterly,* 3d ser., 38 (1981): 3–34.
Tucker, Robert W., and David C. Hendrickson. *Empire of Liberty: The Statecraft of Thomas Jefferson.* 1990.

LANCE BANNING

KENTUCKY RESOLUTIONS. See *Virginia and Kentucky Resolutions.*

KING, RUFUS (1755–1827), Federalist senator and ambassador to Great Britain. King and Madison were allied by their mutual support for strengthening the national government at the Federal Convention of 1787. King played a central role in the Federalists' ratification strategy in Massachusetts and through frequent letters kept Madison informed about the negotiations to achieve unconditional ratification by that state. Their alliance survived into the first session of the First Congress, in which King, having married into New York City's wealthy Alsop

SEN. RUFUS KING.   Etching by Albert Rosenthal, 1888, after a portrait by John Trumbull.
PRINTS AND PHOTOGRAPHS DIVISION, LIBRARY OF CONGRESS.

family, served as a New York senator, but it disintegrated as the Congress considered locating the federal capital and funding the Revolutionary War debts. As Madison shifted from his centrist position to become a leader of the nascent Democratic Republican party, King's support for a strong central government solidified.

The French Revolution and its aftermath deepened the rift. Distressed by the disorder in France, King pressed for a treaty with Great Britain. He led pro–Jay Treaty forces in the Senate, while Madison attempted to prevent the treaty's implementation. In 1801, while minister to Great Britain, King negotiated a treaty establishing the boundary between the United States and Canada at Secretary of State Madison's request, but was unsuccessful in obtaining Madison's authorization to seek revisions in the Jay Treaty.

Following his unsuccessful candidacy for vice president in 1804, King held no public office until reelected to the Senate in 1813. There he led the opposition to President Madison's foreign and economic policies, but when Britain turned all its forces against the United States after Napoleon's defeat, he pushed for vigorous prosecution of the war. King's fortunes rose at Madison's expense, and some Federalist newspapers even called for the president's resignation in favor of King. By 1816, when King was the Federalist candidate for president, enthusiasm for him had subsided with the victory over Britain and he was soundly defeated. King remained in the Senate until 1825, after Madison had retired to the position of elder statesman.

BIBLIOGRAPHY

Ernst, Robert. *Rufus King: American Antifederalist.* 1968.

CHARLENE BANGS BICKFORD

L

LAFAYETTE, MARQUIS DE (1757–1834), major general in the American Revolution, French soldier and statesman. Following his volunteer service in the Continental army, Marie Joseph Paul Yves Roch Gilbert du Motier de Lafayette remained a lifelong advocate of the young republic. He corresponded often with figures in every part of America, yet Virginia and Virginians always held a special place in his heart. He commanded Virginian troops in 1777; in the dark months before Yorktown, the only forces defending Virginia from the depredations of Cornwallis were led by Lafayette. That service alone seemed to assure that leading Virginians were to be lifelong advocates and supporters of Lafayette.

Among the first of these was Madison. After Yorktown, he urged the Virginia Assembly to "pay some handsome compliments to the Marquis for his judicious & zealous services whilst the protection of the Country was entrusted to him." The Assembly responded by commissioning duplicate busts of Lafayette: one was presented to the city of Paris; the other still occupies a niche in the capitol at Richmond. When Lafayette returned to France in 1781, it was Madison who wrote the congressional resolution thanking him for his "attachment to the cause" and his "judgement, vigilance and gallantry . . . in its defense."

Lafayette returned to the United States for six months in 1784. Madison joined him for a week in upstate New York, where they attended a meeting with the Oneida Indians at Fort Schuyler. He then gave Jefferson an appraisal of Lafayette's character, "with great natural frankness of temper he unites much address with very considerable talents, a strong thirst of praise and popularity. . . . I take him to be as amiable a man as his vanity will admit and as sincere an American as any Frenchman can be." A year later the ever-judicious Madison sent Jefferson a revision, "On closer inspection he certainly possesses talents which might figure in any line. If he is ambitious it is rather of the praise which virtue dedicates to merit than of the homeage which fear renders to power . . . and his attachment to the United States [is] unquestionable."

Madison and Lafayette did not meet again for forty years. Lafayette became a leader early in the French Revolution. He was proscribed in 1792; he fled France, was captured by the Prussians, and spent five years in their prisons. Returning to France in 1800, he spent the next two decades in straitened circumstances.

Madison, in his official capacities as congressman, secretary of state, and president, often led or joined in American efforts to assist Lafayette and his family during and after the French Revolution. When, in 1803 Congress awarded Lafayette a grant of land reserved for Virginia veterans, he then gave Madison powers of attorney. Thus Madison became Lafayette's agent until 1814, when the Frenchman was able to sell the land to clear his debts. Their correspondence during those years was, on Lafayette's side, lengthy and affectionate; from Madison, it was brief and businesslike.

The two met again during Lafayette's tour of America in 1824–1825. The General stayed at Montpelier and was feted at the courthouse, where Madison offered many of the thirteen toasts honoring "the nation's guest." Upon Lafayette's departure for France, Madison wrote, "he carries with him the unanimous blessings of a free nation which has adopted him."

It may not have occurred to Madison that for nearly forty-five years he had been a chief initiator of these benisons, sponsoring assistance and honors for Lafayette because he believed both Virginia and the nation should always be ready to show gratitude for Lafayette's services in the Revolution and for his unwavering devotion to the principles of the Republic.

MARQUIS DE LAFAYETTE.   Engraving by J. De Mare
after a drawing by Alonzo Chappel.
PRINTS AND PHOTOGRAPHS DIVISION, LIBRARY OF CONGRESS.

BIBLIOGRAPHY

Idzerda, Stanley J., ed. *Lafayette in the Age of the American Revolution: Selected Letters and Papers, 1776–1790.* 5 vols. 1977–.
Loveland, Anne C. *Emblem of Liberty: The Image of Lafayette in the American Mind.* 1971.
MacIntire, Jane Bacon. *Lafayette, the Guest of the Nation: The Tracing of the Route of Lafayette's Tour of the United States in 1824–25.* 1967.

STANLEY J. IDZERDA

LAFFITE, JEAN

LAFFITE, JEAN (1782–1853?), privateer, patriot, adventurer, merchant. Jean Laffite (also spelled Lafitte) was born 22 April 1782 at Port-au-Prince, Santo Domingo, to a French father and a Spanish-Jewish mother. He had a special hatred for the Spanish government, mainly because his grandfather had died at the hands of the Inquisition.

Jean and his brothers Pierre and Alexander (the latter was also known as Dominique You) are best known as privateers who established a base of operations at Barataria Bay, a point south of New Orleans. Laffite was not a pirate, since he held letters of marque from various South American governments. His legal troubles with the United States resulted from his smuggling of both goods and slaves.

During the War of 1812 Laffite was approached by the British with a lucrative offer to join their attack on New Orleans. He refused their proposal, however, and reported it to the American authorities. Laffite later offered his services to the Americans, who readily accepted assistance from the Baratarians. Laffite's contributions included a large number of skilled artillerists, vast amounts of powder and shot, and a detailed knowledge of the approaches to New Orleans. The men from Barataria played a significant role in Andrew Jackson's victory, and as a reward President James Madison on 6 February 1815 ordered smuggling charges against them dropped.

After the war, Laffite and his companions continued to raid Spanish commerce from Galveston. Laffite seemed to disappear from public view around 1825, and it was believed that he had died. In 1958, however, more than 130 years later, a descendant translated and published Jean's memoirs. The work indicates that Jean Laffite, after retiring from the life of a privateer, became a merchant in St. Louis, Missouri, and traveled extensively. The memoir reveals that Laffite died sometime after 1853.

BIBLIOGRAPHY

Arthur, Stanley Clisby. *Jean Laffite Gentleman Rover.* 1952.
De Grummond, Jane L. *The Baratarians and the Battle of New Orleans.* 1961.
Laffite, John A., ed. *The Journal of Jean Laffite: The Privateer Patriot's Own Story.* 1958.

FRANK LAWRENCE OWSLEY, JR.

LAKE CHAMPLAIN, BATTLE OF

LAKE CHAMPLAIN, BATTLE OF (11 September 1814). The Battle of Lake Champlain marked the termination of a British attempt to win control of that strategic lake and thus improve Great Britain's bargaining position at Ghent.

Sir George Prevost, governor general of Canada, had led an invasion force of slightly more than ten thousand men to Plattsburgh on the north bank of the Saranac River. His opponent, Brig. Gen. Alexander Macomb, had only four thousand men, most of them newly arrived militia, but Prevost would not advance against Macomb until the British squadron under Capt. George Downie had engaged the American naval force on Lake Champlain, led by Capt. Thomas Macdonough. For four days, Prevost impatiently awaited Captain Downie's appearance.

Macdonough positioned his squadron in a battle line across Plattsburgh Bay in order to fill much of the two-mile gap from Cumberland Head on the northeast to Crab Island on the southwest. He thus protected Macomb's right flank and compelled the enemy to attack him in a position of his own choosing. His four principal ships—the *Eagle* (twenty guns), the flagship *Saratoga* (twenty six guns), the *Ticonderoga* (seven guns), and the *Preble* (seven guns)—were anchored from north to south with their starboard guns pointing east to face the approaching enemy. The line was reinforced with a number of gunboats. Each major vessel had been equipped with both bow and stern anchors to permit the ship to swing around and bring its portside cannons to bear. This tactic would be a significant key to Macdonough's ultimate success.

Captain Downie's squadron—the recently built *Confiance* (thirty seven guns), the *Linnet* (sixteen guns), the *Chubb* (eleven guns), and the *Finch* (eleven guns), plus a number of galleys—was nearly the equal of its foe. However, Downie had been in command only since 1 Sep-

tember, and both his flagship *Confiance* and its crew were untried. Downie enjoyed an advantage in long-range firepower, but in close action, Macdonough's superior number of short-range carronades would be crucial.

The battle began shortly after eight o'clock on the morning of 11 September and essentially developed into two actions: at the north end of the line, the *Eagle* and the *Saratoga* opposed the *Confiance*, the *Linnet*, and the *Chubb*, while the *Ticonderoga* and the *Preble* took on the *Finch* and the British galleys at the south end. The *Chubb* was soon put out of action. The *Eagle*, under heavy fire, maneuvered to bring her undamaged port guns to bear and took up a new station between the *Saratoga* and the *Ticonderoga*. The American flagship then performed a similar operation, thus presenting the battered *Confiance* and the *Linnet* with fresh guns. Captain Downie had been killed early in the battle. His successor attempted to bring the *Confiance* around, but the latter had lost both her anchors, its sails were in tatters, and she was nearly helpless. It surrendered, followed shortly by the *Linnet* and also by the *Finch*, which had run aground on a reef off

BATTLE OF LAKE CHAMPLAIN.   The American and British fleets battle on the lake as British troops are repelled from Plattsburg on the far shore.

Crab Island. The *Ticonderoga* had successfully fended off attacks from four of the British galleys. The only British success was the meaningless disabling of the *Preble*. The battle had lasted just over two hours and had resulted in a decisive American victory. General Prevost, dismayed by the turn of events, broke off his halfhearted attack on Macomb and withdrew to Canada.

The victory had a considerable impact on the negotiations at Ghent and was a factor in the British diplomatic retreat from a position of a peace based on current military possession to one of status quo ante, thus restoring eastern Maine to the United States. Antiwar sentiment in the northeast was somewhat lessened, most notably in Vermont. Macdonough's triumph would be a source of the strong feeling of national pride that developed after the war.

BIBLIOGRAPHY

Everest, Allan S. *The War of 1812 in the Champlain Valley*. 1981.
Mahan, Captain A. T. *Sea Power in its Relations to the War of 1812*.
Vol. 2. 1905.
Muller, Charles G. *The Proudest Day: Macdonough on Lake Champlain*. 1960.
Roosevelt, Theodore. *The Naval War of 1812*. 1904.

IAN C. B. PEMBERTON

LAKE ERIE, BATTLE OF (10 September 1813). A famous action fought off Put-in-Bay, Ohio, between nine vessels of Oliver Hazard Perry's squadron, spearheaded by the brigs *Lawrence* and *Niagara*, and the six vessels of Capt. Robert Heriot Barclay's squadron, led by the ships *Detroit* and *Queen Charlotte*, the Battle of Lake Erie lasted less than four hours. Perry came perilously close to being beaten in an action in which he overmatched his opponent in weight of metal, seamen, and vessels. Severely damaged, Perry's flagship *Lawrence* struck its colors after Perry transferred his flag to the *Niagara* and redeemed the day.

Perry had 532 men (329 seamen of all ranks; 203 lands-

BATTLE OF LAKE ERIE.   Commodore Oliver Hazard Perry being transferred from the *Lawrence* to the *Niagara*. Engraving by T. Phillibrown after the painting by W. H. Powell.
PRINTS AND PHOTOGRAPHS DIVISION, LIBRARY OF CONGRESS.

men and soldiers) to Barclay's 424 (55 British and 108 Canadian seamen; 150 troops from a British regular regiment, 100 Royal Newfoundland troops, and some landsmen). He also outgunned Barclay, and, mainly because of Perry's pivot guns, the broadside discrepancy considerably favored the Americans. Perry's squadron lost 34 killed and 96 wounded, including 22 killed and 61 wounded on the *Lawrence*. Barclay lost 41 killed and 93 wounded, with 11 killed and 40 wounded on the *Detroit* and 18 killed and 24 wounded on the *Queen Charlotte*.

Perry has been praised for building a powerful squadron and for single-handedly winning the fight. However, he has been criticized as an inferior commodore who gave contradictory fighting instructions and who led a straggling line. The action opened the door for Gen. William Henry Harrison's army to reconquer the western lake region and also generated a long-running factional dispute between rival supporters of Perry and those of his second in command, Jesse D. Elliott.

BIBLIOGRAPHY

Drake, Frederick C. "A Loss of Mastery: The British Squadron on Lake Erie, May–September, 1813." *Journal of Erie Studies* 17, 2 (Fall 1988): 47–75.
Dudley, William S., ed. *The Naval War of 1812.* Vol. 2. 1992.
Mahan, Alfred Thayer. *Sea Power in Its Relations to the War of 1812.* Vol. 2. 1905.
Palmer, Michael A. "A Failure of Command, Control, and Communication: Oliver Hazard Perry and the Battle of Lake Erie." *Journal of Erie Studies* 17, 2 (Fall 1988): 7–26.
Welsh, William J., and David C. Skaggs, eds. *War on the Great Lakes: Essays Commemorating the 175th Anniversary of the Battle of Lake Erie.* 1991.

FREDERICK C. DRAKE

LATIN AMERICA. Several decades after the emergence of the United States as an independent country, much of the vast region in the western hemisphere to the south of the new republic began a protracted series of revolutionary struggles to escape Spanish colonialism. By the mid 1820s, the shape of an independent Latin America had taken clear form. For the most part, citizens of the United States hailed these anticolonial revolutions as the extension and fulfillment of their own republican revolution of 1776. American support of Latin American independence also arose from considerations of interest as well as principle; the demise of Spanish mercantilism in the western hemisphere promised both to enhance the security of the United States and at the same time to create valuable trading partners in the new republics to the south.

Madison followed this emergence of modern Latin America with unusual interest and warm sympathy. As secretary of state and then president, his support of aspiring revolutionaries, including the notoriously reckless Francisco Miranda of Venezuela, had to be tempered by prudent considerations of law and diplomacy. Following his retirement from the presidency in early 1817, when the revolutions entered their climactic phase and when his successor, James Monroe, regularly informed and consulted him on developments in the struggling Spanish colonies, Madison's interest in Latin America deepened. He urged President Monroe to extend every lawful manifestation of American approval and support to the Spanish American insurgents and welcomed formal American recognition of the new republics during the independence movements of the early 1820s. Then, when the European nations making up the reactionary Holy Alliance appeared to threaten Latin American independence, Madison welcomed British overtures for a joint Anglo-American stance against that threat. He understood that Britain's motives were self-interested and quite different from—indeed, from the commercial perspective, antithetical to—those of the United States, but Madison also believed that all available help should be employed in what he called "the great struggle of the Epoch" between republican liberty and autocratic despotism.

Much of Madison's thinking on Latin American independence was conventional. With his characteristically sharp eye, however, he also explored the broader range of likely repercussions for the United States. He suggested, for instance, that the liberation of Spanish America would doubtless accelerate the trend already under way in his own republic toward increased manufacturing. As Madison peered into the future, he saw the new Hispanic-American republics occupying the former place of the United States as the most efficient provider of produce and raw materials for European markets. But Madison did not fear this competition, for he believed that a more mature and developed United States would logically take advantage of the vast, unencumbered Latin American market for imported American manufactures. To this extent Madison's views on Latin America reflected his customary integration of diplomacy, geopolitics, and political economy.

BIBLIOGRAPHY

Johnson, John J. *A Hemisphere Apart: The Foundations of United States Policy toward Latin America.* 1990.
McCoy, Drew R. *The Last of the Fathers: James Madison and the Republican Legacy.* 1989.
Whitaker, Arthur P. *The United States and the Independence of Latin America, 1800–1830.* 1941.

DREW R. MCCOY

LATROBE, BENJAMIN HENRY (1764–1820), foremost engineer and architect in the early Republic. Born in Fulneck, Yorkshire, England, Latrobe was educated there, then in schools in Germany, according to the rigorous tradition of the Moravian (United Brethren) Church. After his return to London in 1783, he worked as an engineer and was trained in and practiced architecture, gaining valuable experience but finding few opportunities to distinguish himself. The death of his first wife in 1793 and the effects of the outbreak of war on public works in England led him into deep emotional and financial distress, and, seeking a new life, he sailed for America in November 1795.

Latrobe spent the next three years in Virginia. He won the competition for the Virginia Penitentiary in 1797, did mapping and surveying for landowners and projectors, and designed one residence in Norfolk, as well as several "castles in the air"—but he found the Virginia gentry tight with their purses and their hospitality in their dealings with professional men. He thus had ample time to sketch and draw, producing during these years a remarkable record of Virginia life and landscape. He found more fertile ground for his livelihood and ambitions in Philadelphia. His designs for the Bank of Pennsylvania, which introduced the neo-Greek architectural style to America, and for the Philadelphia Water Works, a significant technological achievement, won much praise, and he was elected to the American Philosophical Society in 1799.

In 1802 President Jefferson brought Latrobe to Washington to help with the design of dry docks for the U.S. Navy. The next year Jefferson appointed him "surveyor of the public buildings." Latrobe's primary responsibility was to direct construction of the Capitol, but he waged a vigorous campaign against William Thornton's accepted design for the building, criticizing work already completed and pressing for changes in the interiors. Jefferson resisted most of these suggestions, yielding only when convinced that structural necessity required it. He admired Latrobe's talents and work but questioned his estimates, a point of view Jefferson passed on to Madison upon leaving office in 1809.

Latrobe had some advantage in his relations with the new president; his second wife, Mary Elizabeth (Hazlehurst), had been Dolley Madison's friend since childhood. Moreover, the Madisons appreciated his "elegant taste," as Dolley put it, in furnishing the interiors of the White House. But as Latrobe observed to his father-in-law, intending it quite favorably: "Mr. Jefferson is a man out of a book. Mr. Madison more a man of the world." When Congress, judging Latrobe to be extravagant, terminated appropriations for construction at the Capitol in 1811–1812, Madison made no move to intervene. This elicited a salvo

BENJAMIN HENRY LATROBE.   Watercolor by Raphaelle Peale, c. 1810.   MARYLAND HISTORICAL SOCIETY, BALTIMORE.

from the architect: "[H]onest & right intentioned as is our cold-blooded president, you might as well stroke an Armadillo with a feather by way of making the animal feel, as try to move *him* by words from any of his opinions or purposes." Latrobe went off to Pittsburgh to build steamboats for Robert Fulton, a venture begun in hope of financial reward but soon ended in more disputes and debts.

Madison recalled Latrobe to Washington in 1815 to restore the demolished Capitol, yet agreed to proposed alterations, notably to the House chamber (now Statuary Hall), that Jefferson had consistently opposed. Compared to his predecessor, Madison took little interest in design matters. When arguments about changes and costs revived, Madison worked with Congress to put the entire business under a single commissioner and effectively subordinated Latrobe to his new official, Samuel Lane. Differences with Lane, and with President Monroe, caused Latrobe to resign his post in 1817. He died three years later of yellow fever while working to complete the New Orleans Waterworks.

BIBLIOGRAPHY

Carter, Edward C., II, et al., eds. *The Papers of Benjamin Latrobe.* 1977–.

Hamlin, Talbot. *Benjamin Henry Latrobe.* 1955.

Rutland, Robert A., et al., eds. *The Papers of James Madison:* Presidential Series. Vols. 1, 2. 1962–1992.

C. M. HARRIS

LAWRENCE, JAMES

LAWRENCE, JAMES (1781–1813), naval officer. Born in Burlington, New Jersey, James Lawrence was appointed a midshipman in the U.S. Navy on 4 September 1798. He saw active service in both the Quasi-War with France and the Barbary Wars, earning a reputation as a brave and capable officer. In the Barbary Wars, he participated in seven actions, including the destruction of the captured American frigate *Philadelphia.* Following the cessation of hostilities with Tripoli, Lawrence was ordered home, where he commanded a succession of vessels charged with protecting American shipping and suppressing smuggling. In late November 1811 Lawrence was ordered to convey diplomatic dispatches to Europe in the sloop of war *Hornet.* When Lawrence returned aboard the *Hornet* in May 1812, the news he carried dashed remaining hopes that hostilities with England might be averted.

CAPT. JAMES LAWRENCE.   Engraving by William Rollinson after a portrait by Gilbert Stuart.
PRINTS AND PHOTOGRAPHS DIVISION, LIBRARY OF CONGRESS.

On 21 June, three days after war was declared on Great Britain, Lawrence sailed from New York in the *Hornet* as part of a five-ship squadron under the command of John Rodgers. The American squadron cruised the North Atlantic for two months but enjoyed little success, netting only seven prizes, two of which were captured by the *Hornet.*

After refitting the *Hornet,* Lawrence was ordered on a cruise under William Bainbridge, commander of the *Constitution.* On 27 October the two warships left Boston for the coast of Brazil. There they planned to rendezvous with the frigate *Essex* and then attack British shipping in the South Atlantic. Arriving off Salvador in mid December, the Americans discovered the British ship *Bonne Citoyenne* at anchor in the harbor. Despite the departure of the *Constitution* and a formal challenge from Lawrence, the commander of the British warship refused to sail out and engage the *Hornet.* Lawrence blockaded the *Bonne Citoyenne* until the *Hornet* was driven off by the arrival of an enemy ship of the line. Cruising alone now, Lawrence made his way northward along the South American coast. On 4 February 1813 he captured the privateer brig *Resolution.* Twenty days later he engaged the British brig *Peacock* off the Demerara River. The *Hornet*'s well-trained gun crews delivered their fire into the enemy brig with devastating effect. After fifteen minutes, a battered and sinking *Peacock* struck her colors.

The *Hornet*'s victory, the sixth by an American over a Royal Navy vessel in ship-to-ship combat, lifted American morale and made Lawrence a national hero. He arrived home on 24 March to find that he had been promoted to captain; in early April, a grateful Navy Department offered him provisional command of the *Constitution.* It was the first in a series of changing orders that left Lawrence in command, not of "Old Ironsides," but of the frigate *Chesapeake.* Lawrence assumed command of that ship on 20 May and by the end of the month was ready to sail. His cruising orders called for him to attack British shipping in the waters off Newfoundland and Nova Scotia. On 1 June, with an enemy vessel in sight of his anchorage, Lawrence sailed out of Boston Harbor to engage in combat. The *Chesapeake* and the British ship, the frigate *Shannon,* were relatively equal in size and weight of broadside fire, with the *Chesapeake* having the edge in men. The *Shannon*'s one clear advantage was that its captain and crew had served long together and were experts in gunnery. The two frigates dueled yardarm-to-yardarm, with the *Shannon* finally carrying the day in a boarding action. Lawrence was mortally wounded during the battle and died three days later en route to Halifax, where he was buried with full military honors. His remains were later reinterred at Trinity Church, New York. Lawrence's words, "Don't give up the ship," uttered after he was wounded, became a rallying cry for the navy.

BIBLIOGRAPHY

Dudley, William S. *The Naval War of 1812: A Documentary History*. 2 vols. 1985.
Gleaves, Albert. *James Lawrence, Captain, United States Navy, Commander of the "Chesapeake."* 1904.
Roosevelt, Theodore. *The Naval War of 1812*. Repr. 1987.

CHARLES E. BRODINE, JR.

LEE, HENRY (1756–1818), Revolutionary War hero, governor of Virginia, Federalist, friend of James Madison. Member of one of Virginia's first families and father of Robert E. Lee, Henry Lee was born in Prince William County, the son of Henry and Lucy Grymes Lee. He graduated in 1773 from the College of New Jersey (later Princeton), where he and his classmate Madison became close friends. That friendship, which Lee esteemed as "the first blessing of my life," flourished in the years before 1795 but was severely strained thereafter by Lee's political partisanship as a Federalist.

Lee was preparing to study law at London's Middle Temple when the approaching Revolution caused him to cancel his plans and join the patriot struggle for independence. Appointed a captain in a Virginia cavalry unit in 1776, the next year he joined the Continental army. His daring skills as commander of an irregular force of cavalry and infantry known as Lee's legion, which fought brilliantly both in New Jersey and across the Carolinas, earned him the enduring admiration and respect of George Washington. Despondent about the needless cruelty of war and his own failure to obtain the fuller glory he craved, Lee resigned his commission as lieutenant colonel in 1782. His "deep melancholy," as Madison described it, belied reality; his achievements as soldier and patriot had been extraordinary, and his military genius, equaled by few of his generation, made "Light-Horse Harry," as he was now known, one of the Revolution's foremost heroes.

In 1782 Lee married a wealthy cousin, Matilda Lee, heiress to a ten thousand-acre estate that included Stratford Hall, and entered politics. Over the next sixteen years he served successively as a delegate to the Continental Congress, as a member of the Virginia constitutional ratifying convention, as governor of Virginia, as a member of Congress, and, on three separate occasions, as a member of the Virginia legislature. A staunch advocate of union and a strong national government, he was Madison's firm ally in the struggle to ratify the Constitution. At the Virginia convention Lee repeatedly challenged Patrick Henry and helped to blunt his assault on the Constitution. After Virginia ratified, Lee played a leading role in state government. During these years, and in particular during his three one-year terms as governor beginning in 1791, he maintained an active correspondence with Madison. Lee shared his friend's misgivings about the motives and policies of Alexander Hamilton and was especially critical of Hamilton's financial program, which he denounced as a "base perversion of the Constitution." He mirrored the opinions of most Virginians when he asserted that funding, assumption, and the creation of a national bank would create a powerful moneyed interest capable of destroying the experiment in self-government. To promote opposition, Lee joined Madison in encouraging their old Princeton classmate, Philip Freneau, to launch the *National Gazette*.

In 1794 President Washington called for Lee to command the military expedition that suppressed the Whiskey Rebellion in Pennsylvania. Lee was disturbed by that insurgency because he feared it might throw the country into anarchy, where chaos and mob rule would inevitably lead to civil bloodshed and disunion. He returned from the expedition a chastened conservative, convinced that the Federalist party's policies and leaders were the surest guarantors of stability and security. Thereafter he was unwavering in his support of the Federalist party. In 1798 he stoutly defended the Alien and Sedition Acts and led the opposition in the Virginia Assembly to Madison's Virginia Resolutions. Failing to block their passage, he won election to Congress and continued his fight there. Two years later, defeated and discouraged because of Jefferson's accession to the presidency, he quit public life. Though he detested Jefferson, Lee maintained friendly feelings for Madison, whom he considered an honest but misguided patriot.

Lee's retirement was marked by misfortune and tragedy. A poor businessman, he lost a fortune in speculative land ventures and commercial projects, such as the construction of a canal at the Great Falls of the Potomac, in which he tried unsuccessfully to involve Madison as partner. He landed in debtor's prison in 1808–1809. His second wife, Anne Carter of Shirley, whom he had married in 1793 after his first wife died, and their five children were forced to leave Stratford for a more modest residence. In the Baltimore riot of 1812 Lee received injuries inflicted by a Republican mob from which he never recovered. He spent the last five years of his life trying to regain his health in the West Indies, estranged from his family. He died while returning to Virginia and was buried on Cumberland Island, Georgia.

HENRY ("LIGHT-HORSE HARRY") LEE.   Print after a portrait by Alonzo Chappel.
PRINTS AND PHOTOGRAPHS DIVISION, LIBRARY OF CONGRESS.

BIBLIOGRAPHY

Hendrick, Burton J. *The Lees of Virginia: Biography of a Family.* 1935.

Royster, Charles. *Light-Horse Harry Lee and the Legacy of the American Revolution.* 1981.

CHARLES D. LOWERY

LEE, RICHARD HENRY (1733–1794), revolutionary statesman and senator from Virginia. From 1758, when he entered the Virginia House of Burgesses, until 1792, when he resigned his seat in the first Senate convened under the Constitution of 1787, Lee was a major force in the politics of the times. Thirty years after Lee's death, James Madison remembered him as "one of the distinguished worthies of the distinguished times in which his lot was cast." Lee was a man, Madison insisted, of "patriotic zeal," "captivating eloquence," and "polished manners."

On 7 June 1776, Lee made the call in Congress for independence. It was not only the necessary first step toward the Declaration of Independence but set in motion the political events that would culminate in the Constitution of 1787, a document Lee could not bring himself to support.

Throughout his political career, Lee advocated what he called "a regulated Liberty." He saw the necessity of a government sufficient to curb both "the fury of a Mob" and "the art, cunning, and industry of wicked, vicious, and avaricious men"; but liberty also demanded a government limited in scope. In its conception of the purposes and objects of government, Lee's political theory bore a striking resemblance to that of Madison. Yet the two men differed widely on the means best suited to achieve those ends.

In the recesses of his political heart, Lee was an Antifederalist, a foe of big national government, and an ardent defender of state sovereignty. Although Lee thought the Constitution contained many worthy parts,

RICHARD HENRY LEE.
PRINTS AND PHOTOGRAPHS DIVISION, LIBRARY OF CONGRESS.

it would ultimately tend, he said, toward an elective despotism.

To reward his ally and to punish Madison, Patrick Henry orchestrated Lee's election to the new Senate, where Lee fought to keep the new government as limited as possible, in contrast to what he saw as the pretensions of Madison and the Federalists. Lee's writings mark him as a public man committed to what in time would be called a states' rights philosophy.

BIBLIOGRAPHY

Chitwood, Oliver Perry. *Richard Henry Lee: Statesman of the Revolution.* 1967.
McDowell, Gary L. "Richard Henry Lee and the Quest for Constitutional Liberty." In *The American Founding: Politics, Statesmanship, and the Constitution.* Edited by Ralph A. Rossum and Gary L. McDowell. 1981.
Matthews, John Carter. *Richard Henry Lee.* 1978.

GARY L. MCDOWELL

LEIB, MICHAEL (1760–1822), physician, representative, senator. Leib was born in Philadelphia and, after a common school education, studied medicine under Benjamin Rush. He served as a surgeon with the Philadelphia militia from 1780 to 1783 and went on to practice medicine in that city at various hospitals and as a member of the College of Physicians.

Attracted to politics, Leib served three years in the Pennsylvania legislature representing Philadelphia County, then was elected to the House of Representatives in 1798. There he established himself as a forthright, and at times extreme, Republican voice until his retirement from the House in 1806. He supported the Jeffersonian agenda of judiciary reform, reduced military spending, and elimination of internal taxes. He also pressed hard on the patronage question, pushing to replace all Federalists with Republicans, especially in his own Pennsylvania bailiwick. In Philadelphia, Leib wielded tremendous influence in concert with William Duane, the editor of the *Aurora*, probably the most influential Republican newspaper in the country. Their dominance left many Pennsylvania Republicans chafing and led to the emergence of a third party in that state's politics in 1804.

Most of Leib's political decisions from this point on, in both national and state affairs, can be traced to personal animosities in Pennsylvania politics. He enthusiastically supported Madison as a presidential elector in 1808. Elected to the U.S. Senate in 1809, he quickly moved into opposition to the Madison administration over patronage and because of his personal hatred for Secretary of the Treasury Albert Gallatin. As one of the Senate Invisibles, Leib voted for war with Great Britain

MICHAEL LEIB.   Portrait by C. B.-J. Fevret de Saint-Mémin.
PRINTS AND PHOTOGRAPHS DIVISION, LIBRARY OF CONGRESS.

in 1812, although it was said he was privately opposed to it. Similarly, he voted for Madison's renomination in the Republican caucus of 1812 but openly supported DeWitt Clinton for president, backing a short-lived anti-Madison newspaper called the *Whig Chronicle*. Madison retaliated by awarding Pennsylvania political plums to Leib's enemies. In 1814 Postmaster General Gideon Granger appointed Leib Philadelphia postmaster, incurring Madison's displeasure. In short order, Madison removed Granger from office, and Leib was dismissed in early 1815. Despite waning influence, Leib returned to the Pennsylvania legislature from 1817 to 1821 and held local office until his death.

BIBLIOGRAPHY

Higginbotham, Sanford W. *The Keystone in the Democratic Arch: Pennsylvania Politics, 1800–1816.* 1952.
Ketchum, Ralph. *James Madison: A Biography.* 1971.
Stagg, J. C. A. *Mr. Madison's War: Politics, Diplomacy, and Warfare in the Early American Republic, 1783–1830.* 1983.

DAVID B. MATTERN

LELAND, JOHN (1754–1841), Baptist minister, advocate of religious freedom. Leland moved from his Massachusetts home to Culpeper, Virginia, in 1777. Although he felt he "was too young and roving to be looked up to as a pastor," the next year he relocated to Orange County, where he served as a Baptist minister until returning to Massachusetts in 1791. In those years Leland may well have discussed with Madison their mutual concerns for religious freedom. Leland supported Madison's effort in 1784–1785 to defeat the General Assessment Bill to establish a provision for teachers of the Christian religion.

In 1788 Madison was a candidate in Orange County for election to the Virginia convention called to ratify the U.S. Constitution. In February he was warned by friends that opposition to his election was building. In particular, John Leland was said to be opposed to ratification of the Constitution because it lacked a bill of rights and a guarantee of religious freedom. Madison returned to his home on 23 March 1788. It is possible although there is no direct evidence from Madison to suggest it, that Madison, at the suggestion of Joseph Spencer, met on the evening of 22 March with Leland in order to convince him of the wisdom of supporting ratification. Madison won election handily, gaining 202 votes out of a possible 240. In February 1789, Leland wrote to Madison, congratulating him on his election to Congress. He asked but one thing: "that if religious Liberty is in any wise threatened; that I shall receive the earliest Intelligence." Leland's unswerving dedication to religious freedom was a classic manifestation of a fundamental Baptist principle espoused first in the colonies by John Clarke and Roger Williams.

A second lifelong concern for Leland was slavery. Before departing from Virginia, he succeeded in having the Baptist General Committee adopt a resolution resolving "[t]hat slavery is a violent deprivation of the rights of nature, and inconsistent with a republican government."

Leland left Virginia, returning to New England, in 1791. He continued to support full religious freedom in Massachusetts for the remainder of his life and apparently had no further contact with Madison.

BIBLIOGRAPHY

Alley, Reuben E. *A History of Baptists in Virginia.* 1973.
Greene, L. F. *The Writings of John Leland.* 1969.
Hutchinson, William T., et al., eds. *The Papers of James Madison.* Vol. 10. 1962–.

ROBERT S. ALLEY

L'ENFANT, PIERRE-CHARLES (1754–1825), artist, planner of the city of Washington, D.C. Trained as a painter in his native France, L'Enfant came to America with a contingent of French military engineers in 1777. During the American Revolution he became acquainted with George Washington and his circle, who noticed L'Enfant's graphic skills. In the war, L'Enfant attained the rank of major.

L'Enfant's career as an American designer began after the war. He worked in the waning Renaissance tradition of the universal artist, and symbolism was his forte. At first he created allegorical decorations for celebrations and devised official insignia but gradually he became more involved in architecture. He had two particularly important commissions in the 1780s: In 1783 he designed the membership diploma, the badge, and a medal for the Society of the Cincinnati, and in 1788 he redesigned New York City Hall as Federal Hall (now demolished), where the First Federal Congress sat and where Washington took his oath of office as president in 1789.

In 1791 Washington chose L'Enfant to plan the layout and to design the public buildings of the new "federal city" along the Potomac, which Jefferson, Madison, and the city commissioners named for the first president later the same year. Responding to the potential of a bluff rising over lowlands and composing an ingenious program of symbolism, L'Enfant conceived of a city of imperial majesty. He placed the Capitol on the height, looking down over a metropolis of wide, straight streets laid out according to a combination of radial patterns and a grid. But L'Enfant overestimated his own authority and was dismissed in 1792. His plan survived his dismissal, although the possibilities of his conception for the city were not fully realized until the twentieth century.

L'Enfant's known commissions after he left Washington were few and short-lived. For Alexander Hamilton and the Society for Establishing Useful Manufactures, he devised a plan for Paterson, New Jersey, in 1792, but Peter Colt executed a simplified form of L'Enfant's thinking. For the financier Robert Morris, L'Enfant began an extravagant Philadelphia mansion (1793–1795), but Morris went bankrupt, and the unfinished house was demolished around 1800. L'Enfant was occasionally active as a military engineer into the second decade of the nineteenth century. The Digges family of Maryland supported him for the last decade of his life. In 1909 his body was transferred from a Digges estate to Arlington National Cemetery, where it was interred on a site overlooking the city that L'Enfant had shaped.

BIBLIOGRAPHY

Reiff, Daniel D. "L'Enfant, Pierre Charles." In *Macmillan Encyclopedia of Architects.* Edited by Adolf K. Placzek. 4 vols. 1982.
Scott, Pamela. " 'This Vast Empire': The Iconography of the Mall, 1791–1848." In *The Mall in Washington, 1791–1991.* Edited by Richard Longstreth. 1991.

CHARLES E. BROWNELL

LEWIS, MERIWETHER (1774–1809), commander (with William Clark) of the first United States exploration of the Louisiana Territory and the Pacific Coast, governor of the Louisiana Territory.

Lewis was born in Albemarle County, Virginia. In the 1790s he joined the army and soon rose to the rank of captain. In 1801 he became President Jefferson's secretary, and together they planned an exploring venture across the continent. After the Louisiana Purchase in 1803, the exploration took on national importance, as a political gesture and as a scientific endeavor.

The Lewis and Clark expedition started from a camp across from Saint Louis in May 1804. By October the explorers had followed the Missouri River to present-day North Dakota, where they spent the winter. With the return of good weather in the spring of 1805 they continued up the Missouri, crossing the Rocky Mountains in September 1805. The explorers discovered streams that led them to the Columbia River and on to the coast. After a dreary winter on the Oregon coast, they began their trip back in March 1806. On the return journey the party split; Lewis and a small group explored regions to the north, while Clark, accompanied by the main party, went down the Yellowstone. They reached Saint Louis together in September 1806. Throughout the journey Lewis served as the party's naturalist, and he collected a plethora of new plant, animal, and mineral specimens.

Jefferson named Lewis governor of the Louisiana Territory in 1807, but Lewis became frustrated in this work. Later, officials in Madison's administration refused to reimburse some of Lewis's expenditures, and in a state of depression Lewis set out for Washington to correct the situation. While en route he stopped for a night on the Natchez Trace in Tennessee and committed suicide, although some historians still maintain that he was murdered. Perhaps personal problems, as well as his professional difficulties, pushed him to this tragic end. He was thirty-five.

[See also *Clark, William.*]

BIBLIOGRAPHY

Bakeless, John. *Lewis and Clark, Partners in Discovery.* 1947.
Dillon, Richard. *Meriwether Lewis: A Biography.* 1965. Repr. 1988.
Moulton, Gary E., ed. *Journals of the Lewis and Clark Expedition.* 11 vols. 1983–.

GARY E. MOULTON

LEWIS, MORGAN (1754–1844), judge, soldier, governor of New York. Lewis was born in New York City, the son of Francis Lewis, a prosperous merchant and a signer of the Declaration of Independence. One of Madison's classmates at the College of New Jersey (later Princeton), Lewis graduated in 1773 and immediately began to study law under John Jay. He served in the Continental army during the Revolution, rose to the rank of colonel, and worked as a deputy quartermaster in the Northern Department. In 1779 Lewis married Gertrude Livingston, the sister of Robert R. Livingston, and this family alliance determined much of the course of his subsequent political career.

In the 1780s Lewis practiced law in New York City, serving in local offices and in the state assembly (1789–1790) as a Federalist. He soon moved into the Clintonian camp with the Livingston family, however, and Gov. George Clinton appointed him state attorney general in 1791, then to the state supreme court in 1792. As part of the Jeffersonian triumph of 1800, Lewis was elevated to the post of New York's chief justice in 1801. In 1804 Lewis successfully ran for governor against Aaron Burr in a bitterly contested election.

In Lewis's one term as governor he laid the foundations for a common school system for the state, but he aggravated the divisions between the Livingstons and the Clintonians in the Republican party. The party schism resulted in Lewis's defeat in 1807 by the Clin-

tonian Daniel Tompkins. Almost immediately Lewis opened a correspondence with his college friend Madison, keeping him abreast of Clintonian intrigues to wrest the presidential nomination from the Virginian. In May 1812 Madison appointed Lewis a brigadier general and quartermaster general of the U.S. Army. Later, Madison granted Lewis's request for a field commission, promoting him to major general in February 1813 and naming him second-in-command to Henry Dearborn on the New York–Canadian front. Lewis commanded at the capture of Fort George in May 1813 but because of either his own hesitancy or Dearborn's order failed to take advantage of the victory to crush the British forces. After the defeat at Chrysler's Farm in November 1813, Lewis was transferred to command the Third Military District (the New York City area), a post he held until he was replaced in October 1814 despite "strong expressions of personal regard" given to Lewis by Madison in a personal interview shortly after Lewis's removal. After his retirement from the army, Lewis practiced law and remained active in politics until his death.

BIBLIOGRAPHY

Delafield, Julia. *Biographies of Francis Lewis and Morgan Lewis.* 1877.
Harrison, Richard A. *Princetonians, 1769–1775: A Biographical Dictionary.* 1980.

DAVID B. MATTERN

MORGAN LEWIS.
PRINTS AND PHOTOGRAPHS DIVISION, LIBRARY OF CONGRESS.

LIBRARY OF CONGRESS. Delegates attending the First Continental Congress in 1774 were permitted to use the Philadelphia Library Company holdings when they met in Philadelphia, an arrangement that lasted until the First Federal Congress met in New York and had access to a local private library. As early as 1780, however, the Continental Congress had discussed the need for a collection of legal works, books on international law, and other materials that would aid delegates in their legislative roles.

Madison was serving in the Continental Congress in 1782 when a committee was created to compile "a list of books to be imported for the use of the United States in Congress assembled." Madison took his charge seriously, and in January 1783 he offered a compilation of 307 books as the nucleus of a congressional library. The list ranged from the *Encyclopédie méthodique* to a history of Paraguay and emphasized works on international law, natural law, geography, and history. Madison's list tells more about his own intellectual development than about the works available to Congress, for his suggested list was not purchased, because of a lack of funds and the temporary circumstances of the Confederation's legislature.

After the federal government moved from New York back to Philadelphia in 1790, private libraries were still open to members of Congress, but the need for a separate library was evident. In August 1789 Rep. Elbridge Gerry had called for a report that would list books needed for congressional business, and in 1790 a committee recommended a start-up library appropriation of $1,000. Nothing came of this early call for a suitable library, but with a permanent capital in mind and the meager resources of the small village of Washington evident, there was renewed interest in a collection of books for the use of members of the House of Representatives and the Senate. In April 1800 the two branches voted to spend $5,000 on a library, and a year later William Duane (editor of the Philadelphia *Aurora*) wrote to Secretary of State Madison offering to serve as the purchasing agent for this collection. The authorization also called for a librarian of Congress, who was to be paid $2 a day for his trouble, and Jefferson appointed the Republican wheelhorse, John Beckley, to the post as an additional duty for the clerk of the House.

The 1802 catalog of the Library of Congress shows that 243 volumes had been purchased, including a 21-volume set of the *U.S. Statutes-at-Large* and an 18-volume collection of the journals of the House of Commons. The books were shifted from one section of the new Capitol building to another, sometimes because of a lack of space and at other times because the roof leaked. A real disaster struck in August 1814, when the invading British troops placed a torch to the Capitol and the entire first Library of Congress was destroyed.

Upon hearing of the burning, Jefferson wrote to President Madison and Samuel Harrison Smith, offering his Monticello library to replaced the charred volumes. The magnanimous offer soon became a political issue, as Jefferson's enemies in Congress derided the collection as a hodge-podge of books by French philosophers that were lacking in merit, but in time legislation was passed offering Jefferson $23,950 for more than six thousand volumes. The purchase was made by size, with large volumes bringing $10 and the smallest $1. The books were brought in ten wagons from Monticello to Washington with the approval of President Madison. Thus Jefferson's books, bearing his signature and marginalia, became the nucleus of a collection that would eventually comprise more than 60 million items in one of the world's greatest libraries.

JAMES MADISON MEMORIAL. The heroic statue by Walter K. Hancock in the memorial hall in the Madison Building portrays Madison in his thirties, holding in his right hand volume 83 of the *Encyclopédie Méthodique*.

LIBRARY OF CONGRESS.

JAMES MADISON MEMORIAL BUILDING.   The Madison Building is the nation's official memorial to the Father of the Constitution, the Father of the Bill of Rights, and the fourth president. The building, designed by DeWitt, Poor, and Shelton, Associated Architects, was opened in 1980 as the Library of Congress's third major structure (the others are the Thomas Jefferson Building, opened in 1897, and the John Adams Building, opened in 1939).

LIBRARY OF CONGRESS.

The Library of Congress was housed in various sections of the restored Capitol until a new building was finished and occupied in 1897 adjacent to the Capitol grounds. Two additional buildings were required as the holdings expanded; the James Madison Building opened in 1980.

BIBLIOGRAPHY

Johnston, William D. *The History of the Library of Congress.* 2 vols. 1904.
Hutchinson, William T., et al., eds. *Papers of James Madison: Congressional Series.* Vol. 6. 1969.
Malone, Dumas. *Jefferson and His Time: The Sage of Monticello.* 1981.
Rutland, Robert A. *"Well Acquainted with Books": The Founding Framers of 1787.* 1987.

ROBERT A. RUTLAND

LINCOLN, LEVI (1749–1820), politician, attorney general. In 1801 Lincoln, a Republican leader in the Federalist-dominated state of Massachusetts, accepted the office of attorney general from the newly inaugurated president, Thomas Jefferson. When a bout with rheumatism and the need to settle the estate of his recently deceased father delayed Madison's assumption of office as secretary of state for two months, Lincoln acted in his place. In so doing, he spared Madison a huge backlog of paperwork. Lincoln and Madison remained cabinet colleagues until the former resigned at the end of 1804.

In 1801 Jefferson named Lincoln, Gallatin, and Madison to a commission to arrange Georgia's cession of its western lands to the United States. The commission agreed that, in return for $1.25 million, Georgia would surrender most of present-day Alabama and Mississippi. Controversy arose over the commission's decision to compensate landowners in the ceded territory, most of whom had been unwittingly caught up in the Yazoo Lands frauds of 1795. In that scandal, speculators had bribed the Georgia Assembly into selling a huge chunk of Yazoo land at a fraction of its worth. The following year, the legislature nullified the deal, but not before the speculators had resold much of the real estate to unsuspecting customers. To prevent injury to these innocent purchasers, the 1801 commission recommended a generous settlement. Led by John Randolph, a group of extreme states' rights representatives attacked the decision as a corrupt invasion of Georgia's sovereignty. Madison, Lincoln, and Gallatin were vindicated when the Supreme Court ruled, in *Fletcher* v. *Peck* (1810), that Georgia's repeal of the land sale was unconstitutional.

As president, Madison remembered Lincoln's abilities. In 1810, after the death of the Federalist Justice Caleb Cushing opened a seat on the Supreme Court, he offered the post to Lincoln, one of the few prominent Republicans in New England. With his eyesight failing, however, Lincoln declined.

BIBLIOGRAPHY

Brant, Irving. *James Madison.* Vol. 4: *Secretary of State. 1800–1809.* 1953.
Malone, Dumas, ed. *Dictionary of American Biography.* 1927–1936.
Malone, Dumas. *Jefferson and His Time.* Vol. 4: *Jefferson the President, First Term 1801–1805.* 1970.
Malone, Dumas. *Jefferson and His Time.* Vol. 5: *Jefferson the President, Second Term 1805–1809.* 1974.

STUART LEIBIGER

LITTLE BELT. A twenty-gun British sloop-of-war, *Little Belt* was captured from the Danish navy at the battle of Copenhagen in 1801. She was originally named *Lille Belt*, after a body of water (Lille Baelt) off the northeastern Danish coast, but this name was corrupted to *Little Belt* when she was taken into the Royal Navy.

The *Little Belt* achieved fame of a sort when she was mistaken for a much larger ship by Commodore John Rodgers on 16 May 1811. Rodgers had been ordered to intercept a British frigate that was harrassing American shipping off the port of New York. Rodgers's frigate *President* carried more than twice as many guns and men as did *Little Belt*, but he made a not uncommon mistake when he began to chase the frigate in failing light.

By the time *President* overhauled *Little Belt*, it was after dark and Rodgers was still unable to see the number of guns she carried. It was then that confusion reigned, each ship's captain calling for an identification and neither yielding, then one of the ships fired a single gun and this led to several broadsides. Each ship was damaged and the British suffered far more killed and wounded. The ships separated, waited for dawn, and when Rodgers realized he had fired on a much smaller ship, he offered his regrets and assistance, which were refused by his opposite number, Master and Commander Arthur Bingham. In the official inquiries that followed, each captain maintained the other had fired first, and they were upheld by their respective navies. Each side, from then on, was spoiling for a fight, which eventually came when the United States declared war on 18 June 1812.

When Capt. James Dacres of HMS *Guerrière* cruised the North American station in June 1812, he hoisted a sail with the motto "Not the Little Belt." For their part, many American naval officers and the public considered the *President–Little Belt* affair as fair retaliation for HMS *Leopard*'s humiliating attack on USS *Chesapeake* in 1807.

BIBLIOGRAPHY

Dudley, William S., and Michael J. Crawford, eds. *The Naval War of 1812: A Documentary History*. 1985. Vol. 1, pp. 40–50.
Maloney, Linda M. *Captain from Connecticut: The Life and Naval Times of Captain Isaac Hull*. 1986.

WILLIAM S. DUDLEY

LIVERPOOL, LORD (ROBERT BANKS JENKINSON) (1770–1828), prime minister of Great Britain. Lord Liverpool undertook his long premiership (1812–1827) at a time when war raged in Europe and North America and England writhed under an economic depression. Accommodation rather than principled obduracy characterized Liverpool's ministry, and experience molded his outlook more than ideology or tradition; he saw the Bastille stormed and became a lifelong foe of extremism.

Liverpool came to power after Spencer Perceval's

assassination in 1812. Although he had been preoccupied with prosecuting the European war to final victory during his tenure as foreign secretary (1808) and as secretary for war and the colonies (1809–1812), he had also managed to ease Anglo-American tensions. Since he understood Europe better than he did America, as prime minister he wisely left most American affairs to his permanent undersecretary for war, George Hammond, who had spent four years as the British minister in Washington, and then to Viscount Castlereagh. Like them, Liverpool accepted the finality of American independence, treated the young republic respectfully and as an equal, and consistently argued that Britain's economic welfare depended heavily on the goodwill and cooperation of the United States. Even before Madison requested Britain's help during the Tripolitan War in 1815, Liverpool offered use of Britain's naval bases in the Mediterranean. Rufus King and Liverpool settled their nations' differences over outstanding American debts and over the Maine boundary. Liverpool supported Henry Brougham's efforts in Parliament to block the 1808 order in council that violated America's neutral rights. He also tried to avert war with the United States out of an abiding belief in laissez-faire and then, when war came, tried to end it speedily. His chance came in 1814 at Ghent, a sideshow for Britain compared with the critical negotiations taking place at the Congress of Vienna. Liverpool ordered the British commissioners to stop wrangling over contentious issues that had long irritated the Americans, convinced that they could be resolved piecemeal once a treaty had been concluded. Subsequent events proved his judgment entirely correct.

BIBLIOGRAPHY

Derry, John W. *Castlereagh*. 1976.
Gash, Norman. *Lord Liverpool: The Life and Political Career of Robert Banks Jenkinson, Second Earl of Liverpool, 1770–1828*. 1984.
Hilton, Boyd. "The Political Arts of Lord Liverpool." *Transactions of the Royal Historical Society*, 5th ser., 38 (1988): 147–170.

MARTIN J. HAVRAN

LIVINGSTON, ROBERT R. (1746–1813), American statesman, diplomat. Born into a wealthy and powerful New York family, Livingston graduated from King's College (later Columbia University) in 1765 and joined the bar in 1768. A delegate to the Second Continental Congress in 1775, he was one of five members of the committee selected to draw up a declaration of independence, but he neither voted on nor signed the final version, having returned to New York before Jefferson's draft was presented to the Congress.

ROBERT LIVINGSTON.
PRINTS AND PHOTOGRAPHS DIVISION, LIBRARY OF CONGRESS.

Livingston spent the next several years in New York state government, serving on committees for defense and administration and coordinating continental and local military operations. In 1777 he was appointed state chancellor, a position he retained until 1801 while serving in other state and national offices. He returned twice more to the Continental Congress and was one of that body's busiest members, serving on committees dealing with military, legal, financial, and foreign affairs.

In 1781 Livingston was named secretary for foreign affairs, in part because his partiality for France made him acceptable to the French minister, Luzerne. Livingston instructed the American peace commissioners in Paris to cooperate with the French negotiators and urged the extension of American boundaries to the Mississippi. Irked by the close, even restrictive, supervision of Congress, Livingston left office in 1783, having created an efficient, well-organized foreign affairs department for the new nation.

Returning to New York, Livingston again immersed himself in state politics, negotiating the settlement of several territorial disputes with neighboring states. Livingston's experience with the Confederation government made him one of the federal Constitution's strongest supporters at the New York ratification convention in 1788,

and as chancellor he delivered the presidential oath of office to Washington in 1789. The wrangles of state politics led to Livingston's estrangement from the Federalists, and by 1792 he was a confirmed, if aristocratic, Republican who refused an appointment as minister to France because of his differences with Federalist foreign policy. In 1795 he publicly opposed Jay's Treaty with Great Britain, and he supported Jefferson's presidential campaign in 1800.

In 1801 Livingston was named minister to France, since Madison and Jefferson believed his known friendship for that nation would help dispel the animosity remaining after the Quasi-War. Madison directed Livingston to discourage the rumored retrocession of Louisiana to France by Spain or, barring that, to offer to purchase West Florida and to encourage prompt French payment of indemnities agreed to under the Convention of 1800. Livingston's notes pressed American claims so firmly that Napoleon stated he would have invaded a European country that pressured him so aggressively. In memorials to Napoleon through his brother Joseph and through Talleyrand, Livingston portrayed Louisiana as a burden on France, costly to maintain in peace and easily lost in war, and repeatedly suggested the sale of at least part of the country to the United States. Convinced the approaching war with Great Britain would result in British seizure of Louisiana, Napoleon resolved instead to profit from the loss of the territory and instructed Finance Minister Barbé-Marbois to begin negotiations with Livingston and James Monroe, who had arrived with special instructions from Madison to arrange the purchase of New Orleans and the Floridas. Within a month the Louisiana Purchase treaty, which Livingston described as "the noblest work of our whole lives," was completed and signed. Livingston's pleasure at the settlement faded over the next two years as he became involved in squabbles with members of the American claims commission and as he saw the credit he believed he deserved for arranging the treaty go to Monroe and Jefferson. Returning to the United States in 1805, Livingston retired from politics, devoting himself to raising merino sheep and promoting the development of Robert Fulton's steamboat.

BIBLIOGRAPHY

Barbé-Marbois, François. *The History of Louisiana.* Edited by E. Wilson Lyon. 1977.

Brant, Irving. *James Madison.* Vol. 4. 1941.

Dangerfield, George. *Chancellor Robert R. Livingston of New York: 1746–1813.* 1960.

DeConde, Alexander. *This Affair of Louisiana.* 1976.

Malone, Dumas. *Jefferson and His Time.* Vol. 4. 1948.

MARY A. HACKETT

LOCKE, JOHN (1632–1704), English philosopher, political activist. Locke came from a well-to-do Somerset family with Puritan sympathies. He studied at Christ Church, Oxford, in the 1650s, continued there as a tutor until 1665, and joined the household of the radical Whig politician Anthony Ashley Cooper, the first earl of Shaftesbury, in 1667. He fled to Holland in 1683 after the attempt to assassinate Charles II in the Rye House Plot failed. Locke returned to England in 1689 after the Glorious Revolution and in that year published anonymously *A Letter Concerning Toleration* and *Two Treatises of Government*, as well as, under his own name, *An Essay Concerning Human Understanding*, which made him famous. From 1694 to 1700 he was again politically active, especially in matters concerning trade and monetary policy, this time as the confidant of Lord Somers, the chief figure in the government of William III.

His most important work in political philosophy, "An Essay Concerning the True Original, End, and Extent of Government," the second of his *Two Treatises*, was written (but not published) in the early 1680s to counter Robert Filmer's royalist tract, *Patriarcha*. Locke's work can be seen as a theoretical expression of the revolutionary Whig movement that led to the Rye House Plot. Locke's political beliefs were based on the ideas of human equality and the individual's natural rights to life, liberty, and property. Because of these rights, legitimate political authority was necessarily limited and, within its limits, had to be based on individual consent. Locke wrote to defend a people's right to resist and to revolt when their natural rights and representative institutions were violated by a tyrannical executive or government. Because Locke believed that sincere religious belief could not be forced, he argued that religious regulations were beyond the proper limits of government activity. In philosophy he is identified with the idea that the mind starts as a *tabula rasa*, or blank slate.

In the 1770s, as the colonists came to think that their rights were being violated by the British and that resistance might be justified, they found Locke's analysis of tyranny and his defense of revolution in the *Second Treatise* particularly important. In a letter to William Bradford in 1774 Madison wrote that the delegates at the Continental Congress frequently consulted "Vattel, Burlemaqui, Locke, and Montesquieu . . . when settling the rights of the colonies." Locke's works were among the most widely held books on politics and philosophy in the libraries of colonial America.

Locke's works were assigned reading at the College of New Jersey when Madison was a student there, and in 1783 Locke's works on politics and money were on a list of books that Madison suggested for inclusion in a Library of Congress. Madison's respect for Locke's *An Essay Concerning Human Understanding* can be seen in his pairing of Newton and Locke, both of whom he said "established immortal systems, the one in matter, the other in mind." Madison's most obvious debt to Locke's political writings is in his "Memorial and Remonstrance against Religious Assessments," a 1785 essay against the establishment of a state-subsidized religion in Virginia that shows the influence of *A Letter Concerning Toleration*. Yet Madison could also be critical of Locke, as he was in his first "Helvidius" essay in 1793. Here he disagreed with Locke's willingness to give the executive a prerogative power in foreign affairs and argued instead for legislative supremacy in this area.

JOHN LOCKE.   Lithograph by H. Garnier.
PRINTS AND PHOTOGRAPHS DIVISION, LIBRARY OF CONGRESS.

BIBLIOGRAPHY

Ashcraft, Richard. *Revolutionary Politics and Locke's Two Treatises of Government.* 1986.

Dunn, John. *The Political Thought of John Locke.* 1969.

Kramnick, Isaac. "Republican Revisionism Revisited." *American Historical Review* 87 (1982): 629–664.

Lutz, Donald. "The Relative Influence of European Writers on Late Eighteenth Century American Political Thought." *American Political Science Review* 78 (1984): 189–197.

Waldron, Jeremy. *The Right to Private Property.* 1988.

THOMAS A. HORNE

LOGAN, GEORGE (1753–1821), physician, U.S. senator from Pennsylvania. Logan's pursuits—peace, scientific agriculture, antislavery—were admirable but not always successful. As a private citizen Logan sought to cool a simmering war fever between France and the United States. In 1798 bearing letters from Thomas Jefferson and Pennsylvania Chief Justice Thomas McKean, he traveled to Paris. There, with the help of the marquis de Lafayette, he met with the foreign minister, Talleyrand, and Philippe-Antoine Merlin, one of the five French Directors. France soon lifted its embargo and freed American seamen, so Logan can claim at least partial credit for helping to end the Quasi-War. But the Federalist Congress was not appreciative and it passed a measure prohibiting the conduct of diplomacy by private citizens. (Known as the Logan Act, the law is still on the books.)

In 1801 McKean, the Republican governor of Pennsylvania, appointed Logan to fill a seat in the U.S. Senate vacated by Peter Muhlenberg after only one month. His service, from July 1801 to March 1807, exposed the dilemma of a principled pacifist in politics. Logan broke with the radical Duane-Leib Republicans in Pennsylvania and became, with McKean, a moderate member first of the Rising Sun faction and then of the Tertium Quids. Nationally, he quailed at any assertion of aggressiveness in foreign policy. He left the chamber rather than vote for $2 million to buy West Florida. He was the only Republican senator to oppose nonimportation.

Logan's acquaintance with James Madison was of long standing; he had known the widow Dolley Todd in Philadelphia. Nervous about the drift to war, he visited the president in Washington and wrote him in January 1810: "Make use of your power and your influence . . . to arrest the progress of the destruction of your country." Despite the Logan Act, he traveled to England on a second peace mission, less salutary than his first.

BIBLIOGRAPHY

Tolles, Frederick B. *George Logan of Philadelphia*. 1953.

HARRY W. FRITZ

LOUISIANA. Originally inhabited by Native Americans, the area was claimed for France by the explorer Robert Cavelier, sieur de La Salle, in 1682. By treaties of 1762 and 1763 France ceded to Spain the Isle of Orleans (present day New Orleans), along with all other French territory in North America. Until 1800, Louisiana was a defined territory, and the port of New Orleans played a key role in all trade up and down the Mississippi River. By terms of the Treaty of San Lorenzo (1795), Spain granted American traders the right to deposit goods at New Orleans for transshipment. Louisiana's population, which in 1777 was approximately eighteen thousand (about nine thousand white and nine thousand slave and mulatto), grew to about eighty thousand by the achievement of statehood in 1812 and included a large group of Acadian immigrants from Canada who settled along Louisiana's bayous.

Most of Louisiana's population lived on plantations along the Mississippi River and its tributaries, where they grew sugarcane and cotton, which could be conveniently transported by water. Spanish authorities failed to impress upon their government the advantages to be derived from a policy of accommodating this growing business, however, and in October 1802 the Spanish intendant, acting under royal instruction, revoked the right of Americans to deposit goods at New Orleans, an action technically permissible according to the treaty of 1795. This action confirmed rumors coming from Europe that Spain had ceded the territory back to France, a diplomatic action that caught Jefferson and Madison off their guard. Madison had long believed that, as long as Louisiana was in the hands of Spain, it could be obtained by negotiation whenever the United States felt ready to assume the territory. By the secret Treaty of San Ildefonso (1800), Spain had in fact ceded the territory back to France, but it was unclear to Madison whether West Florida had been included in that deal. When the rumor of cession was confirmed, Jefferson sent James Monroe to Paris in 1803 as a special envoy to support ambassador Robert R. Livingston's efforts to secure either New Orleans or an area in West Florida as a place of deposit for American shippers. The diplomats had authority to spend up to $10 million. The administration had secured good relations with France through a treaty known as the Convention of 1800; Madison's immediate role in the affair was to impress the need for a trade zone on France's chargé d'affaires in Washington, Louis Pichon.

Meanwhile, Napoleon's plans to take over Louisiana and other North American territory foundered against a series of natural and political obstacles that increased his need for ready cash. Napoleon therefore instructed his minister, Talleyrand, to offer the Americans the whole of the Louisiana Territory for $15 million, $11 million of which would be cash paid to the French government, with the rest to be paid by the American government directly to satisfy westerners' claims against France. This deal, known as the Louisiana Purchase Treaty, was signed by Livingston and Monroe on 30 April 1803 in Paris. Ratification by Congress secured 560 million acres in the trans-Mississippi West for the United States.

Madison sent William C. C. Claiborne, governor of the Mississippi Territory, to formally accept Louisiana from the French at New Orleans on Tuesday, 20 December 1803. Claiborne was appointed governor of the Orleans Territory formed on 26 March 1804 and became the first

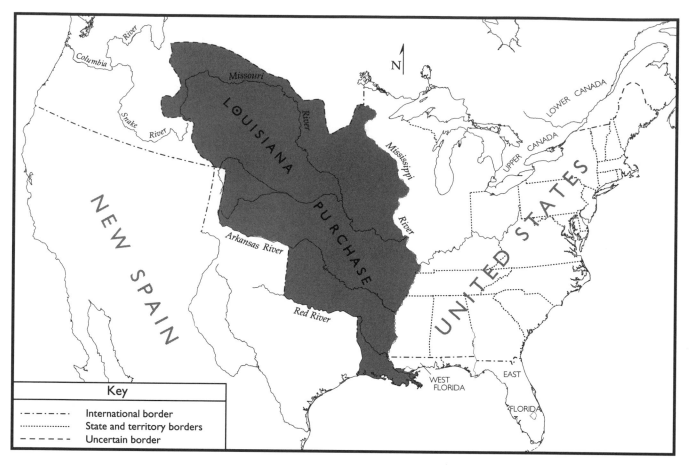

THE LOUISIANA PURCHASE.

governor of the state of Louisiana, the eighteenth state, when it was created from the Orleans Territory on 30 April 1812. After 1812, the District of Louisiana, that part of the territory above the thirty-third parallel, was joined to the jurisdiction of the Indiana Territory. In January 1815 Gen. Andrew Jackson endeared himself to Louisianians with his victory over the British at New Orleans.

BIBLIOGRAPHY

Davis, Edwin Adams. *Louisiana: A Narrative History*. 1961.
Ferrell, Robert H. *American Diplomacy: A History*. 1969.
Peterson, Merrill D. *James Madison: A Biography*. 1974.
Taylor, Joe Gray. *Louisiana: A Bicentennial History*. 1976.

FRANK C. MEVERS

LOUVERTURE, TOUSSAINT. See *Toussaint-Louverture*.

LUNDY'S LANE, BATTLE OF (25–26 July 1814). Misinterpreting directions from Washington that ordered him to attack Kingston, Upper Canada (now Ontario), Maj. Gen. Jacob Brown began a campaign on the Canadian side of the Niagara River in the summer of 1814. When his army won a preliminary victory at the Battle of Chippewa (5 July), Brown moved forward and clashed with a British-Canadian force not far from Niagara Falls. The resulting Battle of Lundy's Lane (or Niagara) probably was the most desperately fought ground engagement of the war.

To succeed, the American advance needed the cooperation of Commodore Isaac Chauncey and the Lake Ontario squadron, who were to endanger the British flank and supply line and to open logistical support for the army. But Chauncey hesitated, not wanting to expose his base at Sackets Harbor to an enemy raid. Brown waited for ten days but received no word from Chauncey. In the meantime, Maj. Gen. Phineas Riall reinforced the British garrisons at Forts George and Mississauga and moved a detachment to the American side of the Niagara River. To offset that threat, Brown ordered Brig. Gen. Winfield Scott to threaten the British at Fort George on the Canadian side. Riall moved forward to Lundy's Lane to meet Scott and was joined by Lt. Gen. Gordon Drummond with reinforcements.

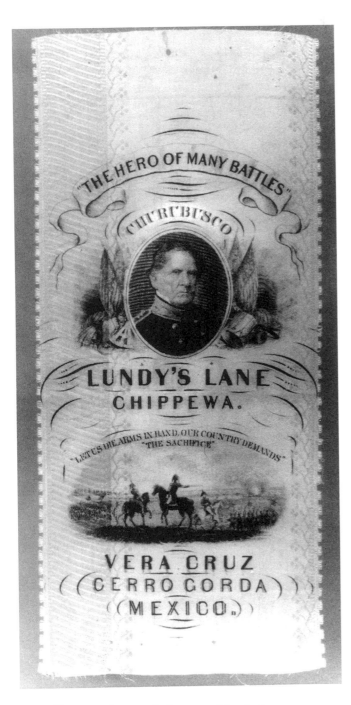

THE HERO OF LUNDY'S LANE.   Nearly forty years after he was severely wounded at the battle of Lundy's Lane, Winfield Scott ran for president on the Whig ticket in 1852 against Democrat Franklin Pierce. His bravery at Lundy's Lane and at Chippewa, and his service in the war against Mexico, are commemorated on this campaign ribbon.
COURTESY OF THE DAVID J. AND JANICE L. FRENT POLITICAL AMERICANA COLLECTION.

Instead of waiting for Brown's two following brigades to come forward, Scott attacked the center of the British-Canadian line, which held brilliantly because of its effective use of field artillery. Meanwhile, a regiment commanded by Col. Thomas Jesup outflanked the British left wing, captured Riall, and pushed the British back. Although the British line bent, it did not break. As darkness began to fall on 25 July, both sides brought up reinforcements. Elements of Brig. Gen. Eleazer W. Ripley's brigade stormed the British artillery at the center of the line and seized the Royal Artillery guns in a bayonet charge. Charge and countercharge ensued during the night until both sides were exhausted and without reserves. Finally, a wounded General Brown ordered withdrawal even though he had won a tactical victory.

Losses on both sides were great. The United States took 850 casualties, the British 875. Approximately 255 British and American soldiers were killed. The bodies were so numerous the British could not bury them; instead, they created three funeral pyres on which they burned the Americans' remains.

Since Brown had to be evacuated because of his wounds and Scott was wounded so severely he was out of the war, command devolved to Ripley, who ordered a precipitous withdrawal to Fort Erie (opposite Buffalo) and gave up the hard-earned ground won at Chippewa. Drummond failed to exploit the situation and instead allowed Ripley's withdrawal to go uncontested; later he would suffer 1,600 casualties trying to take Fort Erie. Chauncey's failure to support Brown undoubtedly contributed to the campaign's failure. More significant, the operation against Kingston was once more postponed.

However strategically insignificant the Battle of Lundy's Lane was, it proved an important factor in the emerging professionalism of the U.S. Army's officer corps and enlisted ranks. Particularly commendable were the performances of the regular troops led by Jesup of the Twenty-fifth U.S. Infantry and by Lt. Col. James Miller of the Twenty-first U.S. Infantry. For the Canadians, Lundy's Lane was an important factor in fostering their emerging sense of nationalism.

BIBLIOGRAPHY

Dudley, William S. "Commodore Isaac Chauncey and U.S. Joint Operations on Lake Ontario, 1813–14." In *New Interpretations in Naval History: Selected Papers from the Eighth Naval History Symposium.* Edited by William B. Cogar. 1989.

Graves, Donald E. *The Battle of Lundy's Lane on the Niagara in 1814.* 1993.

Morris, John D. "General Jacob Brown and the Problems of Command in 1814." In *War along the Niagara: Essays on the War of 1812 and Its Legacy.* Edited by R. Arthur Bowler. 1991.

Stanley, George F. G. *The War of 1812: Land Operations.* 1983.

DAVID CURTIS SKAGGS

LYON, MATTHEW (1750–1822), representative. The first person imprisoned under the Sedition Act of 1798, Lyon was born in County Wicklow, Ireland, and came to America in 1765, covering the costs of transportation by agreeing to a three-year indenture in Connecticut. In 1774 he moved to Wallingford, Vermont, and joined Ethan Allen in 1775 as one of the Green Mountain Boys who seized Fort Ticonderoga from the British. He also served in the Saratoga campaign in 1777.

In 1796 Lyon was elected to the House of Representatives as a Republican. When Roger Griswold, a Connecticut Federalist, made a disparaging remark about Lyon's military record, Lyon replied by spitting in his face. After the Federalists' attempt to expel Lyon from Congress failed, he was denounced by the Federalist press during the Quasi-War with France as *"a seditious foreigner in our council [who] may endanger us more than a thousand Frenchmen in the field."* James Madison thought "the affair of Lyon and Griswold is bad eno' [in] every way, but worst of all in becoming a topic of tedious and disgraceful debates in Congress." After Griswold attacked Lyon with a cane on the floor of the House, Madison called the whole episode "extremely disgraceful" but confessed that he was "curious to see how the zealots for expelling Lyon will treat the deliberate riot of Griswold."

In his campaign for reelection in 1798, Lyon was critical of the administration of John Adams, referring to the president's "unbounded thirst for ridiculous pomp, foolish adulation or selfish avarice." He was promptly indicted under the Sedition Act passed two weeks earlier, becoming the first person charged with libeling the president by remarks that contained "scurrilous, feigned, false, scandalous, seditious, and malicious matters." In October 1798 he was sentenced to four months

MATTHEW LYON AND ROGER GRISWOLD.   In debate in the House, Griswold accused Lyon of cowardice during the Revolutionary War. The two came to blows in February 1798, Lyon defending himself with a pair of fire tongs. Engraving, 1798.
PRINTS AND PHOTOGRAPHS DIVISION, LIBRARY OF CONGRESS.

in jail and fined $1,000 plus court costs. After learning of Lyon's conviction, Jefferson wrote that he did not know "which mortifies me most, that I should fear to write what I think or my country bear such a state of things. Yet Lyon's judges, and a jury of all nations, are objects of national fear."

While serving his prison sentence, Lyon was reelected to Congress by a large majority. Jeffersonian leaders, including Madison, made contributions toward his fine and court costs.

Lyon left Vermont in 1801 and settled in Kentucky, which he represented in Congress. Ever restless, he went on to Arkansas in 1820 and entered the first race for congressional delegate from the Territory of Arkansas but lost the election by sixty-one votes.

BIBLIOGRAPHY

Austin, Aleine. *Matthew Lyon: "New Man" of the Democratic Revolution, 1749–1822.* 1981.

Mott, Frank Luther. *American Journalism: A History, 1690–1960.* 1962.

JAMES MORTON SMITH

M

MACDONOUGH, THOMAS (1783–1825), American naval officer. Born in Delaware, Macdonough joined the navy in 1800 and made his first cruise on board USS *Ganges* in the Caribbean during the Quasi-War with France. He served on the USS *Constellation* in the Tripolitan War in 1801 and on the USS *Philadelphia* at Tripoli in 1803.

Macdonough achieved distinction when, in February 1804, he volunteered with Stephen Decatur for the expedition that sailed into Tripoli harbor and burned *Philadelphia*, which had been captured by the Tripolitans. Macdonough took part in the gunboat actions against Tripoli later that year. As a lieutenant, he was later given command of *Enterprise*, superintended the construction of gunboats at Venice, and sailed as first lieutenant of the brig USS *Syren*.

From 1806 to 1812, Macdonough superintended construction of gunboats, served in USS *Wasp* while carrying despatches to Europe, and cruised the U.S. coastline, enforcing President Jefferson's trade embargo. Needing additional income, Macdonough took furlough in order to command a merchant vessel. He then returned to duty and was commanding gunboats at Portland, in the Maine District, when war broke out in 1812.

Secretary of the Navy William Jones ordered Macdonough to take command of a few naval vessels on Lake Champlain. Macdonough suffered a setback in late May 1813 when the sloops *Growler* and *Eagle* were captured and taken into British service and used in a raid against American-held portions of the lake. The British Lt. Col. John Murray, aided by officers and men from the Royal Navy sloop *Wasp*, looted Plattsburg and other lake towns, and destroyed any lake vessels they could find during a three-day raid that began on 31 July 1813.

Secretary Jones ordered the shipbuilders Noah and Adam Brown, who had recently constructed ships for Perry's squadron on Lake Erie, to travel to Vergennes, Vermont, to build ships for Macdonough. In addition, the Navy Department ordered officers and men to Lake Champlain from blockaded frigates on the Atlantic seaboard. In record time, the Brown brothers' team of shipwrights constructed the ship *Saratoga* and the brig *Eagle*, converted a steamboat to be the schooner *Ticonderoga*, and built six row-galleys.

During August 1814, Macdonough's opponent, Commodore George Downie, commanding a brig, three

COMMODORE THOMAS MACDONOUGH.   Engraving by T. Gimbrede.
PRINTS AND PHOTOGRAPHS DIVISION, LIBRARY OF CONGRESS.

sloops, and thirteen galleys, was engaged in building *Confiance*, a ship of thirty-seven guns. At that moment, Gov. Gen. George Prevost marched fourteen thousand British veterans unopposed toward Plattsburgh. The British army probed the defenses established by Gen. Alexander Macomb around the town. Prevost, however, refused to attack before Downie had defeated Macdonough. In the ensuing action on 11 September, Macdonough anchored his outnumbered vessels under Macomb's protective guns. In an action that lasted an hour and a half and cost the Americans fifty-seven and the British over one hundred men, Macdonough's superior tactics won the day. Without naval support, Prevost retreated, thereby easing the significant British threat.

News of this strategic victory strengthened the hand of the American peace commissioners at Ghent, enabling them to obtain a more equitable peace treaty. Macdonough was rewarded with the thanks of Congress, a gold medal, and a promotion to the rank of captain. In later years, Macdonough served as commandant of the Portsmouth Naval Shipyard and twice as commodore of the Mediterranean Squadron before dying at sea on a return voyage to the United States.

BIBLIOGRAPHY

Everest, Allan S. *The War of 1812 in the Champlain Valley.* 1981.
Macdonough, Rodney. *Life of Commodore Thomas Macdonough, USN.* 1909.

WILLIAM S. DUDLEY

MACKINAC ISLAND. Mackinac (pronounced MACK-i-naw) Island, Michigan, is located at the juncture of Lakes Huron and Michigan and near the mouth of the Saint Mary's River, which drains Lake Superior. The French erected an outpost known as Fort Michilimackinac, on the mainland south of the island around 1715. The British transferred their post to the island in 1781. The Americans took over the post after the signing of Jay's Treaty in 1794 and remained in control at the outbreak of the War of 1812. A leading fur-trading center for the western Great Lakes, the island, which was often called Michilimackinac at this time, was a rendezvous point for Indians and fur traders operating in what is now Michigan, Wisconsin, Minnesota, and western Ontario. Fort Michilimackinac's fifty-seven-soldier army garrison was unaware of the declaration of war when a surprise attack by an overwhelming force of British regulars, Canadian militiamen, and Indian warriors forced its commander to surrender on 17 July 1812. The fall of this small but strategic post emboldened western Indians (Chippewas, Ottawas, Menominees, Winnebagos, Foxes, and Sioux) to join the war against the Americans. From the island, Capt. Charles Roberts directed attacks on American outposts at Green Bay and Prairie du Chien, Wisconsin, and at Fort Dearborn (modern Chicago). The American forces spent most of the next two years of the war trying to reclaim the losses resulting from the fall of Mackinac and Detroit in 1812.

Oliver Hazard Perry's victory at the Battle of Lake Erie (10 September 1813) and William Henry Harrison's at the Battle of the Thames (5 October) turned the strategic situation around. Indian resistance collapsed in southern Michigan and southwestern Upper Canada, but Fort Michilimackinac held on. Bad weather stopped an American assault in the fall of 1813. The following spring the British reinforced the garrison (via waterways and portages that avoided Lake Erie by crossing what is now Ontario to Georgian Bay on Lake Huron) with three hundred regulars commanded by Lt. Col. Robert McDouall. He coordinated a British-Canadian-Indian counterattack to reclaim Prairie du Chien, which had been retaken by an American force sent from Saint Louis. A British expedition from Mackinac retook the post (19 July 1814) and mauled a small American reinforcement effort. The British at Prairie du Chien also assisted Indians in repulsing an American campaign led by Maj. Zachary Taylor to the Rock River region of northern Illinois (5 September).

Meanwhile, a joint army-navy force commanded by Commodore Arthur Sinclair and Lt. Col. George Croghan, the hero of the Battle of Fort Stephenson, Ohio, mounted a counterattack against the British on Mackinac Island. McDouall combined almost his entire garrison with all available Indians to repel the American landing (4 August 1814). To add to the American's embarrassment, two U.S. Navy schooners left to blockade the island were captured through stealth and a ruse by British seamen and Newfoundland infantrymen (3 and 6 September). The British and their allies now controlled the three westernmost Great Lakes.

The capture and holding of this island proved important in frustrating American attempts to regain ground lost to its west and southwest for the remainder of the war. Colonel McDouall was appalled that British negotiators in Ghent failed to modify the boundaries of 1783 to conform to the military realities of 1814. Instead, he found himself "penetrated with grief at the restoration of this fine Island, a Fortress built by Nature for herself," to the Americans. He evacuated the post in July 1815 and left his Indian allies to the mercy of the United States. Henceforth known as Fort Mackinac, the post remained a U.S. Army installation until 1895.

BIBLIOGRAPHY

Allen, Robert S. *His Majesty's Indian Allies: British Indian Policy in the Defense of Canada, 1774–1815.* 1992.

Dunnigan, Brian Leigh. "The British Army at Mackinac, 1812–1815." *Reports in Mackinac History and Archeology.* No. 7. 1980.

Gilpin, Alec R. *The War of 1812 in the Old Northwest.* 1958.

Horsman, Reginald. "The Role of the Indian in the War." In *After Tippecanoe: Some Aspects of the War of 1812.* Edited by Philip P. Mason. 1963.

Stanley, George F. G. *The War of 1812: Land Operations.* 1983.

DAVID CURTIS SKAGGS

MACON, NATHANIEL (1758–1837), Republican congressional leader, senator. Born 17 December 1758 in what is now Warren County, North Carolina, he was the sixth child of Gideon and Priscilla Jones Macon. He enrolled at the College of New Jersey (Princeton) in 1774, but the Revolutionary War interrupted his studies. He served a tour as a volunteer in the New Jersey militia before returning to North Carolina to begin studying law. Unwilling to remain a spectator to the struggle for independence, he reenlisted as a private in a company commanded by his brother and fought the British across the Carolinas.

Macon left the military in 1781 to serve three terms in the state senate, where he came under the influence of

NATHANIEL MACON.
PRINTS AND PHOTOGRAPHS DIVISION, LIBRARY OF CONGRESS.

Willie Jones, an Antifederalist who was largely responsible for North Carolina's initial refusal to ratify the Constitution. Macon shared his mentor's opposition to the Constitution, which he thought gave the federal government too much power. In 1791 Macon was elected to Congress, where he served continuously from October 1791 until December 1828, first in the House of Representatives and then, beginning in 1815, in the Senate. He was Speaker of the House from 1801 to 1807 and was president pro tempore of the Senate in 1827–1828.

Macon was one of President Jefferson's key congressional lieutenants. His unwavering commitment to fundamental Republican principles, especially to the compact theory of government with its corollaries of economy, simplicity, and strict limitations on the power of the federal government, endeared him to Jefferson. Throughout the 1790s Macon stoutly opposed Federalist measures, including Jay's Treaty, the Alien and Sedition Acts, and the building of a navy. He warmly supported the administration of Jefferson, whose presidency coincided with his own tenure as Speaker of the House. An estrangement developed between the two men when Macon joined John Randolph and other conservative Republicans to support James Monroe, rather than James Madison, Jefferson's choice, as the Republican presidential nominee in 1808. Macon supported Monroe not because he disliked Madison but because he thought Monroe was a more conservative Republican. Once Madison became president, however, Macon usually supported his administration. He voted for war against England in 1812, although he tried to make it a defensive war by opposing naval appropriations. He also opposed conscription, the taxes necessary to wage war, and renewal of the national bank's charter.

In the Senate Macon resisted the postwar nationalism enunciated by President Madison in his seventh annual message to Congress. He opposed the national bank, internal improvements, the protective tariff, a stronger military, and almost every political measure that cost money. For Macon, "that government is best which spends least." An outspoken defender of slavery, he opposed the Missouri Compromise and fought against his country's participation in the antislavery Panama Congress of 1826. In the 1824 presidential race his orthodox Republicanism gained him Virginia's electoral vote for the vice presidency. He resigned from office in 1828, after dutifully opposing the nationalist program of President John Quincy Adams.

Macon was an old-fashioned agrarian Republican whose dogmatism and provincialism compelled him to oppose the forces that shaped domestic programs during his congressional career and to resist the democratic changes affecting American society. He favored government by landed gentlemen and opposed liberal voting laws for the unlanded, propertyless class. He quietly opposed the North Carolina suffrage movement that culminated in the constitutional convention of 1835. He presided over the convention but was unable to accept ballot-box democracy and voted against the revised constitution.

Despite his narrow views, Macon was popular among his colleagues, who respected him for his integrity, consistency, and hard work. He died at Buck Spring, his Warren County home, on 29 June 1837.

BIBLIOGRAPHY

Bibliographical Directory of the U.S. Congress, 1774–1989. 1989.
Dodd, William E. *The Life of Nathaniel Macon.* 1903.
Helms, James M., Jr. "The Early Career of Nathaniel Macon." Ph.D. dissertation, University of Virginia. 1962.

CHARLES D. LOWERY

MACON'S BILL NO. 1 AND NO. 2. When Madison became president, he inherited a party rife with internal divisions over personalities and policies. New York Governor George Clinton made an ill-advised attempt to be president, as had James Monroe of Virginia. Within Madison's administration, Secretary of State Robert Smith and Secretary of the Treasury Albert Gallatin fell into open conflict in early 1811 over the Bank of the United States and over foreign affairs.

After a diplomatic settlement of Anglo-American differences (the Erskine Agreement) was repudiated, the president needed a new policy to replace the discredited Nonintercourse Acts. Although North Carolinian Nathaniel Macon's name appeared on the legislation, he claimed only to be "step father" to the bills, introduced in 1810, which he referred to as "a cabinet project." Macon's Bill No. 1 allowed American ships to go anywhere in the world, but British and French goods could enter U.S. ports only in American-owned vessels. The bill passed the House, but was rejected in the Senate. Undaunted, Republican leaders tried again. Macon's Bill No. 2 provided that if either France or Great Britain "cease[d] to violate the neutral commerce of the United States," the other nation would have three months within which to do likewise. If the offending nation did not act by that date, trade with that nation would cease.

When the opportunistic Napoleon issued an ambiguous repeal of his several decrees, in November 1810 Madison closed trade with the British. When British leaders followed with a confirmation that they would not repeal their offensive orders, Congress passed additional legislation placing an embargo on all British goods.

When the French continued to seize American trade, Federalists in Congress raised the cry that Napoleon had duped the president and his party. Macon's Bill, however, forced Great Britain and France either to show respect for America's commercial rights or to reveal their evil intentions by continuing their restrictive measures. Anglophobic Republican congressmen argued that the orders went far beyond an attempt to compete with a trading rival and revealed a diabolical plot by Great Britain's leaders to recolonize America.

For Madison, Macon's Bill No. 2 proved a major turning point. Republican party voting reached a high point following passage of the act during the third session of the Eleventh Congress. At the end of the session, Madison replaced Robert Smith with James Monroe as secretary of state, and during the war session of the Twelfth Congress he used Monroe to communicate with the House Foreign Relations Committee. There, Republican leaders hammered out the major war legislation, bolstered with the language of British diabolism.

The president used Macon's bills to test British intentions. When the British failed the test, he felt justified in asking Congress to declare war.

BIBLIOGRAPHY

Hatzenbuehler, Ronald L., and Robert L. Ivie. *Congress Declares War: Rhetoric, Leadership, and Partisanship in the Early Republic.* 1983.
Kaplan, Lawrence S. *Entangling Alliances with None: American Foreign Policy in the Age of Jefferson.* 1987.
Perkins, Bradford. *Prologue to War: England and the United States, 1805–1812.* 1961.
Stagg, J. C. A. *Mr. Madison's War: Politics, Diplomacy, and Warfare in the Early American Republic, 1783–1830.* 1983.

RONALD L. HATZENBUEHLER

MADDISON, JOHN (d. c. 1682), emigrant from England, great-great-grandfather of President Madison. Both President James Madison and his father, James Madison, Sr., assumed that the first member of their direct family line to live in Virginia was John Madison, or Maddison, an emigrant from England who was in Virginia by the early 1650's. Under the variable spelling of the era, his surname was usually rendered as "Maddison" in contemporary records.

The earliest known record in Virginia citing this John Maddison, is a land patent dated 4 January 1653, granting him six hundred acres of land described as being in Gloucester County in what is now King and Queen County. Over the next dozen years, John Maddison received well over three-thousand acres in land patents. His initial patent, as well as many of his subsequent acquisitions, was located on the north side of the Mattaponi River in present-day King and Queen County.

The exact death date of John Maddison is unrecorded, but he died sometime before 22 September 1682, when a land patent for property in what is now King and Queen County describes an adjoining tract as formerly belonging to "John Maddison, deceased."

The seventeenth-century records for the Virginia counties in which Maddison owned land no longer survive, making it difficult to uncover many facts about his life. However, there is no evidence that Maddison held any major office at either county or colony level. He is frequently described as a ship's carpenter by profession; however, the reference to "John Maddison, ship carpenter," appears in a legal document executed on 6 February 1682 (February 1683 by the modern calendar). John Maddison, the emigrant, was dead by then; the ship's carpenter was in reality his son, also named John Maddison.

The name of John Maddison's wife is undocumented, although traditional accounts have given it as Maria Ambrose. They had at least one child, a son, John Madison (or Maddison), Jr., the great-grandfather of the president.

BIBLIOGRAPHY

Green, Raleigh Travers. *Genealogical and Historical Notes on Culpeper County, Virginia.* 1900. Repr. 1989.
Harris, Malcolm H. *Old New Kent County.* 1977.
Nugent, Nell Marion. *Cavaliers and Pioneers.* Vols. 1 and 2. 1934–1977.

ANN L. MILLER

MADISON, AMBROSE (d. 1732), merchant, planter, county justice, grandfather of President Madison.

Ambrose Madison, son of John Maddison, Jr., and grandson of John Maddison, the emigrant, was a merchant and planter who originally lived in King and Queen County, Virginia. His generation's spelling of the surname with only one "d" was a simplification from the common seventeenth-century spelling of the name, and it was this simplified usage that was adopted by later generations of the family.

On 24 August 1721, Ambrose Madison married Frances Taylor, daughter of Col. James and Martha (Thompson) Taylor of King and Queen County. Three children were born to Ambrose and Frances Madison: a son, James Madison (1723–1801), and two daughters, Elizabeth Madison (1725–ca. 1772) and Frances Madison (1726–1776).

Ambrose Madison was a justice of the peace in the King and Queen County court in 1726. His residence was within that section of King and Queen County that became Caroline County in 1728, and Ambrose Madison, as a leading citizen of the area, was appointed a justice of the new court of Caroline County.

In 1732 Ambrose and Frances Madison moved west from Caroline County to Ambrose's property in Spotsylvania (now Orange) County—the land that would later become known as Montpelier. Ambrose Madison's sojourn in the Virginia Piedmont was brief, for he died on 27 August 1732, only a few months after moving to his new home.

The destruction of the King and Queen County and Caroline County records prevents an accurate assessment of Ambrose Madison's life, landholdings, and economic status while he was a resident of that area. However, his position as a justice in both counties and a few surviving family records indicate that he was a prosperous member of the gentry. He owned more than seven-thousand acres of land in present-day Orange and Greene counties and owned sizable numbers of slaves, cattle, hogs, sheep, and horses.

Ambrose Madison's will divided his property among his children. The bulk of the land was to go to his son James (then aged nine) when the boy reached his eighteenth birthday. After Ambrose Madison's death, Frances Taylor Madison remained at Montpelier and was instrumental in the continued settlement and development of the Madison plantations. She retained a life estate in the plantation and continued to run the Montpelier property and the other Madison holdings until her son came of age. Thereafter, she operated the plantation in concert with her son until her death on 25 November 1761.

BIBLIOGRAPHY

Brant, Irving. *James Madison: The Virginia Revolutionist, 1751–1780.* 1941.
Executive Journals of the Council of Colonial Virginia, vol. 4, 1930. Repr. 1978.
Miller, Ann L. *Historic Structure Report: Montpelier, Orange County, Virginia—Phase II: Documentary Evidence Regarding the Montpelier House.* 1990.

ANN L. MILLER

MADISON, DOLLEY (1768–1849), wife of James Madison.

Dolley Madison was born Dolley Payne on 20 May 1768 in Guilford County, North Carolina. She was one of eight children and had four brothers and three sisters. Although Victorian (and many later) historians later insisted on calling her by the more "proper" names of Dorothea or Dorothy, neither of these names appear in any contemporary documents; in her birth record, as well as in her own usage, her name is given simply as "Dolley," although later in life she frequently signed herself by her initials, "D. P. Madison."

Her parents, John and Mary (Coles) Payne, were Virginians. Mary Coles had been a Quaker when she married, and John Payne, a member of the established Angli-

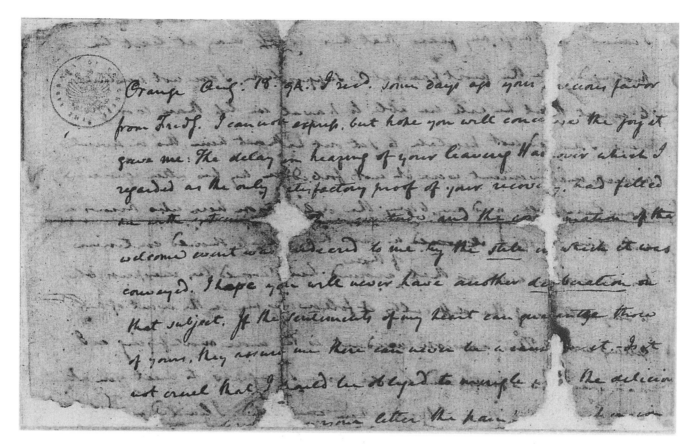

MR. MADISON COURTS MRS. TODD.   Madison's letter to Dolley Payne Todd, 18 August 1794. They were married on 15 September.

JAMES MADISON PAPERS, LIBRARY OF CONGRESS.

can Church, converted to his wife's faith soon afterward. The Paynes later returned to Virginia and lived at Scotchtown in Hanover County, a plantation formerly owned by Mary Payne's cousin Patrick Henry.

Like many Quakers, the Paynes deplored slavery, and in 1782 they freed their slaves. The following year, they moved to Philadelphia to join the large Quaker community there. John Payne tried to earn a living as a starchmaker, but his training and talents lay in managing farms, and he did not prosper. He went bankrupt in 1789, and, unable to pay his debts, he was disowned by his strict Quaker congregation. Broken both physically and mentally by the strain of his business failure and religious rejection, he died in Philadelphia in 1792.

Widowhood and Remarriage. In 1790 Dolley Payne married John Todd, Jr., a prosperous young Quaker lawyer who was a friend of her father's and one of the few Quakers to stand by him after his financial troubles. The couple had two sons: John Payne Todd, born in 1791, and William Temple Todd, born in the summer of 1793.

In October 1793, Dolley Payne Todd lost her in-laws, her husband, and her infant son William in the Philadelphia yellow fever epidemic. Dolley also fell ill and nearly died herself, either of yellow fever or of a similar sickness. Perhaps because of these overwhelming blows, she treated her remaining son, John Payne Todd, with extreme indulgence—something that he quickly learned to exploit.

Attractive, vivacious, and well-to-do, Dolley Payne Todd quickly became one of the most eligible widows in Philadelphia. In the spring of 1794, Rep. James Madison, already acknowledged as the principal Framer of the U.S. Constitution, asked their mutual friend Aaron Burr to introduce them. Perhaps anxious about the prospect of meeting the older, intellectual Madison, Dolley nervously penned a note to her close friend Eliza Collins, asking for her support: "Dear Friend, thou must come to me, Aaron Burr says that the great little Madison has asked to be brought to see me this evening." The shy, slight Madison, considered by some a confirmed bachelor at the age of forty-three, quickly fell in love with the outgoing young widow and soon proposed to her.

Dolley had mixed feelings about remarrying. Her first husband had been dead less than a year, and she would face almost certain banishment from her Quaker congregation for marrying "out of unity" of the Quaker faith—for James Madison was a nominal Episcopalian.

DOLLEY MADISON.   Portrait by Gilbert Stuart, Washington, 1804.
COURTESY PENNSYLVANIA ACADEMY OF THE FINE ARTS, PHILADELPHIA. HARRISON EARL FUND.

Against these considerations, she weighed the respect that she felt for Madison, his strength of character, and the solidity of the home and presence that he would provide for her and her young son.

Madison persisted in his courtship and eventually overcame her objections and resistance. Dolley accepted the proposal of "the man I most admire," noting that "in this union I have everything soothing and grateful in prospect." They were married on 15 September 1794 at Harewood, the home of Dolley's sister and brother-in-law, Lucy and Steptoe Washington (nephew of President George Washington), in what is now West Virginia.

As Dolley had feared, she was turned out of her Quaker congregation because of her marriage. Away from the sober, somewhat grim influences of the Philadelphia Quakers of that period, however, she soon grew to enjoy fashionable gowns, politics, and social events. Kind and gregarious, an extrovert, she was in her element at large gatherings. She was a perfect complement to her shy, retiring, introverted husband, who was more comfortable in small groups or in the company of friends.

In Washington. After James Madison was appointed secretary of state in 1801, Dolley acted as hostess for the widowed President Thomas Jefferson. Her tact and her personal diplomatic talents were important in smoothing the ruffled feathers that sometimes resulted from sectarian politics and from Jefferson's aggressively egalitarian policies for running presidential social events—policies that were sometimes considered insulting by both European diplomats and Americans in an age that was extremely conscious of class and protocol.

Relatively well educated for a woman of her day, Dolley Madison was also an astute judge of human nature, and she had a keen interest in and understanding of politics. (During the summer of 1805, when she had to spend several months in Philadelphia for treatment of a leg ulcer, Dolley frequently wrote to ask her husband for news on events in Washington.) In an age when women were discouraged from, even ridiculed for, interest or involvement in politics, there is evidence that James Madison prized his wife's opinions and judgment in such matters, although understandably both he and Dolley kept her interests and influence hidden to avoid social and political censure. Nevertheless, her understanding and talents were such that later, during James Madison's presidency, she acted as his personal secretary when the holder of that position, Edward Coles, became ill and was unable to work for an extended time. With Madison, she formed a marital and political partnership rare in that era. They were seldom apart for more than a few days throughout their forty-two-year marriage.

As First Lady in her own right, Dolley Madison became noted for the weekly receptions—or "drawing rooms" as she called them—in which she somehow managed tactfully and peacefully to combine government officials, members of rival political factions, diplomats, special guests, and ordinary citizens. Dolley maintained her image and protocol by appearing in deliberately regal costumes, which she then balanced with a friendly, informal manner that set the tone for the receptions. Washington Irving, attending the "blazing splendor" of one of these receptions in 1811, remembered that Dolley had "a smile and a pleasant word for everybody," while another admirer noted that "[she] puts everyone in such a good humour with themselves, that no one who has ever seen her can help being pleased with her, or quit her house without feeling a desire to renew their visit." James Madison, ill at ease in crowds, was remembered as being stiff, taciturn, and overly formal at large gatherings, whereas Dolley, in the eyes of both friends and critics, was an attractive hostess who moved easily through the crowds of guests "with some pretty remark for every lady . . . and gentleman,"—an important part of her talents for smoothing political and diplomatic differences and for providing a measure of intellectual and social cohesiveness in the young nation.

During Madison's first term, Dolley worked with architect Benjamin Henry Latrobe to furnish the White House. They chose elegant classical motifs in furniture and decorative elements, many in the Greek Revival style. Unfortunately, the results of their work were destroyed when the White House was burned by invading British troops in 1814. Left in charge of the White House while Madison was with the army, Dolley Madison had to oversee the evacuation of the building. As the British advanced on the city, she gave first priority to saving vital government papers and the full-length portrait of George Washington and had to abandon most of the furniture, as well as her personal property.

The Madisons were never able to reoccupy the White House during the remainder of Madison's presidency. Instead, they lived in a series of rented dwellings—first the Octagon House and later a portion of the Seven Buildings complex (now demolished), which stood on Pennsylvania Avenue. Dolley Madison managed to reinstitute her "drawing rooms" while buying suitable presidential furnishings within the strict budget allowed by Congress.

James Madison's Retirement. In 1817 James Madison retired to Montpelier at the end of his second term as president. Over the next nineteen years, Dolley Madison helped him organize and prepare his notes on the Federal Convention. She also acted as hostess to family members, neighbors, and the perpetual stream of visitors who came to see the former president.

With no children from their own marriage, the Madisons encouraged younger family members to visit

DOLLEY MADISON, C. 1817.   Engraving by J. F. E.
Prud'homme.
PRINTS AND PHOTOGRAPHS DIVISION, LIBRARY OF CONGRESS.

or live with them for extended periods. Dolley Madison's younger sister Anna Payne had lived with the Madisons for the decade before her marriage to Rep. Richard Cutts in 1804, and later the Cutts children spent long visits at Montpelier. Another niece, Annie Payne, daughter of Dolley Madison's brother John, became virtually an adopted daughter and her aunt's companion in her old age.

In his retirement, James Madison had determined to devote much of his time to running his plantation in the fashion of the idealized American yeoman farmer cherished by himself and other friends, such as Thomas Jefferson. Under Madison's management of Montpelier, his lands were more profitable than those of most of his neighbors, although new agricultural pests, financial recessions, and uncertain weather and markets all caused problems. Still, the Madisons might have had a relatively comfortable retirement except for the financial drains caused by Payne Todd. Dolley Madison remained a doting mother, and James Madison an indulgent stepfather, to the boy who grew up to be an alcoholic, ne'er-do-well, and compulsive gambler. In all, they spent some $40,000 (equivalent to nearly $500,000 today) to cover his debts and expenses and to finance various unsuccessful business ventures.

In addition to these financial problems, by the early 1830s James Madison's health was failing, and he suffered increasingly from crippling arthritis. For the last few years of his life, Dolley Madison seldom left his side, acting as nurse as well as secretary so that he could continue his political correspondence and the editing of his papers. After Madison's death on 28 June 1836, Dolley began to divide her time between Montpelier and a house on Lafayette Square in Washington, D.C. Because of increasing vision problems, her lack of ability as a plantation manager, the continuing debts incurred by her son Payne Todd, as well as Payne's continuing skill in manipulating her and extracting money from her, she found Montpelier too much to run by herself.

Payne Todd was a continuous drain on his mother's resources; he spent most of the $30,000 that she had received from the sale of Madison's constitutional papers to Congress in 1837. In 1842 she mortgaged her Lafayette Square house, hoping to recoup the money through future proceeds from the sale of the remaining Madison papers. The same year she sold part of the Montpelier land to Henry Moncure, a merchant from Richmond, Virginia, and rented part of the house to him. Two years later, in 1844, she finally sold the balance of the property, the house, and much of the livestock, slaves, and furniture to Moncure. By this time she had already settled permanently in Washington with her niece and companion, Annie Payne.

Retirement in Washington. In the early years of her marriage, Dolley Madison apparently retained an allegiance in conscience to the Quaker faith, even though she had been dismissed from her congregation for marrying outside the faith. However, at some point she began to attend Episcopal services with her husband. By the end of James Madison's presidency, both the Madisons attended St. John's Episcopal Church (built 1816) in Washington.

The Episcopal congregation in James Madison's native Orange County, disorganized following the Revolution, had revitalized sufficiently by the early 1830s to construct a new church, St. Thomas' Church, in the town of Orange, the county seat. It is not known if James Madison attended St. Thomas' after the building was finished in 1834; his health was already declining and he may not have been able comfortably to make the ride into town by the time that the building was completed. However, Dolley Madison apparently attended, or at least supported, St. Thomas'. Her name appears on an 1838 list of people who gave money to pay the minister's salary and to meet the cost of erecting the church. After she moved permanently to Washington and sold Montpelier in 1844, her house on Lafayette Square was near St. John's Church, where both she and Annie Payne were baptized in 1846.

For much of her retirement in Washington, Dolley Madison's situation was one of genteel poverty. Washington neighbors and friends such as Daniel Webster quietly sent foodstuffs at times. The year after she moved to Washington, Dolley was reduced to pawning part of the family silver.

Despite these financial difficulties, Dolley Madison spent her last years as a much-loved and honored member of Washington society. She was a frequent guest at government functions and the White House and was voted a seat in the Hall of Representatives in 1844, an unprecedented honor for a woman in that era. The families of later presidents often consulted her on matters of protocol. A fixture at Washington events, she attended the first public exhibition of the telegraph (her greetings to a friend in Baltimore was the next message transmitted after Morse's "What hath God wrought!") and was an honored guest at the dedication of the cornerstone of the Washington Monument in 1848. The same year, the sale of the remainder of Madison's writings to Congress for $25,000 enabled her to live her final days in a measure of security—for one of the conditions of the sale was that a trust fund be set up to keep Payne Todd from gaining control of his mother's money. Of the $25,000, only $5,000 was released to cover Dolley Madison's debts; the remaining $20,000, put at interest, was to provide her with a lifelong annuity.

Dolley Madison had personally known eleven U.S. presidents when she died in Washington, aged eighty-one, on 12 July 1849. Her funeral was held on 16 July at St. John's Church; her funeral procession was the largest yet seen in the city and followed the protocol for state funerals. A contemporary listing of the order of the cortege listed virtually every major governmental figure of the day, along with many private citizens: after the "Reverend Clergy," attending physicians, pallbearers and family members, came "The President and Cabinet, The Diplomatic Corps, Members of the Senate and the House of Representatives . . . and their officers; Judges of the Supreme Court and Courts of the District and their officers; Officers of the Army and Navy; the Mayor and Corporation of Washington." Last were a great number of "Citizens and Strangers," who had come to pay their respects to one of the last remaining figures of the early Republic.

Dolley Madison was first buried in Congressional Cemetery in Washington, but in 1858 she was reinterred beside her husband in the Madison family cemetery at Montpelier.

BIBLIOGRAPHY

Arnett, Ethel Stevens. *Mrs. James Madison: The Incomparable Dolley.* 1972.

Clark, Allen C. *Life and Letters of Dolly Madison.* 1914.

Cutts, Lucia B. *Memoirs and Letters of Dolly Madison, Wife of James Madison, President of the United States: Edited by Her Grand-Niece.* 1886.

Hunt-Jones, Conover. *Dolley and the "Great Little Madison".* 1977.

Ketcham, Ralph. *James Madison: A Biography.* 1971. Repr. 1990.

ANN L. MILLER

MADISON, JAMES (1723–1801), Virginia planter, father of President James Madison. James Madison, Sr., was the great-grandson of John Madison (or Maddison), who immigrated to Virginia in 1653 and acquired lands along the Mattaponi River through the "headright" system: fifty acres for each of twelve immigrants whose passage he had paid from England. The family's Tidewater holdings increased through the next two generations, and the family prospered further when Ambrose Madison (d. 1732), grandfather of the president, acquired rich lands in the Piedmont country (what became Orange County).

James Madison, Sr., was about seven years old when his parents moved to the Piedmont and began the large plantation that came to be known as Montpelier. When Ambrose Madison died, he left management of the plantation (which included twenty-nine slaves) to his young widow, Frances Taylor Madison (1700–1761), until their son James was eighteen.

James Madison, Sr., and his family continued to do business with merchants on the Tidewater, one of whom, Francis Conway (1696–1733), was the father of Nelly Conway (1732–1829), whom James Madison, Sr., married in 1749. The Montpelier mansion was begun about 1760, and twelve children were born to the Madisons between 1751 and 1774, seven of whom, four sons and three daughters, lived to adulthood. Of the others, Nelly and James Madison, Sr., had one stillborn child, one son who lived only a day, another who lived less than a year, and yet another who lived four years, and a daughter who died at age seven. Of the sons who lived to adulthood, two—Francis (1753–1800) and Ambrose (1755–1793)—predeceased their father.

As the Montpelier plantation flourished (it grew to more than five thousand acres worked by more than one hundred slaves), James Madison, Sr., became the model of a Virginia gentleman. He was a vestryman of the local Anglican church, a justice of the peace, and a colonel of the Orange County militia. Madison supported local improvements and helped pay for itinerant schoolteachers and dancing masters for his own and neighboring children, and he enjoyed congenial social relationships with neighboring planters. In his later years he and his wife traveled to spas, to ease the aches and pains of advanced age. He seems not to have had his eldest son James's scholarly leanings, but he enjoyed reading, wrote correct, even sophisticated English in a neat and legible hand, and did all he could to advance the education of his children.

In politics, he approved of Virginia's resistance to the Stamp Act and ordered his Liverpool merchant in 1769 to ship goods only "if the American Revenue Acts should be repealed." He was elected chairman of the Orange County "Committee of Safety" in 1774, and throughout the Revolution he actively supported the patriot cause. After his eldest son became a prominent political leader, Madison, Sr., seems to have followed the younger man's lead as an advocate of ratification of the Constitution in 1788. He was a friend of the Washington administration in its first years and then a supporter of the party his son and Jefferson founded in the 1790s.

Portraits painted about 1798 by Charles Peale Polk of Nelly Conway and James Madison, Sr., reveal a well-dressed, alert, but elderly pair. By then the Madisons had largely turned over management of the Montpelier plantation to their children. Though Nelly would survive until her eldest son's seventy-ninth year, James Madison, Sr., weakened as the century ended, and he died on 27 February 1801; on that morning, as James, Jr., wrote President-elect Jefferson in Washington, his father had "become sensibly worse, and . . . rather suddenly, though very gently, the flame of life went out."

BIBLIOGRAPHY

Account books, letters, and other family papers of James Madison, Sr., are at the Presbyterian Historical Society, Philadelphia. Three biographies of James Madison provide information about his father:
Brant, Irving. *James Madison*. 6 vols. 1941–1961.
Ketcham, Ralph. *James Madison, A Biography*. 1971. Repr. 1991.
Moore, Virginia. *The Madisons, A Biography*. 1979.

RALPH KETCHAM

MADISON, JAMES (1749–1812), educator, Episcopal clergyman, scientist. Madison was born and raised near Staunton, in present-day Rockingham County, Virginia, across the Blue Ridge Mountains from the Orange County home of his second cousin of the same name. After assuming duties as professor of natural philosophy and mathematics, and after being ordained as a minister in the Church of England, Madison successfully served as president of the College of William and Mary from 1777 to his death. In 1778, he received his second cousin James into his Williamsburg home for two years while the latter served as a member of the Council of State. Although never again in physical proximity, the two Madisons remained lifelong friends. Their thirty-year correspondence reveals nearly identical political convictions as revolutionaries, supporters of the Federal Constitution, and Jeffersonian Republicans.

An Enlightenment scholar, Madison performed numerous scientific investigations in fields including astronomy, physics, geology, chemistry, and biology, that gained him membership in the American Philosophical Society in 1779. Consecrated as first Bishop of the Protestant Episcopal Church in Virginia in 1790, Madison had the misfortune to head a church that disestablishment had nearly destroyed. His theology was a reconciliation of orthodox Episcopalianism and republicanism: he viewed the American Revolution as a providential event and he referred to heaven as a "republic," not a "kingdom." In 1800, future president Madison suggested that the bishop purchase a tract of land adjoining his and become a neighbor, but the owner's price was too high. Nearly twenty years after the bishop's death, President Madison remembered his kinsman with undiminished respect for his "intellectual power and diversified learning," his "benevolence," "courtesy," and allegiance to "our Revolution, and to the purest principles of a Government founded on the rights of man."

BIBLIOGRAPHY

Crowe, Charles. "Bishop James Madison and the Republic of Virtue." *Journal of Southern History* 30 (1964): 58–70.
Holmes, David L. "The Decline and Revival of the Church of Virginia." In *Up from Independence: The Episcopal Church in Virginia*. Edited by Brewster S. Ford et al. 1976.

RICHARD RANKIN

MADISON, JAMES (1751–1836). [This entry provides a biography of James Madison in seven articles:

Birth and childhood
Education
American Revolution
Continental Congress
Secretary of State
Presidency
Retirement

For discussion of Madison's participation in the Constitutional Convention of 1787, see *Federal Convention*. For discussion of his service in Congress, see *Congress*, articles on *First Congress, Second Congress, Third Congress*, and *Fourth Congress*. For discussion of biographies of Madison, see *Biographies of James Madison*.]

Birth and Childhood

Nelly Conway Madison was nineteen when she gave birth to her first son, James Madison, Jr., on 16 March

1751 (5 March 1750 O.S.). The young mother was visiting her stepfather's plantation on the banks of the Rappahannock River, which could still accommodate ocean-going vessels at the time of Madison's birth. When Nelly Madison felt well enough, Madison's father took his young family from King George County over the winding Virginia country roads to Orange County, Virginia, where Ambrose Madison (the baby's grandfather) had established a plantation some twenty years earlier. By 1751 James Madison, Sr., had enlarged the original farm to a plantation spread of more than four thousand acres in the foothills of the Blue Ridge Mountains.

Social life on the Madison plantation, which would in time be called Montpelier, moved along as Nelly Madison bore eleven more children in the years through 1774. For playmates James had his brothers Francis (born 1753), Ambrose (born 1755), and William (born 1762). A baby brother, Catlett, lived only one year, and another brother, Reuben, died when he was four. Nelly Conway lost two other children between 1766 and 1770—one was still-born, and one died within twenty-four hours of birth. The first sister, Nelly, was delivered in 1760; after Nelly there were Sarah, Elizabeth, and Frances. All seem to have had tutoring at Montpelier, as the family home was a sometime schoolroom; then around 1760 the family moved to new quarters in the house, which young James would inherit and die in nearly eighty years later.

Small of stature (no certain record of his height or weight ever was kept), Madison probably learned to ride horses while still a toddler, for most Virginia boys from well-to-do parents owned their own steeds early on. The main house was not finished when the family moved in, so over the next few years young Madison dodged carpenters, bricklayers, and painters as the home took shape. Whether young Madison showed his lifelong tendency toward periods of sickness or indisposition is uncertain, but he was well enough to be sent to Donald Robertson's school in the summer of 1762.

Before Madison left Montpelier for schooling in King and Queen County, he had learned the fundamentals of arithmetic, reading, and writing, and unless his father was an exceptional Virginian, the family was acquainted with the New Testament and the Anglican *Book of Common Prayer*. An inventory of the elder Madison's library indicates there was little in the way of belles lettres present in the household as Madison grew up, but once Madison attended Robertson's school, his literary horizon expanded.

Late in life Madison wrote an autobiographical sketch in which he barely alluded to his boyhood. No record was made of childhood games or holidays at Montpelier as Madison skipped from his birth to the year he left home for Robertson's school at "the age of about 12 years." The elder Madison's record book showed that a dancing mas-

ter visited Montpelier to teach the children the minuet and other proper dances. But whether James Madison, Jr., ever learned to dance or played a parlor game during his early years is far from certain.

BIBLIOGRAPHY

Brant, Irving. *James Madison: The Virginia Revolutionist, 1751–1780.* 1941.
Hunt-Jones, Conover. *Dolley and the "Great Little Madison."* 1977.
Ketcham, Ralph. *James Madison: A Biography.* 1971.

ROBERT A. RUTLAND

Education

Madison probably began rudimentary lessons in reading and writing while he was growing up at Montpelier, with his mother or another close relative as a makeshift tutor. Late in life Madison recalled that when he was "the age of about twelve years" he was placed under the tutelage of the Scottish pedagogue Donald Robertson, who maintained a school in King and Queen County, Virginia. Robertson, a native of Aberdeenshire, Scotland, had moved to Virginia in 1753 and had taught on Tidewater plantations until he established his school in 1758. Robertson's own account book indicates that Madison first came to his school in June 1762 and was part of his class of scholars until September 1767.

After an introductory year, Madison concentrated in Latin but was also instructed in Greek, French, arithmetic, algebra, geometry, geography, and literature. Robertson's pupils were required to study Virgil, Terence, and Sallust; Madison's boyhood "Book of Logick" (which was a typical notebook with entries by the youthful Madison) show that he was acquainted with Socrates, Plato, Euclid, and John Locke. The notebook entries include drawings of the Copernican solar system, as well as geometric designs. Other entries indicate Madison was exposed to the works of the popular Anglican bishop of Cloyne, George Berkeley, whose attacks on materialism were widely read in colonial British America. Like Franklin and other impressionable Americans, Madison fell under the spell of Joseph Addison's *Spectator*, whose literary style captivated the young Virginian and which may account (according to the scholar Irving Brant) for Madison's later difficulties in writing a simple, straightforward sentence.

Under Robertson's tutelage Madison also acquired a knowledge of French, which he later confessed to have been almost useless as a conversational vehicle, perhaps owing to the Scottish accents of Robertson and another teacher at the College of New Jersey (later Princeton).

In 1767 Madison was back at Montpelier, where he was taught (along with his brothers and sister) by the Rev-

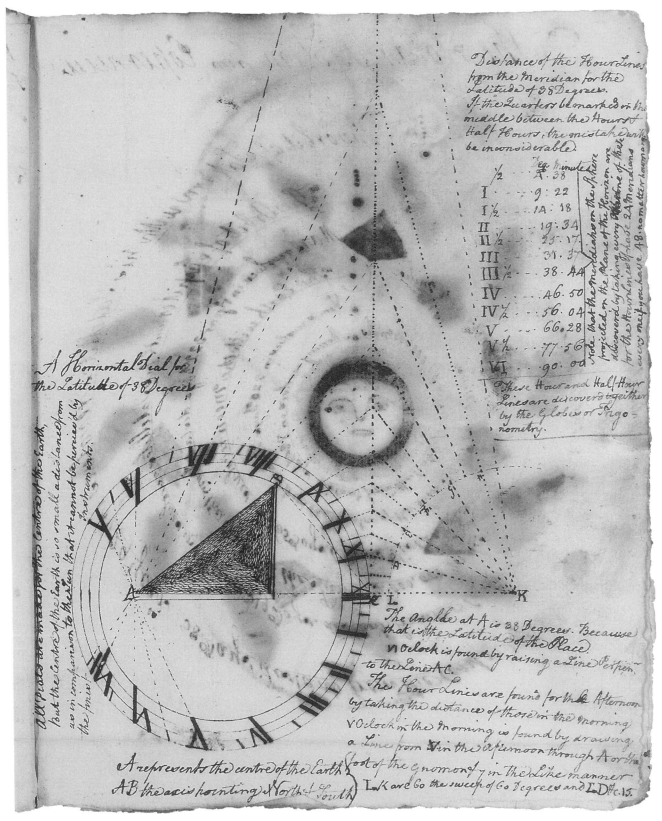

Distance of the Hour Lines from the Meridian for the Latitude of 38 Degrees.

If the Quarters be marked in the middle between the Hours & Half Hours, the mistake will be inconsiderable.

	Deg. Minutes
½	A. 38
I	9 : 22
I½	1A : 18
II	19 : 34
II½	25 : 17
III	31 . 37
III½	38 . AA
IV	A6 . 50
IV½	56 . 04
V	66 . 28
V½	77 . 56
VI	90 . 00

Note that the Meridian or the future projected on the Plane of the Horizon are discovered by taking every other one of these hour lines & these are 2A meridians for these hour lines & these 2A meridians every next you have AB no matter how many

These Hour and Half Hour Lines are discover'd together by the Globes or Trigonometry.

A Horizontal Dial for the Latitude of 38 Degrees

All places the Meridian the centre of the earth, but the centre of the earth is so small a distance from us in comparison to Heaven that it cannot be perceived by Instruments

The Angle at A is 38 Degrees. Because that is the Latitude of the Place.

VI Oclock is found by raising a Line Perpendicular to the Lines AC.

The Hour Lines are found for the Afternoon by taking the distances of those in the morning.

V Oclock in the morning is found by drawing a Line from VI in the afternoon through A or the foot of the gnomon & y in the Like manner

A represents the centre of the Earth

AB the axis pointing North & South

L & K are Go the sweep of Go Degrees and LD Hc. 15.

A STUDENT'S NOTEBOOK. "A Brief System of Logick" dates from 1763–1765, when Madison was a schoolboy in Virginia. "Distance of the Hour Lines" is given for 38 degrees latitude, the latitude of Orange County, Virginia. The sun in the center of the page shows through from the other side of the sheet. JAMES MADISON PAPERS, LIBRARY OF CONGRESS.

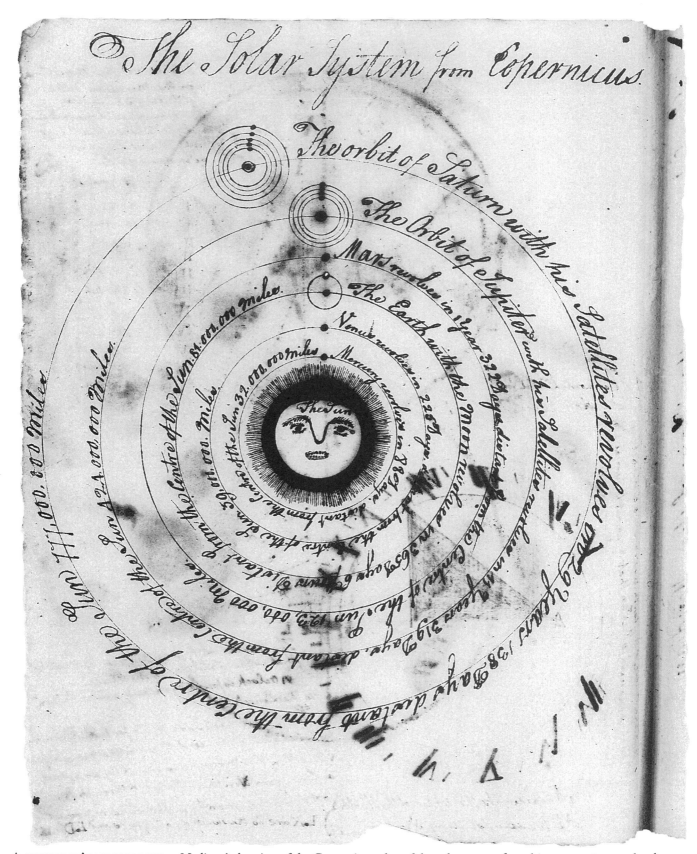

A STUDENT'S NOTEBOOK.   Madison's drawing of the Copernican plan of the solar system from his manuscript notebook, "A Brief System of Logick," c. 1763–1765. This is the reverse of the previous illustration; the circle of Roman numerals shows through at the lower right.

JAMES MADISON PAPERS, LIBRARY OF CONGRESS.

erend Thomas Martin, the recently arrived minister at the Anglican church in Orange County. Martin, who had graduated from the College of New Jersey in 1764, lived with the Madisons at Montpelier and divided his time between teaching and preaching. Little is known of Martin's curriculum, but Martin's influence on Madison was evident, for, two years later, the eighteen-year-old Madison was enrolled at his teacher's alma mater at Princeton. While most of the bright young men in Virginia studied at the College of William and Mary in pre-Revolutionary days, Madison remembered that his choice was also affected by warnings that the Williamsburg climate "was unhealthy for persons going from a mountainous region." Already concerned about his health, Madison sought an intellectual haven at Princeton in all likelihood because the Presbyterian school was known to be "a bulwark against Episcopacy." There were also rumors that William and Mary students were addicted to gambling.

Madison arrived at Princeton in the summer of 1769 and there was instructed by its formidable president, John Witherspoon, and a faculty of three tutors. The curriculum was intended to prepare young men for the ministry, but the broad range of courses appealed to Madison's appetite for knowledge, rather than his religious conviction. He was introduced to Montesquieu, Grotius, and Pufendorf, and his study habits became spartan—he recalled that he sometimes slept "less than five hours in the twenty four" and had his head in a book for most of each waking day. He found time, however, to join the Whig Society, where he knew Philip Freneau and Hugh Henry Brackenridge. As the political storms brewed in nearby Philadelphia, the Princeton students became aware of the tensions between England and British America. Madison witnessed and may have participated in a public burning, outside Nassau Hall, of a letter from New York merchants deploring colonial resistance to parliamentary intimidation.

Madison's rigorous academic regimen allowed him to cram two years of course work into one, so that by September 1771 he was qualified for the baccalaureate degree. Whether Madison hurried his collegiate studies to save money or because of his deepening intellectual curiosity is not clear. Certainly, he took chances with his health, for a contemporary reported that Madison was excused from attending the commencement exercises, probably because of illness. Madison stayed on at Princeton, after gaining his father's permission, until the spring of 1772.

Back at Montpelier, Madison played tutor himself for his brothers and sisters but was restless about his future. As the eldest son, he was by custom in line to succeed his father as the manager of Montpelier, but he complained about his poor health and lamented that he was confined "in an Obscure Corner" where little of importance hap-

pened. Madison began collecting his own library and to a degree became a scholar in the wilderness. As another Princeton graduate, Philip Fithian (class of 1772), observed, Madison's degree from their alma mater was worth £10,000.

"And you might come & go, & converse, & keep company, according to this value," Fithian added, "and you would be despised & slighted if you rate yourself a farthing cheaper." Madison had his Princeton degree, but his future in 1772 depended more on circumstances than on his education.

BIBLIOGRAPHY

Brant, Irving. *James Madison: The Virginia Revolutionist, 1751–1780*. 1941.
Ketcham, Ralph. *James Madison: A Biography*. 1971.
Peterson, Merrill D. *James Madison: A Biography in His Own Words*. 2 vols. 1974.

ROBERT A. RUTLAND

American Revolution

At the forefront of the American Revolution, both in its origins and accomplishments, was James Madison's Virginia, the wealthiest and most populous of Britain's North American colonies. Virginia's House of Burgesses led other provincial legislatures in vigorously denying Parliamentary authority to tax America in the Stamp Act crisis of 1765. A few years later that body strongly opposed Parliament's second effort to raise an American revenue with the Townshend Duties. The provincial political elite also took the lead in calling for colony-wide committees of correspondence, for trade retaliations in response to Parliament's Coercive Acts, and for an intercolonial congress to plan a series of united responses to the continuing threats to American liberties. Moreover, Virginians leading the patriot cause included Peyton Randolph, the first president of the Continental Congress; George Washington, the commander in chief of the Continental army; Richard Henry Lee, the introducer of the congressional resolution for breaking all political ties with Britain; and Thomas Jefferson, the author of the Declaration of Independence.

If young James Madison, recently graduated from the College of New Jersey, was slow to take an active role in the events propelling Virginia toward independence, his few surviving letters certainly voiced support for the colony and its break with the British. But prior to June 1774 his approval came in measured, judicious prose, not in passionate rhetoric. At times, Madison appeared more concerned about his health, his choice of reading matter, and his philosophical development.

Though advocating military preparedness on the part

MADISON'S DIPLOMA. Madison graduated from the College of New Jersey (now Princeton University) on 7 October 1771. The signature of the president of the college, John Witherspoon, appears at the left under the word "Testimonium."

JAMES MADISON PAPERS, LIBRARY OF CONGRESS.

of both the provincial Convention, which had effectively replaced royal government in the colony, and the Continental Congress in Philadelphia, Madison did not take a direct part in the resistance until his prestigious father, James Madison, Sr., provided him specific opportunities. Young Madison was elected in December 1774 to the Orange County Committee of Safety, which the elder Madison chaired. Madison, Sr., also headed the county militia, to which his son—without meaningful military experience—received an appointment as a colonel in October 1775.

No doubt family influence further contributed to Madison's deepening public involvement when he won a seat in the provincial convention in spring 1776. His father's financial resources, together with his own lack of a family, enabled Madison to serve his colony-state and the Revolution in a variety of capacities in subsequent years without facing the domestic concerns that interrupted or permanently cut short some public careers.

In weighing his options, soldiering was never a serious consideration for Madison, nor did he ever seem interested in military affairs except in the broadest sense. "He was restrained from entering into the military service," Madison later recalled, "by the unsettled state of his health and the discourageing [sic] feebleness of his constitution." Instead, the Revolution demonstrated that he had superb abilities as a member of deliberative forums: conventions and legislatures, bodies that crafted laws and instruments of government. His brilliance shone in constitutional matters, particularly in matters of individual rights and liberties. In his capacity for detail, for the business of legislation, and for cool, reasoned debate and discussion—a far cry from Patrick Henry's flamboyance and florid speech—Madison was not unlike the highly respected Edmund Pendleton, a Virginia legislator since 1752. The similarity of their political styles perhaps explains the attraction the veteran Pendleton felt towards advancing Madison's career.

Even so, the political neophyte Madison took a back seat in the Convention to such luminaries as Pendleton and Henry, and George Mason, who was the principal architect of the Virginia Constitution of 1776. But the twenty-five-year-old Orange County representative left a significant mark on the accompanying Declaration of

Rights, the most influential document of its kind adopted in America prior to the federal bill of rights of 1791 (itself introduced by Madison). The subject was religious toleration, a concern of Madison's since 1774 when several dissenting Baptist ministers ran afoul of the law and the Anglican establishment for preaching without a license. He admired the religious toleration of Pennsylvania, where the Quaker founders had never created a state church. Madison would have personally preferred the Virginia Constitution to have provided for absolute separation of church and state, but there was no way in 1776 he could prevail on that issue. He persuaded the Convention to go beyond Mason's language, however, moving beyond mere toleration to the explicit statement that "all men are equally entitled to the free exercise of religion." Completing its momentous work on 5 July, the Convention adjourned and then reassembled in the fall under a new name, the House of Delegates, now part of the legislative branch of an independent state. This session marked the first of the many collaborative undertakings of Madison and Thomas Jefferson, who was back from Congress and a fellow member with Madison of the legislature's Committee on Religion. They met with only modest success when they supported petitions from dissenters seeking the complete disestablishment of the Anglican church. They learned that change is not always easy, even during a revolution. Religious conservatives forced a compromise: Baptists, Presbyterians, and other non-Anglicans were exempted from the annual parish levies, but the Anglican church structure remained in place.

Madison also learned that his family name and his creative and conscientious labors were not enough to ensure his reelection to the House of Delegates. He was defeated in 1777 by another planter candidate, a tavern owner, who did not scruple, as did Madison, to "swill the planters with bimbo," which was the practice of providing strong drink to show the generosity of the candidate for all the gentlemen freeholders. Yet Madison, whose republican creed stressed conduct that was reasonable, moderate, and virtuous (as opposed to what he considered to be his opponent's demagoguery), had gained high marks from his colleagues in the legislature. To retain his services, they picked him for a seat on the eight-man Council of State.

For over two years Madison served as a member of this privy council, an advisory body to the governor with a good deal of authority in its own right, particularly when it dealt with a welter of wartime problems. Virginia had been spared the ravages of a British invasion, although Loyalists led by Lord Dunmore, the colony's last royal governor, caused trouble in the Norfolk-Portsmouth area because they received temporary support from British naval forces. Nevertheless, the council spent long hours, especially when the legislature was not in session, dealing with the day-to-day wartime problems. The Continental Congress and General Washington repeatedly called on the Old Dominion to increase its contributions of men and supplies to the war effort. Meanwhile, Virginians complained about inflation and high taxes, although in fact both the states and the Congress endeavored to pay for most of the war costs not through taxes but by printing paper money, which by 1779 had depreciated to the point of being almost worthless. Madison concluded that neither state nor Congressional governments were working well. At the state level governors were all but impotent, while at the federal level Congress was too dependent on the goodwill and cooperation of the states.

Elected to Congress in December 1779, Madison learned still more about the problems of federal-state relations, staying at his post without returning to Virginia until his term expired in December 1783. Madison's important committee assignments indicated his growing influence in Congress, which existed as an extralegal body prior to the ratification of the Articles of Confederation, the nation's first constitution, in 1781. An increasing number of congressmen were committed to enhancing the authority of a central government, that had no executive and judicial branches and only limited powers under the Articles. These so-called Nationalists, though hardly a cohesive faction, believed that Congress needed authority to raise revenues independently of the states and to enforce its legitimate legislative acts. While Madison defended the interests of Virginia in such matters as its proposal to cede western lands to the Confederation, he also saw the need to cement a firmer American union. Virginia's own inability to protect itself from a succession of British raiding parties along its coasts, followed by the arrival of Cornwallis's army in May 1781, only reinforced his convictions, which remained fixed even after Cornwallis's surrender to Franco-American forces in October of that same year.

Madison's final two years of his first service in the Continental Congress were devoted principally to offering qualified support for Superintendent of Finance Robert Morris's financial program and drafting an acceptable compromise on securing federal revenues through an impost on foreign goods. Madison retired from Congress before a decision was made on reforming the Confederation, but the prospects that the states would give up authority to Congress looked dim.

[For discussion of the continuation of Madison's career, see *Annapolis Convention; Federal Convention;* and *Congress.*]

BIBLIOGRAPHY

Banning, Lance. "James Madison and the Nationalists, 1780–1783." *William and Mary Quarterly*, 3d ser., 40 (1983): 227–255.

Brant, Irving. *James Madison, the Virginia Revolutionist, 1751–1780.* 1941.

Ketcham, Ralph. *James Madison: A Biography.* 1971.

Rakove, Jack N. *James Madison and the Creation of the American Republic.* 1990.

Selby, John E. *The Revolution in Virginia, 1775–1783.* 1988.

DON HIGGINBOTHAM

Continental Congress

Madison's years in the Continental Congress, 1780–1783 and 1787–1788, were a small but formative part of a long and distinguished career. He arrived in Philadelphia on his twenty-ninth birthday in March 1780, just in time to witness Congress's repudiation of the Continental dollar, the collapse of congressional finances, and the failure of the "in-kind" system of state requisitions for provisioning the Continental army. As a result, he endorsed vigorous measures for sustaining the war and

MADISON IN 1783. Madison exchanged miniatures with Catherine Floyd. Miniature by Charles Willson Peale. [For her portrait, see *Floyd, Catherine.*]

RARE BOOK AND SPECIAL COLLECTIONS DIVISION, LIBRARY OF CONGRESS.

restoring public credit, eventually urging a number of proposals to ensure Congress a dependable revenue, and even offering a motion for compelling states "to fulfill their federal engagements." If Madison was the father of the Constitution, the Continental Congress was surely the political father of Madison.

Yet Madison came to Congress a faithful son of Virginia, without the centralizing vision or agenda for change that characterized other nationalistic leaders with whom he eventually became identified. Madison was never an ideologue—his transformation was the product of experience, of events and circumstances that reshaped the perceptions of his generation of Americans.

His first year in Congress saw the capture of Charleston, the collapse of the Continental army in the southern department, renewed Indian attacks on the frontier, the treason of Benedict Arnold, mutinies of Pennsylvania and New Jersey regiments, and almost weekly reports of hardships suffered by Continental troops inadequately fed, clothed, and supplied by Congress. Madison readily identified the principal cause of these embarrassments—the evaporation of Continental fiscal authority. "The situation of Congress has undergone a total change from what it originally was," he explained to Jefferson soon after his arrival. "Since the resolution passed for shutting the press, this power [of emitting money] has been entirely given up and they are now as dependent on the states as the King of England is on parliament. They can neither enlist, pay nor feed a single soldier." To support the army various expedients were tried and discarded. A special congressional committee was sent to Washington's headquarters to work out in-kind state requisitions and impressment of supplies by Continental commissaries and quartermasters. Trial and error loomed large in Madison's congressional experience.

Simultaneously Congress struggled with the more fundamental problem of the lack of a constitutional foundation, an acute issue once the money supply had failed. As the British invasion of the South became more dire in 1780, ratification of the Articles of Confederation acquired urgency. Attention focused on Maryland's refusal to join the Union unless states with vast western claims ceded their unappropriated western lands to the entire United States. Virginia wanted assurance that land companies based in other states did not exploit such concessions, and Madison resolutely opposed all attempts to override his constituents' demands until Virginia's conditions were accepted nearly three years later.

Madison also tenaciously defended the Franco-American alliance. France had provided vital credit, arms, and the naval aid that prevented enemy troops from overrunning Virginia, and Madison never forgot the debt owed America's ally. He often worked closely with the

MADISON AT 30.   Silhouette by Joseph Sansom, Philadelphia, c. 1781.
COURTESY HISTORICAL SOCIETY OF PENNSYLVANIA, PHILADELPHIA, PEROT COLLECTION.

French minister La Luzerne and his assistant, the marquis de Barbé-Marbois, to represent French views sympathetically to Americans, and staunchly defended Benjamin Franklin's Paris diplomacy against such congressional Francophobes as Arthur Lee.

It would be folly, Madison believed, for Americans to turn their backs on their powerful benefactor once the war ended. He appealed for a French naval presence in the Chesapeake to protect the tobacco trade, and remained faithful to the vision of a flourishing postwar commerce with France as the best means open to escape the domination of Britain. He denounced early British overtures for a separate peace designed to divide the allies and he opposed keeping an article of the peace treaty secret from France on the grounds that it would breed distrust.

He had arrived in Congress in 1780 a shy young man whose earliest assignment was the narrow routine of the marine department, but within the year Madison was considered for the post of secretary for foreign affairs and was repeatedly assigned to the most significant congressional committees. His steady congressional attendance was nearly unrivaled, and when James Lovell returned home early in 1782 after five years consecutive attendance, Madison stood alone as the most experienced delegate in Congress. This fact illustrated his philosophy that congressional debility was rooted in congressional instability. He often bridled at the irresponsibility of delegates such as New Jersey's Abraham Clark, who denied being bound to honor decisions of previous Congresses, or Connecticut's Eliphalet Dyer, whose constituents wished to ignore earlier congressional commitments to Continental army officers concerning half pay, commutation, and depreciation allowances. "The idea of erecting our national independence on the ruins of public faith and national honor," Madison noted, "must be horrid to every mind."

Judged from the perspective of 1789, Madison and his congressional colleagues were builders of an American nation, but his career in the Continental Congress was more precisely one of frustration and even failure. Independence had been won, but at an unnecessarily high price. American sacrifices had been inequitably shared, and poor leadership had contributed to excessive hardship. Congress simply lacked the will, vision, and means to discharge the country's obligations to those who had borne the heaviest burdens. Fiscal reform was absolutely essential if the Continental army and public creditors were to be paid, or the foreign debt adequately serviced, but Congress was as far from realizing this goal in 1784 as it had been in 1780.

Madison and his colleagues thrice begged the states for requisitions or new fiscal powers and were as often disappointed. They attempted unsuccessfully to resolve a number of festering interstate disputes, such as the status of Vermont or Connecticut's claims in Pennsylvania's Wyoming Valley, to establish frontier security through friendly relations with most of the Indian tribes, and to gain recognition of their southwestern boundary claims. The right to navigate the Mississippi River was Madison's overriding concern. Other nagging failures rooted in Continental weakness and instability included the provisioning and exchange of prisoners of war; illicit trade with the enemy; state and local violations of Continental flags of truce and export agreements; restitution of slaves evacuated by the British in violation of the treaty of peace; and effective courts for resolving appeals from state admiralty decisions.

Despite this legacy of congressional futility, Madison struggled to the end to find equitable and effective fiscal solutions for upholding Continental authority and reviving national honor. He opposed several state efforts to assume responsibility for payment of their own troops, which threatened Continental fiscal control, and he played a key role in the deliberations sparked by the army's unrest at Newburgh in winter 1783. And he was the author of both the landmark fiscal report and the Address to the States of April 1783 that asked the states to vest Congress with an independent source of revenue—authority to levy a 5 percent impost similar to that proposed and rejected in 1781. The revival of Continental fortunes was once more left to a decision of the states.

Congressman Madison's hopes were to remain unfulfilled, however, for the states again refused to grant the authority requested. In summer 1783 Congress suffered the ultimate humiliation of intimidation by its own troops, who escaped punishment, and a flight from Philadelphia that sent the vagabond Congress—unable to reach agreement on a site for the federal government—to Princeton, Annapolis, Trenton, and New York in the space of eighteen months. Finally, before leaving Congress in fall 1783, Madison suffered a crushing psychological blow when his fiancée, sixteen-year-old Kitty Floyd, daughter of his New York colleague William Floyd, broke off their engagement.

Madison rallied from these disappointments, public and private. From Virginia he later launched himself into new initiatives for rescuing national fortunes. His tenure in Congress taught him the difficulty of trying to harmonize the interests of thirteen competing American jurisdictions and the complexity of creating an American nationhood. He experienced firsthand the growing pains of the new nation, and repeatedly offered enlightened leadership and policies, although few Americans saw the necessity for the changes he advocated.

He devoted his final brief tenure in Congress to the establishment and ratification of a new federal constitution, whose nature he brilliantly elucidated in his *Federalist* essays, written while in New York in 1787–1788, serving out the final days of the old Confederation Congress.

BIBLIOGRAPHY

Banning, Lance. "James Madison and the Nationalists, 1780–1783." *William and Mary Quarterly* 3d ser., 40 (1983): 227–255.

Hutchinson, William T., et al., eds. *The Papers of James Madison.* 18 vols. 1962–.

Ketcham, Ralph L. *James Madison: A Biography.* 2d ed. 1990.

Rakove, Jack N. *James Madison and the Creation of the American Republic.* 1990.

Smith, Paul H., et al., eds. *Letters of Delegates to Congress, 1774–1789.* 20 vols. 1976–.

PAUL H. SMITH

Secretary of State

James Madison began his duties as secretary of state on 2 May 1801 amid a variety of personal anxieties. For months he had suffered ill health, and then on 27 February his father had died. His trip from Virginia to Washington through heavy rains and quagmires had been unpleasant, but his political and intellectual relationship with the new president, Thomas Jefferson, was firm. Throughout the policy debates of the Federalist era, the two men had stood together in their opposition to Alexander Hamilton's proposals on both domestic and foreign policy. Now in command of the country's foreign relations, Jefferson and Madison limited their exchanges on external issues largely to conferences, rather than to letters. The State Department that Madison inherited was small. To maintain his correspondence with over fifty American representatives abroad, Madison relied on a chief clerk, six copying clerks, and a messenger.

Conditions abroad were scarcely more reassuring than those that had confronted George Washington in 1789. The Barbary states continued to prey on American commerce in the Mediterranean. Throughout eight years of European war the U.S. government had been unable to protect American shipping from marauding British and French privateers and cruisers. Then, in March 1801, the rumor reached Washington that Napoleon had wrested Louisiana from Spain.

The Louisiana Purchase. Jefferson's initial venture into foreign affairs augured well for the future. Napoleon indeed had dispatched a special mission to Madrid in 1800 to acquire Louisiana. Finally, in the spring of 1802, Robert R. Livingston, the American minister in Paris, confirmed the existence of a treaty that transferred Louisiana to France. Jefferson's famed response of 18 April acknowledged that the United States and France had few interests in conflict, but he added: "There is on the globe one single spot, the possession of which is our natural and habitual enemy. It is New Orleans. . . . The day that France takes possession of New Orleans . . . we must marry ourselves to the British fleet and nation." When in October the Spanish intendant at New Orleans closed that port to American shippers, Jefferson and Madison assumed that Napoleon was behind the move, which threatened all American commerce on the western rivers. The Mississippi, wrote Madison, was "the Hudson, the Delaware, the Potomac, and all the navigable rivers of the Atlantic States formed into one stream."

What drove the administration to act, however, was less the fear of France's possession of New Orleans than Alexander Hamilton's public demand that the United States seize New Orleans by force if negotiations failed to acquire it peacefully. Jefferson responded by sending James Monroe on an extraordinary mission to France, explaining to Livingston that he expected little of the mission but hoped to counter Congress's inflammatory resolutions. Jefferson anticipated no territorial expansion of the republic; the Louisiana Purchase was a windfall that was neither sought nor pursued. Napoleon's dream of a New World empire collapsed when yellow fever destroyed much of his army in Santo Domingo, permitting natives to regain control of the island. Convinced that Louisiana had become a burden, he then offered it to the United States. Monroe and Livingston signed the treaty transferring Louisiana to the United States for $15 million on 30 April 1803. Madison regarded the purchase as highly advantageous but, like Jefferson, wondered whether the transaction was constitutional. So popular was the acquisition, however, that Jefferson accepted it without a constitutional amendment.

Negotiations with Britain. When Jefferson and Madison assumed command of U.S. foreign policy in the spring of 1801, war was still raging in Europe. After long negotiations, the Treaty of Amiens, signed on 2 March 1802, brought a general peace to Europe for the first time in almost a decade. The peace was short-lived, and the fighting resumed in May 1803 as France and Great Britain, one supreme on land, the other supreme on the oceans, again ventured onto the Atlantic to challenge American neutral rights. Jefferson responded in his annual message of 17 October by restating America's determination to avoid war by treating the belligerent nations fairly and by restraining American citizens "from embarking individually in a war in which their country takes no part." Jefferson had not lost his faith in the power of American neutral commerce to coerce the European belligerents to respect American neutral rights. He restated that faith in his October message: "[W]ith productions and wants which render our commerce and friendship useful to them and theirs to us, it cannot be the intent of any to assail us, nor ours to disturb them."

To Madison fell the burden of convincing the British that their interest lay in recognizing American rights on the high seas. He demanded that the British give way on four issues: impressment, blockade, contraband, and trade with France's West Indian possessions. Madison instructed Monroe in London to remind the British that failure to respond would close the American market for "certain important and popular classes of British manufactures."

Madison demanded essentially the relaxation of Britain's infringements on American commerce through its naval blockades. The British reach deprived the United States of even the lucrative trade with French and Spanish colonial possessions, behavior that Madison regarded as overly demanding, capricious, and arbitrary. U.S. trade with the European continent hinged on the British definition of importation. The British *Polly* decision of 1800 had granted neutral countries the right to carry noncontraband goods between all ports, including the colonial possessions of belligerents except those

MADISON AND THE EMBARGO.   Secretary of State Jemmy Madison is devoured by his unpopular creation. Woodcut by Alexander Anderson after John Wesley Jarvis. [For a later use of this image, see *Embargo Act of 1807.*]

PRINTS AND PHOTOGRAPHS DIVISION, LIBRARY OF CONGRESS.

under direct blockade. But that decision required that a voyage be broken (by unloading goods and paying duties) before transshipment to a belligerent.

To the British government, it was apparent that U.S. officials often cleared unloaded cargoes for ports in continental Europe or the West Indies. In the *Essex* prize case of 1805, the British judge declared that the owner of a ship that had landed at Charleston, paid duties, and continued to Havana had regarded Havana as his destination from the beginning. The *Essex* ruling declared that a cargo's ultimate destination determined its nationality and thus determined whether it was subject to blockade. Defending the decision in his pamphlet *War in Disguise; or, The Frauds of Neutral Flags,* James Stephen accused the United States of war profiteering at Britain's expense. The decision reestablished Britain's own Rule of 1756, which held that trade prohibited in time of peace could not be opened in time of war. No longer would Britain permit neutrals to carry enemy goods with impunity. In 1806 the British government extended its assault on neutral commerce by declaring a blockade of much of the European coast.

Jefferson faced the choice of accepting the *Essex* decision as a reasonable expression of British interests or countering it with argument, economic retaliation, or diplomacy. Since argument appeared the most promising and least expensive response, Madison prepared to enter the fray with his pen. His 204-page pamphlet, *An Examination of the British Doctrine, Which Subjects to Capture a Neutral Trade, Not Open in Time of Peace,* appeared in January 1806. Jefferson was delighted with Madison's demolition of the *Essex* ruling. "I send you a pamphlet," he wrote a friend in February, "in which the British doctrine that a commerce not open to neutrals in peace shall not be pursued by them in war is logically and unanswerably refuted." Others were less convinced; Madison's assertion that belligerents had no right to interfere in the commerce of neutral countries not at war scarcely defined a doctrine. Federalists complained that the argument was tedious, and Virginia's John Randolph accused Madison of "hurling a shilling pamphlet" against eight hundred ships of war.

For Monroe in London, Britain's disguised war against the United States demanded some retaliation, even at the risk of war. He wrote to Madison in December 1805: "It seems to be a question, simply, whether we will resist their unjust pressures at this time or defer it to some future opportunity." If his fears were justified, Monroe argued, the country might as well fight instead of sending more diplomatic notes. Monroe wondered, as did Jefferson and Madison, whether the economic value of the shipping involved was worth more than winning the argument. Economic retaliation carried risks, and southerners engaged in a direct commodity trade with Britain opposed any threat to exclude British vessels from American ports. They accepted the Jeffersonian principle that commerce contributed to social welfare only if it encouraged American productivity. On the other hand, northern Republicans, led by Andrew Gregg of Pennsylvania, believed that Congress should counter the *Essex* rule with a complete boycott of British imports. Britain, they believed, understood its economic interests too well to accept the loss of the American market. Congress did not care to see either American commerce or the southern staple market injured by an embargo, but a majority agreed that successful diplomacy with Britain required some action. The Nonimportation Act of April 1806 was a halfhearted congressional attempt at economic coercion, with the implementation date postponed until December. To Randolph the measure was merely "a dose of chicken broth to be taken nine months hence."

Compelled by the necessity to protect American commerce against the *Essex* decision and to forestall nonimportation, Jefferson and Madison sought some defense of American shipping via a treaty. In April 1806 the president sent William Pinkney of Maryland to join Monroe in negotiating an arrangement that would include British recognition of American neutral rights as well as curbs on the practice of impressment. Madison instructed Monroe and Pinkney to reestablish the principle of the broken voyage and to secure indemnity for all illegal seizures under the *Essex* ruling. Both Jefferson and Madison doubted that the negotiations would succeed, for in 1806 the British were not dealing from weakness. Yet as late as July Jefferson argued that the British recognition of American neutrality would benefit Britain by giving that country an open market for its manufactured goods and allow France a safe carriage of its productions, both metropolitan and colonial. If Britain accepted Jefferson's definition of useful neutrality, the United States could again enjoy unrestricted trade at little cost.

There were no grounds for much hope. Monroe and Pinkney faced determined resistance as the British now demanded that a broken voyage be defined to require the storage of cargo for a month and reshipment in a different vessel. In effect, the American threat of nonimportation had no meaning. When the American negotiators raised the question of impressment, the British promised to moderate their practices but would not concede in a treaty the right to impressment.

When word reached Washington that Monroe and Pinkney intended to sign a treaty that did not terminate impressment, Madison, on 3 February 1807, informed them that the president would reject such a treaty. But the treaty, signed in December, was already on its way across the Atlantic and reached Washington on 3 March. Jefferson informed Congress, about to adjourn, that he would not recall the Senate to consider the treaty and blamed the absence of a satisfactory article on impressment. In addition, the president discovered that Monroe and Pinkney had agreed to make any removal of British restrictions contingent on American resistance to French commercial policy. For Jefferson, that provision would compel the United States to join Britain in a common cause against France. Later, Monroe explained that he and Pinkney had violated their instructions out of fear that their failure to negotiate some sort of agreement would bring a war for which the United States was not prepared.

The European War. During 1807 American commerce became trapped in a massive commercial war between Britain and France. In November 1806 Napoleon responded to the British blockade with his Berlin Decree, which proclaimed a paper blockade, the Continental System, of the British Isles that would prohibit all neutral trade with Great Britain. London responded with its order in council of 7 January 1807, which outlawed all neutral commerce between ports under French control. Madison complained in late March that such restrictions would destroy the profitability of American trade by denying neutral captains the right to visit a series of European ports. Neither Jefferson nor Madison could explain Britain's continued rejection of American neutral rights as other than an inexcusable demonstration of anti-Americanism.

Jefferson's continuing conflict with Britain over impressment reached a crisis in the *Chesapeake* affair of 22 June 1807. That day, the American warship *Chesapeake* sailed from Hampton Roads, only to be fired on and stopped by the British frigate *Leopard* in American territorial waters. The British removed four American sailors, then permitted the badly damaged *Chesapeake* to return to port. In seizing the *Chesapeake*, the British had denied the immunity of a national ship of war, had seized the ship in American waters, and had removed men who claimed to be American citizens. Madison immediately ordered Monroe to demand a formal disavowal of the incident, the return of the four seamen, and the cessation of impressment from vessels sailing under the flag of the United States. On 17 July Madison complained to Monroe that the British continued to detain and examine merchant vessels in American waters. In September Madison still anticipated a diplomatic settlement of the *Chesapeake* affair, but Monroe, who conducted the negotiations in London, failed to achieve agreement when Madison instructed him to seek satisfaction for all impressments, not merely those on the *Chesapeake*. In October the British government issued a proclamation reaffirming that country's right to search vessels for British seamen.

Jefferson's troubles with Europe were only beginning. Following his great victory over Russia at Friedland in June 1807, Napoleon believed that he had at last gained

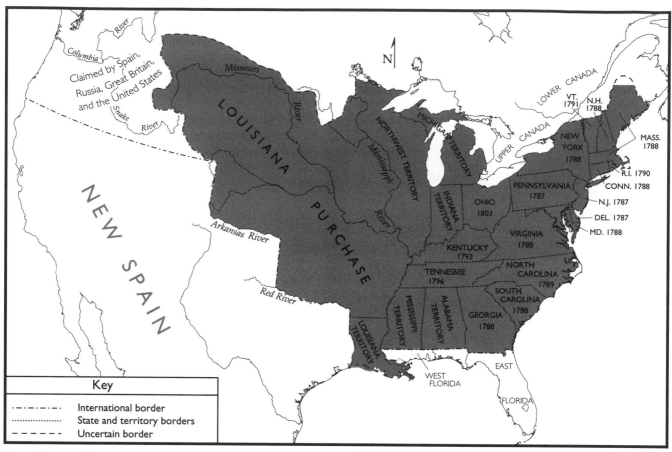

THE UNITED STATES IN 1808.

mastery over Europe, especially when he persuaded Tsar Alexander I to extend the Continental System to Russian ports. During the late summer of 1807 Napoleon began to enforce his Berlin Decree with numerous seizures in the ports of Europe. The British retaliated with their famous order in council of 11 November 1807, which declared a blockade of all countries in the Napoleonic system, as well as their colonies, and condemned their products as lawful prizes. In reaction, Napoleon tightened French restrictions on British trade with his Milan Decree of 17 December. Now any neutral ship sailing from a British port or subjected to British search lost its neutral character and became vulnerable to French seizure. Five days after the issuance of Napoleon's Milan Decree, Jefferson recommended to Congress an embargo on all American vessels departing for foreign ports. With little debate Republican majorities in Congress adopted the president's program.

Jefferson hoped that the Embargo would postpone the outbreak of war until the country could build its strength sufficiently to meet any European challenge. Meanwhile, the embargo, he observed in March 1808, would keep "our ships and seamen out of harm's way." By keeping American ships at home, the Embargo did affect the European economy, but it scarcely undermined Britain's dominance in the Atlantic or its command of neutral commerce. The Embargo destroyed much of the European market for southern agriculture and granted Britain a virtual monopoly over world trade. Its impact on northern shipping was disastrous. For Jefferson the Embargo was always a temporary measure, to be continued or terminated as conditions demanded. Still, he knew that any abandonment of the Embargo before the British repealed their orders in council would leave American policy nowhere to go. Still, dissident Republicans and New England Federalists favored abandonment, convinced that the Embargo's ineffectiveness, aggravating the country's frustrations, would eventually trap it in war.

When Jefferson's administration finally turned the Embargo into a weapon of coercion, it sought the power to coerce, not in the Embargo itself, but in the threat of war against the country responsible for its failure. To determine which European power would be the victim, the administration informed London and Paris in April 1808 that the Embargo would end in December. Thereafter the United States would resume trade with the belligerent that removed its restrictions and would declare war on the other. If both belligerents responded favorably, the United States would have its trade without the price of war; if neither did, the United States, in Jefferson's words, would take its choice of enemies. The offers to Britain and France were ostensibly identical, yet very unequal. The requirement that the two powers repeal all restrictions that infringed on American neutral trade on the high seas touched Britain's entire commercial war against the United States; it did not challenge Napoleon's Continental System, where enforcement occurred in port. The British navy had long reduced France's commercial warfare on the high seas to a nullity. In effect, therefore, the administration asked France to revoke only that aspect of its commercial program that it was powerless to enforce.

Both Britain and France rejected the American offers, but Madison wondered why the French would reject an arrangement that demanded so small a sacrifice. Napoleon angered Madison further with his Bayonne Decree, in which France proclaimed its commitment to the success of the American Embargo by promising to capture all American merchant vessels on the high seas or in European ports. Jefferson and Madison had adopted a futile policy because every alternative permitted by British and French commercial policy made matters worse. In his final message to Congress in November 1808, Jefferson assigned to Congress the responsibility for defining the next response to Europe's challenge.

After a long debate, Congress, on the eve of Madison's presidency in early March 1809, embarked on a potentially effective policy by adopting the Nonintercourse Act. This law terminated all commerce with Britain and France but promised to restore trade with either belligerent upon its recognition of American commercial rights on the oceans. Madison had pressed for the inclusion of the latter provision and quickly assured the European belligerents that the United States would respond to favorable action by either power by retaliating against the other. In practice, nonintercourse injured Britain, with its dominance of the seas, more than France. Madison reminded British minister David M. Erskine that adequate British concessions would effectively direct American animosity toward France, and so Erskine reported to London. Foreign Minister George Canning wondered how the United States, following a British-American accord, would keep its vessels, cleared for Britain, from entering the ports of France. Canning informed Erskine that Britain would withdraw its orders of January and November 1807 if the United States would cancel its trade restrictions regarding Britain, leaving them in force against France; renounce its wartime carrying trade with the French colonies; and permit Britain to capture American vessels attempting to trade with continental ports in violation of American law. Madison accepted the first of Britain's three conditions but rejected the other two. What appeared reasonable to the British seemed degrading to Madison. As president, Madison discovered early that the quest for an effective American policy toward Europe's warring powers had scarcely begun.

BIBLIOGRAPHY

Brant, Irving. *James Madison: Secretary of State, 1800–1809*. 1953.
Burt, A. L. *The United States, Great Britain, and British North America from the Revolution to the Establishment of Peace after the War of 1812*. 1940.
Perkins, Bradford. *Prologue to War: England and the United States, 1805–1812*. 1968.
Rutland, Robert A. *James Madison: The Founding Father*. 1987.
Spivak, Burton. *Jefferson's English Crisis: Commerce, Embargo, and the Republican Revolution*. 1979.

NORMAN A. GRAEBNER

Presidency

Since occupants of the White House are judged in a variety of contexts, the usual criteria of strong leadership, forceful decisiveness, and unimpeachable integrity bring to mind visions of a Washington, a Jefferson, or a Lincoln. Adhering to this high standard, history and historians rarely have accorded Madison more than a modicum of acclaim. The tendency has been to speak of Madison's service at the Federal Convention and to hail him as "the father of the Constitution" but to see him as a disappointment once he donned the presidential mantle. There is no record of any protest made when the outstanding presidents chosen for the Mount Rushmore monument were announced: Washington, Jefferson, Lincoln, and Theodore Roosevelt. Madison, to the popular notion, was not in their company.

Madison's presidency came at a crucial time in the history of the young republic, and perhaps it would be fairer to look at the accomplishments of his eight years in the office. He was Jefferson's handpicked successor and inherited a mass of congressional discontent that had accumulated during Jefferson's two terms. From the outset, Jefferson had a willing Congress and the goodwill of the nation; his cabinet was so able that he never needed to change it, and until 1807 his relations with Congress were so amicable that he never once exercised his veto power. The Louisiana Purchase added to the nation's vast western reserve, and the war in Europe proved troublesome but never demanded U.S. involvement in a way that required a declaration of war.

A Difficult Beginning. Consider the sharp contrast from early 1809 onward. President-elect Madison, an

PRESIDENT JAMES MADISON.   Engraving by David Edwin after the portrait by Thomas Sully.
PRINTS AND PHOTOGRAPHS DIVISION, LIBRARY OF CONGRESS.

eyewitness to the cordiality of Jefferson's halcyon days in the White House, was confronted by angry senators and representatives weeks before his inaugural. Jealous, ambitious senators feared the presence of Albert Gallatin and wanted him out of the cabinet. Others, mindful of the disaffection of New England during the Embargo crisis, were eager to see geographical balance in the president's official family, even if that meant sacrificing competence for convenience.

Thus Madison was not accorded the peaceful interim that usually precedes an inaugural "honeymoon" when goodwill reigns at both ends of Pennsylvania Avenue. From the outset, Madison strove to preserve unity and was so eager to keep peace within Republican ranks that he sacrificed his independent judgment when he allowed critics to deny him the choice of his trusted ally, Gallatin, as secretary of state. The appointment of Robert Smith, who had been secretary of the navy in Jefferson's cabinet, was a mistake that Madison would regret. And there were others, for the secretaries of war and of the navy—

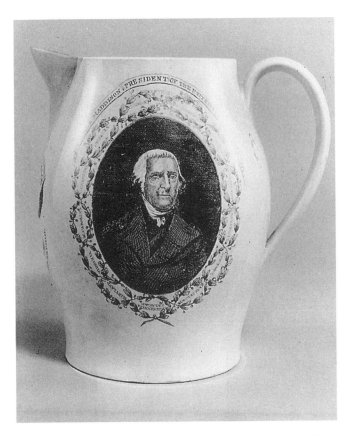

MADISON'S IMAGE.   Lest the beholder not recognize the portrait, purportedly of James Madison, his name adorns the banner over his image; it is misspelled. Creamware jug made in England for export to America; such creamware was sometimes called Liverpoolware.   COURTESY DAVID J. AND JANICE L. FRENT POLITICAL AMERICANA COLLECTION.

William Eustis and Paul Hamilton—were has-beens of limited talents, so that in effect Gallatin (who had been appointed by Jefferson, so no confirmation was needed to keep him as secretary of the Treasury) was to wear a variety of hats as he tried to serve Madison loyally. One is tempted to recall the 1806 British coalition cabinet "of all talents" and to speak of Madison's first cabinet as one of no talents, Gallatin excepted.

Madison also kept a Jeffersonian appointment, Caesar Rodney, as his attorney general. In 1809 that position was not of cabinet rank, however, and was so lowly regarded as a part-time job that Rodney was "on call" at his home, not a resident of Washington unless pressed to come down from Delaware for urgent business.

Madison's troubles did not end there, either. A small coterie of surly senators, nicknamed the Invisibles by colleagues who saw them as devious workers-by-stealth, labored overtime to thwart Madison's programs in the upper house. Their match in the House of Representatives, in a sense, was the obstreperous John Randolph, the erratic Virginian who had once been a Jeffersonian favorite. Randolph had broken with Jefferson and took potshots at Madison whenever possible, hinting at one time that Madison stood to profit from the miserable Yazoo Lands fraud and at another time persuading James Monroe to stand for the presidential office when all knew the suggestion was ludicrous, if not futile, or both.

Madison could depend on the loyal Republicans in the Congress, but for aid he relied on Gallatin to serve as a go-between; the Treasury chief drafted laws and kept fences mended so that the national Treasury could remain solvent. Gallatin's job would have been much easier if the Bank of the United States had won recharter; although the bank had been a sore point with Madison in 1790 when Hamilton proposed it, Madison had dropped his constitutional objections and saw the wisdom of creating a central bank that could control the country's credit system. But there was trouble ahead, for after the House took the bait and passed the rechartering bill, Vice President George Clinton (who had presidential pretensions) broke a tie vote in the Senate and defeated the bill. This was a setback Madison had not expected, and he was as dejected and powerless as Gallatin.

Challenges from Abroad. Clinton's vote showed how little control Madison had over his Republican friends in Congress. However, neither the bank bill nor other domestic affairs were a key concern when Madison was inaugurated in March 1809. The Embargo died as Madison's tenure began, and loyal Republican farmers who made up the nation's largest voting bloc looked for relief from depressed prices but believed their patriotism required patience. A young group of newly elected representatives was less subtle—they were restless and ready

A sketch for the REGENTS speech on MAD-ASS-SON's insanity.

A BRITISH VIEW OF PRESIDENT MADISON.   James Mad-Ass-Son, supported by the devil and Napoleon Bonaparte, reacts to the angel of judgment, who trumpets "Bad news for you" and carries a banner referring to Gen. William Hull's surrender of Detroit and Commissary General of Ordnance Decius Wadsworth's failed attack on a British flotilla on the Patuxent River in Maryland. Colored etching of a drawing by the English caricaturist George Cruikshank, London, December 1812.

PRINTS AND PHOTOGRAPHS DIVISION, LIBRARY OF CONGRESS.

to twist the British lion's tail after repeated British insults to the American flag had raised doubts about Britain's respect for the independence of the United States. If British ships could fire on American naval vessels, impress seamen, hang alleged "deserters," and impose the orders in council that strangled Yankee trade to continental ports, what must the United States do to prove worthy of the events of 1776? Was the country still, in effect, a mere British colonial outpost with pretensions to sovereignty? And what of Napoleon, with his stranglehold on Europe threatened by the Royal Navy so that he too ran roughshod over American rights, seized Yankee ships, and imprisoned hapless American seamen?

Madison faced these problems as president after having wrestled with them as Jefferson's secretary of state. The unfortunate beginning of his presidency, the Erskine affair that was revealed as one blunder compounded by a diplomatic reprimand, put Madison on the defensive. Erskine, the British minister in Washington, told Madison that the detested orders in council could be revoked if Madison would cancel the Nonintercourse Act provisions applying to Great Britain. Erskine had overstepped his authority, but Madison did not know that, so he grabbed at the straw Erskine offered.

When the foreign minister, George Canning, backtracked, Madison saw this disavowal as more evidence of British duplicity. Long noted for his Anglophobia, Madison found nothing in the conduct of the British cabinet to alter his judgment that the main source of U.S. troubles sprang from the environs of Westminster in London. The impressment issue, which had never been solved despite diplomatic protest and the ill-timed Pinkney-Monroe treaty (which Jefferson repudiated), seemed to raise doubts about the ability of Americans to stand up for their rights at a time when the American mercantile fleet was challenging the best shipping that Europe or Great Britain could offer. The contempt shown by the Barbary corsairs as they attacked ships flying the stars and stripes and tried to hold American sailors for ransom was another problem that arose from the outreach of American commerce into world markets.

Madison looked to Congress for help, since his idea of a president's duties as spelled out in the Constitution required a partnership between the president and the legislature; Congress would pass laws and set national goals in the process, and the president would approve the laws and see that they were executed. Congress could even delve into the field of foreign policy, and Madison welcomed cooperation because of his conception of the presidency. As the historian Jack Rakove has observed, in this case Madison was "a prisoner of his constitutional convictions."

Months and years passed, and Madison's frustration was compounded by the slowness of communications; sometimes six months would go by before a strongly worded note to one of the belligerents had been answered. Meanwhile, the presidential election of 1812 loomed, and within his official family Madison discovered that Robert Smith was double-dealing, leaking stories about internal bickering, and displaying disloyalty with arrogance. Madison fired Smith and replaced him with James Monroe. Monroe had accepted an olive branch from Madison, whose magnanimous gesture restored integrity to the cabinet. Reports that Secretary of the Navy Hamilton was often drunk heralded a change there. But Madison, innately conservative, was reluctant to make wholesale cabinet changes, and with Gallatin and Monroe by his side, Madison recognized the combination of intellect and loyalty he sorely needed.

As the United States inched toward war, Madison stood aside and allowed Congress to shape foreign policy. With Republicans in a majority in both the House and the Senate, Congress resorted to patchwork laws meant to steer the country outside the shoals of war by maintaining U.S. neutrality. Nothing seemed to work, for the British would not permit American ships to trade through their blockade of Napoleon's continental ports, and Napoleon was clever enough to pretend that he was doing exactly what Congress wanted and insisted that America "put up or shut up" by boycotting Great Britain and, in effect, becoming a French ally. Plagued by British intransigence and by his own anxieties, Madison fell into Napoleon's trap.

Before his patience ran out, Madison tried one last time to gain British recognition of American rights; the return to America of a diplomatic courier ship, empty-handed, led Madison to believe he had no choice. Reluctantly, but with an optimism that seemed foolhardy, Madison took the nation into war in June 1812.

The War of 1812. The war did not go well. Early on, boisterous representatives had bragged that Canada would fall to American troops at the first feint, but in fact, the U.S. armies were poorly led, ill equipped, and confused as to war aims. If Canada was to become a bargaining chip in a diplomatic poker game, its conquest had to be swift and sure. Instead, the disgraceful surrender of Detroit and the obstinate attitude of Federalist New England somewhat tied Madison's hands. He could not mount a successful land campaign, and, except for some spectacular and isolated successes, the navy was bottled up in Atlantic coastal ports for most of the war. The U.S. flotilla in the Great Lakes, nearly equal in number to the British and Canadian foe, was another matter, for the courage of the seamen proved that Yankees could fight and win against their opponents.

The presidential election of 1812 hardly mattered. De Witt Clinton tried to mount a campaign to appeal to the anti-Madison crowd, but he made contradictory promises and wound up carrying New England but losing nearly everything else. Madison never made a campaign speech and won a second term as the nation first showed its preference for a tested president in a wartime election.

Congress, for all its bluster, refused to approve a wartime taxing program and left Gallatin the unhappy task of raising money to prosecute the war through loans. New England bankers retaliated by almost refusing to help finance the war, and Gallatin was able to keep the nation's cash register full enough to pay the bills but had to drop the old Jeffersonian dream of retiring the national debt. Congress was ready to vote to raise armies but not for the taxes needed to recruit and train men or to equip them. As in the darkest days of the Revolution, foreign bankers and financiers supplied the money when Congress would not or could not.

All the mismanagement and inefficiency became glaringly apparent when the British army, no longer needing to battle the now exiled Napoleon, was free to concentrate on the American conflict. A force of British marines landed in Chesapeake Bay and almost without opposition marched into Washington, burned the White House, burned the Capitol, and left behind a good deal of ill will and mythology. Dolley Madison's dramatic rescue of Washington's portrait became symbolic—the Madison administration's ineptness had brought on a national disgrace, but a proud lady had kept the humiliation from being total. In August 1814 the capital was a shambles, and so was Madison's reputation.

No American thought that the country was whipped, but the outlook was dismal. And then, as salt in the nation's wound, the Federalists held a convention at Hartford and shaped an arrogant set of demands that would make sectionalism the watchword in postwar America. Some dis-

Stop, Stop Stop Brother Jonathan, or I shall fall with the loss of blood — I thought to have been too heavy for you — But I must acknowledge your superior skill — two blows to my one! — And so well directed too! Mercy mercy on me, how does this happen!!!

Ha - ah Johnny! you thought yourself a Boxer did you! — I'll let you know we are an Enterprizeing Nation. and ready to meet you with equal force any day.

A BOXING MATCH, or Another Bloody Nose for JOHN BULL.

BROTHER JONATHAN V. JOHN BULL. "A Boxing Match" between Brother Jonathan (James Madison) and John Bull (George III) refers to the defeat of HMS *Boxer* by the American frigate *Enterprise* in September 1813. Brother Jonathan was the personification of the United States in the early republic. Hand-colored etching by William Charles, 1813.

PRINTS AND PHOTOGRAPHS DIVISION, LIBRARY OF CONGRESS.

tant settlements in upper New England even treated British invaders with deference and spoke of seceding from the Union to become British protectorates.

Madison moved back to Washington and took up temporary quarters in a borrowed mansion. The only ray of hope rested on the diplomatic mission he had sent to Russia, grasping at a straw thrown out by Tsar Alexander I, who had offered to serve as mediator between the United States and Britain. As peace talks opened, Madison's choice of negotiators, including John Quincy Adams, Gallatin (on leave from the cabinet), and Henry Clay, was inspired. Their negotiating sites changed, but the mettle of the negotiators did not. They seemed to ignore the campaign results and overlook lost battles as they jockeyed for advantages for America at the bargaining table. Luck was with them, for the British lion roared at one time and purred at another, until by December 1814 a miracle was in the making. On Christmas Eve, 1814, a peace treaty was signed that left most matters where they had stood at the war's start. No territory was lost, no indemnities paid, and minor matters relating to boundaries and fishing rights were left to be worked out later.

The Madison administration and the nation were ignorant of these happenings, for the British invasion army near New Orleans was aimed at the southern heartland of American commerce at the mouth of the Mississippi. Then the news exploded on a delirious nation. The British had been routed at New Orleans, with terrible casualties for the redcoats and only a few loses for the tobacco-chewing American marksmen. Andrew Jackson was a new and much-needed American hero. First came the news from New Orleans, then more joyous reports from Ghent and London. It was all over, and the president who had looked like a beaten man in August 1814 was beaming in February 1815. The Federalists took their Hartford ultimatum and their party into oblivion.

Peace and Laurels. Once the effect of peace sank in on the American consciousness, the laurels denied to Madison for so long began to appear. Gallatin perceived a radical change in the nation's self-assessment. "The war has renewed and reinstated the national feelings and charters which the Revolution had given, and which were daily lessened," he observed. "The people have now more general objects of attachment. . . . They are more American; they feel and act more as a nation; and I hope the permanency of the Union is thereby better secured." Even the New Englander Justice Joseph Story was amazed by the new spring in the American step: "Never did a country occupy more lofty ground; we have stood the contest, single-handed, against the conqueror of Europe; and we are at peace, with all out blushing victories thick crowding on us."

Madison, the object of so much scorn six months earlier, was hailed as the worthy successor of great men. Embarrassed by the recalcitrant New England stand dur-ing the fighting, former president John Adams looked about and noted (as Madison prepared for retirement) how much the United States had advanced during the Madison years: "Notwithstanding a thousand faults and blunders, his Administration has acquired more glory, and established more Union, than all three Predecessors, Washington, Adams and Jefferson put together." High praise, from a discerning source.

By the time that John Adams had decided Madison deserved high marks, the nation had not only returned to a peacetime prosperity but was headed toward an era that would soon be described as one of "good feeling." With a more cooperative Congress, Madison had at last solved the national banking riddle, made his own statement about the limits of constitutional powers on domestic matters, and seen the Barbary pirates humbled in their own lair by American warships. The Indian tribes on the western frontier were at peace, the gridlock on trans-

THE CAPTURE OF WASHINGTON.   Fleeing the burning city, the epicure Madison stuffs Napoleon's promises in his pockets. At left, Brother Jonathan suggests that he join Napoleon in exile. "The Fall of Washington, or Maddy in full flight," colored engraving by Charles Williams, London, 1814.   COURTESY PRINTS AND PHOTOGRAPHS DIVISION, LIBRARY OF CONGRESS.

THE FIRST SIX PRESIDENTS.   James Madison (far right) appears on a printed fabric with (from left) Thomas Jefferson, James Monroe, John Quincy Adams, George Washington, and John Adams. Engraving roller-printed on textile, France, c. 1827.
COURTESY OF THE DAVID J. AND JANICE L. FRENT POLITICAL AMERICANA COLLECTION.

portation for farm products was soon to be replaced by new canals and turnpikes, and in the Treasury there was a surplus of $9 million. When Madison went back to Montpelier in retirement, his old friend Francis Corbin (who had assisted Madison at the fateful Richmond ratifying convention in 1788) was euphoric in his praise. Corbin told Madison his White House tenure was the fitting climax to a brilliant career. "The End," Corbin observed, "has indeed crowned the Work!"

Madison's Reputation. Harbors were full of ships, harvests were bountiful, and the American flag commanded new respect on the world's oceans. Not a bad record for the president who would later be ridiculed by a New England historian, Henry Adams, as a hapless, vacillating chief executive. Adams mesmerized a whole generation of historians with his charges of "executive weakness" and wartime mismanagement in a multivolume *History of the United States during the Administrations* *of Thomas Jefferson and James Madison.* Adams's harsh judgment did incalculable damage to Madison's reputation as president, convincing several generations of readers and students that Madison was a Founding Father who had stayed on the stage too long for his own good. The negative image of Madison's presidency was so persistent that a widely adopted American history college text in 1977 described the fourth president as an executive who "inspired little affection and no enthusiasm."

Adams's views on Madison were at wide variance with those of his distinguished grandfather but in keeping with sweeping judgments rendered only a few years after Madison died in 1836. When an edition of Madison's papers was prepared for publication in 1840, the editor, Henry Gilpin, concentrated on Madison's service as a legislator and as a delegate at the Federal Convention and ignored his presidency completely. A four-volume edition of Madison's *Letters and Other Writings* published after the Civil War skipped over most of Madison's presidential papers, and a nine-volume edition of Madison's *Writings* issued early in the twentieth century had only one devoted to Madison's White House years.

Since World War II much of the scholarship devoted to Madison's presidential years has taken a more elevated tone. Irving Brant's six-volume biography found little fault with Madison at any level. A biography by the historian Harold Schultz was generally sympathetic to Madison's handling of problems but reminded readers that those stands that had been virtues in Madison's early career (favoring restrictions on the powers of government, shaping opposition to political opponents) became liabilities when he entered the White House. Madison, Schultz said, realized "that circumstances could produce both failures and successes for which an individual in office might undeservingly be blamed or praised." No harsher judgment on Madison as president was voiced than that leveled by Leonard White, who insisted that Madison "would have been much more at home as president of the University of Virginia" than as president of the United States.

Despite this blight caused by historians' hindsight, Madison has remained a benign presence in the nation's consciousness. The annex to the Library of Congress dedicated in 1981 was designated as the James Madison Memorial Building, but the revival of interest that followed—particularly in 1987 (the Constitutional Bicen-

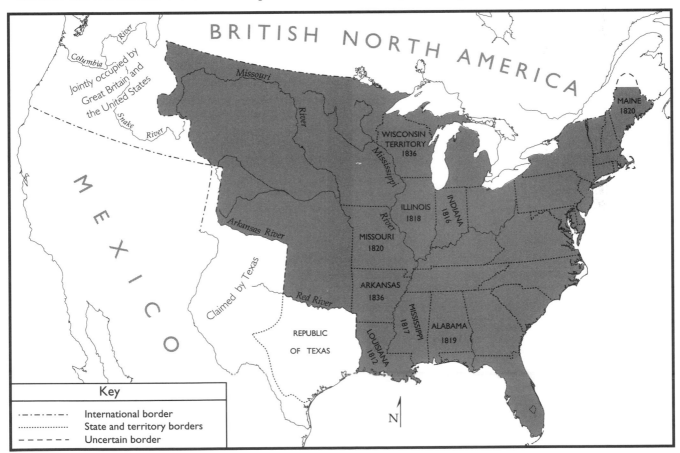

THE UNITED STATES IN 1836.

tennial)—centered more on Madison's contributions to *The Federalist Papers* than on any other aspect of his career.

Madison's presidency was full of ordeals, and presidents make their reputations by the way they handle adversity. Buchanan walked away from trouble, whereas Madison gritted his teeth and believed that the United States could not be treated as a third-rate power in a world full of conflicts. Polk set forth a program and then sought to keep all his campaign promises and almost achieved the unachievable; Madison had no program but neutrality, and he abandoned that makeshift approach only when it seemed unrealistic. In 1817 he left the United States a far stronger nation than it had been in 1809. The new nation was poised for a half-century of expansion, the Constitution was still the polestar of his country's conduct, and he believed that the Union he had done so much to preserve was firmly in place. Madison left Washington and headed for Montpelier a happy man.

BIBLIOGRAPHY

Brant, Irving. *James Madison.* 6 vols. 1941–1961.
Ketcham, Ralph. *James Madison: A Biography.* 1971.
McCoy, Drew R. *The Last of the Fathers: James Madison and the Republican Legacy.* 1989.
Rakove, Jack. *James Madison and the Creation of the American Republic.* 1990.
Rutland, Robert A. *James Madison: The Founding Father.* 1987.
Schultz, Harold. *James Madison.* 1970.

ROBERT A. RUTLAND

Retirement

Madison's lengthy and unusually productive retirement offers inspiring commentary on the possibilities of old age. For the last nineteen years of his life, from the end of his second term as President in early 1817 to his death in 1836 at the age of eighty-five, the "Sage of Montpelier" remained intellectually active and vibrant while retaining his customary even-temperedness in the face of mounting private and public troubles. In short, Madison's retirement was far from being a period of dotage. Madison had always been an avid reader, and his retirement afforded him ample time to indulge that pleasure. He continued to develop his longstanding intellectual pursuits, and through his avid perusal of newspapers, he remained remarkably well informed about current affairs. Above all he was, as always, deeply and passionately involved in his country's ongoing experiment in republican government.

Madison entered his retirement riding the wave of personal popularity that he had enjoyed during the final two years of his presidency. Notwithstanding the string of military and political disasters that had brought the federal government to the brink of collapse by the fall of 1814, Americans had emerged from the War of 1812 in an ebullient, self-confident mood that cast a warm and lasting glow on the man who had led them through that national rite of passage. Madison in retirement could not have avoided playing the role of elder statesman if he had wanted to, and all evidence suggests that he was happy, if not eager, to oblige. He began his retirement at a time when a profound generational shift in American public affairs was already well under way, indeed when public awareness of that shift and its significance was increasing. The almost simultaneous deaths of John Adams and Thomas Jefferson on 4 July 1826 was an especially poignant, powerful reminder that the Revolutionary generation had passed from the scene. But Madison survived for another ten years. As early as 1831 the last of the Founding Fathers seemed bemused by his longevity, quipping to the historian Jared Sparks that "having outlived so many of my cotemporaries I ought not to forget that I may be thought to have outlived myself."

Playing the role of elder statesman was anything but relaxing for Madison. He entertained a steady stream of visitors at Montpelier, foreign as well as American, many of whom regarded their journey to rural and remote Orange County, Virginia, as a pilgrimage of sorts. The records they kept of their visits, sometimes including detailed accounts of conversations with their host, constitute an important source of information about the elderly statesman and his views. The volume of Madison's correspondence during these twilight years is daunting, even staggering. He was besieged with requests for information, opinions, and advice about a wide range of matters past and present. Gracious as always, and wanting to offer guidance to a new generation, Madison was remarkably accommodating. He scrupulously avoided becoming involved in what he considered strictly partisan issues and controversies, but he rarely refrained from offering his opinion on matters vital to the enduring health of the republic he had done so much to create.

Madison's principal contribution to the transmission of his generation's legacy to posterity during these years was the countless hours he spent preserving, organizing, and to some extent editing the documentary records at his disposal. This included his own correspondence dating back to the Revolution, but much more important to him were the voluminous notes he had taken of the debates at the Federal Convention of 1787. Historians will be eternally grateful to Madison for having made those records and for having taken such scrupulous care of them. He had decided, for a number of reasons, not to publish them while any of the Framers were still alive, but he did everything possible during his

MADISON IN RETIREMENT.   Engraving by T. B. Welch from a oil sketch by James Barton Longacre done at Montpelier in July 1833.
PRINTS AND PHOTOGRAPHS DIVISION, LIBRARY OF CONGRESS.

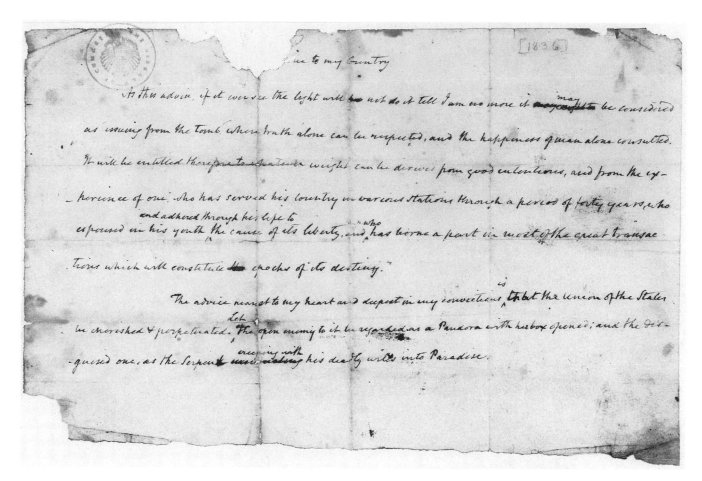

ADVICE TO MY COUNTRY.   James Madison dictated this text to Dolley Madison in 1834; this copy is in Madison's own handwriting. The second paragraph reads: "The advice nearest to my heart and deepest in my convictions is that the Union of the States be cherished and perpetuated. Let the open enemy to it be regarded as a Pandora with her box opened; and the disguised one, as the Serpent creeping with his deadly wiles into Paradise." Edward Coles supplied a copy of this text to Henry Clay in 1850, as the Senate debated the status of slavery in territories acquired after the Mexican War.

JAMES MADISON PAPERS, LIBRARY OF CONGRESS.

retirement to assure their eventual appearance, in good form, shortly after his own death. Madison was confident that these records would afford future citizens, and above all historians, unique and invaluable insight into how his generation had endeavored, through the creation of a modern federal republic, to change the course of human history. Madison was not interested in promoting his own fame (or that of his generation) as much as he was in expanding the evidentiary basis for what is today called political science.

It is important to understand that Madison did not regard the debates at the Federal Convention as any kind of sacred text. He insisted that the views of the Framers contained in his notes had in no way determined or fixed the meaning of the Constitution. But he also believed that posterity must have a sound understanding of the history of the early republic in order to make any meaningful sense of their government. What saddened Madi-

son most during his retirement was having to confront the extent to which the Constitution lacked any fixed meaning for Americans and indeed continued to be a source of controversy, not consensus. Invoking the past, which Madison hoped would serve as a necessary source of stability, only seemed to complicate matters, since the past could be read or interpreted in strikingly different ways according to the needs and inclinations of different groups in the present.

On a few occasions the elderly Madison actually found himself being told by younger Americans that he lacked a sound understanding of his own earlier words and deeds. During the nullification controversy, especially, Madison learned that he was not necessarily considered a reliable guide or authority when it came to interpreting himself. He bore these insults with somewhat bemused chagrin, and seems to have accepted the larger fact that the kind of subtle distinctions and

In consideration of the particular and valuable aids received from my brother-in-law, John C. Payne and the affection which I bear him I devise to him and his heirs two hundred and forty acres of land on which he lives including the improvements, on some of which he has bestowed considerable expense to be laid off adjoining the lands of Reuben & James Newman in a convenient form for a farm so as to include woodland and by the said Mr Newmans.

I bequeath to my stepson John Payne Todd the case of medals presented me by my friend George W. Irving, and the walking staff made from a timber of the frigate Constitution and presented me by Commodore Elliot her present Commander.

I desire the gold mounted walking staff bequeathed to me by my late friend Thomas Jefferson be delivered Thomas J. Randolph as well in testimony of the esteem I have for him as from the knowledge I have of the place he held in the affections of his grandfather.

To remove every doubt of what is meant by the terms of tract of land whereon I live, I here declare it to comprehend all land owned by me and not herein otherwise devised away.

I hereby appoint my dear Wife to be sole executrix of this my Will and desire that she may not be required to give security for the execution thereof and that my estate be not appraised. In testimony hereof I have this fifteenth day of April one thousand eight hundred and thirty five signed, sealed, published and delivered this to be my last

MADISON'S WILL.   The second-last page of Madison's will details the distribution of mementos to his brother-in-law, John C. Todd, his stepson, John Payne Todd, and Thomas Jefferson's grandson, Thomas J. Randolph. Madison's gift to Randolph was significant, since by 1836 most of the furniture, books, and art at Monticello had been scattered by legacies and forced sales. This copy of the will is not in Madison's handwriting.   JAMES MADISON PAPERS, LIBRARY OF CONGRESS.

Will and Testament. We have signed in presence of the Testator and of each other.

(Signed) James Madison.   {Seal}

Robert Taylor.
Reuben Newman Senr.
Reuben Newman Junr.
Sims Brockman.

I James Madison do annex this codicil to my last will as above and to be taken as part thereof It is my will that the nine thousand dollars to be paid by my wife and distributed among my nephews & nieces may be paid into the Bank of Virginia, or into the Circuit Superior Court of Chancery for Orange, within three years after my death

I direct that the proceeds from the sale of my Grist mill & the land annexed sold at the death of my wife shall be paid Ralph Randolph Gurley Secretary of the American Colonization Society, and to his Executors & Administrators in trust and for the purposes of the said Society, whether the same be incorporated by law or not.

This codicil is written wholly by and signed with my own hand, this nineteenth day of April 1835.

(signed) James Madison.

The last Will of James Madison, not to be opened till his death written by his

89-51

CODICIL TO MADISON'S WILL.   On the last page of his will, Madison added a codicil, dated 19 April 1835, arranging for the distribution of bequests to his nephews and nieces and leaving the proceeds from the sale of a mill to the American Colonization Society. This copy is not in Madison's handwriting.   JAMES MADISON PAPERS, LIBRARY OF CONGRESS.

The President of the United States having communicated to the two Houses of Congress the melancholy intelligence of the death of their illustrious and beloved fellow Citizen, James Madison, of Virginia, late President of the United States; and the two Houses sharing in the general grief which this distressing event must produce —

Resolved, by the Senate and House of Representatives of the United States in Congress assembled, That the Chairs of the President of the Senate and of the Speaker of the House of Representatives be shrouded in black during the residue of the session, and that the President of the Senate, the Speaker of the House of Representatives, and the members and officers of both Houses, wear the usual badge of mourning for thirty days. —

Resolved, That it be recommended to the people of the United States to wear crape on the left arm, as mourning, for thirty days. —

Resolved, That the President of the United States be requested to transmit a copy of these Resolutions to Mrs Madison, and to assure her of the profound respect of the two Houses of Congress for her person and character, and of their sincere condolence on the late afflicting dispensation of Providence.

Passed the Senate of the U.S. June 30th 1836. Attest   Walter Lowrie
                                                          Sec. Senate

Passed House of Representatives U.S. June 30. 1836. Attest. Walter S. Franklin, clerk.
                                                          Pr. Robt. M. Johnston asst.

DEATH OF MADISON.   Tribute by Congress to the recently deceased James Madison, 30 June 1836.

HONOR TO THE DEAD.
August 25, 1836.

LIBERTY

JAMES MADISON.
EX-PRESIDENT OF THE UNITED STATES.
Born 17th March, 1750.
Died 28th June, 1836.

MEMORIAL RIBBON.   A silk ribbon dating from August 1836 commemorates Madison. The birthdate is incorrect: Madison was born on 5 March 1750 according to the Julian calendar; when Britain adopted the Gregorian calendar and moved the beginning of the year from 25 March to 1 January, Madison's birthday became 16 March 1751.

DAVID J. AND JANICE L. FRENT
POLITICAL AMERICANA COLLECTION.

refinements that were the distinctive trademark of his constitutional thought were for the most part lost upon a new generation of politicians and partisans who were all too often incompetent historians. Whether that new generation of passionate individualists would be able to preserve the republic under his beloved Constitu-

tion was the question that increasingly haunted him during his final years.

sDuring his retirement Madison also came to see much more clearly than he had earlier the significance of slavery for the future of the republic. In this area as in others, his personal experience intersected and illuminated larger public concerns. Madison was one of many Revolutionary-era statesmen who embodied a paradox that later generations of his countrymen have found difficult to fathom: he was a slaveholder vehemently opposed to the institution of slavery. As a young man in the years immediately after the war for American independence, Madison had pondered possible ways of escaping his inherited role as a Virginia planter and a master of slaves. But he accepted his legacy, misgivings and all, and over the years gradually accommodated himself to that identity without compromising either his principled opposition to slavery or his commitment to abolishing it in the United States. By all accounts he was a generous, even loving, master who always tried to do the best that he could for his slaves. During his retirement, however, Madison the planter found himself caught in the same economic squeeze that was ruining scores of his fellow Virginians, with one consequence being his decision in 1834 to do something he had apparently resolved never to do: sell off to more prosperous planters in the deep South some of his work force. Meanwhile, none of his slaves appears to have had any interest in participating in what Madison believed was central to a larger national strategy for emancipation: emigrating to the new colony of Liberia, on the west coast of Africa, where colonizationists like Madison believed America's former slaves would be best off. The Sage of Montpelier had also hoped to emancipate his slaves in his will. But much to the dismay of some of his admirers, he did not, in part because he could in good conscience neither force them to go to Africa nor turn them loose, unprepared for freedom, in a hostile white world at home.

By the end of his life Madison needed to look no further than his own plantation to understand his country's predicament. Despite his anxiety, he never succumbed to the despair that circumstances would have warranted. His stoical optimism is a telling measure of the depth of his faith in Americans and their republic.

BIBLIOGRAPHY

Brant, Irving. *James Madison: Commander in Chief, 1812–1836.* 1961.

Ketcham, Ralph. *James Madison: A Biography.* 1971.

McCoy, Drew R. *The Last of the Fathers: James Madison and the Republican Legacy.* 1989.

DREW R. MCCOY

GRAVE OF JAMES MADISON, MONTPELIER.
PRINTS AND PHOTOGRAPHS DIVISION, LIBRARY OF CONGRESS.

MADISON, NELLY CONWAY (1731–1829),

mother of President James Madison. Nelly Conway was born 9 January 1731/2, the daughter of Francis Conway and Rebecca (Catlett) Conway. She married James Madison, Sr., on 15 September 1749 at Mount Scion (also spelled Mount Sion and Mount Zion), the Conway plantation in Caroline County. The first of their twelve children, born 16 March 1751, was a son, James Madison, Jr., later fourth president of the United States.

Family records, and her own signature, invariably give her name as Nelly Conway Madison. The usage of "Eleanor Conway" and "Eleanor Rose Conway" in many older sources are Victorianisms, products of an age when the simple name "Nelly" was not considered genteel enough for the mother of a president.

For much of her life, Nelly Conway Madison was plagued by health problems, particularly recurrent fevers and a malaria-like condition. Her family often despaired of her recovery after the most serious of these episodes. However, after "taking the cures" at mineral springs in Orange County and western Virginia in the late eighteenth century, she experienced a dramatic improvement

in her health. In spite of her twelve pregnancies and the many illnesses she endured for most of her first seventy years, she survived her husband by twenty-eight years and outlived eight of her children.

At his death in 1801, James Madison, Sr., left his wife a life interest in the Montpelier house and the Madison plantations. Sharing the house with James and Dolley Madison, with whom she maintained a close and warm relationship, she continued to occupy most of the original (ca. 1760) dwelling. Known affectionately as "The Old Lady," she had her own staff of slaves, her own furnishings, her own kitchen and garden, and her own household schedule. In deference to Nelly Madison's position as mother of an American president and because her longevity made her something of a marvel, visitors to James and Dolley Madison at Montpelier frequently called upon Nelly Madison as well. She lived to a vigorous and mentally active old age, dying at Montpelier on 11 February 1829 at the age of 97.

BIBLIOGRAPHY

Brant, Irving. *James Madison.* 6 vols. 1941–1961.
Ketcham, Ralph. *James Madison: A Biography.* 1971. Repr. 1990.
Miller, Ann L. *Historic Structure Report: Montpelier, Orange County, Virginia—Phase II: Documentary Evidence Regarding the Montpelier House.* 1990.

ANN L. MILLER

MADISON FAMILY.

The Madison family name is found in a number of English counties, especially Northumberland, Durham, and Lincoln. However, there is no known documentation for the exact English ancestry or origins of the family of President James Madison.

The first recorded individual of the Madison name in Virginia was Isaac Maddison, who came to Virginia ca. 1608 and who was dead by early 1624. Although a number of genealogies have cited Isaac as an ancestor of President James Madison, no children of Isaac Madison have been documented, and there is no known evidence that Isaac Madison was a direct forebear of President Madison.

Seventeenth-century Virginia records include more than a half dozen individuals or families with the Madison surname, but because of gaps in the surviving documents from most of that century, the relationships of these individuals or families to each other—if indeed there are relationships—cannot be proven.

Early Family in Virginia. Family memoranda left by President James Madison and his father, James Madison, Sr., state that the first member of their direct family line in Virginia was John Madison, or Maddison (great-great-grandfather of the president), an emigrant from England who was granted land in Gloucester County (now King

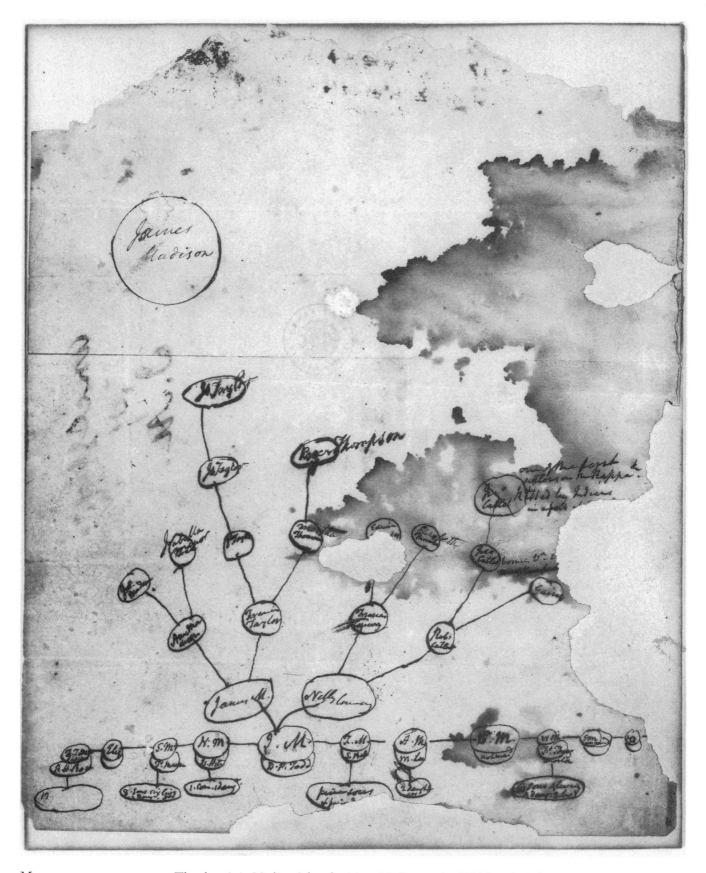

MADISON FAMILY TREE.   The chart is in Madison's handwriting. Madison is the "J.M." to the left of center at the bottom of the chart. His wife, "D. P. Todd," is below him and his brothers and sisters spread out to either side. Above him are his parents, James Madison and Nelly Conway; to the left, he traces the Madisons back only two more generations, to Ambrose Madison and John Madison. To the right, he notes that his mother's grandfather was "one of the first settlers on the Rappa[hannnoc]k. Killed by Indians."

and Queen County), Virginia, in 1653. His wife's name is not recorded, although some traditional accounts say she was Maria Ambrose, thus giving an origin for the use of the given name Ambrose in later generations of the family. The only documented child of this John Maddison was a son, John Maddison, Jr. (d. ca. 1717), the great-grandfather of the president.

John Maddison, Jr., was appointed a justice of the court of King and Queen County, Virginia, in 1707. He had become sheriff of the county by 1714. According to the genealogical chart prepared by President Madison, John Maddison, Jr., married Isabella Minor Todd. The couple had at least three sons: Henry Madison, John Madison, and Ambrose Madison (the president's grandfather); there may have been other children as well.

Of the known children of Sheriff John Madison, Henry Madison remained in Tidewater; he lived in King William County and in Caroline County, and his descendants include members of the Madison families of Charlotte County and the surrounding region. The second son, John, was the progenitor of the Madison family of the Shenandoah Valley, west of the Blue Ridge.

Ambrose Madison, a merchant, planter, and county justice in King and Queen County and in Caroline County, Virginia, married Frances Taylor, daughter of Col. James and Martha (Thompson) Taylor of King and Queen County, in 1721. The couple later moved to Ambrose's Montpelier property in Spotsylvania (now Orange) County. The couple had three children prior to Ambrose's death in 1732: James Madison (1723–1801), father of the president; Elizabeth Madison (1725–ca. 1772); and Frances Madison (1726–1776). All three of these children married and had children.

The elder daughter, Elizabeth Madison, first married John Willis (d. 1750), son of Col. Henry Willis of Fredericksburg. The couple had one child, a daughter, Mary Willis, who married William Daingerfield. Elizabeth Madison's second marriage, to Richard Beale (d. 1771), produced two daughters: Molley Beale and Ann Beale, who married John Whitaker Willis. Frances Madison married Taverner Beale (1713–1756), brother of Richard Beale, and had the following children: Charles Beale, Taverner Beale, Jr. (who married Elizabeth Hite, daughter of his stepfather, Jacob Hite), Frances Beale (who married Thomas Hite, son of her stepfather, Jacob Hite), Elizabeth Beale, and Ann Beale.

Frances Madison Beale's second husband, whom she married in 1760, was Jacob Hite (1719–1776), a widower with children by his first marriage. The children of the marriage of Jacob and Frances Madison Hite were Eleanor Hite, George Hite (1761–1816), who married Deborah Rutherford, and Susan Hite. In the early 1770s, the Hite family moved to South Carolina. Jacob and

Frances Hite and most of their family were killed there during an Indian attack in mid 1776.

President Madison's Immediate Family. Ambrose and Frances Taylor Madison's only son was James Madison, Sr. (27 March 1723–27 February 1801). He married Nelly Conway (9 January 1731/2–11 February 1829), daughter of Francis Conway and Rebecca (Catlett) Conway, on 15 September 1749, and the couple lived on the Madison plantation, Montpelier, in Orange County, Virginia.

An active, entrepreneurial, and public-spirited individual, James Madison, Sr., not only managed and improved Montpelier and his other landholdings (totaling more than five thousand acres) but ran a number of other diverse businesses: he was a merchant, distiller, building contractor, and proprietor of a major plantation ironworks. In his public career, which spanned more than fifty years, he served as Orange County justice, sheriff, and militia colonel, as well as serving as a vestryman of St. Thomas parish in Orange County.

James and Nelly Madison's eldest son and the first of their twelve children was James Madison, Jr., later fourth president of the United States. Their next eleven children, in order of birth, were Francis Madison (1753–1800); Ambrose Madison (1755–1793); Catlett Madison (born and died 1758); Nelly Conway Madison (1760–1802); William Madison (1762–1843); Sarah Catlett Madison (1764–1843); a boy (born and died the same day in 1766); Elizabeth Madison (1768–1775); a stillborn child (1770); Reuben Madison (1771–1775); and Frances Taylor Madison (1774–1823).

James Madison, Jr. (16 March 1751–28 June 1836) married the widowed Dolley (Payne) Todd (20 May 1768–12 July 1849) on 15 September 1794. Although no children were born of this marriage, Dolley Madison had two sons by her first marriage: John Payne Todd (1792–1852) and William Temple Todd (born and died 1793). John Payne Todd, the president's stepson, never married and left no known descendants.

Of President Madison's six brothers and sisters who survived to adulthood, all left children of their own. The Madisons were a close-knit family, and the names of many family members, including siblings, nieces, and nephews appear in the president's papers.

Francis Madison (18 June 1753–5 April 1800) married Susanna Bell in October 1772. The couple lived at Prospect Hill (now called Greenway) in Madison County, Virginia, and had nine children: Frances T. Madison, married Thompson Shepherd; Elizabeth Madison, married Alexander Shepherd; Mary C. B. (Polly) Madison, married William H. Smith; Catherine (Kitty) Bell Madison (d. ca. 1855), married Alexander Spotswood Taliaferro; Elinor (Nelly) Madison, married William B. Wood; James Madison, died unmarried; Catlett M.

THE MADISON FAMILY

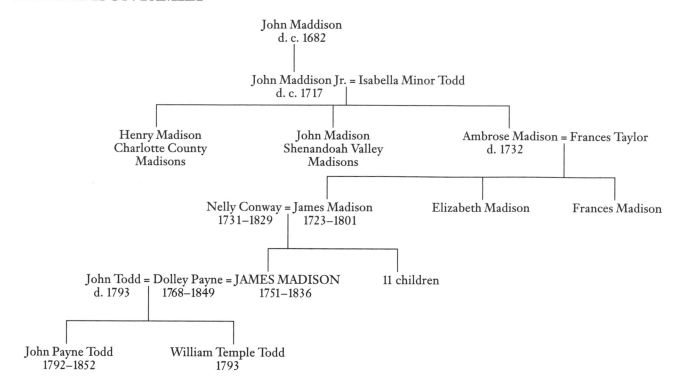

Madison, married Winny Routt; Reubin Conway Madison, married Winna [maiden name unknown]; and William Madison, died unmarried.

Ambrose Madison (27 January 1755–October 1793) was married ca. 1780 to Mary Willis Lee (d. 1798). They lived at their plantation, Woodley, south of Montpelier in Orange County, Virginia, and had one daughter, Nelly Conway Madison (1783–c. 1862), who married Dr. John Willis.

Nelly Conway Madison (14 February 1760–24 December 1802) married Isaac Hite, Jr. (7 February 1758–24 November 1836) in 1783. They lived at Belle Grove, Frederick County, Virginia, and had three children: James Madison Hite (1788–1791); Nelly Conway Hite (b. 1789), married Cornelius Baldwin; and James Madison Hite (1793–1860), married Caroline Matilda Irvine. After Nelly Conway Madison Hite's death in 1802, Isaac Hite married Anne Tunstall Maury and had ten additional children.

William Madison (1 May 1762–20 July 1843) married Frances Throckmorton (1765–1832) in 1783. They lived at Woodberry Forest, Madison County, Virginia, and had eleven children: Rebecca Conway Madison (1795–1860), married Reynolds Chapman; John Madison (1787–1809), died unmarried; William F. Madison (1789–1812), died unmarried; Alfred Madison (1791–1811), died unmarried; Robert Lewis Madison (1794–1828), married [name unknown]; Maj. Ambrose Madison (1796–1855), married

Jane Bankhead Willis; James Edwin Madison (1798–1821), died unmarried; Lucy Frances Madison (1800–1813), died unmarried; Elizabeth Madison (b. 1802), married Lewis Willis; Letitia Madison (b. 1804), married Daniel French Slaughter; and John Madison (d. 1833), died unmarried.

William Madison married Nancy Jarrell as his second wife in 1834. William Madison may have had a son or an adopted son by his second wife, as he mentions a John, or Jack, Madison as a legatee in his will. This John R. Madison [dates unknown] married Lucy B. Rout.

Sarah Catlett Madison (17 August 1764–17 October 1843) married Thomas Macon (11 June 1765–26 February 1838) in 1790. They lived in Hanover County and later at Somerset in Orange County, Virginia, and had eight children: James Madison Macon (1791–1877), married Lucetta Todd Newman; Conway Catlett Macon (1792–1860), married Agnes Mayo; Lucy Hartwell Macon (1794–1871), married Reuben Conway; William Ambrose Macon (1797–1856), died unmarried; Edgar Macon (1802–1829), married [name unknown]; daughter [name unknown] (1803–1805), died unmarried; Reuben Conway Macon (1808–1853), died unmarried; and Henry Macon [dates unknown], died unmarried.

Frances Taylor Madison (4 October 1774–October 1832) married Dr. Robert Henry Rose (d. 1833) in 1801 and had eleven children: Hugh Francis Rose (1801–1856), married Emma Taliaferro Newman; Ambrose James Rose

(b. 1802), married [first name unknown] Kelly; James Madison Rose, died in infancy; Henry Rose (b. 1804), married Sarah Smith; Samuel Jordan Rose (1805–1868), married, first, Prudence W. Jones and, second, Dorothy W. Jones; Erasmus Taylor Rose (1806–1874), married Mary Louise Rose; Ann Fitzhugh Rose [dates unknown], died young; Nelly Conway Rose [dates unknown], married John Francis Newman; Frances Rose [dates unknown], died young; Mary Rose [dates unknown], died young; and Robert H. Rose [dates unknown], married [name unknown].

BIBLIOGRAPHY

Brant, Irving. *James Madison.* 6 vols. 1941–1961.
Ketcham, Ralph. *James Madison: A Biography.* 1971. Repr. 1990.
Meade, William, *Old Churches, Ministers, and Families of Virginia.* 1857. Repr. 1978.
Montgomery-Massingbird, Hugh, ed. *Burke's Presidential Families of the United States of America.* 1975.

ANN L. MILLER

MAINE, DISTRICT OF. The District of Maine, once the easternmost province of the Commonwealth of Massachusetts, like most of New England defied the Madison administration during the War of 1812. The separatist sentiments of the district, developing since the American Revolution, were strengthened by the war and its antecedents. The Embargo of 1807–1809 severely hurt the seaboard, which was dependent on shipping and shipbuilding. Some 60 percent of the workers in coastal communities were reported unemployed by the end of the Embargo.

When "Mr. Madison's War" was declared, the Federalists of Massachusetts and of the Maine District were quick to condemn it, and they continued to trade with the British in defiance of the Madison administration. Smuggling across the border from New Brunswick to Maine flourished until Gen. George Ulmer, commander of the American garrison at Eastport, curbed it. Irate Maine citizens, angered by this interruption of their illegal traffic, retaliated by imprisoning Ulmer at Machias. Only after political intervention from Washington was Ulmer released.

The British, who hoped to recover that portion of Maine lost to them by the treaty of 1783, did not wage active war in the district until the fighting was nearly over. They then occupied Eastport and Castine, captured Bangor and Belfast, and effectively controlled Maine east of the Penobscot River. American vessels, however, continued a brisk trade in the area, reportedly contributing £13,000 to royal customs officials in Castine.

The animosity that existed between the Madison administration and the Federalists of Massachusetts, personified by Gov. Caleb Strong, had repercussions in the district. Strong refused to allow the militia to go outside the state as requested by the War Department. The department retaliated by ordering U.S. garrisons in the district to be moved to the Great Lakes theater of war. This development left the district virtually defenseless, but when the Massachusetts General Court voted money for defense, the needs of the district were ignored in favor of Boston and its suburbs.

When President Madison decided to use an act of 1795 to nationalize part of the Massachusetts militia to serve as an expeditionary force against the British in Castine, the extent of the split between the Federalists and Madison's Republican followers was reflected in the Boston banks' unwillingness to meet Secretary of War James Monroe's request for a temporary loan. Claiming they were limited by their charters, they similarly rejected a request from the Massachusetts legislature. When William King, a Republican businessman and a military leader from the district, requested funds from Governor Strong, he was denied. The deteriorating situation was further exacerbated when a Federalist newspaper published a letter from Secretary Monroe to Governor Strong outlining plans for attacking Castine. As a result of the disclosure, the British were given ample warning of the Americans' intentions.

Strong, who endorsed the secessionist spirit of the ill-fated Hartford Convention, was prepared to give up a portion of Maine occupied by the British. A group of moderate Federalists and Republicans meeting in Portland in December 1814 concluded that only a direct appeal to President Madison could save the district from the treacherous policies emanating from Boston; in their appeal they pointed out that the district had been left defenseless and that revenue laws were being violated with impunity. Their effort was made irrelevant, however, by the fact that a peace treaty was signed that same month, ending the war (although the news did not reach the district until mid February 1815).

The War of 1812, pitting Federalists against Republicans and Massachusetts against the Maine District, had revealed to residents of that district the danger of depending on either Boston or Washington. Although the separationist fever subsided temporarily after the coming of peace, the lessons of the war contributed to the arguments for separation of Maine from Massachusetts. Maine became a state in 1820 as part of the Missouri Compromise, and William King became its first governor.

BIBLIOGRAPHY

Adams, Henry. *History of the United States of America during the Administrations of Thomas Jefferson and James Madison.* 2 vols. 1986.

Banks, Ronald F. "The War of 1812: A Turning Point in the Movement to Separate Maine from Massachusetts." In *A History of Maine, A Collection of Readings on the History of Maine, 1600–1974*. Edited by Ronald F. Banks. 3d ed. 1974.

ARTHUR M. JOHNSON

MARBURY v. *MADISON*. In this case, decided in February 1803, the Supreme Court for the first time declared an act of Congress void because it was contrary to the Constitution. As the leading precedent for judicial review, the power of courts to pass upon the constitutionality of legislative acts, *Marbury* is regarded as a landmark, perhaps the most prominent decision in the history of American constitutional law. It is no less important for asserting the courts' right to bring certain executive actions under judicial scrutiny.

The case began at the December 1801 term of the Supreme Court, when attorney Charles Lee moved for a rule to show cause why a writ of mandamus should not be issued commanding Secretary of State Madison to deliver the commissions of William Marbury and others as justices of the peace for the District of Columbia. Marbury and his cocomplainants were "midnight" appointments, nominated by outgoing President Adams on 2 March 1801 and confirmed by the Senate the same day. Adams signed the commissions on 3 March and sent them to his secretary of state, John Marshall, to affix the presidential seal and send out. Ironically, Marshall, who as chief justice subsequently ruled on the application for a mandamus, did not send out the commissions. On taking office on 4 March, President Jefferson, assuming that he had discretion to revoke these appointments because the commissions had not been delivered, made his own appointments. Although he reappointed many of those named by his predecessor, Jefferson did not nominate Marbury and others.

Chief Justice Marshall granted the rule and ordered a hearing for the next term, which, because of the repeal of the Judiciary Act of 1801, was postponed until February 1803. The only argument presented to the Court was Lee's in support of issuing a mandamus. Attorney General Levi Lincoln was present at the hearing, but he declined the Court's invitation to speak, stating that he had not been instructed. As the nominal defendant, Madison did not personally appear at this proceeding. Neither did he comment on the case in writing, though surely he and Jefferson discussed its implications in private conversations.

As was recognized at the time and ever since, Marbury's application for a mandamus was more than a private legal dispute. It arose directly from the victorious party's resentment at the outgoing administration's effort to make eleventh-hour appointments to a host of new judi-cial offices created by the Judiciary Act of 1801 and the act concerning the District of Columbia, both of which had been enacted during the waning days of Adams's presidency by the lame-duck Federalist Congress. The bringing of the action, which coincided with the meeting of the first session of the new Congress under a Republican majority, hastened the repeal of the Judiciary Act of 1801.

The Supreme Court ultimately denied Marbury's application, but Chief Justice Marshall's accompanying opinion infuriated Jefferson and members of the Republican party, who were not mollified by the technical victory for the administration. The ground for denying the writ of mandamus was that section 13 of the Judiciary Act of 1789, which empowered the Supreme Court to issue that writ to persons holding federal office, was an unconstitutional enlargement of the Court's original jurisdiction. This ruling came in the latter part of the opinion. In the preceding sections, however, Marshall affirmed that Marbury had a legal right to his commission, expressing his opinion in terms that unmistakably rebuked the administration for violating Marbury's right. Republicans denounced this part of the opinion as obiter dicta, entirely unnecessary for deciding the point directly before the Court. The chief justice, they complained, improperly reversed the normal order by first discussing the merits of Marbury's claim and then deciding that the Court had no jurisdiction to hear the case. Such an unusual disposition of the case was ascribed to partisan motives—a Federalist judiciary gratuitously interfering with the legitimate prerogatives of a Republican executive.

Given the circumstances of the case, Chief Justice Marshall faced a formidable task in writing an opinion that breathed disinterested judicial statesmanship. There was an inherent difficulty in assimilating this highly political case into the realm of legal rights and remedies. A reading of the whole opinion on its own terms leaves little doubt that the Court intended the mandamus case to be the occasion of a major statement of the judiciary's role in the American constitutional system. In this regard, the Court was less concerned with asserting its power to review acts of Congress than with discovering and applying a principle for reviewing executive acts. This task constituted the "peculiar delicacy" and "real difficulty" of the case, according to Marshall. More than half the opinion, the part usually dismissed as dicta, is devoted to an inquiry into the nature of executive acts, which were found to fall into two categories: "political," or discretionary, which were not examinable by courts, and "ministerial," those in which the law imposes a duty on an officer to perform a certain act on which individual rights depend. Acts of this class were properly reviewable by courts in the course of enforcing legal rights. Even this limited claim, as Marshall anticipated, would be "considered by some, as an attempt to intrude into the cabinet, and to intermeddle with the prerogative of the executive." The Court's disclaiming "all pretensions to such a jurisdiction" failed to mute partisan criticism of the opinion as an unwarranted judicial trespass upon executive functions.

By contrast, the exercise of judicial review over an act of Congress provoked little commentary at the time. Indeed, in this respect, the Court in *Marbury* was not boldly asserting a claim to a controversial power but merely reaffirming an established doctrine. That courts possessed at least a limited power of judicial review was already accepted doctrine in America before the mandamus case.

[See also *Judicial Review; Judiciary Act of 1789*.]

BIBLIOGRAPHY

Clinton, Robert Lowry. *Marbury v. Madison and Judicial Review.* 1989.

Dewey, Donald O. *Marshall versus Jefferson: The Political Background of Marbury v. Madison.* 1970.

Haskins, George Lee, and Herbert A. Johnson. *Foundations of Power: John Marshall, 1801–15.* 1981.

Warren, Charles. *The Supreme Court in United States History.* 2 vols. Rev. ed. 1926.

CHARLES F. HOBSON

MARSHALL, JOHN (1755–1835), lawyer, statesman, fourth chief justice of the United States. His father was a planter of middling circumstances whose ambition, good marriage, and success in land speculation made him one of the leading men of Fauquier County, Virginia. Through his mother Marshall was connected to such Virginia "first families" as the Randolphs and the Lees. Educated largely at home, Marshall interrupted his law studies in 1775 to take up arms, first in the state militia and then in the Continental army. Eventually attaining the rank of captain, he participated in the battles of Brandywine Creek, Germantown, Monmouth, and Stony Point and also survived the harsh winter at Valley Forge in 1777–1778.

With the coming of peace, Marshall turned his attention to law with great success. In 1784 he moved permanently to Richmond to practice in the superior courts and by the end of the decade had secured a place at the top of the bar. During these years he participated in state politics, serving six terms in the House of Delegates between 1782 and 1790 and as a delegate to the Virginia ratifying convention of June 1788. The paths of Marshall and Madison first crossed in 1784 (if not earlier) when they served together in the Virginia legislature. As legislators in post-Revolutionary Virginia, they shared a continental outlook acquired during the war and an increasing disgust at the tendency of state politics. Following the lead of Madison,

CHIEF JUSTICE JOHN MARSHALL.   As Chief Justice of the United States, Marshall delivered the Supreme Court's opinion in *Marbury* v. *Madison* in 1803. Engraving by W. G. Jackman. PRINTS AND PHOTOGRAPHS DIVISION, LIBRARY OF CONGRESS.

whom he regarded as "the enlightened advocate of Union and of an efficient federal government," Marshall became an enthusiastic supporter of the Constitution. At the ratifying convention, he ably assisted Madison in the debates, notably in defending the judiciary article.

During Washington's administration Marshall declined to run for Congress and turned down federal appointments, unwilling to give up his lucrative law practice. He largely withdrew from politics, even giving up his seat in the state legislature. When Madison and Jefferson split with the administration and formed the Republican party, Marshall remained a loyal supporter of Washington. His public defense of the administration at the time of the Neutrality Proclamation in 1793 and in the wake of the 1794 Jay's Treaty propelled him into a leading role in the Federalist party. In 1797 he accepted a commission from President Adams to serve as a special envoy to France, in which capacity he won national acclaim for his role in the episode known in American history as the XYZ Affair. After returning from France, he served one term in the Sixth Congress and in May 1800 entered the cabinet as secretary of state. Nine months later Adams nominated him to be chief justice to succeed Oliver Ellsworth.

During Marshall's long tenure as chief justice (1801–1835), the Supreme Court successfully assumed its peculiar function as preeminent interpreter of the Constitution and umpire of the American federal system. Marshall elaborated a constitutional interpretation that strove to give full effect to the powers conferred on the federal government and to the restraints and prohibitions placed on the state governments. Except for *McCulloch* v. *Maryland* (1819), which set forth a broad construction of Congress's implied powers, Marshall's constitutional pronouncements provoked little critical comment from Madison, who fully accepted the Supreme Court's exercise of judicial power to check state legislative power and to revise the judgments of state judiciaries.

Despite many years in political opposition, Marshall and Madison more often than not during the 1820s and 1830s agreed on fundamental questions touching the nature of the American union. When Madison publicly denounced nullification in 1830, Marshall was delighted to note that Madison "is himself again." Nullification and the recollection of their cooperation during the 1780s brought the two elder statesmen closer together in their last years.

BIBLIOGRAPHY

Faulkner, Robert Kenneth. *The Jurisprudence of John Marshall.* 1968.

Newmyer, R. Kent. *The Supreme Court under Marshall and Taney.* 1968.

Stites, Francis N. *John Marshall: Defender of the Constitution.* 1981.

CHARLES F. HOBSON

MARTINEAU, HARRIET (1802–1876), English radical writer, social theorist. Born in Norwich, England, the sixth of eight children of a textile manufacturer, she overcame profound deafness and an unhappy childhood to become one of nineteenth-century England's best-known authors. Her ear trumpet and her unconventional opinions were equally renowned among her contemporaries.

Martineau first achieved fame in 1832 with a series of booklets, titled *Illustrations of Political Economy*, which demonstrated the principles of political economy within the format of fictional stories. In 1834 she visited the United States, where her opposition to slavery and her abolitionist sympathies caused widespread denunciation of her in the press. In February 1835 she visited Madison at Montpelier and spent two days discussing politics, property rights, and slavery with the aged former president. After her return to England in 1836, she published *Society in America* and *Retrospect of Western Travel*, devoting a chapter in the latter to her visit to Montpelier. Martineau described Madison as a believer in free trade, inter-

HARRIET MARTINEAU.
PRINTS AND PHOTOGRAPHS DIVISION, LIBRARY OF CONGRESS.

national copyrights for the protection of authors' rights, and the dissemination of popular literature as a means of public education. She described his deep concern over the burden slavery laid on the country and his belief in colonization as a solution. She reported his conviction that the proliferation of religious sects had caused the strengthening of religion in the United States and that a strong central government monitoring the conflict between political factions had kept the country from degenerating into either absolutism or chaos.

Martineau later wrote a history of England and several other books dealing with subjects as varied as religion, atheism, labor relations, mesmerism, Malthusian population studies, and women's rights. Her ability to sense what was of immediate interest to her contemporaries made her the expositor of most of the controversial issues that arose during her lifetime.

BIBLIOGRAPHY

Martineau, Harriet. *Retrospect of Western Travel.* 2 vols. 1838.

Pichanick, Valerie Kossew. *Harriet Martineau: The Woman and Her Work, 1802–76.* 1980.

Webb, R. K. *Harriet Martineau: A Radical Victorian.* 1960.

MARY A. HACKETT

MASON, GEORGE (1725–1792), Virginia planter, statesman. The son of a well-to-do planter, Mason was educated by tutors and forced into early responsibilities by the accidental drowning of his father when Mason was seventeen. Mason became a careful head of the family and prospered during the period when Virginia tobacco brought considerable profits to the plantation economy of colonial Virginia. He developed a friendship with his neighbor George Washington and became an active advocate of American rights when the Stamp Act crisis flared in 1765. In a notable essay written for a London newspaper, Mason warned that the British colonies must not be treated like wayward children but as nearly equal partners in an expanding British empire. To Mason and other Virginians, the imposition of taxes by Parliament was a kind of powder keg that demanded close and careful watching. At the same time, Mason professed he was an admirer of the British Constitution and gloried in his English heritage.

Such loyalty dissolved in the crisis that followed the Townshend duties enacted by Parliament in 1767. When the port of Boston was closed by Parliament in 1774, Mason advocated a closing of colonial ranks with a boycott on British goods that would be enforced by local committees. His Fairfax Resolves, which Washington took to the Virginia colonial legislature in 1774, was a clarion call for united action by the colonists against their parliamentary oppressors. When Washington was called to command the Continental army, Mason took his place in the colonial legislature. There his broad knowledge and his ability to grasp important issues and confront them with rational argument impressed fellow delegates.

At the Virginia Convention of 1776, Mason played a key role on the committees that drafted a declaration of rights and a constitution as the colonies headed toward a complete rupture with Great Britain. Impatient with the cumbersome legislative process, Mason, serving in the drafting committee, wrote a declaration of rights that spoke of the rights of Americans to "life, liberty, & the Pursueing and Obtaining of Happiness & Safety." A young delegate later recalled that Mason's plan "swallowed up all the rest," giving the convention a document that enumerated the rights most convention members believed to be the heritage of free-born English-Americans. Most of Mason's draft was accepted by the convention, but his call for toleration in religious practice was modified at the suggestion of James Madison to become a stronger statement granting "the free exercise of religion." Thus did Mason, a vestryman and a lifelong Anglican, plant the seeds for complete separation of church and state in the new nation. His explicit statements on freedom of the press, on the rights of accused persons, and on other civil liberties

GEORGE MASON.
PRINTS AND PHOTOGRAPHS DIVISION, LIBRARY OF CONGRESS.

were adopted by a complaisant convention and quickly published in other colonies during the summer of 1776. By 1780, eight of the former British colonies had a similar prefatory bill of rights or included civil rights guarantees in their constitutions.

Mason also had drafted a constitution that remained the fundamental law in Virginia until 1829. A disciple of Montesquieu, Mason wrote a document that prescribed a weak executive branch, a court system of limited powers, and a two-house legislature that was all-powerful. Mason's constitution was modified by other states but provided a powerful example to them. His own dislike of slavery was not written into either of these powerful documents, although he was outspoken in his condemnation of the slave trade and believed that every slave master was potentially "a petty Tyrant."

During the Revolution Mason served on the Virginia Committee of State that kept the war effort moving until the successful conclusion at Yorktown in 1781. Thereafter, he eschewed public life until 1787, when he was named to the Virginia delegation to the Federal Convention in Philadelphia. Mason considered the crisis facing the young republic a grave matter and left his home at

Gunston Hall to serve with Madison and Washington through that fateful summer.

At the convention Mason was a frequent debater; a fellow delegate noted that "Mr. Mason is a Gentleman of remarkable strong powers, and possesses a clear and copious understanding. He is able and convincing in debate, steady and firm in his principles, and undoubtedly one of the best politicians in America." Mason spoke often, served on important committees, and left his mark on the final draft of the Constitution as his suggestions (such as making new states enter the Union as equal partners) often appeared on the final draft. But Mason attempted to vitiate a perceived threat to southern agriculture from restrictive commercial regulations in the new Constitution and, when his idea was rejected, declared he would not sign the document.

In opposition, Mason proved a formidable foe. His pamphlet attack on the Constitution, during the ratification struggle, began: "There is no Declaration of Rights." This motto became the tocsin of the opposition, and pro-Constitution forces never were able to overcome its power. The result was a compromise, in which the Federalists promised to enact a bill of rights if only the ratification might take place. Mason still held out and tried to block outright ratification at the 1788 Virginia convention. In defeat he was bitter but later recanted when his old friend James Madison introduced a series of amendments in 1789 that became the Bill of Rights in 1791.

During his last months, Mason said that Madison's amendments made the Constitution a document he could now "chearfully put my Heart & Hand to," and he resumed his friendly relations with Jefferson and Madison. He died at Gunston Hall in October 1792 and was mourned as one of the leading figures who had plotted the nation's course since 1776.

BIBLIOGRAPHY

Miller, Helen Hill. *George Mason: Gentleman Revolutionary*. 1975.
Rutland, Robert A. *George Mason: Reluctant Statesman*. 1992
Rutland, Robert A., ed. *The Papers of George Mason*. 3 vols. 1970.
Sydnor, Charles S. *American Revolutionaries in the Making: Political Practices in Washington's Virginia*. 1962.

ROBERT A. RUTLAND

MASON, JOHN

MASON, JOHN (1766–1849), Georgetown merchant, banker, businessman. When George Mason of Gunston Hall came to Philadelphia to attend the Federal Convention in May 1787, he was accompanied by his son John. Over the next few months, Madison and the younger Mason probably became well acquainted. Years later, while Madison was secretary of state, Mason served as superintendent of Indian trade. During Jefferson's and Madison's administrations, Mason, who lived in a mansion on Analostan Island in the Potomac River, often lavishly entertained Washington society.

In 1802 Mason became a brigadier general in the Washington militia, and, during the War of 1812, he served as the commissioner general of prisoners. On the evening of 24 August 1814, Mason, Secretary of the Navy William Jones, and Attorney General Richard Rush helped Madison escape the capital to avoid capture by the British. As they retreated across the Potomac River into Virginia at Little Falls, Madison, Mason, Rush, and Jones saw the city's public buildings burning in the distance. Mason remained at Madison's side for the next three days, during which the president was reunited with his wife, Dolley, who had departed the federal district before her husband.

In 1802 Mason became a director of the Potomac River Company, which Madison had helped charter as a member of the Virginia legislature in 1785. Mason accepted the company's presidency in 1817 and served until 1828, when the corporation was succeeded by the Chesapeake and Ohio Canal Company. Mason later befriended Mrs. Madison when she returned to the capital in 1837.

BIBLIOGRAPHY

Copeland, Pamela C., and Richard K. McMaster. *The Five George Masons: Patriots and Planters of Virginia and Maryland*. 1975.
Ketcham, Ralph. *James Madison: A Biography*. 1971.
Rutland, Robert A., ed. *The Papers of George Mason*. 3 vols. 1970.

STUART LEIBIGER

MATHEWS, GEORGE

MATHEWS, GEORGE (1739–1812), revolutionary soldier, representative, governor of Georgia. Born in Augusta County, Virginia, George Mathews had his first military experience in 1774 when, as a militia captain, he clashed with Indians along the Ohio River. In 1775 he became colonel of the Ninth Virginia Regiment, and he served under the command of George Washington at the battles of Brandywine and Germantown. Captured at Germantown, Mathews was exchanged in time to lead the Third Virginia Regiment in the Carolina campaigns under Gen. Nathanael Greene.

In 1785 Mathews moved to Oglethorpe County, Georgia, where he became a brigadier general in the militia two years later. In 1787 he was elected governor of Georgia, and in 1789 he was elected to the House of Representatives. In 1793 he served another term as governor, but his reputation was badly tarnished when he signed the corrupt Yazoo Land Act.

In 1810 Mathews was employed as an agent of the United States. As a longtime supporter of the annexation of Florida, Mathews represented the United States that year in a negotiation with Gov. Vincente Folch of West Florida. At first Folch seemed willing to surrender West Florida to the United States, since he did not believe that Spain had the forces to hold it. Early in 1811 Folch made an offer to cede West Florida, but in March he withdrew the offer. It is likely that Folch was simply negotiating to prevent American filibusterers from Baton Rouge from taking the territory by force; with the filibuster group gone, Folch withdrew the offer.

Mathews, outraged by Folch's change of heart, began to equip an irregular force in an effort to seize East Florida. While he had the support of Sen. William H. Crawford for this operation, the existence of any authorization from Washington was unclear. Mathews appealed in vain to the local commander of U.S. army forces at Saint Mary's, Georgia, claiming that he had orders from President Madison authorizing his request for aid. Although government authorities later denied the existence of any such orders, Mathews must have had some official encouragement, since he received aid from both army and navy commanders who claimed to have seen Mathews's orders.

By April 1812, Mathews reported that the Americans controlled all of East Florida except the town of Saint Augustine. On the basis of this occupation, Mathews claimed that the Americans were now in control of East Florida and sought immediate annexation to the United States. Instead of annexing the area, however, President Madison recalled and dismissed Mathews. In August, feeling betrayed, Mathews began a journey to Washington, apparently planning to protest his dismissal in person, but he died at Augusta.

The dismissal of Mathews was almost certainly a political maneuver to satisfy New England Republicans. Madison's real objectives were not changed, for he promptly replaced Mathews with Gov. David B. Mitchell of Georgia. Mitchell's instructions seem to have been identical to Mathews's alleged instructions.

BIBLIOGRAPHY

Cox, I. J. *The West Florida Controversy, 1798–1813: A Study in American Diplomacy.* 1818.

Patrick, Rembert W. *Florida Fiasco: Rampant Rebels on the Georgia-Florida Border 1810–1813.* 1954.

Peters, Virginia Borgman. *The Florida Wars.* 1979.

Pratt, Julius William. *Expansionists of 1812.* 1925.

Smith, Joseph B. *The Plot to Steal Florida: James Madison's Phony War.* 1983.

FRANK LAWRENCE OWSLEY, JR.

MAURY, JAMES (1746–1840), Tidewater merchant, Liverpool factor, U.S. consul. After an active business life in Fredericksburg, Virginia, where he often represented the Madison family in its sales of tobacco and purchase of goods, Maury moved to England around 1785 and became an agent for Virginia planters involved in the tobacco trade centered in the port at Liverpool. He sold tobacco for the Madison family and made reports on the condition of the tobacco market, advising Madison when the market was glutted and recommending the delay of shipments until prices stabilized.

In 1790 Maury was appointed the U.S. consul in Liverpool. From there he made periodic reports on the seizure of American vessels by British authorities, particularly after the Anglo-French wars brought on a rash of captures by the Royal Navy. In April 1801 Maury reported that six American cargo vessels had been boarded by the British, with four subsequently released after paying a fine and two still "under seizure." Maury wanted Madison, as secretary of state, to warn the commanders of other American vessels of the dangers that awaited them in British waters.

After Madison became president, Maury sent news of the British reaction to the repeal of the Embargo Act and other information, including the current prices for cotton and tobacco. He also performed small favors for Madison, such as shipping to the White House delicacies and cigars. George Joy, an Englishman who fancied himself a source of inside information on British politics, also used Maury's diplomatic pouch to send letters to President Madison.

BIBLIOGRAPHY

Brugger, Robert J., et al., eds. *Papers of James Madison:* Secretary of State Series. Vol 1. 1986.

Hutchinson, William T., et al., eds. *Papers of James Madison:* Congressional Series. Vols. 8, 13. 1973–1981.

ROBERT A. RUTLAND

MEIGS, RETURN JONATHAN (1764–1824), governor, senator, postmaster general. Born in Middletown, Connecticut, Meigs graduated from Yale College in 1788 and moved to Marietta in the Ohio Territory, where he practiced law, served as the town's first postmaster, and in 1798 was appointed a territorial judge. When Ohio achieved statehood in 1803, Meigs was elected chief justice of its supreme court. He resigned in 1804 to accept appointment as commandant of the Upper District of Louisiana and in 1805 won appointment as its chief judge. Meigs's health apparently failed temporarily, but he accepted a judgeship in the Michigan Territory in 1807 and in the same year won election as governor of Ohio. The state legislature rejected his election on the basis of his prolonged absence from the state and instead named him to the U.S. Senate in 1808 to fill the term of John Smith. He won the governorship in 1810 and 1812.

POSTMASTER GENERAL RETURN J. MEIGS.
PRINTS AND PHOTOGRAPHS DIVISION, LIBRARY OF CONGRESS.

As governor during the War of 1812, Meigs ardently supported the Madison administration by responding immediately to Secretary of War Eustis's call for twelve hundred militia and for supplies to support Gen. William Hull. Despite Hull's setback at Detroit, which dampened the spirit of Ohioans, Meigs rallied support during the war to implement Madison's decision to retake Detroit. Although his zealous efforts to support the administration aggravated his local military relationship with Gen. William Henry Harrison, a fort was named in Meigs's honor where the Maumee River empties into Lake Erie. After President Madison fired Gideon Granger, he called on Meigs to resign the governorship to accept appointment as postmaster general in 1814. Meigs took over the postal position and continued in that post under Monroe, taking care that the president was aware of his appointments. In 1823 ill health forced him to resign and return to Marietta, where he died.

BIBLIOGRAPHY

Dexter, Franklin B., ed. *Biographical Sketches of the Graduates of Yale College.* 5 vols. 1885–1941. Volume 4. 1913.

Meigs, H. B. *Records of the Descendants of Vincent Meigs.* 1901.

FRANK C. MEVERS

MEMORIAL AND REMONSTRANCE (1785). Madison's *Memorial and Remonstrance* is the classic statement of his position on religion and the state. Later correspondence makes it clear that the author considered the *Memorial* his definitive statement of the arguments for freedom of conscience and for ecclesiastical disestablishment.

The *Memorial* was Madison's carefully constructed response to a 1784 debate waged in the Virginia General Assembly concerning two proposed bills. One bill proposed the incorporation of the Episcopal Church in the state; the other, the General Assessment Bill, sought to raise public funds "for the support of Christian teachers" in order "to correct the morals of men, restrain their vices and preserve the peace of society." Both proposals were reactions to the Virginia Convention of 1776, which adopted measures exempting dissenters from contributing to the established Anglican Church. However, delegates at the convention, responding to Madison's arguments, put off a vote on the "question of a general assessment, or voluntary contribution," because it was "thought most prudent to defer this matter to the discussion and final determination of a future assembly, when the opinions of the country in general may be better known."

The Virginia debate over religious liberty was rooted in a clash of ideas and wills that emerged in the 1740s. Virginia, like its neighbors, had inherited from English practice the concept of established religion (a church supported by the state). Because some of the earliest colonists—Puritans and Separatists—had adopted religious services that conflicted with the Anglican pattern that prevailed in Virginia, it was inevitable that no one norm of establishment would dominate in the colonies. Massachusetts created a theocratic structure within a secular system of government, and other colonies adopted systems that subordinated religious institutions to temporal power.

With the striking exception of Roger Williams's tenure in Rhode Island, the universal practice in the 1600s was the establishment of some form of worship. By 1700 a variety of Protestant denominations were demanding some degree of toleration, even in the most restrictive colonies. In Virginia the Church of England (the Anglican Church) was the established church, but, by the 1740s, a growing population of Presbyterians in the mountains in the western part of the colony, combined with a surge of interest in dissenting sects in the eastern part, created pressure on colonial officials to adopt more lenient policies. In the 1760s, as the Baptist population grew, many of that sect insisted upon total religious freedom; Baptist ministers who refused to seek licenses to preach were beaten or jailed.

Responding to an increase in the persecution of religious dissenters in Virginia, young Madison wrote in 1774 to a friend, William Bradford, concerning "that diabolical Hell conceived principle of persecution," noting "there are at this [time] in the adjacent County not less than 5 or 6 well meaning men in close gaol [*sic*] for publishing their religious Sentiment." Madison said he was "without common patience" on the subject and begged Bradford "to pity me and pray for Liberty of Conscience."

In 1776, after being elected to the Virginia Convention, Madison served on a committee chaired by George Mason and charged with developing a Virginia Declaration of Rights. The final draft was largely the work of Mason, but Madison accomplished one critical change, convincing Mason and the convention to replace "toleration" with "the free exercise of religion." Madison thus advanced a radical departure from paternalistic toleration, anticipating Jefferson's affirmation of religious freedom as a "natural right of mankind."

When, in 1784, the Virginia Assembly took up unfinished business relating to religious establishment, an enthusiastic Patrick Henry supported establishment of the Episcopal Church and the passage of the General Assessment Bill. Madison recognized the danger in the bill, which promised something for all Protestant churches, and its likely passage. The politically adroit Madison supported the establishment of the Episcopal Church, a move he described to his father as having "parried for the present the Genl. Assesst. which would otherwise have certainly been saddled upon us." He was certain that a single established church would quickly be rejected by the diverse population of the state, but he feared a tax-supported de facto establishment might remain a permanent fixture.

The assessment bill debate carried over to 1785, as the Assembly authorized the circulation of the bill among the general population. When the broadsides of the bill reached the public, Baptist and Presbyterian groups flooded the Assembly with petitions and memorials signed by thousands. George Nicholas and Mason, seeing the swell of public opinion, urged Madison to write an attack on the bill to undermine Henry's influence. He agreed, and the *Memorial and Remonstrance* was the result. Madison feared that his authorship would be a potential liability in the anticipated debate in the House of Delegates. His document was therefore distributed for signatures anonymously, leading to speculation about its authorship. However, Madison privately identified himself as the author in a 1785 letter to Jefferson, stating, "I drew up the remonstrance herewith enclosed."

When the Assembly returned in the fall of 1785, numerous petitions awaited, but so dramatically had the mood changed in the Assembly that the assessment bill never reached the House floor. The reversal of sentiment proved so startling that Madison introduced Jefferson's "Revised Code" for the state, including an "Act for Establishing Religious Freedom." After the act's preamble was revised, the House passed Jefferson's bill on 16 January 1786. It was signed into law on 19 January. From Paris, Jefferson wrote to Madison that the new law had been received with "infinite approbation in Europe," adding, "[I]t is comfortable to see the standard of reason at length prevail."

The *Memorial and Remonstrance* affirmed the principle of religious freedom and offered fifteen "remonstrances" against the assessment bill. In his introduction, Madison explained that the petition's signers took action because they believed the assessment bill would constitute a "dangerous abuse of power."

The first remonstrance made three points: 1. religion can be directed only by conviction and reason; 2. "Civil Society" has no role to play with respect to religion; 3. permitting the majority to rule absolutely can result in the destruction of rights of the minority. In the second remonstrance, Madison contended that if the legislature passed the bill it would be exceeding its lawful authority. In the third argument, which began, "Because it is proper to take alarm at the first experiment on our liberties," Madison warned against any government interference with human rights. An authority that taxes for the support of Christianity, he wrote, may "with the same ease" later choose to establish a single Christian sect. Next Madison insisted that all individuals possess natural rights to their chosen religious beliefs and that coercion in religion is an offense against God.

In remonstrance four, Madison addressed the issues of establishment and free exercise, including a strong argument for protection of the state from religion, and labeled as a "perversion" of religion its use to achieve political ends. His sixth point focused upon Baptists and Presbyterians. He appealed to their concerns by making the Christian argument for religious freedom, asserting that Christianity does not require state support to flourish and that seeking such support demeans religion's divine nature. He concluded that state support historically has damaged the Christian cause.

Remonstrance eight is Madison's strongest statement against allowing religious institutions to work their will on civil government. If religion does not require state assistance, then good government, in turn, does not need assistance from established religion. Turning to a practical consideration, Madison noted that the "generous policy" of freedom from religious establishment in the nation offered asylum to persecuted persons abroad. For Virginia to tax for support of religion would drive potential immigrants to other states and encourage native Virginians to leave, he suggested. In the eleventh argument Madison insisted that only religious freedom and equality among religions ensure domestic peace.

Madison further argued that making Virginia a Christian state would discourage non-Christians from migrating there, diminishing opportunity for missionary work. In remonstrance thirteen he stated that the assessment bill would prove so "obnoxious" that it would be unenforceable. He followed this point with a suggestion that the majority of citizens opposed the bill (a risky argument, given his contention that the majority should not decide in matters of natural rights). Madison was banking on overwhelming popular opposition to the bill.

Madison concluded with a defense of natural rights, warning the Assembly that it had no authority to "sweep away all our fundamental rights." If government could establish a religion, he argued, it could, if it wished, eliminate trial by jury. Religious freedom is, he wrote, in its origin, "the gift of nature." In Madison's view of religion, freedom of conscience was the only policy consistent with the concept of the deity. He drew a portrait of a creator consistent with the establishment of fundamental rights.

Four years later, arguing before the First Congress on behalf of religious freedom in his proposed bill of rights, Madison reflected the spirit and letter of the *Memorial*. In 1947, when the Supreme Court delivered its decision in *Everson* v. *Board of Education*, the five-justice majority and the four dissenters alike relied upon the *Memorial* as a determinative document, along with the First Amendment and Jefferson's Act to Establish Religious Freedom in Virginia.

[See also *Anglican Church; Baptists; Religion, establishments of;* and appendix for text.]

BIBLIOGRAPHY

Alley, Robert S. *James Madison on Religious Liberty.* 1985.
Brant, Irving. *James Madison.* 6 vols. 1941–1961.
Buckley, Thomas E. *Church and State in Revolutionary Virginia, 1776–1787.* 1977.
Hening, William Waller. *The Statutes at Large; A Collection of All the Laws of Virginia.* Vol. 9. 1821.
Hutchinson, William T., et al., eds. *The Papers of James Madison.* Vols. 1, 8, 9, 10. 1962–.
Levy, Leonard. *The Establishment Clause.* 1986.
Rutland, Robert A. *The Birth of the Bill of Rights.* 1991.

ROBERT S. ALLEY

MERCANTILISM. The great Scottish political economist Adam Smith used the term "the mercantile system" (rendered in more recent times as "mercantilism") to refer to a specific pattern of governmental intrusion into a nation's economy that he categorically condemned as corrupt and unproductive. For Smith, the system involved an elaborate system of privileges extended to two groups—merchants and manufacturers—who had deceived policymakers into believing that the advancement of their private interests coincided with both the interest of the state and the general or public good. Mercantilism, a system that benefited the industry of the towns, came at the specific expense of the countryside, or agriculture, which received no similar protection and which was denied access to the capital that government was diverting into commerce and industry.

Smith's position, which was shared in its broad outline by contemporary French reformers known as physiocrats, presented an entirely different logic and case from that of the mercantilists—namely, that investment in agriculture was intrinsically more productive, hence generally beneficial, and that the mercantile system succeeded only in upsetting a natural order or sequence of economic development that truly advanced the common good or general welfare. Writing in the second half of the eighteenth century, Smith pointed to England's North American colonies as empirical evidence of the advantages of what he called a contrasting system of "natural liberty," in which the unimpeded investment of capital in agriculture promoted unprecedented growth and prosperity.

James Madison was sympathetic to Smith's indictment of the mercantile system and shared his analysis of what was best for America's economy. Madison agreed that for a youthful, land-rich, and relatively undeveloped country like the United States to follow the logic of mercantilism by having government promote and even subsidize manufactures and the carrying trade would be a tragic perversion of both nature and good sense. In Madison's view, this ill-advised policy was precisely what Alexander Hamilton and others in the 1790s were proposing, and his opposition to the Federalist economic program can fairly be described (from Madison's vantage point) as an attempt to defeat mercantilism.

While Madison proclaimed himself a friend of Smith's doctrine of economic freedom, he also believed that the United States had to protect itself and its best interests in a world shaped much more by European nations that practiced mercantilism than by Smith's lofty ideals. He therefore advocated using the power of the federal government to protect both American commerce and American manufactures against foreign, especially British, domination. He was also willing to make exceptions to what he called the general rule of free industry when the national interest, especially in matters of defense, so dictated. Madison's willingness to use government policy in such a fashion has led some modern historians to call him a "mercantilist" in spite of his broad philosophical commitment to Smith's antimercantilist ideals.

BIBLIOGRAPHY

McCoy, Drew R. *The Elusive Republic: Political Economy in Jeffersonian America.* 1980.

Nelson, John R., Jr. *Liberty and Property: Political Economy and Policymaking in the New Nation, 1789–1812.* 1987.

Williams, William Appleman. *The Contours of American History.* 1961.

DREW R. MCCOY

MISSISSIPPI RIVER.

By terms of the Treaty of Paris, which ended the French and Indian War, Great Britain retained control of the east bank of the Mississippi and thus had navigational rights to New Orleans. The United States in 1776 claimed these rights, but Spain refused to recognize the American claims when Spain declared war on the British in 1779. Virginia, with its claims to territories that included the present states of Illinois, Kentucky, and West Virginia, was the foremost exponent of the American diplomatic position. Before the Revolutionary War ended, the American position was upheld by the Virginia delegation in the Continental Congress. Madison was appointed to a committee that drafted instructions to John Jay in Madrid, where the American envoy pleaded for free navigation on the vital waterway. Madison utilized all of his knowledge of international law in preparing the letter of instruction, which insisted that the Mississippi formed a natural boundary and that, by the law of nature, free use of the river to New Orleans served "the general good of mankind."

For a variety of reasons, a coalition of other states backed away from Madison's adamant position and forced the Virginia legislature to instruct its delegation not to insist on navigation rights to New Orleans if the claim jeopardized a pending treaty with Spain. In 1784 the matter still remained unsettled, and Jay became involved in negotiations that would have surrendered the Mississippi claims in exchange for a Spanish market for New England fish. Madison was incensed by the proposition and sought a strong coalition, headed by Virginia, to kill the scheme; meanwhile, Kentuckians threatened secession if the Jay-Gardoqui treaty went into effect. Madison was returned to the Continental Congress in 1787 to carry on his fight against the prospective treaty.

Armed with the resolutions from the Virginia General Assembly denouncing any surrender of navigational rights to the Mississippi, Madison reached the temporary national capital in New York early in 1787 and reported to Jefferson that all the southern states now supported the Virginia position. The mid-Atlantic state delegations were inclined to "do the same. I am told that Mr. Jay has not ventured to proceed in his project and I suppose will not now do it." There the matter rested as Madison began preparing for the forthcoming Federal Convention, and one of the implied virtues of the strong central government he envisioned was a unified insistence on the nation's right to navigate the Mississippi without restrictions.

With the admission of Kentucky as a state in 1792, the Mississippi question was no longer a vital concern for Virginians alone, since the entire western United States needed access to the river and therefore national policy required a firm stand with Spain. Creation of the Mississippi Territory in 1798 reinforced this need, but the Spanish threatened to close the river (and finally did) as the world learned that the Louisiana Territory had been ceded to France by the secret Treaty of San Ildefonso. Madison, now secretary of state, must have consulted Jefferson on this surprising turn of events. Jefferson's reaction was immediate. "The day that France takes possession of New Orleans," he wrote the American minister in Paris, condemning the diplomatic maneuver, ". . . we must marry ourselves to the British fleet and nation." Within months the Americans approached Napoleon with a plan to purchase the vital port, and ultimately the French emperor handed over the entire western area in the negotiated Louisiana Purchase (1803). Thus the Mississippi River moved from a potential cause of war into the geographic center of the United States, in the nation's first venture into dollar diplomacy as an alternative to war.

[See also *Jay-Gardoqui Negotiations; Louisiana Purchase.*]

BIBLIOGRAPHY

Brant, Irving. *James Madison: The Nationalist, 1780–1787.* 1948.

Hutchinson, William T., et al., eds. *Papers of James Madison: Congressional Series.* Vols. 2, 3, 9. 1962–1975.

Ketcham, Ralph. *James Madison: A Biography.* 1971.

Whitaker, A. P. *The Spanish-American Frontier, 1783–1795.* 1927.

ROBERT A. RUTLAND

MISSISSIPPI TERRITORY.

Hernando De Soto entered the boundaries of the present state of Mississippi in 1539, and other explorers opened parts of the territory, which was claimed successively by France, Britain, Spain, and the United States (after the Treaty of Paris of 1783). A congressional act of 7 April 1798 provided for organization of the Mississippi Territory, extending from the thirty-first parallel to the mouth of the Yazoo River and east from the Mississippi River to the Chattahoochee River.

The territorial government was to be based on the plan set forth in the Northwest Territory Act, except that slavery was to be permitted. Winthrop Sargent, secretary of the Northwest Territory since 1788, was appointed governor. Quarrels over the territorial constitution resulted in Sargent's downfall and the appointment by President Jefferson of William C. C. Claiborne as governor in 1801. In 1802 Claiborne signified his desire to wrest control of New Orleans from Spain, writing to Madison that six hundred militia should be sufficient to open that port to free trade. When Jefferson ordered Claiborne, representing the United States, to accept Louisiana from France in 1803 and then to serve as its governor, the post was to be only an additional duty for the governor of the Mississippi Territory, but Claiborne never returned to Mississippi as governor and shifted his base to the Orleans Territory.

Cato West, secretary of the Mississippi Territory, acted as governor from 1803 to 1806 when Jefferson appointed Robert Williams to the post. In January 1807, while Williams was temporarily away from the territory, Aaron Burr landed north of Natchez, and was arrested on the plantation of the territorial judge Peter Bruin. Burr, whom Jefferson believed to be a traitor for intending to establish a separate nation in the southwest territory, was evading Jefferson's proclamation seeking his arrest. The territorial supreme court refused to indict Burr for treason; Burr journeyed on to Alabama before being again arrested and taken to Richmond, Virginia, for trial. In 1809 Jefferson appointed as governor the Virginian David Holmes, whose personality served to calm tensions throughout the remainder of the territorial period.

In 1804 the area south of Tennessee was added to the territory, and in 1812 the area between the Pearl and Perdido rivers (which had been West Florida) was also included, so that the territory comprised all of what today is the states of Mississippi and Alabama. The state of Mississippi was admitted to the Union on 10 December 1817; the eastern portion of the territory was known as the Alabama Territory until its admittance as a state on 14 December 1819.

The Mississippi Territory was home to the Muskhogean, or Creek, linguistic family of Native Americans. The first large influx of white settlers arrived during and immediately after the Revolution, when Tories from the English colonies established plantations along the Mississippi River. The territorial population climbed from five thousand in 1798 to thirty-one thousand in 1810; there were seventy-five thousand people in the state of Mississippi alone in 1820. Black slaves were brought in early in the eighteenth century to cultivate fields of rice and tobacco, which, along with indigo, constituted the commercial crops during the territorial period. Cotton took on commercial significance after the invention of the gin in 1792 and the importation of an improved seed from Mexico in 1806. The proliferation of steamboats on the Mississippi River, which occurred toward the end of the territorial period, made transportation of bulk quantities practical.

The development of public education lagged, but Jefferson Military College, which served as the site of the preliminary treason trial of Aaron Burr in 1807, was founded in 1802 in the town of Washington. In 1810 the Supreme Court settled the long-pending question of rights to the Yazoo Land Company territory around the Yazoo River by upholding the constitutional guarantee of the grants [see *Yazoo Lands Frauds*]. President Jefferson, and presumably Secretary of State Madison as well, favored a settlement that would accommodate both the investors and the state of Georgia, but the decision sided firmly with the investors. In the War of 1812 the Choctaws aided Gen. Andrew Jackson in quelling the Creeks.

BIBLIOGRAPHY

Rowland, Dunbar, ed. *The Mississippi Territorial Archives, 1798–1803.* 1905.
Skates, John Ray. *Mississippi: A Bicentennial History.* 1979.

FRANK C. MEVERS

MISSOURI COMPROMISE.

The question of the future of slavery in the United States arose almost simultaneously with the founding of the Union itself. It surfaced first when the Continental Congress enacted the Ordinance of 1787, prohibiting slavery from expanding into the Northwest Territory. The Federal Convention grappled with the question as it pertained to representation in the House of Representatives. But the issue truly caught fire in 1819 when Missouri, with a population of some sixty-six thousand, including ten thousand slaves, sought entry into the Union. When the Missouri enabling bill was introduced in the House of Representatives, Rep. James Tallmadge of New York offered an amendment that would have prohibited the further introduction of slaves into Missouri while freeing the children of slaves resident there when the children reached the age of twenty-five.

During the debate Sen. Rufus King of New York gave two powerful speeches supporting Tallmadge. According to John Quincy Adams, "the great slave-holders gnawed their lips and clenched their fists," while listening to King. But neither King nor others who spoke on that side of the issue opposed slavery on moral grounds. They sought merely to block its expansion. In the circumstances, and given the fact that few public figures at the time wanted to press the issue, compromise was possible.

During the Sixteenth Congress the basis for a peaceful settlement to the dispute materialized when the District of Maine (a part of Massachusetts) applied to be admitted as a free state. Henry Clay, the Speaker of the House, made a political deal likely when he remarked that "if it is right to make the restriction of slavery the condition of the admission of Missouri, it is equally just to make the admission of Missouri the condition of that of Maine."

During the following weeks, a compromise bill admitting Maine as a free state and Missouri as a slave state made its way through Congress. The final compromise also took into account the broader question of slavery's expansion into other, as yet unorganized areas of the Louisiana Territory. A line was drawn at the 36° 30' mark. The area below that line was to be open to slavery expansion; with the exception of Missouri, slavery was to be prohibited in the territory above that line.

The Missouri Compromise temporarily obscured a growing chasm that separated slavery from freedom in the United States. Jefferson described the Missouri debate as "a firebell in the night" that signaled the probable extinction of the Union. He believed that slavery was more likely to disappear if it were allowed to spread than if attempts were made to restrict it. But in the last analysis, Jefferson feared that America's dilemma was insoluble. He could not conceive of blacks and whites living together in the same society as free men: "[W]e have the wolf by the ears, and we can neither safely hold him, nor safely let him go." Madison agreed. Like Jefferson, he was convinced "that an uncontrolled dispersion of the slaves now in the U.S. was not only best for the nation, but most favorable for the slaves, both as to their prospects for emancipation, and as to their condition in the meantime." On the other hand, John Quincy Adams thought it might have been best had the Union split over the Missouri question. A new northern nation of a dozen or more states would then have been created free of the shame of slavery. If the Union were to divide, Adams thought, slavery was the issue on which it ought to founder.

[See also *Slavery*.]

BIBLIOGRAPHY

Dangerfield, George. *The Era of Good Feelings.* 1952.
Moore, Glover. *The Missouri Controversy.* 1953.
Rimini, Robert. *Henry Clay.* 1991.

GERARD CLARFIELD

MITCHILL, SAMUEL LATHAM (1764–1831),

scientist, physician, representative and senator from New York. Mitchill was surely an American anomaly: a politician with an Edinburgh degree. His reputation is as a scientist, not as a politician. "He supported the Republican party because Mr. Jefferson was its leader," reported the New York historian Jabez D. Hammond, "and he supported Mr. Jefferson because he was a philosopher."

Mitchill exemplified "enlightened republicanism"; more of a promoter than a pure scientist, he used his political positions to promote practical projects, such as Robert Livingston's steamboat monopoly and De Witt Clinton's Erie Canal. James Madison was president and Mitchill a vice president (with George Logan) of the American Board of Agriculture, founded in 1803. Both Jefferson and Madison found him a congenial dinner guest.

On occasion Mitchill tempered his Republicanism. Sent to the House in 1801, he remained loyal until the impeachment of U.S. district court judge John Pickering, which he opposed, although he was originally one of the House managers. Sent to the Senate in 1804, he voted against Pickering's conviction on all counts. Mitchill chaired the powerful Committee of Commerce and Manufactures in the Eighth Congress, and became involved in foreign affairs. He supported trade and opposed war— once abstaining by his absence rather than voting for Jefferson's aggressive policy toward Spain. Then he backed the Embargo of 1807 as the lesser of two evils.

In the Senate (1804–1809) and back in the House (1810–1813) Mitchill fell under the influence of Samuel Smith of Maryland and flirted with the Invisibles, a vaguely anti-Madison and anti-Gallatin faction. Mitchill supported Madison for president in 1808 and 1812, decrying "the arts of stratagem and intrigue . . . put in motion to supplant" him, but could not bring himself to vote for war against Great Britain. He talked tough but did not vote accordingly; Roger Brown charitably attributes his opposition to the timing of the declaration.

BIBLIOGRAPHY

Brown, Roger H. *The Republic in Peril: 1812.* 1964.
Hammond, J. D. *History of the Political Parties in the State of New York.* 2 vols. 1852. An old but interesting source of information.

HARRY W. FRITZ

MONROE, JAMES (1758–1831), senator, minister

to France, secretary of state, fifth president of the United States. The friendship between James Monroe and James Madison compares with that of Madison and Thomas Jefferson in longevity, though not in quality and consistency. Jefferson introduced his two closest friends to each other in a letter to Madison in 1784: "The scrupulousness of his honor will make you safe in the most confidential communications. A better man cannot be." Monroe was then a member of Congress, living with the other Virginians at Mrs. House's boardinghouse, but he had recently been a law student of Jefferson's. Jefferson remained a lifelong friend of both Monroe and Madison. He frequently urged them to settle near Monticello; Monroe did so, but Madison remained thirty miles away

JAMES MONROE.   Engraving by Asher B. Durand after a portrait by John Vanderlyn.

COURTESY PRINTS AND PHOTOGRAPHS DIVISION, LIBRARY OF CONGRESS.

at Montpelier. Madison was predisposed to like Monroe, for he was the nephew of Madison's good friend Joseph Jones. The friendship between Madison and Monroe remained warm for most of their long lives, except for brief interruptions caused by the thinness of Monroe's political skin and his readiness to imagine political conspiracies against him.

Madison and Monroe were closely allied in politics and in western land ventures after 1784. When Monroe's financial problems forced him to withdraw from their joint investment in western New York lands, Madison released him from his obligations on generous terms. There was a steady flow of correspondence between them from 1784 to 1787. Monroe for the first time revealed his suspicious nature when the two conflicted in 1788 over ratification of the Constitution. Monroe had been a strong supporter of the Annapolis Convention, urging friends to attend, but when his active support did not lead to an appointment to the Federal Convention in 1787, he blamed the personal hostility of Gov. Edmund Randolph and the suspected connivance of Madison. He thought that Madison had "concurr'd in *arrangements* unfavorable *to me*" and that Madison was "in strict league" with Randolph. If Monroe had been selected, he would have been the second youngest delegate at the convention. Meanwhile, Madison innocently assumed, as the Virginia ratifying convention approached, that Monroe would be a friend to ratification, "though a cool one." Instead, Monroe became a moderate opponent. On the final day of the convention in Richmond, he pleaded unsuccessfully for the adoption of constitutional amendments prior to ratification.

Disappointed by the convention's approval of the Constitution, Patrick Henry schemed to keep Madison out of the First Congress by having Monroe run against him in an Antifederalist district that included Monroe's Spotsylvania County. Though Monroe campaigned extensively, he claimed to be relieved when Madison prevailed in February 1789, winning election to the House of Representatives, and the election did not hinder the resumption of their friendship. By avoiding personal comments as they campaigned together from county to county, Madison claimed that they saved their friendship "from the smallest diminution."

Monroe was later sent to the Senate and cooperated closely with Madison in the House in the early 1790s as the new government and new political parties were forming. They also journeyed together to upstate New York to consider land investments. While Monroe was American minister to France from 1794 to 1796, he often purchased books and furnishings for Madison; meanwhile, Madison kept Monroe's accounts. Monroe was sent to France to offset the anger left by his pro-English predecessor,

but his own pro-French agenda was so blatant that he antagonized both the American and the British governments, and he was recalled in 1796. He asked Madison to publish his letters to vindicate his mission, but no vindication was needed in Virginia, where Monroe was governor from 1799 to 1802.

Monroe was Secretary of State Madison's diplomatic troubleshooter, taking on a role similar to that he would assume as a member of the cabinet in Madison's administration. Because of his great popularity in France, in the American West, and in Jefferson's cabinet, Monroe was sent to France in 1803 to help with negotiations over American claims to the Mississippi River. The American minister, Robert R. Livingston, resented the arrival of a seeming interloper and sought full credit for the Louisiana Purchase. Then, in 1804, Monroe was dispatched to Madrid to help Charles Pinckney with negotiations for eastern Florida. The next year Monroe was sent to London to negotiate for American rights on the Atlantic Ocean during England's bitter war with France. Before Monroe's plea to be allowed to negotiate alone in England had reached Washington, the administration had acquiesced in congressional demands that the American mission be expanded. Monroe was irritated when he learned that William Pinkney would share credit for a treaty; in one of several bitter letters that he wrote but never mailed, he described himself as being "nothing" after Pinkney's appointment. Monroe does not seem to have shared his bitterness with Pinkney, however, and worked well with him, possibly influenced by the shabby treatment he had received from Livingston. The real problem was that the Treaty of 1806 brought both men more blame than credit. Madison had made it clear to Monroe and Pinkney that the most important goal was to stop the impressment of American seamen by the Royal Navy. The British offered only to be careful about impressments, however, and the Treaty of 1806 was not significantly better than Jay's Treaty, which Jefferson, Madison, and Monroe had all scorned and tried to defeat. Ultimately, Jefferson decided not to send the treaty to the Senate; Monroe was crushed by this gesture and for the next several years blamed Madison for the affront.

Disillusioned, Monroe returned to Virginia without informing Madison or Jefferson of his disappointment. Instead, he listened to John Randolph and the handful of Virginia Old Republicans who could never forgive Madison and Jefferson for failing to govern entirely by the philosophy of their own Virginia and Kentucky Resolutions. Randolph had written Monroe that Pinkney was sent to "take from you, the credit for settling our differences with England." Monroe later complained that "circumstances have occur'd during my service abroad, which were calculated to hurt my feelings and actually did hurt them, which may produce a change in the future relation between some of them and myself, unless satisfactorily explained." But Monroe never took the obvious step of asking for an explanation. Instead, he opposed Madison for the presidency in 1808. Eventually, Monroe attributed his anger to Madison's failure to include two minor letters in the diplomatic packet that he sent to the Senate. Monroe's candidacy was rejected by a vote of 136 to 57 in the Virginia legislature, and he received no electoral votes.

In 1810 Jefferson helped his two friends to resume their friendship. In March 1811, only two months after Monroe was again elected governor, Madison persuaded him to become secretary of state; finally, Madison had a secretary capable of writing his own diplomatic correspondence. William Branch Giles described the appointment as "the wickedest of all [of Madison's] contrivances." Trusted completely by Madison, Monroe served, when needed, as acting secretary of war, as secretary of war, and again as secretary of state.

Monroe was an ideal administrative ally. His political ambition was his one notable flaw; his decisions regarding military service and which department he would head often seemed to be determined by their likely impact on his prospects for the presidential nomination in 1816. With Madison's blessing, Monroe was nominated by the congressional caucus, and he was easily elected in both 1816 and 1820.

Madison and Monroe remained close friends for Monroe's remaining years, corresponding often and often visiting each other. They met twice a year at meetings of the Board of Visitors of the University of Virginia. They also agreed in opposing wider suffrage proposed in the Virginia convention of 1829–1830.

BIBLIOGRAPHY

Ammon, Harry. *James Monroe: The Quest for National Identity.* 1971.

Brant, Irving. *The Fourth President: A Life of James Madison, 1809–1812.* 1970.

Ketcham, Ralph. *James Madison: A Biography.* 1971.

DONALD O. DEWEY

MONTESQUIEU (1689–1755), French social and political philosopher. In 1748 "the celebrated" Montesquieu, as Madison called him, published *De l'esprit des lois (The Spirit of the Laws)*, a seminal analysis of governmental separation of powers as a guarantor of political liberty. Charles de Secondat, baron de La Brède et de Montesquieu idealistically viewed the constitution of early-eighteenth-century England, with its distinct legislative and executive powers vested in Parliament and a

MONTESQUIEU.   Engraving by J. Chapman.
PRINTS AND PHOTOGRAPHS DIVISION, LIBRARY OF CONGRESS.

king, as the model of a moderated, ordered rule. His writing influenced the thinkers of the Scottish Enlightenment, especially David Hume, Adam Smith, and Adam Ferguson, whose works in turn were admired by the American Framers. Madison probably read *De l'esprit des lois* for the first time in Robertson's School in 1767–1769 and encountered works of the Scotsmen at Princeton.

In his research for the *National Gazette* essays in the mid 1780s, Madison took extensive notes on "Ancient and Modern Confederacies" and sometimes relied upon Montesquieu's political theories. Perhaps no other writer had more influence on delegates to the Federal Convention in 1787, where Montesquieu was often cited as the leading authority.

Although Madison disagreed with several of Montesquieu's ideas, he regarded him as a meritorious political philosopher and quoted him (and sometimes challenged his theories) in his writings and letters and in *Federalist* 43 and 47. *De l'esprit des lois* may have moved Madison to consider, among other things, the meaning and sources of national character, the influence of size of a nation on its government (Madison rejected Montesquieu's warning that republics could not survive in a large country), the principles of a confederated republic, the division, balance, and separation of governmental powers, and even the beginnings of analysis and criticism of modern democratic society.

BIBLIOGRAPHY

Cohler, Anne M. *Montesquieu's Comparative Politics and the Spirit of American Constitutionalism.* 1988.

Montesquieu, Charles de Secondat, baron de. *The Spirit of the Laws.* Translated and edited by Anne M. Cohler, Basia Carolyn Miller, and Harold Samuel Stone. 1989.

Spurlin, Paul Merrill. *Montesquieu in America, 1760–1801.* 1940.

THEODORE M. VESTAL

MONTPELIER. The area around Montpelier, the Madison plantation in Orange County, Virginia, has a rich history spanning ten millennia. Native American habitation of the area dates back as far as c. 8000 B.C., although westward migrations of Piedmont Virginia Indian groups during the late seventeenth century, as well as European-introduced illnesses to which the native populations had no natural immunity, had cleared most of the native tribes from the area before the beginning of European settlement in the early eighteenth century.

European settlement of the Montpelier land itself began in the early 1720s. Montpelier was included within a patent for 4,675 acres granted to Ambrose Madison (grandfather of President James Madison) and his brother-in-law, Thomas Chew, on 15 November 1723. The region then was still part of Spotsylvania County; it became part of a new county, Orange, in 1734. Ambrose Madison originally called his plantation Mount Pleasant; the name was later changed to Montpelier. The choice of name, presumably of French origin, was apparently a common contemporary reference to a pleasant, healthful place.

Ambrose Madison spent most of the next decade on more cultivated properties to the east, directing the settlement of his Montpelier lands by resident overseers and slave crews. He and his family moved permanently to Montpelier in early 1732. His house, near what is now the Madison family cemetery, no longer stands, but, given the standards of the time, it was probably a relatively small and simple dwelling—likely a 1½-story frame structure

MONTPELIER.   Print from *Family Magazine*, 1830.

PRINTS AND PHOTOGRAPHS DIVISION, LIBRARY OF CONGRESS.

with fewer than a half-dozen rooms. Upon Ambrose Madison's death in August 1732, the property passed to his widow, Frances Taylor Madison, and to his nine-year-old son, James Madison, Sr. Under Ambrose and Frances Taylor Madison, tobacco was the primary market and cash crop. Other crops and livestock—corn and other vegetables, cattle, sheep, and hogs—were raised to provide sustenance for the family and plantation work force.

For a decade after his marriage in 1749, James Madison, Sr., continued to live in his father's house or in another structure, which was the first home of his son James Madison, Jr., the future president. It was James Madison, Sr., who built the nucleus of the present Montpelier mansion (c. 1760), and the family moved from the old house to the new, President Madison remembered, when he was barely old enough to carry lighter items of furniture.

Since James Madison, Sr., was in business as a building contractor during this time, he may have designed his own house. In its original form, the Montpelier house was a two-story brick Georgian structure, with a main-floor center passageway and two rooms on either side. To the south of the house was an extensive domestic complex, including a kitchen and other support buildings. To the north was an industrial site, the plantation ironworks. Surviving plantation records for James Madison, Sr.'s tenure (the last half of the eighteenth century) show a diversified Montpelier economy, combining agriculture, commerce, and industry. In addition to agricultural products (corn, tobacco, hay, hemp, wheat, cows, oxen, horses, hogs, and sheep), the senior Madison was a merchant and a distiller; he also had a building contracting business, a gristmill, and the ironworks.

Between 1797 and 1800, an addition thirty feet long was made to the north end of the house to provide a residence for James Madison, Jr., and his family; the front portico was added at this time as well. All additions were designed by the younger Madison. The senior Madisons continued to occupy most of the original portion of the house.

Inheriting Montpelier after his father's death in 1801, James Madison eliminated his father's commercial and industrial businesses and returned Montpelier to a solely agricultural base, in keeping with his devotion to the Republican ideal of America as primarily a nation of yeoman farmers, each working his own land. Between 1809 and 1812 he enlarged the house a second time to serve as his retirement home, adding a rear portico and one-story wings to both ends. Madison apparently consulted both Dr. William Thornton and Benjamin Latrobe regarding the design, which was carried out by three builders recommended by Thomas Jefferson: James Dinsmore, John Neilson, and Hugh Chisholm.

President Madison devoted much of his retirement to running his plantation and to continuing his earlier experiments with progressive agricultural techniques. He corresponded widely on these subjects with friends and relatives, including Jefferson and Madison's brother-in-law Isaac Hite, Jr. Under Madison's management, Montpelier showed greater profits than the plantations of many of his neighbors, although new pests, recessions, bad weather and markets, and Madison's increasing age and illness all took their toll. Following Madison's death in 1836, the widowed Dolley Madison was unable to manage the plantation on her own, and she sold Montpelier in 1844.

Over the next half-century, Montpelier had half a dozen owners, and the house was remodeled several times before being purchased by William du Pont, Sr., in 1900. The du Ponts further enlarged the house and added extensive landscaping and buildings. Montpelier remained in the duPont family until 1983, when it passed to the National Trust for Historic Preservation, which operates it as a museum property and is undertaking various research projects to determine more about the history of the house and land.

BIBLIOGRAPHY

Miller, Ann L. *Historic Structure Report: Montpelier, Orange County, Virginia—Phase II: Documentary Evidence Regarding the Montpelier House.* 1990.
Scott, W. W. *A History of Orange County, Virginia.* 1907.

ANN L. MILLER

MONTREAL. History and its location at the confluence of water routes to the Great Lakes basin made Montreal the principal city of the British North American provinces and a strategic commercial link between Upper Canada and Great Britain. The fur trade brought prosperity to the city by the 1790s, and the city's wealthiest citizens were its leading fur merchants. Finance and timber, along with trade with areas to the west and south, broadened the city's economic base.

English and Scottish merchants and officials dominated Montreal's social and political life, while the French in the city remained an economic underclass. Americans in the upper Champlain Valley and in northern New York looked to Montreal for markets and supplies, and in 1796 direct trade between Montreal and New York City began. Montreal attracted the attention of men with grand schemes; John Jacob Astor sought partnerships with Montreal fur traders and with the Northwest Company in order to create his continental empire, and the American businessman Horatio Gates settled in the city and became a founder of the Bank of Montreal. In 1812 some thirty-five American merchants operating in Montreal took an oath of allegiance to the crown in order to retain their businesses.

By 1812 Montreal had more than sixteen thousand

inhabitants, who saw the War of 1812 as primarily an Upper Canadian (Ontarian) affair. The city's walls were dilapidated and its outer defensive works weak and underprotected. Both French and English militia units mustered to defend against potential American invasions. Early on, Madison nullified Henry Dearborn's local armistice with Gov. George Prevost, and a hastily organized, hesitantly led American force moved against Champlain, then stalled and withdrew. Despite American threats, Montreal never felt the fall of shot during the war.

In 1813 British forces raided Burlington, Plattsburgh, and Swanton to delay the Americans. Combined British and Canadian forces stopped a two-pronged advance under Wade Hampton and James Wilkinson at the battles of Chateaugay in October and Chrysler's Farm in November. In 1814 Montreal was the principal British staging area for an unsuccessful assault on Plattsburgh.

Throughout the War of 1812, American farmers sold livestock and supplies to British rather than American commissary agents as smuggling, prevalent before the outbreak of war, continued. The city prospered from the work and the spending occasioned by the war but suffered a mild depression after 1815. American internal canal building in the 1820s reduced Montreal's economic significance for the United States, but continuing development in Upper Canada sustained the city as British North America's principal commercial center.

BIBLIOGRAPHY

Jenkins, Kathleen. *Montreal: Island City of the St. Lawrence.* 1966.
Rich, Edwin. *Montreal and the Fur Trade.* 1966
Rumily, Robert. *Histoire de Montréal.* 3 vols. 1970.

REGINALD C. STUART

MORRIS, GOUVERNEUR (1752–1816), revolutionary statesman and diplomat. Morris was elected to New York's first provincial congress in 1775 and three years later to the Continental Congress, where he served for two years before becoming assistant superintendent of finance under Robert Morris.

In 1787 Morris was elected as a delegate from Pennsylvania to the Federal Convention, where he and James Madison participated in the debates more often than any other speakers, with Morris edging out Madison for high honors. According to Madison, Morris had "a fondness for saying things and advancing doctrines that no one else would." Morris did not believe in the perfectibility of man, and his aristocratic views led Madison to describe him as "a member who on all occasions, had inculcated so strongly, the political depravity of men, and the necessity of checking one vice and interest by opposing them to another vice and interest."

Both Morris and Madison supported a strong national government, but Morris favored one controlled by the wealthy, whereas Madison advocated popular representation. Both men proposed allowing a congressional veto of state laws, but they differed over whether to admit new states on terms of equality with the original states, with Morris favoring a subordinate role for the western territories as provinces under eastern control. Both men also served on the Committee on Style, but the committee asked Morris to prepare its final report, and he therefore became the member chiefly responsible for the literary form of the Constitution. Writing late in life, Madison praised Morris for "the brilliancy of his genius" at the convention, noting that "he added, what is too rare, a candid surrender of his opinions, when the lights of discussion satisfied him, that they had been too hastily formed, and a readiness to aid in making the best of measures in which he had been overruled."

In 1792 President George Washington appointed Morris as minister to France, where he served until 1794, when he was recalled at the request of the French government after Washington had dismissed Citizen Genet as the French minister to the United States. Morris served briefly as a Federalist senator from New York between 1800 and 1802 and became increasingly opposed to the Republicans. He was hostile to "Mr. Madison's War" between 1812 and 1815 and suggested that Congress refuse to support the war loans of the Madison administration. He finally advocated secession by New York and the New England states and denounced the Hartford Convention for not calling for that extreme step.

BIBLIOGRAPHY

Mintz, Max M. *Gouverneur Morris and the American Revolution.* 1970.

JAMES MORTON SMITH

MORRIS, ROBERT (1734–1806), financier, senator, superintendant of finance. Morris was born in England but soon joined his father in Maryland and engaged in the tobacco export trade. He spent some years employed by the Willing family of Philadelphia and in 1754 became a partner in Willing, Morris and Company. This association catapulted him to a position among the leading merchants of the American colonies. Morris became increasingly interested in the resistance politics of his colony and occupied important committee positions in the Pennsylvania legislature.

In 1775 he was chosen a member of the Continental Congress and soon became an important and active delegate, serving on the committees of secret correspon-

GOUVERNEUR MORRIS AND ROBERT MORRIS.   Robert Morris (right), superintendent of finance in the Continental government under the Articles of Confederation, points to his plan for establishing public credit. As assistant to Robert (no relation) from 1781 to 1785, Gouverneur Morris (left), planned the decimal system of American currency. Double portrait by Charles Willson Peale, 1783.   PENNSYLVANIA ACADEMY OF THE FINE ARTS, PHILADELPHIA. BEQUEST OF RICHARD ASHHURST.

dence, ways and means, naval armament, and others. He was a signer of the Declaration of Independence (1776) and the Articles of Confederation (1778). After he left Congress, Morris was accused of profiteering on government contracts held by his trading companies, but several investigations absolved him of illegal actions. In 1781 Morris was appointed superintendant of finance for the new national government formed under the Articles of Confederation. He launched a program to rationalize the finances of the national government by establishing public credit through taxation for current expenses and debt service and by establishing controls on spending through,

among other items, contracts for supplying the army. Early on, Madison, then a delegate in Congress, supported Morris's program for a central government powerful enough to carry on the war. Morris's efforts were defeated eventually, but not before he had provided the resources, through his personal credit and with the help of French and Dutch loans, to see the war through to its successful conclusion. He resigned his post in 1784. He was a member, along with Madison, of the Annapolis Convention (1786) and the Federal Convention (1787), and he was chosen one of Pennsylvania's first two U.S. senators, serving from 1789 to 1795.

After his retirement from politics, Morris plunged into reckless western land speculation, lost his fortune, and was arrested in 1798 and sent to debtor's prison. There he remained until released by the new federal bankruptcy law in 1801. He never regained his former wealth or eminence.

BIBLIOGRAPHY

Dictionary of American Biography. 1928–1958.

Ferguson, E. James, et al. *Papers of Robert Morris.* 7 vols. to date. 1973–.

Ver Steeg, Clarence L. *Robert Morris: Revolutionary Financier.* 1954.

DAVID B. MATTERN

MURRAY, WILLIAM VANS (1760–1803), legislator, diplomat. Born in Cambridge, Maryland, to well-to-do parents, Murray was sent to England for legal training at the Middle Temple in 1784. While in England he married and wrote a book on politics that he dedicated to the American minister in Great Britain, John Adams.

Murray brought his bride to Maryland and began practicing law in 1787. He was elected to the Maryland state legislature but resigned to accept a seat in the U.S. House of Representatives, where he served from 1791 to 1797 as a Federalist. President Washington valued Murray's judgment, and his appointment of James McHenry as secretary of war and of Samuel Chase to the Supreme Court may have been at Murray's urging. Murray also defended the president when the House of Representatives debated a move to bring Washington's correspondence on Jay's Treaty before the House.

When John Adams was nominated for the presidency in 1796, Murray was an early supporter, writing essays for a Federalist newspaper on Adams's behalf. Early in 1797 Washington appointed Murray to serve as the American minister to the Netherlands, then in 1799 Adams named Murray as minister to France, and in Paris, Murray worked to heal the Franco-American rupture that caused both ill feeling and some bloodshed in 1798–1800. After the French blunder in the XYZ Affair became notorious, Talleyrand worked through Murray for a reconciliation, and Adams appointed Murray (with Oliver Ellsworth and William R. Davie) to the commission that negotiated a treaty, signed in October 1800, that ended the 1778 Franco-American alliance but kept the favorable commercial arrangements in the original pact.

Madison wrote Murray in June 1801 informing him that President Jefferson had decided "to discontinue the establishment of a Public Minister at the Hague." Murray realized his political affiliation had not helped him but pleaded for the continuance of an American diplomat in Holland and was affronted that his recall was known in Paris before he had heard the news. Murray's post was left vacant when he resigned in September 1801.

BIBLIOGRAPHY

Murray's papers are in the Manuscripts division of the Library of Congress.

Brugger, Robert J., et al., eds. *Papers of James Madison: Secretary of State Series.* Vol. 1. 1986.

Graebner, Norman A., *The Foundation of American Foreign Policy . . . from Franklin to McKinley.* 1985.

ROBERT A. RUTLAND

N

NAPOLEON I (1769–1821), French general, first consul, emperor of the French (1804–1815). Napoleon was not involved in American politics until the spring of 1803, when he renewed his ongoing war with Great Britain and sold the French territory of Louisiana to the United States to help finance the renewed Anglo-French struggle. In May of that year, Napoleon took advantage of an American offer for part of the territory and offered the whole area to the United States for $15 million. The action surprised the American negotiators, but Jefferson and his cabinet saw the purchase as a great boon to American interests, although the president and Madison both wondered about the constitutionality of acquiring new territory in such an unorthodox manner. Undoubtedly they discussed the purchase in private conversations, and Madison came to look on the transaction as a "bargain . . . highly advantageous" to the United States. Once the bargain was sealed, Madison as secretary of state was involved in implementing the treaty ratified by the Senate to confirm the sale.

When the European war intensified, England issued orders in council that forbade neutral commerce with France. The Royal Navy soon began capturing Yankee ships, impounding their crews, and auctioning off their cargoes. Napoleon retaliated with a series of decrees dated at Berlin, Milan, and Bayonne that warned neutrals not to trade with England; those that did would suffer the consequences—French seizure of all vessels engaged in breaking Napoleon's "paper" blockade (the French fleet had been destroyed at Trafalgar in 1805). Dozens of American vessels were interdicted by the French coastal fleet, their cargoes seized, and the Yankee crews imprisoned. Napoleon ignored American protests until he decided to risk a diplomatic ploy. After hearing the terms of Macon's Bill No. 2, Napoleon purportedly issued a letter to his foreign minister declaring an end to all French restrictions, provided the British also rescinded their orders in council.

The skeptical British insisted that the French order was spurious, for in fact the French had continued to seize American vessels within their jurisdiction. President Madison had fallen into Napoleon's trap but would not admit it. Instead, he called on the British to follow Napoleon's lead. When he heard the British were delaying any action until the French offer was proved valid, Madison's patience ran out. He sent a war message to Congress in April 1812, thus proving Napoleon's cunning maneuver had been the bait needed to force the issue of neutral rights.

The American declaration of war made the United States, technically, an ally of France. But the disastrous French invasion of Russia and its aftermath left Napoleon more concerned with European military matters. Clearly, the British considered the American war of secondary importance as long as Napoleon's army was intact. However, after the Russian disaster, Napoleon was forced to abdicate. When the French emperor was sent into exile, there was mounting pressure in Great Britain to use the experienced British army for an extensive campaign in Louisiana, including the invasion at New Orleans. British public opinion turned against the United States and demanded a punitive strike at the Americans for what was regarded as a bumbled effort to stab the British in the back as they fought off the menace of a Napoleonized Europe. Albert Gallatin was in London and reported that the British "thirst for a great revenge, and the nation will not be satisfied without it." Meanwhile, Madison may have welcomed Napoleon's replacement by Louis XVIII, particularly when it was learned that the monarch apparently accepted the credentials of William H. Crawford as the American minister to France.

With Napoleon's decline the American bargaining position at the treaty table was weakened. Pessimistic

NAPOLEON I, EMPEROR OF THE FRENCH, 1804–1815. Napoleon Bonaparte abdicated in April 1814 and again in June 1815; he was exiled to the island of Saint Helena in the South Atlantic, where he died in 1821. Stipple engraving published by G. Virtue, London, 1827.
PRINTS AND PHOTOGRAPHS DIVISION, LIBRARY OF CONGRESS.

Federalist newspapers even predicted that, with Napoleon gone, the British would proceed to recolonize their former North American possessions. The American commissioners gave up their insistence that the British renounce the impressment of American seamen, and a peace treaty was signed as Napoleon languished at Elba. When Napoleon returned and summoned an army (that would eventually be defeated at Waterloo), Americans were at peace with the British. Napoleon's duplicity had drained Americans of any sympathy for the deposed emperor, and his final exile to Saint Helena was regarded by most Americans with indifference.

BIBLIOGRAPHY

Brant, Irving. *James Madison: Commander in Chief.* 1961.
Castelot, André. *Napoléon.* 1971.
Ketcham, Ralph. *James Madison: A Biography.* 1971.
Stagg, J. C. A. *Mr. Madison's War.* 1983.
Tulard, Jean, ed. *Dictionnaire Napoléon.* 1987.

ROBERT A. RUTLAND

NATIONAL GAZETTE.   Disturbed by the influence of the arch-Federalist *Gazette of the United States,* Secretary of State Thomas Jefferson sought to promote a rival newspaper in the nation's temporary capital in Philadelphia that would support Republican causes. Madison and Jefferson decided that Philip Freneau, a college classmate of Madison's, had the qualifications to edit such a journal, and they began seeking subscriptions from friends to support the enterprise. On 31 October 1791 the *National Gazette* began publication as a semiweekly newspaper under Freneau's editorship. Jefferson's backing for the new newspaper was thinly disguised, for Freneau was a clerk in the State Department; coinciding with the efforts to start an opposition journal were Madison's efforts in Congress to encourage the circulation of newspapers by lowering postal rates.

Freneau's mission was to publish a newspaper that would provide a forum for attacks on Alexander Hamilton's growing influence in the Washington administration. Once the *Gazette* was launched, Jefferson hailed Freneau as a hero. "His paper has saved our constitution which was galloping fast into monarchy," Jefferson exulted. Encouraged by Jefferson, Madison began contributing to the *Gazette* columns, and between the issues of 19 November 1791 and 20 December 1792 he prepared eighteen essays for Freneau's newspaper. Madison's essays were unsigned and ranged from comments on public opinion to blatant attacks on Federalists. "Public opinion sets bounds to every government, and is the real sovereign in every free one," Madison began his first essay, and he consistently polarized contrasts between the Republicans and the Federalists. Washington became a target of the *Gazette,* and the controversy was further exacerbated when Citizen Genet arrived in Philadelphia as the newly appointed French minister. Genet ignored Washington's proclamation of neutrality, and the *Gazette* charged that the president was the dupe of "speculators, tories and British emissaries." Washington lost his patience and denounced "that rascal Freneau."

Jefferson resigned as secretary of state as a yellow fever epidemic swept through Philadelphia. Though Jefferson denied Federalist charges that he was the driving force behind Freneau, the epidemic and Jefferson's withdrawal from the cabinet left Freneau's newspaper in a precarious financial state. The embarrassing Genet affair caused both Jefferson and Madison to cease their active support for Freneau, and the *Gazette* ceased publication on 26 October 1793.

BIBLIOGRAPHY

Hutchinson, William T., et al., eds. *Papers of James Madison: Congressional Series.* Vols. 14–15. 1983–1985.
Mott, Frank L. *American Journalism: A History 1690–1960.* 1962.

ROBERT A. RUTLAND

NATIONAL INTELLIGENCER. Established in October 1800 in Washington, D.C., by Samuel Harrison Smith, the *National Intelligencer* soon became recognized as the outstanding voice of the Jefferson administration. Federalists regarded the triweekly journal as the official paper of the administration, although Jefferson insisted that he had no formal connection with Smith or his newspaper. In truth, Jefferson endorsed Smith's newspaper and used its columns to print reports and unofficial information, as well as to promote his policies.

Madison's nomination for president by the congressional caucus in February 1808 was first announced in the *National Intelligencer,* and Smith was a steadfast supporter of Madison in the campaign. Although Federalists accused Smith of favoritism in the reporting of debates, the *National Intelligencer's* coverage of Congress was fuller than that of any other newspaper and thus widely reprinted. Smith depended on a stenographer and on obliging members of Congress for his reports of debates at a time when the official proceedings were little more than outlines of the actions taken.

Madison's friendship with Smith was useful in helping him disseminate widely information such as the arrival of the dispatch ship *Hornet* from England in 1812. Expectations of some concession by the British were high, and the *National Intelligencer* hinted that, unless the ship carried news of a fundamental change in British policy, the Madison administration would take decisive action; when no such change was revealed, Madison soon had a war message ready.

Republican newspapers, particulary in the South, borrowed heavily from the *National Intelligencer* and it, along with Thomas Ritchie's *Richmond Enquirer* and William Duane's Philadelphia *Aurora,* constituted the holy trinity of Republican journalism.

Smith sold the newspaper in 1810, but the new owners continued its close link with Madison, and the paper was one of the first to endorse Madison for reelection in 1812. The firm of Gales & Seaton continued the *National Intelligencer's* reputation as a Republican outlet for the executive branch and converted it into a daily newspaper in 1813. Helped by printing contracts from Congress, the newspaper kept its place in party circles until the election of Andrew Jackson as president in 1828. Other newspapers then took over its role as a presidential mouthpiece, but the *National Intelligencer* continued publishing until 1869.

BIBLIOGRAPHY

Cunningham, Noble E., Jr. *The Jeffersonian Republicans in Power: Party Operations, 1801–1809.* 1974.

Mott, Frank L. *American Journalism: A History 1690–1960.* 1962.

Rutland, Robert A. *The Newsmongers: Journalism in the Life of the Nation, 1690–1972.* 1973.

ROBERT A. RUTLAND

NATIONAL ROAD. See *Cumberland Road.*

NATIVE AMERICANS. See *Creek Indians; Shawnee Indians.*

NAVY, BRITISH. See *Royal Navy.*

NAVY, UNITED STATES. See *United States Navy.*

NEUTRALITY. Neutrality presumes that the avoidance of an ongoing war would serve the country better than entering it. James Madison, like Americans generally in the period after the Revolution, believed that the young republic should remain neutral toward European wars in which U.S. interests were minimal, especially when contrasted to those of the warring European powers. The United States had managed to maintain a precarious neutrality during the French revolutionary wars of the 1790s. When war returned to Europe in 1803, Thomas Jefferson and Madison remained officially aloof. As Napoleon prepared to crush his opponents on the continent, England countered by destroying the French fleet at Trafalgar in October 1805. In December Napoleon defeated the combined Austrian and Russian armies at Austerlitz. Supreme on land, he could not invade England or challenge Britain's control of the seas nor could Britain invade the continent. Frustrated by this standoff, France and England resorted to commercial warfare in an effort to weaken one another through seizures and blockades.

For this assault the United States, a leading neutral carrier, was not prepared. Jefferson and Madison were determined to protect America's lucrative commerce with all belligerents and still maintain the country's official neutrality. One highly profitable U.S. trade consisted of carrying cargoes from the French West Indies to France, a trade that France had not permitted in peacetime. In the *Essex* decision of 1805, the British government declared the West Indian trade illegal and subject to seizure under the Rule of 1756, which declared that trade closed in time of peace could not be opened in time of war. American ship captains cleared French colonial cargoes through an American port in accordance with the earlier British *Polly* decision, but often failed to break the voyage by unloading and reloading. The British had little respect for American claims to neutral rights; they regarded American neutrality merely a cover for wartime profiteering. A British admiralty court reaffirmed the *Essex* ruling with a decree that "set aside the Pretensions of the Americans to legalize their cargoes by fictitious landing & reshipping." Then in May 1806 the British cabinet tightened American commerce further by declaring the north coast of Europe under blockade. Jefferson and Madison soon discovered that their country's capacity to wage commercial warfare was no match for the power and determination of the British and French governments to restrict American commerce in their quest for victory. Jefferson, in December 1807, finally imposed an embargo on U.S. exports to Europe to protect American goods and shipping from the gauntlet of French and British power. As President, Madison continued the nation's efforts to protect its neutral trade against European encroachments. Those efforts gained little protection, but they fanned the spirit of American nationalism, unleashed a crusade against Britain, and ultimately compelled Madison to accept congressional demands for war, a war for which the country was not prepared.

External events trapped Madison as president in another controversy over neutral rights when the Spanish American colonies demanded U.S. material and moral support in their revolt against Spain. President Madison, under pressure from the Madrid government, which sought to preserve its empire, introduced legislation in January 1816 to enforce American neutrality. Henry Clay of Kentucky accused Madison of taking up the cause of the Spanish king. In December 1816 Madison sent a special message to Congress calling for legislation to prevent the employment on the high seas of vessels armed in the United States. In January 1817 Clay again entered the neutrality debate, pointing to Spain's advantages over the Latin Americans in exerting pressure in Washington. What others might do with vessels armed in the United States, Clay argued, should not be the administration's concern. After March 1817 President James Monroe could no longer prevent the outfitting of privateers under existing neutrality legislation. Finally in April 1818 Congress enacted a neutrality law that empowered the government to suppress the outfitting of privateers. Again Madison's experience revealed the special difficulty that the United States confronted in defending its neutrality.

[See also *Blockades by England and France; Embargo Act of 1807; Privateers; Rule of 1756.*]

BIBLIOGRAPHY

Brant, Irving. *James Madison: Secretary of State, 1800–1809.* 1953.
Peterson, Merrill D. *The Great Triumvirate: Webster, Clay, and Calhoun.* 1987.

NORMAN A. GRAEBNER

NEW ENGLAND.   During the administration of James Madison, New England consisted of five states: Rhode Island, Connecticut, Massachusetts, Vermont, and New Hampshire. With the exception of Vermont (admitted to the Union in 1791), all these states were among the original thirteen. Until 1820, when it was admitted as a separate state, Maine was part of Massachusetts. New England is bounded on the east by the Atlantic Ocean, to the north by the Canadian provinces of New Brunswick and Quebec, to the west by the Hudson River Valley and New York state and to the south by New York. Altogether the region encompasses slightly more than 63,000 square miles. In 1800 the population was 941,000, about 25 percent of the nation's total population.

Connecticut, the most southern state of the region, was also the most agricultural. With gentle, rolling hills in the east and the broad expanse of the Connecticut River, the state produced a variety of agricultural products, many of them exported along the Connecticut River to either New York City via Long Island Sound or south to the West Indian islands. Nicknamed the "Land of Steady Habits," Connecticut was firmly in the Federalist camp. In 1808, at the time of Madison's first election, it was the only New England state with a congressional delegation composed entirely of Federalists.

Rhode Island, the last of the original thirteen states to join the Union under the Constitution and the smallest, was dominated by the city of Providence. Sitting at the head of Narragansett Bay this community dominated the state as did no other city in New England. Although it was a port, by 1800 Providence was showing clear signs of industrialization. Samuel Slater, financed by money drawn from Providence merchants, had established the first cotton mill in America at nearby Pawtucket.

Massachusetts, the most populous of the New England states, was still heavily dependent upon maritime commerce and therefore anti-Republican after the Embargo of 1807. During the War of 1812 the state militia did not take part in the Canadian campaign because of opposition to Madison's administration. After the war, she began to develop considerable industry, particularly a textile industry, as water power became a major source of energy in the region. Maine, not admitted as a state until 1820, was a district of Massachusetts. She had the longest and most forbidding coastline in the region. Some shipbuilding and trading took place near towns such as York, Portland, and Bath, where deep water and an abundance of timber was available.

Vermont was carved out of territory claimed by both New York and New Hampshire. Mountainous, except in the Connecticut River Valley and near the shores of Lake Champlain, the state was the most isolated and least populous state in New England, the only one without direct

JOSIAH QUINCY.   Quincy, an opponent of the War of 1812, declares himself king of New England and grand master of the Order of Two Cod fishes. Etching by William Charles, 1812 or 1813.

PRINTS AND PHOTOGRAPHS DIVISION, LIBRARY OF CONGRESS.

access to the sea. The greatest concentration of population was in the south, where farming was the principal occupation, which may account for Republican strength among Vermont's yeoman farmers.

New Hampshire too was somewhat isolated. Her coastline stretched for only a few miles between two parts of Massachusetts. The state exported some timber, floating it down the Piscataqua River to Portsmouth, but for the most part she relied on small farms tucked away in the hills toward the southern part of the state.

Long accustomed to complain about the Virginia dynasty despite the success of the Adams family, New England witnessed its relative importance in the nation decline in the years following the War of 1812. As population moved west and new states entered the Union, New England found itself with less political influence. Many parts of the region held to Federalism long after that party had ceased to be a viable national force. Politics, however, were not monolithic. In the presidential elections of 1808 and 1812 Vermont voted for Madison while all the remaining New England states cast their ballots in favor of Charles Cotesworth Pinckney in 1808 and De Witt Clinton in 1812. Divisions within the region could also be discerned in the contest over the Tariff of 1816; the New England congressional delegation split by a margin of 17 to 10 in favor. Those voting against were allied with the Federalists, who were keen on protecting maritime interests, while those voting in favor were reflecting the growing interests of those committed to protecting newly emerging industries. New England in the early decades of the nineteenth century was clearly a region undergoing a fundamental transformation.

BIBLIOGRAPHY

Bruchey, Stuart. *The Roots of American Economic Growth, 1607–1861.* 1965.
Russell, Howard S. *A Long, Deep Furrow: Three Centuries of Farming in New England.* 1976.
Weeden, William B. *Economic and Social History of New England, 1620–1789.* 2 vols. 1890.

WILLIAM M. FOWLER, JR.

NEW JERSEY, COLLEGE OF. See *Princeton University.*

NEW JERSEY PLAN. At the beginning of the Federal Convention, Edmund Randolph introduced what became known as the Virginia Plan, calling for a radical restructuring of the government. The plan was a distillation of James Madison's ideas as discussed at the Virginia caucus held before the Federal Convention began.

Under the Virginia Plan (also called the Randolph Plan), representation in Congress would be based on population. On 15 June 1787 William Paterson introduced the New Jersey Plan (or Paterson Plan). This plan was a response to the fear of the small states that a population-based legislature would be dominated by a few large states. The plan retained the apportionment of Congress that already existed under the Articles of Confederation, allowing one vote per state. But New Jersey's proposal was not a states' rights plan. Except for the "one state, one vote" rule, the plan reflected the nationalism of the Virginia Plan, although it did not go as far as the Virginia Plan in strengthening the national government.

Under Paterson's plan, members of Congress would elect a national executive with a fixed term of office, a salary paid by Congress, and the power to appoint national officeholders. The plan also created a national judiciary with appellate jurisdiction and with the power to review cases from state courts. The plan gave Congress new and significant taxing powers and the power to regulate interstate and international commerce and provided a supremacy clause making all acts of Congress and all treaties the supreme law of the land. The convention vigorously debated this plan for four days before defeating it on 19 June. Only New Jersey, New York, and Delaware supported the plan, with Maryland's delegation divided.

The New Jersey Plan stimulated extensive debate. James Wilson spent most of 16 June attacking the plan. On Monday, 18 June, Alexander Hamilton gave his first major speech of the convention. In a day-long attack, Hamilton expressed his dislike of both plans but opposed New Jersey's in particular. During this speech Hamilton presented his own plan of government, a radically nationalist proposal in which senators and a chief executive would serve for life and the national government would have the power to overrule state laws. In his speech Hamilton praised the English system of government as the "only good one." Hamilton's proposals were far too extreme for the convention and for the nation. They provided a foil for the New Jersey Plan, however, and thus may have made the Virginia Plan seem more palatable to the smaller states.

Madison remained silent until the day of the vote on the New Jersey Plan. Then he gave one of his longest speeches of the convention. Madison dissected the New Jersey Plan to show why it was inadequate for the needs of the nation. He began by placing Paterson on the defensive, noting that New Jersey was "notorious" in refusing to pay its share of the nation's expenses. Madison pointed out that the New Jersey Plan did not have any mechanism for compelling the states to implement national treaties and "left the will of the States as uncontrouled as ever." Drawing on ancient Greek history, as well as Swiss, Germany, and Belgian history, Madison argued that the states would be too strong under the New Jersey Plan and that this flaw would ultimately destroy the nation. He thought the plan too weak to prevent states from fighting with each other or to prevent insurrections within states. After Madison's speech the convention voted on the New Jersey Plan and defeated it.

The defeat of the New Jersey Plan left the Virginia Plan on the table, but without the support of a number of states. For the rest of the month the convention drifted, until the Great Compromise resolved the split between large and small states. That compromise incorporated the idea of state equality embodied in the New Jersey Plan for the Senate, while retaining the idea of population-based representation in the House of Representatives.

[See also *Federal Convention; Virginia Plan.*]

BIBLIOGRAPHY

Farrand, Max, ed. *The Records of the Federal Convention of 1787.* Rev. ed. 1966.

Onuf, Peter S., ed. *The New American Nation, 1775–1820.* Vol. 5. *The Federal Constitution.* 1991.

PAUL FINKELMAN

NEW ORLEANS, BATTLE OF (8 January 1815). The Battle of New Orleans was the last great battle of the War of 1812. Although fought on 8 January 1815—two weeks after an Anglo-American peace treaty had been signed in Europe but five weeks before the treaty reached America—the battle was such a lopsided American victory that it helped generate the myth that the United States had won the war.

Although a British attack on New Orleans was widely expected, when Gen. Andrew Jackson arrived in the city on 1 December 1814, he found that few defensive preparations had been made and that people throughout Louisiana radiated disloyalty and defeatism. Galvanizing

BATTLE OF NEW ORLEANS.   PRINTS AND PHOTOGRAPHS DIVISION, LIBRARY OF CONGRESS.

the residents to action, Jackson initiated defense measures and established an intelligence system to keep abreast of enemy movements.

Meanwhile, the British transported a large army— 7,500 strong—commanded by Gen. Edward Pakenham (the Duke of Wellington's brother-in-law) from Jamaica to the Gulf Coast. After arriving on the coast in November 1814, the troops were ferried to Lake Borgne. There a small British naval force defeated a fleet of American gunboats, enabling the British to move their troops to a spot on the Mississippi River south of New Orleans.

Jackson was determined to meet the enemy well beyond New Orleans. Hence, when he learned in late December that the British had made it to the river, he launched a series of attacks. These engagements proved inconclusive, but they bought Jackson enough time to establish a fortified defensive line, anchored by heavy naval guns, that blocked the road to New Orleans on the eastern side of the river. Jackson also ordered the establishment of a defensive line on the western side of the river to ensure that he would not be outflanked.

The British dispatched six hundred troops under Col. William Thornton to storm the American positions (held by seven hundred ill-trained militia) on the west bank. Thornton's men completely routed the militia, but they were so far behind schedule that the main battle ended before they could threaten American positions on the east bank.

Meanwhile, the main British force (about 5,300 strong) advanced across an open plain in three columns against Jackson's main line, which was defended by 4,700 men. A fog covered the British advance, but when the fog lifted suddenly, the redcoats were completely exposed to American fire. The effect of this fire—particularly the grape and canister from the American cannons—was utterly devastating.

Only a small column advancing along the river got to the American line, but these troops endured such withering fire that they had to fall back. The fire was so intense that many hardened British veterans turned and fled. Others hit the ground and remained there until the battle was over. Pakenham, a conspicuous target on his horse, was killed by cannon fire.

Gen. John Lambert, who took command after Pakenham fell, broke off the engagement. It had lasted only a half hour on the eastern side of the river, and yet the toll was terrific. In all, the British lost over two thousand men (including close to five hundred captured). The United States, in contrast, lost only about seventy men, and only thirteen on Jackson's side of the river.

Republicans across the country celebrated the great victory, asserting that the United States had single-handedly defeated Wellington's "invincibles" and had delivered a crushing blow to the conqueror of Napoleon and the mistress of the seas. Although the United States had not achieved its war aims, in the wake of the victory at New Orleans President James Madison proclaimed the war a success, and he was echoed by Republican orators and editors everywhere.

BIBLIOGRAPHY

Brooks, Charles B. *The Siege of New Orleans.* 1961.

Brown, Wilbert S. *The Amphibious Campaign for West Florida and Louisiana, 1814–1815: A Critical Review of Strategy and Tactics at New Orleans.* 1969.

Owsley, Frank L., Jr. *Struggle for the Gulf Borderlands: The Creek War and the Battle of New Orleans, 1812–1815.* 1981.

DONALD R. HICKEY

NEW YORK STATE. Madison first became involved in New York state political matters when he agreed in 1787 to join Alexander Hamilton and John Jay in writing the "Publius" papers (later collected as *The Federalist*) for New York newspapers supporting ratification of the Constitution. Thus he joined with the opponents of Gov. George Clinton, who was against ratification.

New York politics was dominated at that time by various family alignments and landholding alliances strengthened by intermarriage, a hangover from the days of colonial rivalries of the wealthy patroons. Madison took no sides but was friendly with Aaron Burr, who became a senator from New York and a key figure in Clinton's plans for national prominence. Throughout the period 1792–1799 New Yorkers cultivated political ties with Virginians, and Jefferson in particular. The Livingston family was also allied with the Jeffersonian Republicans and clearly had more influence in Washington after Burr's near-election as president in 1800 ruined his standing with Jefferson's friends.

The Burr-Jefferson tie vote in the House of Representatives early in 1801 came as a result of the 'duplicity' of New York Republicans, who had sought an alliance with Virginia supporters of Jefferson, ostensibly to make Burr the vice president—but they reneged and tried to reverse the outcome. Ultimately, Burr became vice president under the then-existing provisions of the Constitution, but his political career was at an end. Jefferson and Madison overlooked local attachments to Burr when the time for patronage came, and the appointment of Burr's friend David Gelston to the lucrative New York customs collector's post helped keep the New York–Virginia alliance intact. Gov. George Clinton was unable to attract national support for his ambitions and had to take a place on the 1804 and 1808 tickets as the vice presidential candidate.

Thomas Ritchie, editor of the Richmond *Enquirer*, cultivated the political alliance between Virginia, Pennsyl-

FEDERAL HALL, NEW YORK, IN 1789.   The Confederation Congress met in this building on Wall Street in the 1780s. Pierre-Charles L'Enfant renovated it for the use of the First Federal Congress in 1789. Lithograph after engraving by Cornelius Tiebout.

PRINTS AND PHOTOGRAPHS DIVISION, LIBRARY OF CONGRESS.

vania, and New York Republicans as a sure means of controlling national policies, and he had able newspaper allies in Clinton's faction. But the alliance was strained by George Clinton's odd moves in the 1808 presidential election, and the New Yorkers went their own way when De Witt Clinton challenged Madison in the 1812 presidential contest. New York voted for Clinton; Madison would have lost the election had not the Pennyslvania Republicans remained loyal to the president. Thereafter the attenuated Republican alliance linking southern planters with New York merchants was strained, partially restored by Martin Van Buren, and finally torn asunder in the embattled years following the Kansas-Nebraska Act.

BIBLIOGRAPHY

Alexander, De Alva S. *A Political History of the State of New York, 1774–1882.* 3 vols. 1906–1909.
Young, Alfred F. *The Democratic Republicans of New York: The Origins, 1763–1797.* 1967.

ROBERT A. RUTLAND

NICHOLAS, GEORGE (ca. 1749–1790), Virginia legislator, drafter of the first Kentucky constitution.

Nicholas was one of four sons of Robert Carter Nicholas and thus destined for a role in Virginia politics. After graduating from the College of William and Mary in 1772, he studied law, and when fighting between the British and the Americans started in 1775, he soon joined the Continental army. Nicholas rose to the rank of lieutenant colonel, left the army briefly to be admitted to the bar, then served as aide-de-camp to Gen. Thomas Nelson.

In 1781 Nicholas was elected to the House of Delegates from Hanover County. He was probably influenced by Patrick Henry when he criticized Gov. Thomas Jefferson's conduct after the British invasion of Virginia. Then Nicholas moved to Albemarle County, became friendly with Jefferson, and was elected to the House of Delegates from Albemarle in 1783 and 1786. He helped muster support for Madison when Jefferson's bill for establishing religious freedom was revived in 1785 and was active in distributing Madison's *Memorial and Remonstrance*, which helped achieve passage of Jefferson's bill.

Nicholas was a delegate at the 1788 Richmond Convention and voted to ratify the Constitution. At the convention he was a firm supporter of Madison's efforts to strengthen the national government, and he frequently corresponded with Madison after moving to Kentucky. Despite his initial inclination to stay aloof from politics in Kentucky, Nicholas was soon playing a major role in the steps that led to Kentucky's admission to the Union. Nicholas became involved in drafting a constitution for the new state, and he received a copy of Madison's "Observations on Jefferson's Draft of a Constitution for Virginia," which Madison wrote to aid transplanted Virginians seeking Kentucky statehood. Thus, Madison's views on framing a new government passed through Nicholas's friendly hands, but the constitution adopted by the Kentucky convention of 1792 showed few marks of Madison's influence. After Kentucky was admitted into the Union, Nicholas served as the first state attorney general.

BIBLIOGRAPHY

Hutchinson, William T., et al., eds. *Papers of James Madison: Congressional Series.* Vols. 6, 10, 11, 12. 1969–1979.

ROBERT A. RUTLAND

NICHOLAS, WILSON CARY (1761–1820), United States representative and senator, governor of Virginia. Born in Williamsburg to a politically and socially elite Virginia family, Nicholas was the son of Robert Carter and Anne Cary Nicholas. After studying at the College of William and Mary, in 1779 he joined the Revolutionary army and served until war's end as commanding officer of George Washington's Life Guard.

After the Revolution, Nicholas married Margaret Smith of Baltimore and settled in Albemarle County near Thomas Jefferson, his lifelong friend and patron. For nearly four decades Nicholas alternated periods of public service with time spent in private life, moving from one to the other as circumstances dictated. He entered public life in 1784 as a member of the Virginia House of Delegates, where he began his long political alliance with James Madison by joining him in support of Jefferson's bill supporting religious freedom. At the 1788 state ratifying convention he again joined with Madison to champion adoption of the proposed federal Constitution. During the crisis following the passage of the Alien and Sedition Acts, he served as consultant and intermediary for Jefferson and Madison as they formulated a response to the objectionable laws. In getting Jefferson's Protest Resolutions before the Kentucky legislature and in steering Madison's Resolutions through the Virginia General Assembly, Nicholas performed yeoman service.

Elected to the United States Senate in 1799, Nicholas was an effective spokesman and a leader of the Jefferson forces. His retirement to private life in 1804 was brief, for in 1806 Jefferson persuaded him to enter Congress and

to assume House leadership of a Republican party weakened by John Randolph's defection. Although he won election to the House, Nicholas was unsuccessful in uniting the party, but, as a confidant and as campaign manager for Madison in the 1808 caucus, he helped ensure his friend's succession to the presidency. Elected governor of Virginia in 1814, he urged the state to support internal improvements and to charter the University of Virginia. Then Nicholas's personal financial crisis left him destitute; the difficulties spread to his friends, including Jefferson. He died 10 October 1820, and was buried at Monticello.

BIBLIOGRAPHY

Malone, Dumas. *The Sage of Monticello.* 1981.
Weeder, Elinor Janet. "Wilson Cary Nicholas, Jefferson's Lieutenant." M.A. thesis, University of Virginia, 1946.

CHARLES D. LOWERY

NONINTERCOURSE ACTS. Madison's views on foreign affairs during the closing months of the Jefferson administration are difficult to reconstruct precisely. He persisted in his belief that increased pressure from the Embargo would eventually bring the British to terms, but he was willing to leave Congress to find its own way early in the second session of the Tenth Congress. Left to itself, Congress repealed the Embargo in March 1809 and replaced it with various Nonintercourse Acts.

The acts barred British and French ships from U.S. ports and prohibited American trade with either nation. All other trade was allowed, subject to penalties, forfeitures, and seizures of ships or cargoes not conforming to the provisions of the act. In an attempt to entice the British or the French to trade openly with Americans, the acts authorized the president to renew commerce with whichever nation "shall cease to violate the neutral commerce of the United States."

Madison opposed the nonintercourse policy because he felt it left American trade at the mercy of the British and believed its failure would move the nation closer to war. When the British minister David Erskine promised that the orders in council would be withdrawn, President Madison complied with the law and opened trade with Great Britain. With the disavowal of Erskine's agreement in late July 1809, however, the president and the nation returned to the difficult situation of either trading with the two great belligerents on their own terms or finding a new way to assert American rights.

BIBLIOGRAPHY

Spivak, Burton. *Jefferson's English Crisis: Commerce, Embargo, and the Republican Revolution.* 1979.

Stagg, J. C. A. *Mr. Madison's War: Politics, Diplomacy, and Warfare in the Early American Republic, 1783–1830*. 1983.

RONALD L. HATZENBUEHLER

NULLIFICATION DOCTRINE. In the late 1820s disgruntled South Carolinians, led by Vice President John C. Calhoun, developed an extreme states' rights formulation of the United States Constitution. Suffering from economic hard times that they blamed on federal protective tariffs, they sought a way of legitimating their desire to revoke, or nullify, the most recent tariff legislation, the so-called Tariff of Abominations of 1828. In the South Carolina "Exposition and Protest," Calhoun articulated a formal theory of the Constitution whereby an aggrieved state might exercise individually its sovereign right to take such action and nullify federal legislation.

The doctrine of nullification was predicated on the idea that the Constitution was a compact among sovereign states that allowed each state to retain sovereign authority within its borders and therefore the right, under the Constitution, to "interpose" that authority and declare null and void any federal law. The implications were broad, but the theory had a target—the despised protective tariff—that outspoken southern leaders judged to be a violation of the original compact, hence unconstitutional.

Calhoun also devised a set of formal procedures for implementing this interpretation of the Constitution. Once an individual state had "nullified" a federal law within its borders and received support for its actions from one-fourth of all the states, that verdict would stand unless and until the Constitution was formally amended to grant the disputed power—at which time the protesting state could either acquiesce or withdraw from the Union.

Calhoun and his fellow nullifiers denied that they were inventing a new theory of the Constitution. They claimed, on the contrary, that they were merely reviving an honorable tradition. The nullifiers based their interpretation squarely on historical precedent, most notably the Virginia and Kentucky Resolutions of the late 1790s that had provided a vehicle for Jeffersonian opposition to the Federalist Alien and Sedition Acts. They thus invoked Madison, a principal author of the Virginia Resolutions and of a subsequent legislative report defending those resolutions, as an authority in support of nullification. But whereas Jefferson had urged "interposition" in his Kentucky Resolution, Madison had included no hint of nullification in his 1798 Virginia Resolutions.

Unfortunately for the nullifiers, Madison was still alive in 1833 and able to interpret his own writing when the South Carolina legislature adopted an Ordinance of Nullification. The "Father of the Constitution" condemned the nullification doctrine as "a preposterous and anarchical pretension" that fundamentally misconstrued both the Constitution and Madison's own writings from the late 1790s. Madison believed that the nullifiers were attempting nothing less than a redefinition of the Union that would have catastrophic repercussions. Put into practice, nullification would subvert and undo the greatest achievement of Madison's career, the founding of the republic under the Constitution during the late 1780s, and plunge the United States into the chaos that adoption of the Constitution had so barely averted. Madison was so alarmed by the nullification doctrine and by the erroneous argument that federal tariffs were unconstitutional that he broke with his practice of public silence on political controversies and openly, unequivocally condemned as heretical a body of constitutional theory whose proponents were invoking him in their support.

[See also *Virginia and Kentucky Resolutions*.]

BIBLIOGRAPHY

Ellis, Richard E. *The Union at Risk: Jacksonian Democracy, States' Rights, and the Nullification Crisis*. 1987.

McCoy, Drew R. *The Last of the Fathers: James Madison and the Republican Legacy*. 1989.

Peterson, Merrill D. *The Jefferson Image in the American Mind*. 1960.

DREW R. MCCOY

O

ORANGE COUNTY, VIRGINIA. In 1714 the Virginia Council established a fort at Germanna on the Rapidan River, in what is now Orange County. Settlement proceeded slowly through the 1710s, when the region was part of the western reaches of Essex, King and Queen, and King William counties.

In 1720 Spotsylvania County was formed from this area. In its original form, it included the present-day counties of Spotsylvania, Orange, Culpeper, Rappahannock, Madison, and Greene, as well as the area west of the Blue Ridge Mountains to the Shenandoah River. An express purpose of the new county was to foster settlement of the Virginia Piedmont—that area between the fall line (the point beyond which the rivers are no longer navigable to oceangoing ships) and the Blue Ridge Mountains. Increasing numbers of settlers moved onto the new lands; some came directly from Europe, but many, including Ambrose Madison, grandfather of President James Madison, were members of established Tidewater families that had acquired lands in the Piedmont.

In response to the increased population, Orange County was created in 1734 from the western portion of Spotsylvania County. The new county was named for William IV, prince of Orange-Nassau, whose marriage to Anne, eldest daughter of King George II, had been celebrated earlier that year. As created, Orange County was a giant county, stretching from the western border of present-day Spotsylvania County west "to the utmost limits of Virginia"—the vicinity of the Mississippi River, with settlement extending into what is now West Virginia. Again, its purpose was to foster westward expansion of British colonial settlement. As the population of Orange County grew, new counties were formed in their turn: the Shenandoah Valley and points west were cut off as the original forms of Frederick (1743) and Augusta (1745) counties. East of the Blue Ridge, Culpeper County (comprising the modern counties of Culpeper, Madison, and Rappahannock) was created in 1749 from the area north of the Rapidan River, and the present county seat, the town of Orange, was founded the same year. With the creation of modern Greene County in 1838, Orange assumed its present boundaries. Today it is a medium-size central Virginia county, bounded on the north by the Rapidan River and the counties of Madison and Culpeper, on the east by Spotsylvania County, on the south by Albemarle and Louisa counties, and on the west by Greene County.

BIBLIOGRAPHY

Scott, W. W. *A History of Orange County, Virginia.* 1907.

ANN L. MILLER

ORDERS IN COUNCIL. Orders in council were declarations of policy by the British cabinet, that carried the force of law even though they were not acts of Parliament. They loomed large in early U.S. history because they regulated British commercial relations with the young republic. London's first major imposition on American commerce took the form of an order in council of 2 July 1783, which denied the United States its former lucrative trade with the British West Indies. At the outset of the wars of the French Revolution, an order in council of 8 June 1793 commanded the capture of any neutral vessel carrying flour, corn, or meal to any French port. In Congress James Madison introduced a series of discriminatory countermeasures. Jay's Treaty of 1794 temporarily resolved the Anglo-American conflict on the high seas and halted the drift toward war.

The U.S. effort to defend its neutral commerce—and still remain at peace—after war returned to Europe in 1803 proved to be futile. Napoleon, in control of the continent, relied on neutral coasting vessels to satisfy France's commercial needs. Britain, in an order in council of 16 May 1806, declared a blockade of the European coast from Brest to the Elbe, to be enforced between the Seine and Ostend. Following his victory over the Prussian forces at Jena in October 1806, Napoleon issued his Berlin Decree, which proclaimed a paper blockade of Britain and closed the continent to British trade by threatening to confiscate any neutral vessel within his reach that had visited a British port. London responded with two orders in council. The first, on 7 January 1807, prohibited neutral trade between ports under French control. The second, on 11 November 1807, declared a blockade of all countries in the Napoleonic system and condemned their products as lawful prizes. For Madison, as secretary of state, these British assaults on American commerce were unacceptable; he argued against them without success because commerce, in itself, possessed little power to coerce powerful belligerents whose interests centered on victory. When Britain dropped its orders in council in 1812, after the United States had already declared war, the belated action seemed to confirm Madison's policy. But the declaration of war made the issue moot.

[See also Blockades by England and France; Jay's Treaty.]

BIBLIOGRAPHY

Burt, A. L. The United States, Great Britain, and British North America From the Revolution to the Establishment of Peace after the War of 1812. 1940.
Perkins, Bradford. The First Rapprochement: England and the United States, 1795–1805. 1955.

NORMAN A. GRAEBNER

OTIS, HARRISON GRAY (1765–1848), Massachusetts Federalist, senator. He was the son of Samuel Allyne Otis, secretary of the Senate from 1789 to 1814, and a nephew of James Otis, the patriot orator. Otis graduated from Harvard in 1783 and prospered as a lawyer and investor in Boston real estate. He first distinguished himself politically in 1794, speaking against Madison's proposed commercial resolutions. Otis was elected to the House of Representatives in 1796 from the district previously represented by Fisher Ames, but his federalism was less strident.

Otis declined reelection to Congress in 1800 but won a seat in the Massachusetts Assembly, where he quickly assumed a leading role, although the extremist Federalists of the Essex Junto never accepted him as one of their own. He accused the Republicans of admitting Louisiana as a state in order to diminish the influence of New England in Congress. Otis opposed Jefferson and Madison on most issues, and as early as 1808 he favored a convention of the "commercial states" to resist the Embargo Act of 1807. In 1811 Otis accused Madison of being a Napoleonic pawn and unsuccessfully promoted a scheme for permitting states to nullify the Nonintercourse Act.

After June 1812 Otis was a leading critic of "Mr. Madison's War," which was highly unpopular in Boston. His speeches at town meetings encouraged all measures of opposition that were not clearly unlawful. The growing threat of a British invasion of New England in 1814 stirred Federalist opponents of the war to even stronger efforts. Otis played a major role in calling the Hartford Convention in December 1814. He was unquestionably the leader of its sessions, wrote most of its report, but for the rest of his life denied that it had even discussed secession or a separate peace with Great Britain. The Hartford Convention report was published on 6 January 1815; three weeks later Otis served as one of the three Massachusetts commissioners sent to Washington to arrange for a stronger defense of the state. The double news of Andrew Jackson's startling victory at New Orleans and the Treaty of Ghent made the mission pointless. Otis was politely received by President Madison in Washington, his mission a total failure.

When President Monroe visited Boston in 1817, Otis delivered the welcoming speech and entertained him at his Beacon Hill mansion, a signal that bitter partisanship was fading. He served as a senator from 1817 to 1822.

BIBLIOGRAPHY

Banner, James M. To the Hartford Convention: The Federalists and the Origins of Party Politics in Massachusetts, 1789–1815. 1970.
Morison, Samuel Eliot. Harrison Gray Otis, 1765–1848: The Urbane Federalist. 1969.

PATRICK J. FURLONG

OTTO, LOUIS-GUILLAUME, count of Mosloy (1754–1817), French diplomat. Otto, who was born and educated in Germany, was regarded as an astute observer of the American scene. He accompanied the chevalier de La Luzerne to the United States in 1779 and became legation secretary, serving as chargé d'affaires from 1785 to 1788 and from 1789 to 1791. His tact and charm, his marriage to Elizabeth Livingston of New York, and his membership in the American Philosophical Society brought friendships with leading statesmen that allowed him to return detailed reports on American affairs to the Foreign Ministry. He described Madison as a "well-educated, wise" man whose speech proposing discriminatory reimbursement of public debt holders was "the best speech which has ever been made in America."

After his return to France in 1792 Otto opposed the seizure of American provision ships trading with England, suggesting that a friendlier attitude toward the United States might lead to joint commercial action against Great Britain. He lived in obscurity after the Girondin collapse until 1798, when he was named legation secretary at Berlin. In 1801 he was entrusted with the negotiations that culminated in the signing of peace preliminaries between England and France. Jefferson had approved Otto's appointment as chargé in 1785 because of his friendship for the United States but came to consider him too susceptible to Federalist influence and in 1802 objected to his suggested appointment as minister to the United States. Otto was named count of Mosloy as a reward for his intelligence activities while ambassador to Munich from 1801 to 1809. As minister to Vienna from 1809 to 1813 he participated in negotiations for Napoleon's marriage to Marie Louise. He held a minor post during the first Bourbon restoration, but his service in Napoleon's Ministry of Foreign Affairs during the Hundred Days led to his retirement from public life after the second restoration.

BIBLIOGRAPHY

Bowman, Albert. *The Struggle for Neutrality.* 1974.

Michaud, Joseph François. *Biographie universelle, ancienne et moderne: ou, Histoire, par ordre alphabétique, de la vie publique et privée de tous les hommes qui se sont fait remarquer par leurs écrits, leurs actions, leurs talents, leurs vertus ou leurs crimes.* Vol. 31. 1843–[1865].

O'Dwyer, Margaret M. "A French Diplomat's View of Congress, 1790." *William and Mary Quarterly,* 3d ser., 21 (1964): 408–444.

MARY A. HACKETT

P

PAGE, JOHN (1743–1808), United States representative, governor of Virginia. Born 17 April 1743, at Roswell in Gloucester County, Page was the son of Mann and Alice Grymes Page, both from wealthy Tidewater Virginia families. Page was educated at the College of William and Mary, where he became part of a cultivated circle that included George Wythe and Thomas Jefferson. For half a century, Page and Jefferson were intimate friends. Twice married, first to Frances Burwell and then to Margaret Lowther, Page fathered twenty children, and his large family constituted a heavy drain on his resources. In addition to running his plantation, which was worked by more than 150 slaves, Page dabbled in many areas, including astronomy and science, interests he shared with both Jefferson and Madison.

During the Revolution, in addition to serving on the Virginia Committee of Public Safety, Page raised and led a militia unit from Gloucester County. He attained the rank of colonel before leaving the service to enter politics.

Throughout his adult life, Page was politically active. He served in the House of Burgesses; was councilor to two royal governors; was lieutenant governor of Virginia under Patrick Henry, during which time he and Madison became fast friends; attended the Virginia Convention of 1776; and was a leader in the state legislature during the 1780s. Elected as a Federalist to the U.S. House of Representatives, where he served from 1789 to 1797, he strongly backed Madison's efforts to establish the new government on a solid footing. When a political fissure occurred in Congress, Page remained firmly committed to the political creed articulated by Jefferson and Madison.

After leaving Congress, Page served four more terms in the Virginia legislature before being elected governor in 1802. After completing three successful terms, he accepted a federal appointment from President Jefferson as commissioner of loans. He died 11 October 1808 and was buried in Richmond.

BIBLIOGRAPHY

Biographical Directory of the United States Congress, 1774–1989. 1989.

Biographical Directory of Governors of the United States, 1789–1978. 1978.

CHARLES D. LOWERY

JOHN PAGE.   Portrait by Charles Willson Peale.
INDEPENDENCE NATIONAL HISTORICAL PARK, PHILADELPHIA.

PAKENHAM, SIR EDWARD (1778–1815), major general, British commander at the Battle of New Orleans. Son of the second Baron Longford of Westmeath, Ireland, and brother-in-law of Arthur Wellesley, duke of Wellington, Pakenham had a career punctuated by rapid promotion and conspicuous success. He served during the Napoleonic Wars in the West Indies, Denmark, and Spain, winning distinction at the battle of Salamanca (July 1812). Following the Peninsular War the British concentrated their efforts in America. Adm. Alexander Cochrane launched a campaign in August 1814 in the Chesapeake that was aimed at destroying military installations and distracting the Americans along the Canadian frontier. Maj. Gen. James Ross defeated the Americans at Bladensburg and the British occupied Washington, but Ross was killed in the attack on Baltimore. Pakenham replaced Ross as the land commander.

In October Cochrane left the Chesapeake for Jamaica, where an expedition was launched on 26 November 1814, heading for Louisiana. While the fleet was en route, carrying 7,500 troops under Pakenham's command (weather delayed his arrival at New Orleans until late December), Gen. Andrew Jackson invaded Spanish Florida and reached New Orleans about two weeks before the British disembarked at Lake Borgne, fifteen miles away. The British seized American gunboats and fought preliminary engagements before Pakenham could take personal command. Pakenham's failure to press his advantage allowed Jackson to strengthen his defenses on the Mississippi's left bank and disable the British artillery. Finally, on 8 January 1815, the British twice attacked frontally over the morass separating the two armies and were devastated by sharpshooters. Within two hours Pakenham and two of his adjutants lay dead on the field. More than two thousand British died or were wounded; only about seventy Americans were killed or wounded. The battle ensured Jackson's fame but was meaningless as a military victory, since the Treaty of Ghent had been signed on 24 December.

BIBLIOGRAPHY

Chichester, Henry Manners. "Sir Edward Pakenham." In vol. 15 of *The Dictionary of National Biography.* Edited by Sir Leslie Stephen and Sir Sidney Lee. 63 vols. 1885–1900.

Coles, Harry L. *The War of 1812.* 1971.

Reilly, Robin. *The British at the Gates: The New Orleans Campaign in the War of 1812.* 1974.

MARTIN J. HAVRAN

PANIC OF 1819. The dramatic reversal in 1819 of the economic boom that followed the War of 1812 has been described as the first true financial panic in the nation's history. As such, this event portended subsequent nineteenth-century periods of boom and bust.

Expansion and optimism were the rule from 1815 through 1818 in the United States. Settlers streamed west in ever-increasing numbers to develop new lands in the upper Midwest, while soaring cotton prices spurred unprecedented growth in the cultivation of that crop in the South and the Southwest. Meanwhile, European nations, their economies deranged by more than two decades of warfare, provided a brisk market for American staple products. Led by grain and cotton, U.S. exports grew from $52,557,753 in 1815 to $93,281,133 in 1818. The latter figure was not surpassed until 1834.

To finance this economic surge, the nation's banking system expanded apace. State banks, which numbered 204 in 1815, had grown to nearly 400 establishments by 1819, and the reestablished Bank of the United States began operation in 1817. The western branches of the bank, rather than seeking to curb the potential excesses of the state banks, vied with the latter in providing loans and capital for investments.

The increase in banknote issue resulting from the rapid increase in the number of banks fueled the inflation of land and commodity prices. Land sales in five southern states rose from $332,000 in 1815 to $9,063,000 in 1818, while the price of cotton in New York climbed from 15 cents per pound in 1815 to 29.5 cents per pound in 1816 and leveled off at about 24 cents per pound in 1818–1819. Western land sales in seven states more than doubled from $2,078,000 in 1815 to $4,556,000 in 1818.

As this period of expansion neared its end, events conspired to turn the inevitable readjustment into a debacle. In Europe, the postwar adjustment process saw food production rise, and the demand for American surpluses fell. English manufacturers and exporters moved quickly after 1815 to reestablish American export markets.

Wholesale prices in the United States, which had risen to a level of 187 (1830 = 100) by 1815, declined to 137 by 1819 and reached 112 in 1821. Land sales plummeted. Cotton prices fell to one-half their 1818–1819 level and stood at 11.4 cents per pound in 1823.

The expansion and the growing interdependence of the nation's financial structures served to intensify, rather than ameliorate, the readjustment process. As part of the compromise proposed by Madison to obtain approval of the recharter of the bank, the House and Senate ordered the resumption of specie payments by all state banks in 1817. Secretary of the Treasury Alexander J. Dallas won agreement from the state banks on resumption as of 20 February 1817. After that date, payments to the U.S. government for taxes, land purchases, and tariffs would be accepted only in the notes of the Bank of the United States or of specie-paying state banks. This arrangement forced state banks to curtail lending drastically. The rechartered Bank of the United States had played a role in the expansion of state bank lending, if only by its permissive stance and the irresponsible activities of its western branches. Thus, the decision to restrict credit came at the worst possible time. Langdon Cheves, who succeeded William Jones as president of the bank in 1819, pushed policies that further restricted the supply of money and credit as the nation's economy faltered.

The result of these economic forces and policies was a wave of bank failures and bankruptcies caused primarily by bad loans based on inflated prices. As unemployment rose and agricultural expansion slowed, American producers demanded and received tariff protection from foreign goods. The reputation of the Bank of the United States was permanently (and, as it turned out, mortally) wounded as a result of its poor performance, and the weaknesses of the unregulated and decentralized American banking system, which tended to promote the boom-and-bust character of the nineteenth-century American economy, were exposed.

BIBLIOGRAPHY

Dangerfield, George. *The Awakening of American Nationalism, 1815–1828.* 1965.
North, Douglass C. *The Economic Growth of the United States, 1790–1860.* 1966.
Smith, Walter B., and Arthur H. Cole. *Fluctuations in American Business.* 1935.

DONALD R. ADAMS, JR.

PARISH, DAVID (d. 1826), financier. The son of John Parish, a wealthy Hamburg merchant with commercial ties throughout Europe, Parish started his own firm in Antwerp in 1803. His successes there brought him to the attention of a consortium founded to transport safely the bullion of the Spanish crown from its American colonies to Europe in the midst of the Napoleonic Wars. The syndicate included Great Britain, Spain, and the banking houses of Hope & Co. of Holland and Baring Brothers of Great Britain, with the trade to be carried out in neutral American ships. To abet the scheme, the syndicate needed an agent in the United States, and for this post it chose David Parish. Parish arrived in New York in January 1806 and soon set up operations in Philadelphia, where he entertained lavishly. By mid 1808 the combine's operations had been successfully concluded and Parish had reaped more than $1 million for his agency. In December of that year he bought an immense tract of land in northern New York state and proceeded to invest in its development, but the outbreak of war in 1812 slowed his operations. In February 1813 Congress authorized a $16 million war loan, but Albert Gallatin's initial attempts to interest Parish and other financiers were unsuccessful. In March, however, Gallatin proposed a quarter-percent commission to anyone buying $100,000 or more in subscriptions, and this proved enough to entice Parish, Stephen Girard, John Jacob Astor, and others to take up $10 million of the 6 percent stock at a price of $88, thus saving the loan from failure. Parish proposed a similar arrangement for the much larger loan that the United States attempted to float in 1814, but this suggestion was turned down by Secretary of the Treasury George Campbell. In 1814 Parish also played a key role in lobbying the government for the establishment of a national bank, but his efforts failed when Madison vetoed the bank bill. He returned to Europe in 1816. Facing bankruptcy in 1826, he drowned himself in the Danube River.

BIBLIOGRAPHY

Walters, Philip G., and Raymond Walters, Jr. "The American Career of David Parish." *Journal of Economic History* 4 (1944): 149–166.

DAVID B. MATTERN

PATERSON, WILLIAM (1745–1806), delegate to the Federal Convention of 1787, U.S. Supreme Court justice. William Paterson's parents came from Ireland when he was an infant, settled in New Jersey, and saw their son become prominent as a lawyer and as state attorney general. He graduated from the College of New Jersey (later Princeton), where in 1769 he was a founding member of what became the Cliosophic Society, a debating club that was attacked with attempted humor by James Madison on behalf of a rival society. During his student days Madison kept an account at the general store owned by Paterson's father. Paterson served on the state Provincial Council in 1775–1776 and attended the state constitutional convention in 1776. He was selected as attorney general that same year and remained in that office until 1783. He would have begun his congressional career in 1780, the same year as Madison, but he declined to serve.

Paterson was practicing law in New Brunswick when he was elected to the Federal Convention, where he was leader of the small-state opposition to Madison's Virginia Plan. The New Jersey Plan, which he introduced on 15 June, was a modification of the Articles of Confederation that strengthened Congress and made its acts "the supreme law of the respective states." The major flaw of Paterson's plan was that it maintained legislative equality among the states, a proposition that was unacceptable to Madison and his allies. Madison met Paterson's challenge by devoting his longest speech at the Convention to a detailed repudiation of the New Jersey Plan.

WILLIAM PATERSON.   Etching by Albert Rosenthal, 1888.
PRINTS AND PHOTOGRAPHS DIVISION, LIBRARY OF CONGRESS.

After approval of the compromise affording each state, regardless of its population, two senators, Paterson supported a strong central government, both in the Federal Convention and for the rest of his life. Elected to the first U.S. Senate, he was a major author of the Judiciary Act of 1789, writing at least the first nine sections. He was governor and chancellor of New Jersey from 1790 to 1793, when he was appointed to the U.S. Supreme Court. On the judicial circuit, he presided over several Whiskey Rebellion trials and the sedition trial of Matthew Lyon in 1798; his conduct in these cases made him unpopular among the Jeffersonian Republicans but a darling to "High Federalists." These same conservatives were outraged when John Adams appointed John Marshall, rather than Paterson, as chief justice in 1801. Paterson's political realism was demonstrated in his decision in *Stuart* v. *Laird* (1803), which upheld the Republican repeal of the Judiciary Act of 1801, thus acquiescing to the "Revolution of 1800."

Paterson's path crossed with Madison's in his final judicial act, only weeks before his death. In a circuit court trial at New York City in June 1806, two adventurers implicated in an attack on Venezuela insisted that Madison, Henry Dearborn, and Robert Smith be subpoenaed as witnesses. President Jefferson directed his cabinet members to decline to appear because they were needed in Washington. Paterson wanted to hold them in contempt, but the district judge disagreed, so there was no majority. Because of his illness, Paterson was unable to complete the trial, leaving Judge Matthias Tallmadge to proceed alone.

BIBLIOGRAPHY

O'Connor, John E. *William Paterson: Lawyer and Statesman, 1745–1806.* 1979.
Wood, Gertrude S. *William Paterson of New Jersey, 1745–1806.* 1933.

DONALD O. DEWEY

PEALE, CHARLES WILLSON (1741–1827), painter. A painter, patriot, tinkerer, and museum pioneer, Charles Willson Peale founded America's first artistic dynasty as a half-dozen of his seventeen children became artists.

Peale, the son of a Cambridge-educated schoolteacher exiled to America, was born in Queen Anne's County, Maryland. At thirteen he was apprenticed to a saddler, thus beginning a varied career as an artisan and artist that included silversmithing, watch repairing, and innovations in farm machinery, fireplaces, and false teeth. Peale took his first painting lessons in Philadelphia in the early 1760s; he later studied briefly in Boston with John Singleton Copley before training with Benjamin West in London. Upon his return to Annapolis in 1769, Peale established himself as a portraitist, specializing in the Maryland gentry.

A political radical, Peale was living in Philadelphia at the outbreak of the Revolution. He soon enlisted as a private in the city militia and rose to the rank of captain of volunteers. His lifelong friendship with George Washington, begun when Peale painted the hero's portrait at Mount Vernon in 1772, solidified during the war years. During his career, Peale painted Washington from life more often than any other artist.

Following the war, Peale became a museum entrepreneur. In 1782 he opened a public gallery, the first in America to be illuminated by skylights, where he exhibited the series of portraits of heroes of the Revolution that he had begun during the war. Peale's Gallery of Great Men evolved along with the young republic, as the artist added likenesses of the Founding Fathers and of other patriots. Peale frequently moved his portrait gallery, which at one time included a sensitively painted image of James Madison (now in the collection of the Gilcrease Museum, Tulsa), and in 1802 he installed

CHARLES WILLSON PEALE.   Self-portrait with Spectacles, c. 1804.
PENNSYLVANIA ACADEMY OF THE FINE ARTS, PHILADELPHIA.
HENRY D. GILPIN FUND.

his expanded collection, which now also included natural history specimens, useful inventions, and Indian artifacts collected by Lewis and Clark, in the second floor of the State House (now Independence Hall). Peale refined gallery lighting, introduced naturalistic "habitats" for his stuffed birds, and experimented with taxidermy. The first reconstructed skeleton of a mastodon, which he had excavated in Newburgh, New York, in 1801, was a sensation of the era. Peale entertained the public with lectures, concerts, "moving pictures" (painted transparencies), and an exotic collection of living creatures that included a hyena, grizzly bears, and a five-legged cow.

A true son of the Enlightenment, Charles Willson Peale embodied the practical, rational, and optimistic ideals of his age.

BIBLIOGRAPHY

Miller, Lillian B. *The Collected Papers of Charles Willson Peale and His Family: A Guide and Index to the Microfiche Edition.* 1980.
Richardson, Edgar P., Brooke Hindle, and Lillian B. Miller. *Charles Willson Peale and His World.* 1982.
Sellers, Charles Coleman. *Charles Willson Peale.* 1969.
Sellers, Charles Coleman. *Mr. Peale's Museum: Charles Willson Peale and the First Popular Museum of Natural Science and Art.* 1980.

JOAN CARPENTER TROCCOLI

PENDLETON, EDMUND (1721–1803), Virginia jurist, political mentor of Jefferson and Madison. His impressive legal knowledge, consummate political skill, and exceptional strength of character made Pendleton, in Jefferson's opinion, one of the greatest men of his age. He was born 9 September 1721 in Caroline County. Both his father and his grandfather, prominent leaders in Virginia politics, died in 1721, leaving him without paternal guidance and with little or no property. Without means for a formal education, he was apprenticed at the age of fourteen to Benjamin Robinson, clerk of the Caroline County Court and a relative of Virginia's influential treasurer, John Robinson. For the next six and a half years Pendleton lived with his master's family, worked in Robinson's law office, and devoted himself to studying the law. At the age of sixteen he became parish clerk, at twenty he was admitted to the local bar, and at twenty-four he qualified to practice before the General Court. In 1751 he became a justice on the Caroline County Court, where he served until his election to the High Court of Chancery in 1777. His distinguished judicial career spanned half a century.

In 1752 the freeholders of Caroline elected Pendleton to the House of Burgesses. During his twenty-two-year tenure there he served on most of the important committees and gained recognition for his exceptional gifts as debater, parliamentarian, and leader. Conservative by nature, he opposed sudden or radical change. When Virginia became embroiled after 1763 in the controversy with Great Britain over the Stamp Act and other tax measures, Pendleton was more cautious than Patrick Henry and other radical representatives, whose inflammatory rhetoric he disliked. Reconciliation, not separation, was his goal.

In working for that goal, however, Pendleton was not willing to compromise colonial rights. A decade before Patrick Henry proposed his Stamp Act resolutions, Pendleton protested the crown's imposition of a tax without the consent of the House of Burgesses. As the Revolution approached, he served on the Committee of Correspondence created in 1773 and represented Virginia at the First Continental Congress in 1774. He participated in all five of Virginia's prerevolutionary conventions between August 1774 and July 1776 and presided over the two that met in 1775. He was also elected president of the Committee of Public Safety, which in effect placed him at the head of the province's temporary government. In this capacity Pendleton continued on his conservative course—seeking a redress of grievances rather than independence.

Nevertheless, it was Pendleton who as president of the Virginia convention of 1776 drew up the resolves instructing Virginia's delegates in Congress to propose a declaration of independence. Madison, who joined his state's councils for the first time in 1776, was delighted to find "this trusted family connection and friend" in a leadership position. Pendleton served on the committee that framed a new state constitution. On one of the few occasions when he ever differed with Jefferson or Madison on an important political issue, Pendleton opposed Jefferson's plan to disestablish the church in Virginia.

When the new state government was organized in 1776, Pendleton was elected Speaker of the House of Delegates. The following year, after a riding accident that left him crippled for life, he was appointed presiding judge of the newly organized chancery court. In 1778 he became president of the Supreme Court of Appeals, a position he held until his death.

To Madison's delight, Pendleton was chosen president of the Virginia constitutional ratifying convention of 1788. Pendleton aided Madison by challenging and blunting some of Patrick Henry's criticisms of the proposed frame of government. Then, after Madison assumed a leadership role in the House of Representatives, Pendleton corresponded with him regularly and offered him valued advice about the problems of the new government. Distrustful of the centralizing tendencies of Alexander Hamilton and committed to the idea of a truly federal government, he urged Madison to curb the growing powers of the national government. In 1799 he published a campaign document supporting Jefferson and lauding the principles of the Republican party; he followed that in 1801 with a pamphlet entitled "The Danger Not Over," calling upon Republican party leaders to restrain executive power, limit the central government's borrowing power, respect the power of the states, and construe the Constitution narrowly.

Pendleton declined all proffers of national office, choosing instead to devote his talents to serving Virginia. Among Virginians his popularity and stature were extraordinary: he never lost a political election, and invariably he was chosen presiding officer of whatever assembly he attended. An eighteenth-century epitome of leadership, he was unassuming and unpretentious. Indeed, Pendleton never bothered to preserve his writings for posterity or tried to extend his reputation into the national arena. However, Pendleton's powerful influence on his fellow Virginians—Washington, Jefferson, and Madison—helped to set the course for nationhood. He died on 23 October 1803.

BIBLIOGRAPHY

Grigsby, Hugh Blair. *The Virginia Convention of 1776.* 1855.

Grigsby, Hugh Blair. *The History of the Federal Convention of 1788, with some account of the eminent Virginians of that era who were members of the body.* 2 vols. 1890–1891.

Hilldrup, Robert Leroy. *The Life and Times of Edmund Pendleton.* 1939.

Ketcham, Ralph. *James Madison. A Biography.* 1971.

Mays, David John. *Edmund Pendleton, 1721–1803. A Biography.* 2 vols. 1952.

CHARLES D. LOWERY

PERCEVAL, SPENCER (1762–1812), barrister, prime minister of Great Britain. Perceval, a younger son of the second earl of Egmont, was educated at Cambridge and Lincoln's Inn in preparation for a career in law and government. He won celebrity early during his law practice in the Midlands, leading to his filing briefs in prominent cases as crown counsel and to advancement through the intervention of Prime Minister William Pitt. One of Perceval's cases involved the fiery champion of political rights Thomas Paine, who attended meetings in London led by supporters of French radicalism and English reform. Perceval read the indictment at Paine's trial in 1792 and prosecuted publishers of his *Rights of Man* in a trial that attracted Madison's attention.

Perceval became an expert on maritime affairs while

SPENCER PERCEVAL.
PRINTS AND PHOTOGRAPHS DIVISION, LIBRARY OF CONGRESS.

serving as counsel to the Admiralty Board, as a member of Parliament (from 1796), and as chancellor of the exchequer in the earl of Portland's cabinet. As chancellor of the exchequer, a position he also filled during his own ministry (1809–1812), he managed Britain's finances during a period of massive war expenditure and economic decline resulting from the Napoleonic Continental System and from the interdiction of commerce with the United States. Perceval drafted the order in council in 1808 that heightened Anglo-American tensions; ironically, Madison had helped devise the Jefferson administration's Embargo Act (1807) and other interdictions of foreign commerce partly to avert war with France or England, while Perceval believed that the orders might forestall war with America.

Anglo-American issues worried Perceval in 1812. Civil unrest and complaints over declining manufacturing and commerce threatened to overwhelm his ministry and led him to reconsider the wisdom of sustaining the unpopular orders. On 11 May, during heated debate in Parliament concerning the orders, a deranged petitioner, John Bellingham, assassinated Perceval. When Foreign Secretary Castlereagh finally announced the suspension of the orders on 23 June, it was too late; the United States had declared war on Britain four days earlier.

BIBLIOGRAPHY

Gray, Denis. *Spencer Perceval the Evangelical Prime Minister, 1762–1812.* 1963.
Horsman, Reginald. *The Causes of the War of 1812.* 1961.
Middleton, Charles R. *The Administration of British Foreign Policy, 1782–1846.* 1977.

MARTIN J. HAVRAN

PERRY, OLIVER HAZARD (1785–1819), U.S. naval officer, victor at the Battle of Lake Erie. Son of a naval officer and one of four brothers to serve with the U.S. Navy, Oliver Hazard Perry began service as a teenage midshipman on his father's ship, the *General Greene.* He served on several vessels during the Tripolitan War (1801–1806). For six years he directed the construction of President Jefferson's gunboats; he was in command of a gunboat flotilla at his hometown of Newport, Rhode Island, when the War of 1812 began. Here Perry first demonstrated a tendency to shield his subordinates from facing discipline for incompetence. Newly promoted to the rank of master commandant and frustrated in his desire to serve on one of the nation's saltwater frigates, he accepted appointment to construct and command the Lake Erie squadron under the overall direction of Commodore Isaac Chauncey, who stayed on the more strategically critical Lake Ontario. Perry replaced Lt. Jesse Duncan Elliott, who was below him in rank although older in years and an acclaimed hero because of his recent capture of British vessels in the Niagara River.

In early 1813 Perry began construction of the Lake Erie squadron at Presque Isle (now Erie), Pennsylvania, where he brought supplies from Pittsburgh. Before construction was finished, Perry demonstrated a commitment to joint operations by cooperating with army units during the attack on Fort George at the mouth of the Niagara River on 27 May 1813. After this successful operation on Lake Ontario, Perry returned to Presque Isle and completed the construction of his squadron. Although his fleet was ready by early summer, Perry waited six weeks before he had enough men to staff the squadron, thereby delaying Gen. William Henry Harrison's advance to retake Detroit.

Perry's manpower problems were resolved when Harrison attached a number of his soldiers to the fleet (about 40 percent of the crews), supplemented by additional sailors finally sent by Chauncey. His command problems may have increased, however, since the officer sent as second in command was the newly promoted master commandant, Jesse Duncan Elliott, who still chafed at not being named the Lake Erie commander. During early August Perry's fleet, consisting of two brigs—his flagship, the *Lawrence,* and the *Niagara,* commanded by Elliott—and several smaller vessels sailed onto Lake Erie and gained dominance over a smaller British squadron commanded by Robert Heriot Barclay. For five weeks the British remained anchored at the Detroit River hamlet of Amherstburg awaiting the completion of their flagship, the *Detroit.* Perry moved his squadron to Put-in-Bay, Ohio, where he finally cooperated closely with General Harrison on the latter's Detroit campaign. With his troops and Indian allies cut off from supplies brought via ship, the British army commander, Brig. Gen. Henry Procter directed Barclay to attack Perry's fleet.

In the resulting Battle of Lake Erie (10 September 1813), Perry had a decided five-to-three advantage in long guns and a five-to-two advantage in ship-killing carronades. During the battle Perry fought close action with the *Detroit* and two other vessels, while the *Niagara* and most of the squadron remained out of the battle for over two hours. Elliott obviously followed too closely his instructions to maintain his place in the battle line, behind the slow-sailing *Caledonia,* and failed to engage his assigned vessel in battle, allowing it to join in the attack on the *Lawrence.* Perry has been criticized for not signaling Elliott to close up; he was, as one commentator put it, "a better captain than a commodore." With his flagship nearly defenseless, Perry took a longboat to the *Niagara,* sent Elliott to bring up the trailing vessels, and

OLIVER PERRY.   Engraving after a painting by Alonzo Chappel.

captured the entire Royal Navy squadron. Perry was immediately promoted to captain and hailed as the "hero of the lake" by a nation grateful for a military victory. Subsequently, Perry's squadron ably assisted Harrison's army in its recapture of Detroit and in the victory in the Battle of the Thames.

Perry sought to protect Elliott from charges of misconduct by writing a moderately favorable after-action report on Elliott's role. Elliott thought himself maligned, however, and began a thirty-year campaign to vindicate his name that ended in bitter recriminations. Perry's premature death from yellow fever in 1819 foreclosed a probable court-martial of Elliott. As counties, towns, and townships were named in his honor, Perry became a symbol of the fighting tradition of the U.S. Navy.

BIBLIOGRAPHY

Drake, Frederick C. "Artillery and Its Influence on Naval Tactics: Reflections on the Battle of Lake Erie." In *War on the Great Lakes: Essays Commemorating the 175th Anniversary of the Battle of Lake Erie.* Edited by William Jeffrey Welsh and David Curtis Skaggs. 1991.

McKenzie, Alexander Slidell. *The Life of Commodore Oliver Hazard Perry.* 2 vols. 1840.

Palmer, Michael A. "A Failure of Command, Control, and Communications: Oliver Hazard Perry and the Battle of Lake Erie." *Journal of Erie Studies* 17 (1988): 7–26.

Roosevelt, Theodore. *The Naval War of 1812.* 1882.

Skaggs, David Curtis. "Joint Operations during the Detroit-Lake Erie Campaign, 1813." In *New Interpretations in Naval History.* Edited by William B. Cogar. 1989.

DAVID CURTIS SKAGGS

PICHON, LOUIS-ANDRÉ, BARON (1771–1850), French diplomat and public official. In 1791 Pichon visited the United States, where he served as second secretary of the French legation. He returned to France in 1795, became division subchief in the department of foreign relations, and was sent to Holland after the XYZ Affair to convince American minister William Vans Murray of France's desire for peace.

Named consul general and chargé d'affaires to the United States in 1801, Madison's first year as secretary of state, he worked toward improving French-American relations following the signing of the convention of 1800, which ended the Quasi-War. After the Spanish retrocession of Louisiana to France became known in the United States, Pichon, an astute observer of the American scene, reported often to Talleyrand, the French foreign minister, on the intensity of American feelings regarding free access to the Mississippi, the right of deposit at New Orleans, and the prospect of a strong France replacing weak Spain as a western neighbor. He attempted to alleviate tensions between the French army and American merchants trading with Haitian rebels in defiance of French laws and was also charged with negotiating the financial arrangements for the Louisiana Purchase.

He remained in the United States until 1805, when he was recalled and dismissed from office after having been accused of opposing the imperial system of government and the expedition to reconquer Haiti. He attached himself to Napoleon's brother Jerome, king of Westphalia, whom he had known in America and who appointed him counselor of state and intendant general of finance in 1809. He resigned these positions in 1812 and returned to France, where he held office under Louis XVIII. Assigned in 1817 to regulate the administrations of Martinique and Guadeloupe, he later became one of the first civil commissioners of Algeria. In 1832 he returned to Paris and was counselor of state under Louis-Philippe.

BIBLIOGRAPHY

Brant, Irving. *James Madison, Secretary of State, 1800–1809.* Vol. 4. 1941.

Egan, Clifford L. *Neither Peace nor War: Franco-American Relations, 1803–1812.* 1983.

Hoefer, Jean Chrétien Ferdinand, ed. *Nouvelle biographie générale depuis les temps plus reculés jusqu'à nos jours, avec les renseignements bibliographiques et l'indication des sources à consulter.* 1852–1865.

MARY A. HACKETT

PICKERING, TIMOTHY (1745–1829), Federalist politician, secretary of state. Pickering was reared in Salem, Massachusetts, and educated at Harvard; he was a lawyer by profession. By 1777 Colonel Pickering was adjutant general of the Continental army. He later became a member of the congressional Board of War, and in 1780–1783 he reluctantly served as quartermaster general. He was stubborn, arrogant, and suspicious, characteristics that carried over into his political career.

Upon leaving the army Pickering engaged in western land speculations. In 1790 President Washington named him postmaster general. Late in 1794 Pickering joined the cabinet as secretary of war, advancing within a year to secretary of state. (Six others declined the office before Washington turned, with grave misgivings, to Pickering.)

As secretary of state, Pickering consistently favored good relations with Great Britain. Dominated by Alexander Hamilton, Pickering opposed Madison on every issue. When President Adams considered Madison for a diplomatic mission to France in 1797, Pickering threatened to resign in protest. Pickering was secretly hostile to Adams, regarding him as deluded for seeking

TIMOTHY PICKERING.   Line-and-stipple engraving by
T. B. Welch from a drawing by James Barton Longacre after a
portrait by Gilbert Stuart.
PRINTS AND PHOTOGRAPHS DIVISION, LIBRARY OF CONGRESS.

peaceful relations with revolutionary France. He was
humiliated when Adams removed him from office in
1800. In 1802 he narrowly lost a race for the House, but
a year later the Massachusetts legislature elected him to
the Senate. Bitterness and ill temper soon made him
unpopular even among Federalists, while Republicans
ridiculed his belief that Jefferson led a diabolical plot to
make himself president for life. Pickering supported the
British in the *Chesapeake* affair and met often with
George Rose, the British envoy.

In the spring of 1809 Pickering surprised friends and
foes by supporting Madison's efforts to smooth relations with Britain and dined several times with the new
president. A few months later, after David Erskine's
superiors in London rejected the conciliatory agreement he had signed in Washington, Pickering resumed
his customary denunciation of the Republicans and
became an intimate friend of the new British minister,
Francis Jackson, whose hostility toward Madison was
notorious. In retirement from the Senate, Pickering
vigorously denounced Madison's policies and after the
outbreak of the War of 1812 easily won election to the

House. Pickering described Madison's war policy as a
mixture of "wickedness and stupidity" and argued for
secession by the New England states. He remained in
Congress until 1817.

BIBLIOGRAPHY

Clarfield, Gerard H. *Timothy Pickering and American Diplomacy, 1795–1800.* 1969.
Clarfield, Gerard H. *Timothy Pickering and the American Republic.*
1980.

PATRICK J. FURLONG

PINCKNEY, CHARLES (1757–1824), soldier, congressman, diplomat. Born in Charleston, S.C., to wealthy
parents, Pinckney had to cope with his father's loyalism
during the Revolution. Pinckney served with the American force captured at the fall of Charleston and remained
a British prisoner of war until 1781.

In postwar Charleston he became a lawyer and was
elected a delegate to the Continental Congress, where
he served with Madison; they also served together at the
Federal Convention. His claim (made in 1818) to have

CHARLES PINCKNEY.   Pinckney was the second cousin of
Charles Cotesworth Pinckney.
PRINTS AND PHOTOGRAPHS DIVISION, LIBRARY OF CONGRESS.

submitted a plan for a new constitution that was remarkably close to the document finally adopted has been discredited, but internal evidence indicates that Pinckney was a busy, innovative delegate who made many valuable suggestions that survived in the final draft.

Pinckney was an active Federalist in the successful South Carolina ratification campaign. He then served on the state privy council and took office as governor in 1789. He had married the daughter of wealthy Henry Laurens in 1788, which allowed him to maintain a lavish lifestyle. He was elected as a Federalist to a second term as governor.

Disappointed by Washington's failure to appoint him the American minister to Great Britain, his commitment to Federalist policies waned, and in 1795 he was outspoken in his opposition to the Jay Treaty. In 1796 he returned to the governor's seat. In 1798 he drew support from the western part of his state to win election to the U.S. Senate.

Now a convert to Republicanism, Pinckney successfully managed Jefferson's presidential candidacy in South Carolina in 1800 and was rewarded with an appointment to serve as the American minister in Madrid. There he negotiated a treaty favorable to the United States' western interests, including the American right of deposit at New Orleans. Ratification of the treaty was delayed, however, after Napoleon sold Louisiana to the United States. Pinckney endeavored to placate the Spanish court so that the territorial transfer did not cause an international incident; but because Spain feared that the United States would seek Florida, his treaty languished. He was replaced by James Monroe in 1805. The two American envoys failed in their mission to assuage Spanish fears and gain approval of the treaty. Frustrated, Pinckney headed for home.

Back in Charleston, Pinckney returned to public life and became governor again in 1806. During his absence Pinckney's estate had dwindled, owing to poor management, but Pinckney remained personally popular with voters and his liberal support for universal white male suffrage in 1808 was in the Republican tradition. He was sent to Congress in 1818 and became an outspoken opponent of the Missouri Compromise. In 1820 he declined renomination for the House, citing the unhealthy climate in Washington and his frail health as justification. He died four years later.

BIBLIOGRAPHY

Abernathy, Thomas P. *The South in the New Nation, 1789–1819.* 1961.
Wallace, David D. *South Carolina: A Short History.* 1951.
Wright, Louis B. *South Carolina: A Bicentennial History.* 1976.

ROBERT A. RUTLAND

PINCKNEY, CHARLES COTESWORTH

(1746–1825), soldier, statesman, presidential candidate. The son of a rich planter and an English-born mother, Pinckney was reared in England and educated at Christ Church, Oxford. After reading law, Pinckney was admitted to the English bar, but returned to America in 1769. He identified with the patriot cause and was soon involved in the tug-of-war between the colonies and England. He took an active part in the resistance movement, joined the American forces, served with Washington as an aide-de-camp, and was captured at the fall of Charleston.

With peace restored, Pinckney became a conservative force in South Carolina politics. He attended the Federal Convention in 1787, where several of Pinckney's suggestions were incorporated in the Constitution, including the 1808 cutoff date for the slave trade. Pinckney turned down several high offices in the Washington administra-

CHARLES COTESWORTH PINCKNEY.   On a special diplomatic mission to France in 1797 with John Marshall and Elbridge Gerry, Pinckney turned down a French request for a bribe with the words, "No, no, not a sixpence!" His response inspired Robert Goodloe Harper's toast to Marshall in June 1798, "Millions for defense, but not one cent for tribute!" Pinckney stood as the Federalist candidate for president against Madison in 1808. He was a second cousin of Charles Pinckney. Engraving by E. Wellmore after a miniature by Edward Greene Malbone.
PRINTS AND PHOTOGRAPHS DIVISION, LIBRARY OF CONGRESS.

tion before he was sent to France as a diplomatic minister. Rejected by the French Revolutionary government, Pinckney stayed in Europe and served on the commission attempting to resolve Franco-American differences, and was thus involved in the XYZ Affair. Pinckney's outspoken views of the French bribery attempts made him a hero in America. He then served in the army two years as a major general.

Federalists esteemed his reputation and southern connections and made him their vice presidential nominee in 1800 and presidential nominee in both 1804 and 1808. After 1808, Pinckney gave up his political connections, retired, and became noted for his hospitality and his role as a promoter of southern agriculture.

BIBLIOGRAPHY

Wallace, David D. *South Carolina: A Short History, 1520–1948*. 1961.
Zahniser, Marvin R. *Charles Cotesworth Pinckney: Founding Father*. 1967.

ROBERT A. RUTLAND

PINKNEY, WILLIAM (1764–1822), lawyer, minister to Great Britain, U.S. attorney general. Pinkney was one of the most brilliant and flamboyant legal figures of the early republic. Widely acknowledged by his peers as the foremost lawyer of his times, Pinkney thrilled courtroom audiences with his eloquent oratory and his elaborate sartorial display. A pompous individual of excessive vanity, Pinkney nevertheless served the public in a long and distinguished career.

Born in Annapolis, Maryland, Pinkney studied law in the office of Samuel Chase and followed the lead of his mentor in 1788 and voted against the ratification of the Constitution. Pinkney served in the lower house of the Maryland Assembly (1788–1792) and on the state Executive Council (1792–1795). He spent eight years (1796–1804) as a commissioner to London under Jay's Treaty to adjust American claims for maritime losses and then returned to the practice of law in Baltimore. His experience with British maritime law proved valuable to the merchants of Baltimore. In January 1806 he sent to Congress a powerful protest against British attacks on American merchant ships that was published as *Memorial of the Merchants of Baltimore, on the Violation of Our Neutral Rights*. Jefferson's appointment of Pinkney as a special commissioner to negotiate a treaty with Great Britain surprised and enraged Republican leaders who themselves coveted the position. Since Pinkney was now a Federalist, many Republicans viewed Jefferson's choice as reflecting the influence of Secretary of State Madison, who was seeking bipartisan support for the impending Anglo-American treaty.

WILLIAM PINKNEY. Portrait by Charles B. King.
MARYLAND HISTORICAL SOCIETY, BALTIMORE.

The thrust of Pinkney's mission, undertaken jointly with James Monroe, was to gain a halt to the impressment of American seamen and to secure a more liberal treatment of the American reexport trade. During months of negotiation, Pinkney and Monroe managed to win several significant concessions on the reexport trade but found the British unwilling to budge on the crucial issue of impressment. Believing an agreement with some gains for American commerce superior to none at all, Pinkney and Monroe signed a treaty in December 1806. Jefferson, however, rejected the Monroe-Pinkney Treaty outright, refusing even to send it to the Senate. By his action Jefferson, some historians believe, missed a valuable opportunity to reach a useful accommodation with the British that could have formed the basis for commercial prosperity and future negotiation.

Despite the failure of the Monroe-Pinkney Treaty, Jefferson appointed Pinkney minister to Great Britain in 1807. Pinkney again faced the difficult task of attempting to gain concessions from Britain in its undeclared war on American shipping. He proved an extremely capable minister. The publication of Pinkney's diplomatic dispatches helped Madison mobilize public opinion for war and refute the ultra-Federalist charges of excessive

French influence over administration policy. Pinkney left London abruptly in February 1811 convinced that the settlement of American grievances could not be achieved through diplomacy. Soon after his return to Baltimore, Madison appointed his former minister U.S. attorney general. In June 1812 Pinkney drafted the American declaration of war.

Pinkney became an important political supporter of the embattled Madison. During Madison's reelection campaign in 1812, Pinkney penned a series of four articles published in Baltimore as a pamphlet, *Decius to the Republican Citizens of Maryland*, in which the attorney general defended Madison against the attacks of the supporters of his presidential rival De Witt Clinton. Madison rewarded Pinkney by making him the Republican party's chief patronage agent in Baltimore.

Pinkney remained in Madison's cabinet until February 1814, when the introduction of legislation requiring the residence of the attorney general at the seat of government led him to resign his office. The following year he was elected to the House of Representatives. He served in the House for a single year (1815–1816) until he was sent to Saint Petersburg as the American minister to Russia (1817–1818).

In 1819 Pinkney, in association with Daniel Webster and William Wirt, represented the Bank of the United States in the case of *McCulloch v. Maryland* (1819). Pinkney was also principal counsel in *Cohens v. Virginia* (1821), another critical case defining the powers of the federal government against those of the states.

During his term as senator from Maryland (1820–1822), Pinkney played an influential role in the debate over the admission of Missouri to the Union. Siding with the southern states, Pinkney contended that it was unconstitutional for Congress to forbid slavery in admitting a new state.

Pinkney died at the height of his career while in Washington in 1822. Ironically, although he refused to reside in the nation's capital during his lifetime, he was buried in the Congressional Cemetery.

BIBLIOGRAPHY

Hickey, Donald R. "The Monroe-Pinkney Treaty of 1806: A Reappraisal." *William and Mary Quarterly* 3d ser., 44 (1987): 65–88.

Ireland, Robert M. "William Pinkney: A Revision and Reemphasis." *American Journal of Legal History* 14 (1970): 235–246.

Papenfuse, Edward C., et al., eds. *A Biographical Dictionary of the Maryland Legislature, 1635–1789.* 2 vols. 1979–1985.

Perkins, Bradford. *Prologue to War: England and the United States, 1805–1812.* 1961.

Wheaton, Henry. *Some Account of the Life, Writings, and Speeches of William Pinkney.* 1826.

TINA H. SHELLER

POLITICAL ECONOMY. The concept of political economy was commonly used during Madison's lifetime to refer specifically to the economic policy of the state and more generally to the necessary interdependence of government, economy, and society. As a segment of the emerging social sciences, political economy was subsumed under the broader rubric of moral philosophy, and thus the expression suggested a fusion of empirical issues and ethical concerns that was common during the second half of the eighteenth century. Americans of Madison's generation were keenly attentive to the moral dimension of economic life because they tended to assume that the success of their experiment in republican government was directly linked to the character of the American people. Hence Madison sought to define, and then to secure, an economic, political, and social order for the United States that would sustain a virtuous citizenry.

Following the intellectual lead of Scottish thinkers who conceived of social development in terms of movement through regular phases or stages from the simplest hunting communities to modern commercial society, Madison himself believed that Americans would be healthy, happy, and republican so long as they continued at a predominantly agricultural stage of development. If population density remained sufficiently low to permit the widespread ownership of land, Americans would be an independent, virtuous people who could make self-government work. Commerce was also an integral part of Madison's agricultural vision, because industrious, virtuous farmers in the fertile territories of the United States would necessarily produce a bountiful surplus for export to foreign markets, mainly Europe. Finally, Madison believed that securing the republic required the support, but not the systematic intervention, of the state. Unlike monarchical governments in Europe, which behaved in ways that both Adam Smith and Madison depicted as corrupt and unproductive, Madison's ideal government would intervene in the natural order of things only if necessary to defend and promote the broader conditions conducive to his vision of republican success.

Following adoption of the Constitution in 1788, Madison wanted the new federal government he had been instrumental in creating to do whatever seemed necessary to secure the twin guarantors of that success: unobstructed access to an open supply of fresh land (which would permit continuous waves of a regenerative expansion across space) and a relatively open international commercial order. The latter point was consistent with Adam Smith's belief that free trade would provide sufficient markets to sustain the republican industry of America's farmers. Madison's was thus an expansive vision requiring both the support of the new government under the Constitution and the cooperation of foreign peoples, although neither proved easy to obtain. During the 1790s he and his colleague Thomas Jefferson resisted the efforts of Alexander Hamilton and other Federalists to implement a quite different system of political economy that challenged Republicans' most basic assumptions about the nature and shape of America's republican revolution.

After the great electoral victory of the Jeffersonians in 1800, Madison and Jefferson had the opportunity to put their system into practice. During the next sixteen years, they reversed the thrust of Hamilton's fiscal programs, which they believed threatened to impose on the United States a corrupt British precedent; they acquired a vast expanse of territory for future generations of Americans to expand into, through the Louisiana Purchase of 1803; and they tried through both peaceful and ultimately forcible means to shape the open international commercial order that lay at the heart of their vision. The latter challenge, made acute by the international commercial conflict attending the Napoleonic Wars in Europe, prompted Madison, as secretary of state, to support the Embargo of 1807–1809 and, as president, to lead the United States into war with England in 1812.

By the time he retired from public life, after this second war for American independence, Madison understood the need to make adjustments and accommodations in his vision. His political economy had always included a place for manufactures, but principally of the simpler household and small workshop varieties appropriate to a predominantly agricultural stage of development. But the failure of the Jeffersonians to secure a world of international free trade, combined with their recognition that America's agricultural surplus was simply too large to be absorbed by available foreign markets, steadily pushed Madison toward acceptance of increased manufacturing of all kinds and a more balanced domestic economy. His original vision was never fully abandoned; rather, it was adapted to the demands and conditions of a world that could not be fully molded in the shape of his revolutionary dreams.

During his final years, as he stoically contemplated America's future, Madison remained guardedly optimistic that republicanism would survive the kinds of social and economic changes that were, in some vital respects, least conducive to its success.

[See also *Louisiana; Public Lands; Republicanism.*]

BIBLIOGRAPHY

Appleby, Joyce. *Capitalism and a New Social Order: The Republican Vision of the 1790s.* 1984.

McCoy, Drew R. *The Elusive Republic: Political Economy in Jeffersonian America.* 1980.

Nelson, John R., Jr. *Liberty and Property: Political Economy and Policymaking in the New Nation. 1789–1812.* 1987.

DREW R. MCCOY

PORTER, DAVID (1780–1843), U.S. naval officer. Born in Boston and nurtured by a seafaring family, Porter entered the navy as a midshipman in 1798. He served in the frigate *Constellation* during the Quasi-War with France, and in the brig *Enterprise* during the Barbary Wars. He was captured in the frigate *Philadelphia* when she ran aground off Tripoli in 1803. Porter commanded the New Orleans naval station as a master commandant during 1809–1811.

At the beginning of the War of 1812, Porter commanded the thirty-two-gun frigate *Essex.* Sailing independently, he captured nine prizes off Nova Scotia and Newfoundland during July and August 1812. One of these was HMS *Alert,* the first British naval prize of the war, taken on 14 August. Because *Essex* was being refitted, Porter missed participating in one of the three naval squadrons sent out by Secretary of the Navy William Jones to attack British merchant shipping during the fall. Porter sailed into the eastern Pacific, where he ranged widely, attacking British merchant and whaling ships. He eventually commanded a small flotilla of prizes, which he sailed to the Marquesas Islands for refitting in late 1813.

Learning that the British had sent some warships to hunt him down, Porter went to meet them in *Essex* and *Essex Junior,* one of his smaller prizes. Owing to a partial dismasting, Porter was trapped by HMS *Phoebe* and HMS *Cherub* in Chilean waters north of Valparaiso. On 28 March 1814, Porter valiantly fought these ships, but suffered the destruction of his ship and capture. He was paroled and allowed to return with his men in the diminutive *Essex Junior,* arriving off New York in July 1814. He took with him those men who could travel and joined the effort to defend Washington, Alexandria, and Baltimore against British raids in August and September.

After the war, Porter was one of three men named to the Board of Navy Commissioners who advised the secretary of the navy on professional and technical matters. Restless ashore and unable to get along well with his colleagues, Capt. John Rodgers and Capt. Stephen Decatur, he resigned from the Board in 1823 to become commodore of the West India Squadron, which was then engaged in suppressing piracy in the Caribbean. Porter's aggressive personality led him astray in the Fajardo Incident, during which he attacked a Spanish town on the island of Puerto Rico whose inhabitants were sheltering some pirates. The administration of President John Quincy Adams censured Porter for endangering relations with Spain.

Porter resigned from the navy in 1826 and accepted the post of commander in chief of the Mexican Navy. In 1829 President Andrew Jackson invited him to return to the navy, but instead Porter accepted diplomatic posts in the Mediterranean, the longest held being that of U.S. minister to Turkey from 1839 to 1841. Porter died in Turkey;

DAVID PORTER.   Portrait by Charles Willson Peale.
INDEPENDENCE NATIONAL HISTORICAL PARK, PHILADELPHIA.

his remains were shipped to the United States for interment at Philadelphia.

Porter was one of those men, found in all military services, who are born fighters, but who languish unhappily and unappreciated in times of peace. His exploits in the Pacific during the War of 1812 became an indelible part of the American naval heritage. The best aspects of his character were inherited by his natural son David Dixon Porter and his foster son David Glasgow Farragut, both of whom reached the highest rank of the U.S. Navy.

BIBLIOGRAPHY

Long, David F. *Nothing Too Daring: A Biography of Commodore David Porter, 1780–1843.* 1970.
Roosevelt, Theodore. *The Naval War of 1812.* 1882.

WILLIAM S. DUDLEY

PRESIDENT. In response to the depredations committed by the Algerian corsairs, Congress on 27 March

1794 authorized the president to provide for six frigates. Peace with Algiers in 1796 temporarily suspended construction of three of the ships, the *President* included. By 1798, however, Congress reinstated a naval building program because of the undeclared war with France. The forty-four-gun *President* sailed from New York for the West Indies on 4 September 1800 under Commodore Thomas Truxtun but had an uneventful cruise before peace ensued in 1801.

The *President* had two tours of duty in the Mediterranean during the war with the Barbary states. It was Commodore Richard Dale's flagship from June 1801 to April 1802 and Commodore Samuel Barron's from July 1804 to September 1805, after which it returned to Washington, where it was laid up for three years.

After undergoing repairs, the *President* engaged in coastal cruising under Capt. William Bainbridge from 1809 to 1810. As Commodore John Rodgers's flagship beginning in June 1810, the *President* cruised the eastern seaboard to protect American commerce against British and French depredations. On 16 May 1811, the *President* and the British vessel *Little Belt* exchanged broadsides off Cape Henry, Virginia, further exacerbating tensions between the United States and Great Britain.

The *President* sailed on five cruises during the War of 1812, and, although it never achieved spectacular naval victories, it succeeded in harassing British commerce. Commodore John Rodgers commanded the *President* during its first four cruises from June 1812 to February 1814, capturing twenty-two merchant vessels and the British schooner *Highflyer* and recapturing two American merchantmen.

Unaware that the peace commissioners had signed a treaty ending the war, the new commander of the *President*, Commodore Stephen Decatur, set sail from New York on 14 January 1815. The frigate ran aground, causing serious damage to the hull. The next day the *President* encountered a British squadron and surrendered after a six-hour struggle. The British took the *President* back to England, where it was brought into government service, until being broken up in 1818.

BIBLIOGRAPHY

National Archives. Naval Records Collection of the Office of Naval Records and Library. Record Group 45. Letters Received by the Secretary of the Navy from Captains, 1 January 1805–31 March 1815 (National Archives Microfilm Publication M-125, reels 1–43).

Paullin, Charles O. *Commodore John Rodgers: Captain, Commodore, and Senior Officer of the American Navy, 1773–1838.* 1909. Repr. 1967.

U.S. Office of Naval Records and Library. *Naval Documents Related to the Quasi-War between the United States and France.* 7 vols. 1935–1938.

U.S. Office of Naval Records and Library. *Naval Documents Related to the United States Wars with the Barbary Powers.* 6 vols. 1939–1944.

CHRISTINE F. HUGHES

PREVOST, GEORGE (1767–1816), soldier, governor general of Canada. Born in Switzerland, Prevost bought a commission in the British army as a captain in 1783. He rose in military rank during service in the West Indies and achieved the governorship of Saint Lucia in 1798. After another decade of military service in the West Indies (during which he was created a baronet in 1805), he was appointed commander in chief of Nova Scotia in 1808 and governor general of British North America in 1811. The Battle of Tippecanoe in November 1811 convinced Prevost that war with the United States was inevitable. He welcomed Tecumseh and his warriors into the British fold at Amherstburg in 1812 and further enlarged his force by enlisting the local population into the militia.

Prevost provoked the Madison administration by lead-

SIR GEORGE PREVOST.   From a mezzotint by S. W. Reynolds.
PRINTS AND PHOTOGRAPHS DIVISION, LIBRARY OF CONGRESS.

ing attacks at Sackets Harbor in May 1813 and at Platts-burg in September 1814. To gain control of Lake Champlain, Prevost led an army of more than a thousand regulars and Indians, combined with a naval force, against the American base at Sackets Harbor which had nearly equal forces. The Americans stalled the British attack. When the American forces were bolstered by the arrival of reinforcements, Prevost ordered a withdrawal. Sixteen months later Prevost attempted another combined army-navy attack, this time at Plattsburg, but he lost his fleet and was forced back to Montreal. The repulse resulted in his recall to England. He arrived there to find that the naval court had already condemned his actions. He was allowed a court-martial in person but died a week before it commenced. He is buried in Hertfordshire.

BIBLIOGRAPHY

Dictionary of National Biography. Vol. 46. 1896.
Mahon, John K. *The War of 1812.* 1972.

FRANK C. MEVERS

PRINCETON UNIVERSITY. Princeton University was founded as the College of New Jersey in Prince-ton, New Jersey, in 1746 and retained that name until 1896. Although affiliated with the Presbyterian Church, the institution housed in Nassau Hall was independent of church control. During Madison's student days, as a consequence of the direction given by the influential Scottish divine Dr. John Witherspoon, president from 1768 to 1794, the college exhibited a strong Whiggish bias, standing firmly, in Witherspoon's words, against both "lordly domination and sacerdotal tyranny."

James Madison, Sr.'s decision to send his son to Princeton is probably best explained by his confidence in young James's tutor, the Rev. Thomas Martin, rector of the Brick Church in Orange, Va. Accompanied by Martin and his brother Alexander, both Princeton graduates, and the slave Sawney, Madison set out from Montpelier in June 1769 and matriculated at Nassau Hall the following month. Because Madison had been well prepared, and perhaps because of his father's insistence on economy, he was permitted to take additional classes and to complete requirements for the bachelor's degree in two, rather than four, years. He stayed on through the winter of 1771–1772 to learn some Hebrew and to pursue "miscellaneous" subjects, including law.

At Princeton Madison continued his studies in mathematics and the classics and took courses in natural phi-

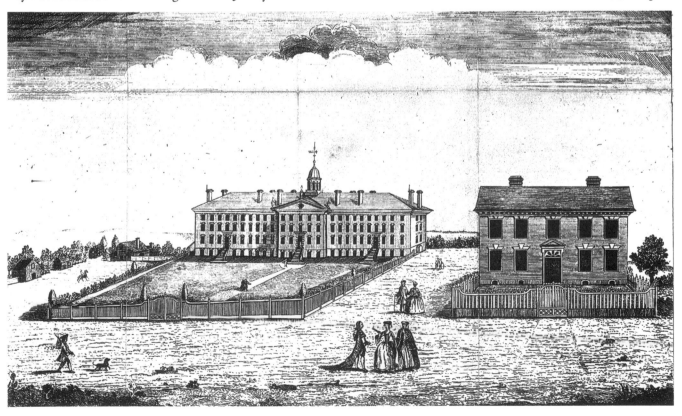

NASSAU HALL.   The main building of the College of New Jersey (Princeton University). Engraving by Henry Dawkins after a drawing by W. Tennant, 1764.   PRINTS AND PHOTOGRAPHS DIVISION, LIBRARY OF CONGRESS.

losophy, moral philosophy, and law. He also read the great treatises and the philosophical works of the Enlightenment. Here, where opposition to British colonial policy was openly championed, he first sensed the high calling of the lawgiver in his own time and an inclination for politics and law (as well as for religion). Madison's physical debilities, made worse by excessive studying, made him doubt his fitness for an active life. But his confidence grew during the lively and uninhibited "paper wars" of wit waged between the American Whig Society, of which he was a member, and its rival, the Cliosophic, or Clio, Society. It was further strengthened, and his outlook broadened, by friendships he formed with fellow students from the middle and northern colonies, notably Aaron Burr, William Bradford, Philip Freneau, and Hugh Henry Brackenridge.

Twelve students, including Madison, were awarded degrees during the college's graduation in September 1771, but accounts indicate that he did not take an active part in the proceedings. Princeton conferred a doctor of laws degree on Madison in 1787.

BIBLIOGRAPHY

Alexander, Samuel Davies. *Princeton College during the Eighteenth Century.* 1872.
Brant, Irving. *Madison: The Virginia Revolutionist.* Vol. 1. 1941.
Hutchinson, William T., et al., eds. *The Papers of James Madison: Congressional Series.* Vol. 1. 1962.

C. M. HARRIS

PRIVATEERS. Privateers were authorized by the United States during the War of 1812. Exposed to European privateering, both as practitioners and as victims, the North American colonies borrowed the British version of the privateering system during the American Revolution. No longer a means of redress for individual grievances in peacetime, privateering evolved into a wartime device for the rapid expansion of maritime raiding forces; after issuing letters of marque and reprisal authorizing shipowners to seize an opponent's merchantmen, the government shared prize proceeds with the ships' crews and owners. At first the Continental Congress and the states both issued such licenses, but after 1787, the new Constitution prohibited the issuance of state commissions. The federal government operated a privateering system during its undeclared war with France between 1795 and 1800.

The 18 June 1812 declaration of war against Great Britain authorized President Madison "to issue private armed vessels of the United States commissions of marque and reprisal." This freed the public navy from commerce raiding by substituting armed merchantmen, act-

ing individually but not without regulation. Congress passed an Act Concerning Letters-of-Marque, Prizes, and Prize Goods that created procedures to be followed by would-be privateers, explained all steps from the application process to the workings of prize auctions and prize money distributions, and detailed "Instructions for the Private Armed Vessels of the United States" from the commander in chief. All regulations were enforceable in federal courts, as were owners' instructions to their commanders and articles of agreement signed by the crew. The administration made every effort to regulate the 1,100 commissions it assigned to about 600 registered vessels.

The new commerce raiders operated in two overlapping phases. The first phase was ruled by opportunism, as eager owners cleared even one-gun boats to seize unsuspecting and unarmed British merchantmen. Soon, larger, sturdier seagoing vessels, such as the eighteen privateers outfitted at Baltimore (the leading privateer's nest, Baltimore sent out 122 vessels, or an average of one a week for thirty months), also scoured the nearby sealanes. This initial surge produced a parade of prizes, condemnation decrees, auctions, and prize distributions. Some fortunes were made, but only after heavy duties, costs, and fees were deducted from the owners', officers', and crews' shares.

A second phase of privateering evolved after the easy pickings disappeared. Armed merchantmen often sailed in escorted convoys far from American ports. Investors (200 in Baltimore) built large fifty-thousand-dollar privateers (fully armed warships) and twenty-five-thousand-dollar letter-of-marque traders with identical commissions for longer cruises in more distant seas. The traders, or "flyers," used fewer guns and men but carried cargoes and took prizes of opportunity while paying wages and, sometimes, prize money. Conversely, those manning the privateers risked all under a "no prize, no pay" rule. Both types of vessels were typically brig- or schooner-rigged vessels of 150 to 450 tons armed with one long gun plus six to ten carronades (shorter guns) and up to 149 men (to avoid paying the higher bond required for 150 or more men). These larger, better designed raiders cruised English and Irish waters, off Africa, in the south Atlantic and Indian Oceans, and even off China.

During the two phases, American privateers captured between 1,300 and 1,700 prizes. If ships burned, fishing vessels, and prisoner cartels are included, this meant two losses per day for British shipowners. Some cruises garnered twenty or more prizes (although not all prizes got into port, as some goods may have been divested), while others made limited profits, covered only their cost, or lost money. Unlike a letter-of-marque flyer carrying cargo on a voyage, a privateer without a prize did not even meet its costs, the minimal expectation of shipping ventures. The owners might auction their arms, sails, supplies, and vessel to recoup their expenses, but the crew got nothing. Successes, however, greatly outnumbered failures.

The Madison administration became dependent upon licensed vessels for exports, imports, and income and for its sea force. It motivated raiders by lowering duties on prize goods, quickening the auction process, and multiplying fivefold its prisoner bonus. Government cannons were transferred to privateers as the administration strained to keep forty or fifty raiders in action each month throughout the war, even during the perilous year of 1814.

One criticism of the privateer system was that it competed with the navy for seamen. Some sailors preferred the shorter tours, less deadly combat, and promise of a small bonanza that privateering offered. This competition eased after 1813 as the naval forces declined in size. Complaints of illegal land incursions by privateers were settled by the commander in chief, and federal courts adjudicated disputed claims for prize goods and tickets, seizures of alleged neutral vessels, and captures in neutral waters. One serious complaint never resolved by the Madison administration was the postwar charge by Spain that American-owned, -outfitted, and -manned privateers were raiding its commerce under illegal South American revolutionary commissions.

During the war, some crew members enjoyed prize incomes from 90- or 120-day cruises that exceeded a year's peacetime wages. Others died, languished in prisons, or received no prize money. A sole owner of a successful raider and those who bought shares in a number of commissioned vessels realized great profits, although their earnings may not have exceeded their peacetime incomes from trade over an equivalent period. Ports, shipyards, wharves, sailmakers, and caulkers were kept active as investors and traders sought wartime substitutes for peacetime income. At times, privateering was the only source of income available to some individuals. The war effort was the greatest beneficiary of Madison's efforts to create and nurture private armed vessels, because the privateers' exploits turned frustrated British merchants into opponents of the war. Unlike Madison's other two maritime achievements—his superfrigates and his 1814 successes on the northern lakes—only his private armed vessels performed successfully from the outset of war until months after the peace treaty was signed. As one of the best privateering performances in history, the effort was a credit both to the participants and to Madison's leadership.

BIBLIOGRAPHY

Chapelle, Howard I. *The Baltimore Clipper: Its Origin and Development.* 1930,

Coggeshall, George. *History of the American Privateers and Letters-of-Marque during Our War with England in the Years 1812, 1813, and 1814.* 1856.
Dudley, William S., ed. *The Naval War of 1812: A Documentary History.* Vol. 1. 1985.
Garitee, Jerome R. *The Republic's Private Navy: The American Privateering Business as Practiced by Baltimore during the War of 1812.* 1977.
Maclay, Edgar Stanton. *A History of American Privateers.* 1899.

JEROME R. GARITEE

PRIVY COUNCIL OF VIRGINIA. The Privy Council, or Council of State, as it was called in the Virginia Constitution of 1776 that created it, consisted of eight members elected for indeterminate terms by joint ballot of the two houses of the General Assembly. The Constitution required the General Assembly to remove and replace two members every third year and to fill vacancies caused by deaths and resignations. Unlike the colonial council, to which it was in some measure a successor, the Council of State possessed no legislative or judicial powers. The councillors and the governor together formed a plural executive, and the councillors each year chose a president to serve as lieutenant, or acting, governor during the absence or incapacity of the governor or in the event of his death. The governor presided at council meetings and could take no significant action without the council's advice, making it, in theory, both an aid to the governor and a check on executive misconduct. When no quorum could be assembled, as happened during the British invasion in the spring of 1781, the executive branch of government virtually ceased to function.

The Council of State was a cumbersome institution that most of the governors grew to despise. Rather than attracting the valuable services of wise and experienced men, it became a training ground with salaries for young men hoping to advance their careers. The Constitution of 1830 reduced the council to three members, and the Constitution of 1851 abolished it. James Madison was elected to the Council of State on 15 November 1777 and served from 14 January 1778 until December 1779. In 1784 he described the Council of State as "a grave of useful talents." Nevertheless, Madison's service on the council led to the firming of his friendship with Gov. Thomas Jefferson, whom Madison had known only slightly before Madison's appointment to the post.

BIBLIOGRAPHY

There is no scholarly history of the Council of State. The most extensive treatment of James Madison's term on the council is in vol. 1 of Irving Brant, *James Madison,* 6 vols. (1941–1961). The fragmentary surviving journals and letterbooks covering Madison's term have been published in vol. 2 of H. R. McIlwaine et al., eds., *Journals of the Council of the State of Virginia*, 6 vols. (1931–1982), and in vol. 2 and 3 of H. R. McIlwaine, ed., *Official Letters of the Governors of the State of Virginia*, 3 vols. (1926–1929). The incoming letters to the council are in Record Group 75, Virginia State Library and Archives, and those for the period of Madison's service have been abstracted in part in vol. 1 of William P. Palmer and Henry W. Flournoy, eds., *Calendar of Virginia State Papers*, 11 vols. (1875–1893), and printed in part in vol. 3 of Julian P. Boyd et al., eds., *The Papers of Thomas Jefferson* (1950–).

BRENT TARTER

PROPHET, THE (Tenskwatawa, Lalawethika, the Shawnee Prophet) (c. 1775–1836), Indian religious leader. Born near present-day Piqua, Ohio, Lalawethi-

ka lost an eye in an accident as a child and led a dissolute early life. In 1805 he experienced a vision in which he claimed to have received a message from the Master of Life. Renouncing alcohol, he took the name Tenskwatawa, meaning "the open door," and preached a doctrine of religious revitalization. Denouncing white Americans as a poison in the land, he urged his followers to eschew intermarriage with whites, abstain from alcohol, cast off white's clothing, reject Christianity and corrupt shamans, and return to the ways and beliefs of their ancestors.

The teachings of the Shawnee messiah attracted a following among many tribes as the Indian peoples of the Great Lakes region confronted a new world of chaos and dispossession. The Treaty of Fort Wayne in 1809, in which a number of chiefs ceded 2.5 million acres of land

THE PROPHET WITH TECUMSEH.   From Augustus Mason, *Romance and Tragedy of Pioneer Life.*
PRINTS AND PHOTOGRAPHS DIVISION, LIBRARY OF CONGRESS.

to the United States, helped galvanize opposition to both the Americans and the government chiefs. The Prophet's brother Tecumseh broadened the movement of cultural and religious revitalization into a movement of political and, when necessary, military resistance to American expansion. The growing confederacy alarmed the United States, and in 1811, while Tecumseh was away in the South, William Henry Harrison, the governor of Indiana Territory, launched a preemptive strike against the Prophet's village at Tippecanoe. Confident in the power of his medicine, the Prophet allowed himself to be drawn into battle. While Tippecanoe was not the victory that Harrison claimed, the battle was a disaster for the Prophet, whose warriors died despite his claims that they would be invulnerable to the soldiers' bullets. Discredited, the Prophet played little part in the War of 1812. He remained in Canada until 1826, returned to Ohio for a short time, then migrated to the West. George Catlin painted his portrait in 1832, but the Prophet died in obscurity.

BIBLIOGRAPHY

Edmunds, R. David. *The Shawnee Prophet.* 1983.

Kinietz, Vernon, and Erminie Wheeler-Voegelin, eds. "Shawnese Traditions: C. C. Trowbridge's Account." *Occasional Contributions from the Museum of Anthropology of the University of Michigan* 9 (1939). Includes Trowbridge's interviews with the Prophet in the 1820s.

COLIN G. CALLOWAY

PROTESTANT EPISCOPAL CHURCH. See *Anglican Church.*

PUBLIC LANDS.

James Madison's long public career and extended retirement spanned the half-century when the public domain was created and when the terms and circumstances of its distribution became one of the salient issues for the new, independent American nation. From his election to the Continental Congress in 1780 until his death at Montpelier in 1836, Madison was witness to and observer of, if not active participant in the westward expansion of the American people. Through most of his public life, Madison was involved in the attendant struggle over the acquisition of the public lands and their distribution.

Madison was a leading figure in the establishment of the public domain. As a member of the Continental Congress (1780–1783) and of the Virginia House of Delegates (1784–1786), he arranged for Virginia's cession of its western claims and persuaded other states to do likewise. Indeed, Virginia's cession of its claims north of the Ohio River in 1781 laid the basis for the creation of the public domain.

In response to these cessions, the Continental Congress enacted an ordinance laying down guidelines for the disposal of the public lands. Confirmed by the new government under the Constitution, the Ordinance of 1785 provided for survey along rectangular lines to precede sale, for public sale by auction at a specified minimum price, and for several reservations to enrich the government and to support education. The Ordinance became a guide for Madison during his long public service. He energetically guarded its provisions and refused to support special appeals that would bypass the land system and offer special advantages to some groups.

After his significant role in the writing and the adoption of the Constitution, Madison served in Congress (1789–1797), where his interests centered on the new national government. He saw the public domain as a great national resource, especially in generating revenue for the new nation and retiring the debt. Like his colleague and fellow Virginian Thomas Jefferson, he was suspicious of a government based on the allegiance of debtors.

The diplomatic crisis with Great Britain and the subsequent war dominated Madison's presidency, but the final two years (1815–1816) of his second administration witnessed the first great surge of population moving west. As the demand for public lands rose to unprecedented levels and prices rose to unheard-of levels, Congress responded with an expanded land system. Soon the president and his administration had to confront the problem of widespread evasion of law and trespassing on the public domain. Madison found this disorderly aspect of westward expansion disturbing. In an attempt to control trespassing, in December 1815 he issued a proclamation against it and threatened to use military force. Of course, a recourse to force was politically impossible, but the incident defines Madison's attitude toward the public domain.

In the years after his return to private life, Madison became increasingly interested in the public domain as a resource to support the emancipation of the slaves. Concerned about the growing intrusion of slavery into the national political life in the 1820s, he proposed that slave owners who voluntarily emancipated their slaves be compensated by public monies raised through the sale of public lands. The voluntary provision doomed his proposal to failure before it could be seriously considered, but he continued to write about his ideas. Later he expanded his uses of revenue from the public lands to include the removal of Native Americans.

Whether as elected representative, appointed official, or elder statesman, Madison lacked empathy for the land hunger that tied the public domain to the lives of ordinary citizens, particularly those living in the West. Yet he well understood the importance of the public lands as a resource for the nation. In the final years of his life, he vigorously resisted any attempt to return portions of the public domain to individual states. In this respect, he remained a nationalist to the end.

[See also *Indians; Kentucky and the Western Country; Slavery*.]

BIBLIOGRAPHY

Hutchinson, William T. et al., eds. *The Papers of James Madison: Congressional Series*. 17 vols. 1962–.

Rohrbough, Malcolm J. *The Land Office Business: The Acquisition and Administration of the American Public Lands*. 1989.

Rutland, Robert A., et al., eds. *The Papers of James Madison. Presidental Series*. 2 vols. 1984.

MALCOLM J. ROHRBOUGH

R

RAISIN RIVER, BATTLES OF. See *River Raisin, Battles of.*

RANDOLPH, EDMUND (1753–1813), revolutionary statesman, lawyer, first attorney general of the United States. Born to a distinguished Virginia family, Randolph was the son and grandson of prominent lawyers, both of whom had served as king's attorneys in the colony. Although his father was a loyalist, Randolph cast his lot with the patriot cause. Despite his youth, Randolph rose rapidly to prominence in the new state government, serving as attorney general, governor, and member of the legislature. He also held appointments as delegate to Congress, the Annapolis Convention, and the Federal Convention and was elected to serve in the Virginia ratifying convention. In 1789 President Washington appointed Randolph first attorney general of the United States, an office he held until 1794, when he succeeded Thomas Jefferson as secretary of state. After resigning the latter office under fire in August 1795, Randolph left public life for good.

Beginning in 1776, when they served together in the state constitutional convention, Randolph and Madison enjoyed a lifelong friendship. They were particularly close during the 1780s, and their correspondence is rich in substance concerning the early history of the United States and the framing and ratification of the Constitution. As fellow delegates to the Continental Congress, the Annapolis Convention, the Federal Convention, and the Virginia ratifying convention, Randolph and Madison collaborated in the movement for federal reform. In May 1787 Randolph presented to the Federal Convention the Virginia Plan (chiefly Madison's work), which he introduced in a speech that persuasively argued the necessity of scrapping the existing confederation in favor of an "energetic" government formed on national and republican principles. Randolph was a conspicuous participant in the debates, particularly during the first half of the convention. By September, however, he was unhappy with the direction the proceedings had taken and refused to sign the Constitution. He believed the plan was insufficiently republican, principally in distributing too much power to the executive and to the Senate. At the same time he insisted that withholding his signature did not mean he was unalterably opposed to the Constitution but merely reflected his wish to remain free "to act according to the dictates of his judgment." Ultimately, as a delegate to the ratifying convention in June 1788, Randolph supported unconditional ratification, ably assisting Madison in championing the plan. The popular governor's vigorous advocacy of the Constitution was crucial in securing a close vote in favor of adoption.

Randolph's vacillating conduct toward the Constitution, whether reflecting a temperamental irresolution or a principled attempt to maintain his independence, earned him a reputation as a political trimmer. Serving in Washington's cabinet, Randolph found it increasingly difficult to steer a middle course through the emerging party divisions between Federalists and Republicans. At the height of the controversy over Jay's Treaty in the summer of 1795, he was forced under humiliating circumstances to resign as secretary of state. Captured dispatches—supplied by the British to well-placed Federalists, evidently as part of a plot to bring down the secretary of state for his lukewarm support of the treaty—seemed to indicate that Randolph had solicited a bribe from the French minister. Although historians have completely exonerated him of wrongdoing, at the time Randolph was unable to dispel the cloud of suspicion.

Returning to private life, Randolph spent his remaining years practicing law in Richmond. In 1807 he served as counsel for Aaron Burr in his celebrated trial for treason. In retirement Randolph also wrote a history of Vir-

EDMUND RANDOLPH.
PRINTS AND PHOTOGRAPHS DIVISION, LIBRARY OF CONGRESS.

ginia, the surviving portion of which was published many years after his death.

BIBLIOGRAPHY

Reardon, John J. *Edmund Randolph: A Biography.* 1975.

CHARLES F. HOBSON

RANDOLPH, JOHN (OF ROANOKE) (1773–

1833), Republican gadfly and onetime leader of the House of Representatives. John Randolph of Roanoke was a brilliant orator who used his voice and his powerful personality to dominate a lackluster Republican-dominated House of Representatives during the first administration of his distant cousin Thomas Jefferson. Even while he was chairman of the Committee on Ways and Means and a handpicked administration leader, Randolph developed a personal animosity toward Madison that inspired him to take every conceivable step to thwart Madison's political career, including the creation of the presidential candidacy of James Monroe in 1808. To Randolph, Madison personified the degeneration of those Republican principles that had defined the party before its rise to power; Randolph insisted that it was due to the "baleful influence of the Secretary of State that we have been gradually relax-

ing from our old principles." To Randolph and his handful of followers, Republicans in power were little better than the Federalists they had supplanted.

Randolph's public assault began early in 1805, in response to the "Articles of Agreement and Cession" that Madison, Albert Gallatin, and Levi Lincoln had negotiated to resolve the sectional crisis caused by the Yazoo Lands frauds. Randolph was so outraged that the speculators, many of them New England Federalists, were to receive benefits that he successfully blocked the appropriations of funds to pay the investors until 1814, when he was temporarily out of Congress. Even though he had to know that the compromise was largely the work of his dear friend Gallatin, Randolph chose to blame Madison, persistently and unfairly branding him as a "Yazoo man." By the end of 1805 Madison was attacked for his (and Jefferson's) efforts to acquire discretionary funds to facilitate the acquisition of West Florida. Randolph insisted that the Mobile area already belonged to the United States because of the Louisiana Purchase, that it should be taken by war, if necessary, and that it was morally corrupt of Secretary of State Madison to attempt to acquire it by bribery. Madison's delight at Randolph's mishandling of the Chase impeachment trial contributed to Randolph's rage. The final straw was Madison's entirely accurate remark in 1806 that Randolph was not qualified to be ambassador to Great Britain.

Beginning in October 1805, Randolph's Old Republicans, called the "Tertium Quid" (or Quids) by others, worked unceasingly to prevent Madison from becoming president. Despite his peculiar appearance and manner (he was tall, gaunt, oddly shaped, and pale and had a shrill voice that was often mistaken for a woman's), Randolph was a formidable adversary. He was a brilliant and vitriolic orator, and anyone who resisted him could expect a torrent of abuse. Randolph's attacks were described by a contemporary as comparable only to those of Robespierre for their "abusive strain of invective." The historian Henry Adams referred to the "public and personal war which he waged" against Madison, "in a temper and by means so revolting as in the end to throw the sympathies of every unprejudiced man on the side of his victim." Early in the campaign, Randolph declared that if Madison's "cold and insidious moderation" was vindicated by the electorate, "we are gone, forever." After failing in his efforts to prevent "Mr. Madison's War," Randolph described "Mr. Madison's dictatorship" as "one vast prison-house." In 1816 he would claim that Madison "out-Hamiltons Alexander Hamilton." As Madison left office, Randolph uncharacteristically described him as "a great man" and "wished him all happiness in his retirement."

Randolph's deceptive letters persuaded Monroe to mount a fruitless presidential campaign in 1808; Monroe did not receive a single electoral vote, despite Randolph's assurance that Virginia was solidly behind him. Randolph refused Monroe's request for advice on whether he should end his isolation from his party leaders, but when Monroe sought a rapprochement with Madison, Randolph wrote in his diary that he had been "betrayed and deserted" by "a Judas and a Traitor."

Despite Randolph's expressed revulsion against the Federalists, whom he accused of co-opting Madison, it is difficult to draw a clear line between the Quids and the Federalists as the United States progressed toward war with Great Britain. Randolph contemptuously hurled Madison's lengthy *Examination of the British Doctrine, Which Subjects to Capture a Neutral Trade, Not Open in Time of Peace* on the floor of the House in 1806, calling it a "shilling pamphlet hurled against eight hundred ships of war." He joined the Federalists in opposition, first to nonimportation, then to the Embargo, which he regarded as truckling to France by the Jefferson administration. In 1810 and 1811 he continually attempted to undercut military preparations and once contemptuously described soldiers as vagabonds recruited in brothels. Even in 1812 he waged a private war against the Madison administration from his seat on the House Foreign Relations Committee. He declared it would be "gross and unparalleled treason" for Madison to take the country into war against England. When Madison finally asked Congress for a declaration of war, Randolph spoke for hours, even defending the British blockade of the United States and attacking Madison for subservience to France.

Randolph lost his seat in the House in 1813 but returned again in 1815 in time to oppose all the nationalistic postwar measures of Madison's final years in Washington. He was in Congress throughout the 1820s, including a brief period of Senate service. During these years, Randolph reached new peaks of intemperance and irrelevance. He served with Madison and Monroe in the Virginia constitutional convention of 1829–1830, where he persistently supported the overrepresentation of the eastern counties.

BIBLIOGRAPHY

Brant, Irving. *The Fourth President: A Life of James Madison.* 1970.

Bruce, William C. *John Randolph of Roanoke, 1773–1833.* 2 vols. 1922.

Dawidoff, Robert. *The Education of John Randolph.* 1979.

Ketcham, Ralph. *James Madison: A Biography.* 1971.

DONALD O. DEWEY

RELIGION, ESTABLISHMENTS OF.
When in 1789 Madison proposed to the First Federal Congress the amendments that became the Bill of Rights, the section on religion read: "The civil rights of none shall be abridged on account of religious belief or worship, nor shall any national religion be established, nor shall the full and existing rights of conscience be in any manner, or on any pretext, infringed." By "national" Madison meant the result of an act of Congress; he was distinguishing an act of the national government from that of a state. His next recommended amendment restricted state powers. In debate he declared, "Congress should not establish a religion." What did he mean by an establishment of religion?

At the Virginia ratifying convention in 1788 Madison declared that the people of Virginia opposed "any exclusive establishment" and added, "There is not a shadow of right in the general government to intermeddle with religion." Was a national religion an exclusive establishment of one religion by Congress? Madison's remarks must be understood in context. The previous speaker, Patrick Henry, had opposed ratification of the Constitution. Because the Constitution lacked a bill of rights, Henry claimed, Congress might establish one religion in preference to others. Madison replied that the worst fear, an exclusive establishment, would not materialize even if the Constitution lacked a bill of rights, because Congress had no power to act on the subject of religion.

In 1785 Madison had opposed Henry's general assessment bill, which would have required a tax for the support of the Christian religion or some Christian church, each person's tax to go to the church of his choice. The bill declared that all sects and denominations being equal before the law, none could be preferred over others. In effect it would have established all Protestant churches in the state, for there were few Jews or Catholics in Virginia at the time.

In Europe an establishment of religion meant a union between government and a single church, as in Catholic Spain, Lutheran states in Germany, or Anglican England. In America, however, single preferential establishments were disappearing and being replaced, in states that maintained establishments, by multiple nonpreferential establishments. Virginia had supported an exclusive establishment of the Anglican Church before 1776; thereafter, Madison opposed any public aid to religion, whether on a preferential or a nonpreferential basis. He repeatedly condemned Henry's proposal as an "establishment," the "ecclesiastical establishment," and "the establishment in question." Madison's opposition was not based on the fact that the bill failed to support Catholicism, Hinduism, and Judaism, as well as all Protestant denominations. He did not oppose it because it benefited only Protestantism. His "Memorial and Remonstrance" against the bill offered fifteen reasons for defeating the general assessment, none of which concerned the inclusiveness or exclusiveness of the proposed establishment, which he said differed from the Inquisition only in degree, not in principle. Madison argued that religion is a private voluntary affair not subject to government in any way; any public aid to religion violates religious freedom and threatens public liberty. Christianity did not stand in need of government support, which history showed would damage religion, and the government did not need the support of religion. Religion itself, as well as religious liberty, benefited from the absence of government aid. The public concerns of the state did not extend to matters of conscience.

In 1785 Madison led the fight to enact into law Jefferson's Virginia Statute of Religious Liberty, which provided, in part, that "no man shall be compelled to frequent or support any religious worship, place, or ministry whatsoever." Such compulsion or support constituted an establishment of religion. The statute became law in 1786, thanks to Madison's efforts.

In 1790 Madison argued that a census should omit the number of ministers because "the general government is proscribed from interfering, in any manner whatever, in matters respecting religion." As president, Madison vetoed a bill intended to remedy the unique situation of a church that had been built on federal land as a result of a surveying error. He saw a dangerous precedent in the bill because it appropriated funds for the church contrary to the First Amendment, "which declares that Congress shall make no law respecting a religious establishment." That the Father of the Bill of Rights in a formal veto misquoted the amendment shows his belief that the amendment prohibited Congress from making *any* law touching or respecting religious institutions. A "religious establishment" is a religious institution; it involves no government recognition or assistance as does an establishment of religion. Madison again misquoted the amendment in the same way when he vetoed a bill that would have incorporated a church in the District of Columbia, showing, once more, that he believed that even simple recognition without financial support constituted a violation of the amendment.

In his "Detached Memoranda," written some time after his retirement from the presidency in 1817, Madison denounced congressional chaplaincies as "an establishment of a national religion," contrary to the First Amendment. He classified chaplainships for the military "in the same way" as a prohibited "establishment of a national religion":

The Constitution of the U.S. forbids everything like an establishment of a national religion. The law appointing Chaplains establishes a religious worship for the national representatives, to be performed by Ministers of religion, elected by a majority of them, and these are to be paid out of the national taxes. Does not this involve the principle of a national establishment, applicable to a provision for a religious worship for the Constitutent as well as of the representative Body, approved by the majority, and conducted by Ministers of religion paid by the entire nation.

Obviously, a man who regarded as unconstitutional the use of public monies for nonpreferential, interfaith invocations and benedictions would consider as unconstitutional the use of public funds for any purpose respecting religion. The Constitution, he repeated, misquoting again, "forbids everything like an establishment of a national religion." And obviously, a man who believed that chaplains paid with public taxes constituted a national religion did not mean by national religion merely an exclusive establishment of one church. Madison also considered presidential proclamations "recommending fasts & thanksgivings" as examples "of a national religion."

Madison had been a member of the joint committee of the First Federal Congress that established congressional chaplaincies. The only indication of how he voted on that issue in 1790 derives from a letter of 1822 in which he said, speaking of "the immunity of religion from civil jurisdiction," that "it was not with my approbation, that the deviation from it took place in the Congress when they appointed Chaplains, to be paid from the National Treasury." Nevertheless, Madison violated consistency when as president he proclaimed days of fast and thanksgiving. In the same letter of 1822 he extenuated his inconsistency on the ground that he was president when a war was fought on national soil. Moreover, he said, he had merely recommended, rather than designated, the days of fast and thanksgiving when he had deviated from "strict principle." In the same letter he announced himself as favoring "a *perfect separation* between ecclesiastical and civil matters." He believed that exempting churches from taxation also violated the First Amendment.

Madison, in sum, believed that, even in the absence of the First Amendment, the United States lacked all authority over the subject of religion. Congress, therefore, was powerless to pass laws benefiting one religion or church in preference to others or benefiting all of them equally and impartially. The First Amendment reinforced that constitutional fact. In Madison's thinking, no circumstances existed that could legitimately or reasonably allow legislation that nonpreferentially assisted all religions.

[See also *Anglican Church; Memorial and Remonstrance*.]

BIBLIOGRAPHY

Alley, Robert S., ed. *James Madison on Religious Liberty*. 1985.
Curry, Thomas J. *The First Freedoms: Church and State in America to the Passage of the First Amendment*. 1986.
Levy, Leonard W. *The Establishment Clause: Religion and the First Amendment*. 1986.

LEONARD W. LEVY

REPUBLICANISM. In *Federalist* 39, as he began the long succession of related essays that would constitute his central contribution to the series, Madison posed the "first," most fundamental question to be asked about the Constitution: "whether the general form and aspect of the government be strictly republican?" "No other form," he wrote, "would be reconcilable with the genius of the people of America, with the fundamental principles of the Revolution, or with that honorable determination which animates every votary of freedom to rest all our political experiments on the capacity of mankind for self-government." Madison intended to convince his compatriots that the Federal Convention's plan was not just perfectly republican in form but also perfectly republican in "spirit"—indeed, that by providing a republican corrective for the problems most destructive to republics, the Constitution promised to redeem the great experiment in popular self-governance from the vices that disheartened its supporters and endangered its survival. With Antifederalists insisting that the remedy proposed by the convention was more dangerous than the disease, a firm assurance on these points was probably as critical for Madison himself as for the readers he was seeking to convince. A fixed determination to be sure that all American experiments were fundamentally consistent with republican objectives animated his entire career.

In eighteenth-century terminology, few words were more elastic or disputed. *Republic* had been used before the Revolution to describe the city-states of ancient Greece, the oligarchy of contemporary Holland, and even, on occasion, Britain's mixture of the one, the many, and the few. After 1776, nearly all Americans reserved the term for governments without hereditary parts, with all authority derived entirely from the people. But because societies or even policies could also seem consistent or at odds with the commitment to equality and popular consent, the word proved so flexible that nearly anything within the public realm (*res publica*) could be praised by calling it "republican" or condemned by not. To bring some clarity to this confusion was the task that Madison intended to accomplish.

In order to facilitate a close examination of the Constitution, the authors of *The Federalist* insisted on distinguishing between the modern, representative republics established in the states and the direct democracies of ancient Greece, in part because they wanted to reject the aristocratic overtones that Montesquieu and others included in classical republican thought. In *Federalist* 14, Madison defined a modern representative republic as a government in which the people do *not* "meet and exercise the government in person." Europe had invented representation, he exulted, but America could "claim the merit of making the discovery the basis of unmixed and extensive republics"—governments, that is, without a will or power independent of the people. (The argument is also advanced in *Federalist* 51.)

Few critics of the Constitution could have faulted Madison for insufficient rigor in his effort to define a genuine republic, since Americans never advocated anything except a representative regime. A republic, he began, "derives all its powers directly or indirectly from the great body of the people, and is administered by persons holding their offices during pleasure, for a limited period, or during good behavior." But in America at least, it was agreed that "it is *essential* to such a government that it be derived from the great body of the people, not from an inconsiderable proportion or a favored class of it," as was the case in Holland (No. 39). More than that, he argued, while a lasting and effective government required "stability and energy," which could be inconsistent with immediate responses to majority demands, "the genius of republican liberty" required "not only that all power should be derived from the people, but that those entrusted with it should be kept in dependence on the people by a short duration of their appointments, and that, even during this short period, the trust should be placed not in a few but in a number of hands" (No. 37).

Madison insisted that the Constitution would secure the requisite stability and energy without endangering the "genius" or the "spirit" of the system. The House of Representatives would be elected by the body of the people, and any adult male might serve. The representatives would enter office with affection for the voters; before that sentiment had been effaced, they would face the prospect of a new election. The president and the Senate would be chosen indirectly and for longer terms of office, providing some restraint on the majority's immediate desires. But after all the checks and balances had been applied, the product of successive distillations of the people's will was still to be the well-considered wishes of the people.

Indeed, the Constitution offered every guarantee of a "diffusive sympathy" between the rulers and the ruled that human ingenuity could possibly contrive, every safeguard for official faithfulness that any true republican could wish. For, in the end, a true republican relied upon the people, whose vigilance and public spirit were the ultimate securities for any free regime. "As there is a degree of depravity in mankind which requires a certain degree of circumspection and distrust, so there are other qualities in human nature which justify a certain portion of esteem and confidence. Republican government presupposes the existence of these qualities in a higher degree than any other form" (No. 55).

To Madison, however (as would become increasingly apparent after the adoption of the Constitution), "the vigilant and manly spirit which actuates the people of America, a spirit which nourishes freedom and in return is nourished by it" (*Federalist* 57), had preconditions of its own. Sound republics, he believed, are incompatible with huge disparities between the wealthy and the poor, which foster undue influence on the one side and an unrepublican dependence on the other. The archetypal citizen of a republic was the independent farmer-owner, who did not depend on any other individual for the necessities of life and, by that fact, was free to vote (or even to defend his liberty by force of arms) according to his own autonomous desires. As with Thomas Jefferson, Madison, the most important Framer and defender of the Constitution, came to be increasingly disturbed about the consequences for the revolutionary order of the policies of Washington's (or Hamilton's) administration. "Republicanism" also had a Jeffersonian agrarian dimension to it.

On the other hand, Hamiltonian finance, as Madison conceived it, forged corrupting links between the federal government and special-interest, moneyed factions dependent on the federal treasury or on a national bank for the promotion of their interests. Thus, government programs enriched a moneyed few at popular expense. Federal encouragement of manufacturing and commerce, if permitted, would compound the unrepublican disparities between the many and the few, and broad construction of the Constitution would encourage an increasing concentration of authority in federal hands and in the governmental branches least responsive to the people. All of this was incompatible with a republican regime.

After 1800 Jefferson and Madison pursued a very different course. Hamilton had hoped to foster rapid and intensive economic change. In contrast, Republican administrations were intent on securing world markets for the country's agricultural producers, even at the risk of confrontation with Great Britain. In combination with expansion to the west, these open markets, they assumed, would guarantee that a republic resting on the sturdy stock of independent farmers would be constantly revitalized as it expanded over space.

Hamilton had hoped to found a potent nation-state. Jefferson and Madison were determined to retire the national debt, reduce taxation, and confine the federal government to the responsibilities that they believed had been intended by the Constitution. After 1800, as before, as president and even during his retirement, Madison remained intent on the objective that had guided him throughout the founding of the federal republic. The underlying theme of his forty years of active public life—the single theme that best explains his career's many twists and turns—was his determination to perpetuate the Revolution.

[See also *Constitution Making; Constitution of 1787; Federalist, The.*]

BIBLIOGRAPHY

Banning, Lance. *The Jeffersonian Persuasion: Evolution of a Party Ideology.* 1978.
Cooke, Jacob E., ed. *The Federalist.* 1961.
McCoy, Drew R. *The Elusive Republic: Political Economy in Jeffersonian America.* 1980.
McCoy, Drew R. *The Last of the Fathers: James Madison and the Republican Legacy.* 1989.
Rahe, Paul A. *Republics Ancient and Modern: Classical Republicanism and the American Revolution.* 1992.
Wood, Gordon S. *The Creation of the American Republic, 1776–1787.* 1969.

LANCE BANNING

REPUBLICAN PARTY. At the time of the adoption of the Constitution of the United States, most of the founders of the American republic looked upon political parties as dangerous evils to be avoided. During the nation's first decade under the Constitution, however, two national political parties formed and adopted the names Federalist and Republican. Champions of President George Washington's administration used the name Federalist, which had identified supporters of the Constitution, and sought to label all opposition as Antifederalist. Claiming equal allegiance to the Constitution and to a federal form of government, members of the emerging opposition called themselves Republicans to emphasize their commitment to the new republic.

The earliest partisan alignments emerged in Congress and coincided with a growing division in Washington's cabinet between Secretary of State Thomas Jefferson and Secretary of the Treasury Alexander Hamilton. Although Jefferson had cooperated with Hamilton's early efforts to establish the financial stability and national credit of the new government, he broke openly with Hamilton over the plan to create a national bank. When Washington asked both Jefferson and Hamilton to provide written opinions on the constitutional power of Congress to establish a national bank, Hamilton justified such a step on the ground of implied powers, whereas Jefferson applied strict construction to the Constitution and found no power to create banks.

This was but one of the numerous policies on which Jefferson and Hamilton differed. In foreign affairs, Hamilton favored closer ties to Great Britain; Jefferson was sympathetic to the French Revolution and to the French Republic that was proclaimed while he was secretary of state. Before Washington's first term ended, Jefferson and Hamilton were differing on almost everything. It is tempting to see political parties emerging solely from this conflict, but the Republican opposition had a broader base. In Congress a group formed around Madison in opposition to Hamilton's policies and in support of Jefferson's positions. Jefferson and others referred to the "republican interest" in Congress, and this group became the base from which the Republican party gradually formed throughout the nation. In the origins of the early Republican party, Madison was as important as Jefferson.

By 1792 Republicans were strong enough to challenge the reelection of John Adams as vice president. Though not able to deny Adams reelection, Republicans marshaled a substantial vote for Gov. George Clinton of New York. By 1796, when Washington decided to retire at the end of his second term, party divisions were sharp enough to produce a close contest between Adams and Jefferson to succeed Washington, though neither man campaigned for the office. Indeed, Jefferson, who had retired as secretary of state at the end of 1793, seemed reluctant to leave Monticello to return to politics. Adams's victory over Jefferson by only three electoral votes, however, brought Jefferson—elected vice president—back into national political life and stimulated the Republican party to increased activity.

As the election of 1800 approached, Republicans were increasingly active in creating party organizations in various states. They conducted a vigorous campaign in 1800 to challenge Adams's bid for reelection and to elect Jefferson as president. Republicans also worked to elect a Republican majority in Congress to replace the Federalist majority that had built up the military forces in response to a threatened war with France, raised taxes, passed the alien and sedition laws, and tightened naturalization laws.

The election of 1800, a hard-fought party contest between the Federalists and the Republicans, demonstrated that the Republican party was well organized in a number of states and effective in conducting a national campaign. In Virginia, Republicans set up a state party committee, as well as creating committees in most counties throughout the state. In New Jersey, Republicans created township and county committees. Unlike 1796, when Jefferson did nothing to promote his election, in 1800 Jefferson was active in writing letters, seeing that party literature was distributed, and encouraging his supporters to work for the Republican cause. Jefferson became the Republican nominee for president by consensus, and Republican members of Congress, in a nominating caucus, selected Aaron Burr as their candidate for vice president. (Burr received the nomination as a reward for organizing the Republican victory in New York City that ensured Republicans a majority in the New York legislature, which would choose the state's presidential electors. Burr's nomination also strengthened the Republican New York–Virginia alliance that went back to 1792, when Virginians supported Clinton for vice president.)

The congressional nominating caucus would assume the function of nominating presidential and vice presidential candidates of the Republican party until 1824, and until 1824 the nominees of the Republican nominating caucus would be elected president.

In the election of 1800, the Republicans appealed to voters who sought change. The party had a diverse constituency, but Jefferson's appeal to the agrarian interest was strong, whereas the Federalist party was supported by the banking, manufacturing, and commercial interests represented by Hamilton's economic programs. Although Jefferson was no friend of banks or manufacturers, he was supportive of commerce. The Republican party also appealed to artisans and workers in cities, where Jefferson was hailed as a man of the people. Republicans presented their party as the party of the people and pictured the Federalist party as the friend of the rich and powerful, who were distrustful of the people.

By 1800, party loyalty within Republican ranks was stronger than even party leaders expected, and the party was embarrassed when every presidential elector who voted for Jefferson also voted for Aaron Burr, the vice presidential nominee. Prior to 1804, electors each cast two votes without distinguishing between president and vice president; the candidate coming in second became vice president. Because Jefferson and Burr received the same number of electoral votes, the election went to the House of Representatives, where it took thirty-six ballots to resolve the deadlock and elect Jefferson president.

The Republican party under President Jefferson became an important tool in his administration of the executive office. The Republicans had a majority in both houses of Congress, and Jefferson was both the president and the head of the party. By Jefferson's second term, as Federalist strength faded, Republican party unity also weakened, and after Madison succeeded Jefferson as president, divisions within the party mounted. Though party affiliation was the major influence in the vote for the declaration of war against Great Britain in 1812, Madison's bid for reelection was challenged by a fellow Republican, De Witt Clinton of New York.

Federalist opposition to the War of 1812 and, especially, the Federalist-led Hartford Convention signaled the demise of the Federalist party as a national force. By the time Monroe succeeded Madison as president in 1817, the Republican party had no significant national opposition, and Monroe joined others in proclaiming a new era of good feelings in which party divisions would fade away. By the beginning of Monroe's second term, the Republican party as a unified national force had largely vanished, replaced by factions that supported various contenders to succeed Monroe as president. The congressional nominating caucus met and nominated William

H. Crawford for the presidency in 1824, but the caucus nomination no longer had the influence of earlier years. In the new party system that emerged in the 1820s, the Jacksonian Democrats claimed the heritage of the Jeffersonian Republican party, thus enabling the modern Democratic party to trace its origins to the early Republican party formed while Washington was president.

[See also *Democratic-Republican Societies; Federalist Party; Republicanism.*]

BIBLIOGRAPHY

Appleby, Joyce. *Capitalism and a New Social Order: The Republican Vision of the 1790s.* 1984.
Banning, Lance. *The Jeffersonian Persuasion: Evolution of a Party Ideology.* 1978.
Cunningham, Noble E., Jr. *In Pursuit of Reason: The Life of Thomas Jefferson.* 1987.
Cunningham, Noble E., Jr. *The Jeffersonian Republicans: The Formation of Party Organization, 1789–1801.* 1957.
Cunningham, Noble E., Jr. *The Jeffersonian Republicans in Power: Party Operations, 1801–1809.* 1963.

NOBLE E. CUNNINGHAM, JR.

RIPLEY, ELEAZAR WHEELOCK (1782–1839), soldier, representative. Born in Hanover, New Hampshire, the grandson of Eleazar Wheelock, the founder of Dartmouth College, Ripley graduated from Dartmouth in 1800, read law, and opened a practice in Maine. He was elected to the Massachusetts legislature in 1807 as a Jeffersonian and served several terms, including one as Speaker of the House (1811).

Ripley was a state senator in 1812 when Madison appointed him a lieutenant colonel in the U.S. Army. He was promoted the next year and led a regiment in the attack on York, Ontario, in April 1813 and in the capture of Fort George. Following the disappointments of the 1813 campaign, Secretary of War John Armstrong cleaned house, appointing a number of younger men to leadership positions in the army. Ripley was made a brigadier general and attached to Maj. Gen. Jacob Brown's army at Niagara. There, in 1814, he fought in the battles of Chippewa and Lundy's Lane and participated in the siege of Fort Erie, where he was severely wounded. At Lundy's Lane, Brown accused Ripley of failing to secure the battlefield after the British had retreated; Ripley maintained that he was only following Brown's orders. The dispute was not resolved until 1815, when Congress voted Ripley its thanks and a gold medal. Ripley remained in the army until 1820, when he began to practice law in Louisiana. He was elected to the House of Representatives in 1834 as a Jacksonian and was reelected in 1836. He died while in office.

BIBLIOGRAPHY

Baylies, Nicholas. *Eleazar Wheelock Ripley, of the War of 1812.* 1890.
Elting, John R. *Amateurs, to Arms!: A Military History of the War of 1812.* 1991.
Johnson, Allen, ed. *Dictionary of American Biography.* 1928.

DAVID B. MATTERN

RITCHIE, THOMAS (1778–1854), editor, publisher, political leader. A member of a prominent Virginia family, Thomas Ritchie entered journalism in May 1804, when he founded *The Enquirer* at Richmond as the voice of the Virginia Republican party. In his political principles and in his vision of the press as an agency for public education, he was a disciple of Thomas Jefferson, who in 1823 called Ritchie's newspaper "the best that is published or ever has been published in America." The Richmond paper (renamed the *Richmond Enquirer* in 1815) circulated throughout the state, but its influence was even broader, for its editorials and articles were reprinted throughout the nation as party gospel.

Ritchie supported the presidential administration of James Madison as he had supported that of Jefferson. An advocate of party unity, he strongly criticized dissident Republicans who accused Madison of being too sympathetic to Federalist principles. However, after 1819, when Ritchie began to promote a more rigid states' rights position that opposed the "consolidating" tendencies of the federal government, Madison and Ritchie clashed over the interpretation of the Constitution. While Madison did oppose the actions of the federal government that alarmed Ritchie, he saw them as abuses of legitimate powers, rather than as unconstitutional acts, and he feared that the states' rights movement would undermine the federal compact. He first tried to sway Ritchie and other like-minded Republicans, including Jefferson, through private letters, but in 1828 he made public his position on the constitutionality of the federal tariff. Ritchie disagreed politely in his editorials, but he opened his newspaper to writers who attacked Madison more forcefully.

On other public issues of the 1820s and 1830s, especially the need for state support of the University of Virginia, Ritchie and Madison generally agreed. Ritchie was a leader in forming the Jacksonian Democratic party and remained a force in national politics until the end of his life.

BIBLIOGRAPHY

Ellis, Richard E. *Jacksonian Democracy, States' Rights, and the Nullification Crisis.* 1987.
McCoy, Drew R. *The Last of the Fathers: James Madison and the Republican Legacy.* 1989.

Richmond Enquirer. 1804–1856.

STEVEN H. HOCHMAN

RIVER RAISIN, BATTLES OF.

RIVER RAISIN, BATTLES OF.   The military engagements in southeastern Michigan on 18 and 21 January 1813, also known as the Battles of River Rasin, were part of an attempt by the United States to regain Detroit through a winter campaign. Early in 1813 Maj. Gen. William Henry Harrison advanced his troops from southern Ohio toward Michigan. His advance party of untrained regulars and volunteers, mostly from Kentucky, was led by Brig. Gen. James Winchester, a regular army officer who thought he, not Harrison, should be in command. Directed to stop at the Maumee Rapids (west of modern Toledo), Winchester instead advanced to the hamlet of Frenchtown (modern Monroe, Michigan), where he dispersed a small British detachment on 18 January 1813. Winchester failed to send out scouts or set up security outposts, and casually deployed his troops throughout the village located along the River Raisin.

Upon learning of the situation, British Lt. Col. Henry Procter at Fort Malden, located near the mouth of the Detroit River, decided to counterattack. Taking all the forces he could muster from Malden and Detroit, Procter crossed the frozen Detroit River to Brownstown with his artillery. Procter also commanded a band of Wyandot Indians headed by Chief Roundhead so that his total force reached approximately 1,300, compared to Winchester's 934. In addition, his artillery gave Procter superior firepower.

On 21 January a combination of artillery fire and Indian attack crushed the hastily formed American right and led to Winchester's capture as he sought to reach his forces from his comfortable quarters some distance from the battlefield. Although his troops were still giving a good account of themselves, Winchester surrendered in order to avoid a massacre of his troops. Nonetheless, of the Americans engaged, only thirty-three escaped death or capture. When Procter withdrew twenty-five miles to Brownstown, he left wounded Americans in Frenchtown under Indian guards, who soon executed between thirty and sixty (depending upon the source) of the prisoners. The incident led American newspapers to label the engagement the "River Raisin Massacre."

Winchester's surrender canceled Harrison's winter offensive. Instead, he began constructing a defensive and logistical outpost at the Maumee Rapids known as Fort Meigs. "Remember the River Raisin" became a western rallying cry, but Winchester's misconduct only increased antiregular sentiment among frontiersmen. Procter was rewarded with a brigadier generalship, but his inability to control the Indians brought severe censure upon him by many of his own officers.

BIBLIOGRAPHY

Au, Dennis. *War on the Raisin.* 1981.
Carter-Edwards, Dennis. "The War of 1812 along the Detroit Frontier: A Canadian Perspective." *Michigan Historical Review* 13 (1987): 25–50.
Clift, G. Glen. *Remember the Raisin.* 1961.
Gilpin, Alex. *The War of 1812 in the Old Northwest.* 1958.
Stanley, George F. G. *The War of 1812: Land Operations.* 1983.

DAVID CURTIS SKAGGS

RIVES, WILLIAM CABELL

RIVES, WILLIAM CABELL   (1793–1868), Virginia planter, politician, biographer of Madison. W. C. Rives was a prominent figure in American politics during the Jacksonian era, serving as a representative and a senator from Virginia as well as minister to France. The evolution of his political ideas was decisively shaped by Madison's influence during the late 1820s. Madison's tutoring of Rives on the tariff issue paved the way for Rives's emergence as a Jacksonian Unionist during the nullification crisis of 1832–1833. Rives's strong stance against John C. Calhoun and the South Carolina nullifiers, consistent with Madison's public position, separated him from more

W. C. RIVES.   Lithograph by Charles Fenderich, 1839.
PRINTS AND PHOTOGRAPHS DIVISION, LIBRARY OF CONGRESS.

extreme advocates of states' rights in Virginia for many years to come. Indeed, his strong bond with Madison, which developed during the elder statesman's final decade of life, affected Rives's private and public career throughout the antebellum and Civil War years.

Rives self-consciously attempted to uphold Madison's legacy in many areas, most notably as a defender of the Union created by the Constitution. By the 1850s Rives's influence in Virginia and national politics had significantly eroded, which contributed to his decision to quit politics and become an editor-historian. Working with Madison's papers, he constructed a flattering, filiopietistic portrait of his mentor that was designed both to instruct and to rebuke the present generation of demagogic Democrats who were blundering their way toward disunion and civil war.

Ironically, Rives, who resisted secession in Virginia until the final moment of President Lincoln's call for troops, reentered politics as a member of the Confederate Congress. His biography of Madison, which reached three volumes, remained unfinished at his death in 1868.

BIBLIOGRAPHY

Dingledine, Raymond C. "The Education of a Virginia Planter's Son." In *America: The Middle Period; Essays in Honor of Bernard Mayo.* Edited by John B. Boles. 1973.
McCoy, Drew R. *The Last of the Fathers: James Madison and the Republican Legacy.* 1989.

DREW R. MCCOY

ROANE, SPENCER (1762–1822), judge of the General Court of Virginia, judge of the Virginia Supreme Court of Appeals. There is an apocryphal story that holds that Roane would have been appointed chief justice of the U.S. Supreme Court if President Adams had delayed longer in the appointment of John Marshall and left the position to be filled by President Jefferson. Jefferson came to appreciate Roane, but, as Patrick Henry's son-in-law, Roane was an unlikely candidate for a warm reception by Jefferson or Madison in 1801.

Madison had worked with Roane in Virginia politics over several decades. Roane was Madison's ally in the campaign for religious freedom in 1784, when they were together in the Virginia House of Delegates. Roane voted against his future father-in-law on the bill to incorporate the Episcopal Church and on the assessment to support churches. (Ironically, the incorporation bill was one of the rare occasions when Madison and Henry voted together, for Madison temporarily supported incorporation as a strategy to head off the assessment bill.) Roane stood between Madison and Henry in the Virginia ratification convention of 1788. He opposed ratification of the Constitution largely because of the lack of a bill of rights, but he was no advocate of the Articles of Confederation. Roane's principal contribution to the convention probably was his sarcastic criticism of Gov. Edmund Randolph's inconsistency in his public statements.

Roane was an admirer of the Virginia and Kentucky Resolutions, though the terminal illness of his wife in 1799 kept him from actively supporting them in public. When he learned that Washington had persuaded Henry to return to state politics to oppose Madison's Virginia Resolutions, Roane hastily informed James Monroe that his chagrin at his father-in-law's political conversion had "given place to an ardent desire on my part, to counteract him, by every means tending to defeat his schemes." Roane added that he hoped that Monroe and "your illustrious friend Madison will not hesitate in coming into the legislature." Roane's writings, both on and off the bench, contain frequent references to the Resolutions, which came to form the core of his political philosophy. Madison's Virginia Resolutions he praised as "the Magna Carta on which the Republic settled down after the great struggle in the year 1799." Roane was also a strong supporter of Madison's presidential candidacies, both in 1808 and in 1812.

Roane favored an influential federal judiciary, but he consistently opposed John Marshall's expansive use of judicial nationalism and insisted that the federal judiciary could not overturn decisions of state courts. When Roane became a political essayist in response primarily to Marshall's *McCulloch* v. *Maryland* (1819) and *Cohens* v. *Virginia* (1821) decisions, he turned to Madison for support, describing him as "the only certain antidote to the ingenious and fatal sophistries of Marshall. Other and inferior pens may no doubt take up the subject; but to yours an universal homage would be paid." Whereas Jefferson publicly supported Roane's essay (signed "Algernon Sidney"), Madison cautiously expressed his concern that its principles might make the Constitution "different in every State." But Madison agreed with Roane's "Hampden" essay, which held that Marshall's "latitudinarian mode of expounding the Constitution" was inappropriate (Madison added that state claims must yield to federal supremacy). Madison, like many other Republicans, agreed with Marshall's rulings but disliked the obiter dicta that Marshall used to arrive at them. Shortly before he died, Roane served with Madison on the commission planning the University of Virginia.

BIBLIOGRAPHY

Brant, Irving. *James Madison: Commander in Chief, 1812–1836.* 1961.
Horsnell, Margaret E. *Spencer Roane: Judicial Advocate of Jeffersonian Principles.* 1986.

DONALD O. DEWEY

RODGERS, JOHN (1772–1838), U.S. naval officer. A native of Havre de Grace, Maryland, Rodgers entered the navy in 1798 after several years in merchantmen. He was released from service when the navy was reduced in size in 1800 and returned to the merchant service.

With the outbreak of the Barbary Wars, Rodgers commanded first the frigate *John Adams* and then the frigate *Congress* in the Mediterranean. When Commodore Samuel Barron's health failed, he reluctantly yielded command of the squadron to the ambitious Rodgers, who forced the bey of Tunis to grant the United States most-favored-nation status.

Almost simultaneously, the bashaw (pasha) of Tripoli signed the treaty that ended the war on 3 June 1805. Rodgers's exercise of naval force and Tobias Lear's conciliatory diplomacy combined to bring a temporary peace for the United States in the frustrating Barbary Wars. Rodgers returned home in 1806, having commanded USS *Constitution* off Tripoli and Tunis.

From 1808 to 1812, Rodgers commanded the squadron that enforced the embargo of foreign trade. In 1811, as commander of the *President*, Rodgers fought a night action against the *Little Belt*, a ship half *President*'s size. Rodgers claimed that he could not discover the ship's size or name and that *Little Belt* fired first. A court-martial found Rodgers blameless, but the episode exacerbated the relations between the two navies and many U.S. naval officers felt that *Chesapeake* had been avenged.

With the declaration of war in 1812, Rodgers immediately set sail with his squadron in search of British merchantmen. His squadron spent two months cruising but returned to Boston with but few prizes, though, from a strategic viewpoint, the existence of the American squadron had compelled the few British ships on station to combine, thereby weakening their blockade of American ports. During 1813, Rodgers's *President*, in company with the frigate *Congress*, made two more cruises that took him as far as the North Cape of Norway and to the Caribbean. Returning to New York in February 1814, Rodgers was offered the new frigate *Guerrière*, under construction at Philadelphia. When the British launched their attacks on Washington, Alexandria, and Baltimore in August 1814, Rodgers assisted in the defense of the capital, bringing with him three hundred sailors. Rodgers constructed fire ships on the Potomac to harass the British squadron that looted Alexandria and then assisted Gen. Samuel Smith in strengthening the seaward defenses of Baltimore and Fort McHenry.

After the war, President Madison recognized the need to strengthen the navy by creating a staff of professional advisers to assist Secretary of the Navy Benjamin Crowninshield in technical decisions. When the Board of Navy Commissioners was created in February 1815, Rodgers

JOHN RODGERS.   Portrait by Charles Willson Peale.
PRINTS AND PHOTOGRAPHS DIVISION, LIBRARY OF CONGRESS.

became its first president. In 1824, he was chosen to initiate discussions of a commercial treaty with Turkey. In late 1827, Rodgers was restored to the Board of Navy Commissioners and continued to dominate that body as it cautiously considered innovations such as the use of the exploding shell and steam power in the fleet. During a cholera epidemic that hit Washington in 1832, Rodgers was afflicted and never recovered. His health gradually deteriorated and he died at the Philadelphia Naval Asylum on 1 August 1838.

BIBLIOGRAPHY

Bauer, K. Jack. "John Rodgers: The Stalwart Conservative." In *Command under Sail: Makers of the American Naval Tradition, 1775–1850.* Edited by James C. Bradford. 1985.

Paullin, Charles O. *Commodore John Rodgers: Captain, Commodore, and Senior Officer of the American Navy, 1773–1838.* 1910.

WILLIAM S. DUDLEY

RODNEY, CAESAR A. (1772–1824), Delaware lawyer, attorney general of the United States. Rodney

CAESAR RODNEY.

was born in Dover and admitted to the bar in 1793. He served in the Delaware House of Representatives from 1796 until 1802, when he was elected to the U.S. House of Representatives as a Republican. On 20 January 1807 he joined President Thomas Jefferson's cabinet as attorney general, a part-time office that allowed him to live and practice law in Wilmington.

When James Madison became president in 1809, he retained Rodney as attorney general. Rodney's most significant achievement came in the first months of Madison's administration, when the president sent him to Pennsylvania to represent the United States in resolving the federal-state imbroglio over the Olmstead case. During the American Revolution, Gideon Olmstead and other American prisoners aboard a British sloop had overpowered their captors and were taking the ship into port as a prize when the vessel was seized by a state-owned Pennsylvania ship and sold, with the proceeds going to the state. As the real captor, Olmstead sued the state of Pennsylvania and won, but Pennsylvania then defied the Continental Congress and its Court of Appeals, as well as an 1803 decision by a federal district court.

On the eve of Madison's inauguration in 1809, after thirty-two years of litigation, the U.S. Supreme Court issued a mandamus directing Pennsylvania to pay the prize money to Olmstead. On 25 March 1809 state troops under Gen. Michael Bright prevented the federal marshal from serving a writ on the state treasurer, and Madison dispatched Rodney to see that the U.S. writ prevailed. The president explained that he was "expressly enjoined, by statute, to carry into effect any such decree where opposition may be made to it." Pennsylvania then complied with the order and paid the prize money to Olmstead.

Reacting to criticism that he had not moved from Wilmington to Washington, Rodney in 1811 shipped his furniture and law library by sea, but they were lost when the ship was wrecked off the Eastern Shore of Virginia. On 5 December 1811 Rodney resigned and returned to Delaware.

BIBLIOGRAPHY

Brant, Irving. *James Madison, The President: 1809–1812*. 1956.
Munroe, John A. *Federalist Delaware, 1775–1815*. 1954.

JAMES MORTON SMITH

ROSE, GEORGE HENRY (1771–1855), British diplomat and politician. Rose, the son of a government official, was named first secretary of the British embassy at the Hague in 1792 and in 1793 went to Berlin, where he was also chargé d'affaires. From 1794 to 1813 he was a member of Parliament. In 1813 he was appointed minister at Munich and was later transferred to Berlin. In 1818 he returned to Parliament, where he served until 1844.

In 1807 Rose was sent as envoy to the United States to negotiate the settlement of the *Chesapeake* affair, the latest in a series of incidents stemming from the behavior of British naval commanders in American waters. In June 1807 the frigate *Leopard*, while searching for deserters, had attacked the American warship *Chesapeake* off Cape Henry, Virginia, wounding eighteen men, killing three, and forcibly removing four crew members. As indignant Americans cried out for war, President Jefferson issued a proclamation, heavily edited by James Madison, barring British warships from American ports. Madison demanded British disavowal of the action, restoration of the crewmen, and payment of reparations, as well as an immediate end to the impressment of American seamen.

Rose arrived in Washington in January 1808 with instructions that forbade any discussion of impressment. The British were willing to disavow the action and forgo their pretensions to take deserters from American warships, but insisted that the proclamation be recalled before reparations could be discussed. Madison suggested that the recall of the proclamation and the preliminary agreement to discuss reparations could take place the same day, thus removing the issue of priority. Rose agreed but then began releasing details of other British demands that implied that the *Chesapeake*'s commander bore some responsibility for the incident. When Madison rejected these new demands as unwarranted, Rose returned to England in March 1808 and the issue remained unsettled until 1810.

BIBLIOGRAPHY

Brant, Irving. *James Madison.* Vol. 4. 1941.
Dictionary of National Biography. Vol. 17. 1950.
Malone, Dumas. *Jefferson and His Time.* Vol. 5. 1948.

MARY A. HACKETT

ROSS, ROBERT (1766–1814), British major general. In the spring of 1814, the British ministry, hoping to divert American troops from the Canadian theater of war, ordered Gen. Ross to lead a combined military and naval assault on the Atlantic coast of the United States. By August, Ross's four thousand-man force had reached the Chesapeake Bay. After sailing up the Patuxent River, Ross landed at Benedict, Maryland, on 19 August. While the British fleet cleared the waterway of American shipping, Ross rapidly marched to within a dozen miles of Washington, D.C. At Bladensburg, Ross found the road to the capital blocked by three poorly deployed lines of American militia, totaling perhaps seven thousand troops, which Gen. William H. Winder had hastily assembled. The defenders were joined by President Madison, who rode out to rally the troops and to survey the situation firsthand.

On 24 August Ross attacked, driving the Americans back toward Washington. Realizing that defeat was imminent, Madison hurriedly returned to the White House. Finding that his wife had already fled, Madison also escaped across the Potomac. The British arrived in the city only a few hours after the commander in chief's hasty departure. Ross noted that "so unexpected was our entry and capture of Washington, and so confident was Madison of the defeat of our troops, that he had prepared a supper for the expected conquerors; and when our advanced party entered the President's house, they found a table laid with forty covers." After helping themselves to the waiting dinner, Ross and Adm. George Cockburn torched the public buildings. The next day, 25 August, the British abandoned the federal district. Two weeks later, the British struck Baltimore. During preliminary skirmishing, Ross received a mortal wound from an American sharpshooter. Before his men could remove him to the British fleet, he was dead.

BIBLIOGRAPHY

Dictionary of National Biography. 1928.
Hickey, Donald R. *The War of 1812: A Forgotten Conflict.* 1989.
Ketcham, Ralph. *James Madison: A Biography.* 1971.

STUART LEIBIGER

ROYAL NAVY. At the outset of the War of 1812 the Royal Navy concentrated on the strategic task of containing Napoleon's ambitions and ability to utilize the 122 battleships and 85 frigates ready for sea at various ports around the coast of Europe. The British had 584 cruising warships in sea service, with another 39 on service reserve, for a total of 623 vessels. An additional 355 vessels were in harbor duty or ordinary (reserve), or building. A building program in 1812 and 1813 increased naval strength by almost 15 percent in varying classes of ships, from one-hundred-gun ships to eighteen-gun ships. Fleet concentrations in the Mediterranean were from 112 to 120 vessels; off the Texel, from 57 to 60 vessels; off the Scheldt estuary and the approaches to Antwerp, 35 vessels; in the Baltic, 62 vessels; and in the North Sea and the western channel patrol grounds, from 37 to 40 vessels. Smaller squadrons operated overseas, and the navy also supported Wellington's campaign in the Iberian peninsula.

The American declaration of war on 18 June 1812 created significant additional naval responsibilities. The new naval theater was huge. Off Newfoundland were one frigate, two sloops, and one gunbrig. At Halifax the North American squadron was commanded by Rear Adm. Herbert Sawyer. A branch of the British army operated the Canadian Provincial Marine on the Great Lakes and the Saint Lawrence River. In the Caribbean, the navy had 25 vessels off Jamaica and 31 off the Leeward Islands. Neutralizing French vessels in French and Dutch ports, keeping Russian vessels out of French hands, ensuring the neutrality of the Swedish and Turkish forces, and, after 18 June 1812, preventing the small but efficient American navy and large numbers of privateers from disrupting British ocean commerce were the Royal Navy's main tasks. In the western Atlantic theater, that meant containing the American attempt to overrun British control of the northern provinces before adequate reinforcements arrived and protecting British trade routes. The Royal Navy protected West Indian convoys of from 100 to 200 ships as they sailed to England three times a year, as well as numerous smaller Quebec and Newfoundland convoys on the run across the Atlantic. An American sea frontier of more than 3,500 coastal miles was patrolled in 1812 and partially blockaded in 1813. (This total represented a larger coastline, extending some 1,200 miles farther north, than that patrolled by the Union navy during the Civil War and does not include the Saint Lawrence and the Great Lakes, which the Royal Navy also monitored.) Early American sweeps in 1812 led to the capture of one British frigate, the destruction of two others, and the loss of three sloops. In each case the more heavily armed and larger American vessels prevailed.

DEATH OF ROBERT ROSS.   Print published by T. Kunnersley, 1816.

GEORGE III BAKING SHIPS.   John Bull, who strongly resembles George III, and his helpers bake ships to replace those destroyed by the Americans on the Great Lakes in 1813 and 1814. Etching by the American artist William Charles, 1814.

PRINTS AND PHOTOGRAPHS DIVISION, LIBRARY OF CONGRESS.

In September 1812 Adm. Sir John Borlase Warren combined the Halifax, Jamaica, and Leeward Island stations, and a party of 460 men under Sir James Lucas Yeo was sent in March 1813 to man the ships of the Canadian Provincial Marine on the Great Lakes. Based at Halifax and Bermuda, Warren fought a defensive war to relieve pressure on the Canadas from September 1812 to April 1814. Not a convoy was lost or successfully attacked. In summer 1813 Warren extended the blockade from the Chesapeake to New York and supported small raiding parties in the Chesapeake under Rear Adm. Sir George Cockburn. After 1 June 1813, when the British frigate *Shannon* captured the American *Chesapeake*, the Royal Navy shut down American raiders. It later captured two more American frigates and burned two others. Additional ships were blockaded for the duration of the war. Early in 1813, the American navy laid up ships and sent

their crews to the Great Lakes. After an extensive American building program initiated by the Madison administration, Robert H. Barclay's inferior British squadron on Lake Erie, outgunned and manned mainly with troops from the Forty-first and Royal Newfoundland regiments, was defeated by Oliver Hazard Perry's more powerful force on 10 September 1813.

In January 1814 the maritime forces on the Great Lakes, the Saint Lawrence, and Lake Champlain were brought under Admiralty jurisdiction. Reinforcements were sent to Yeo, who made the contest a holding action and a shipbuilding war while working closely with army forces in Upper Canada. Warren was eventually relieved by Vice Adm. Sir Alexander Cochrane in April 1814, and the combined stations were separated. A close blockade of the American coast was extended to include New England after the summer of 1814, and an embargo severely hampered American ocean commerce except for that allowed under British licenses.

By summer 1814 the Admiralty had six flag officers on the American coast. They were Rear Adm. Edward Griffith at Halifax and Rear Admirals Sir George Cockburn, Pulteney Malcolm, Edward Codrington, and Henry Hotham serving under Cochrane. With over 100 vessels, Cochrane's aggressive campaign used two raiding squadrons in the Chesapeake under Cockburn and Sir Robert Barrie, and, after August 1814, combined operations with 2,300 soldiers and 800 marines supported by 25 warships of various classes and 25 transports and storeships. In August and September 1814, Washington was captured, the public buildings burned, and President Madison and his cabinet forced to flee the city. A successful attack and capture of shipping at Alexandria by Capt. Charles Gordon in August and an unsuccessful attack on Baltimore by Admiral Cochrane and Col. Arthur Brook completed operations.

On Lake Champlain in September 1814 an ill-conceived British invasion of the Champlain River valley by Sir George Prevost, commander in chief in the Canadas, was turned back after the defeat of Capt. George Downie's hastily improvised British naval squadron by Master Commandant Thomas Macdonough's squadron (11 September 1814). However, the Royal Navy's retention of Lake Ontario and the Saint Lawrence and increasing British reinforcements after the fall of Napoleon in April 1814 denied Madison the war goal of capturing the Canadas.

The last major combined operation of the war, a landing at New Orleans supported by 8,000 troops sent out from Bordeaux, failed. Cochrane had extensive plans to continue the war along the Gulf, the southern Atlantic, and the Chesapeake coasts in 1815 when peace was ratified in February 1815.

BIBLIOGRAPHY

Drake, Frederick C. *The War of 1812: Naval Operations.* Forthcoming.

Dudley, William S., ed. *The Naval War of 1812.* Vol. 1. 1985. Vol. 2. 1992.

Hickey, Donald R. *The War of 1812: A Forgotten Conflict.* 1989.

Mahan, Alfred Thayer. *Sea Power in Its Relations to the War of 1812.* Vols. 1 and 2. 1905.

Welsh, William J., and David C. Skaggs, eds. *War on the Great Lakes: Essays Commemorating the 175th Anniversary of the Battle of Lake Erie.* 1991.

FREDERICK C. DRAKE

RULE OF 1756. The Rule of 1756 was a British maritime doctrine that held that trade closed to a nation in time of peace could not be opened in time of war. During the French revolutionary and Napoleonic Wars (1793–1815), the British repeatedly invoked this rule to prevent American vessels from participating in France's colonial and coastal trade.

In 1793–1794 the British seized several hundred American ships in the West Indies for violating the Rule of 1756, but the shipowners were later compensated under a provision in Jay's Treaty (1794). Thereafter, American merchants trading between France and its West Indian colonies circumvented the rule by making a stopover in the United States. In the *Polly* decision (1800), the British held that this indirect trade did not violate their doctrine. As a result, American re-exports soared from $2 million in 1792 to $53 million in 1805.

In England there was considerable resentment over this mushrooming trade, especially since mounting evidence suggested that the stopover made by American ships in the United States was often nominal. Accordingly, the British government modified its policy in the *Essex* decision (1805), which demanded that ships stopping over in the United States provide additional, though unspecified, proof that they actually had broken their voyages. A new round of ship seizures ensued, though most of these vessels were later released by the British courts.

In early 1806 Secretary of State James Madison published a learned critique of the Rule of 1756 entitled *An Examination of the British Doctrine, Which Subjects to Capture a Neutral Trade, Not Open in Time of Peace.* Although Madison's treatise was ignored in Britain, the British government in May 1806 set the *Essex* decision aside in a decree proclaiming the Fox Blockade. The British offered further protection for the re-export trade in the Monroe-Pinkney Treaty of 1806, but the United States declined to ratify the treaty. Thereafter, controversy over the Rule of 1756 subsided, largely because the British captured most of France's colonies.

BIBLIOGRAPHY

Burt, A. L. *The United States, Great Britain, and British North America from the Revolution to the Establishment of Peace after the War of 1812.* 1940.

Hickey, Donald R. *The War of 1812: A Forgotten Conflict.* 1989.

DONALD R. HICKEY

RUMIANTSEV, COUNT NIKOLAI (1754–1826), Russian diplomat, statesman. A member of one of Russia's most prominent families, Rumiantsev had held several diplomatic positions abroad before being named minister of commerce in 1802. He assumed the duties of foreign minister in 1807 and became state chancellor in 1809. Rumiantsev sponsored Russian economic development through agricultural improvements, canal construction, and the growth of foreign trade.

A self-proclaimed friend to American interests, he strove constantly to improve Russian-American relations. When British shipping was banned from Russian ports following the Tilsit treaty in 1807, Rumiantsev substituted American commerce for British by relaxing restrictions on American imports. Although he complained that "Bostonians" were supplying natives in Russian fur trading territories north of the Columbia River with arms and liquor, he accepted Madison's argument that the American government had no control over its citizens' activities abroad. He responded favorably to Madison's 1811 proposal of a commercial treaty but postponed negotiations when the approach of war between the United States and Great Britain and between Russia and France presaged the cessation of international commerce.

Eager to forestall hostilities between two allies, Rumiantsev offered Russia's services as mediator when news of the outbreak of war between England and America reached Saint Petersburg in 1812. Madison quickly accepted but the British rejected the offer, believing that Rumiantsev's sympathy for America's position precluded the possibility of unbiased arbitration. An ardent Francophile, Rumiantsev had deplored the collapse of the Franco-Russian alliance under Napoleon's expansionist policies and when Tsar Alexander I allied himself with England, Count Nesselrode replaced Rumiantsev in the tsar's confidence. Rumiantsev was gradually excluded from important diplomatic dealings and was formally removed from office in 1814. He was widely read in Russian and Slavic history and, following his death, his extensive library was housed in the Rumiantsev Museum, which later became the core of the Russian State Library at Moscow.

BIBLIOGRAPHY

Bemis, Samuel Flagg. *John Quincy Adams and the Foundations of American Foreign Policy.* 1949.

Grimsted, Patricia Kennedy. *The Foreign Ministers of Alexander I: Political Attitudes and the Conduct of Russian Diplomacy, 1801–1825.* 1969.

Michaud, Joseph, et al. *Biographie universelle, ancienne et moderne: ou, Histoire, par ordre alphabétique, de la vie publique et privée de tous les hommes qui se sont fait remarquer par leurs écrits, leurs actions, leurs talents, leurs vertus ou leurs crimes.* 1843–1865. Vol. 36.

MARY A. HACKETT

RUSH, BENJAMIN (1745 O.S.–1813), physician, reformer. Born in a rural community in Pennsylvania, Rush was educated at the College of New Jersey (later Princeton) and the University of Edinburgh. His broad

interests and his appointment in 1777 as surgeon general of the American army brought him into contact with a number of patriot leaders, including Thomas Jefferson.

After the Revolution, Rush resumed his practice in Philadelphia, then the home of the Continental Congress, and became acquainted with Rep. James Madison. Although Rush found the shy Virginian a cultivated and amiable companion, and although the two men corresponded throughout the course of their long lives, they never developed a close friendship; as president of the Pennsylvania Society for Promoting the Abolition of Slavery, Rush was a bitter critic of Virginia's "peculiar institution."

Rush and Madison did agree on the defects in the Articles of Confederation. Although he was not a delegate to the Annapolis Convention, Rush helped to publicize the meeting. Like Madison, he hoped the convention would do more than merely remedy Congress's lack of authority over taxes and trade. In a series of essays, Rush called for "a uniform currency" to facilitate commerce between the states and the creation of a bicameral assembly. In the days after the Federal Convention, Rush again publicly supported ratification of the new Constitution. As a

BENJAMIN RUSH. Engraving by R. W. Dodson after a portrait by Thomas Sully.

result, he was rewarded with a seat in the Pennsylvania ratifying convention.

Rush's support for the new government quickly gave way to dismay over Treasury Secretary Alexander Hamilton's financial policies. Funding and assumption, Rush confided to Madison, would discredit the cause of reform by proving that the Revolution had been fought by the "*many* for the benefit of the *few.*" Weary of politics, Rush accepted a position at the University of Pennsylvania. By his death in 1813 he had trained more than 3,000 students.

BIBLIOGRAPHY

Corner, George W., ed. *The Autobiography of Benjamin Rush.* 1948.
Goodman, Nathan G. *Benjamin Rush, Physician and Citizen, 1746–1813.* 1934.
Hawke, David Freeman. *Benjamin Rush, Revolutionary Gadfly.* 1971.

DOUGLAS R. EGERTON

RUSSELL, BENJAMIN (1761–1845), journalist. Russell edited the *Columbian Centinel,* a Boston biweekly, for more than forty years. He learned his trade during the American Revolution working for the *Massachusetts Spy* and in 1784 helped establish the *Centinel,* of which he soon became sole owner. Although the first issue proclaimed its independence of all political affiliations, there was never any doubt as to where the *Centinel*'s editor's sympathies lay. He registered alarm at Shays's Rebellion, welcomed the drafting of the federal Constitution, and campaigned for its ratification. In 1791 he published a series of articles by Publicola (John Quincy Adams), which identified Jefferson with the views expressed in Paine's *Rights of Man,* thereby drawing attention to the ideological divisions within Washington's cabinet.

Russell's own style of journalism was robust. He gave his unqualified support to the policies of the Washington and Adams administrations, representing their critics as "Jacobinic foxes, skunks and serpents." He regarded the outcome of the election of 1800 as a national disaster but found consolation in the scope it gave for Jefferson-baiting, which he undertook with characteristic gusto. The Republicans were "ridiculous, despicable, weak-minded, weak-hearted." Madison proved a less ready target than Jefferson, but the *Centinel* took a strong stand against the War of 1812, which it portrayed as arising out of an attempt to encourage "British, Irish and Jersey runaway sailors, to enter on board American vessels, and then to be PROTECTED, while they are underworking the native born American Seamen and Navigators."

Under Russell's editorship, the *Centinel* became the acknowledged voice of New England Federalism. It was also notable for its innovative style, layout, and coverage of European events. The *Centinel*'s influence declined with that of the Federalist party it supported, and sometime after Russell's retirement in 1828 the paper merged with its archrival, the Boston *Independent Chronicle.*

BIBLIOGRAPHY

Banner, James M. *To the Hartford Convention: The Federalists and the Origins of Party Politics in Massachusetts, 1789–1815.* 1970.
Rutland, Robert A. *The Newsmongers: Journalism in the Life of the Nation, 1690–1972.* 1973.

HOWARD TEMPERLEY

RUSSELL, JONATHAN (1771–1832), American merchant and diplomat. Russell was born in Providence, Rhode Island, and graduated from Brown University. He studied law but did not practice, devoting himself to business and to Republican politics. Twenty editions of his 1800 Fourth of July speech were published and in 1808 he produced a pamphlet supporting James Madison's election to the presidency.

In 1810 Madison named Russell secretary of the American legation at Paris, where he served as chargé d'affaires following John Armstrong's departure. Russell pressed the French to clarify their restrictions on American shipping but his originally optimistic outlook on Franco-American relations faded as French equivocations continued. When Joel Barlow was appointed minister in 1811, Russell was named chargé d'affaires at London where he served as agent for American prisoners following the American declaration of war against Great Britain in 1812. Madison instructed him to initiate armistice negotiations, with authority to agree to a truce if the orders in council were revoked and impressment stopped, but Lord Castlereagh refused to yield on the impressment issue.

In 1814 Russell was appointed minister to Sweden and was also named, with Henry Clay, Albert Gallatin, John Quincy Adams, and James A. Bayard, commissioner to the peace treaty negotiations in Ghent, where he supported Clay in whatever disagreements arose among the Americans. After the signing of the treaty on 24 December 1814, he returned to Sweden and served until his recall in 1818.

He moved to Massachusetts, which he represented in Congress from 1821 to 1823; during this time he attempted to weaken John Quincy Adams's support among Clay's western followers by accusing him of having been ready to concede navigation rights on the Mississippi to the British in exchange for restoration of fishing rights on the Gulf of Saint Lawrence. Adams's proof that Russell had released altered copies of his own letters effectively ended Russell's public career.

BIBLIOGRAPHY

Bemis, Samuel Flagg. *John Quincy Adams and the Foundations of American Foreign Policy.* 1949.

Brant, Irving. *James Madison.* Vols. 4 and 5. 1941, 1961.

Egan, Clifford L. *Neither Peace nor War: Franco-American Relations, 1803–1812.* 1983.

MARY A. HACKETT

RUSSIA. Madison's relationship with Russia began in 1780 when he helped draft Francis Dana's commission as minister to Catherine the Great; his concern for amicable Russian-American relations deepened during his terms as secretary of state and as president. Tsar Alexander I, who came to power in 1801, admired American statesmen and wanted closer commercial relations, while Madison and Jefferson believed Russia's role in the Armed Neutralities of 1780 and 1800 made it a natural ally in the struggle with Great Britain over neutral shipping rights.

In 1803 Madison sent consul Levett Harris to Saint Petersburg, where he was warmly received by Alexander and his commerce minister, Nikolai Rumiantsev. Alexander also assisted the United States by requesting Turkish intervention in negotiations for the release of the crew of the captured warship *Philadelphia* in 1804 and for an Algerian peace treaty in 1815. In a move toward formalizing diplomatic relations, Alexander appointed Andrei Daschkoff chargé d'affaires in 1808 and Fedor Pahlen minister in 1810. In 1809 Madison named John Quincy Adams, who had been Dana's secretary, minister to Russia, where he immediately sought and obtained Russian aid in arranging the release of American merchant ships seized by Denmark. The Russians responded enthusiastically to Adams's 1811 overtures for a commercial treaty and proposed another treaty regulating American access to Russian fur-trading colonies in North America. Madison's reluctance to acknowledge Russian territorial rights in the region delayed agreement on the fur trade and discussion of the commercial treaty was postponed when the approaching wars between Russia and France and the United States and Great Britain foreshadowed a decrease in all international trade. Russia, concerned over hostilities between friendly nations, offered its services as mediator when Congress declared war on Great Britain in 1812. After Madison accepted the offer and sent Albert Gallatin and James Bayard as commissioners to Saint Petersburg, the British refused the offer, preferring to deal directly with the Americans. Russia's diminished support for neutral rights after the defeat of Napoleon led Madison to mod-

SAINT PETERSBURG, RUSSIA.   The view is south across the Neva River toward the Winter Palace and the Hermitage.
Engraving after an aquatint by J. A. Atkinson, c. 1801–1812.   PRINTS AND PHOTOGRAPHS DIVISION, LIBRARY OF CONGRESS.

erate American demands in the peace negotiations at Ghent in 1814.

BIBLIOGRAPHY

Bashkina, Nina N., et al., eds. *The United States and Russia: The Beginning of Relations, 1765–1815.* 1980.

Bemis, Samuel Flagg. *John Quincy Adams and the Foundations of American Foreign Policy.* 1949.

Stagg, J. C. A. *Mr. Madison's War: Politics, Diplomacy, and Warfare in the Early American Republic, 1783–1830.* 1983.

MARY A. HACKETT

S

SANTO DOMINGO. A West Indian island also known as Hispaniola, Santo Domingo was the keystone of Napoleonic policy in North America. Santo Domingo, a French possession, gained American attention in 1791 when the island's slave majority, under the leadership of François-Dominique Toussaint, later known as Toussaint-Louverture, won control of the island. The influx of white and mulatto refugees struck terror into the hearts of Americans, most notably southerners, who saw in the French debacle the realization of their own deepest fears.

The administrations of Washington and Adams hoped to see the rebellion crushed and even hinted that the United States might assist British forces fighting Toussaint for control of the island. However, as it became clear that the British could not defeat Toussaint, and as the more practical considerations of trade assumed greater urgency, the United States sought accommodation with the rebel government. Working with the British, Secretary of State Timothy Pickering and the American consul, Edward Stevens, forged an agreement with Toussaint in 1799 that opened the island to British and American ships and assured nervous Americans that the former slaves of Santo Domingo would not engage in ocean commerce or privateering or even leave the island, except on diplomatic missions to the United States or to England.

Affairs in Santo Domingo shifted dramatically in 1801. For Napoleon, control over Santo Domingo was crucial to the establishment of a French New World empire in Louisiana and in the Floridas. In 1801 he sent his brother-in-law, Gen. Charles Leclerc, and 28,000 troops to reestablish French rule.

The Jefferson administration reacted cautiously. Jefferson and Madison supported French claims of dominion over the island but also sought to maintain valuable commercial links to the Toussaint regime. But within a year the French army had been nearly destroyed by Toussaint's army and an epidemic of yellow fever. France's failure to conquer Santo Domingo proved an important factor in Napoleon's decision to sell Louisiana to the United States in 1803.

Despite its military defeat, France continued to claim sovereignty over Santo Domingo. In the years following the victory of the former slaves, American trade with the island rebels strained Franco-American relations. Hoping to improve those relations and thereby win Napoleon's assistance in securing West Florida from Spain, Jefferson, in 1806 and 1807, pushed through Congress legislation prohibiting trade between the United States and those portions of Santo Domingo not under French control. Jefferson's gamble failed as the French emperor refused to lend support to the president's expansionist aims. The French government's presence on Santo Domingo ended in 1809 when the native black army and an English expeditionary force together drove the remnants of Leclerc's army off the island. Afterward, control of the island was divided. The inhabitants of the eastern, formerly Spanish, portion of the island accepted the rule of Spain until 1821, when the Dominican Republic declared its independence. In the formerly French western territory, where the Republic of Haiti had been proclaimed in 1804, a group of black generals vied for control. In 1820 Jean Pierre Boyer emerged as the lone ruler of Haiti. Two years later, he conquered the young republic to the east and declared himself sovereign over all Santo Domingo.

BIBLIOGRAPHY

Brant, Irving. *James Madison: Secretary of State, 1800–1809.* 1953.
Perkins, Bradford. *The First Rapprochement: England and the United States, 1795–1805.* 1955.
Tansill, Charles C. *The United States and Santo Domingo, 1798–1873: A Chapter in Caribbean Diplomacy.* 1938.

TINA H. SHELLER

SCOTT, WINFIELD (1786–1866), U.S. general, presidential candidate. The most important American military leader between the American Revolution and the Civil War, Winfield Scott began his military career as an artillery captain. When the War of 1812 began, he rose to lieutenant colonel and performed well at the Battle of Queenston Heights (13 October 1812), although he was taken prisoner.

After his exchange, he was promoted to colonel and appointed adjutant general to Maj. Gen. Henry Dearborn's Northern Army. Scott led the successful American assault on Fort George (27 May 1813).

In an army overloaded with dawdlers, Scott earned a reputation as a fighter. He received an order from President James Madison to come to Washington in late 1813, where Madison consulted with him on the conduct of the war. Scott was advanced to brigadier general in early 1814 and was sent to New York, where, as a liaison for Madison, he met with leading New York Republicans. He then led a brigade in Maj. Gen. Jacob Brown's army, where he was a stern drillmaster. Scott's drilling paid off when his brigade encountered and defeated a British force on the Niagara frontier at the Battle of Chippewa (5 July 1814), causing the British commander to remark, "Those are

MAJ. GEN. WINFIELD SCOTT. Stipple engraving by David Edwin after a portrait by Joseph Wood. PRINTS AND PHOTOGRAPHS DIVISION, LIBRARY OF CONGRESS.

regulars, by God!" Scott also performed signally at Lundy's Lane (25 July 1814), where he was seriously wounded. In late 1814, as a brevet major general, he assumed command of the Tenth Military District headquartered at Baltimore, sometimes traveling to Washington to provide Madison and Secretary of War James Monroe with advice on military affairs. He was marked for high command had the war continued into 1815.

After the war, Scott enjoyed a long career and even greater fame, participating in the Seminole War, the Mexican War, and the Civil War. He was also an unsuccessful Whig candidate for president in 1852.

BIBLIOGRAPHY

Elliot, Charles Winslow. *Winfield Scott: The Soldier and the Man.* 1937.
Scott, Winfield. *Memoirs of Lieut.-General Scott, LL.D., Written by Himself.* 2 vols. 1864.

MARK PITCAVAGE

SEATON, WILLIAM S. See *Gales and Seaton.*

SECTIONALISM.

As a southerner and one of the leading nationalists of his generation, Madison was keenly aware of the dangers posed by sectional differences and conflicts within the American republic. During his forty years of public service he labored to create and then preserve a viable union of the states. The Constitution that he was instrumental in drafting at the Philadelphia convention of 1787 became the principal vehicle for achieving this necessary measure of regional or territorial integration. Madison's nationalist vision was itself regionally based—which is to say that it was clearly connected to his background and experience as a Virginia planter—and his understanding of what endangered the Union was perforce colored by that bias. But as a politician and a statesman he consistently sought to transcend narrow sectional allegiances and interests in favor of a broader common good.

This attachment to the Union as a priority was strengthened during the crisis of the 1780s that led to the adoption of the Constitution. Madison became convinced that the weak Union under the Articles of Confederation was on the brink of collapse, in large part because of the extreme tension and conflict between the southern states, led by his native Virginia, and the northeastern, or New England, states. Although Madison commented on the importance of slavery as a source of regional distinctions, he did not, at this time, view this issue as the principal source of division between the regional extremities of the republic. He saw instead a conflict between the relatively constricted, maritime-based economy of the northeastern states, tied to the vagaries of a larger Atlantic commercial world, and the much more expansive agricultural economy of the southern states, focused on the settlement and development of a vast inland frontier. Madison saw the Jay-Gardoqui negotiations as an alarming sign of the potential for this conflict to sunder the Union; at the Federal Convention he desperately sought some means of accommodating such divergent interests and the contrasting visions of the future they engendered. Compromise on immediate conflicts of interest was essential—most notably regarding representation and slavery—but so too was Madison's broader vision of westward expansion. As he imagined the future of the republic under the Constitution, sustained population growth would ensure the prompt settlement and development of the vacant western lands. Expansion would lead to a successful experiment in republican nationality, he believed, once all the original states, north and south, overcame their narrow sectional inclinations and joined hands to participate and hence share an interest in that imperial growth. Madison's vision was southern-based, but he was staking a great deal on the common expectation (false, as it turned out) that the southern or agricultural states were growing in population (and power) at a much faster rate than the northeastern states. But his political vision was not so much of a narrow or partisan southern majority under the new Constitution, as it was of an agricultural, republican majority.

During the 1790s Madison became instrumental in forging the political organization that, in his judgment, represented that intersectional majority. The Democratic-Republican party, which unseated the New England–based Federalist party in the election of 1800, triumphed at the national level when the Jeffersonians successfully broadened their predominantly southern base to include substantial support in other regions of the country, most notably in the so-called middle states of New York and Pennsylvania. But the political triumph of the Jeffersonians, which became permanent with the rapid demise of the Federalist party during Madison's presidency, by no means solved the problem of sectionalism. Within a few years of Madison's retirement, the Missouri controversy of 1819–1821 aroused renewed fears of disunion that remained with him until his death in 1836. Ironically, westward expansion, rather than promoting regional accommodation as Madison had earlier hoped, became a source of intersectional tension and discord once it became tied to the newly explosive issue of slavery.

[See also *Kentucky and the Western Country; Missouri Compromise; Public Lands.*]

BIBLIOGRAPHY

Cooper, William J., Jr. *Liberty and Slavery: Southern Politics to 1860.* 1983.

Koch, Adrienne. *Madison's Advice to My Country.* 1966.

McCoy, Drew R. "James Madison and Visions of American Nationality in the Confederation Period: A Regional Perspective." In *Beyond Confederation: Origins of the Constitution and American National Identity.* Edited by Richard Beeman, et al. 1987.

Robinson, Donald. *Slavery in the Structure of American Politics, 1765–1820.* 1971.

DREW R. McCoy

SHAWNEE INDIANS.

The Algonquian-speaking Shawnees traditionally comprised five divisions: the Chillicothe, Thwakela, Kispoki, Maquachake, and Piqua. Each division was responsible for a particular aspect of tribal life, such as warfare, ritual, or health. Forced, like other Ohio Valley tribes, to relocate by the Iroquois Indians in the seventeenth century, the Shawnees were again located in southeastern Ohio by the mid eighteenth century, where they came under heavy pressure from the influx of white settlers. Despite the Shawnees' defeat in Lord Dunmore's War (1774), many continued to fight to limit white expansion to the Ohio River. During the American Revolution, some Shawnees tried to steer a neutral course, but American aggression and the murder of the Shawnee chief Cornstalk drove most Shawnees to cast their lot with the British. George Rogers Clark and other American commanders launched regular campaigns into Shawnee country, burning villages and crops, but the Shawnees and their allies more than held their own in the west.

By the end of the Revolution, however, the Shawnee bands had undergone serious dislocation. Part of the nation had migrated west of the Mississippi to take up lands in territory claimed by Spain. The Ohio Shawnee bands had retreated northwest, beyond the reach of American campaigns, and they continued their fight against the United States for a dozen years more until Anthony Wayne defeated the Indian confederacy at Fallen Timbers, Ohio, and secured the cession of most of Ohio at the Treaty of Greenville in 1795. After the signing of the treaty, many Shawnee chiefs, such as Black Hoof, followed a path of accommodation with the Americans, and a new generation of warriors took up the war of resistance.

With the emergence of a significant religious following for the Shawnee Prophet, the Shawnee leader Tecumseh began to form a multitribal confederacy in the first decade of the nineteenth century. The growing Indian activism alarmed the American authorities. Gov. William Henry Harrison of Indiana Territory took steps to stifle the movement and dealt both the Prophet's reputation and the Indian confederacy a serious blow at the Battle of Tippecanoe in 1811. Tecumseh and his followers united with the British in the War of 1812 and won some significant victories early in the war, but Tecumseh's death at the Battle of the Thames in 1813 robbed the Indian confederacy of its leader and effectively ended united Indian resistance to American expansion east of the Mississippi. In subsequent years, more Shawnees followed the path of migration taken in earlier years by their relatives, relocating to Missouri, Kansas, Oklahoma, and Texas.

BIBLIOGRAPHY

Edmunds, R. David. *The Shawnee Prophet.* 1983.

Howard, James. *Shawnee: The Ceremonialism of a Native Indian Tribe and Its Cultural Background.* 1981.

Kinietz, Vernon, and Erminie Wheeler-Voegelin, eds. "Shawnese Traditions: C. C. Trowbridge's Account." *Occasional Contributions from the Museum of Anthropology of the University of Michigan* 9 (1939).

COLIN G. CALLOWAY

SHAWNEE PROPHET. See *Prophet, The.*

SHELBY, ISAAC

(1750–1826), governor of Kentucky, militia general. Isaac Shelby was an exemplar of the second-rank Chesapeake gentry who were so critical to the evolution of the young republic's politics. In his first term as governor he ably brought a new state into being and directed its contribution to Anthony Wayne's Indian wars (1792–1795). In his second, he focused the commonwealth's efforts on the Detroit campaign despite military losses and again demonstrated both his political appeal and his military skills. Few other governors provided Madison's administration more effective support during the War of 1812 than did Shelby.

The Maryland-born son of a prominent North Carolina–Tennessee politician and militia general, Isaac Shelby gained steadily in experience and reputation as a leader in the American Revolution and in Indian wars fought between 1774 and 1795. He is credited with devising the unusual tactics used by the Americans to defeat decisively a Loyalist force at the Battle of Kings Mountain, South Carolina, on 7 October 1780.

Moving to Kentucky in 1783, Shelby soon became a major political figure and served as the first governor of that commonwealth (1792–1796). Reflecting Kentucky's desire for free navigation of the Mississippi, Shelby provided lukewarm support for the Washington administration's attempt to curtail the activities of George Rogers Clark in behalf of revolutionary France against Spanish-held New Orleans. A leader in the moderate Republican wing of Kentucky politics, Shelby in the last months of his administration became involved in the bitter struggle with the radical Republicans over the role of the courts in deciding the validity of land titles. This was a critical issue in a region where, as Shelby said in one address, "the happiness and welfare of the country depends so much on the speedy settlement of our land disputes." After completing his term, Shelby for fifteen years pursued his own business and family affairs from his home near Danville, returning to public life when the imminent war with Great Britain brought him back to the governorship in 1812.

Shelby was instrumental in securing William Henry Harrison's appointment as a major general first in the Kentucky militia and then in the U.S. Army so that Harrison might lead the campaign to reclaim Detroit (1812–1813). Despite the loss of some of Kentucky's finest young men at the Battle of the River Raisin, Michigan (21 January 1813), Governor Shelby was able to raise more than 3,000 Kentuckians to reinforce Harrison for his 1813 campaign. The sixty-three-year-old Shelby pleaded with young Kentuckians that he would personally lead them "to the field of battle and share" with them "the dangers and honors of the campaign." His willingness to subordinate himself to the much younger and less experienced Harrison in this campaign says much about Shelby's self-discipline.

Major General Shelby brought his Kentuckians northward to join Harrison on the Lake Erie shore, supervised their transport across the lake to Amherstburg, Upper Canada (now Ontario), conducted them in the pursuit of the fleeing British and Indians along the Thames River, and led them in the Battle of the Thames (5 October 1813), where both the British and the Indian threats to Kentucky were eliminated. Shelby's Kentuckians also campaigned on the Indiana-Illinois frontier and in Andrew Jackson's New Orleans defense in January 1815.

After Shelby's term ended in 1816, he retired to his Danville, Kentucky, home. He declined James Monroe's offer to make him secretary of war in 1817.

BIBLIOGRAPHY

Beasley, Paul W. "The Life and Times of Isaac Shelby, 1750–1826." Ph.D. dissertation, University of Kentucky. 1968.

Coward, Joan Wells. *Kentucky in the New Republic: The Process of Constitution Making.* 1979.

Hammack, James W., Jr. "Kentucky and Anglo-American Relations, 1803–1815." Ph.D. dissertation, University of Kentucky. 1974.

Sprague, Stuart Seely. "Kentucky and the Navigation of the Mississippi: The Climactic Years, 1793–1795." *Register of the Kentucky Historical Society* 71 (October 1973): 364–392.

Tachau, Mary K. Boonsteel. *Federal Courts in the Early Republic: Kentucky, 1789–1816.* 1978.

DAVID CURTIS SKAGGS

ISAAC SHELBY. Shelby was governor of Kentucky in the 1790s and again during the War of 1812. Engraving by Asher B. Durand after a portrait by Matthew Harris Jouett.
PRINTS AND PHOTOGRAPHS DIVISION, LIBRARY OF CONGRESS.

SHERMAN, ROGER (1721–1793), Connecticut patriot, member of Congress, delegate to the Federal Convention. Born in Massachusetts, Sherman moved to Connecticut and prospered as a land speculator, lawyer, and merchant. He was elected to the legislature in 1764 and soon rose to prominence as an opponent of the Stamp Act.

Sherman was named to the Continental Congress in 1774, remained a delegate until 1784, and was a jealous guardian of Connecticut's western land claims.

At the Federal Convention in Philadelphia in 1787 Sherman spoke more often than any other delegate except Madison. Madison's Virginia Plan displeased Sherman, who favored a Congress chosen by the state legislatures, in order to protect the interests of the smaller states. When the Convention deadlocked in early July, Sherman suggested formation of a committee comprising one delegate from each state to devise a compromise on the question of representation, a proposal adopted over Madison's objections. Sherman opposed the inclusion of a bill of rights in the Constitution as unnecessary.

ROGER SHERMAN.   Engraving by S. S. Jocelyn.
PRINTS AND PHOTOGRAPHS DIVISION, LIBRARY OF CONGRESS.

Although Sherman and Madison often differed, there was no hostility between them.

Sherman was elected to the first House of Representatives, where he voted for adequate federal revenues but argued against Madison's efforts to protect Virginia's interests. He vigorously opposed a federal bill of rights, arguing that Madison's proposals were unnecessary and disruptive of the new government. Sherman served on the committee for a bill of rights, however, and his motion to list amendments to the Constitution separately, rather than within the original text, was accepted.

Madison and Sherman clashed sharply in 1790 on the assumption of state debts, and Sherman forcefully opposed locating the national capital along the Potomac. He was elected to the Senate in 1791 and served until his death. Sherman was regarded as a simple and honest legislator, firm in his opinions but never bitter in debate.

BIBLIOGRAPHY

Collier, Christopher. *Roger Sherman's Connecticut: Yankee Politics and the American Revolution.* 1971.

McDonald, Forrest. *Novus Ordo Seclorum: The Intellectual Origins of the Constitution.* 1985.

Rossiter, Clinton. *1787: The Grand Convention.* 1966.

PATRICK J. FURLONG

SLAVERY. James Madison was seriously involved with the institution of chattel slavery, both personally and publicly, throughout his life. As the eldest son of a prominent, well-to-do Virginia slaveholder, Madison inherited what he identified as a major problem. He grew up in an environment substantially shaped by the presence of slaves, and he owned close to one hundred of them at the time of his death. Moreover, as a Republican statesman and a Founding Father, he was forced to grapple with the issue on a larger scale. Although he firmly believed that slavery must be ended in the United States and consistently did what he thought possible to promote its demise, the institution was thriving and expanding in many areas of Madison's beloved republic during his later years. In short, on both a personal and a public level, Madison failed to meet his own expectations regarding slavery.

We have evidence that Madison was at least somewhat reluctant during his younger years to accept his inherited identity as a Virginia planter. Along with religious intolerance, slavery was part of a larger pattern of oppression in his native state that he found abhorrent. Soon after the Revolution, when Madison was in his thirties, he appears to have sought (largely through speculation in land outside of Virginia) some means of establishing himself, independent of his father, so that he might not have to rely on the labor of slaves for his own support. All such efforts failed, however; he became the owner of both land and slaves through paternal bequests and gradually accommodated himself to a role and an identity that he reluctantly embraced. For the rest of his adult life Madison was a kind and even a benevolent master of slaves, some of whom had been in his family for several generations and who collectively remained an integral part of the Montpelier community.

Madison sincerely wished to honor his slaves' best interests, but his understanding of what was best for them was controlled by his own assumptions about the importance of race and above all by larger social and political circumstances over which he had little control. As a supporter of both emancipation and colonization, he attempted in his later years to persuade at least some of his slaves to migrate to the new colony of Liberia on the west coast of Africa. But his blacks at Montpelier appear to have had little interest in this escape from slavery, preferring to remain in generally comfortable and familiar surroundings, no doubt hoping that better times in America lay ahead. Madison also hoped to follow the example of George Washington by emancipating his slaves in his will. But he did not, apparently for a number of practical reasons having to do with his concern for his much younger wife's financial well-being and with his understanding of the almost impossibly difficult conditions faced by free blacks in Virginia (and elsewhere in the United States) by the 1830s. It is a tragic comment on the limitations of Madison's vision, and even more on the racist structure of his republic, that his definition of his own slaves' best interests was, in the end, remaining in bondage under his widow's benevolent control.

Madison's personal dilemma neatly parallels his frustration and failure as a statesman on this thorny issue. Viewed from one perspective, Madison's antislavery credentials are impeccable. He never qualified his fundamental belief that slavery was wrong in principle and therefore had to be eliminated from an American republic that offered a moral and political example for the rest of the world. He knew that African American slaves, as human beings, were entitled to all the natural rights enumerated in the Declaration of Independence and that justice demanded that those rights be granted. Thus for Madison, the question was never whether slavery should be abolished but rather when and how it could be eradicated. The when and how were the rub.

Madison believed that a general emancipation of the slaves was feasible only under certain circumstances made necessary by the racial character of American slavery. Madison's acceptance of those conditions as necessary tended to make emancipation extremely difficult, if not impossible, and may have also helped excuse his own (and his society's) relative inaction.

Like so many other members of the revolutionary generation, Madison initially placed great stock and hope in what he regarded as a major antislavery reform—the abolition of the foreign slave trade. Madison believed that eliminating the further importation of slaves from abroad was a necessary first step toward abolishing the institution altogether. At the Federal Convention in 1787 he only reluctantly accepted the necessary compromise of delaying a national program of outlawing the slave trade for at least

SLAVERY IN VIRGINIA.   *An Overseer Doing His Duty.* Watercolor, ink, and ink wash by Benjamin Henry Latrobe near Fredericksburg, Virginia, 13 March 1798.   MARYLAND HISTORICAL SOCIETY, BALTIMORE.

twenty years. But any hopes that slavery in the United States could be strangled by cutting off the supply of laborers from Africa proved to be naive and illusory. Even in the absence of a large external source of supply, the numbers of African Americans in bondage dramatically expanded after the Revolution, notably as the institution became a primary source of labor on the southwestern cotton frontier.

Nevertheless, Madison stubbornly clung to his belief that the greatest impediment to emancipation was not the continuing profitability of the institution but rather the larger dilemma of racial adjustment. Unlike his friend Thomas Jefferson, he never stated his own belief or suspicion that blacks were intrinsically inferior to whites, nor did he express alarm about the threat of miscegenation in a biracial society. However, Madison accepted as permanent the widespread prejudice against blacks held by virtually all white Americans, a prejudice that he assumed made impossible the integration of free blacks as equal citizens into the republic. In other words, prudence dictated that slavery be abolished only when the former slaves, always with their own consent, could be colonized outside the United States.

Madison sincerely believed that colonization was the best solution for the blacks and, even more important, that his fellow white Americans would never voluntarily accept emancipation on a large scale if freeing the slaves meant having to find a place for increasing numbers of free blacks within the United States. Toward the end of his life, in the 1830s, in the face of an emerging proslavery argument that he found morally repugnant, Madison clung desperately, and perhaps pathetically, to his faith in colonization—a hopelessly impractical program on any substantial scale—as a necessary vehicle for sustaining, not merely the hope of emancipation, but even principled opposition to slavery itself. Madison avoided abject despair about the future of slavery and the republic, and this faith in a rational solution to the slavery dilemma became Madison's only triumph in these troubled final years.

[See also *American Colonization Society*.]

BIBLIOGRAPHY

Davis, David Brion. *The Problem of Slavery in the Age of Revolution, 1770–1823*. 1975.

Jordan, Winthrop D. *White over Black: American Attitudes toward the Negro, 1550–1812*. 1968.

McColley, Robert. *Slavery and Jeffersonian Virginia*. 2d ed. 1973.

McCoy, Drew R. *The Last of the Fathers: James Madison and the Republican Legacy*. 1989.

MacLeod, Duncan J. *Slavery, Race, and the American Revolution*. 1974.

Miller, John Chester. *The Wolf by the Ears: Thomas Jefferson and Slavery*. 1977.

DREW R. McCOY

SMITH, ADAM (1723–1790), seminal figure of modern economics. Although there were a few stalwarts before Smith, the Scottish scholar was highly influential as the leader of the classical school of economics.

The underlying concerns of Smith and his varied liberal predecessors and followers were the nature of real wealth, the conditions necessary for the creation of wealth, and the processes and consequences of economic growth. Smith's major—and monumental—book was *An Inquiry into the Nature and Causes of the Wealth of Nations* (1776), a work familiar to Madison.

It was not entirely fortuitous that Smith's magnum opus appeared almost simultaneously with Thomas Jefferson's Declaration of Independence, for *The Wealth of Nations*, too, was a pronouncement of liberty. Smith lived in the third century of stultifying mercantilism, with its orientation of economic constraint and direction and its selective subsidization by government in alliance with commercial and manufacturing sectors. Smith railed against state-dominated mercantilism—and also against monopolizing businessmen.

The classical economists decidedly were not anarchists, but they consciously were reformers. They envisioned

ADAM SMITH.
PRINTS AND PHOTOGRAPHS DIVISION, LIBRARY OF CONGRESS.

an economy composed of numerous independent consumers and producers, each pursuing his own interests with his own resources according to his own criteria in open, competitive markets. A price-directed economy based on private rights to the use of property was seen to be not only coherent and self-equilibrating but productive and efficient in responding to consumer preferences, with people "led by an invisible hand" to channel energies of personal betterment into activities of reciprocal gain and social well-being. Individuals are not devoid of sympathy and a sense of justice, Smith explained in *The Theory of Moral Sentiments* (1759), but he saw self-interest as the basis for complex market coordination.

The community lives better with a greater ratio of production to the number of those who use and consume the national output. That ratio is determined by the productivity of workers and the proportion of the population in the work force. The first of those determinants is the more important, and the essential analytic theme is how to achieve high and ever-rising productivity.

"Division of labor" is critical to Smith's theory. His discussion at the level of the producing *plant* is not innovative, and he did not develop the concept of "comparative advantage" to explain personal or regional specialization on the basis of differing relative productivities. Much more significant to Smith was broad *social* division of labor. He saw society as a complex interdependency of self-interested, would-be autonomous individuals, productive specialists linked through mutually beneficial exchanges. The more each member of society produces, the more he can offer in the market and obtain from others.

Behind the division of labor in Smith's theory is capital accumulation, which provides subsistence and tools to workers during time-consuming productive processes. Continuing capital accumulation requires much saving and appropriate investment, which in turn leads to better, as well as more, capital. Smith argued that society will save more, invest better, and work harder if it is free to respond to the incentives generated by open markets, free of bungling misdirection by intrusive government.

The work of Smith was appreciated by Madison and other American Founding Fathers. And Smith was intrigued by the potential of an American empire that could become "one of the greatest and most formidable that ever was."

On grounds of morality and propriety, as well as of economics, Smith vigorously opposed mercantilistic imperialism and colonialism. He hoped that the American colonies would become fully integrated into British society and government or that Britain would voluntarily give up all authority over them. "To prohibit a great people . . . from employing their stock and industry in the way that they judge most advantageous," wrote this sometime professor of moral philosophy, "is a manifest violation of the most sacred rights of mankind."

BIBLIOGRAPHY

Campbell, Roy H., and Andrew S. Skinner. *Adam Smith.* 1982.
Coase, Ronald H. "Adam Smith's View of Man." *Journal of Law and Economics* 19 (1976): 529–546.
Skinner, Andrew S. "Adam Smith." In vol. 4 of *The New Palgrave, A Dictionary of Economics.* Edited by John Eatwell, Murray Milgate, and Peter Newman. 1987.
Viner, Jacob. "Adam Smith and Laissez Faire." *Journal of Political Economy* 35 (1927): 198–232.

WILLIAM R. ALLEN

SMITH, MARGARET BAYARD (1778–1844), writer, social leader, diarist. Only a month before he began publishing the powerful Jeffersonian newspaper the *National Intelligencer and Washington Advertiser,* Samuel Harrison Smith returned briefly to Philadelphia in September 1800 to marry his second cousin, Margaret Bayard. Mrs. Smith was a cultured and charming hostess in a new capital city that was then little more than a frontier town. Together with Dolley Madison, her entertainments provided an oasis of social grace that was eagerly sought by diplomats and statesmen of every political leaning during the administrations of Jefferson and Madison.

Margaret Smith's novels, her articles in several literary journals, and especially her stream of letters (collected in *The First Forty Years of Washington Society*) give a descriptive personal picture of the city where she resided from her marriage in 1800 until her death. Generations of American political leaders were guests at the Smiths' home, which stood on what is now the site of Catholic University. In addition, she visited Monticello and Montpelier and described in detail the home life of Presidents Jefferson and Madison. Jefferson outranked Madison in Margaret Smith's mind, for Madison could not make her heart "beat with pleasure" as did Jefferson. She does, however, provide a rare glimpse of Madison's reactions to social gatherings, both as president and in retirement. Her detailed description of the 1809 inaugural ball is one of the earliest records of the Madisons' social life, including the report that Madison told her, "I would much rather be in bed." She even described Madison's mother shortly before Mrs. Madison's death in 1829. Her description of the burning of Washington in 1814 and her observations of the conduct of Madison while his government was stalked by the British invaders is a unique account often used by historians.

BIBLIOGRAPHY

Green, Constance M. *Washington: Village and Capital, 1800-1878.* 1962.

Smith, Margaret Bayard. *The First Forty Years of Washington Society*. Edited by Gaillard Hunt. 1906.

DONALD O. DEWEY

SMITH, ROBERT (1757–1842), secretary of the navy, secretary of state. Born in Lancaster, Pennsylvania, Smith attended the College of New Jersey (later Princeton) and graduated in 1781. Shortly thereafter he moved to Baltimore, where his father and his older brother Samuel, a former brigadier general in the Maryland militia, operated a profitable shipping business.

Although affable and ambitious, Robert was a man of only average talents; his fate was to stand in the long shadow of his able and charismatic older brother. By 1793, when Smith obtained a seat in the Maryland Senate, Samuel was already a member of Congress and an ardent Republican. Upon his election to the presidency, Thomas Jefferson offered Samuel Smith the position of secretary of the navy, but Smith understood that Jefferson and Secretary of the Treasury Albert Gallatin were committed to budgetary retrenchment and to cuts in the navy. As a mercantile man who desired a naval force strong enough to protect his city's commerce, Samuel Smith therefore declined Jefferson's offer. After three others refused the position for similar reasons, the new president, out of desperation, offered the post to Robert Smith. Although the younger Smith had limited experience with naval affairs, Jefferson prayed the appointment would appease the increasingly influential Maryland wing of the party. Smith accepted and remained in the position until 1809.

As president-elect, James Madison planned to name Albert Gallatin to the State Department, but this move was opposed by Samuel Smith, now a senator, who feared Gallatin would cut further naval strength at a time of growing tension with Britain. In hopes of winning the senator's support for his administration, Madison suggested promoting Robert Smith to the Treasury Department, where he would be assisted in his affairs by Secretary of State Gallatin. Regarding Smith as inept and uncooperative, the Swiss-born financier refused. Faced with a hostile Smith-led Senate cabal, known as the Invisibles, Madison had little choice but to retain Gallatin at Treasury and to appoint Robert Smith as secretary of state.

The appointment proved an unhappy one. Robert Smith no more shared Madison's agrarian vision than did his brother, and the secretary publicly differed with Madison's futile attempts to stop British depredations on American shipping through commercial restrictions. Madison, in turn, found fault with Smith's clumsy prose. The secretary's dispatches were "so crude and inadequate" that the president was "generally obliged to write them anew" himself. The inevitable explosion came in March 1811 when Smith hinted to the British chargé d'affaires that American sanctions would soon collapse for lack of congressional support. To avoid political embarrassment, Madison tried to get Smith out of the way by appointing him to a diplomatic post at Saint Petersburg. When Smith countered by requesting a seat on the Supreme Court, Madison removed him from office and nominated James Monroe to replace him.

Three months later Smith retaliated with a venomous pamphlet, *Address to the People of the United States*, in which he charged, with some justification, that Madison's policies toward Britain and France were naive and inconsistent. Furious at this "wicked publication," Madison wrote but never published a sixteen-page rebuttal. A public reply was unnecessary; Smith's malicious tone and his obvious incompetence only served to damage his prestige and to end his public career. He died in 1842.

BIBLIOGRAPHY

Armstrong, Thom M. *Politics, Diplomacy, and Intrigue in the Early Republic: The Cabinet Career of Robert Smith, 1801–1811*. 1991.
Cassell, Frank A. *Merchant Congressman in the Young Republic: Samuel Smith of Maryland, 1752–1839*. 1971.
Pancake, John S. *Samuel Smith and the Politics of Business, 1752–1839*. 1972.
Tansill, Charles C. "Robert Smith." In *American Secretaries of State and Their Diplomacy*. Edited by Samuel Flagg Bemis. 1927.

DOUGLAS R. EGERTON

SMITH, SAMUEL (1752–1839), soldier in the Revolution and the War of 1812, senator and representative, and leader of the Republican party in Maryland. Born in Lancaster, Pennsylvania, Smith moved to Baltimore as a child in 1759. By the beginning of the Revolutionary War he had become active in his father's commercial firm and had traveled extensively in Europe to learn about trading opportunities. Commissioned a lieutenant colonel in the Continental army, Smith earned the thanks of Congress and a ceremonial sword for his role in defending Fort Mifflin on the Delaware River in 1777. Smith resigned his commission in 1779 and spent the remainder of the war managing a fleet of privateers.

By 1789 Smith was among the richest merchants in Baltimore. Economically secure, he entered politics as a member of the Maryland House of Delegates in 1790 and, two years later, won election to the U.S. House of Representatives. Although affiliated with George Washington and the Federalist party, Smith balked at Jay's Treaty and switched his allegiance to the Republican party in 1794. His wealth and political influence and his position as a general in the Maryland militia soon made him the most powerful political figure in the state.

Smith represented the urban commercial wing of the Republican party and frequently disagreed with Madison, who championed agrarian and southern interests in the House. Although members of the same party, the two men often clashed over trade and military policies. While Smith held little affection for Madison, he genuinely liked Thomas Jefferson and actively campaigned during the presidential election of 1800. When Jefferson and Aaron Burr received the same number of electoral votes, throwing the election into the House of Representatives, Smith brokered a settlement that brought Jefferson the victory. The new president thanked Smith by appointing him as acting secretary of the navy, a post he held for only a few months. Jefferson then named Smith's brother, Robert, to the post.

In 1803 Smith became a U.S. senator at a time when a renewal of war between France and England led to significant infringements on American commercial rights. Smith became increasingly critical of Jefferson and Secretary of State Madison, whose policies he believed had left the United States defenseless and unable to protect its commerce. Although Smith supported the president during the *Chesapeake-Leopard* affair of 1807 and helped pass the Embargo Bill in the Senate, he became increasingly estranged from the administration.

When Madison assumed the presidency in 1809, he tried to placate Smith by appointing his brother secretary of state. Despite this gesture, relations between the two men deteriorated rapidly. Madison came to believe that the Smith brothers stood at the head of a political cabal, sometimes known as the Invisibles, that sought to frustrate his policies. In retaliation, Albert Gallatin, the secretary of the Treasury, orchestrated an effort to prevent Samuel Smith's reelection as senator and accused the two brothers of mishandling government funds. By 1810 the Smiths were completely in opposition to Madison, and within a year the president dismissed Robert Smith, replacing him with James Monroe, and denied Samuel Smith access to government patronage positions.

Although weakened, Samuel Smith continued to be a political force for decades both in Maryland and in Congress. His most famous exploit, however, came as a soldier in the War of 1812. As major general of Maryland's third militia division, Smith had primary responsibility for protecting Baltimore. He organized the city's defenses and led the army that successfully repulsed Gen. Robert Ross's British troops in September 1814. Smith left Congress in 1832 after forty years of continuous service. After leading the citizens of Baltimore in suppressing a major riot in 1835, he was elected mayor. Four years later he died at age 87.

BIBLIOGRAPHY

Cassell, Frank A. *Merchant Congressman in the Young Republic: Samuel Smith of Maryland, 1752–1839.* 1971.

Cunningham, Noble E., Jr. *The Jeffersonian Republicans in Power: Party Operators, 1801–1809.* 1963.

Pancake, John Silas. *Samuel Smith and the Politics of Business, 1752–1839.* 1972.

FRANK A. CASSELL

SMITH, SAMUEL HARRISON (1772–1845), Republican newspaper editor, banker. Samuel Harrison Smith, secretary of the American Philosophical Society and a minor Republican journalist in Philadelphia, became a major political and journalistic figure in 1800 when he accepted Vice President Jefferson's request that he establish a party newspaper at Washington, D.C. Smith had edited the *New World* and the *Independent Gazetteer* in the late 1790s.

The year 1800 was a banner year for Smith. First he started a Washington weekly, the *Universal Gazette;* on 29 September he married Margaret Bayard Smith; and on 31 October he founded the *National Intelligencer and Washington Advertiser,* which would be published three times a week and would become the principal voice of the Jefferson-led Republican party. Madison was not extolled by Smith in the *Intelligencer* as Jefferson was, but he could always rely on Smith's support. When James Monroe mounted a weak opposition to Madison in the presidential election of 1808, Smith editorialized that Madison "has invariably displayed a dignity and moderation which are at once the best evidence, and the surest preservative of republican principles."

Smith's style was much less extreme in its partisanship than that of other Republican (or Federalist) editors; some Republicans called him "Silky-Milky Smith," and to the vulgar editor James T. Callender he was "Miss Smith." But he spoke with authority about the views of the Republican administrations, and he was influential because his remarks were copied extensively by other Republican newspapers. The status of the *Intelligencer* was demonstrated at the outset when it published Jefferson's first inaugural address before it had been delivered. Smith sold the *Intelligencer* in August 1810, but the newspaper remained influential until the Jackson administration. In July 1813 Madison appointed Smith to be the first commissioner of revenue. Later Smith served as president of the Bank of Washington, and in 1828 he became president of the Washington branch of the Second Bank of the United States. The Smiths remained close to the Madisons and were frequent visitors to Montpelier during Madison's retirement years.

BIBLIOGRAPHY

Green, Constance M. *Washington: Village and Capital, 1800–1878*. 1962.

Rutland, Robert A. *The Presidency of James Madison*. 1990.

DONALD O. DEWEY

SMITH, WILLIAM LOUGHTON (1758–1812), Federalist politician, diplomat. Smith was born in Charleston, South Carolina, and was educated in England and Switzerland between 1770 and 1782. He returned to South Carolina in November 1783 and was admitted to the bar in 1784. In 1788 he was elected to the state ratification convention and then to the First Federal Congress, where his election was contested by David Ramsay on the ground that Smith was not an American citizen as required by the Constitution.

James Madison supported Smith's election, but the two men seldom agreed thereafter. Smith opposed the president's removal power over executive appointees and led the opposition to Madison's proposal for discrimination against nations that did not have commercial treaties with the United States. When Madison moved that a bill of rights be added to the Constitution, Smith thought it impolitic to consider amendments before the government was fully organized.

Smith became a leading spokesman for Alexander Hamilton's financial program and opposed Madison's motion to discriminate between original public creditors and later purchasers of such debts, many of whom were speculators. Smith backed the assumption of state wartime debts by the federal government, a policy Madison opposed. Smith wanted the nation's capital to remain in New York, but Madison preferred a site along the Potomac. In a classic compromise, Hamilton's program passed the House, which then voted to locate the capital on the Potomac. Smith also favored the Bank of the United States and Jay's Treaty with England.

After winning his fifth consecutive election to the House of Representatives as a Federalist in 1796, Smith wrote a slashing attack titled *The Pretensions of Thomas Jefferson to the Presidency . . .* (1796). In 1797 Smith was appointed by President John Adams as minister to Portugal. His political career ended on 1 June 1801 when Secretary of State Madison informed him that he had been dismissed by President Jefferson.

BIBLIOG3RAPHY

Rogers, George C., Jr. *Evolution of a Federalist: William Loughton Smith of Charleston, 1758–1812*. 1962.

JAMES MORTON SMITH

SMYTH, ALEXANDER (1765–1830), lawyer, military officer, congressman. Born on the island of Rathlin off the Irish coast, Smyth came with his family to southwest Virginia shortly before the outbreak of the Revolution. Son of an Episcopal clergyman, and a county clerk at the age of 20, Smyth read law and began practicing in 1789. After marriage he moved to Wythe County, Virginia, where he maintained his legal practice until his death. In the 1790s he began service as a loyal Jeffersonian in the Virginia House of Delegates and moved to the state senate in 1808.

During the expansion of the U.S. Army in 1808, President Jefferson commissioned Smyth a colonel in a newly formed regiment. Despite Smyth's inexperience, his appointment reflected Jefferson's political desire for Republican senior officers rather than appointments based on military expertise. At the outbreak of war in 1812, President Madison named Smyth inspector general with the rank of brigadier general. At the same time, Smyth published his *Regulations for the Field Exercise, Manoeuvers, and Conduct of the Infantry of the United States* copied from the French manual of 1791. Smyth's formal, European military system drew the wrath of another of Jefferson's 1808 appointees, Lt. Col. William Duane. In response, Duane drafted his

ALEXANDER SMYTH. Profile by C. B.-J. Fevret de Saint-Mémin.
PRINTS AND PHOTOGRAPHS DIVISION, LIBRARY OF CONGRESS.

own simplified version of the French original; but Smyth's version predominated in training throughout the army, and Winfield Scott's 1815 manual followed Smyth's approach.

As a commander of a brigade on the Niagara frontier, Smyth refused to coordinate his activities with his superior, Maj. Gen. Stephen Van Rensselaer of the New York militia, despite specific orders placing him under the New Yorker's authority. Smyth claimed his regular commission superseded Van Rensselaer's militia one; thus, placing military punctilio above national interest, he refused to meet or to cooperate with Van Rensselaer and his militia force. Thus, when Van Rensselaer launched the abortive Queenston Heights offensive on 13 October 1812, Smyth and his sixteen hundred regulars were idle in Buffalo. Such inaction was a major contributing factor to Van Rensselaer's defeat.

Smyth then assumed command of the Niagara frontier and immediately began issuing bombastic proclamations, offending many of his militia troops, who felt Smyth imputed cowardice to them. His prolix general orders caused his troops to nickname him "van Bladder." Smyth soon proved as militarily unfit for command as his predecessor. His attempted river crossing at the Niagara River headwaters on 28 November and 1 December suffered from poor staff work, a lack of boats, indecision, and confusion. Subsequently, Smyth's militia deserted and his regulars went into winter quarters, where they lost their discipline. Smyth never recognized that the issue was competent leadership rather than tensions between regular army and militia. The Niagara campaign of 1812 ended disastrously, owing to inept leadership, personality clashes, and interservice animosities.

When on 8 December 1812 New York Brig. Gen. Peter B. Porter published a letter in the *Buffalo Gazette* accusing his superior of cowardice, Smyth challenged the congressman-turned-general to a duel. Neither duelist was injured, but Smyth's reputation was lost. After his request for leave was quickly granted, Smyth was soon dropped from the army rolls without either a resignation or court martial.

Jefferson, observing all this from retirement, said that "our men are good and want only generals." The former president failed to acknowledge that most of the army leaders of the various incompetent expeditions of 1812 were men he either commissioned or promoted to high rank. Smyth's fellow Virginians were more forgiving of him than history has been. Elected congressman from southwest Virginia in 1816, he served almost continuously in the House of Representatives until his death. Ironically, among those serving with him was Congressman Stephen Van Rensselaer of New York.

BIBLIOGRAPHY

Crackel, Theodore J. "The Battle of Queenston Heights, 13 October 1812." In *America's First Battles, 1776–1965*. Edited by Charles E. Heller and William A. Stofft. 1986.

Graves, Donald E. " 'I Have a Handsome Little Army . . .': A Re-Examination of Winfield Scott's Camp at Buffalo in 1814." In *War along the Niagara: Essays on the War of 1812 and Its Legacy*. Edited by R. Arthur Bowler. 1991.

Stanley, George F. G. *The War of 1812: Land Operations*. 1983.

DAVID CURTIS SKAGGS

SNYDER, SIMON (1759–1819), state legislator, governor of Pennsylvania. The son of German emigrants to Pennsylvania, Snyder was apprenticed to a tanner when he was seventeen. He became active in local Republican party politics, then was elected to the Pennsylvania legislature, where he served from 1797 to 1807. Snyder served three terms as Speaker and supported affordable legal services for working-class, merchant, and farmer litigants. In 1805 he sought the gubernatorial nomination on the "anti-judicial" ticket but lost to his rival, Thomas McKean.

Snyder campaigned as a Republican and stressed the fact that he was not a lawyer; he did not try to conceal the

SIMON SNYDER.   Portrait by Charles Willson Peale.
INDEPENDENCE NATIONAL HISTORICAL PARK, PHILADELPHIA.

fact that he had not served in the military at a time when officeseekers usually stressed their army or navy connections. His simple lifestyle also appealed to voters. Within his own party, Snyder suffered at times because of his feud with William Duane and Sen. Michael Leib. He was elected governor in 1808 and reelected in 1811, despite the *Olmstead* case, which had erupted in the spring of 1809 and had drawn Snyder into public conflict with Madison.

The *Olmstead* case went back to 1778, when a British sloop had been captured and taken to Philadelphia as a prize ship. The dispute over the disposition of the ship's cargo dragged on until 1809, when Chief Justice John Marshall ordered a federal judge to enforce Marshall's (1803) decision in favor of Capt. Gideon Olmstead, who had captured the British prize. Snyder ordered the state militia to protect the daughters of an original litigant. In April Snyder wrote Madison, pleading for a solution "to adjust the present unhappy collision of the two governments," but Madison replied that he could not interfere with a Supreme Court ruling. Both sides were relieved when a Pennsylvania court ruled that Capt. Gideon Olmstead deserved the prize money and that the state had erred in becoming a party in the lawsuit. Several state militiamen charged with resisting federal officers were convicted, but Madison pardoned them, and the case was finally closed.

After his reelection, Snyder took pains to show his support for Madison when war was declared in June 1812. Snyder was ahead of his time in his outspoken opposition to the death penalty. In 1817 he was elected to the state senate.

BIBLIOGRAPHY

Higginbotham, Sanford W. *The Keystone of the Democratic Arch: Pennsylvania Politics, 1800–1816.* 1952.

Kehl, James A. *Ill Feeling in the Era of Good Feeling.* 1956.

Rutland, Robert A., et al., eds. *Papers of James Madison:* Presidential Series. Vol 1. 1984.

ROBERT A. RUTLAND

SPAIN. Spain played a lesser role in James Madison's public life than either Britain or France. But in the 1780s, as the young republic attempted to establish itself as an independent nation, Spain's possession of the Floridas, Louisiana, and the lower Mississippi created troubling issues of boundaries, commerce, and security. Spain demonstrated its determination to curtail the movement of American settlers into the Ohio and Mississippi valleys by refusing, in the Jay-Gardoqui negotiations of 1785–1786, to grant Americans the unrestricted right to navigate the Mississippi. Madison, as the South's spokesman in Congress, opposed Jay's decision of 1786 to accept Spain's prohibition of American navigation on the Mississippi for twenty-five to thirty years in exchange for a generous commercial treaty with the Madrid government. In April 1787 Madison secured an indefinite postponement of the Mississippi question. Not until 1795, in the Treaty of San Lorenzo (Pinckney's Treaty), did Spain open the Mississippi to western commerce and grant Americans the right of deposit at New Orleans.

When Madison reached Washington in 1801 as secretary of state, Spain again challenged a variety of American interests in the Southwest. Rumors from France suggested that Napoleon desired Louisiana. Such an acquisition would place continental Europe's most powerful nation in control of the highly strategic lower Mississippi. That possibility troubled Jefferson and Madison deeply. "The day that France takes possession of New Orleans," Jefferson wrote in April 1802, "we must marry ourselves to the British fleet and nation." When, in 1802, Spanish officials at New Orleans withdrew the American right of desposit, Americans attributed the unwelcome decision to French influence. Jefferson confronted the challenge by dispatching his fellow Virginian James Monroe to Paris to join the American minister, Robert R. Livingston, in an effort to acquire New Orleans. Napoleon, who indeed had secretly acquired title to Louisiana in 1800, was now prepared to sell, not only New Orleans, but all Louisiana as well. Taken by surprise, the two American diplomats required some convincing; eventually they signed a treaty that transferred Louisiana to the United States for $15 million. When Madison saw the terms, he observed that "the bargain will be regarded as on the whole highly advantageous." In 1803 Spanish officials in New Orleans formally turned the city over to the French, who, assigned it to the United States the same day.

Madison had hoped to add Florida to the bargain, but Spain would not agree. What complicated the question of Florida's future was the boundary separating Florida from Louisiana. French Louisiana before 1763 included Florida as far east as the Perdido River, but British officials, in turning Louisiana over to Spain in the Treaty of Paris (1763), granted title only to Louisiana west of the Mississippi, while Britain acquired all of Florida east of the Mississippi. In 1764 Britain divided Florida at the Apalachicola River east of the Perdido, the historic line between French Louisiana and Spanish Florida. This created two separate provinces, East and West Florida. All Florida reverted to Spain in the Versailles Treaty of 1783.

During the spring of 1805 Monroe, then in London, traveled to Madrid to negotiate a new border for Florida, claiming that the Perdido River marked the eastern boundary of Louisiana. That boundary would give the United States command of both banks of the lower Mississippi. Monroe reported to Madison that his offer of money brought only expressions of anger and resentment. Then in October, John Armstrong, the new U.S. minister in Paris, informed Washington that the United States could obtain all Florida and part of Texas for a $7 million bribe. Jefferson regarded Florida under Spanish control a nuisance because it harbored smugglers and border ruffians, as well as fugitive slaves. Acquiring Florida by purchase, moreover, would be less costly than fighting for it. Jefferson sent a secret request to Congress for $2 million. Despite some vocal opposition, Congress passed the appropriation. Madison informed Paris that the United States was prepared to deal. Spain again resisted French pressure; there would be no deal.

If the Madrid government could resist American pressures on both Floridas, Spanish officials in West Florida could not. In 1810 a group of West Floridians revolted against Spanish rule and attacked the garrison at Baton Rouge. They killed the commander, took possession of the post, declared their independence, and asked the United States to recognize their new republic. Madison had long desired the acquisition of Florida, but he was troubled by such procedures. Before Congress could offer advice, Madison condemned the revolutionaries for their actions and, on 27 October 1810, ordered U.S. forces to enter West Florida and advance to the Perdido River. With Spanish garrisons in control of Mobile and Pensacola, the Americans halted at the Pearl. Madison's critics denied that the United States had the right to occupy foreign territory. When Great Britain protested the American action, Congress, at Madison's request, passed a resolution on 15 January 1811 declaring that the United States could not, "without serious inquietude, see any part of the said territory pass into the hands of any foreign power." Congress authorized the President to take control of East Florida should the province face the danger of foreign occupation, preferably with Spanish cooperation but by force if necessary. While Madison continued to solidify the American position in West Florida, no foreign power created the occasion to justify U.S. occupation of East Florida. In April 1812 Congress annexed West Florida west of the Pearl River to Louisiana; a month later Congress added West Florida east of the Pearl to Mississippi Territory. The disposition of East Florida awaited the continuing decline of Spanish authority and the diplomacy of John Quincy Adams during the succeeding administration. The United States acquired what remained of Spanish Florida in the Transcontinental Treaty of 1819.

[See also *Florida*; *France*; *Jay-Gardoqui Negotiations*; *Louisiana*; *Mississippi River*; *Mississippi Territory*.]

BIBLIOGRAPHY

Cox, I. J. *The West Florida Controversy, 1798–1813.* 1918
Whitaker, Arthur P. *The Mississippi Question, 1795–1803.* 1934.
Whitaker, Arthur P. *The Spanish-American Frontier, 1783–1795.* 1927.

NORMAN A. GRAEBNER

STATES' RIGHTS. Few terms in American history have been so overused and misused as "states' rights." Building on the biography by Irving Brant and on the work of Martin Diamond, some recent authorities have discerned a sudden shift in Madison's position on states' rights after the adoption of the Constitution. During his years in the Confederation Congress, Brant maintains, Madison conducted a deliberate campaign to expand the boundaries of federal authority by means of a doctrine of implied congressional powers. An eager advocate of centralizing change, he stood throughout the 1780s for a federal power to coerce the states, for independent federal taxes, and for federal authority to regulate the country's trade. In *Federalist* 44, he laid the groundwork for a broad construction of the Constitution. Not until Secretary of the Treasury Alexander Hamilton proposed a national bank did Madison reverse himself and advocate a strict interpretation. Modern scholarship indicates that Madison's commitment to states' rights, which culminated in the compact theory of the Constitution, started as a tactical maneuver. After 1800 he relaxed his stand again, and during his retirement he denied that the Virginia and Kentucky Resolutions could be used to justify the nullifiers' theory of the Constitution.

A closer look at the evidence, however, permits a different understanding. According to more recent studies, Madison was not an early or a consistent advocate of centralizing change. In the Confederation Congress he was usually as ready to resist unauthorized extensions of congressional authority as to support a vigorous exertion of the powers clearly granted by the Articles of Confederation. Although he considered a power to coerce delinquent states to be implicit in the Articles, he did not approve of acting on that basis. Because the Articles did not include a power of incorporation, he resisted the creation of a bank. In 1783 he separated from the other advocates of independent federal funds when it became apparent that they hoped to imitate an English model of political consolidation. From the beginning of his national career, a genuine respect for written limitations of authority was near the center of Madison's creed, as was a conviction that excessive central power could endanger popular control.

By 1787, Madison had concluded that the powers of the states were inconsistent with survival of the Union. The Virginia Plan was premised on the supposition that the general government should rise directly from the people and would have to be equipped with plenary authority to act without recourse to intervening actions by the states. As Madison wrote in *Federalist* 20: "a sovereignty over sovereigns, a government over governments, a legislation for communities as contradistinguished from individuals" was as insupportable in practice as in theory. Accordingly, from the beginning of the Federal Convention, he attempted to exclude the states from any role in choosing federal officials or in executing federal decisions. He was disappointed when the delegates decided that the upper house would be elected by the legislatures of the states, which would retain their equal votes in one branch of the Congress.

Madison's defeat on the makeup of the Senate, together with his famous argument that fundamental rights are safer in a large than in a small republic, have been emphasized repeatedly as evidence that he preferred a more complete consolidation of authority than the convention finally proposed. In fact, Madison's determination to create a central government that would be wholly national *in structure* was accompanied throughout the Federal Convention by a relatively moderate position on the powers or responsibilities that were to be confided to its hands. Madison was determined, he insisted, to "preserve the state rights, as carefully as the trials by jury." In *Federalist* 10, he noted that the federal representatives had been entrusted only with decisions they were qualified to make. In *Federalist* 14, he made the point again: "The general government is not to be charged with the whole power of making and administering laws. Its jurisdiction is limited to certain enumerated objects which concern all the members of the republic but which are not to be attained by the separate provisions of any."

Whatever one thinks about Madison's private judgment of the Constitution, it is undeniably the case that the division of responsibilities between the central government and the states became a leading topic of the Framer's contributions to *The Federalist*. In *Federalist* 39, he offered an elaborate discussion of the partly "national" but also partly "federal" features of the finished Constitution. In essays 41–45, he sought to show that every power granted to the general Congress was "absolutely necessary" for a more effective union. Next, he argued that the mass of federal powers would not imperil the remaining powers of the states, that state encroachments on the federal sphere would be the greater danger, and that federal encroachments, should they happen, would produce a general alarm. In that event, he reasoned, "plans of resistance would be concerted," as they were against the British. A handful of ambitious federal usurpers would be faced with "thirteen sets of representatives" and "the whole body of their common constituents."

Madison was not content to demonstrate that local liberties and interests were protected by the Constitution. Rather, as the central theme of these related essays, he insisted that the federal structure would be a positive force for the country. Governmental sovereignty, whatever "theoretic politicians" said, *could* be successfully and lastingly divided, provided that the state and general governments were both the creatures of a common master, who was ultimately sovereign over both. The state and the general governments, he argued, were both to be the people's "agents and trustees," but neither would be able to absorb the other if the people disapproved. Instead, each would help control the other, and, as each was charged exclusively with duties suited to its nature, both liberty and the public good would be safer in the large, compound republic than in any simpler system.

Madison's denunciations of a Hamiltonian construction of the Constitution should not be seen as covers for an opposition that originated, fundamentally, in other disagreements. He had always been suspicious of deducing governmental powers from the implications of a constitution. As he wrote in the letters of Helvidius in 1793, the consequences of this doctrine were apparent. "Every power that can be deduced . . . will be deduced and exercised sooner or later. . . . A people, therefore, who are so happy as to possess the inestimable blessing of a free and defined constitution, cannot be too watchful against the introduction, nor too critical in tracing the consequences, of new principles and new constructions that may remove the landmarks of power." By 1793, moreover, Madison regarded Hamilton's interpretation of the Constitution as an integral component of a broader plan to transfer power to the federal level and, within the federal level, to the branches least responsive to the people. In *Federalist* 14, Madison had implied that the critics of the Constitution would have been on better grounds for their objection that the Union was too large to be administered as a republic if, in fact, the Constitution had entrusted comprehensive jurisdiction to a single set of hands. He was convinced that an increasing concentration of authority was certainly the tendency, and probably the object, of administration measures. Beginning with his essays for the *National Gazette* ("Consolidation" and "Government of the United States"), he warned repeatedly that Hamilton's designs could have no other end than "schism or consolidation; both of them bad, but the latter the worst, since it is the high road to monarchy, than which nothing worse, in the eye of republicans, could result from the anarchy implied in the former."

The Virginia Resolutions of 1798, calling on the legislatures of the other states to join in condemning the Alien and Sedition Acts, were an extreme, yet logical, development of Madison's continuing concern with "forced constructions" of the Constitution: with employment of the sweeping clauses "so as to destroy the meaning and effect of the particular enumeration which necessarily explains and limits the general phrases; and so as to consolidate the states by degrees into one sovereignty, the obvious tendency and inevitable consequence of which would be to transform the present republican system of the United States into an absolute, or at best a mixed monarchy." Madison's insistence that the Constitution was a compact, "that in case of a deliberate, palpable, and dangerous exercise of . . . powers not granted by the said compact, the states who are the parties thereto have the right, and are in duty bound, to interpose for arresting the progress of the evil," was rooted in the understanding of the Constitution that was first advanced in *Federalist* 39.

More thought confirmed the view, as Madison explained in the Virginia Report of 1799–1800. This major clue to Madison's thoughts was a reply to the objection that the local legislatures lacked the authority to judge the constitutionality of national laws and argued that the federal government had been created by the peoples of the several states. Those peoples had compacted, each with all the others, to entrust the general government with delegated portions of their power, reserving the remainder for themselves or for their states. And in the last analysis, the peoples of the states, acting in their highest, sovereign capacity as parties to this compact, were the only agency that could deliver a definitive decision on its meaning.

Madison never tired of telling the nullifiers during his retirement that no single state could unilaterally retract its compact with the others. His doctrine did not imply that any single legislature (which was not itself the sovereign) could undo a federal measure. It did imply, however, that as agents of the people, local representatives were constitutionally entitled to express their views and to appeal to others to unite with them "in maintaining unimpaired the authorities, rights, and liberties reserved to the states respectively, or to the people." This was all, he said, that the Virginia Resolutions were intended to achieve.

[See also *Federalist, The; Helvidius; Nullification Doctrine; Virginia and Kentucky Resolutions; Virginia Plan; Virginia Report of 1799–1800.*]

BIBLIOGRAPHY

Banning, Lance. "James Madison and the Nationalists, 1780–1783." *William and Mary Quarterly*, 3d ser., 40 (1983): 227–255.

Banning, Lance. "The Practicable Sphere of a Republic: James Madison, the Constitutional Convention, and the Emergence of Revolutionary Federalism." In *Beyond Confederation: Origins of the Constitution and American National Identity*. Edited by Richard Beeman et al. 1987.

Brant, Irving. *James Madison.* 6 vols. 1940–1962.

Cooke, Jacob E., ed. *The Federalist.* 1961.

Diamond, Martin. "The Federalist's View of Federalism." In *Essays in Federalism.* Edited by George C. S. Benson et al. 1961.

Dietze, Gottfried. *The Federalist: A Classic on Federalism and Free Government.* 1960.

Hutchinson, William T., et al., eds. *The Papers of James Madison: Congressional Series.* Vols. 14, 17. 1962–.

Ostrom, Vincent. *The Political Theory of a Compound Republic: Designing the American Experiment.* 2d ed. 1987.

LANCE BANNING

STORY, JOSEPH (1779–1845), member of Congress, Supreme Court justice. Born at Marblehead, Massachusetts, the eldest of twelve children, Story was the son of an ardent patriot who was one of the boarding party that brewed the Boston Tea Party. Like Madison, Story taxed his health by cramming four years of college study into three, and he graduated from Harvard with the class of 1798. Also like Madison, Story found his first reading of *Coke on Littleton* so difficult he despaired of becoming a lawyer—but where Madison turned to politics for a full-time career Story persisted and became a lawyer. Among his clients were the New England Land Company, speculators whose claims involved the Yazoo lands frauds.

Like his father before him, Story was a Jeffersonian Republican at a time when most of his friends and neighbors were committed Federalists. In 1803 Jefferson appointed Story to a customs post at Salem, but Story declined the job and stayed with his law practice. In 1805–1807 he served in the state legislature, where he drafted legislation intended to create a court of equity in Massachusetts; and although his report on a court of chancery was not accepted, it became a landmark in the development of equity jurisprudence in the United States.

Elected without opposition to Congress in 1808 as a Republican, Story was caught in the crossfire created by the enforcement of the Embargo Act. Jefferson believed Story was a "pseudo-Republican" who helped repeal the law, which was despised in Story's home district with a passion. Story was, in fact, a lame duck who was not renominated. He soon returned to the state legislature, where he was elected Speaker in 1811.

Convinced that a Supreme Court vacancy must be filled by a New England man, Madison first appointed Levi Lincoln to the position. Lincoln turned it down; a vengeful Senate rejected Alexander Wolcott; and appointee John Quincy Adams refused to quit his post in Saint Petersburg. Almost in desperation, Madison named Story to the vacancy, an act Madison later regretted because Story's commitment to Republican principles was tenuous at best. Under John Marshall's influence, Story voted

ASSOCIATE JUSTICE JOSEPH STORY. Engraving by G. Parker after a portrait by Chester Harding.
PRINTS AND PHOTOGRAPHS DIVISION, LIBRARY OF CONGRESS.

regularly with the high priest of Federalism and consistently favored national interests over state matters.

After the War of 1812 began, Story became an expert on maritime law and his opinions in key cases helped establish the admiralty jurisdiction of the federal courts. His opinion in *Martin* v. *Hunter's Lessee* (1816) firmly fixed the appellate jurisdiction of the high court over state courts. After Marshall's death in 1835 he was mentioned as Marshall's successor as chief justice, but Andrew Jackson passed over the one-time Democrat to select Roger Taney.

Story was able to serve on the high court and hold a professorship in law at Harvard from 1829 until his death. His lectures were the basis for his twelve-volume *Commentaries* on various aspects of the law. The final volume, on *Promissory Notes*, was published in the year of his death.

BIBLIOGRAPHY

Dunne, Gerald T. *Justice Joseph Story and the Rise of the Supreme Court.* 1970.
McClellan, James. *Joseph Story and the American Constitution: A Study in Political and Legal Thought.* 1971.
Newmeyer, Kent. *Supreme Court Justice Joseph Story, Statesman of the Old Republic.* 1985.
Weston, Alan. *Joseph Story and the Comity of Errors: A Case Study in Conflict of Laws.* 1992.

ROBERT A. RUTLAND

STRONG, CALEB (1745–1819), lawyer, politician. Born in the western part of Massachusetts in the town of Northampton, Strong graduated from Harvard College in 1764 and after studying law with Joseph Hawley was admitted to the bar. Strong began his political career in Massachusetts with his election as selectman in 1774. He supported the Revolution and during the war he took an active part in local and state politics. He served as county attorney and as a representative in the General Court and in 1779–1780 he helped draft the Massachusetts state constitution that is still in force.

In 1787 Strong was elected one of the Massachusetts delegates to the Federal Convention, where he met James Madison. Strong played only a small role in the proceedings at Philadelphia and it is by no means clear that

CALEB STRONG. Etching by Albert Rosenthal after a portrait by Gilbert Stuart.
PRINTS AND PHOTOGRAPHS DIVISION, LIBRARY OF CONGRESS.

he was a supporter of the Constitution. Pleading ill health, he returned to Massachusetts in August and thus was not present to cast a final vote or sign the document.

During the Massachusetts ratifying convention held at Boston, Strong spoke in support of the document. As a delegate from the western part of the commonwealth, where support for the Constitution was weakest, his voice was critical in the final vote, in which the Constitution was ratified by a narrow margin.

Strong was elected to the first session of the United States Senate and remained in that body as a firm Federalist until he resigned in 1796. In 1800 he was elected governor and was reelected each year until 1807, when he was defeated by the Jeffersonian James Sullivan. Although he maintained his Federalism, Strong earned a reputation as a moderate and as a result he regained the governor's office in 1812. Strong opposed the War of 1812 and repeatedly refused President Madison's request for troops. He was accused of making separate peace overtures to the British and he approved the calling of the Hartford Convention, but did not support secession. He remained governor until 1816, when he declined to run for reelection.

BIBLIOGRAPHY

Banner, James. *To the Hartford Convention: The Federalists and the Origins of Party Politics in Massachusetts, 1789–1815*. 1970.

Hart, Albert B., ed. *Commonwealth History of Massachusetts, Colony, Province, and State*. 5 vols. 1927–1930.

Lodge, Henry Cabot. "Memoir of Honorable Caleb Strong." *Proceedings of the Massachusetts Historical Society 17* (1879): 290–316.

WILLIAM M. FOWLER, JR.

STUART, GILBERT (1755–1828), painter. Stuart was born near Kingston, Rhode Island, the son of a snuff maker. Educated at the parish school of Newport's Trinity Church, Stuart became a pupil of the Scottish Jacobite painter Cosmo Alexander at the age of fourteen. Alexander took him to Edinburgh, where Alexander's sudden death in 1772 left Stuart bereft of a protector. He returned to America and worked for about a year in Boston but then hastily departed for London when the American Revolution curtailed his prospects for patronage.

In London, Stuart lived in poverty for several years until he became a copyist and a pupil of Benjamin West, the Pennsylvania-born artist who was First Painter to George III. By 1780 Stuart was West's principal assistant. *The Skater*, commissioned by the Scotsman William Grant, was Stuart's first portrait to win critical and popular praise. Its exhibition at the Royal Academy in 1782 marked the beginning of Stuart's rapid rise to acclaim as one of London's leading portraitists. Stuart's image of

GILBERT STUART.   Self-portrait (detail).
PRINTS AND PHOTOGRAPHS DIVISION, LIBRARY OF CONGRESS.

Grant's elegant figure, boldly silhouetted against the London skyline, is considered one of the greatest masterpieces of American portraiture (it is now in the National Gallery of Art in Washington, D.C.).

In 1787 Stuart, pressed by his creditors, fled to Dublin. He enjoyed success there until 1793, when France's declaration of war on Britain prompted his return to the United States. Following residencies in New York (1793–1795), Philadelphia (1795–1803), and Washington, D.C. (1803–1805), Stuart settled in Boston. Chief Justice John Jay sat for him in 1794, the first in a series of luminaries of the early republic, including Thomas Jefferson, John and Abigail Adams, John Jacob Astor, Albert Gallatin, James and Dolley Madison, John Randolph, James Monroe, Paul Revere, and Josiah Quincy, to have their portraits painted by Stuart. Stuart's best-known works are his many portraits of George Washington, of which the "Atheneum" version (named for the Boston museum that acquired it after Stuart's death) quickly achieved iconic status. Dolley Madison rescued one of Stuart's full-length portraits of Washington from the White House in August 1814.

Stuart was a painter's painter. No drawings by him are known to exist; he improvised his compositions directly on the canvas. In the final, American, phase of his career, Stuart increasingly concentrated his acute perception and masterful brush on the sitter's face, creating straightforward likenesses unencumbered by the aristocratic trappings of the European grand manner. Although Stuart disavowed any interest in history painting, he produced one of the greatest historical monuments of his age through his portraits of its leading personages, who seem, in his work, our contemporaries rather than our ancestors.

BIBLIOGRAPHY

McLanathan, Richard. *Gilbert Stuart.* 1986.
Mount, Charles Merrill. *Gilbert Stuart: A Biography.* 1964.
Park, Lawrence. *Gilbert Stuart: An Illustrated Descriptive List of His Works.* 4 vols. 1926.
Whitley, William T. *Gilbert Stuart.* 1932.

JOAN CARPENTER TROCCOLI

SUPREME COURT. The Supreme Court is at the heart of James Madison's conception of a system of checks and balances structured to prevent any single branch from dominating the United States government. In fact, while Madison was still a major factor in American government, he would see the Supreme Court assume powers that far transcended his own conception of its role. Yet Madison remained more tolerant of Chief Justice John Marshall's innovations than most of his fellow Republicans, including their leader, Thomas Jefferson. So long as judicial gains were viewed as a limit on the legislature, the branch in Madison's view most vulnerable to corruption, he was relatively content.

Madison's Virginia Plan, in 1787, presented at the Federal Convention proposed that "a National Judiciary be established to consist of one or more supreme tribunals" and that "the Executive and a convenient number of the National Judiciary, ought to compose a Council of revision with authority to examine every act of the National Legislature before it shall operate, & every act of a particular [meaning state] Legislature before a Negative thereon shall be final." When the council of revision was not included in the Constitution, even after Madison's second attempt, he turned consistently to the Supreme Court as the final arbiter of conflicts between the states and the central government. In *Federalist* 39 he argued that a national "tribunal is clearly essential to prevent an appeal to the sword and a dissolution of the compact." In February 1795, Madison chaired a committee of the U.S. House of Representatives that was reviewing an appeal filed by the New Hampshire legislature asking that Congress uphold the state judiciary against the U.S. Supreme Court decision in *Penhallow* v. *Doane's Administrator.* He asserted that

the committee could not conceive of "any ground, on which legislative interference could be proper" when there had been a "final decision by the Supreme Court."

The only time that Madison strayed from this position was in his response to the Alien and Sedition Acts of 1798. He argued in his Virginia Resolutions that states "have the right and are duty bound to interpose for arresting the progress of the evil." "Interposition" was to be a term used by advocates of state sovereignty beginning in the 1820s, but Madison insisted that interposition, and even Jefferson's more flamboyant word "nullification" in the Kentucky Resolutions, could not justify nullification as it was being threatened in the 1820s. Madison was more in character in 1809 when he declined to intervene in a comic-opera rebellion resulting from Pennsylvania's pique over *United States* v. *Peters* (the *Olmstead* case). He declared then that the president was "unauthorized to prevent the execution of a decree sanctioned by the Supreme Court of the United States."

Madison did not willingly extend this arbiter's role to cover intervention in disputes between the branches of the central government. Reviewing congressional legislation would make the judiciary "paramount in fact to the Legislature, which was never intended and can never be proper." In Madison's view, the Supreme Court was to review legislation primarily to protect the judiciary from encroachments by the other branches. This is probably the reason Madison was not as concerned by the Marshall Court's precedential ruling in *Marbury* v. *Madison* (1803) as his prominence in the title might imply that he should be. In voiding Section 13 of the Judiciary Act of 1789, the Court was at least formally acting in its own sphere. Moreover, Madison was really a bystander in "his" case, since Jefferson was the real target of the Court; Madison was the defendant only because he had not completed an action that was really the responsibility of his predecessor, then-Secretary of State John Marshall. Madison was less comfortable with Marshall's greatest decision regarding congressional powers, *McCulloch* v. *Maryland* (1819), for the Court's expansive (and Hamiltonian) reading of the "necessary and proper clause" of the Constitution seemed to be telling Congress what to do—and in particular to expand its use of that clause.

Late in life, probably in 1834, Madison wrote that, "when happily filled," the judiciary was "the surest expositor of the Constitution, as well in questions within its cognizance concerning the boundaries between the several departments of the Government as in those between the Union and its members." Unfortunately, Madison failed to set a good example for future presidents regarding the "happy" filling of seats on the bench. Madison's only appointments to the Supreme

Court were made in 1811, when he replaced William Cushing and Samuel Chase. One selection was outstanding. He was Joseph Story, who was Marshall's greatest supporter until Story died in 1845. The second appointment was as weak as Story's was strong. Gabriel Duvall lived until 1844 and served on the Court until 1835, but he left almost no mark on the Court's history. Earlier, Madison had appointed a political ally, Alexander Wolcott, Jr., to Cushing's seat, but Wolcott was so heartily detested by northern merchants that he was rejected, 24 to 9, by the Senate. Madison next appointed a recent convert to Republicanism, John Quincy Adams, who was approved unanimously by the Senate but then declined the appointment. Still, history confirms that Madison's judgment was probably better than Jefferson's, for Jefferson opposed Story as too young and "unquestionably a Tory." When Jefferson endorsed Postmaster General Gideon Granger's abilities, Madison responded that Granger's legal talents were meager. Fortunately, neither of them supported the inept Robert Smith, who offered to step aside to make room for James Monroe as secretary of state, provided he was assured of an appointment as an associate justice.

BIBLIOGRAPHY

Brant, Irving. *James Madison: The President, 1809–1812*. 1956.

Haskins, George Lee, and Herbert A. Johnson. *The Oliver Wendell Holmes Devise History of the Supreme Court of the United States*. Vol. 2. 1981.

Hutchinson, William T., et al., eds. *The Papers of James Madison: Congressional Series*. Vols. 11, 15. 1977, 1985.

Meyers, Marvin. *The Mind of the Founder: Sources of the Political Thought of James Madison*. 1981.

DONALD O. DEWEY

T

TAGGART, SAMUEL (1754–1823), Presbyterian minister, member of Congress. Born in New Hampshire, Taggart graduated from Dartmouth College in 1774, studied theology, and served as pastor of the Presbyterian church in Coleraine, Massachusetts, from 1777 to 1818. As a Federalist member of the House of Representatives from 1803 until 1817, he opposed Madison and Republican policies.

On 17 December 1808 Taggart dissented *"in toto"* from Republican foreign policy toward Great Britain and France, objecting especially to what he saw as the unconstitutional, inefficient, and ruinous (to the United States) "permanent embargo." He chastised President Jefferson and Secretary of State Madison (whom he supposed was "Chief Magistrate elect") for threatening American liberty by assuming "new, unusual or unconstitutional powers" in enforcing the Embargo. In June 1812 Taggart prepared a lengthy speech (which, although not delivered in the House, was published) critical of what he asserted was the unnecessary, impolitic, and potentially disastrous decision to declare war on Great Britain.

In a series of private letters to the Rev. John Taylor of Enfield, Connecticut, Taggart sarcastically attacked Madison. In 1808 Taggart called Madison "a visionary, theoretic, closet politician" and opposed his election as president. Once the election results were known, Taggart exclaimed, "James the first of America will take possession of the throne the fourth of March [1809]. . . . I think Friend James will have rather a troublesome reign." Taggart portrayed Madison as a weak and indecisive president, "a mere puppet or a cypher managed by some chiefs of the faction who are behind the curtain." Although Taggart believed Madison personally favored rechartering the First Bank of the United States, he maintained that Madison "was overawed by a powerful party against the bank and dared not recommend it. The truth is as a President

he is but little better than a man of straw and has no independence in anything." Again in March and April 1812 Taggart was harshly critical of the president. Threatening war to obtain new commercial restrictions against Britain, Taggart asserted, Madison was trapped by his ambition to be reelected and swept along by the war party. Madison's "crooked insidious policy," Taggart insisted, had brought the nation to the brink of ruin.

BIBLIOGRAPHY

Haynes, George Henry, and Mary Robinson Reynolds, eds. "Letters of Samuel Taggart, Representative in Congress, 1803–1814." *Proceedings of the American Antiquarian Society*, n.s. 33 (1923): 113–226, 297–438.

Packard, Theophilus, Jr. *A History of the Churches and Ministers, and of Franklin Association in Franklin County, Mass.* 1854.

CHARLES H. SCHOENLEBER

TARIFF OF 1789. Madison had been working to establish federal revenues since he first entered the Continental Congress in 1780. No issue confronting the First Federal Congress required more of his time and leadership skills. On 8 April 1789 he introduced the resolution that led to the impost or tariff act, the tonnage act, and the first collection act. Between then and 15 June, debate on these three bills dominated the attention of the House. Madison spoke with greater frequency than anyone else during the debate.

Madison, who favored the immediate establishment of a temporary system in order to provide the federal government with revenue as rapidly as possible, based his resolution on the revenue plan of 1783, which the Confederation Congress sent to the states as an amendment to the Articles of Confederation. Madison wanted a permanent system and argued for international free trade except with those nations that discriminated against American goods; consequently, he unsuccessfully sought higher duties on distilled spirits imported from Great Britain and from other countries not in treaty with the United States. He also supported protection for American manufacturing, but not at the expense of revenue. Madison successfully resisted pressure to reduce duties in most cases; after a lengthy debate between northerners and southerners, the duty on molasses was reduced.

Madison expected that the debate would be difficult because of conflicting state and sectional interests. While regional conflicts were evident, Madison was delighted at the moderate tone of the debates and at the fact that differences appeared within state delegations as much as among the different states. He found the spirit of accommodation among the members reassuring and concluded that those who had supported the Constitution's provision requiring a simple majority, rather than a two-thirds vote, for the adoption of laws regulating commerce had been vindicated.

The congressional debate, the first held under the new Constitution, was widely reported in the American press. Among the issues addressed by Madison and his colleagues were the relative importance of encouraging shipping and developing a navy against maintaining the primacy of agriculture; the effect of taxation on different social classes and on the settlement of the West; the tension between the consumption of luxury goods and republican theories; and the role of the federal government in regulating public morality by heavily taxing the consumption of alcohol.

BIBLIOGRAPHY

Bickford, Charlene B., and Kenneth R. Bowling. *Birth of the Nation: The First Federal Congress, 1789–1791.* 1989.
Bickford, Charlene, Kenneth Bowling, and Helen E. Veit, eds. *Debates in the House of Representatives, Documentary History of the First Federal Congress, 1789–1791.* 1992.
Hobson, Charles F., and Robert A. Rutland, eds. *The Papers of James Madison.* 1979.

KENNETH R. BOWLING

TARIFF OF 1816. Early in 1816 Congress passed a bill that is probably best described as a moderate or mild protective tariff. Its supporters, including President Madison, defined a number of purposes linked to the emergence of a new world order in the wake of Napoleon's final renunciation of his throne. After decades of military and commercial upheaval in Europe, as well as its own recent war with Great Britain, the United States had to take into account the changes that had occurred and the adjustments that were so clearly in order. In his

Seventh Annual Message to Congress in late 1815, his first since the end of the War of 1812, President Madison alerted Congress to the need for protection of U.S. manufactures that had been established during the recent years of embargo and war and that had become acutely vulnerable to British dumping and competition in the postwar market. The Jeffersonians had always been keen on household and small-scale manufactures, but Madison explicitly suggested that large-scale, public manufacturing establishments now deserved legislative support. That support soon took the form of import duties on competitive foreign goods, especially cottons and woolens, in the tariff of 1816.

These duties were modest, and the tariff law itself was not particularly controversial, enjoying support from all regions of the country, including the South. To a considerable extent, particularly among southerners, support for the new law arose from a concern for the republic's security in the light of recent experience. Many Jeffersonians, following Madison's lead, were principally concerned with protecting manufactures that were of prime necessity and essential to the public defense. In their cases especially, support for the tariff of 1816 was thus in no way tantamount to embracing a modern industrial society or to the protectionism supported by northern manufacturers from Hamilton's time on.

BIBLIOGRAPHY

Dangerfield, George. *The Awakening of American Nationalism, 1815–1828.* 1965.
McCoy, Drew R. *The Elusive Republic: Political Economy in Jeffersonian America.* 1980.
Preyer, Norris W. "Southern Support for the Tariff of 1816—A Reappraisal." *Journal of Southern History* 25 (1959): 306–322.

DREW R. MCCOY

TAYLOE, JOHN, II (1721–1779) prominent planter from the Northern Neck of Virginia. Born to one of Virginia's oldest and wealthiest families, Tayloe was educated in England. He returned to Virginia and married Rebecca Plater of Maryland in 1747. From his father (also named John), who himself was a great landowner and an influential member of the colonial government, he acquired land overlooking the Rappahannock River, where in 1748 he began construction of his home, Mt. Airy. Ten years in construction, Mt. Airy was considered one of the finest mansions in Virginia, rivaled in its day only by William Byrd's Westover. The magnificence of its imported French cut-glass chandeliers, its mahogany wainscoting capped with sterling silver, and its white sandstone exterior was matched by the beauty of the surrounding terraced gardens, bowling green, deer park, and racetrack.

Mt. Airy's racetrack was a gathering place for members of the Virginia gentry. George Washington frequented the races there and greatly admired the Tayloes' thoroughbred horses. Indeed, the most prominent characteristic of the Tayloe family, apart from its wealth, was its success on the turf. The first John Tayloe began importing Arabian horses about 1740, and his son, as master of Mt. Airy, continued the practice. John Tayloe III (1770–1838), who inherited Mt. Airy upon his father's death in 1779, became the undisputed leader of American thoroughbred racing and was founder of the Washington Jockey Club. It was his son, Benjamin Tayloe, who built the Octagon House in Washington where James and Dolley Madison took quarters after the British burned Washington in 1814.

John Tayloe II, like his father, was active in political life. He served on the county court and in the House of Burgesses and was appointed to the Council of State by Gov. Robert Dinwiddie in 1756. He continued as a member of this governing body for many years and was still active in its deliberations when Madison became a member during Patrick Henry's governorship. His political association with Madison was quite limited, however, for Tayloe died on 12 April 1779, barely more than a year after Madison became a member of the Council.

BIBLIOGRAPHY

Ryland, Elizabeth Lowell, ed. *Richmond County, Virginia.* 1976.

CHARLES D. LOWERY

TAYLOR, JOHN (OF CAROLINE) (1753–1824), political theorist, scientific farmer, champion of southern agrarianism. Taylor was born in either Orange or Caroline County, Virginia, the boundaries being obscure. An infant when his father died, he was reared by his uncle, Edmund Pendleton. Taylor attended Donald Robertson's private boarding school in King and Queen County, where Madison was among his classmates. He studied for two years at the College of William and Mary and then returned home to study law with Pendleton, one of the most distinguished jurists in Virginia. Upon gaining admission to the bar in 1775, Taylor set up practice in Caroline County.

Taylor fought in the Revolution, serving as a major in the Continental army and as a lieutenant colonel in the Virginia militia. In 1779 he was elected to the Virginia General Assembly and served intermittently from 1779 to 1800. He was elected in 1792 to the U.S. Senate to fill a vacancy created by the resignation of Richard Henry Lee. Reelected in 1793, he resigned the following year to pursue other interests. In 1803 and 1822–1824 he served in the Senate as a replacement for an incumbent who had either resigned or died, but he never sought the office. The simple pleasures of his splendid Rappahannock River plantation, Hazelwood, were far more appealing to him than politics.

Taylor devoted his life to farming. One of the leading scientific farmers of his day, he labored to promote an agricultural society and to protect the security of the agricultural freeholders on which the agrarian society rested. This accounted for his devotion to the Republican philosophy, with the yeoman farmer as its ideal citizen. By precept and example, he advocated progressive farming techniques; Taylor's essays reporting the favorable results of numerous agricultural experiments at Hazelwood were collected and reprinted in 1813 under the title *The Arator* and became something of a bible for progressive southern farmers.

Taylor was the foremost political theorist of Jeffersonian republicanism, at least as it was interpreted by its conservative, orthodox wing. A resolute critic of Hamiltonian finance, he opposed any type of individualistic capitalism that threatened the idyllic agrarian community he idealized. America's Edenic age, he believed, was the revolutionary era. The constitutional principles embodied in the Articles of Confederation guaranteed that sovereignty resided with the people, with government merely the vehicle for implementing the people's will. Taylor opposed ratification of the Constitution because he thought it concentrated too much power in the national government. His first political treatises, published in 1794, grew out of his fear of Federalist programs, particularly Alexander Hamilton's funding and banking measures. Those measures, he asserted, would promote the emergence of a powerful moneyed aristocracy that would tyrannize and plunder society, transferring property from those who earned it to those who held the reins of political power. Over and over, Taylor warned his compatriots that if they abandoned the virtues of the Revolution, their experiment in self-government and human liberty would surely fail.

A lifelong friend of Thomas Jefferson, Taylor occasionally worked closely with Madison. During the mid 1780s he collaborated with Madison in the Virginia General Assembly to gain passage of Jefferson's Statute for Religious Freedom (1786). Several years later, however, Taylor opposed Madison on ratification of the Constitution. In 1798 Taylor introduced Madison's Virginia Resolutions and worked for their passage, despite his belief that they were not bold enough because they did not declare the Alien and Sedition Acts null and void. In fact, Taylor never fully trusted Madison's republicanism. Taylor was a staunch supporter of Jefferson's presidency, but after 1805 he began to drift into the conservative, doctrinaire wing of the party led by the dissident John Randolph. In the presidential election of 1808 Taylor was an unsuccessful elector for James Monroe, whom he favored over Madison because the latter was "too much of a federalist."

Taylor's most important political publications were *An Inquiry into the Principles and Policy of the Government of the United States* (1814), *Construction Construed and Constitutions Vindicated* (1820), and *Tyranny Unmasked* (1822). As he grew older, his voice became increasingly strident. His defense of states' rights, strict construction of the Constitution, slavery, and minimal government became more strident, and his jeremiads warning of impending doom, of decline and decay, did much to create a sectional mood that in turn contributed to the disaster he prophesied. He died on 21 August 1824, and was buried at Hazelwood.

BIBLIOGRAPHY

Craven, Avery O. "John Taylor and Southern Agriculture." *Journal of Southern History* 4 (1938): 137–147.

Hill, C. William, Jr. *The Political Theory of John Taylor of Caroline*. 1977.

Mudge, Eugene Tenbroeck. *The Social Philosophy of John Taylor of Caroline: A Study in Jeffersonian Democracy*. 1939.

Shalhope, Robert E. *John Taylor of Caroline: Pastoral Republican*. 1980.

Simms, Henry Harrison. *Life of John Taylor: The Story of a Brilliant Leader in the Early Virginia States' Rights School*. 1932.

CHARLES D. LOWERY

TECUMSEH (1768–1813), Shawnee war chief, Indian leader. Born in 1768, near Piqua, Ohio, to a Shawnee father and a Creek mother, Tecumseh was raised amid the warfare of the American Revolution. His father was killed at the Battle of Point Pleasant, and his mother accompanied other Shawnees to Missouri in 1779, leaving Tecumseh in the care of an older sister, Tecumpease. As an adolescent, Tecumseh was heavily influenced by an older brother, Chiksika, a successful young Shawnee warrior. Tecumseh first fought against the Americans during November 1792, when he joined with other Shawnees to oppose an expedition of Kentuckians who had invaded Ohio. During the postrevolutionary decade he continued to fight in skirmishes that flared throughout southern Ohio and Kentucky. In November 1791 he led a party of scouts who monitored Gov. Arthur St. Clair's ill-fated campaign to the headwaters of the Wabash. Three years later he fought in the Indian attack upon Fort Recovery, and in August 1794 he led a party of warriors who were defeated by Anthony Wayne's army at Fallen Timbers. Embittered by the Indian defeat, Tecumseh refused to participate in the subsequent negotiations and did not sign the Treaty of Greenville.

After 1795 Tecumseh emerged as a village chief with a small but growing band of followers. Between 1796 and 1800 he resided at several villages in western Ohio, but by 1805 he had established a village on the White River in eastern Indiana. During this period he occasionally met with officials in Ohio to mediate quarrels between the Shawnees and local settlers.

In April 1805 Tecumseh's younger brother, Lalawethika, experienced the first of a series of visions that transformed his life. A former alcoholic, Lalawethika emerged as Tenskwatawa (The Open Door), the Shawnee Prophet, and began to preach a doctrine of revitalization. Combining traditional Shawnee beliefs with certain Christian doctrines, the Prophet urged his followers to renounce all contacts with Americans and to return to a more traditional way of life. By 1807 Indians from throughout the Old Northwest had flocked to a new village that Tecumseh and the Prophet had established near modern Greenville, Ohio, causing both state and federal officials to express alarm. Hard-pressed to feed the visitors, in the spring of 1808 the Shawnee brothers abandoned their village in Ohio and established Prophetstown, at the juncture of the Tippecanoe and Wabash rivers in western Indiana.

By 1808 Tecumseh had begun to utilize the Prophet's religious movement as the basis for a pantribal political and military alliance. Adopting the doctrine that all tribes held lands in common, Tecumseh argued that no individual tribe or leader could cede land to the United States. During 1808 Tecumseh met with British officials in Canada, then traveled among the tribes of Ohio, Indiana, and Illinois, seeking recruits for his new confederacy. He was opposed by many older tribal chiefs who saw his movement as a threat to their leadership, and in 1809 many of these leaders met with William Henry Harrison and signed the Treaty of Fort Wayne, relinquishing Indian claims to almost three million acres in northern Indiana.

In response, Tecumseh met with Harrison in August 1810 and declared the Fort Wayne Treaty invalid, with a warning to Harrison not to occupy the lands. In the autumn of 1810 he met again with the British and visited Potawatomi and Ottawa villages in Michigan, where he recruited additional warriors. During the following summer he met again with Harrison in Vincennes, then traveled across the South, attempting to recruit followers among the Choctaws, Chickasaws, and Creeks. In November 1811, while Tecumseh was in the South, Harrison attacked Prophetstown, destroying Indian supplies and dispersing Tecumseh's followers.

Tecumseh returned from the South in January 1812 and attempted to rebuild his confederacy. He met with

DEATH OF TECUMSEH.   The Shawnee chief and head of the united Indian confederation that resisted American expansion in the first decade of the nineteenth century was killed, reportedly by Richard Mentor Johnson, at the battle of the Thames, 5 October 1813. Lithograph published by Currier and Ives, 1841.   PRINTS AND PHOTOGRAPHS DIVISION, LIBRARY OF CONGRESS.

American officials on the Mississinewa River in May, but one month later he journeyed to Amherstburg, in Canada, where he learned that war had been declared between Britain and the United States. On 5 August 1812 Tecumseh directed the Indian force that defeated the Americans at the Battle of Brownstown, but four days later he was wounded at the Battle of Monguagon. On 16 August he led the Indian warriors who accompanied the British at the surrender of Detroit, and in September he joined the British expedition that ascended the Maumee Valley, but he turned back before capturing Fort Wayne.

Tecumseh spent the winter of 1812–1813 in northern Indiana recruiting additional warriors, and in May 1813 he assisted in the British siege of Fort Meigs, near modern Toledo. Although the siege failed, the Indians defeated a force of Kentuckians en route to relieve the fort. In the aftermath, Tecumseh interceded on the American prisoners' behalf after some of the Indians began to kill their captives. In July 1813 he led the Indian warriors who again assisted in a second unsuccessful attack on Fort Meigs and an assault on Fort Stephenson. Aware that Col. Henry Procter planned to retreat after the American victory on Lake Erie, in September Tecumseh denounced the British commander but was forced to accompany him as the British withdrew toward Toronto. On 3 October 1813 Tecumseh was slightly wounded in a skirmish at McGregor's Creek, but two days later he led those Indians who supported the British at the Battle of the Thames. Although the British fled after the initial American attack, Tecumseh and the Indians stood and fought, and during the subsequent battle Tecumseh was shot and killed, possibly by Richard M. Johnson, a militia officer from Kentucky. Following the battle his body was mutilated by the Americans and then inadvertently interred on the battlefield.

A courageous and honorable man, much devoted to his people, Tecumseh was praised by his American adversaries during his lifetime, and following his death Tecumseh's life story was embellished with apochryphal incidents. In the twentieth century Tecumseh remains a Native American hero but also has emerged as an American folk hero, perhaps the most admired Native American leader in U.S. history.

BIBLIOGRAPHY

Drake, Benjamin. *Life of Tecumseh, and of His Brother the Prophet; with a Historical Sketch of the Shawanoe Indians.* 1858; 1969.
Edmunds, R. David. *The Shawnee Prophet.* 1983.
Edmunds, R. David. *Tecumseh and the Quest for Indian Leadership.* 1984.
Sugden, John. *Tecumseh's Last Stand.* 1985.

R. DAVID EDMUNDS

TERRE AUX BOEUFS.   Terre aux Boeufs, an army camp site twelve miles south of New Orleans, was the scene of an American military disaster in 1809. In late 1808, the Jefferson administration received word that the British were assembling troops to send to the West Indies, possibly en route to an attack on New Orleans. To meet this threat, Jefferson and Secretary of War Henry Dearborn arranged to reinforce the New Orleans garrison. Brig. Gen. James Wilkinson was put in charge of these reinforcements and ordered to defend New Orleans.

Eventually, more than two thousand troops had arrived at New Orleans. Many of the troops were sick from drinking river water during the journey to New Orleans or from other causes, and Orleans Territorial Gov. William C. C. Claiborne and other civilian leaders disliked having the troops in the city.

Back in Washington, neither the new president, James Madison, nor his secretary of war, William Eustis, felt as strongly about the expedition as had their predecessors. Sickness rates were already high, and the unhealthy summer months were fast approaching. Accordingly, Eustis in late April ordered Wilkinson to transport the troops to high ground to preserve their health.

Wilkinson, however, had other ideas, and decided to encamp the army twelve miles south of New Orleans at a place called Terre aux Boeufs, on the left bank of the Mississippi, which enjoyed a commanding position on a bend in the river known as the English Turn. By 10 June the main force had arrived at the camp, only to discover highly inhospitable conditions. The waters had risen so high that they had overflowed the levee at certain places, rendering parts of the camp unsuitable for use. Moreover, the troops—mostly new recruits raised in 1808–1809—had no idea how to police the camp properly, thus increasing sanitation problems. The location of the camp, combined with the lack of camp police and various shortages caused by a lack of money, turned the encampment into a sickhouse. Everything went wrong. Flies and mosquitoes were everywhere; the drainage ditches overflowed in July, when the river was in full flood, covering the camp with raw sewage; rain damaged the tents; and there were few supplies of medicine. Perhaps worst of all was the food, supplied through the contract system, which mainly consisted of moldy flour and spoiled meat.

Despite these conditions, Wilkinson saw no need to move, although his army was now decimated. Madison and Eustis grew more concerned and in July ordered Wilkinson to move to Fort Adams and Natchez, up the Mississippi. Still Wilkinson dawdled, noting in mid August that he was having problems finding transports. In late August the condition of the army was measured: 632 could march with full pack, 350 could march without a load, 382 could not march, and 178 required personal assistance. Finally in September the army moved north, but conditions did not improve. The open, crowded boats were more unhealthy than the camp, and the army had no money with which to purchase food or medicine. By 20 September the army had reached New Orleans. Wilkinson ordered paymasters not to pay the troops, fearing they would desert if they had money. The army did not reach Natchez until 31 October. No arrangements had been made for hospitals to care for the ill; the sick lay on the ground, and soldiers died every day. Not until the middle of December did the number of deaths begin to decrease.

From 1 May 1809 to 28 February 1810, out of a total force of 2,036, there were 852 casualties—686 deaths, 108 desertions, and 58 discharges. Proportionately, this was the worst peacetime disaster ever to have struck the U.S. Army.

BIBLIOGRAPHY

Jacobs, James Ripley. *The Beginnings of the U.S. Army, 1783–1812.* 1947.
Risch, Erna. *Quartermaster Support of the Army: A History of the Corps, 1775–1939.* 1965.
Wilkinson, James. *Memoirs.* 3 vols. 1816.

MARK PITCAVAGE

TERTIUM QUIDS. The term *Tertium Quid*, Latin for "third something," was applied to Republican party factions in the states and the nation. These Quid factions—in Pennsylvania, New York, and elsewhere—formed no national party, considered themselves regular Republicans, supported President Jefferson, and backed James Madison for president in 1808.

On the national level the Tertium Quid schism of 1806 was the first serious intraparty division in Republican history. The defection of John Randolph and his followers, however, bore no relation to state party splits and must not be confused with the larger Old Republican (arch-conservative, strict-constructionist) opposition to Presidents Jefferson and Madison. Randolph's small band of supporters—only thirteen members in the House—believed their leaders were stretching the Constitution too far in the direction of Federalism. These country, or old-fashioned, Republicans mistrusted Madison because of his nationalist past, his support of the Yazoo compromise, and the administration's policy toward West Florida. According to Madison's biographer, Irving Brant, Randolph's inveterate hostility to "the weak and pusillanimous spirit of the keeper of the Cabinet—the Secretary of State," caused the break.

Randolph's troublesome Quids controlled key committees, displayed able parliamentary and oratorical skills, and swayed numerous other Republicans to their side. On one or another occasion, 72 of 115 Republican congressmen voted with the Quids. With the addition of 27 Federalists, the Quids had the potential to defeat the administration. But Randolph's tempestuous abuse and harassment often alienated his colleagues, and in time the Quids dwindled to a vexatious few. Under Jefferson's tactful persuasion, the administration's lines stiffened. Randolph and most Quids supported James Monroe for president in 1808 and were among the opponents of the War of 1812.

BIBLIOGRAPHY

Cunningham, Noble E., Jr. "Who Were the Quids?" *Mississippi Valley Historical Review* 50 (1963): 252–263.
Risjord, Norman K. *The Old Republicans: Southern Conservatism in the Age of Jefferson.* 1965.

HARRY W. FRITZ

THAMES, BATTLE OF THE (5 October 1813). Oliver Hazard Perry's defeat of the British Lake Erie squadron on 10 September 1813 cleared the way for William Henry Harrison's army to invade Upper Canada. This army landed from Perry's vessels near Fort Malden on 23 September, and four days later Harrison approached Amherstburg in battle formation, only to find the enemy gone.

The British general Henry Procter had been trying to feed several thousand people, both soldiers and Indians, but, because of drought, little food was available locally. Supplies had to come by water from Long Point, 150 miles to the east, but because the Americans dominated Lake Erie, this route was cut off. Procter decided that his alternatives were to retreat or to starve. He chose to retreat, a move that Tecumseh denounced as cowardly. Procter, in his haste, did not destroy bridges as he crossed them or fell trees to obstruct the road.

On 1 October Col. Richard Mentor Johnson, commanding a regiment of 1,200 Kentucky mounted riflemen, entered Canada and joined in the pursuit of the British force (Johnson's was the only American unit permitted to bring its horses into Canada), and Master Commandant Perry joined the march. Both the British and the Americans carried extra baggage up the Thames River in boats as long as they could. Even so Procter averaged only nine miles a day.

On 4 October the Indians created the only obstacle able to deter their American pursuers by wrecking the bridge over McGregor's Creek. Cannon fire drove the Indians away, but not before they had killed two of Johnson's men and wounded seven.

Early on 5 October, Harrison reached the enemy.

The British troops stood in two lines, with the Thames on the left and a small swamp on the right. One cannon was placed in the road beside the river. The space was too limited to permit troops trained only in close-order combat to maneuver. Beyond the small swamp on the British right were five hundred Indians led by Tecumseh.

Harrison had 140 regulars of the Twenty-seventh Infantry Regiment, 1,000 of Johnson's mounted riflemen, and 2,300 Kentucky volunteers, led by their governor, Isaac Shelby. The inflamed Kentuckians hated Procter, for he had commanded at the River Raisin on 22 January 1813, when his Indians massacred helpless Kentuckians who had been captured.

The Kentucky mounted riflemen carried a deadly long rifle, plus a hatchet and a knife for close fighting. The mounted riflemen, shouting "Remember the River Raisin," galloped through the two British lines, dismounted, and opened fire. The battle lasted only five minutes, as the cannoneers failed to get off a single round.

Half of Johnson's regiment veered left to attack the Indians. Because the brush was too thick for horsemen, combat there became hand-to-hand. The Kentucky volunteers entered that melee, but when Tecumseh was killed, the Indian defense dissolved. Colonel Johnson later advanced his political career by claiming that he had killed Tecumseh. Kentuckians cut strips of skin as souvenirs from a body they believed was Tecumseh's, but the Indians claimed they had removed their chief's body. No white man ever saw Tecumseh's corpse.

Procter himself rode away in retreat at the first fire, taking no part in the combat. Seven of his soldiers were killed, twenty-two wounded, six hundred taken prisoner. The American loss was seven killed, twelve wounded. This battle destroyed Britain's western army, but the U.S. victory was tactical, rather than strategic, for Harrison could stretch his supply line no deeper into Canada and was forced to return to Detroit.

BATTLE OF THE THAMES.   Engraving by W. Wellstood after a painting by Alonzo Chappel.
PRINTS AND PHOTOGRAPHS DIVISION, LIBRARY OF CONGRESS.

BIBLIOGRAPHY

Cleaves, Freeman. *Old Tippecanoe: William Henry Harrison and Time.* 1939.

Coffin, William F. *1812: The War and Its Moral; A Canadian Chronicle.* 1864.

Stanley, George F. G. *The War of 1812: Land Operations.* 1983.

JOHN MAHON

THORNTON, WILLIAM (1759–1828), architect and civil servant. Thornton, one of the founders of Washington, D.C., was born on a sugar plantation in the British Virgin Islands and was educated in Britain in the Quaker tradition. He studied medicine at the University of Edinburgh (receiving his M.D. in 1784 from the University of Aberdeen), in London, and in Paris but throughout his life was more inclined to the design arts than the medical.

Thornton arrived in Philadelphia in October 1786 and during the next four years attempted unsuccessfully to enlist free northern blacks to join the settlement of black poor that was being organized in Sierra Leone by London abolitionists. While in Philadelphia he stayed at Mrs. Mary House's establishment and came to know several delegates to the Federal Convention, including Madison, who took an interest in his colonization ideas and who even inserted an anonymous note on the subject in a letter dated 7 November 1789 that Thornton directed to the Société des Amis des Noirs in Paris. During these years Thornton was also active in the American Philosophical Society and in John Fitch's steamboat company, and in 1789 he designed the new hall of the Library Company of Philadelphia.

Thornton is best known for his design of the U.S. Capitol. His unfinished competition drawings for a neo-Roman republican temple elicited enthusiastic endorsements from President Washington and Secretary of State Jefferson when they were presented in late January 1793 and gained official approval four months later. The design was later modified but still formed the basis for the plan adhered to by both Jefferson and Madison during their presidencies.

In September 1794 Thornton was appointed one of three commissioners of the federal district, a position he held until the board's dissolution in 1802. In his private capacity he contributed to the embellishment of the Federal City with designs for town residences, notably that for John Tayloe, now known as The Octagon, located at New York Avenue and 18th Street, N.W., which served as President Madison's official residence from September 1814 until March 1815. In 1801, at Madison's request, he negotiated the lease and reworked the interiors of the

WILLIAM THORNTON.
PRINTS AND PHOTOGRAPHS DIVISION, LIBRARY OF CONGRESS.

rowhouse on F Street (later 1333 F Street, N.W.), next door to his own, that the Madisons occupied between 1801 and 1809.

Thornton supported Jefferson in the presidential elections of 1796 and 1800 and in 1801 sought an official position from his friend Madison. Passed over for treasurer of the United States, he was given a special clerkship in the State Department for the issuance of patents in the summer of the following year. With the blessings of Secretary of State Madison and his successors, he organized the first distinct U.S. Patent Office within that department and supervised its business and collections of models (known as the National Museum of the Arts) effectively, if not without controversy, until his death in 1828. His repeated attempts to upgrade the Patent Office, as well as his open support for republican revolutionaries in Latin America, occasionally caused Madison political embarrassment.

The Thorntons were personal friends of the Madisons and saw them almost daily when they were neighbors on F Street, and Mrs. Thornton recorded two visits to Montpelier, in September 1802 and September 1806. During the first stay Thornton made a drawing of the house, which Madison told Margaret Bayard Smith in September

1830 was the only drawing he had of Montpelier (the drawing is believed to survive in private hands but has never been displayed or published). Madison surely drew in part on Thornton's ideas and knowledge of materials when he began to remodel Montpelier in 1808, at which time Thornton was working on the design of Tudor Place for Thomas Peter of Georgetown; Thornton's plans for that residence incorporated a temple quite similar to that built at Montpelier in the center of its principal front.

BIBLIOGRAPHY

Harris, C. M. *The Design of the U.S. Capitol: Politics, Architecture, and the Founding of the American Republic.* Forthcoming.
Harris, C. M., ed. *The Papers of William Thornton.* 2 vols. Forthcoming.
Harris, C. M., and Daniel Preston, eds. *Papers Relating to the Administration of the Patent Office during the Superintendency of William Thornton.* National Archives: Federal Documentary Microfilm Edition No. 1, 1987.

C. M. HARRIS

TIPPECANOE, BATTLE OF (7–8 November 1811). William Henry Harrison, governor of the Indiana Territory, by 1809 concluded a series of treaties by which some Indian tribes of the Old Northwest ceded large tracts of land in Indiana and Illinois to the United States. Two Shawnee brothers, Tecumseh and Tenskwatawa, known as the Prophet, had united hostile Indians throughout the transappalachian frontier in a movement based on spiritual renewal. They advocated an end to intertribal warfare and a return to traditional Indian values. Contact with Europeans had resulted in sweeping changes in the life-style of the Indians, who had gone from a self-sufficient culture to one heavily dependent on European trade goods. In the spring of 1808 the Prophet moved his camp from Greenville, Ohio, to a site that came to be called Prophetstown, located near the junction of the Tippecanoe and Wabash rivers, approximately 150 miles north of Vincennes, Indiana. In August the Prophet visited Harrison at Vincennes and explained his plans for spiritual renewal among the Indians. Harrison recognized that the Indians had genuine grievances, such as the unwillingness of American juries to convict whites charged with murdering Indians. He acknowledged also that the Prophet had reduced drunkenness among the Indians and encouraged them to practice agriculture. But Harrison also suspected that British agents were supporting and encouraging the Prophet. Harrison was implementing the ambivalent policies of the Jefferson and Madison administrations—driven by the dual realities that the government wanted peace with the Indians but also wanted their land—and those policies ultimately proved to be irreconcilable. The Treaty of Fort Wayne (1809), which ceded more than 3 million acres, particularly alarmed Tecumseh. The threat of further land cessions transformed the religious movement led by the Prophet into a political and military confederacy led by Tecumseh. He opposed the land cessions, contending that all the tribes commonly owned the remaining Indian land and that no one group of Indians could cede it to the United States. At conferences at Vincennes in 1810 and 1811, Tecumseh and Harrison both professed to want peace but came to regard conflict as inevitable. While Tecumseh traveled among the southern tribes recruiting additional warriors to his cause, Harrison mobilized a military force and moved against Prophetstown. Meanwhile, Secretary of War William Eustis communicated to Harrison President Madison's desire for peace with the Indians if possible. However, Eustis also authorized Harrison to order the Prophet to disperse his followers and to use force if the Prophet refused.

On 26 September Harrison led from Vincennes a combined force of regular infantry, Indiana militia, and Kentucky volunteers. The army stopped for a month to build Fort Harrison at the site of present-day Terre Haute, then arrived at Prophetstown. Harrison chose not to initiate hostilities and accepted the Prophet's suggestion to negotiate the following day. He made his encampment for the night, knowing that an attack was probable. Despite Harrison's preparations, Indians from several tribes almost overran his camp in a fierce predawn attack on 7 November 1811. The American force of about one thousand troops rallied and repulsed several assaults, suffering 188 casualties, of which at least sixty-two were killed. The Indians suffered comparable losses, but Harrison claimed victory because the Americans held the field, and on the following day, his troops burned Prophetstown. When Tecumseh heard of the battle's outcome, he regarded it as a severe setback to his Indian confederacy. The Prophet lost influence over his followers, although they soon rebuilt their village on a site near the destroyed Prophetstown. In the message submitting Harrison's reports to Congress, Madison optimistically predicted that the battle of Tippecanoe would produce "a cessation of the murders and depredations committed on our frontier." Harrison advocated a general war against the Indians of the Northwest, but the escalating conflict with Great Britain soon resulted in the War of 1812, which superseded in importance the campaign against the Indians.

BIBLIOGRAPHY

Edmunds, R. David. *The Shawnee Prophet.* 1983.
Edmunds, R. David. *Tecumseh and the Quest for Indian Leadership.* 1984.

BATTLE OF TIPPECANOE.   PRINTS AND PHOTOGRAPHS DIVISION, LIBRARY OF CONGRESS.

Hoffnagle, Warren M. "Road to Fame: William Henry Harrison and National Policy in the Northwest from Tippecanoe to River Raisin." In *Papers on the War of 1812 in the Northwest*, no. 6. 1959.

Smelser, Marshall. "Tecumseh, Harrison, and the War of 1812." *Indiana Magazine of History* 65 (March 1969): 25–44.

THOMAS A. MASON

TODD, JOHN PAYNE (1792–1852), son of Dolley Payne Madison and her first husband, John Todd, Jr. Todd was born in Philadelphia 29 February 1792. The calamities that descended on his family the following year—his father's death in the yellow fever epidemic, his mother's near death of the disease, and the death of his infant brother—had important consequences for his adult life. Dolley was henceforth disposed to dote on her only son, and her inability to deal firmly with him compounded the difficulty of Madison's role as "papa," for which, by the time of his marriage, he was not ideally suited.

Payne Todd's formal schooling began at the Alexandria Academy in 1803. Two years later the Madisons enrolled him at St. Mary's Academy (later College), a Roman Catholic boarding school in Baltimore run by French-speaking Sulpician priests. The boy's unruliness probably explains the decision, but Madison also wished his stepson to gain the fluency in French that had eluded him. Payne remained at St. Mary's until 1812, doing well in French and natural philosophy and growing into a handsome young man. "We intend to send him in a few months to Princeton," Dolley Madison told her sister Anna in May 1812, but events presented other opportunities.

When Edward Coles became ill, Todd temporarily replaced him as President Madison's private secretary. In the spring of 1813 Todd went to Europe as one of three secretaries to the American peace mission, attached to Albert Gallatin. As the president's son he was accorded special status in Europe, and he took pleasure in playing the role of "the American prince." Toward the end of his two-year assignment his behavior became erratic and irresponsible. He left the American mission on two occasions to go to Paris, then lingered there after the other diplomats had returned home. While in Europe he ran up large bills, including gambling debts and the costs of an art collection (intended for Montpelier), against Madison's personal credit.

Back home, Todd continued in this pattern. He served again briefly as the president's private secretary and displayed his continental polish at his mother's last White House entertainments. But he soon began to drift from city to city, often remaining out of touch with his parents, and successfully evaded all of his mother's attempts to find him a suitable wife. His gambling problem, compounded, it would appear, by alcoholism, persisted; he was imprisoned for unpaid debts on at least two occasions. Between 1813 and 1836, Madison expended more than $40,000 to cover Todd's debts, keeping the information from Dolley.

Todd's destructive habits (and his limited capital) led him into a series of get-rich schemes. He obtained a French patent for using a mixture of cologne and spring water as priming fluid for firearms, and at various times pursued ventures in gold mining, stone quarrying, railroads, and silk production. His experiment in sericulture, not discouraged by Madison, led him to purchase land near Montpelier in 1818, but this, like his other ventures, came to nothing. At Toddsberthe, as he called his plantation, he constructed an unusual group of buildings about a central "Rotunda" that housed a ballroom, the design of the ensemble reflecting his expectations for entertaining and accommodating his and his mother's guests.

After Madison's death, Todd took over management of his mother's affairs and of the Montpelier estate. He negotiated its sale and tried without success to gain favorable terms for the commercial publication of Madison's private correspondence. His debts, combined with his mother's, kept them both on the brink of ruin. He sold off many family objects, as well as hundreds of Madison's letters from the collection of papers that Congress purchased in 1848. His death in Washington on 17 January 1852 (ascribed to dropsy) ended what Madison had summed up twenty five years earlier as a "strange and distressing career."

BIBLIOGRAPHY

Arnett, Ethel Stephens. *Mrs. James Madison: The Incomparable Dolley.* 1972.
Hunt-Jones, Conover. *Dolley and the "Great Little Madison."* 1979.
Moore, Virginia. *The Madisons: A Biography.* 1979.

C. M. HARRIS

TOMPKINS, DANIEL D. (1774–1825), governor of New York, vice president of the United States. Born in Westchester County, New York, Tompkins graduated from Columbia College in 1795 and read law in New York City. In 1797 he married Hannah Minthorne, whose father was a prominent Republican party activist, and a few years later he launched his political career, serving as a Republican member of the state constitutional convention of 1801 and then in the state legislature, joining the Tammany Society in 1803. In 1804 Tompkins was elected to the House of Representatives but resigned to become an associate justice of the state supreme court.

Popular and ambitious, Tompkins, with strong backing from De Witt Clinton, defeated Morgan Lewis for the governorship in 1807. Despite Clinton's support, Tompkins was a friend of the Jefferson and Madison administrations, backing Madison's runs for the presidency in 1808 and 1812. When war loomed in 1812, Tompkins, often without the cooperation of the War Department or the state legislature, used his authority as commander in chief of the state militia to prepare New York for the coming clash. He vigorously supported the

DANIEL D. TOMPKINS.   Engraving by T. Woolnoth after the painting by J. W. Jarvis.

PRINTS AND PHOTOGRAPHS DIVISION, LIBRARY OF CONGRESS.

War of 1812, even using personal assets at critical moments of financial necessity.

During a cabinet shakeup in 1814 Madison offered Tompkins the post of secretary of state and was angered by Tompkins's refusal. Tompkins wrote that he was better able to aid the war effort from Albany than from Washington, but he also feared losing the governorship to Clinton. He also feared losing his personal fortune, which was tied up in state accounts. Madison appointed him to succeed Morgan Lewis as commander of the Third Military District (New York City area). Thus Tompkins, a man with presidential ambitions, failed to position himself for president in 1816. Nonetheless, the Republican caucus that year nominated James Monroe for president and Tompkins for vice president. In 1820, Vice President Tompkins ran once again for the governorship of New York but was defeated. Depressed by his financial problems and the attacks on his integrity, Tompkins slipped into alcoholism. Unable to carry out his duties as president of the Senate any longer, Tompkins left Washington in January 1822 and died three years later.

BIBLIOGRAPHY

Johnson, Allen, ed. *Dictionary of American Biography.* 1928.
Niven, John. *Martin Van Buren: The Romantic Age of American Politics.* 1983.
Stagg, J. C. A. *Mr. Madison's War: Politics, Diplomacy, and Warfare in the Early American Republic, 1783–1830.* 1983.

DAVID B. MATTERN

TOUSSAINT-LOUVERTURE, FRANÇOIS-DOMINIQUE (c. 1743–1803), Haitian revolutionary leader. Born a slave on the Breda plantation in the colony of Saint Domingue, Toussaint became the manager's coachman and lived quietly until the blacks, espousing the revolutionary principles of liberty and equality, rebelled in 1791. His talents for leadership and military strategy soon propelled him into the top ranks of the revolutionary army, and after the French National Assembly abolished slavery in 1793, he joined the whites fighting against Spanish and British invaders. By 1797 the French commissioners had named him governor-general, and the constitution of May 1801 made him governor for life. In 1800 he expelled the British and in 1801 defeated the Spanish in Santo Domingo, obtaining control of the whole island. Toussaint had signed an agreement granting exclusive trading rights to Britain and America, but when peace returned to Europe in 1801, Napoleon made plans to reconquer the colony and end all foreign trade.

In February 1802 the French expeditionary forces under Gen. Charles Victor Leclerc landed at Cap Haitien. Following several months of fierce resistance, Toussaint, Henri Christophe, and Jean-Jacques Dessalines surrendered after being promised amnesty. In spite of that promise, Toussaint was transported to France and imprisoned in the Jura Mountains, where he died of cold and neglect in April 1803.

The question of American relations with Saint Domingue provided Secretary of State Madison with one of his first difficult foreign policy decisions. Desiring both friendship with France and trade with Saint Domingue, the Republicans withdrew the strong support given Toussaint by the Federalists but refused to forbid merchants to deal with the rebels. Madison instructed the American consul to cooperate with Toussaint as long as this could be done without conflict with the French government. Satisfying neither Leclerc nor Toussaint, Madison's balanced approach managed to avoid direct conflict with either side in the civil war.

BIBLIOGRAPHY

Alexis, Stephen. *Black Liberator: The Life of Toussaint Louverture.* 1949.
Korngold, Ralph. *Citizen Toussaint.* 1944.
Ott, Thomas. *The Haitian Revolution, 1789–1804.* 1973.

MARY A. HACKETT

TREATY OF GHENT. Within a week after Congress declared war against Great Britain in June 1812, Secretary of State James Monroe relayed to Jonathan Russell, the American minister in London, the administration's conditions for peace. Monroe observed that the country had just cause for war but wished, if possible, to avoid a long or costly one. Indeed, wrote Monroe, if Britain would repeal its orders in council and discontinue its impressments, there was "no reason why hostilities should not immediately cease." By this time, the British government had already revoked the orders in council, but Russell failed to win the debate over impressment with Lord Castlereagh, the British foreign minister, and so the war continued.

When, in late 1812, the emperor of Russia, Alexander I, offered to mediate an agreement to end the war, President Madison not only accepted the offer but proceeded to appoint commissioners to represent the United States in Saint Petersburg. Monroe's long instructions of 15 April 1813 focused on neutral rights and impressment, the central issues in the coming of the war. The American commissioners, Albert Gallatin and James A. Bayard, joined John Quincy Adams in Saint Petersburg on 21 July. Britain declined the offer of mediation but on 4 November proposed direct peace negotiations with the United States. Washington and London found Gothenburg (Göteborg) in neutral Sweden an acceptable site for the negotiations.

With the fall of Paris in April 1814, Gallatin and Bayard, then in Amsterdam, traveled on to London and there gained an agreement with British officials to facilitate the negotiations by moving them to the Flemish city of Ghent. During June the other American commissioners—Henry Clay, Jonathan Russell, and Adams—reached Ghent from Sweden. The British commissioners—Lord Gambier, Henry Goulburn, and William Adams—arrived on 6 August. William Crawford, the new U.S. minister in Paris, warned the American commissioners to expect little. Britain's great victory over Napoleon, added to the generally inadequate performance of U.S. forces fighting the war in America, gave the United States little diplomatic leverage. Indeed, on 27 July Monroe instructed the commissioners to omit impressment from their agenda in the interest of terminating the war.

At the first meeting in Ghent on 8 August, Lord Gambier expressed his country's regret over the war and its desire for peace. John Quincy Adams responded that the American people also sought an early peace. Henry Goulburn then presented the British agenda: the continuation of the right of impressment, the pacification of Britain's American Indian allies and their protection via an adequate and permanent revised boundary between the United States and Canada, and the termination of the special American rights to the northern fisheries, as embodied in the peace treaty of 1783, without an equivalent British concession. The American agenda scarcely touched these items. Adams asked for time to confer with his colleagues. The American commission had received instructions to discuss impressment and boundaries, but none regarding the fisheries or the critical question of the Indians. The Americans were determined to pursue two additional subjects—the definition of blockade and other neutral rights and American claims for indemnity arising from captures both before and during the war. At the meeting on 9 August the American commissioners announced that they had no instructions regarding Indians and fisheries, neither of which issue had been a cause of the war. But the absence of instructions, the Americans added, did not rule out the insertion of such items in the agenda.

On 19 August Goulburn presented the British case for an Indian defense line, arguing that Britain could not terminate the war leaving its Indian allies exposed to the encroachments of the United States. The British insisted that a durable peace required a permanent reservation for the Indians, which would serve as a neutral barrier between the territories of Britain and the United States. Goulburn suggested the area established by the Treaty of Greenville, signed on 3 August 1795, after Gen. Anthony Wayne's victory over the Indians of the Northwest. That treaty granted the United States all of Ohio except the northwest quarter. Britain did not demand the southern shores of the Great Lakes but did insist on the exclusive rights to fortify its positions and to maintain war vessels on the lakes. Britain also demanded a revision of the border between Lake Superior and the Mississippi that would grant it the right to navigate the great western river. Last, the British demanded territory from Maine that would permit a direct passage between Halifax and Quebec.

Adams noted in his diary entry of 19 August that the British "tone was more peremptory and their language more overbearing than in former conferences. . . . Mr. Clay has the inconceivable idea, that they will finish by receding from the ground they have taken." Clay saw clearly that the British had assumed an untenable position and that the Americans had only to await the impact of history, time, and space.

For five days the American commissioners struggled and searched for an effective defense against the British diplomatic assault. Adams feared that a long American note sent on 24 August would bring the negotiations to a close. In large measure the note focused on the critical Indian boundary question, reminding the British that the causes of the war had been maritime, without reference to Indians or boundaries. The British effort to establish rights and boundaries for Indians residing in the United States, the Americans argued, was contrary to principles of public law acknowledged by all nations. Britain itself had always adhered inflexibly to the maxim that no country with possessions in the New World had the right to interfere in the relations between a sovereign power and the Indians residing in its territories. The American commissioners rejected totally the British proposals for the cession of military sovereignty over the Great Lakes as well as the British demand for new boundaries—issues again that had no relation to the war itself. Recognizing the strength of the American note, the British commissioners sought a delay so that they might consult officials in London.

Adams regarded the British notes delivered during September as overbearing and insulting, but he also observed that the British were retreating from their earlier stands. Already they had acknowledged that their demands for exclusive military possession of the lakes and for boundary changes were negotiable. Both issues could be adjusted on the basis of Indian pacification, upon which they continued to insist. The Americans countered by attacking the fundamental British position that U.S. power and ambition rendered Canada insecure. They reminded the British that the United States had entered the war with no intention of conquering Canada and had sought peace from the commencement of hostilities. The British plenipotentiaries were wrong in presuming that the United States wanted more than the mutual restoration of territories. The American delegates believed that the recognition of any boundary included the relinquishing of any influence over the status of the Indians within that boundary. The Indian tribes of North America could not be compared, as the British argued, to the independent states of Germany. Thus the British had no choice but to recognize the Indians as they were situated at the commencement of the war—as wandering tribes within the boundaries of the United States.

Late in October the American commissioners agreed to prepare a treaty projet with articles regarding boundaries, Indians, impressment, blockades, and indemnities. The commissioners based their peace plan on the *status quo ante bellum*, leaving the issues in dispute to future settlements. For them there was no longer any alternative. Adams doubted that the British would accept the American articles; Clay feared that the British would laugh at the American attempt to escape the consequences of an unsuccessful war. From the outset the American commissioners had resisted every British effort to create an Indian barrier south of the 1783 boundary line. They now presumed victory on that issue by ignoring it altogether. The American article on Indian pacification called for the two countries to agree to stop any continuing hostilities against the Indians and to restore to the Indians all the "possessions, rights, and privileges" that they had enjoyed before the war, provided the Indians did not renew hostilities against either the United States or Britain.

The Americans presented their treaty projet to the British commissioners on 10 November. They informed the British that they were not authorized to discuss the rights and liberties that the United States enjoyed in relation to the fisheries under the treaty of 1783. At the same time the Americans expressed their conviction that possession was irrelevant to the determination of boundaries. British officials were prepared to agree; they had no greater interest than the Americans in the continuance of the war. The prime minister, Lord Liverpool, informed the Foreign Office on 18 November:

> I think we have determined, if all other points can be satisfactorily settled, not to continue the war for the purpose of obtaining or *securing* any acquisition of territory. We have been led to this determination by the *consideration of the unsatisfactory state of the negotiations at Vienna, and by that of the alarming situation of the interior of France.* We have also been obliged to pay serious attention to the state of our finances. . . . [U]nder such circumstances, it has appeared to us desirable to bring the American war if possible to a conclusion.

Before the end of the month the British accepted the basic American proposal for a peace based on the *status quo ante bellum*, with the exception of an unresolved dispute over certain islands especially in the more confined waters of Passamaquoddy Bay, in the Bay of Fundy, that were claimed by both countries. On 1 December the British accepted the American proposal to omit articles that related to the fisheries and to the navigation of the Mississippi. The negotiators provided for the establishment of commissions to settle the disputed claims to the islands in Passamaquoddy Bay and to study the northeast boundary and the river and lakes boundary west of Lake Superior. The American and British commissioners signed the Treaty of Ghent on 24 December 1814. Writing to Monroe the following day, Clay passed judgment on the American achievement, saying that in view of "the pretensions of the enemy at the opening of the negotiation, the conditions of peace certainly reflect no dishonor on us."

News of the treaty reached Washington early in 1815, and the Senate hastily ratified the document on 16 February 1815. Madison proclaimed the war officially at an end the following day.

BIBLIOGRAPHY

Brant, Irving. *James Madison: Commander-in-Chief.* 1961.
Burt, A. L. *The United States, Great Britain, and British North America from the Revolution to the Establishment of Peace after the War of 1812.* 1940.
Engleman, F. L. *The Peace of Christmas Eve.* 1962.
Perkins, Bradford. *Castlereagh and Adams.* 1964.

NORMAN A. GRAEBNER

TRIPOLI. See *Barbary States.*

TRIST, ELIZABETH HOUSE (1751–1828), called Eliza, daughter of Mary (Stretch) House. Mary House was the proprietress of the boarding residence that stood at the southwest corner of Fifth and Market Streets in Philadelphia, one block from the Pennsylvania State House (Independence Hall). This congenial establishment was highly regarded by members of Congress, especially Washington, Jefferson, and Madison, who referred to those under its roof as "our family." Mrs. House's residence thus played a significant role, in an informal way, during the crucial events of the constitutional and early federal period (it was closed after her death on 28 May 1793).

Madison was well acquainted with the House-Trist family. He knew Eliza's brothers Samuel House, a merchant, who in the mid 1780s became his tobacco buyer and agent, and Capt. George House, a privateer-merchant in the Revolution. There were other connections, including the "runaway" slave William (Billey) Gardner (1759–1795), who worked at Mrs. House's after Madison manumitted him in 1783, and the boarders Col. William

Floyd and his young daughter Catherine (Kitty), to whom Madison was briefly engaged in 1783–1784.

Eliza Trist was assisting her mother when Madison, newly elected to the Continental Congress, first lodged at Mrs. House's in March 1780. She had married Lt. Nicholas Trist, a British medical officer, in 1774. After the Revolution, Trist purchased land in Louisiana and went there in late 1781 to establish a plantation. Two years later Eliza made the arduous journey to Pittsburgh and then down the Ohio and the Mississippi to join him, only to learn as she reached Natchez in July 1784 that he was dead of yellow fever; she returned to Philadelphia in August 1785. Their son, Hore Browse Trist, appointed collector of New Orleans by Jefferson, died of yellow fever in 1804.

Eliza's friendship with Madison was close and long-standing. It may have taken a romantic turn in the late 1780s but remained always thoughtful and sympathetic. Eliza spent her later years in the Jefferson family circle. Her grandson, Nicholas Philip Trist, married Jefferson's granddaughter Virginia Jefferson Randolph in 1824 and on Jefferson's death became head of the Monticello household. Eliza Trist died at Monticello 9 December 1828 and was buried there in the family graveyard.

BIBLIOGRAPHY

Brant, Irving. *Madison.* 6 vols. 1949–1961.
Hutchinson, William T., et. al., eds. *The Papers of James Madison:* Congressional Series. 1962–.
Kolodny, Annette. *The Land before Her: Fantasy and Experience of the American Frontiers, 1630–1860.* 1984.

C. M. HARRIS

TRIST, NICHOLAS P. (1800–1874), private secretary to President Andrew Jackson, U.S. diplomat during the Mexican War. Nicholas Trist left a permanent mark on American history during the war with Mexico, when he ignored the recall orders of President James K. Polk and negotiated a peace, accepted by Congress, that limited American acquisition of Mexican territory to California and New Mexico. The present-day boundaries of the United States in the Southwest were thus largely determined by Trist's courageous defiance of a president whose expansionist impulses at times seemed out of control. Trist's preparation for his Mexican mission included previous service as a clerk in the State Department and a lengthy stint as U.S. consul in Havana, Cuba. His success in acquiring government positions owed something to his long-standing family ties to both Madison and Thomas Jefferson—indeed, he was married to one of Jefferson's granddaughters and was a frequent visitor at Monticello and Montpelier.

Trist appropriately considered himself a disciple of the two great Virginians. Madison's influence on Trist can be most clearly discerned in the development of the younger man's constitutional thought during the critical era of the late 1820s and the early 1830s. With Madison's advice and coaching, Trist published a number of articles condemning the nullification doctrine and the threat it posed to the Constitution and to the Union. When Trist became the private secretary to President Andrew Jackson, he became the informal conduit between Madison, in retirement at Montpelier, and the inner circle of the Jackson administration as it prepared to deal with the nullification crisis. As one of Madison's self-appointed legatees, Trist would attempt to explain and defend Madison's constitutional ideas for the remainder of his life, most notably during the great sectional crisis of the 1850s.

BIBLIOGRAPHY

Drexler, Robert W. *Guilty of Making Peace: A Biography of Nicholas P. Trist.* 1991.
McCoy, Drew R. *The Last of the Fathers: James Madison and the Republican Legacy.* 1989.

DREW R. MCCOY

NICHOLAS P. TRIST.   Photograph by Matthew Brady.
PRINTS AND PHOTOGRAPHS DIVISION, LIBRARY OF CONGRESS.

TURREAU DE GARAMBOUVILLE, LOUIS-MARIE (1756–1816), French soldier, diplomat. An infantry captain at the outbreak of the French Revolution in 1789, Turreau joined the revolutionary army, where his campaign against Royalist counterrevolutionaries in the Vendée during 1793 led to his trial on charges of unnecessary cruelty. Following his acquittal, he fought in Switzerland and the Piedmont, where Napoleon named him commander in 1800.

In 1804 the flamboyant Turreau was named minister plenipotentiary to the United States, and his dramatic arrival caused a sensation. His red whiskers, ostentatious dress, gilded carriage, and sumptuous dinners, his rumored penchant for wife beating, his reputation as "butcher of the Vendée," and his harsh and uncompromising attitudes presented a sharp contrast to his amiable predecessor, Louis-André Pichon. Turreau's 1805 demand that the exiled French general Jean Victor Moreau not be welcomed as a hero in the United States was resented as interference with American internal affairs. He rejected Madison's contention that Louisiana's eastern boundary was at the Perdido River and included most of West Florida, while Madison, citing French trade with the rebellious American colonies as precedent, rejected Turreau's request that American merchants be forbidden to send armed ships to trade with the black rebels at Saint Domingue. Turreau commented caustically on the Jefferson administration's maneuvers to avoid war as British and French attacks on American shipping increased after the resumption of war in 1803. He noted that an inadequate navy and northern merchants' resistance to any interference with trade profits would prevent Americans from mounting a strong offensive war but speculated that the large U.S. land area and the use of local militia would enable the Americans to fight a strong defensive guerrilla war, especially since the outrage caused by an invasion by a foreign power would overcome greed for foreign trade and unite the population. Recalled in 1811, he fought in the 1813 German campaign and retired from public affairs after the Bourbon restoration in 1814.

BIBLIOGRAPHY

Brant, Irving. *James Madison.* Vols. 4, 5. 1941.
Egan, Clifford L. *Neither Peace nor War: Franco-American Relations, 1803–1812.* 1983.
Michaud, Joseph François. *Biographie universelle, ancienne et moderne: ou, Histoire, par ordre alphabétique, de la vie publique et privée de tous les hommes qui se sont fait remarquer par leurs écrits, leurs actions, leurs talents, leurs vertus ou leurs crimes.* 1843–1865. Vol. 42.

MARY A. HACKETT

TWENTY-SEVENTH AMENDMENT. James Madison drafted the Twenty-seventh Amendment, which was one of twelve proposed by Congress on 25 September 1789. That amendment provides: "No law, varying the compensation for the services of the Senators and Representatives, shall take effect, until an election of Representatives shall have intervened." Madison argued that allowing Congress to establish its own salary was "an indecent thing and might in time prove a dangerous one."

Between 1789 and 1791, only six of the required nine states ratified the amendment. In response to concern over then recent congressional raises, Ohio ratified the amendment in 1873; Wyoming did so in 1978. As the issue became more controversial, the lack of a deadline for the 1789 proposal generated new interest. Between 1983 and 7 March 1992 thirty-one additional states ratified the amendment. It was certified as being adopted by the archivist of the United States on 18 May 1992. Subsequently, both houses of Congress, by passing a concurrent resolution, expressed their view that the ratification of the amendment was valid.

Doubts about the legality of ratifying a 203-year-old amendment are most likely to arise in questions about whether the amendment prohibits cost-of-living increases. The Constitution does not set time limits for ratification. The Supreme Court, first in 1921 and again in 1939, suggested that ratifications must be "sufficiently contemporaneous" so that they express the will of the people "in all sections at relatively the same period." A modern court could, following the 1921 decision (which used this amendment as an example of one that was no longer valid), hold that the amendment was not properly ratified. On the other hand, following the suggestion in the 1939 case that the question of contemporaneous ratification was political, rather than judicial, a court could hold that this matter had been resolved by Congress in favor of the ratification.

The most lasting contribution of the Twenty-seventh Amendment may be to point up the need for specific legislation to implement the provisions stipulated by Article V for amending the Constitution.

BIBLIOGRAPHY

Dellinger, Walter. "The Legitimacy of Constitutional Change: Rethinking the Amendment Process." *Harvard Law Review* 97 (1983): 386–432.
Huckabee, David C., and Thomas M. Durbin. *The Congressional Pay Constitutional Amendment: Issues Pertaining to Ratification.* Congressional Research Service, Library of Congress. 1992.

RICHARD L. AYNES

TYLER, JOHN (1747–1813) legislator, jurist, governor of Virginia. Tyler was born in York County, Virginia, and attended the College of William and Mary; after reading law in the offices of Robert Carter Nicholas, he became an attorney. He was befriended by Thomas Jefferson while a student and was an eyewitness to Patrick Henry's famous attack on George III during the Stamp Act crisis in 1765. In 1774 Tyler served on the Charles City County committee of safety and was thus thrust into an active role with the patriots, including a part in Henry's seizure of the gunpowder that had been spirited away from Williamsburg by the royal governor.

In 1776 Tyler married Mary Armistead and established Greenway plantation as his York County home. In rapid succession he was elected to the state admiralty court, the House of Delegates, and the Virginia privy council. In 1781 he resigned from the council and was soon elected Speaker of the House of Delegates, a post he held from 1781 to 1785. Tyler was Henry's loyal legislative ally until they differed over treatment of wartime Tories (Henry favored a lenient policy, Tyler sought tougher penalties). Madison and Tyler were in the House of Delegates in 1785, where they agreed that the Articles of Confederation needed drastic mending, and Madison was Tyler's coadjutor in submitting the resolution that eventually led to the calling of the Annapolis Convention of 1786.

After the Federal Convention of 1787, Tyler returned to Henry's political camp and at the Richmond ratifying convention of 1788 he joined with the Antifederalists to oppose approval of the Constitution. In the ensuing years Tyler saw his admiralty court dissolved, but he moved to the Virginia General Court, where he advocated the power of courts to overturn legislative acts that were deemed unconstitutional. In 1795 he resumed his friendship with Jefferson and became a leading advocate of the newly formed Republican party. Tyler steadfastly supported Jefferson and Madison as they tried to assert the United States' sovereignty when both England and France coerced American shipping on the high seas.

Tyler left the bench to become governor in 1808 and served as the Virginia chief executive until 1811, when he became a federal district judge in Richmond. He died while his son (who became the tenth president of the United States in 1841) was following in his footsteps in the Virginia legislature as a loyal supporter of President Madison's wartime policies.

BIBLIOGRAPHY

Grigsby, Hugh Blair. *The History of the Virginia Convention of 1788.* 2 vols. 1890.

Jordan, Daniel P. *Political Leadership in Jefferson's Virginia.* 1983. In *The Papers of James Madison.* Edited by William T. Hutchinson et al. 1962–. Vol. 8, pp. 406–409.

ROBERT A. RUTLAND

U

UNITED STATES ARMY. The United States Army under Thomas Jefferson and James Madison was a small, relatively unprofessional force usually employed in small garrisons scattered across a large country. A traditional republican dislike for a standing army combined with powerful incentives to economy mandated a small army. Forced to expand to fight a war against the more powerful and experienced British army, the army did so with relatively little success. However, the war did cause nationalist politicians such as John C. Calhoun to realize the need for reform, and thus provided the nucleus of a reasonably professional officer corps.

In 1809, as Madison took office as president, prospects were poor for the army. It numbered less than 10,000, and its entire disposable force of 2,000 men under Brig. Gen. James Wilkinson languished near New Orleans at Terre aux Boeufs, guarding against British invasion. Though Madison took steps to remove that garrison to safer ground, half of the soldiers would become casualties in an unparalleled peacetime catastrophe.

Moreover, after his administration had seemingly negotiated an end to Anglo-American problems with British minister David Erskine in the spring of 1809, Madison gave notice to Congress that a decrease in the size of the army might be in order. Despite the subsequent British repudiation of Erskine, the army only narrowly avoided substantial reductions advocated by Secretary of the Treasury Albert Gallatin and many members of Congress. Expenditures did drop in 1811. Not until the War Hawk Congress of 1811–1812 were any substantial military reforms or measures debated, and even then Republican infighting—between supporters and opponents of Madison's administration—and vocal Federalist opposition prevented unanimity and thwarted attempts by Congress to prepare the army for war. The U.S. Army in early 1812 numbered only 6,744—far less than its authorized 10,000.

By the time Congress declared war against Great Britain on 18 June 1812, the authorized strength of the army had risen to over 35,000, not including volunteer regiments also authorized, though there was no hope of its actually reaching that strength. Its highest-ranking officers were in general elderly Revolutionary War veterans such as Henry Dearborn, Thomas Pinckney, and James Wilkinson. The average age of general officers was sixty. The military academy at West Point, created while Jefferson was president, had produced few officers, and some were of dubious quality. Moreover, Secretary of War William Eustis had little administrative or leadership ability, and the awkward structure for supplying and feeding the American forces proved to be entirely inadequate. An inefficient recruiting system could not supply the needed manpower for offensive actions.

The army that took the field in 1812 to invade Canada, supplemented by state militia and some volunteers, was thus far less strong than the population and wealth of the country could provide. Ill-led and ill-provisioned, the army met with military disasters in the summer and fall of 1812 at Detroit and Queenston Heights, even though the British had relatively few troops with which to defend Canada. One nonbattle casualty of the 1812 campaigns was Eustis, whose inadequacies as an administrator lay revealed for all to see.

Following a series of failures, the administration and Congress made a redoubled effort to build an army that could bring victory. The paper strength of the army rose to forty-four infantry regiments with 57,351 troops, though the number of soldiers in actual service never amounted to anything near that force. Eustis's replacement as secretary of war was John Armstrong, an ambitious and energetic official who made some substantial improvements to the army, foremost among them the creation of a general staff to oversee administrative duties.

Armstrong also helped to promote some of the better American commanders to come out of the war, including William Henry Harrison, Zebulon Pike, Jacob Brown, Andrew Jackson, and Winfield Scott. Harrison, Brown, and Jackson were initially militia officers.

Still, 1813 did not bring victory. Though American forces secured some limited successes, they could never muster enough force or initiative to be decisively successful. Older generals such as Dearborn and Wilkinson were slow and passive, while Secretary of War Armstrong's interference only worsened matters, with the result that the following year, Americans would be on the strategic defensive against an enemy who no longer had to worry about its more powerful foe, Napoleon. Moreover, Madison and his administration, relying upon loans to finance the war and facing greater public opposition to the conflict as well, faced increasing difficulties in maintaining American forces. Though the U.S. Army and state militia forces met with success against Native American forces allied with the British in the Old Northwest and in the South, they had more difficulty coming up against British regulars.

The army along with the militia engaged mostly in defensive battles in 1814, trying to turn back British invasions. Again, its paper strength of 62,274 bore little relation to the number of troops in actual service. Nor was its performance substantially better than that of the state militias. However, the hard-fought battles of Chippewa and Lundy's Lane in the summer of that year were actions that the postwar army recalled with pride, as regulars trained largely by the rapidly rising Winfield Scott held their own against British veterans.

Perhaps the most lasting effect of the War of 1812 on the army was its impetus to reform. John C. Calhoun became James Monroe's Secretary of War in 1817, and energetically worked to remove or reduce many of the defects that the army and the War Department had shown during the war. Among his more notable achievements were the strengthening of the general staff system, the improvement of the military academy at West Point, the postwar reorganization of the army, and the creation of coastal fortifications. To many, the War of 1812 demonstrated that the United States needed a more capable and dependable army.

BIBLIOGRAPHY

Horsman, Reginald. *The War of 1812.* 1969.
Jacobs, James Ripley. *The Beginning of the U.S. Army, 1783–1812.* 1947.
Skelton, William B. *An American Profession of Arms: The Army Officer Corps, 1784–1861.* 1992.
Stagg, J. C. A. *Mr. Madison's War: Politics, Diplomacy, and Warfare in the Early American Republic, 1783–1830.* 1983.
Weigley, Russell F. *History of the United States Army.* 1984.

MARK PITCAVAGE

UNITED STATES MILITARY ACADEMY. By an act of Congress in 1802, the United States Military Academy was established at West Point, New York, which, because of its strategic location, had been an army facility most of the time since 1775. Initially opposed to a school for officers, President Thomas Jefferson changed

FORT PUTNAM AT WEST POINT. Aquatint from *Portfolio Magazine*, 1811.
PRINTS AND PHOTOGRAPHS DIVISION, LIBRARY OF CONGRESS.

his mind and pushed Congress to create such a facility as a means of finding "republican" officers for the army. Because the academy would offer a free education, paid for by the government, the cadets, in Jefferson's view, would henceforth come from the broad middling segment of society, and thus the officer corps would not become a preserve of aristocratic Federalists. The administration also showed favoritism to young men from recently acquired Louisiana as a way of winning the support of major provincial leaders. These developments, as well as the weeding out of Federalist officers on active duty, were a part of what Jefferson called a "chaste reformation" of the military establishment.

The academy made slow but steady progress under its early superintendent, Jonathan Williams. Though science and engineering became important parts of the curriculum, they were not stressed in the initial years, contrary to traditional accounts. At the time Madison became president, the course of study emphasized practical knowledge required of officers—mathematics, mapping, artillery skills, and French. As part of Jefferson's expansion of the army in 1808 in response to the Embargo crisis, the authorized size of the cadet corps jumped from forty-four to two hundred. But Madison and his first secretary of war, William Eustis, failed to implement the maximum increases at West Point and in the army in general.

During the War of 1812, West Point graduates were still junior in army rank, but several drew praise for their well-constructed fortifications. None of the works designed by West Pointers fell to the British. Borrowing colors from one of Winfield Scott's successful American units fighting in Canada—gray jackets and white trousers—academy officials made them the standard dress for West Point students.

BIBLIOGRAPHY

Ambrose, Stephen E. *Duty, Honor, Country: A History of West Point.* 1966.
Crackel, Theodore J. *Mr. Jefferson's Army: Political and Social Reform of the Military Establishment, 1801–1809.* 1987.

DON HIGGINBOTHAM

UNITED STATES NAVY. During the American Revolution Madison was one of two congressional representatives on the three-man Board of Admiralty (1780–1781). His role on that body is unclear, but he seems by the end of the war to have developed some appreciation for naval power because he opposed the sale of the *Alliance*, the last ship of the Continental navy, at the end of the war.

Madison first addressed naval affairs when he listed the ability to support a navy as one of the improvements offered by the Constitution over the Articles of Confederation. In the Virginia ratifying convention Madison argued that a navy was necessary to protect American shipping and to gain respect for the United States abroad. When the new congress debated tonnage duties in 1789, Madison supported preferential duties for American ships as a way to promote an American merchant marine that would "form a school for seamen [and] lay the foundation of a navy."

Only five years later, however, Madison abandoned support for the establishment of a navy. Whether motivated by partisan politics, sectional interest, or a change of mind concerning the value of a navy, Madison led the opposition to the Naval Act of 1794, arguing that "the expense of [a naval building program] would be immense, and [that] there was no certainty of reaping any benefit from it." These considerations—expense and doubts about the efficacy of the small navy the United States could afford to build—were to be the hallmarks of Madison's opposition to naval appropriations for almost twenty years and became part of Republican party philosophy.

As secretary of state in the administration of Thomas Jefferson, Madison showed no disagreement with Jefferson's reduction of the blue-water navy and the building of a purely defensive gunboat navy. When president himself, Madison included a number of recommendations concerning the army and the militia in his first four annual messages to Congress, but none concerning the navy. Throughout his term he delegated administration of the service to his secretaries of the navy and deferred to Congress in matters of naval policy. By default Madison continued his predecessor's policy of building gunboats for coastal defense. In the years before the War of 1812 he made only the tepid recommendation of December 1811 that Congress authorize the purchase of naval supplies which "are imperishable in their nature, or may not at once be attainable." On the very eve of war, most of Madison's cabinet proposed laying up the navy's ships or using them for harbor defense, but Madison acted on the advice of senior naval officers and approved the offensive strategy of sending the navy's ships to sea to raid enemy commerce.

In December 1812 Paul Hamilton resigned as navy secretary, and Madison replaced him with William Jones, a Philadelphia merchant who had served in a privateer during the American Revolution. Madison could rely on Jones, whom he later called "the fittest minister who had ever been charged with the Navy Department," to make the most of America's meager naval resources. Jones reorganized the Navy Department and supported building programs that brought morale-boosting victories on the inland lakes.

Madison's reference to "the signal services . . . rendered

by our Navy" in his seventh annual address (1815) and his recommendation to Congress "[t]o preserve the ships now in a sound state, to complete those already contemplated, . . . and to improve the existing arrangements into a more advantageous establishment for the construction, the repairs, and the security of vessels of war" are the strongest endorsements he ever rendered the navy during his nearly fifty years of public service.

After the War of 1812, Madison signed into law two far-reaching pieces of naval legislation. First was the February 1815 establishment of the Board of Naval Commissioners, a body of three senior captains charged with superintending "the procurement of naval stores and materials, and the construction, armament, equipment, and employment of vessels of war." Only three months later a dispute arose when the naval officers on the board claimed that the phrase "employment of vessels" meant that the secretary of the navy had to follow their advice concerning personnel assignments and squadron organization. Madison supported his new navy secretary, Benjamin Crowninshield, in opposing this infringement of the naval secretary's authority and thereby reaffirming the principle of civilian control of the military.

The second piece of legislation was the April 1816 act calling for the "gradual increase of the Navy" and authorizing the expenditure of $1 million a year for eight years on ship construction. This allocation reflected Madison's 18 February 1815 recommendation for a "gradual advancement of the naval establishment" and Crowninshield's 7 December 1816 report to Congress entitled "report relative to the gradual and permanent increase of the Navy." Only a portion of the ships were completed, but the act laid the basis for the first systematic naval building program since Jefferson's gunboats and produced several vessels that would serve the United States until after the Civil War.

Thus the War of 1812 brought Madison's attitude toward the navy full circle. During the American Revolution he developed an appreciation for the flexibility and power provided by a navy, but during the decades between the establishment of the government under the Constitution and the outbreak of the War of 1812 he doubted both the wisdom of constructing a blue water service and the ability of a navy to defend American maritime and commercial interests. The experience of a second war with Great Britain combined with the rapid chastisement of the Barbary corsairs in the brief campaign that followed that war led Madison to support again naval preparedness in 1816 as he had in 1783.

BIBLIOGRAPHY

Dudley, William S., ed. *The Naval War of 1812: A Documentary History.* 2 vols. to date. 1985–1992.

Eckert, Edward K. *The Navy Department in the War of 1812.* 1973.
Fowler, William M., Jr. *Jack Tars and Commodores: The American Navy, 1783–1815.* 1984.
Symonds, Craig L. *Navalists and Anti-Navalists: The Naval Policy Debate in the United States, 1785–1827.* 1980.

JAMES C. BRADFORD

UNIVERSITY OF VIRGINIA. In his effort to establish and sustain the University of Virginia, Thomas Jefferson drew upon the support of his longtime collaborator James Madison. Both Jefferson and Madison were convinced that the ultimate success of a republican system of government depended upon expanding educational opportunities in their state and in the nation. In the 1780s, while Jefferson served in France, Madison unsuccessfully attempted to move through the Virginia legislature Jefferson's "Bill for the More General Diffusion of Knowledge," which would have established a complete system of public education for the state. It took thirty years before the legislature became receptive to a proposal from Jefferson for public education.

In retirement, Jefferson convinced his Albemarle County neighbors to propose to the Virginia legislature the establishment near Charlottesville of an institution of higher learning that he named Central College. He drafted a bill and provided documents in support of the college as well as of his ultimate goal of a comprehensive system of public education. The bill was passed in the 1816 session without the financial support for which he had asked, but the legislature also instructed the governor of the state to prepare for the next legislature a report on a desirable plan of education for the state, from primary schools to a university. This provided hope for future resources.

Jefferson arranged for the appointment of a governing body for Central College that included himself and both the outgoing and the incoming U.S. presidents, Madison and James Monroe, respectively. This involvement of three presidents brought nationwide attention. Madison and Jefferson each pledged one thousand dollars to launch a fund-raising campaign. The board purchased land and approved Jefferson's architectural plans, and on 6 October 1817 the cornerstone for the first building was laid.

In February 1818 the legislature passed an act providing for a university. The location was to be determined by a commission appointed by Gov. James Preston. Jefferson and Madison were both named as members, and, at a meeting at Rockfish Gap, they succeeded in getting the commission to select the Central College site and to endorse Jefferson's educational and architectural plans. The legislature granted the University of Virginia a charter in January 1819, which is considered the official date

UNIVERSITY OF VIRGINIA IN THE 1830S.   Engraving after a drawing by W. Goodacre in I. T. Hinton's *History*, c. 1830.
PRINTS AND PHOTOGRAPHS DIVISION, LIBRARY OF CONGRESS.

of founding, although the university would not open for students until March 1825.

Jefferson and Madison both accepted appointments to the Board of Visitors, and Jefferson was elected rector, or head of the board. Jefferson's vision for the university was ambitious and highly innovative. He not only insisted that its faculty, library, equipment, and buildings be first-rate, he designed a curriculum, a governing structure, and a campus that were unique. Obtaining adequate financial resources proved difficult, especially as the economic climate worsened during 1819. Madison's support and advice were extremely valuable to Jefferson.

Before he died, Jefferson entrusted the care of the university to Madison. Madison accepted the responsibility, becoming rector in 1826 and continuing in that position until 1834, when he believed himself incapable of serving.

He did his best to see that the university maintained the stamp of Jefferson's genius. Madison revered the university as "a temple dedicated to science and liberty" and at his death left $1,500, as well as the bulk of his personal library, to the university. Madison's memory has been honored at the institution, which sponsors the *Papers of James Madison* editorial project and has a James Madison professorship in American history. The university administration is located in Madison Hall, and the student public service association is named Madison House.

BIBLIOGRAPHY

Koch, Adrienne. *Jefferson and Madison: The Great Collaboration.* 1950.

Malone, Dumas. *Jefferson and His Time.* Vol. 6. *The Sage of Monticello.* 1981.

STEVEN H. HOCHMAN

V

VAN RENSSELAER, STEPHEN (1764–1839), politician, soldier, landowner. Educated at Harvard, where he received his B.A. degree in 1782, Van Rensselaer, the fifth in descent from Killian Van Rensselaer, the first patroon, was descended from a distinguished and wealthy landowning family. His mother was the daughter of Philip Livingston, a signer of the Declaration of Independence, and his wife was a daughter of Philip Schuyler. Reputedly the richest man in New York state, Van Rensselaer was often referred to as "the patroon," a reference to his large rent rolls. He served in the New York Assembly and then in the Senate in the early 1790s and was the lieutenant governor from 1795 to 1801. In 1801 he ran unsuccessfully as the Federalist candidate for governor, losing to George Clinton.

During the War of 1812, Van Rensselaer served as a major general of the New York militia, although he had no previous military experience. His political appointment and his assignment to defend the Niagara frontier was the responsibility of Gov. Daniel D. Tompkins, who may have been seeking to attract Federalist support for the War of 1812, although his effort may have been a political ploy; Tompkins may have anticipated a failure that would damage the reputation of his rival for the governorship in the next election.

The difficulty of service on the Niagara frontier in 1812 would have tested the most gifted military leader, and Van Rensselaer's conduct during the fall of 1812 reflected his inexperience. Although he was ably assisted by his relative Col. Solomon Van Rensselaer, who did have military experience, Stephen Van Rensselaer chose to attack British troops across the Niagara River at Queenston in October 1812 before his troops were properly prepared. After an initial American success, the British rushed in reinforcements and pinned the Americans down. The outcome hinged on Van Rensselaer's call for the New York militia to cross the river which was met with outright refusal, and thus the battle was lost. Shortly thereafter, Van Rensselaer resigned. His support for the war may have lost him some Federalist support for governor in 1813, but his defeat at the polls resulted primarily from

STEPHEN VAN RENSSELAER   Engraving by G. Parker from a miniature by C. Fraser.
PRINTS AND PHOTOGRAPHS DIVISION, LIBRARY OF CONGRESS.

the popularity of Tompkins, who defeated him by 3,606 votes out of 83,000 cast.

Van Rensselaer's reputation revived when he supported the project to build the Erie Canal. In 1810 he became a member of the first Canal Commission, and he served as a canal commissioner from 1816 until his death in 1839. He supported the Federalist party even in its decline and in 1823 backed the organization of the "People's Party," a mixture of Federalists and Clintonians, that swept De Witt Clinton into the governorship in 1824.

Van Rensselaer served in the U.S. House of Representatives from 1822 to 1829. He is often remembered for his role in deciding the outcome of the presidential election of 1824, in which he cast the pivotal vote in the New York delegation that swung the vote and the election to John Quincy Adams.

BIBLIOGRAPHY

Alexander, De Alva Stanwood. *A Political History of the State of New York*. Vol. 1. 1906.
Johnson, Allen; ed. *Dictionary of American Biography*. 1936.
Fox, Dixon Ryan. *The Decline of Aristocracy in the Politics of New York, 1801–1840*. Repr. 1965.

C. EDWARD SKEEN

JOSEPH B. VARNUM.   Painting by Charles L. Elliott.
ARCHITECT OF THE CAPITOL.

VARNUM, JOSEPH BRADLEY (1750–1821), soldier, representative, senator. Varnum was born, grew up, and died on the farm he inherited from his father in Dracut, Massachusetts. A farmer by occupation, Varnum received a common-school education. Appointed captain of militia during the American Revolution, he served at Saratoga (1777), in Rhode Island (1778), and in the expedition that supressed Shays's Rebellion (1787). He was a strong supporter of the institution of the militia and maintained his military ties throughout his life, reaching the rank of major general in 1805. He served in the Massachusetts legislature from 1780 to 1795 and voted to ratify the U.S. Constitution at the 1788 state ratifying convention.

In 1794 Varnum defeated, by the slimmest of margins, the prominent Federalist lawyer Samuel Dexter for a seat in the House of Representatives. He held this seat without interruption until 1811, when he resigned after being elected to the Senate. In the House, Varnum was one of the strongest New England Republican voices, denouncing direct taxation, government expenditures on the navy and standing army, and the expansion of the federal judiciary. In 1807 Varnum was chosen Speaker of the House to replace Nathaniel Macon, whose continued support of John Randolph of Roanoke as chairman of the House Ways and Means committee had irritated the Jefferson administration. Varnum promptly sacked Randolph,

replacing him with George Campbell. He was reelected Speaker in the next Congress.

In 1811 Varnum was elected to the Senate, where he became chairman of the Committee on Military Affairs and a supporter of the Madison administration's war policy, this despite the unpopularity of the War of 1812 in New England. He ran on a war platform and was defeated in the race for the Massachusetts governorship in 1813, but he kept his Senate seat until 1817, when he retired from national politics.

BIBLIOGRAPHY

"Autobiography of General Joseph B. Varnum." *Magazine of American History* 20 (November 1888): 405–414.
Johnson, Allen, ed. *Dictionary of American Biography*. 1928.
Smith, William Henry. *Speakers of the House of Representatives of the United States*. 1928.

DAVID B. MATTERN

VETO POWER. Madison's proposal to give Congress a veto (or, as he called it, a "negative") over the laws of the state legislatures was central to his plan of constitutional reform in 1787. Madison believed such a veto power was essential to solving two interrelated problems of reform, "federalism" and "republicanism." The problem of federalism referred to the need to ensure the supremacy of the general government over the individual state governments. Personal observation and historical research convinced him that the mortal disease of confederacies was the federal head's lack of sufficient power to control the centrifugal tendencies of the members, which constantly evaded, defied, or encroached on the general authority. If the United States was to avoid the fate of other confederacies, Madison warned, a negative on the laws of the states was an indispensable requirement in order to eliminate such "vices" as encroachments by the states on the federal authority and upon each other and to ensure uniformity in matters of general concern, such as commerce and foreign affairs.

The idea of the negative as a device for implementing federal supremacy and uniformity was suggested to Madison by the prerogative of the British crown to disallow acts of the colonial legislatures deemed to be injurious to the general interests of the empire. Far from being a potential instrument of tyranny over the states, Madison argued, the negative was "the least possible encroachment on the State jurisdictions," a purely "defensive" weapon to enable the general government to resist state aggressions on its proper authority.

Effective as the veto promised to be in maintaining a due subordination of the states to federal authority, Madison was even more enthusiastic about its potential to control and moderate the internal policies of the states. In this respect, the negative was to be "a republican remedy for the diseases most incident to republican government," a device for reconciling popular government with the virtues of stability and justice. On the eve of the Federal Convention, Madison was deeply troubled by the instability and injustice of the ultrarepublican state governments. States such as Rhode Island enacted a proliferation of confusing, contradictory, and often unnecessary laws that not only disrupted the economy and stifled commercial development but, worse, violated the private rights of individuals and minorities. Indeed, the insecurity of private rights seemed to arise from the very nature of republicanism, for these unjust laws were enacted by popularly elected legislative majorities.

Madison's veto was designed to cure the mischiefs of republicanism by placing ultimate guardianship of private rights in the hands of the general government. Given its broad jurisdiction, the general government would be less likely to fall into the hands of a majority dominated by a single interest or passion. Enlarged electoral districts, moreover, would probably produce national representatives who were disinterested statesmen animated by a broad concern for the public good. The national legislature, in brief, would be less vulnerable to factionalism and therefore a relatively safe repository of the negative power.

Madison conceived of the negative as the means of uniting the advantages of a single enlarged republic and the existing American state system. In effect, the national legislature (Congress) would, in his words, become "an essential branch of the State Legislatures." Instead of state representation in the national government, as provided by the Constitution, he wished to have national representation in the state governments.

Madison was surely disappointed when the Federal Convention ultimately rejected his negative proposal as both inappropriate and impractical. Still, the essential idea behind the negative was embodied in the Constitution in the form of the "supreme law" clause, the judiciary article, and the specific restrictions and prohibitions on the state legislatures—which together constituted a judicial substitute for a legislative negative on state laws. Madison, to be sure, was far from satisfied with this judicial remedy, although he lived long enough to see the Supreme Court become an effective institution for preserving a Constitution that mixed federalism and republicanism.

BIBLIOGRAPHY

Hobson, Charles F. "The Negative on State Laws: James Madison, the Constitution, and the Crisis of Republican Government." *William and Mary Quarterly*, 3d ser., 36 (1979): 215–235.
Hutchinson, William T., et al., eds. *The Papers of James Madison: Congressional Series*. Vol. 10. 1977.

CHARLES F. HOBSON

VIRGINIA AND KENTUCKY RESOLUTIONS.

The Virginia Resolutions, secretly written by James Madison, and the Kentucky Resolutions, secretly drafted by Thomas Jefferson, denounced the Alien and Sedition Acts of 1798 as unconstitutional usurpations of rights reserved to the states or to the people and urged the other state legislatures to join in seeking repeal of these repressive laws. In "a political resistance for political effect," Vice President Jefferson devised the protest strategy to rally the American people against the Federalist party, allowing the voters "to rejudge those who, at present, think they have all judgment in their own hands."

Both sets of resolutions argued that the Union had originated as a compact among the states, that the general government possessed only delegated powers, that acts beyond the enumerated powers were unconstitutional and therefore void, and that, there being no final arbiter of the Constitution (the doctrine of judicial review had not yet been established), each party had "an equal right to judge for itself, as well of infractions as of the mode and measure of redress." Jefferson concluded that the rightful remedy was "nullification," although the Kentucky legislature dropped that designation. Madison used a milder term, asserting the right of each state to "interpose" to combat the evil.

The Kentucky Resolutions. Jefferson did not say that the rightful remedy was the constitutional remedy, however. Instead, that remedy was based on natural right: "Every state has a natural right in cases not within the compact . . . to nullify of their own authority all assumptions of power by others within their limits." But he backed off from this essentially revolutionary and extraconstitutional step, suggesting instead that Kentucky communicate its views to the other contracting parties—that is, the other states—inviting them to declare "whether these acts are or are not authorized by the federal compact." He expressed confidence that "the co-states, recurring to their natural right in cases not made federal, would concur in declaring these acts void and of no force," and would each take measures "providing that neither . . . shall be exercised within their respective territories."

This sweeping claim in the name of states' rights, had it been implemented, would have placed Kentucky in open defiance of federal laws; it was an extreme argument that was potentially as dangerous to the Union as the oppressive laws were to individual liberty. But Kentucky did not go that far. John Breckinridge, who introduced Jefferson's resolutions in the Kentucky legislature, kept the real author's name a secret and made one significant alteration in the text. He dropped all references to nullification and any suggestion that the obnoxious laws could not be enforced within the state. Instead, he followed a proposal that he and the local leaders of an earlier series of county protests in the state had put forward, calling for a double-barreled campaign to repeal the "unconstitutional and obnoxious acts." The resolutions were to be transmitted to the Kentucky senators and representatives in Congress, who were to work for repeal, and the governor was instructed to send the resolutions to the legislatures of the other states to seek their support in requesting "repeal at the next session of Congress."

The Virginia Resolutions. Like Breckinridge, the judicious Madison did not think it prudent to go as far as Jefferson had gone. The Virginia Resolutions were shorter, more moderate, and quieter in tone. They were more carefully couched in Madison's understanding of the constitutional tradition; they made no reference to natural law theory and, therefore, omitted any mention of the "rightful remedy" of nullification, a word that Madison came to abhor. Madison's resolutions opened with a declaration of Virginia's warm attachment to the Union created by the constitutional compact; denounced the Alien and Sedition Acts as "alarming infractions" of the Constitution; cited other federal measures that enlarged governmental powers and threatened "to transform the present republican system of the United States, into an absolute, or at best a mixed monarchy"; and proposed that the legislature "interpose" by urging the other states to concur in declaring the obnoxious laws unconstitutional and to take necessary and proper measures for cooperating with Virginia "in maintaining the authorities, rights, and liberties, reserved to the States respectively, or to the people."

Madison later explained to Jefferson his grounds for differing on proposed remedies by states in cases of unconstitutional acts:

> Have you ever considered thoroughly the distinction between the power of the *State* and that of the *Legislature*, on questions relating to the federal pact. On the supposition that the former is clearly the ultimate Judge of infractions, it does not follow that the latter is the legitimate organ especially as a Convention was the organ by which the compact was made. This was a reason of great weight for using general expressions that would leave to other States a choice of all the modes possible of concurring in the substance, and would shield the General Assembly against the charge of Usurpation in the very act of protesting against the usurpations of Congress.

Not a single state legislature endorsed either set of resolutions, so Jefferson proposed to Madison in 1799 that they renew "the principles already advanced by Virginia and Kentucky." In November 1799 Kentucky adopted a second set of resolutions that introduced the word "nullification" into the political vocabulary. In Virginia Madison was elected to the legislature, where he became chairman of the committee to prepare a vindication of the resolutions that he had written secretly the year before, defending them against "the replies of the other States, and the sophistries from other quarters," including the congressional defense of the Alien and Sedition Acts. Madison's "Report of 1800" was a brilliant exposition that argued that the Sedition Law was unconstitutional; that free speech and a free press are fundamental to republican government—indeed, that "the right of freely examining public characters and measures" is "the only effectual guardian of every other right"; that a popular, or free, form of republican government cannot be libeled; that the federal government possessed no jurisdiction over common-law crimes; and that the First Amendment superseded the common law on speech and press, guaranteeing freedom of both against the federal government, which had no authority to abridge them.

To support this argument, Madison noted that freedom of religion and freedom of the press were "both included in the same amendment, made at the same time, and by the same authority." He concluded, therefore, that "liberty of conscience and the freedom of the press, were *equally* and *completely* exempted from all authority whatever of the United States." The relationship of a free press to a free, elective, and responsible government made political criticism essential if an informed electorate was to make intelligent decisions. The resolutions of 1798 had been based on that proposition, he argued; they were expressions of political opinion "unaccompanied with any other effect, than what they may produce . . . by exciting reflection." Unlike judicial decisions, which were judges' legal opinions, they could not be "carried into immediate effect by force." Instead, they were legitimate verbal appeals that called on the other states for their concurrence "in making a like declaration." Madison's "Report of 1800" has been hailed by the scholar Leonard Levy as "a characteristically brilliant exposition" of "uncommon authority," "a major step in the evolution of the meaning of the free speech-and-press clause."

An Assessment. The principal purpose of the Virginia and Kentucky Resolutions was to reaffirm the right of political opposition, freedom of debate, and change through the electoral process. Although the election of Jefferson and a Republican Congress in 1800 was based on public support of those principles, the state resolutions were quickly forgotten. In practice, the resolutions had worked. But their theory had not been fully debated. "In the final analysis," the historian-biographer Merrill Peterson has observed, "it is impossible to say precisely what Jefferson's theory was in the Resolutions of '98," but he concluded that "he and his associates were somewhat careless on points of constitutional theory." The historian Drew McCoy goes further, charging Jefferson with "intellectual sloppiness" in dashing off his resolutions without more careful constitutional thought. The use of the word "nullification" made it possible for a later generation, led by John C. Calhoun, to resurrect the "Resolutions of '98" as a states' rights defense, not of freedom but of slavery.

[See also *States' Rights; Virginia Report of 1799–1800.*]

BIBLIOGRAPHY

Koch, Adrienne, and Harry Ammon. "The Virginia and Kentucky Resolutions: An Episode in Jefferson's and Madison's Defense of Civil Liberties." *William and Mary Quarterly*, 3d ser., 5 (1948): 145–176.

Levy, Leonard W. *Emergence of a Free Press.* 1985.

McCoy, Drew R. *The Last of the Fathers: James Madison and the Republican Legacy.* 1991.

Malone, Dumas. *Jefferson and the Ordeal of Liberty.* 1962.

Smith, James Morton. "The Grass Roots Origins of the Kentucky Resolutions." *William and Mary Quarterly*, 3d ser., 27 (1970): 221–245.

JAMES MORTON SMITH

VIRGINIA CONVENTION OF 1776. The convention, also known to history as the Fifth Revolutionary

Convention and as the Constitutional Convention of 1776, met in the Capitol in Williamsburg from 6 May through 5 July 1776. It consisted of two delegates from each of Virginia's sixty-one counties, two from the western district of Augusta County, and one each from Jamestown, Norfolk, Williamsburg, and the College of William and Mary. Of the 128 delegates eligible to attend, Benjamin Harrison and Thomas Jefferson were absent because they were representing Virginia in the Continental Congress; three others—Richard Henry Lee, Thomas Nelson, Jr., and George Wythe—each missed all but about two weeks of the convention for the same reason. During the absences of the five members of Congress, their seats were filled by alternate delegates elected at the same time the delegates had been chosen. Edmund Pendleton served as president of the convention, which provided a showcase for such distinguished Virginia statesmen as Richard Bland, Archibald Cary, Patrick Henry, and George Mason; the convention was also the first legislative service for two young men with distinguished futures, Edmund Randolph (George Wythe's alternate for Williamsburg) and James Madison, who, with William Moore, was elected on 25 April 1776 to represent Orange County.

Declarations of Independence and Rights. Delegates from a number of the counties had instructions from their constituents to declare Virginia independent of Great Britain, and the convention unanimously adopted resolutions on 15 May directing the Virginia members of Congress "to propose to that respectable body to declare the United Colonies free and independent states." It was the first such formal instruction to a state delegation in Philadelphia, and the ranking member of the Virginia delegation, Richard Henry Lee, made the motion on 7 June that Congress declare "[t]hat these United Colonies are, and of right ought to be, Free and Independent States."

The resolutions of 15 May also called for the appointment of a committee "to prepare a Declaration of Rights and such a plan of government as will be most likely to maintain peace and order in this colony and secure substantial and equal liberty to the people." Pendleton named Archibald Cary chairman of a committee that included both skilled veterans of the House of Burgesses and several newcomers, including both Randolph and Madison. The leading member was George Mason, who prepared the first drafts of what became the Virginia Declaration of Rights and the Virginia Constitution of 1776.

Mason introduced in committee a draft Declaration of Rights that asserted the equality of all men, set out the principles of republican government, justified the right of revolution, and contained provisions that listed the rights of persons accused of crimes, protecting the right to

8. That all power of suspending laws, or the execution of laws, by any authority without consent of the representatives of the people, is injurious to their rights, and ought not to be exercised.

9. That laws having retrospect to crimes, and punishing offences, committed before the existence of such laws, are generally oppressive, and ought to be avoided.

10. That in all capital or criminal prosecutions a man hath a right to demand the cause and nature of his accusation, to be confronted with the accusers or witnesses, to call for evidence in his favour, and to a speedy trial by an impartial jury of his vicinage, without whose unanimous consent he cannot be found guilty, nor can he be compelled to give evidence against himself; that no man be deprived of his liberty except by the law of the land, or the judgment of his peers.

11. That excessive bail ought not to be required, nor excessive fines imposed, nor cruel and unusual punishments inflicted.

12. That warrants unsupported by evidence, whereby any officer or messenger may be commanded or required to search suspected places, or to seize any person or persons, his or their property, not particularly described, are grievous and oppressive, and ought not to be granted.

13. That in controversies respecting property, and in suits between man and man, the ancient trial by jury is preferable to any other, and ought to be held sacred.

14. That the freedom of the press is one of the great bulwarks of liberty, and can never be restrained but by despotick governments.

15. That a well regulated militia, composed of the body of the people, trained to arms is the proper, natural, and safe defence of a free state; that standing armies, in time of peace, should be avoided, as dangerous to liberty; and that, in all cases, the military should be under strict subordination to, and governed by, the civil power.

16. That the people have a right to uniform government; and therefore, that no government separate from, or independent of, the government of Virginia, ought, of right, to be erected or established within the limits thereof.

17. That no free government, or the blessing of liberty, can be preserved to any people but by a firm adherence to justice, moderation, temperance, frugality, and virtue, and by frequent recurrence to fundamental principles.

18. That religion, or the duty which we owe to our C R E-A T O R, and the manner of discharging it, can be directed only by reason and conviction, not by force or violence; and therefore, that all men should enjoy the fullest toleration in the exercise of religion, according to the dictates of conscience, unpunished and unrestrained by the magistrate, unless, under colour of religion, any man disturb the peace, the happiness, or safety of society; And that it is the mutual duty of all to practice Christian forbearance, love, and charity, towards each other.

VIRGINIA DECLARATION OF RIGHTS. Madison's notes to his copy of the proposed declaration of rights (8 June 1776) reflect his commitment to religious liberty. In paragraph 18 he replaces the phrase "all men should enjoy the fullest toleration in the exercise of religion" to "all men are equally intitled to the full and free exercise of it." [For other discussions of Madison's change, see *Mason, George,* and *Memorial and Remonstrance.*]

jury trials in both criminal and civil cases and restating the provision in the British Act of Toleration of 1689 that all men "shou'd enjoy the fullest Toleration in the Exercize of Religion, according to the Dictates of Conscience." The committee added provisions to protect the right of suffrage for landowners, extolled freedom of the press and the citizen militia, condemned executive suspension of laws ex post facto, proscribed bills of attainder, and copied from the English Bill of Rights the provision "[t]hat excessive bail ought not to be required, nor excessive fines imposed, nor cruel and unusual punishments inflicted."

During debate on the convention floor during the first full week of June, the delegates made a number of stylistic and substantive amendments. They toned down Mason's language about the equality of all men because it contained an implicit condemnation of slavery, and they deleted the prohibition against bills of attainder. On about 10 June they adopted the second of two amendments prepared by James Madison to the final paragraph; Madison's changes transformed the grant of religious toleration into an outright affirmation for the first time that "all Men are equally intitled to the free exercise of Religion according to the Dictates of Conscience." The convention unanimously adopted the amended Declaration of Rights on 12 June 1776.

The Virginia Constitution. Mason's draft constitution was marked up in committee during the second and third weeks of June. On the weekend of 22–23 June the committee added a long preamble and some provisions adapted from a draft constitution that Thomas Jefferson had sent down from Philadelphia. The committee introduced the draft on 24 June; it was debated and amended by the convention and then unanimously adopted on 29 June 1776. It provided for a General Assembly composed of a House of Delegates, elected annually with two members from each county and one from each incorporated city, and a Senate of twenty-four members, with each member serving a four-year term and with the terms staggered so that one-fourth expired each year. The constitution did not permit the Senate to originate any legislation or to make amendments to "money bills." The constitution also provided for a plural executive composed of a governor and a "Privy Council, or Council of State." The General Assembly annually elected the governor, who could not act in important matters without the concurrence of the Privy Council. In order to provide the council with stability and in hopes of encouraging it to act without political motivations, the convention set no term limits for its members, but at the same time, in order to provide the General Assembly with some influence, the constitution required the General Assembly to remove and replace two members every third year and to fill any vacancies that occurred because of

deaths or resignations. The constitution also provided for the creation of an independent judiciary, its members to be elected by the General Assembly.

The Constitution of 1776 made few substantial changes in the institutional or political structures of Virginia's government and in effect secured for another half-century the domination of public life by the same class of landed gentlemen who had controlled the county governments and the House of Burgesses during the colonial period. Without question, the most potent agency of government under the Constitution of 1776 was the popularly elected House of Delegates; it was by placing the bulk of governmental power in that branch of the legislature that the convention members hoped to secure and retain their liberties.

The convention also adopted a number of important resolutions and ordinances designed to curb mischievous loyalists, prevent counterfeiting of the paper currency of Virginia and of the Continental Congress, enable the new government to go into effect, and provide money and arms for an enlarged Virginia army and navy. The delegates also passed an apportionment bill for the new twenty-four-member Senate of Virginia.

More than at any previous time, Patrick Henry and those who supported him carried the day in the major decisions. Circumstantial evidence confirms the contemporary supposition that Henry engineered the 20 June reduction of the Virginia delegation to the Continental Congress from seven members to five in order to displace Carter Braxton and Benjamin Harrison, with whom Henry had been at political odds during the previous two years. On 29 June 1776 the convention, by a vote of sixty to forty-five, elected Henry governor of Virginia over the former president of the colonial council, Thomas Nelson, Sr. One vote was cast for John Page of Rosewell, who went on to become president of the Council of State and was frequently acting governor during the ensuing months when Henry was ill.

The convention adjourned on the afternoon of Friday, 5 July 1776. Most of the members, including James Madison, returned to Williamsburg early in October to serve as members of the first House of Delegates in the General Assembly of the Commonwealth of Virginia.

BIBLIOGRAPHY

The best account of the convention is in chapters 5 and 6 of John E. Selby, *The Revolution in Virginia, 1775–1783* (1988). The convention's journals and papers have been printed in vol. 7 of William J. Van Schreeven, Robert L. Scribner, and Brent Tarter, eds., *Revolutionary Virginia, the Road to Independence: A Documentary Record*, 7 vols. (1973–1983). James Madison's participation is most thoroughly described in chapters 11 through 13 of vol. 1 of Irving Brant, *James Madison*, 6 vols. (1941–1961).

BRENT TARTER

VIRGINIA CONVENTION OF 1829. In the autumn of 1829 James Madison journeyed to Richmond as an elected delegate to a state constitutional convention charged with revising the original Virginia constitution of 1776. This was to be his last public performance in a deliberative body. Nearing his eightieth year, Madison was the only delegate to have participated in the drafting of the earlier framework of state government that he, along with many others, including his good friend Thomas Jefferson, had almost immediately judged to be flawed. Two aspects of the original document were especially controversial: a freehold suffrage requirement, which restricted voting in state elections to landowners, and an apportionment mechanism for the state legislature that heavily favored the eastern, Tidewater region of the state. The 1829 convention represented the culmination of longstanding, chronically frustrated efforts on the part of reformers, principally from the western parts of the state where the economy was not based heavily on slave labor, to remedy these inequities. The reformers were staunchly opposed by conservatives, principally from the east, who felt a compelling interest in protecting the political power of slaveholders and the institution they were wedded to.

Madison's influence in the convention, and for that matter even his precise position on the key issues, is difficult to judge. He enjoyed a great deal of ceremonial deference, and some delegates appear to have believed that his authority carried great weight. But he spoke infrequently, sometimes appeared to change his position, and never enjoyed the confidence of either contending faction. On the grounds of republican principle alone, Madison concurred, in general, with the reformers. However, he felt constrained both by the will of his Orange

VIRGINIA CONVENTION OF 1829.   Madison stands in the center addressing the convention. James Monroe sits in the president's chair (at left). Watercolor by George Catlin, Richmond, 1830.   VIRGINIA HISTORICAL SOCIETY, RICHMOND, VIRGINIA.

County constituents and even more by the very real threat that the bitterly contentious delegates might fail to arrive at a satisfactory consensus. By the time he delivered his one major speech in early December, Madison's fear of impasse—indeed, that the convention might abort—prompted his efforts to find a workable basis for compromise among parties passionately wedded, as he saw it, to powerful local interests. In a sense he attempted to invoke the central lesson of the Federal Constitutional Convention of 1787: that the framers of constitutions must look beyond any immediate, passionate differences of interest and even principle, and accept compromise in order to sustain the larger cause of stable republican government. The dynamics of this state convention gradually pushed Madison toward greater accommodation of the eastern delegates and their interest in protecting property in slaves.

Although Madison appears to have had little measurable influence in shaping the outcome of the convention, which generally favored the conservatives, he expressed satisfaction with the result. The new constitution included a number of disappointments, but the larger point remained that a consensus had been reached; the convention had not collapsed. Hence for Madison, the cause of self-government had been vindicated once again, this time in the face of extraordinary difficulties connected to the vexing institution of slavery.

BIBLIOGRAPHY

Bruce, Dickson D., Jr. *The Rhetoric of Conservatism: The Virginia Convention of 1829–30 and the Conservative Tradition in the South.* 1982.
Freehling, Alison Goodyear. *Drift toward Dissolution: The Virginia Slavery Debate of 1831–1832.* 1982.
McCoy, Drew R. *The Last of the Fathers: James Madison and the Republican Legacy.* 1989.

DREW R. MCCOY

VIRGINIA HOUSE OF DELEGATES. For discussion of Madison's service in the Virginia House of Delegates in 1784 to 1786, see *Madison, James,* article on *American Revolution.*

VIRGINIA PLAN. The Virginia Plan, a set of fifteen resolutions presented by Gov. Edmund Randolph to the Federal Convention on 29 May 1787, established the agenda of debate in the crucial early weeks of the convention. It proposed a "national" plan of union to replace the "confederal" system of equal and sovereign states embodied in the Articles of Confederation. Enlarged, significantly revised, and then organized into articles, sections, and clauses, the Virginia resolutions were transformed into the Constitution adopted by the convention in September. Madison never claimed to be the sole author of the Virginia Plan, but his guiding influence in the Virginia caucus, which drafted the resolutions, is beyond dispute. Moreover, some weeks before the Philadelphia meeting, Madison had sketched the main features of the plan in letters to Jefferson, Randolph, and Washington.

The leading idea of the Virginia resolutions was a national government, consisting of a legislature, an executive, and a judiciary, that would operate directly upon individuals. Representation in the national legislature was to be proportional (according to either free population or wealth); one house was to be elected by the people, and the other was to be chosen by the first from persons nominated by the state legislatures. In addition to the legislative powers vested in the Continental Congress, the national legislature was "to legislate in all cases to which the separate States are incompetent, or in which the harmony of the United States may be interrupted by the exercise of individual Legislation." The legislature was also to have a "negative," or veto, over state laws deemed contrary to the articles of union and to have the authority to employ "the force of the Union" against recalcitrant states. The plan proposed a national executive, elected by the legislature and ineligible for reelection, and a national judiciary, consisting of supreme and inferior courts, with judges holding office during good behavior. Together, the executive and a select number of judges were to compose a "council of revision," with a qualified veto over acts of the national legislature. Other parts of the plan covered the admission of new states, provided a guarantee of a republican government for each state, and described procedures for the passage of amendments, and for the ratification of the new Constitution by special conventions chosen by the people.

The finished Constitution departed from the Virginia Plan in important ways. Proportional representation became the rule for only one house of the legislature, the congressional veto over state laws was omitted entirely, and instead of a council of revision, the president alone was to have a qualified veto over acts of Congress. Moreover, the method of electing the Senate and the president varied significantly from the resolutions. Madison was unhappy with some of these changes, notably the loss of proportional representation in the Senate and the rejection of the veto over state laws. For all its differences from the original resolutions, the Constitution did embody the essential idea of the Virginia Plan, namely, the national principle. Both the plan and the Constitution provided for a national government, acting directly on individuals, to replace the existing confederal government that operated through the states. The Framers also adopted the plan's provision for submitting the Constitution for approval to conventions elected by the people, a method of ratification that became a distinctive feature of American constitutionalism.

[See also *Federal Convention; New Jersey Plan.*]

BIBLIOGRAPHY

Hutchinson, William T., et al., eds. *The Papers of James Madison: Congressional Series.* Vol. 10. 1977.
Kammen, Michael, ed. *The Origins of the American Constitution: A Documentary History.* 1986.

CHARLES F. HOBSON

VIRGINIA RATIFYING CONVENTION. See *Antifederalists.*

VIRGINIA REPORT OF 1799–1800.

Disturbed because not one state supported the Virginia and Kentucky Resolutions of 1798, Madison wrote a lengthy Report on the Alien and Sedition Acts for the Virginia House of Delegates. The resolutions of 1798 were brief statements expressing a constitutional theory of the Union and denouncing the acts of 1798 as unconstitutional. Although the resolutions stated that the Sedition Act violated freedom of the press, they did not declare the act void on the broad libertarian grounds that a free republican government was powerless to punish seditious libel or severe criticism of the government. In his "Address of the General Assembly," written in early 1799, Madison had counted on state criminal prosecutions to correct seditious libels.

At year's end, when he wrote his Report, Madison revealed a significant change in his ideas. The Report is a brilliant exposition of the meaning and scope of freedom of the press. In a tract of about eighty pages, Madison argued that the Sedition Act was unconstitutional, that the United States possessed no jurisdiction over common-law crimes such as seditious libel, that a popular or republican government cannot be libeled, that the First Amendment was intended to supersede the common law on speech and press, that the amendment guaranteed an absolute freedom against the federal government because no authority of the United States could abridge it, and that at the state level the only recourse against libel of public officials should be civil suits for damages.

Madison repudiated the contention that a sedition act that did not establish a prior restraint on the press did not abridge its freedom. He argued that "this idea of the freedom of the press can never be admitted to be the American idea of it" because a law inflicting penalties would have the same effect as a law authorizing a prior restraint. "It would seem a mockery to say that no laws should be passed for preventing publications from being made, but that laws might be passed for punishing them in case they should be made."

Madison discoursed on the differences between the British and the American constitutional systems. In the United States the people, not the government, possessed "absolute sovereignty" and placed the legislature as well as the executive under constitutional limitations. The security of the press required that it be exempt, not only from previous restraints, but also from legislative impositions of subsequent punishments. An elective, limited, and responsible government required a much greater freedom for criticism or attack than might be tolerated in Britain. A wide latitude for political criticism was indispensable for keeping the electorate free, informed, and capable of making rational choices. The relationship of the press to the elective principle necessitated that the press, "checkered as it is with abuses," be exempt from punishment. Abuse was inseparable from proper use, and wisdom dictated leaving the press's "noxious branches to the luxurious growth," rather than "by pruning them away, to injure the vigor of those yielding the proper fruits." The laws of the United States were "destitute of every authority for restraining the licentiousness of the press."

Because officers of the government could not be made responsible unless their conduct and motives were freely examined, it was no defense of the Sedition Act that it allowed the truth to be proved and that it punished only falsehoods. Proof of the truth of political opinions, inferences, and conjectures is exceptionally difficult, perhaps impossible. That the act required proof of intent to defame or bring into contempt meant little because one who believes he has discovered error or corruption means to bring the offending official or measure into contempt. In sum, the Sedition Act violated the rights of election and expression protected by the First Amendment. Often overlooked, Madison's Report stands out as one of the great documents in the history of the fight for freedom of expression.

[See also *Virginia and Kentucky Resolutions.*]

BIBLIOGRAPHY

Levy, Leonard W. *Emergence of a Free Press.* 1985.
Madison, James. *The Virginia Report of 1799–1800 Touching the Alien and Sedition Laws.* Edited by L. W. Levy. 1970.

LEONARD W. LEVY

VIRGINIA STATUTE FOR RELIGIOUS FREEDOM.

Foremost among Thomas Jefferson's many proposed revisions to Virginia laws in 1777 was a bill providing for religious freedom. The bill was dormant throughout the war. When Jefferson became the U.S. minister to France, he urged Madison to press the issue in the Virginia General Assembly. Jefferson chose the perfect legislative lieutenant. Madison's battle was waged throughout 1784 and 1785, primarily against Patrick Henry. At Henry's urging, petitions flooded into Richmond in 1784, calling for the legislature to provide fiscal support to churches. After winning state support for all churches, Henry next focused on the incorporation of the Episcopal Church as the official state church. A distraught Jefferson wrote to Madison, "What we have to do, I think, is devotedly to pray for [Henry's] death." Madison's solution was more humane; he campaigned successfully to remove Henry from the legislature by electing him as governor. Supported by both friends and enemies, Henry was elected unanimously. Madison's supporters then were able to stall the church tax bill until after the April 1785 elections, which added several new opponents of the tax to the legislature.

Madison's July 1785 *Memorial and Remonstrance against Religious Assessments*, listing fifteen reasons for branding as tyrants rulers who intrude on religious freedom, is widely regarded as one of humankind's greatest defenses of religious liberties. In October 1785 Madison persuaded the legislature to consider the revived Bill for Establishing Religious Freedom. Although he had to compromise on some of Jefferson's more extreme philosophical language, Madison could proudly inform Jefferson on 16 January 1786 that the General Assembly had just passed legislation that had "in this Country extinguished for ever the ambitious hope of making laws for the human mind." Jefferson was delighted, and in December 1786 he boasted to Madison that the act was "received with infinite appro-bation in Europe & propagated with enthusiasm." It was translated into French and Italian and already was mentioned in Diderot's *Encyclopédie*. Jefferson himself was its principal propagator and publisher. He boasted that it was "honorable for us to have produced the first legislature who had the courage to declare that the reason of man may be trusted with the formation of his own opinions."

Madison kept his legislative triumph secret until 1826, but anyone who knew him well would not have been surprised by his strong convictions regarding religious freedom. He had studied at the College of New Jersey (Princeton) under its president, John Witherspoon, who had begun battling against church authority while he was still living in Scotland. In 1774 Madison envied a Philadelphia friend who lived far from Virginia's religious constraints. Madison's contribution to the Virginia state constitution in 1776 was to replace the words "fullest toleration" with "free exercise" of religion. Even his War of 1812 proclamations suggesting prayer were directed only to persons "who shall be piously disposed." He felt that "the Holy and Omniscient Being" would respond only to supplicants "guided by their free choice, by the impulse of their hearts and the dictates of their consciences."

[See also *Baptists*; *Anglican Church*; *Memorial and Remonstrance*.]

BIBLIOGRAPHY

Alley, Robert S., ed. *James Madison on Religious Liberty*. 1985.
Brant, Irving. *James Madison: The Nationalist, 1780–1787*. 1948.
Hutchinson, William T., et al., eds. *The Papers of James Madison: Congressional Series*. Vol. 8. 1973.
Malone, Dumas. *Jefferson the Virginian*. 1948.

DONALD O. DEWEY

W

WAGNER, JACOB (1772–1825), chief clerk of the State Department, newspaper editor. Wagner was brought into the State Department by Timothy Pickering in 1798. A confirmed Federalist, Wagner offered to resign on Madison's accession to the office of secretary of state, but the chief clerk's knowledge of the office and his language proficiency outweighed political considerations. For his part, Wagner promised a "neutrality of *conduct* between the belligerant [*sic*] parties." Madison came under a great deal of pressure from Republicans to remove Wagner, but even when the chief clerk was ill and absent for six months in 1802 and once again offered to resign, Madison kept the position open for his return. The post of chief clerk became in Wagner's hands something like that of an assistant secretary of state, especially in the summer months, which Madison spent at home in the Virginia Piedmont. At such times Wagner offered advice (not always taken), observations, and explanations that were more like those of a colleague than a subordinate. According to Wagner, Madison's conduct toward him was always politely correct, even amiable; it seems that despite each man's strong political beliefs, the two were able to maintain a good working relationship. There were rumors, no doubt prompted by Wagner's subsequent newspaper career, that, while in the State Department, the chief clerk ghostwrote editorials for the *Washington Federalist*, but no proof has been found to confirm the suspicion. Wagner resigned his post in 1806 and moved to Baltimore, where in 1808 he established the fervently Federalist newspaper, the *North American*, which soon became the *Federal Republican*. In these papers, Wagner and his coeditor, Alexander Contee Hanson, achieved new depths of political scurrility in their attacks on Madison and his administration. After the declaration of war in 1812, a Baltimore mob destroyed Wagner's press, and he was forced to flee to Georgetown, where he set up shop and continued to publish his newspaper until 1816.

BIBLIOGRAPHY

Cunningham, Noble E., Jr. *The Process of Government under Jefferson.* 1978.

Fischer, David Hackett. *The Revolution of American Conservatism.* 1965.

Timothy Pickering Papers. Massachusetts Historical Society microfilm.

DAVID B. MATTERN

WAR HAWKS. The War of 1812 was the central focus in Madison's second term, but its roots lay in the first term. The struggle in the United States for national identity pitted Federalists and Republicans against each other over the question of foreign relations. As the European war grew in intensity, the French and the British imposed odious conditions upon American trade and shipping, interrupting the free use of sea lanes. As leaders in the United States pondered responses to such foreign interference, several alternatives emerged. A minority in Congress seemed sympathetic with the British cause. John Randolph of Virginia was a leader of the pro-British faction in the House of Representatives. After 1810, Republican representatives from the western states contributed to a majority that saw British actions as threatening to the integrity of the United States. It was this contingent that gained the name "War Hawks."

Few persons favored war with both France and England, and cautious members of Madison's cabinet sought peaceful solutions. By 1810 the president, torn between his deep desire for a peaceful resolution of the strife and a growing conviction that war was inevitable, actively supported a program to strengthen national defense. As

A Scene on the FRONTIERS *as Practiced by the* HUMANE BRITISH *and their* WORTHY ALLIES____

Bring me the Scalps
and the King our master
will reward you__

Reward for
Sixteen
Scalps

Arise Columbia's Sons and forward press,
Your Country's wrongs call loudly for redress;
The Savage Indian with his Scalping knife,
Or Tomahawk may seek to take your life;

By bravery aw'd they'll in a dreadful Fright,
Shrink back for Refuge to the Woods in Flight;
Their British leaders then will quickly shake,
And for those wrongs shall restitution make.

WAR HAWKS' COMPLAINTS.   *A Scene on the Frontiers.* Southern and western members of Congress supported the declaration of war because of their belief that the British encouraged Indian attacks on American settlements. Colored etching by William Charles.   PRINTS AND PHOTOGRAPHS DIVISION, LIBRARY OF CONGRESS.

late as April 1812, Madison wrote to Jefferson, saying of a proposed embargo that "it is a rational and provident measure. . . . Whether if adopted for 60 days, it may beget apprehensions of a protraction, and thence lead to admissible overtures, before the sword is stained with blood, cannot be foreknown with certainty."

As the election of 1810 progressed, Madison was urged by his fellow Virginian Light-Horse Harry Lee to "draw the sword." Henry Clay, representative from Kentucky, considered war with Great Britain inevitable. When newly elected members of Congress assembled in Washington, the War Hawks, young and eager, began to plan a strategy to capture control of the House. Clay, upon his arrival in the capital, found that along with his old associates, Richard Johnson, Peter Porter, and Langdon Cheves, he had a number of newly elected allies, including William Lowndes, John C. Calhoun, Felix Grundy,

and John Adams Harper. Most of these men held a strong enmity toward England. They saw a threat to national sovereignty in the provocative actions employed by the British. Many of these hawks found lodging in the same Washington boarding house. As they discussed their concerns, their conversations were reported to have been so heated that their gatherings became known as the War Mess.

These young lawmakers found a natural leader for their opposition to Great Britain in Clay, a politician who had a remarkable gift of persuasion and could, it was believed, control the pro-British Randolph. After careful planning, when Congress convened on 4 November 1811, Clay's allies nominated and secured on the first ballot Clay's election as Speaker of the House by a margin of two to one.

Clay immediately appointed War Hawks to important

committees. As the session advanced, the debate over war accelerated, and there was discussion about increasing both troop levels and financing. Madison sent Congress a message accusing England of "hostile inflexibility" and noting that the time had arrived to put the country "into an armor and an attitude demanded by the crisis." Congress agreed, and Dolley Madison wrote in December, "I believe there will be war. . . . Mr. Madison sees no end to the perplexities without it, and [Congress] seem to be going on with the preparations."

The president faced a difficult division among the War Hawks over his proposal for enlarging the navy. Madison wanted to construct twelve ships of the line and ten frigates. Representatives from landlocked western states, including War Hawks, opposed the plan as catering to coastal interests. Among the western saber rattlers, only Clay supported plans for an expanded navy. The president's proposal was defeated by a vote of 62 to 59. Upon learning of this rebuke, Jefferson wrote Madison "that a body containing 100 lawyers in it, should direct the measures of a war, is, I fear, impossible."

Madison continued to negotiate with both France and England, presuming that one of them would recognize America's neutrality on the oceans. However, on 19 May 1812 news came that France, despite earlier hopes among the Americans, still refused to give guarantees. England was adamant. In some parts of the country, there was a cry for war against both nations. Madison was determined to face what he considered the greater enemy in this confrontation. Clay agreed, predicting that "the Government will proceed in its course against England, [but] wait a while longer before it takes any measure of hostile character against France."

Madison prepared a war message. On 1 June that message was read to a closed session of Congress. The president's complaints against England included its impressment of American seamen, its attacks on American commercial shipping, and its orders against neutral ships. The rhetoric in the House in support of war was particularly strident from Clay and Calhoun. On 4 June the House of Representatives voted 79 to 49 in favor of a declaration of war, and on 17 June the Senate did so by a vote of 19 to 13. Recent scholarship suggests that there was no War Hawk group as such, and the debate over this distinction became active among historians of congressional behavior during the 1990s. On 4 March 1813 the War Hawk Congress adjourned and Madison turned to prosecuting the conflict.

BIBLIOGRAPHY

Brant, Irving. *James Madison.* Vol. 5. 1956.
Fritz, Harry W. "The War Hawks of 1812: Party Leadership in the Twelfth Congress." *Capital Studies* V (Spring 1977).
Hatzenbuehler, Ronald L. "The War Hawks and the Question of Congressional Leadership in 1812." *Pacific Historical Review* 14 (1976).
Hunt, Gaillard. *The Writings of James Madison.* Vol. 8. 1908.
Ketcham, Ralph. *James Madison.* 1990.
Remini, Robert V. *Henry Clay.* 1991.

ROBERT S. ALLEY

WAR OF 1812. From the outbreak of the Franco-British war in 1793, the young American republic's leaders had fretted and fussed, hoping to guide the nation (still on its own shaky path) through the shoals of a global conflict. Washington, Adams, and Jefferson used a variety of stratagems to avoid an outright rupture with either France or Great Britain—shots were exchanged on many occasions—and there was even a halfhearted shooting war with the French as the century ended. Few men were as aware of these circumstances as James Madison when he became president in 1809. Disappointment followed every frustrated effort to keep America at peace, and Madison believed his patience was a formidable weapon in avoiding war.

The return of the messenger ship *Hornet* without word of British concessions at a time when Madison was hoping for some British accommodation to American demands, led Madison to conclude that war with Great Britain was inevitable. The president therefore asked Congress for a declaration of war, and, not without some dissent (the New England delegations were dead set against war with England), Congress did declare war on 18 June 1812. The nationhood of the United States was at stake.

Even when President Madison learned on 12 August that the British government had repealed the orders in council two days before the United States' declaration of war, he still did not choose to halt the conflict. As he saw it, there were issues that could be compromised, but impressment was not one. Impressment remained his major reason for war.

Ever since, historians have repeatedly altered the interpretation of the causes of the war. Nineteenth-century historians stressed national honor; the trading rights of neutral nations violated by the orders in council; and impressment of sailors. Early in the twentieth century historians added incitement of the Indians by the British and the national hunger for land in Canada and Florida. The detested orders in council seemed to control American overseas commerce, as if the United States were still a colony.

The struggle for nationhood was probably the prime cause for the American declaration. The Republicans, who pushed the nation into war, believed that only a victory over Great Britain would preserve the national honor.

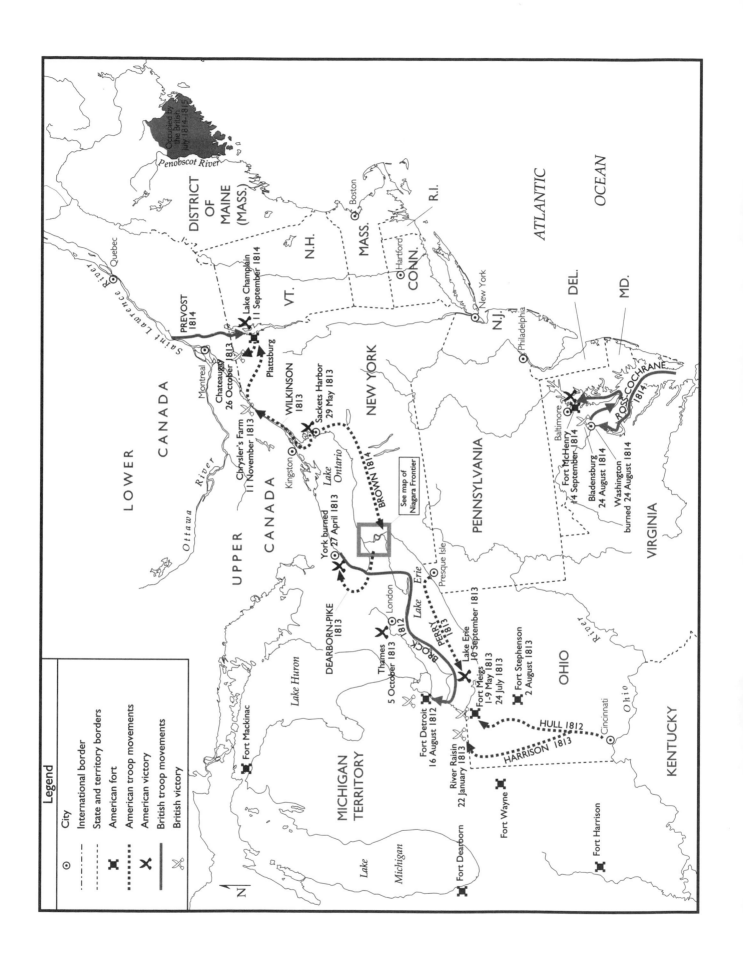

Legend

- ⊙ City
- International border
- State and territory borders
- ✖ American fort
- American troop movements
- ✖ American victory
- British troop movements
- British victory

N

Occupied by the British July 1814–1815

Penobscot River

DISTRICT OF MAINE (MASS.)

Boston

N.H.

VT.

MASS.

R.I.

Hartford CONN.

ATLANTIC

OCEAN

New York

N.J.

DEL.

MD.

Philadelphia

Saint Lawrence River

Quebec

LOWER CANADA

Montreal

PREVOST 1814

Lake Champlain 11 September 1814

Plattsburg

Chateaugay 26 October 1813

Ottawa River

Chrysler's Farm 11 November 1813

WILKINSON 1813

Sackets Harbor 29 May 1813

Kingston

Lake Ontario

NEW YORK

PENNSYLVANIA

Baltimore

Fort McHenry 14 September 1814

Bladensburg 24 August 1814

Washington burned 24 August 1814

VIRGINIA

ROSS-COCHRANE 1814

BROWN 1814

See map of Niagara Frontier

York burned 27 April 1813

UPPER CANADA

London

DEARBORN-PIKE 1813

BROCK 1812

Thames 5 October 1813

Lake Huron

Fort Mackinac

MICHIGAN TERRITORY

Lake Michigan

Fort Dearborn

Fort Detroit 16 August 1812

River Raisin 22 January 1813

Fort Wayne

Lake Erie

PERRY 1813

Lake Erie 10 September 1813

Presque Isle

Fort Meigs 1–9 May 1813 24 July 1813

Fort Stephenson 2 August 1813

OHIO

Ohio River

Cincinnati

HULL 1812

HARRISON 1813

KENTUCKY

Fort Harrison

Since the United States was the sole republic in the world, republicanism itself was in danger. Republicans further believed that the pro-British Federalists would crawl back into the womb of British mercantilism and feared that the Federalists would regain political control if the nation did not fight for its honor. Recent interpretations leave out the acquisition of Florida, discount the Indian menace, and see the effort to conquer Canada as only a bargaining chip to gain concessions in peace negotiations.

The Failed Canadian Campaign (1812). Britain had been at war almost steadily since 1793, piling up a staggering debt and imposing heavy taxes on the influential propertied classes. With Britain's military and diplomatic resources concentrated on Napoleon, British generals and admirals assigned to conduct the American war largely determined British military strategy for the conflict. Their goal was to keep the United States away from Quebec, Montreal, and the Saint Lawrence River lifeline.

On land the United States had no place to strike but at Canada. The traditional route for invading Canada was via Lake Champlain and the Richelieu River, but that route required the cooperation of the Massachusetts and Connecticut citizens who opposed the war. Nevertheless, Madison's administration determined to send one invading column along that route, a second into the Niagara area, and a third to the western tip of Lake Erie.

In a vague way, Madison charged Henry Dearborn with coordination of the three invading columns. Dearborn, a respected veteran of the Revolution whose highest rank had been lieutenant colonel, had served as secretary of war in Jefferson's cabinet. He was elevated to the rank of major general in January 1812 in order to assume high command when war came.

The western column was the first to move. Madison picked William Hull to command it. Hull had limited but honorable service during the Revolution, reaching the rank of lieutenant colonel. He had been governor of the Michigan Territory since 1805 and was promoted to brigadier general just a week before the declaration of war. In the summer of 1812 Secretary of War William Eustis ordered Hull to advance to Detroit. Hull's forces had to cut a road two hundred miles north through heavy timber and swamp. Hull counted on diversions by the other two armies, but none developed. In fact, Dearborn made no effort to coordinate the columns.

With about two thousand men under his command, Hull reached Detroit on 5 July. British-allied Indians had interdicted his long supply line, and they prevented relief parties from reaching supplies at the River Raisin. Meanwhile, Maj. Gen. Sir Isaac Brock, governor and commander of Upper Canada, positioned cannons that threatened the fort in Detroit, but Hull made no move to dislodge them. Brock then warned Hull that in case of a fight he would not be able to restrain his Indians. With real bravado, on 15 August 1812 he summoned Hull to surrender. When Hull refused, Brock ordered bombardment to begin, damaging the interior of the fort. He did not really expect Hull to surrender but did anticipate a sortie. To Brock's surprise Hull on 16 August unaccountably offered to surrender the fort, its forty cannons, and all the American forces in the vicinity. Brock had achieved a magnificent bluff with 330 regulars, 400 militia, and 600 Indians. Hull, after a trial, was cashiered in April 1814.

Hull's surrender jeopardized four forts west and north of Detroit. Fort Mackinac, on Lake Huron, which was vital to the western Indian trade, fell. British Indians massacred the garrison at Fort Dearborn as the troops marched out. Fort Wayne and Fort Harrison repulsed attacks, but Britain now controlled the Michigan Territory and three of the Great Lakes: Huron, Erie, and Ontario.

Two months after the Hull fiasco, the army at Niagara finally moved. Badly commanded, it failed twice to establish a beachhead on the Canadian side. Finally, on 13 October 1812, Americans scaled the bluff 310 feet above the river to Queenston Heights. Brock galloped from Fort George, having ordered out the main force there, and reached Queenston alone. Without waiting for the column from Fort George, Brock organized a small force to drive the Americans from the heights. Conspicuous in leading the charge, Brock was killed in the fighting. But the American militia refused to cross over into Canada. Thus, when eight hundred British regulars reached Queenston from Fort George, they were able to overrun the American position and capture around one thousand soldiers. The last United States attempt to invade Canada in 1812 had failed.

Florida, the Fleet, and the Election of 1812. In Florida, Madison had secretly fomented a revolution against Spanish rule. After they achieved success, the revolutionaries were to offer East Florida to the United States. But as war with Britain loomed, fighting along a front in Florida seemed too risky, so the president decided to disavow all connection with the disturbance in Florida, and East Florida remained Spanish for a few more years.

Although the *London Times* denigrated the American navy as "a few fir built frigates with strips of bunting manned by sons of bitches and outlaws," in fact seven of the frigates in the American navy were the finest in the world. Superbly commanded, those frigates gave the Madison administration its only triumphs in 1812. The *Constitution*, commanded by Capt. Isaac Hull, captured the British vessel *Guerrière*; the *United States*, under Capt. Stephen Decatur, wrecked the *Macedonian*; and, on the

WAR OF 1812 *(left)*.

last day of the year, the *Constitution*, this time under William Bainbridge, conquered the *Java*. Thereafter, the Admiralty ordered British frigates to engage the American frigates only in pairs.

In the midst of a military fiasco, Madison ran for a second term in 1812. The election amounted to a referendum on the war. Madison won all of the South and West, with his 128 electoral votes overwhelming De Witt Clinton's 89 electoral votes.

The Canadian Theaters (1813). Because Britain had only 8,100 soldiers in Canada, it relied heavily on its Indian allies. Using the Indians complicated British supply problems, for Gen. Henry Procter at the western end of the supply line vainly tried to feed several thousand people, more Indians than whites. Controlling the Indians was another problem, for they committed some atrocities, the most damaging at Frenchtown on the River Raisin on 22 January 1813. In this incident the American force under Brig. Gen. James Winchester lost three hundred killed. This number included thirty prisoners who were massacred by the Indians. Since the fallen were primarily Kentuckians, the massacre gave Kentucky a battle cry—"Remember the River Raisin!"

General Procter made three attempts to overpower the Americans after the Frenchtown killings. The garrison at Fort Meigs repulsed his attack on 4 May but lost four hundred casualties because of undisciplined action outside the fort by inexperienced troops. Maj. Gen. William Henry Harrison turned back a second attack on Fort Meigs late in July. Harrison ordered Col. George Croghan to evacuate Fort Stephenson, but Croghan disobeyed orders, defended the fort, and managed to inflict 150 casualties.

Master Commandant Oliver Hazard Perry, under orders to place an American squadron on Lake Erie, reached Presque Isle on 27 March 1813. By grit and good luck, he launched nine ships and sailed out to engage the British squadron headed by Capt. Robert Barclay at Amherstburg. Barclay had to come out and fight or face starvation. The ensuing battle resulted in the annihilation of the British squadron on 10 September 1813.

Harrison, waiting for this moment, crossed on Perry's vessels with an army of 5,600, entered Canada, and pursued the retreating British force. He caught up with Procter on 5 October at Moraviantown on the Thames River and routed Procter's army in the Battle of the Thames. Britain thus lost control of the Michigan Territory and of part of Upper Canada, and its hold on the Indians was reduced. Tecumseh, the charismatic Indian leader, died during the battle. Harrison, lacking the resources to march northwest to the head of Lake Ontario, could only return to the United States.

General Dearborn developed an attack on York (now Toronto), the capital of Upper Canada, but was too ill to go ashore. He turned command over to Brig. Gen. Zebulon M. Pike, a rising regular officer. Pike was killed, but his forces captured the Upper Canadian capital, burned the public buildings, and departed on 2 May 1813. The strategic value of this campaign was questionable.

The Americans next turned to the British forts along the Niagara River. In a gallant action led by Brig. Gen. Winfield Scott, they took Fort George on 27 May. Under pressure from the British, however, the Americans had to abandon the fort on 10 December. The enemy then crossed to the American side of the Niagara River and captured Fort Niagara. At the south end of the river the United States abandoned Fort Erie on 9 June. Late in 1813 the enemy crossed over into New York and laid waste Black Rock and Buffalo.

There was no further advance into western New York by the British. Instead, two offensives were planned for the Saint Lawrence area. Late in May the British moved from Kingston against the American naval base at Sackets Harbor. The attempt failed and the British took heavy losses, largely because of the leadership of the American commander, Brig. Gen. Jacob Brown. Two months later General Prevost sent vessels into Lake Champlain. These ranged at will around the lake, which was of great strategic value partly because of the great quantities of contraband goods, including herds of cattle that were used to feed the British army that passed over it into Canada.

Secretary of War John Armstrong, Eustis's successor, finally directed an American offensive against Canada's strategic center, down the Saint Lawrence from Sackets Harbor. President Madison belatedly relieved General Dearborn, and Armstrong summoned Maj. Gen. James Wilkinson to replace him. Wilkinson, like Dearborn and Hull, was a veteran of the Revolution. As a brigadier general he had been senior officer in the army; his duplicity (receiving a retainer fee from Spain while in the American army) was as yet unknown.

Secretary Armstrong accompanied Wilkinson to Sackets Harbor and for two months ran the War Department from there. It was early November before Wilkinson's command reached the Saint Lawrence. Gunboats from Kingston pressed the rear of his flotilla while shore parties dogged his flanks. The major battle of the campaign took place on the farm of John Chrysler on 11 November 1813. There, eight hundred British soldiers held off one thousand eight hundred Americans, disastrously fed piecemeal into the battle by Brig. Gen. John Boyd. American casualties were 434, British only 170.

Brig. Gen. Wade Hampton, another Revolutionary War veteran, was expected to join Wilkinson for an attack on Montreal, but the Canadians stopped him in a battle at Chateaugay on 26 October. Wilkinson, learning that Hampton would not join him, called off the offensive and

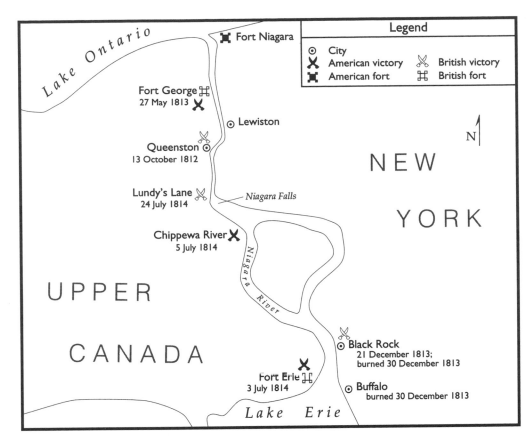

WAR OF 1812: THE NIAGARA FRONTIER.

sulked in winter quarters. Thus ended the sole American attempt to strike at the strategic center of Canada.

Wilkinson and Hampton both left active service after this campaign, and Dearborn was gone, so the way was clear for generals too young to have taken part in the Revolution: Jacob Brown, Edmund P. Gaines, Andrew Jackson, Alexander Macomb, and Winfield Scott.

On Lake Ontario, Isaac Chauncey and his opponent, Sir James Yeo, cautiously jockeyed for position, engaging at the same time in a continuous ship-building duel. Most of the seagoing American frigates were bottled up by the Royal Navy in East Coast harbors. The *Essex*, commanded by David Porter, harassed British shipping in the Pacific Ocean during 1813 but was finally captured outside a Latin American harbor in March 1814.

The Niagara and Chesapeake Campaigns (1814). Napoleon abdicated on 4 April 1814, freeing Britain to concentrate on the United States. Admiral Sir Alexander Cochrane crossed the Atlantic with a powerful fleet and three thousand of Wellington's army veterans. In July 1814 all of Maine east of the Penobscot River returned to British control, and in August Nantucket declared itself neutral. Leading New England Federalists cheered every British victory.

During the winter of 1813–1814 Winfield Scott had trained the U.S. regulars until they were the equal of the British in linear combat. In late March and early April the primary American force in the northern theater, led by Gen. Jacob Brown, marched from Sackets Harbor to the southern end of the Niagara River. Brown's army easily captured Fort Erie in July, withstood assaults by the British in August, but abandoned it late in the fall. On 5 July the American army met the British south of the Chippewa River on the Canadian side, forcing the British to withdraw from the battlefield and inflicting heavy casualties. A more violent action took place on 24 July five miles north of the Chippewa at Lundy's Lane. With 2,600 hundred men involved on each side casualties totaled 855 American and 880 British.

This bloody Niagara campaign failed to secure a foothold for the United States in Canada, but it stopped the enemy and left the security of Canada in question.

The arrival of Admiral Cochrane shifted the center of conflict from the Northeast further south along the East Coast. Moving into the Chesapeake Bay, the invading army, commanded by Maj. Gen. Robert Ross, one of the Duke of Wellington's protégés, moved against Washington. At Bladensburg on 24 August, it faced an improvised

438

438

JOHNNY BULL AND THE ALEXANDRIANS.   After burning Washington, the British army moved against Alexandria, Virginia, whose citizens paid a ransom of supplies to spare their town the torch. Cartoon by the American artist William Charles.
PRINTS AND PHOTOGRAPHS DIVISION, LIBRARY OF CONGRESS.

army of regulars, militia, and a few sailors. The British routed the Americans and marched unchecked into the capital. There they remained long enough to burn some of the government buildings—the White House and the Capitol among them—then returned to their ships.

The British objective then shifted to Baltimore. The Maryland militia was ready. Sharpshooters killed General Ross, the British bombardment was ineffective, and a determined defense prevented the invaders from entering Baltimore. After a brief exchange, the Royal Navy sailed back down the Chesapeake.

The British were not done, however. They launched another offensive in the north, this one up the Richelieu

BURNING OF WASHINGTON (left).   Gen. Robert Ross is at the upper right. Immediately to the left of the American cannons he has captured is the "President's Palace on fire." Print published by G. Thompson, October 1814.
PRINTS AND PHOTOGRAPHS DIVISION, LIBRARY OF CONGRESS.

River toward Lake Champlain. Sir George Prevost himself, in command of twelve thousand men, led this excursion, which tried to take Plattsburg, the key to control of the lake. The British were foiled at Plattsburg; their naval defeat brought about by the efforts of Lt. Thomas Macdonough and his squadron. Seeing that he was outflanked on the lake, Prevost opted to march his untested army back to Canada. After the failure at Baltimore and Plattsburg, Great Britain shifted its main offensive to the Gulf Coast, focusing on New Orleans.

The Battle of New Orleans.   Madison's administration, having somewhat frustrated Andrew Jackson's desire to be in the midst of the fighting, finally gave him command at New Orleans. His opponent in the struggle for the rich port was another of Wellington's generals, Lt. Gen. Sir Edward Pakenham, who controlled fourteen thousand men. A portion of Packenham's force passed through the waterways east of New Orleans, reaching the right bank of the Mississippi seven miles from the city before Jackson

JOHN BULL and the BALTIMOREANS.

JOHN BULL AND THE BALTIMOREANS.   Having burned Washington and terrified the Alexandrians, the British moved against Baltimore, which put up a stiffer resistance. In the distance, an American sniper kills Gen. Robert Ross. Etching by the American artist William Charles.
PRINTS AND PHOTOGRAPHS DIVISION, LIBRARY OF CONGRESS.

knew they were close. Then he acted with characteristic decisiveness. As the invaders advanced on a strip of land one thousand yards wide wedged between the river and a swamp, Jackson, aided by two schooners on the river, met them in three severe battles. In the final combat on 8 January 1815, Pakenham could employ only 5,600 men. Jackson faced them with 4,200 militia, regulars, volunteers, sailors, and even pirates—plus twelve cannons behind earthworks. Pakenham and two of his generals were killed; the army had no choice but to retreat. The three battles, fought on 23 December 1814 and 1 January and 8 January 1815, produced grotesquely uneven casualties: 336 American to 2,444 British, an astonishing ratio of seven to one.

The Treaty of Ghent. Before the outcome at New Orleans was known, delegates from Massachusetts, Connecticut, Rhode Island, one county from Vermont, and two counties from New Hampshire met in Hartford, Connecticut, for a three-week Federalist antiwar convention. These New England Federalists drew up reso-

lutions to amend the Constitution, allotting more military power to the states. Commissioners carrying the resolutions hurried to Washington, but upon hearing of the victory at New Orleans and of a peace signed at Ghent, they left without submitting the resolutions. The Hartford Convention was the last gasp of the Federalist party.

Diplomatic representatives from the two belligerents had signed a treaty on Christmas Eve, 1814. The document was remarkable more for what it left out than for what it contained. Impressment, over which Americans had fought, was not mentioned; neither was a territory for the Indians in the northwest (a quixotic British idea at Ghent). Boundaries remained untouched—the status quo ante bellum prevailed.

What were the consequences of the second war with England? It quickened nationalism in the United States and left Americans with a lasting residue of Anglophobia. The war gave Canada a sense of identity and strengthened its bond with England. It broke the power of the

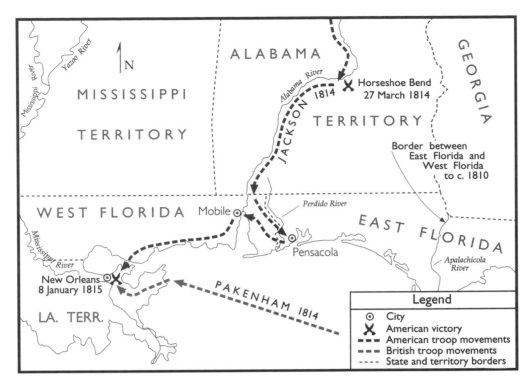

THE WAR OF 1812: THE GULF COAST AND THE CREEK WAR.

Indians in the northwest, clearing the way for westward American expansion. In spite of dismal military failures and the shortcomings of Madison as a war president, the war increased the international stature of the United States. American soldiers, trained while the war went on, showed themselves equal to the best troops in the world. Ships, ship captains, and crews excelled.

Perhaps most notable was the ability of the United States to reorganize its military in the midst of wartime operations. The administration belatedly replaced the secretaries of war and navy, shunted aside aging generals, and replaced them with younger, more aggressive men. These replacements were to shape American military affairs until the Civil War. In May 1813 the War Department drew together the combat-supporting agencies into a general staff, which vastly improved military housekeeping. Finally, with the passage of time, Americans viewed the war as a national triumph, brought about in part by four men who would later became president: James Monroe, John Quincy Adams, Andrew Jackson, and William Henry Harrison.

[See also *Armistice of 1812; Great Britain; Impressment; Indians; Orders in Council; Treaty of Ghent; United States Army; United States Navy;* biographies of figures and entries concerning battles, places, and ships mentioned herein.]

BIBLIOGRAPHY

Brant, Irving. *James Madison: Commander in Chief.* 1961.
Brown, Roger H. *The Republic in Peril: 1812.* 1964.
Brown, Wilbert S. *The Amphibious Campaign for West Florida, 1814–1815.* 1969.
Hickey, Donald R. *The War of 1812.* 1989.
Lord, Walter. *The Dawn's Early Light.* 1972.
Mahon, John K. *The War of 1812.* 1972.
Roosevelt, Theodore. *The Naval War of 1812.* 1927.
Stanley, George F. G. *The War of 1812: Land Operations.* 1983.

JOHN MAHON

WASHINGTON, GEORGE (1732–1799), commander in chief of the Continental army and first president of the United States. Although the friendship and close political association between Washington and Madison lasted only about ten years before foundering on the shoals of partisan politics, no other personal relationship was more vital to the establishment of a strong, effective federal government. Between 1784 and 1794 Washington, the preeminent soldier-politician of his day, worked hand in glove with Madison, the scholar-politician, in an evolving effort to consolidate and institutionalize the gains of the Revolutionary War. Madison's senior by nineteen years but his inferior in point of formal education, Washington relied heavily on the younger man's expertise in dealing with questions of constitutional theory and political precedence, and he frequently sought Madison's advice in the more practical matters of filling offices and writing addresses. Their obvious differences aside, the two men shared an unshakable commitment to creating a respectable American republic, and both possessed a deep understanding of human behavior and political power.

Washington and Madison also had a common interest in western development, and it was a plan to make the Potomac River a navigable route to the West that first brought them together as a political team. In the fall of 1784 both men traveled into the wilderness and were impressed by the rich resources of the western region. Madison's trip to the Mohawk Valley was his first and only visit to the West. For Washington his journey to the Ohio Valley was not a new experience, because he had been a successful frontier surveyor in his youth; by 1784 he owned about forty thousand acres of land between the Blue Ridge and the Ohio. He returned from his trip newly enthused, nevertheless, about the "rising world" beyond the mountains and determined to bind it forever to the Atlantic states by convenient inland routes. In November he and Madison discussed legislation for establishing a Potomac company to open one such route. Because the Potomac lay between Virginia and Maryland, action by both states was required. While Washington lobbied the Maryland assembly for a Potomac navigation bill, Madison managed the legislation on the floor of the Virginia Assembly. Coordinating their efforts between Annapolis and Richmond, they succeeded by January 1785 in obtaining passage of identical Potomac acts by the two assemblies.

Washington's subsequent retreat into private life at Mount Vernon was disrupted in the fall of 1786 by news of Shays's Rebellion. "We are fast verging to anarchy & confusion!" he wrote Madison on 5 November. "Will not the wise & good strive hard to avert this evil?" The only remedy, Washington said, was "a liberal, and energetic Constitution, well guarded, & closely watched, to prevent incroachments." Washington was equally distressed, however, to learn several days later from Madison that his name was first among the Virginia delegates nominated to attend the Federal Convention at Philadelphia that was to meet the following May. In the crisis Washington was willing to break the vow to quit public life that he had made at the end of the war, but he was acutely embarrassed by his recent announcement that he would not appear at a meeting of the Society of the Cincinnati scheduled for the same city and month as the Federal Convention. Madison handled Washington's sensitivity on that point with superb tact. Leaving the ultimate decision about Washington's attendance to him, Madison steadfastly insisted on keeping the general's name at the head of Virginia's delegation in order to secure the participation of the best people from each state. Unable to say no to Madison, Washington went to Philadelphia in the spring of 1787 and served as president of the Federal Convention, a fact that gave the gathering his implicit endorsement

from the outset. Thereafter, Washington's unqualified support for the Constitution was an important factor in its ratification, for it was a widespread assumption that the hero of the Revolution would lead the new government.

Accepting the presidency after anguishing further over the dictates of patriotism and duty, Washington promptly turned to Madison as his principal adviser. A member of the newly created House of Representatives, Madison acted as a sort of prime minister for Washington during the early months of his administration by bridging the gap between the executive and the legislative branches. Madison may have assisted in writing Washington's first inaugural address, and he certainly wrote several of the president's early addresses to Congress, as well as many congressional replies to the president. Thus, between them, Washington and Madison set important precedents for presidential communication with Congress. Madison also advised Washington on a variety of appointments and on matters of etiquette and ceremony, pushing Washington toward forms of republican simplicity and away from self-conscious monarchical trappings. Their working relationship during this period was marked by the same free and easy camaraderie that Washington had enjoyed with his young military aides during the Revolution. "I am very troublesome," Washington wrote Madison in September 1789, after asking his opinion about judicial appointments, "but you must excuse me. Ascribe it to friendship and confidence, and you will do justice to my motives."

Madison's influence in the Washington administration declined somewhat after cabinet officers were appointed, and it decreased even more sharply as Madison began to oppose the policies of the secretary of the Treasury, Alexander Hamilton. Washington, nevertheless, sought confidential advice from Madison in 1792 when he contemplated retiring after his first term as president. Influenced in part at least by Madison's argument that he should remain in office to continue giving "tone & firmness to the Government," Washington served a second term, but he soon encountered opposition from a congressional party led by Madison.

Although increasingly at odds on specific issues of domestic and foreign policy, the two men remained personally cordial and always avoided open criticism of one another. Their final political break apparently did not come until November 1794 when Washington denounced the Democratic-Republican societies in his annual address to Congress, a speech that Madison deemed "perhaps the greatest mistake of his political life." By then their mutual work was done, however. The federal government was strong enough to endure debate and dissent.

BIBLIOGRAPHY

Abbot, W. W., et al., eds. *The Papers of George Washington.* Confederation Series. 2 vols. to date. 1992–.

GEORGE WASHINGTON.   This portrait, painted by Gilbert Stuart in 1797, hung in the White House. On 23–24 August 1814, as British troops approached Washington, Dolley Madison wrote hastily to her sister, Lucy Todd, "I have ordered the frame to be broken, and the canvass taken out it is done,—and the precious portrait placed in the hands of two gentlemen of New York for safe keeping." The British burned the White House on 24 August. The portrait now hangs in the East Room.

Freeman, Douglas Southall. *George Washington: A Biography.* 7 vols. 1948–1957.

Hutchinson, William T., et al., eds. *The Papers of James Madison: Congressional Series.* 1962–.

Ketcham, Ralph. *James Madison: A Biography.* 1971.

Twohig, Dorothy, et al., eds. *The Papers of George Washington. Presidential Series.* 9 vols. 1987–.

PHILANDER D. CHASE

WASHINGTON, D.C. Among the most controversial issues facing Congress after the Revolutionary War was the location of the national capital, since almost all the states sought the much coveted prize of the new nation's seat of government. Newly independent Americans envisioned the young republic's capital as the vital center of national life, a thriving metropolis of commerce and culture comparable to the great capital of the ancient republic of Rome. Amid the economic depression and disarray of the postwar period, the prospect of winning the seat of the future American empire, the Rome of the New World, was compelling.

For the leaders of Virginia, securing the federal city was part of their larger goal of creating a major port in northern Virginia, thus ending the state's dependence on Baltimore and Philadelphia and guaranteeing its future prosperity. During the 1780s, Madison attempted to improve the commercial prospects of the Potomac through legislation limiting foreign commerce to designated ports on the river (the Port Bill of 1784) and through legislation chartering the Potomac Company, formed to improve the river's navigation.

The intensity of the Virginians' desire became evident during the meeting of the First Federal Congress (1789–1791). In a long and heated struggle that increasingly assumed sectional overtones, Madison led the southern states in the House in pressing for the Potomac site as the most central and convenient location for the government. Madison won congressional approval for the Potomac site in 1790. As part of the Compromise of

WASHINGTON IN 1801.   *George Town and Federal City, or City of Washington,* engraving by T. Cartwright after a drawing by G. Beck, 1801.   PRINTS AND PHOTOGRAPHS DIVISION, LIBRARY OF CONGRESS.

1790 in which Jefferson acted as broker, Madison pledged to Alexander Hamilton southern votes in favor of the latter's bill providing for federal assumption of state debts in exchange for northern votes in support of a permanent federal capital on the Potomac. The Seat of Government Act, signed by Washington on 16 July, authorized the president to place the ten-square-mile federal district on a site anywhere along the Potomac River between the Eastern Branch (Anacostia River) and Conococheague Creek.

In August 1790 both Madison and Jefferson submitted memoranda to the president with suggestions on possible sites for the new federal city. In January 1791 Washington announced as his choice for the location of the district the area between Georgetown and the Eastern Branch. Soon after, he engaged the French-born engineer Pierre-Charles L'Enfant to prepare a plan. At a meeting in Philadelphia in August 1791 Washington, Jefferson, Madison, and L'Enfant bestowed the name of the first president upon the city and "District of Columbia" upon the entire federal territory. Reflecting republican aspirations to recall the greatness of the Roman republic, Jenkins Hill was renamed Capitoline Hill, while Goose Creek became the Tiber.

Even as the Virginia triumvirate laid plans for the new seat of government, its dreams for a grand capital on the Potomac began to fade. The great influx of wealth, commerce, and population that they had expected to accompany the founding of the federal city failed to materialize. At the first auction of lots, held in October 1791, only thirty-five out of ten thousand lots then owned by the government were sold. Subsequent auctions fared little better. Because funding for construction of the public buildings depended on the sale of these lots, the city commissioners found themselves without the financial resources to proceed. Only the last-minute provision of loans from Maryland and Virginia enabled work on the public buildings to go ahead.

When members of the federal government arrived in Washington in 1800, the glorious capital envisioned by L'Enfant existed only on paper. The federal city was a wilderness, punctuated by a series of residential enclaves centered on the unfinished Capitol, the President's House, and the Navy Yard on the Anacostia bluffs. With poor roads, inadequate housing, an unpleasant climate, and few of the urban amenities to which eighteenth-century Americans had become accustomed, Washington was a city that legislators merely tolerated during the legislative session and then fled immediately upon adjournment.

During the Jeffersonian era, the capital grew slowly as Congress and the government bureaucracy expanded in size. The population of the city of Washington increased from 3,210 in 1800 to 13,117 in 1820, and the population of the entire federal district, including Georgetown and Alexandria, rose from 14,093 in 1800 to 33,039 in 1820. The new residents of Washington, however, included few merchants, financiers, and other businessmen needed for urban development. As late as 1829, according to a Washington handbook, the "greatest and most respectable business" in the nation's capital was "keeping boarding-houses." Throughout the Jeffersonian era, Washington remained an isolated seat of government, not the grand center of commerce and power envisioned by its Virginia founders.

[See also *Capital, Location of the.*]

BIBLIOGRAPHY

Bowling, Kenneth R. *The Creation of Washington, D.C.: The Idea and Location of the American Capital.* 1991.
Green, Constance McLaughlin. *Washington: Village and Capital, 1800–1878.* 2 vols. 1962.
Young, James Sterling. *The Washington Community, 1800–1828.* 1966.

TINA H. SHELLER

WASP. *Wasp* was the name of two American naval vessels that served in the U.S. Navy during the presidency of James Madison.

The first was a sloop of war constructed in 1806 at the Washington Navy Yard and placed in commission in 1807, under the command of Master Commandant John Smith. From 1810 to 1811, she was on embargo patrol on the southeastern coast of the United States. In 1811, *Wasp* sailed to Norfolk, joining the cruising squadron of Commodore Stephen Decatur. On 13 October 1812, under the command of Master Commandant Jacob Jones, *Wasp* sortied from the Delaware River to attack English shipping. After running through a storm, *Wasp* overtook a convoy of six English merchant ships under the escort of HMS *Frolic,* a twenty-two-gun sloop of war. *Wasp* outfought *Frolic,* but, because of battle damage, was captured by HMS *Poictiers.* Jones and his men were carried to Bermuda, where they were soon paroled and exchanged.

Another USS *Wasp,* the fifth to carry the name, was constructed at Newburyport, Massachusetts, and was commissioned in early 1814. Under the command of Master Commandant Johnston Blakeley, *Wasp* cruised in the western approaches to the English Channel. She had captured five prizes when she encountered the twenty-one-gun sloop of war HMS *Reindeer* about 225 miles west of Plymouth. Blakeley's men captured *Reindeer* after a hard fight but had to burn their prize. *Wasp* finally made the port of L'Orient in early July and remained there refitting until 27 August. Blakeley intercepted the sloop of war HMS *Avon* and fought her until she was a helpless wreck.

The arrival of two powerful British ships prevented the capture of *Avon*, but she sank soon afterward.

On 21 September, *Wasp* captured the brig *Atlanta* and put a prize crew on board her under command of Midshipman David Geisinger. *Wasp* was last seen headed for the Caribbean about three weeks later, but is presumed to have been lost in a storm with all hands. Johnston Blakeley's *Wasp* was the most renowned of the early *Wasp*s of the U.S. Navy because of her defeat of two British naval vessels of similar force in the span of only two months.

BIBLIOGRAPHY

Chapelle, Howard I. *History of the American Sailing Navy.* 1949.
Mooney, James L., ed. *Dictionary of American Naval Fighting Ships.* 8 vols. Vol. 8. 1980.

WILLIAM S. DUDLEY

WEBSTER, DANIEL (1782–1852), representative, senator, secretary of state. Born in Salisbury, New Hampshire, Webster graduated from Dartmouth College in 1801 and was admitted to the New Hampshire bar in 1805. In 1807 he moved to Portsmouth where, as a Federalist, he struggled to obtain local office. In 1812 he won election to the House of Representatives, where he opposed war with Britain. Webster successfully introduced resolutions regarding the war's origins, and he delivered them personally to President Madison.

Webster won reelection to the House in 1814, and in January 1815 he opposed Madison with his partisan minority vote against the purchase of Thomas Jefferson's library. By 1816 he had decided to move to Boston, where his annual income immediately tripled from what it had been in Portsmouth, his clientele proved more enticing, and the workload proved less arduous. He returned to New Hampshire in September 1817 to argue the case of *Dartmouth College* v. *Woodward* and won it the next year before the U.S. Supreme Court. In 1819 he won *McCullouch* v. *Maryland*—another case—before the Supreme Court. Webster holds the distinction of having argued 178 cases before the Supreme Court—more than any other lawyer.

Webster served in the Massachusetts constitutional convention of 1820–1821, was elected to the House of Representatives 1822, 1824, and 1826, and visited Madison at Montpelier in December 1824.

In 1827 Massachusetts sent Webster to the Senate, where he refuted Sen. Robert Y. Hayne of South Carolina on nullification. He failed to obtain recharter for the Second Bank of the United States in 1836. William Henry Harrison appointed him secretary of state in 1841, and Webster settled the boundary with Canada in skillful negotiations with his British counterpart Alexander Baring, first baron Ashburton. Webster returned to the Senate in 1845, supported the Compromise of 1850, and served as Millard Fillmore's secretary of state. He died at Marshfield, Massachusetts, on 24 October 1852.

BIBLIOGRAPHY

Baxter, Maurice G. *One and Inseparable: Daniel Webster and the Union.* 1984.
Fuess, Claude M. *Daniel Webster.* 2 vols. 1930.
Shewmaker, Kenneth E., et al., eds. *The Papers of Daniel Webster: Diplomatic Papers.* 2 vols. 1983–1987.
Wiltse, Charles M., et al., eds. *The Papers of Daniel Webster: Correspondence.* 7 vols. 1974–1987.

FRANK C. MEVERS

DANIEL WEBSTER.   The thirty-year-old Webster was elected to the House of Representatives from New Hampshire in 1812. Engraving by J. A. J. Wilcox.

WEST POINT. See *United States Military Academy.*

WHEATON, HENRY (1785–1848), authority on international law, Supreme Court reporter. Henry Wheaton was one of the few prominent contemporary legal scholars who leaned toward James Madison's politics. After studying law in France, Wheaton edited a New York City newspaper, the *National Advocate*, that ardently supported the wartime policies of Madison's administration, especially justifying the legitimacy of the steps that had brought the United States into the War of 1812. Established by the Tammany Society, the *National Advocate* was branded in New York as the administration "mouthpiece" from 1812 to 1815. Wheaton also published articles in two Rhode Island newspapers supporting Madison and his wartime policies. Wheaton was court reporter for the U.S. Supreme Court from 1816 to 1827, through John Marshall's era of judicial nationalism. His annual volumes set the standard for future reporters. (He was first paid for his efforts in 1817, after learning the process as a newspaper reporter.)

Wheaton solicited Madison's diplomatic correspondence and views on international law in 1824, when he began research for his book *Some Account of the Life, Writings and Speeches of William Pinkney* (1826). Remaining true to his views as a newspaper editor, Wheaton planned to justify Madison's resistance to the bullying diplomacy of Great Britain. Two of Madison's letters, he felt, fully justified American policies. In addition to forwarding his correspondence with Pinkney, Madison praised Wheaton for an address Wheaton had given at the New York Athenaeum. Wheaton drew upon Madison's writings for the definition of international law that was basic to his 1836 treatise, *The Elements of International Law*. Wheaton began his own diplomatic career as chargé d'affaires in Denmark and later took similar assignments in Prussia and Berlin.

BIBLIOGRAPHY

Baker, Elizabeth F. *Henry Wheaton, 1785–1848*. 1971.
Hicks, Frederick C. *Men and Books Famous in the Law*. 1921.

DONALD O. DEWEY

WHITE, ALEXANDER (1738–1804), lawyer, representative, commissioner for the design and development of the District of Columbia. The son of a British navy doctor in Frederick County, Virginia, White graduated from Edinburgh University and studied law in London in 1762–1763. He returned to Virginia in 1765 and began a law practice in the northwestern part of the colony, serving as a representative of Hampshire County (now West Virginia) in the House of Burgesses in 1772 and as king's attorney. Despite his lack of enthusiasm for the American Revolution, he was elected to the Virginia House of Delegates (1782–1786, 1788) and served several terms with Madison as his colleague. On most questions he sided with Madison, including the payment of British debt and the reform of the state legal code. He mobilized support in Virginia's northwest for the ratification of the Constitution and cast his vote for the new government in the state ratifying convention.

Elected to the first two federal congresses, White was an advocate of a strong national government, breaking with Madison on some issues. Probably his most important vote was the support he gave to Hamilton's plan for the assumption of state debts, a vote that became part of the Compromise of 1790, the bargain that traded assumption for a national capital on the banks of the Potomac River. White was not a doctrinaire Federalist, for he voted against the bill to establish the Bank of the United States. Nonetheless, he lost his reelection bid in 1793 to a rising tide of Antifederalist fervor in Virginia. Despite Madison's relief at White's defeat, the two continued to correspond regularly. In 1795 President Washington appointed White one of three commissioners to carry out the design and construction of the public buildings in Washington, D.C. White served in this post until 1802 and in this capacity corresponded with Madison on the district's affairs, including plans for the establishment of a national university.

BIBLIOGRAPHY

Hutchinson, William T., et al. eds. *The Papers of James Madison: Congressional Series*. 1962.
Johnson, Allen, ed. *Dictionary of American Biography*. 1928.
Risjord, Norman. *Chesapeake Politics, 1781–1800*. 1978.

DAVID B. MATTERN

WHITE HOUSE. The White House, formally the President's House in the early republic, was specified in the Residence Act of 16 July 1790, which required the commissioners of the Federal District to provide buildings for the accommodation of the federal government by December 1800. Acting under President Washington's authority, Pierre-Charles L'Enfant fixed the President's Square at the current location in 1791 and began preparing the foundations of what he called the President's Palace, which was to have spanned nearly seven hundred feet. The scale of the projected structure and of its surrounding park had distinct political implications that were alarming to Jefferson, undoubtedly to Madison, and even to the commissioners, who were presidential appointees.

After reluctantly dismissing L'Enfant for insubordination in February 1792, President Washington authorized architectural competitions to obtain designs for the principal public buildings and recruited the architect James Hoban to submit an entry for the President's House. Hoban's competition drawings, more modest in scale, were selected. They proposed a three-story stone build-

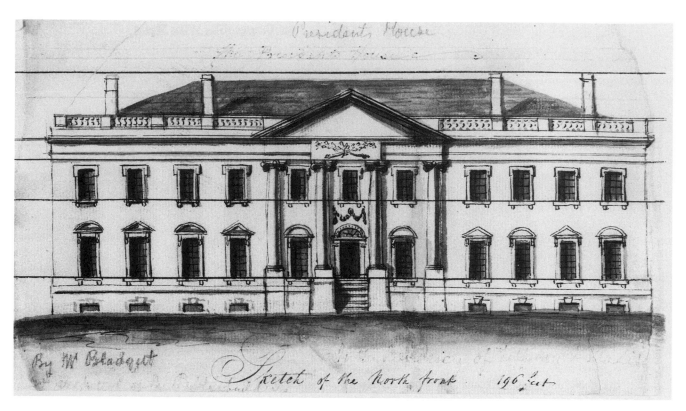

THE WHITE HOUSE.   The north facade of the President's House in the time of Jefferson and Madison. Drawing by
Samuel Blodget, c. 1814.   WHITE HOUSE COLLECTION. COURTESY OFFICE OF THE CURATOR, THE WHITE HOUSE.

RUINS OF THE WHITE HOUSE.   Saint John's Church on Lafayette Square stands in the
foreground. Print after a drawing by Benjamin Henry Latrobe.
                    PRINTS AND PHOTOGRAPHS DIVISION, LIBRARY OF CONGRESS.

ing with a classical frontispiece, or a shallow portico of engaged elements. At Washington's direction, the design was enlarged, then reduced to two stories in a series of modifications made in 1793–1794.

Under Hoban's supervision, construction progressed to the point that President and Mrs. Adams were able to occupy the building when the government removed to the Federal City in 1800. During Jefferson's residence, the architectural interiors were completed and embellished and many changes introduced, most noticeably the addition of east and west wings, which were begun in 1805 under architect Benjamin Latrobe. The Madisons were witnesses to these improvements. They resided briefly with Jefferson at the President's House in 1801, and, during the next eight years, Dolley Madison served as hostess for their widowed friend. Jefferson in fact led her into dinner on that notable evening in December 1803 when Anthony Merry, the British minister, and his wife, much to their surprise, joined the first "pêle-mêle" procession to the state dining room. Merry's steward, Jean-Pierre Sioussat (French John), would become the Madisons' "master of ceremonies" and household when they took residence in 1809 upon Madison's inauguration.

The Madison years began brilliantly. Latrobe reworked the public rooms for large entertainments, and his elegant "Grecian" furnishings helped make the White House fashionable, and a center of society, for the first time. Mrs. Madison's Wednesday drawing-room receptions became an institution and served her husband's politics well. This all ended in August 1814 when British forces moved on Washington. After taking personal belongings of the Madisons as "souvenirs" and contemptuously toasting the president, Adm. George Cockburn and his men torched the building 24 August, two days after Mrs. Madison had hurriedly removed George Washington's portrait and other objects before fleeing the city.

In 1815 Hoban was engaged to reconstruct the building, the progress of which President Madison had to observe from temporary quarters. Madison's successor, Monroe, pushed the architect to complete the public rooms in time for the traditional New Year's Day reception in January 1818. Hoban finished the private apartments later that year; he completed the south portico in 1824 and the north portico in 1829–1830. On her return to Washington as a widow in 1837, Dolley Madison renewed her association with the White House and maintained a residence on Lafayette Square, across from the White House.

BIBLIOGRAPHY

Hunt-Jones, Conover. *Dolley and the "great little Madison."* 1977.
Seale, William. *The President's House.* 2 vols. 1986.

C. M. HARRIS

WILKINSON, JAMES (1757–1825), soldier. Born in Benedict, Maryland, the son of a planter, Wilkinson was educated by private tutors and briefly studied medicine. Joining the Continental army, he served under Benedict Arnold and later as an aide-de-camp to Gen. Horatio Gates. He carried the message of the victory at Saratoga to the Continental Congress, which then brevetted him a brigadier general. Wilkinson's involvement in the Conway Cabal (an effort to replace Washington as commander), however, forced him to resign. Later he served as clothier general, but irregularities in his accounts again forced his resignation in 1781.

Wilkinson had married Ann Biddle of the prominent Philadelphia family in 1778, and he now briefly became a farmer. He also served as brigadier general of the Pennsylvania militia, and in 1783 he was elected to the state assembly. The following year Wilkinson moved to Kentucky, where he soon became a leader of a movement favoring Kentucky's separation from Virginia. Wilkinson took advantage of the Spanish desire to foster western discontent to ingratiate himself with Spanish authorities in New Orleans in order to gain exclusive trading rights and a secret pension of $2,000 a year.

Wilkinson's commercial ventures and land speculations were failures, and in 1791 he returned to military service in the Indian wars. By 1792 he was given the rank of brigadier general under Gen. Anthony Wayne. Wilkinson intrigued incessantly against Wayne to replace him in command. Only after Wayne's death in 1796 did Wilkinson become the commanding general of the U.S. Army.

In the years that followed, Wilkinson retained his position through the changes in presidential administrations. He also maintained his relationship with Spanish authorities and continued to receive secret payments from them. In 1803, with Gov. William C. C. Claiborne, Wilkinson took possession of the new Louisiana Purchase. Wilkinson then became the governor of the Louisiana Territory (all the area above the Territory of Orleans), while retaining his military position.

Wilkinson was a valuable ally of Aaron Burr in the latter's intrigues. Wilkinson facilitated Burr's movements in Burr's first visit to the West in 1805 by giving him letters of introduction to many prominent individuals. Wilkinson's controversial actions as governor, not his connections with Burr, forced President Thomas Jefferson to relieve Wilkinson of that post in May 1806 and to assign him to the southwestern frontier. When Burr returned to the West for a second time in 1806, Wilkinson turned against Burr. He warned Jefferson about Burr's activities, rushed to New Orleans, where he declared martial law, and acted arbitrarily against individuals supposedly connected with Burr.

Ultimately, Burr was arrested and, in Richmond in

1807, tried for treason. Wilkinson was the chief prosecution witness, but he was roundly attacked, not only for his involvement with Burr but also for his previous intrigues with the Spanish.

After Burr's trial, Wilkinson faced a court of inquiry, but he was eventually acquitted. Jefferson ordered Wilkinson to New Orleans, but new accusations were soon lodged against him. Wilkinson so mismanaged his command by placing his troops in an extremely unhealthy situation in a camp at Terre aux Boeufs, below New Orleans, that more than 1,000 of the 2,036 men in the camp died in 1809. President Madison ordered a court-martial to deal with these and other charges, many of which were old and could not be substantiated. Wilkinson was again acquitted,

JAMES WILKINSON.   Portrait by Charles Willson Peale, c. 1797.
INDEPENDENCE NATIONAL HISTORICAL PARK, PHILADELPHIA.

and Madison with some reluctance approved the verdict.

After war was declared in 1812, Wilkinson, early in 1813, took over Mobile, but such was his unpopularity that Madison was warned that the Louisiana senators would join the opposition unless Wilkinson was removed from his command. Wilkinson was now called to take command of the northern front with the rank of major general. He was reluctant to come north, but the new secretary of war, John Armstrong, urged Wilkinson to take the northern command and "renew the scenes of Saratoga." There is no doubt that President Madison also shared in this decision.

The attack on Montreal was long delayed, because of Wilkinson's ill health and his reluctance to take the offensive. Wilkinson also bickered with Armstrong, who had come to the front in part to serve as a coordinator between Wilkinson and Gen. Wade Hampton, who shared part of the command on the northern frontier. Moving down the Saint Lawrence in November 1813, Wilkinson's force suffered a setback at Chrysler's Farm, and he called off the planned attack against Montreal, citing the refusal of Hampton to cooperate. After an ineffectual attack on Canada in the spring of 1814, Secretary of War Armstrong ordered Wilkinson to face another court-martial. When it met in 1815, however, Armstrong was out of favor, and the administration did not press the case. Wilkinson was again acquitted, but he was not given another command.

Wilkinson spent part of his last years publishing his *Memoirs of My Own Times*. They were self-serving and omitted many controversial aspects of his career. There is little doubt that Wilkinson was a damaged character. Gen. Winfield Scott called Wilkinson an "unprincipled imbecile," and John Randolph of Roanoke, another enemy, declared that Wilkinson was "from the bark to the very core a villain." One of Wilkinson's biographers termed him a tarnished warrior, and another called him a finished scoundrel. Yet despite his obvious faults, Wilkinson charmed many prominent Americans, and he received many high offices from them. Undoubtedly he had abilities of value to his country, but his contribution to his country was limited by his rapacity, his devious dealings with the Spanish, and his self-serving attitude.

BIBLIOGRAPHY

Hay, Thomas. *Thomas Admirable Trumpeter: A Biography of General James Wilkinson*. 1941.

Jacobs, James Ripley. *Tarnished Warrior: Major-General James Wilkinson*. 1938.

Shreve, Royal Ornan. *The Finished Scoundrel: General James Wilkinson*. 1933.

Wilkinson, James. *Memoirs of My Own Times*. 3 vols. 1816.

C. EDWARD SKEEN

WILSON, JAMES (1742–1798), jurist, signer of the Declaration of Independence, signer of the Constitution, Supreme Court justice. James Wilson is perhaps best known as one of only six men who signed both the Declaration of Independence and the Constitution. He was a representative from Pennsylvania to the Continental Congress and a delegate to the Federal Convention; a leader in securing ratification of the proposed Constitution in Pennsylvania; active in the drafting of the Pennsylvania Constitution of 1790; and an original justice of the Supreme Court.

Wilson was born in Scotland and pursued a classical education at the University of Saint Andrew's, starting at the age of fifteen. Though he did not finish his studies to become a minister in the Church of Scotland, owing in part to the death of his father in 1762, he was greatly influenced by the Scottish common-sense school of philosophy, particularly by Thomas Reid. The common-sense approach to questions both metaphysical and political is evident in his writings and activities including his famous "Law Lectures" at the College of Philadelphia.

Wilson possessed a coherent and systematic political theory to a degree greater than any other Founding Father. He attempted to advance the key elements of this system throughout his political career. These principles can be seen in his activity in the Federal Convention.

Wilson spoke more than 160 times at the Convention—second only to Gouverneur Morris—addressing every major issue and many minor ones. He served with James Madison on the Committee of Detail, which was charged with framing a "constitution conformable to the Resolutions passed by the Convention." Wilson eagerly engaged in this work and with Madison controlled almost every element of the subsequent report to the Convention. For Wilson, the government that he was helping to frame was required to secure the natural rights of men, which were derived from the natural law or God's will.

In order to secure a government that would promote the happiness of the people, Wilson framed four conditions drawn directly from his belief that "frail and imperfect" men "must be the instruments . . . by which government is administered." The first held that the best and wisest men within society must be elected to serve the people. The second was that the government should promote the good and diminish the bad propensities of human nature. Closely related to the second principle was a third: to "increase, encourage, and strengthen those good propensities" in the general public while discouraging the bad. The fourth looked to structure the government through "particular checks and controls" so that it is "advantageous even for the bad men to act for the publick good." If these conditions were met, Wilson believed that a good government—exhibiting the rule of law—would exist.

Specifically, Wilson was concerned with three features of the proposed government. First, he was a strong proponent of the principle of popular elections and was extremely disappointed with the adoption of popular election for the lower House of Congress only. His second major concern was that the national government be as independent from the state governments as possible (he agreed with Madison that there were no essential differences between large and small states). Finally, and most importantly, Wilson was concerned with the doctrine of separation of powers. He raised serious objections to Madison's Virginia Plan because it made the other branches too dependent on the lower house. Indeed, Wilson opposed the final compromise of a two-house legislature because it violated so many of his principal concerns. However, the compromise was not a complete disaster, since the upper chamber did become independent from the lower one.

Wilson in his Statehouse Address of October 1787 freely admitted that he was not "a blind admirer of this plan of government." However, on the whole, he vigorously defended the new plan as a sufficiently sound "pyramid of government." He was one of the first justices to serve on the Supreme Court.

BIBLIOGRAPHY

Carey, George W. "James Wilson's Political Thought." *Political Science Reviewer* 17 (1987):49–107.
Harlan, John M. "James Wilson and the Formation of the Constitution." *American Law Review* 34 (1900):481–504.
Konkle, Burton A. *James Wilson and the Constitution.* 1904.
McCloskey, Robert G. *The Works of James Wilson.* 2 vols. 1967.
Smith, C. Page. *James Wilson: Founding Father, 1742–1798.* 1956.

JEFFREY D. SCHULTZ

WINCHESTER, JAMES

WINCHESTER, JAMES (1752–1826), merchant, soldier. Born in Carroll County, Maryland, Winchester was privately educated. He joined the Continental army in 1776 and was twice captured by the British. Despite his capture, Winchester rose to captain during the war.

In 1786 Winchester migrated to middle Tennessee, where he quickly established himself as a leader. He became a brigadier general of the militia in 1796 and served one term as state senator, his only political experience.

Winchester was a successful businessman, engaging in mercantile activities and profitable land speculations. After the Battle of Tippecanoe in 1811, he offered his services to the War Department. Supported by members of the Tennessee congressional delegation, Winchester received a commission in March 1812 as brigadier general. He was given command of the Army of the Northwest but was superseded by William Henry Harrison.

Winchester agreed to serve under Harrison. Early in January 1813 Winchester rushed a force to Frenchtown on the River Raisin (now Monroe, Michigan) to relieve American forces under attack by Indians. On 21 January British troops and their Indian allies forced Winchester to surrender. Control over the Indians was lax, and Winchester's troops suffered many atrocities. Winchester was held captive until he was exchanged in April 1814.

In the fall of 1814 Winchester was assigned to serve under Gen. Andrew Jackson and was charged with the defense of Mobile. Again the outcome was unfortunate. Fort Bowyer was forced to surrender on 11 February 1815, but news of the end of the war kept the British from taking Mobile. A chastened Winchester resigned his commission in March 1815.

Winchester's military career was unsuccessful, and in 1817 he published a defense of his actions in the *National Intelligencer* in Washington, D.C. His writing sparked a bitter controversy with Harrison. Later, in 1819, along with John Overton and Andrew Jackson, Winchester became one of the founders of the city of Memphis.

BIBLIOGRAPHY

DeWitt, John H. "General James Winchester." *Tennessee Magazine* 1 (1915): 79–105, 183–205.
Durham, Walter. *James Winchester: Tennessee Pioneer.* 1979.
Harrell, David E. "James Winchester." *Tennessee Historical Quarterly* 17 (1958): 222–249.

C. EDWARD SKEEN

WINDER, WILLIAM H.

WINDER, WILLIAM H. (1775–1824), lawyer, soldier, general. Born in Somerset County, Maryland, Winder was admitted to the Maryland bar around 1802. For the next decade he dabbled in local politics and then was appointed a lieutenant colonel in the Fourteenth Infantry Regiment in 1812 and elevated to brigadier general in June 1813. In the confusion at Stoney Creek, Winder blundered on foot into the British lines, was captured, and was paroled for twelve months.

Winder was President Madison's choice to command the defenses of Washington when the British advanced toward the nation's capital in the summer of 1814. Perhaps Madison's action was based on political considerations, for Winder's uncle was then governor of Maryland and Madison may have figured Governor Winder would cooperate with his kinsman in rounding up the militia and supplies needed to turn back the invaders. Appointed on 5 July, Winder spent a month reconnoitering the area but did little to prepare defenses or bring in sufficient troops;

three thousand militia were called to duty, but fewer than four hundred reported to Winder's command.

On 19 August British troops began their march on Washington from Benedict, Maryland. They moved slowly and by 23 August were still sixteen miles from the capital.

Winder was not sure the British were driving toward Washington. He may have believed that the enemy was making a feint toward the capital and really intended to invade the more tempting port city of Baltimore. Winder continued to ponder his next move when Bladensburg citizens offered to erect a defense of their village. Winder accepted and appears to have ordered a force of nearly two thousand volunteers, infantry regulars, Maryland militia, and light dragoons to take positions around the crossroads village. More militia arrived, and Winder's force of nearly seven thousand outnumbered the forty-five hundred British, who attacked at a bridgehead and were driven back momentarily. The fate of Bladensburg was soon settled, however, when a shower of Congreve rockets and a British counterattack demoralized the American defenders, who began a disorganized retreat. Only the American defense at the Washington Navy Yard organized by Commodore Joshua Barney kept the British temporarily at bay.

After the British finally subdued Barney's small force, their entry into Washington was unimpeded. By the time the British had finished their torching of the capital and begun to withdraw from Washington, Winder was many miles away leading a small band of defeated Americans toward Baltimore. But Winder was finished as the commander. In the welter of accusations and countercharges that followed, Winder insisted he was blameless. A court of inquiry, headed by Winfield Scott, did not find Winder culpable for the rout, but the tarnish on his reputation was indelible.

BIBLIOGRAPHY

Adams, Henry. *History of the United States of America during the Administrations of Thomas Jefferson and James Madison.* 1986.
Coles, Harry L. *The War of 1812.* 1971.
Stagg, J. C. A. *Mr. Madison's War.* 1983.

ROBERT A. RUTLAND

WIRT, WILLIAM (1772–1834), writer, attorney general of the United States, presidential candidate. William Wirt was born at Bladensburg, Maryland, the son of Swiss parents, Jacob and Henrietta Wirt. He studied law with William P. Hunt of Montgomery County, Maryland. In 1795 Wirt married Mildred Gilmer of Virginia; after her death in 1799, he married Elizabeth Washington, also of Virginia, in 1802.

ATTORNEY GENERAL WILLIAM WIRT.
PRINTS AND PHOTOGRAPHS DIVISION, LIBRARY OF CONGRESS.

Wirt served in 1800 as an attorney for James Callender in his trial for violations of the Alien and Sedition Acts. In 1806 Wirt was part of the team that prosecuted Aaron Burr, and the fame he gained from this trial helped him win a seat in the Virginia House of Delegates.

In 1814 Wirt served briefly as captain of artillery in the state militia. In 1816 he argued his first case before the U.S. Supreme Court, and in 1817 President Madison appointed him U.S. attorney for the district of Richmond; later, President Monroe appointed him attorney general of the United States. Wirt participated in *McCullouch* v. *Maryland* and in the Dartmouth College case, and in 1824 he was associated with Daniel Webster in arguing the case of *Gibbons* v. *Ogden*. In 1831 he represented the Cherokees in *Cherokee Nation* v. *Georgia*.

Wirt was reappointed attorney general under John Quincy Adams in 1824 and remained in that office until 1829. Outspoken in his opposition to Andrew Jackson, Wirt was soon identified with the Whig party. He was nominated for the presidency in 1831 by the Anti-Masonic party, a group opposed to Jackson.

Throughout his life, but particularly during his early adulthood, Wirt divided his career between law and literature. He was a superb and logical orator, an attribute that contributed to his fame as a lawyer. At the same time, he was an excellent writer, gaining considerable recognition in literary circles. His literary works include a series of essays (*The Letters of the British Spy*) and *Sketches of the Life of Patrick Henry*. Wirt died in Baltimore on 18 February 1834.

BIBLIOGRAPHY

Gammon, Rhea, Jr. *The Presidential Campaign of 1832*. 1922.
Kennedy, J. P. *Memoirs of the Life of William Wirt*. 2 vols. 1856.
Taylor, William Robert. "William Wirt and the Legend of the Old South." *William and Mary Quarterly*, 2d ser., 14 (1957): 477–493.

FRANK LAWRENCE OWSLEY, JR.

WITHERSPOON, JOHN (1723–1794), educator, Presbyterian clergyman, signer of the Declaration of Independence. The son of a Presbyterian minister and the descendant of numerous other Calvinist divines, Witherspoon was born near Edinburgh, Scotland. After completing his classical education and being ordained to the ministry in 1743, he became an eloquent spokesman and celebrated apologist for the conservative wing of the Scottish Presbyterian Church, which defended traditional orthodoxy against the more moderate cultural influences associated with the Scottish Enlightenment. He and other conservative clergymen also demonstrated democratic views as they defended the right of local congregations, rather than higher church courts, to appoint ministers.

Called to the presidency of the College of New Jersey (Princeton) in 1768, Witherspoon abandoned strict orthodoxy and embraced a more liberal theology that, among other things, emphasized the role of government in promoting social virtue or vice. Convinced that political reform might lead to the moral reformation of society, Witherspoon encouraged students to view their education as preparation for public service. Under his leadership the college achieved a reputation as a nursery of revolutionary ferment, and Witherspoon influenced a generation of national leaders, including James Madison, who enrolled at the Presbyterian college a year after Witherspoon's arrival. Witherspoon supervised most of the work of the senior class and taught a moral philosophy course that combined elements of modern economics, ethics, political science, history, and current affairs. It was here that young Madison encountered important writings from the classical and English Whig traditions that were critical to his development as a republican political thinker. Madison received his B.A. in 1771 and returned the next year for a year of postgraduate work, studying Hebrew and ethics under Witherspoon.

Not an active participant in New Jersey's colonial

JOHN WITHERSPOON.   Witherspoon was president of the College of New Jersey when Madison was a student there. Portrait by Charles Willson Peale.
INDEPENDENCE NATIONAL HISTORICAL PARK, PHILADELPHIA.

resistance movement until 1774, Witherspoon served in various local capacities before being chosen as a delegate to the Continental Congress in 1776. There he pressed for the speedy adoption of the Declaration of Independence. He also supported the revolutionary cause as an able polemicist whose sermons circulated in both the United States and Great Britain. Remaining in Congress until 1782, Witherspoon sat on more than one hundred committees, including two of the most important, the Board of War and the Committee on Secret Correspondence. He also performed valuable congressional duties in the government under the Articles of Confederation, helping to create the executive branch, establishing foreign alliances, and instructing the American peace commissioners in Paris. During his last two years in Congress, Witherspoon worked closely on several committees with his former student and now colleague James Madison.

After retiring from Congress, Witherspoon remained active as college president, state politician, and national leader of the Presbyterian Church. In Princeton he struggled for the remainder of his life with incomplete success to recover the college's prewar vitality. He had not forgotten his former student and expressed great pleasure when the College of New Jersey presented an honorary doctor of laws degree to Madison in 1788. Witherspoon was elected to the New Jersey legislature in 1783 and 1789 and was a delegate to New Jersey's ratifying convention in 1787. His selection in 1789 as first moderator of the General Assembly of the Presbyterian Church was a fitting honor, for he had labored for the four previous years to establish the denomination on a national basis. Blind and impoverished, he spent the last two years of his life in rather pathetic circumstances. Witherspoon's sad last years, however, did nothing to diminish a lifetime of accomplishment, and he and his disciples, particularly Madison, left an indelible mark on the new nation.

BIBLIOGRAPHY

Collins, Varnum Lansing. *President Witherspoon.* Reprint ed. 1969.

Hutchinson, William T., et al., eds. *The Papers of James Madison: Congressional Series.* 1962–.

Noll, Mark A. "The Irony of the Enlightenment for Presbyterians in the Early Republic." *Journal of the Early Republic* 5 (1985): 149–175.

Stohlman, Martha Lou Lemmon. *John Witherspoon.* 1976.

RICHARD RANKIN

WOLCOTT, ALEXANDER, JR. (1758–1828), Republican party manager in Connecticut. Alexander Wolcott, from Middletown, Connecticut, was one of his state's most vigorous (and despised) Jeffersonians. As the district collector of revenue, he reorganized the Republican party in his state into a model for future political machines. His circular letter in 1805, "System of Electioneering established by the democratic party in the State of Connecticut," became a textbook for party reorganization, and Federalist newspapers featured it as a terrible example of the low state of politics in Connecticut.

Wolcott was detested by New England merchants, most of them Federalists, who felt the sting of his vigorous enforcement of the Nonintercourse Act. His attitude was, "If Congress were of his opinion, the merchants might all go to hell in their own way." Wolcott insisted that the unpopular law be vigorously enforced, "let the consequences to the merchants be what they might." He also peppered Connecticut newspapers with articles defending the Nonintercourse Act and the Embargo.

President Madison rewarded Wolcott for his party loyalty in 1810, when he appointed him to one of two existing vacancies on the U.S. Supreme Court. Madison realized the folly of his action when the Senate rejected Wolcott, 24 to 9. Rep. John Randolph gloated over Madison's "great mortification," while Dolley Madison wrote of "some very wicked, & silly doings."

Wolcott's nomination to the Court caused dissent even within Madison's official family. The appointment disappointed Postmaster General Gideon Granger, who thought he was entitled to the position even though he was a covert ally of Madison's political foes. Ironically, in 1807 Jefferson had proposed the appointment of Wolcott as postmaster general in place of Granger. A more credible fellow statesman from Connecticut, Attorney General Levi Lincoln, strongly supported Wolcott, insisting that there were "few men of stronger mind, of greater perceptive and discriminating powers." Whatever Wolcott's potential as a jurist, his legion of enemies made the appointment a political blunder for Madison.

Wolcott remained a force in Connecticut politics and served as a delegate at the 1818 constitutional convention, unsuccessfully opposing the constitution it created.

BIBLIOGRAPHY

Brant, Irving. *James Madison: The President, 1809–1812.* 1956.

Cunningham, Noble E., Jr. *The Jeffersonian Republicans in Power.* 1963.

DONALD O. DEWEY

YATES, ROBERT

YATES, ROBERT (1738–1801), revolutionary jurist, Antifederalist. Yates was born in Schenectady, New York, and was admitted to the bar in Albany in 1760. He represented Albany in four provincial congresses and helped draft the New York state constitution. Appointed a justice of the state supreme court in 1777, in 1790 he became chief justice, a post he held until he resigned in 1798.

In 1787 Yates joined another Antifederalist, John Lansing, and the Federalist Alexander Hamilton to represent New York at the Federal Convention in Philadelphia. Yates and Lansing always outvoted Hamilton, keeping the New York delegation on the states' rights side. Yates took notes on the proceedings until the "Great Compromise" committee, of which he was a member, reported on 5 July 1787. Yates and Lansing then stalked out of the convention, arguing that the meeting, which had been convened to revise the Articles of Confederation, was exceeding its powers by framing a new charter that consolidated the states into a national government, thus impairing the sovereignty of New York. In the contest over ratification, Yates became a leading Antifederalist in 1787 and 1788, writing a series of letters opposing the Constitution and voting against its adoption at the Poughkeepsie convention.

Although Yates's original notes have disappeared, Yates's widow allowed Lansing to make a verbatim transcript after her husband's death in 1801. Edmond C. "Citizen" Genet obtained the Lansing copy from Mrs. Yates about 1808 and published it and other convention documents in 1821 as the *Secret Proceedings and Debates of the Convention Assembled at Philadelphia in the Year 1787 for the Purpose of Forming the Constitution of the United States.* Madison combined Yates's work with his own notes in order to give as thorough a record of the convention as possible, even though he protested against the "extreme incorrectness" of Yates's notes.

BIBLIOGRAPHY

De Pauw, Linda Grant. *The Eleventh Pillar: New York State and the Federal Constitution.* 1966.

Hutson, James H. "Robert Yates's Notes on the Constitutional Convention of 1787: Citizen Genet's Edition." *Quarterly Journal of the Library of Congress* 35 (1978): 173–182.

JAMES MORTON SMITH

YAZOO LANDS FRAUDS. In January 1795 a corrupt Georgia legislature sold 35 million acres, most of what is now Mississippi and Alabama, for $500,000 to four "insider" companies representing land speculators from throughout the United States. The area was named for the Yazoo River, which flows into the Mississippi River at Vicksburg, Mississippi. Every member of the legislature but one was personally involved in the corruption. The scandal was a personal and political nightmare throughout Madison's public career, though he gained nothing but trouble from it and expressed disgust for the speculators from the beginning.

Madison was falsely linked to Yazoo even before the historic scandal occurred. When an earlier Georgia legislature had sold 16 million acres for three cents an acre in 1789, Madison's father warned him of false rumors that he was a partner in a grant "obtained in a dishonest manner." The younger Madison called it "as absolute a falsehood as ever was propagated," adding that the Yazoo grant was "one of the most disgraceful events that have appeared in our public Councils, and such is the opinion which I have ever expressed of it." That first sale fell through before it could become a scandal; the second sale, which went through in 1795, provided the grist for twenty years of corruption, fraud, and accusations.

A reformed Georgia legislature rescinded the sale early

in February 1796, but many of the land titles had already passed to other, some of them innocent, purchasers. The next month Madison chaired the Committee on Privileges that reported that two U.S. senators—James Gunn of Georgia, a leader of the Yazoo speculators, and Frederick Frelinghuysen of New Jersey—had violated the privileges of the House of Representatives by attempting to force a duel with Rep. Abraham Baldwin, one of the Georgia reformers. For the next several years debates raged in Congress regarding the rights of the Yazoo investors, many of them northern Federalists.

President Jefferson attempted in 1801 to resolve this conflict by appointing the leaders of his cabinet—Madison, Albert Gallatin, and Levi Lincoln—to a commission that was to review the issue and to negotiate a solution. None of them had much sympathy for the speculators; Madison remarked that Associate Justice James Wilson, his chief ally in the Federal Convention, was "reprobated by all parties" for his landjobbing. But they knew that compromise was necessary to restore peace between northern and southern factions in Congress. The "Articles of Agreement and Cession," signed in April 1802, provided for the cession of Georgia's western lands to the United States in return for $1.25 million. Five million acres were to be set aside as reimbursement for investors found to have legitimate claims. The commissioners concluded that "the title of the claimants cannot be supported," yet "the interest of the United States, the tranquility of those who thereafter may inhabit that territory, and various equitable considerations . . . render it expedient to enter into a compromise on reasonable terms."

The agreement brought no tranquility to Madison; for John Randolph of Roanoke, Jefferson's floor leader in the House of Representatives, was outraged by concessions to the speculators and turned violently against Madison. He placed all the blame on Madison, even though Randolph's close friend Gallatin was the principal author of the report. Randolph stalled the agreement until 1810, when the Supreme Court decided the issue quite differently in *Fletcher* v. *Peck*. The Marshall Court upheld the claims of the speculators, asserting that the 1796 Georgia legislature had violated the Constitution by depriving investors of their contractual rights. The collusive opponents, Fletcher and Peck, both of whom would profit from the decision, had nothing to show for their efforts until Congress appropriated funds to indemnify the speculators. Randolph and the Georgia delegation prevented this from happening until 1814, by which time Randolph had been defeated in his reelection bid. In March Congress finally passed a compensation bill providing $5 million to end the turmoil; this was already known to be acceptable to the New England Mississippi Land Company, the most insistent and

prominent of the claimants. Madison signed the act almost immediately to close the troublesome incident.

BIBLIOGRAPHY

Brant, Irving. *James Madison: Secretary of State, 1800–1809.* 1953.
Magrath, C. Peter. *Yazoo: Law and Politics in the New Republic.* 1966.

DONALD O. DEWEY

YEO, SIR JAMES LUCAS (1783–1819), British naval officer. Knighted by the Prince Regent of Portugal on 16 March 1810 for restoring Portuguese possessions in South America, Capt. Sir James Lucas Yeo had joined the navy at the age of ten in 1793 and had been promoted to the rank of captain in 1807. On 13 March 1813, Yeo was commissioned as commodore and commander in chief of British naval forces on the lakes of Canada. Instructed to cooperate with Gov. Gen. Sir George Prevost, commander in chief in the Canadas, and to report to Adm. Sir John Borlase Warren, Yeo with 460 officers and men, organized the Lake Ontario station against his opponent, Commodore Isaac Chauncey, improved the escort system for bateaux along the Saint Lawrence, unsuccessfully attacked Chauncey's base at Sackets Harbor (27–28 May 1813), and engaged in several skirmishes in August and September 1813. During the winter of 1813–1814 he began a shipbuilding program. Early in 1814 Yeo blockaded Chauncey in Sackets Harbor, but, after losing some gunboats at Big Sandy in late May 1814, he raised the blockade.

Yeo's activities and his handling of Chauncey, in conjunction with Prevost's defensive war, thwarted President Madison's desires for a joint navy-army sweep into Upper Canada via the Niagara peninsula and Lake Ontario. Ironically, Yeo brought court-martial charges against Prevost for the loss of the British squadron on Lake Champlain, and both were recalled; one to bring, and the other to answer, the charges. Yeo was knighted by the Prince Regent of England and appointed to command the African squadron. He died of fever while fulfilling that office in 1819.

BIBLIOGRAPHY

Drake, Frederick C. "Commodore Sir James Lucas Yeo and Governor General Sir George Prevost: A Study in Command Relations, 1813–1814." In William B. Cogar, ed., *New Interpretations in Naval History: Selected Papers from the Eighth Naval History Symposium.* 1989.
Dudley, William S., ed. *The Naval War of 1812.* Vol. 1. 1985. Vol. 2. 1992.
Spurr, John C. "The Royal Navy's Presence in Kingston, Part I: 1813–1836." *Historic Kingston* 25 (March 1977): 63–64.

FREDERICK C. DRAKE

YRUJO, CARLOS FERNANDO MARTINEZ,

marquis de Casa-Yrujo (1763–1824), Spanish diplomat. In 1795 Yrujo was named minister to the United States, where his struggle to defend Spanish territory against American expansionism began shortly after his arrival in 1796 with his protest against a conspiracy to invade Louisiana, led by William Blount of Tennessee. His 1798 marriage to Dolley Madison's friend Sarah McKean initiated a warm friendship with the Madisons, and in 1802, when the Spanish intendant at New Orleans withdrew the right of deposit guaranteed by the Treaty of San Lorenzo, thereby depriving western farmers of an outlet for their produce, Yrujo cooperated with Madison and the French chargé d'affaires, Louis-André Pichon, to rescind the ban and to forestall military action by the westerners.

Yrujo's protests against the Louisiana Purchase in 1803, as well as his resistance to American designs upon East and West Florida, weakened his friendship with Madison. His involvement in Anthony Merry's quarrel with the administration over diplomatic etiquette and his violent protest against the Mobile Act of 1804 (which he called "an atrocious libel" on Spain) led to a permanent rupture in their relationship.

In 1804 Yrujo moved to Philadelphia without taking formal leave of Secretary Madison and wrote directly to President Jefferson complaining about Madison's behavior. Following Yrujo's authorship of anonymous newspaper articles accusing the government of seeking war with Spain, Madison instructed James Monroe at Madrid to demand Yrujo's recall. The administration rejected the Spanish government's reply that it wished him to stay, and, when Yrujo returned to Washington in early 1806 in violation of Madison's instructions to remain away, Madison insisted that he leave the capital and refused to correspond directly with him. Yrujo's protests against Francisco Miranda's New York-based expedition against Venezuela had to be delivered by the French minister, Louis-Marie Turreau. Yrujo finally left the United States in 1807, when it was clear that his continued presence was harming Spanish-American relations.

BIBLIOGRAPHY

Bleiburg, German, ed. *Diccionario de Historia de España*. Vol. 1. 1968.

Brant, Irving. *James Madison*. 1941–1961.

Michaud, Joseph François. *Biographie universelle, ancienne et moderne: ou, Histoire, par ordre alphabétique, de la vie publique et privée de tous les hommes qui se sont fait remarquer par leurs écrits, leurs actions, leurs talents, leurs vertus ou leurs crimes*. Vol. 31. 1843.

MARY A. HACKETT

Memorial and Remonstrance against Religious Assessments

20 June 1785

To the Honorable the General Assembly of the Commonwealth of Virginia
A Memorial and Remonstrance

We the subscribers, citizens of the said Commonwealth, having taken into serious consideration, a Bill printed by order of the last Session of General Assembly, entitled "A Bill establishing a provision for Teachers of the Christian Religion," and conceiving that the same if finally armed with the sanctions of a law, will be a dangerous abuse of power, are bound as faithful members of a free State to remonstrate against it, and to declare the reasons by which we are determined. We remonstrate against the said Bill,

1. Because we hold it for a fundamental and undeniable truth, "that Religion or the duty which we owe to our Creator and the manner of discharging it, can be directed only by reason and conviction, not by force or violence." [Virginia Declaration of Rights, art. 16] The Religion then of every man must be left to the conviction and conscience of every man; and it is the right of every man to exercise it as these may dictate. This right is in its nature an unalienable right. It is unalienable, because the opinions of men, depending only on the evidence contemplated by their own minds cannot follow the dictates of other men: It is unalienable also, because what is here a right towards men, is a duty towards the Creator. It is the duty of every man to render to the Creator such homage and such only as he believes to be acceptable to him. This duty is precedent, both in order of time and in degree of obligation, to the claims of Civil Society. Before any man can be considered as a member of Civil Society, he must be considered as a subject of the Governour of the Universe: And if a member of Civil Society, who enters into any subordinate Association, must always do it with a reservation of his duty to the General Authority; much more must every man who becomes a member of any particular Civil Society, do it with a saving of his allegiance to the Universal Sovereign. We maintain therefore that in matters of Religion, no mans right is abridged by the institution of Civil Society and that Religion is wholly exempt from its cognizance. True it is, that no other rule exists, by which any question which may divide a Society, can be ultimately determined, but the will of the majority; but it is also true that the majority may trespass on the rights of the minority.

2. Because if Religion be exempt from the authority of the Society at large, still less can it be subject to that of the Legislative Body. The latter are but the creatures and vicegerents of the former. Their jurisdiction is both derivative and limited: it is limited with regard to the co-ordinate departments, more necessarily is it limited with regard to the constituents. The preservation of a free Government requires not merely, that the metes and bounds which separate each department of power be invariably maintained; but more especially that neither of them be suffered to overleap the great Barrier which defends the rights of the people. The Rulers who are guilty of such an encroachment, exceed the commission from which they derive their authority, and are Tyrants. The People who submit to it are governed by laws made neither by themselves nor by an authority derived from them, and are slaves.

3. Because it is proper to take alarm at the first experiment on our liberties. We hold this prudent jealousy to be the first duty of Citizens, and one of the noblest charac-

teristics of the late Revolution. The free men of America did not wait till usurped power had strengthened itself by exercise, and entangled the question in precedents. They saw all the consequences in the principle, and they avoided the consequences by denying the principle. We revere this lesson too much soon to forget it. Who does not see that the same authority which can establish Christianity, in exclusion of all other Religions, may establish with the same ease any particular sect of Christians, in exclusion of all other Sects? that the same authority which can force a citizen to contribute three pence only of his property for the support of any one establishment, may force him to conform to any other establishment in all cases whatsoever?

4. Because the Bill violates that equality which ought to be the basis of every law, and which is more indispensible, in proportion as the validity or expediency of any law is more liable to be impeached. If "all men are by nature equally free and independent," [Virginia Declaration of Rights, art. 1] all men are to be considered as entering into Society on equal conditions; as relinquishing no more, and therefore retaining no less, one than another, of their natural rights. Above all are they to be considered as retaining an "*equal* title to the free exercise of Religion according to the dictates of Conscience." [Virginia Declaration of Rights, art. 16] Whilst we assert for ourselves a freedom to embrace, to profess and to observe the Religion which we believe to be of divine origin, we cannot deny an equal freedom to those whose minds have not yet yielded to the evidence which has convinced us. If this freedom be abused, it is an offence against God, not against man: To God, therefore, not to man, must an account of it be rendered. As the Bill violates equality by subjecting some to peculiar burdens, so it violates the same principle, by granting to others peculiar exemptions. Are the Quakers and Menonists the only sects who think a compulsive support of their Religions unnecessary and unwarrantable? Can their piety alone be entrusted with the care of public worship? Ought their Religions to be endowed above all others with extraordinary privileges by which proselytes may be enticed from all others? We think too favorably of the justice and good sense of these denominations to believe that they either covet pre-eminences over their fellow citizens or that they will be seduced by them from the common opposition to the measure.

5. Because the Bill implies either that the Civil Magistrate is a competent Judge of Religious Truth; or that he may employ Religion as an engine of Civil policy. The first is an arrogant pretension falsified by the contradictory opinions of Rulers in all ages, and throughout the world: the second an unhallowed perversion of the means of salvation.

6. Because the establishment proposed by the Bill is not requisite for the support of the Christian Religion. To say that it is, is a contradiction to the Christian Religion itself, for every page of it disavows a dependence on the powers of this world: it is a contradiction to fact; for it is known that this Religion both existed and flourished, not only without the support of human laws, but in spite of every opposition from them, and not only during the period of miraculous aid, but long after it had been left to its own evidence and the ordinary care of Providence. Nay, it is a contradiction in terms; for a Religion not invented by human policy, must have pre-existed and been supported, before it was established by human policy. It is moreover to weaken in those who profess this Religion a pious confidence in its innate excellence and the patronage of its Author; and to foster in those who still reject it, a suspicion that its friends are too conscious of its fallacies to trust it to its own merits.

7. Because experience witnesseth that ecclesiastical establishments, instead of maintaining the purity and efficacy of Religion, have had a contrary operation. During almost fifteen centuries has the legal establishment of Christianity been on trial. What have been its fruits? More or less in all places, pride and indolence in the Clergy, ignorance and servility in the laity, in both, superstition, bigotry and persecution. Enquire of the Teachers of Christianity for the ages in which it appeared in its greatest lustre; those of every sect, point to the ages prior to its incorporation with Civil policy. Pro-

pose a restoration of this primitive State in which its Teachers depended on the voluntary rewards of their flocks, many of them predict its downfall. On which Side ought their testimony to have greatest weight, when for or when against their interest?

8. Because the establishment in question is not necessary for the support of Civil Government. If it be urged as necessary for the support of Civil Government only as it is a means of supporting Religion, and it be not necessary for the latter purpose, it cannot be necessary for the former. If Religion be not within the cognizance of Civil Government how can its legal establishment be necessary to Civil Government? What influence in fact have ecclesiastical establishments had on Civil Society? In some instances they have been seen to erect a spiritual tyranny on the ruins of the Civil authority; in many instances they have been seen upholding the thrones of political tyranny: in no instance have they been seen the guardians of the liberties of the people. Rulers who wished to subvert the public liberty, may have found an established Clergy convenient auxiliaries. A just Government instituted to secure & perpetuate it needs them not. Such a Government will be best supported by protecting every Citizen in the enjoyment of his Religion with the same equal hand which protects his person and his property; by neither invading the equal rights of any Sect, nor suffering any Sect to invade those of another.

9. Because the proposed establishment is a departure from that generous policy, which, offering an Asylum to the persecuted and oppressed of every Nation and Religion, promised a lustre to our country, and an accession to the number of its citizens. What a melancholy mark is the Bill of sudden degeneracy? Instead of holding forth an Asylum to the persecuted, it is itself a signal of persecution. It degrades from the equal rank of Citizens all those whose opinions in Religion do not bend to those of the Legislative authority. Distant as it may be in its present form from the Inquisition, it differs from it only in degree. The one is the first step, the other the last in the career of intolerance. The magnanimous sufferer under this cruel scourge in foreign Regions, must view the Bill as a Beacon on our Coast, warning him to seek some other haven, where liberty and philanthropy in their due extent, may offer a more certain repose from his Troubles.

10. Because it will have a like tendency to banish our Citizens. The allurements presented by other situations are every day thinning their number. To superadd a fresh motive to emigration by revoking the liberty which they now enjoy, would be the same species of folly which has dishonoured and depopulated flourishing kingdoms.

11. Because it will destroy that moderation and harmony which the forbearance of our laws to intermeddle with Religion has produced among its several sects. Torrents of blood have been spilt in the old world, by vain attempts of the secular arm, to extinguish Religious discord, by proscribing all difference in Religious opinion. Time has at length revealed the true remedy. Every relaxation of narrow and rigorous policy, wherever it has been tried, has been found to assuage the disease. The American Theatre has exhibited proofs that equal and compleat liberty, if it does not wholly eradicate it, sufficiently destroys its malignant influence on the health and prosperity of the State. If with the salutary effects of this system under our own eyes, we begin to contract the bounds of Religious freedom, we know no name that will too severely reproach our folly. At least let warning be taken at the first fruits of the threatened innovation. The very appearance of the Bill has transformed "that Christian forbearance, love and charity," [Virginia Declaration of Rights, art. 16] which of late mutually prevailed, into animosities and jealousies, which may not soon be appeased. What mischiefs may not be dreaded, should this enemy to the public quiet be armed with the force of a law?

12. Because the policy of the Bill is adverse to the diffusion of the light of Christianity. The first wish of those who enjoy this precious gift ought to be that it may be imparted to the whole race of mankind. Compare the number of those who have as yet

received it with the number still remaining under the dominion of false Religions; and how small is the former! Does the policy of the Bill tend to lessen the disproportion? No; it at once discourages those who are strangers to the light of revelation from coming into the Region of it; and countenances by example the nations who continue in darkness, in shutting out those who might convey it to them. Instead of Levelling as far as possible, every obstacle to the victorious progress of Truth, the Bill with an ignoble and unchristian timidity would circumscribe it with a wall of defence against the encroachments of error.

13. Because attempts to enforce by legal sanctions, acts obnoxious to so great a proportion of Citizens, tend to enervate the laws in general, and to slacken the bands of Society. If it be difficult to execute any law which is not generally deemed necessary or salutary, what must be the case, where it is deemed invalid and dangerous? And what may be the effect of so striking an example of impotency in the Government, on its general authority?

14. Because a measure of such singular magnitude and delicacy ought not to be imposed, without the clearest evidence that it is called for by a majority of citizens, and no satisfactory method is yet proposed by which the voice of the majority in this case may be determined, or its influence secured. "The people of the respective counties are indeed requested to signify their opinion respecting the adoption of the Bill to the next Session of Assembly." But the representation must be made equal, before the voice either of the Representatives or of the Counties will be that of the people. Our hope is that neither of the former will, after due consideration, espouse the dangerous principle of the Bill. Should the event disappoint us, it will still leave us in full confidence, that a fair appeal to the latter will reverse the sentence against our liberties.

15. Because finally, "the equal right of every citizen to the free exercise of his Religion according to the dictates of conscience" is held by the same tenure with all our other rights. If we recur to its origin, it is equally the gift of nature; if we weigh its importance, it cannot be less dear to us; if we consult the "Declaration of those rights which pertain to the good people of Virginia, as the basis and foundation of Government," it is enumerated with equal solemnity, or rather studied emphasis. Either then, we must say, that the Will of the Legislature is the only measure of their authority; and that in the plenitude of this authority, they may sweep away all our fundamental rights; or, that they are bound to leave this particular right untouched and sacred: Either we must say, that they may controul the freedom of the press, may abolish the Trial by Jury, may swallow up the Executive and Judiciary Powers of the State; nay that they may despoil us of our very right of suffrage, and erect themselves into an independent and hereditary Assembly or, we must say, that they have no authority to enact into law the Bill under consideration. We the Subscribers say, that the General Assembly of this Commonwealth have no such authority: And that no effort may be omitted on our part against so dangerous an usurpation, we oppose to it, this remonstrance; earnestly praying, as we are in duty bound, that the Supreme Lawgiver of the Universe, by illuminating those to whom it is addressed, may on the one hand, turn their Councils from every act which would affront his holy prerogative, or violate the trust committed to them: and on the other, guide them into every measure which may be worthy of his blessing, may redound to their own praise, and may establish more firmly the liberties, the prosperity and the happiness of the Commonwealth.

The Constitution of the United States

Spelling, capitalization, and punctuation conform to the text of the engrossed copy.

WE THE PEOPLE of the United States, in Order to form a more perfect Union, establish Justice, insure domestic Tranquility, provide for the common defence, promote the general Welfare, and secure the Blessings of Liberty to ourselves and our Posterity, do ordain and establish this Constitution of the United States of America.

ARTICLE. I.

SECTION. 1. All legislative Powers herein granted shall be vested in a Congress of the United States, which shall consist of a Senate and House of Representatives.

SECTION. 2. The House of Representatives shall be composed of Members chosen every second Year by the People of the several States, and the Electors in each State shall have the Qualifications requisite for Electors of the most numerous Branch of the State Legislature.

No Person shall be a Representative who shall not have attained to the Age of twenty five Years, and been seven Years a Citizen of the United States, and who shall not, when elected, be an Inhabitant of that State in which he shall be chosen.

Representatives and direct Taxes shall be apportioned among the several States which may be included within this Union, according to their respective Numbers, which shall be determined by adding to the whole Number of free Persons, including those bound to Service for a Term of Years, and excluding Indians not taxed, three fifths of all other Persons. The actual Enumeration shall be made within three Years after the first Meeting of the Congress of the United States, and within every subsequent Term of ten Years, in such Manner as they shall by Law direct. The Number of Representatives shall not exceed one for every thirty Thousand, but each State shall have at Least one Representative; and until such enumeration shall be made, the State of New Hampshire shall be entitled to chuse three, Massachusetts eight, Rhode-Island and Providence Plantations one, Connecticut five, New-York six, New Jersey four, Pennsylvania eight, Delaware one, Maryland six, Virginia ten, North Carolina five, South Carolina five, and Georgia three.

When vacancies happen in the Representation from any State, the Executive Authority thereof shall issue Writs of Election to fill such Vacancies.

The House of Representatives shall chuse their Speaker and other Officers; and shall have the sole Power of Impeachment.

SECTION. 3. The Senate of the United States shall be composed of two Senators from each State, chosen by the Legislature thereof, for six Years; and each Senator shall have one Vote.

Immediately after they shall be assembled in Consequence of the first Election, they shall be divided as equally as may be into three Classes. The Seats of the Senators of the first Class shall be vacated at the Expiration of the second Year, of the second Class at the Expiration of the fourth Year, and of the third Class at the Expiration of the sixth Year, so that one third may be chosen every second Year; and if Vacancies happen by Resignation, or otherwise, during the Recess of the Legislature of any State, the Executive thereof may make temporary Appointments until the next Meeting of the Legislature, which shall then fill such Vacancies.

No Person shall be a Senator who shall not have attained to the Age of thirty Years, and been nine Years a Citizen of the United States, and who shall not, when elected, be an Inhabitant of that State for which he shall be chosen.

The Vice President of the United States shall be President of the Senate, but shall have no Vote, unless they be equally divided.

The Senate shall chuse their other Officers, and also a President pro tempore, in the Absence of the Vice President, or when he shall exercise the Office of President of the United States.

The Senate shall have the sole Power to try all Impeachments. When sitting for that Purpose, they shall be on Oath or Affirmation. When the President of the United States is tried, the Chief Justice shall preside: And no Person shall be convicted without the Concurrence of two thirds of the Members present.

Judgment in Cases of Impeachment shall not extend further than to removal from Office, and disqualification to hold and enjoy any Office of honor, Trust or Profit under the United States: but the Party convicted shall nevertheless be liable and subject to Indictment, Trial, Judgment and Punishment, according to Law.

SECTION. 4. The Times, Places and Manner of holding Elections for Senators and Representatives, shall be prescribed in each State by the Legislature thereof; but the Congress may at any time by Law make or alter such Regulations, except as to the Places of chusing Senators.

The Congress shall assemble at least once in every Year, and such Meeting shall be on the first Monday in December, unless they shall by Law appoint a different Day.

SECTION. 5. Each House shall be the Judge of the Elections, Returns and Qualifications of its own Members, and a Majority of each shall constitute a Quorum to do Business; but a smaller Number may adjourn from day to day, and may be authorized to compel the Attendance of absent Members, in such Manner, and under such Penalties as each House may provide.

Each House may determine the Rules of its Proceedings, punish its Members for disorderly Behaviour, and, with the Concurrence of two thirds, expel a Member.

Each House shall keep a Journal of its Proceedings, and from time to time publish the same, excepting such Parts as may in their Judgment require Secrecy; and the Yeas and Nays of the Members of either House on any question shall, at the Desire of one fifth of those Present, be entered on the Journal.

Neither House, during the Session of Congress, shall, without the Consent of the other, adjourn for more than three days, nor to any other Place than that in which the two Houses shall be sitting.

SECTION. 6. The Senators and Representatives shall receive a Compensation for their Services, to be ascertained by Law, and paid out of the Treasury of the United States. They shall in all Cases, except Treason, Felony and Breach of the Peace, be privileged from Arrest during their Attendance at the Session of their respective Houses, and in going to and returning from the same; and for any Speech or Debate in either House, they shall not be questioned in any other Place.

No Senator or Representative shall, during the Time for which he was elected, be appointed to any civil Office under the Authority of the United States, which shall have been created, or the Emoluments whereof shall have been encreased during such time; and no Person holding any Office under the United States, shall be a Member of either House during his Continuance in Office.

SECTION. 7. All Bills for raising Revenue shall originate in the House of Representatives; but the Senate may propose or concur with Amendments as on other Bills.

Every Bill which shall have passed the House of Representatives and the Senate, shall, before it become a Law, be presented to the President of the United States; If he approve he shall sign it, but if not he shall return it, with his Objections to that House in which it shall have originated, who shall enter the Objections at large on their Journal, and proceed to reconsider it. If after such Reconsideration two thirds of that House shall agree to pass the Bill, it shall be sent, together with the Objections, to the other House, by which it shall likewise be reconsidered, and if approved by two thirds of that House, it shall become a Law. But in all such Cases the Votes of both Houses shall be determined by yeas and Nays, and the Names of the Persons voting for and against the Bill shall be entered on the Journal of each House respectively. If any Bill shall not be returned by the President within ten Days (Sundays excepted) after it shall have been presented to him, the Same shall be a Law, in like Manner as if he had signed it, unless the Congress by their Adjournment prevent its Return, in which Case it shall not be a Law.

Every Order, Resolution, or Vote to which the Concurrence of the Senate and House of Representatives may be necessary (except on a question of Adjournment) shall be presented to the President of the United States; and before the Same shall take Effect, shall be approved by him, or being disapproved by him, shall be repassed by two thirds of the Senate and House of Representatives, according to the Rules and Limitations prescribed in the Case of a Bill.

SECTION. 8. The Congress shall have Power To lay and collect Taxes, Duties, Imposts and Excises, to pay the Debts and provide for the common Defence and general Welfare of the United States; but all Duties, Imposts and Excises shall be uniform throughout the United States;

To borrow Money on the credit of the United States;

To regulate Commerce with foreign Nations, and among the several States, and with the Indian tribes;

To establish an uniform Rule of Naturalization, and uniform Laws on the subject of Bankruptcies throughout the United States;

To coin Money, regulate the Value thereof, and of foreign Coin, and fix the Standard of Weights and Measures;

To provide for the Punishment of counterfeiting the Securities and current Coin of the United States;

To establish Post Offices and post Roads;

To promote the Progress of Science and useful Arts, by securing for limited Times to Authors and Inventors the exclusive Right to their respective Writings and Discoveries;

To constitute Tribunals inferior to the supreme Court;

To define and punish Piracies and Felonies committed on the high Seas, and Offences against the Law of Nations;

To declare War, grant Letters of Marque and Reprisal, and make Rules concerning Captures on Land and Water;

To raise and support Armies, but no Appropriation of Money to that Use shall be for a longer Term than two Years;

To provide and maintain a Navy;

To make Rules for the Government and Regulation of the land and naval Forces;

To provide for calling forth the Militia to execute the Laws of the Union, suppress Insurrections and repel Invasions;

To provide for organizing, arming, and disciplining, the Militia, and for governing such Part of them as may be employed in the Service of the United States, reserving to the States respectively, the Appointment of the Officers, and the Authority of training the Militia according to the discipline prescribed by Congress;

To exercise exclusive Legislation in all Cases whatsoever, over such District (not exceeding ten Miles square) as may, by Cession of particular States, and the Acceptance of Congress, become the Seat of the Government of the United States, and to exercise like Authority over all Places purchased by the Consent of the Legislature of the State in which the Same shall be, for the Erection of Forts, Magazines, Arsenals, dock-Yards, and other needful Buildings;—And

To make all Laws which shall be necessary and proper for carrying into Execution the foregoing Powers, and all other Powers vested by this Constitution in the Government of the United States, or in any Department or Officer thereof.

SECTION. 9. The Migration or Importation of such Persons as any of the States now existing shall think proper to admit, shall not be prohibited by the Congress prior to the Year one thousand eight hundred and eight, but a Tax or duty may be imposed on such Importation, not exceeding ten dollars for each Person.

The Privilege of the Writ of Habeas Corpus shall not be suspended, unless when in Cases of Rebellion or Invasion the public Safety may require it.

No Bill of Attainder or ex post facto Law shall be passed.

No Capitation, or other direct, Tax shall be laid, unless in Proportion to the Census or Enumeration herein before directed to be taken.

No Tax or Duty shall be laid on Articles exported from any State.

No Preference shall be given by any Regulation of Commerce or Revenue to the Ports of one State over those of another: nor shall Vessels bound to, or from, one State, be obliged to enter, clear, or pay Duties in another.

No Money shall be drawn from the Treasury, but in Consequence of Appropriations made by Law; and a regular Statement and Account of the Receipts and Expenditures of all public Money shall be published from time to time.

No Title of Nobility shall be granted by the United States: And no Person holding any Office of Profit or Trust under them, shall, without the Consent of the Congress, accept of any present, Emolument, Office, or Title, of any kind whatever, from any King, Prince, or foreign State.

SECTION. 10. No State shall enter into any Treaty, Alliance, or Confederation; grant Letters of Marque and Reprisal; coin Money; emit Bills of Credit; make any Thing but gold and silver Coin a Tender in Payment of Debts; pass any Bill of Attainder, ex post facto Law, or Law impairing the Obligation of Contracts, or grant any Title of Nobility.

No State shall, without the Consent of the Congress, lay any Imposts or Duties on Imports or Exports, except what may be absolutely necessary for executing it's inspection Laws: and the net Produce of all Duties and Imposts, laid by any State on Imports or Exports, shall be for the Use of the Treasury of the United States; and all such Laws shall be subject to the Revision and Controul of the Congress.

No State shall, without the consent of Congress, lay any Duty of Tonnage, keep Troops, or Ships of War in time of Peace, enter into any Agreement or Compact with another State, or with a foreign Power, or engage in War, unless actually invaded, or in such imminent Danger as will not admit of delay.

ARTICLE II.

SECTION. 1. The executive Power shall be vested in a President of the United States of America. He shall hold his Office during the Term of four Years, and, together with the Vice President, chosen for the same Term, be elected, as follows

Each State shall appoint, in such Manner as the Legislature thereof may direct, a Number of Electors, equal to the whole Number of Senators and Representatives to which the State may be entitled in the Congress; but no Senator or Representative, or Person holding an Office of Trust or Profit under the United States, shall be appointed an Elector.

The Electors shall meet in their respective States, and vote by Ballot for two Persons, of whom one at least shall not be an inhabitant of the same State with themselves. And they shall make a List of all the Persons voted for, and of the Number of Votes for each; which List they shall sign and certify, and transmit sealed to the Seat of the Government of the United States, directed to the President of the Senate. The President of the Senate shall, in the Presence of the Senate and House of Representatives, open all the Certificates, and the Votes shall then be counted. The Person having the greatest Number of Votes shall be the President, if such Number be a Majority of the whole Number of Electors appointed; and if there be more than one who have such Majority, and have an equal Number of Votes, then the House of Representatives shall immediately chuse by Ballot one of them for President; and if no Person have a Majority, then from the five highest on the List the said House shall in like Manner chuse the President. But in chusing the President, the Votes shall be taken by States, the Representation from each State having one Vote; A quorum for this purpose shall consist of a Member or Members from two thirds of the States, and a Majority of all the States shall be necessary to a Choice. In every Case, after the Choice of the President, the Person having the greatest Number of Votes of the Electors shall be the Vice President. But if there should remain two or more who have equal Votes, the Senate shall chuse from them by Ballot the Vice President.

The Congress may determine the Time of chusing the Electors, and the Day on which they shall give their Votes; which Day shall be the same throughout the United States.

No Person except a natural born Citizen, or a Citizen of the United States, at the time of the Adoption of this Constitution, shall be eligible to the Office of President; neither shall any Person be eligible to that Office who shall not have attained to the Age of thirty five Years, and been fourteen Years a Resident within the United States.

In Case of the Removal of the President from Office, or of his Death, Resignation, or Inability to discharge the Powers and Duties of the said Office, the Same shall devolve on the Vice President, and the Congress may by Law provide for the Case of Removal, Death, Resignation or Inability, both of the President and the Vice President, declaring what Officer shall then act as President, and such Officer shall act accordingly, until the Disability be removed, or a President shall be elected.

The President shall, at stated Times, receive for his Services, a Compensation, which shall neither be encreased nor diminished during the Period for which he shall have been elected, and he shall not receive within that Period any other Emolument from the United States, or any of them.

Before he enter on the Execution of his Office, he shall take the following Oath of Affirmation:—"I do solemnly swear (or affirm) that I will faithfully execute the Office of President of the United States, and will to the best of my Ability, preserve, protect and defend the Constitution of the United States."

SECTION. 2. The President shall be Commander in Chief of the Army and Navy of the United States, and of the Militia of the several States, when called into the actual Service of the United States; he may require the Opinion, in writing, of the principal Officer in each of the executive Departments, upon any Subject relating to the Duties of their respective Offices, and he shall have Power to grant Reprieves and Pardons for Offences against the United States, except in Cases of Impeachment.

He shall have Power, by and with the Advice and Consent of the Senate, to make Treaties, provided two thirds of the Senators present concur; and he shall nominate, and by and with the Advice and Consent of the Senate, shall appoint Ambassadors, other public Ministers and Consuls, Judges of the supreme Court, and all other Officers of the United States, whose Appointments are not herein otherwise provided for, and which shall be established by Law: but the Congress may by Law vest the Appointment of such inferior Officers, as they think proper, in the President alone, in the Courts of Law, or in the Heads of Departments.

The President shall have Power to fill up all Vacancies that may happen during the Recess of the Senate, by granting Commissions which shall expire at the End of their next Session.

SECTION. 3. He shall from time to time give to the Congress Information of the State of the Union, and recommend to their Consideration such Measures as he shall judge necessary and expedient; he may, on extraordinary Occasions, convene both Houses, or either of them, and in Case of Disagreement between them, with Respect to the Time of Adjournment, he may adjourn them to such Time as he shall think proper; he shall receive Ambassadors and other public Ministers; he shall take Care that the Laws be faithfully executed, and shall Commission all the Officers of the United States.

SECTION. 4. The President, Vice President and all civil Officers of the United States, shall be removed from Office on Impeachment for, and Conviction of, Treason, Bribery, or other high Crimes and Misdemeanors.

ARTICLE III.

SECTION. 1. The judicial Power of the United States, shall be vested in one supreme Court, and in such inferior Courts as the Congress may from time to time ordain and establish. The Judges, both of the supreme and inferior Courts, shall hold their Offices during good Behaviour, and shall, at stated Times, receive for their Services, a Compensation, which shall not be diminished during their Continuance in Office.

SECTION. 2. The judicial Power shall extend to all Cases, in Law and Equity, arising under this Constitution, the Laws of the United States, and Treaties made, or which shall be made, under their Authority;—to all cases affecting Ambassadors, other public Ministers and Consuls;—to all Cases of admiralty and maritime Jurisdiction;—to Controversies to which the United States shall be a Party;—to Controversies between two or more States;—between a State and Citizens of another State;—between Citizens of different States;—between Citizens of the same State claiming Lands under Grants of different States, and between a State, or the Citizens thereof, and foreign States, Citizens or Subjects.

In all Cases affecting Ambassadors, other public Ministers and Consuls, and those in which a State shall be Party, the supreme Court shall have original Jurisdiction. In all the other Cases before mentioned, the supreme Court shall have appellate Jurisdiction, both as to Law and Fact, with such Exceptions, and under such Regulations as the Congress shall make.

The Trial of all Crimes, except in Cases of Impeachment, shall be by Jury; and such Trial shall be held in the State where the said Crimes shall have been committed; but when not committed within any State, the Trial shall be at such Place or Places as the Congress may by Law have directed.

SECTION. 3. Treason against the United States, shall consist only in levying War against them, or in adhering to their Enemies, giving them Aid and Comfort. No Person shall be convicted of Treason unless on the Testimony of two Witnesses to the same overt Act, or on Confession in open Court.

The Congress shall have Power to declare the Punishment of Treason, but no Attainder of Treason shall work Corruption of Blood, or Forfeiture except during the Life of the Person attainted.

ARTICLE IV.

SECTION. 1. Full Faith and Credit shall be given in each State to the public Acts, Records, and judicial Proceedings of every other State. And the Congress may by general Laws prescribe the Manner in which such Acts, Records and Proceedings shall be proved, and the Effect thereof.

SECTION. 2. The Citizens of each State shall be entitled to all Privileges and Immunities of Citizens in the several States.

A Person charged in any State with Treason, Felony, or other Crime, who shall flee from Justice, and be found in another State, shall on Demand of the executive Authority of the State from which he fled, be delivered up, to be removed to the State having Jurisdiction of the Crime.

No Person held to Service or Labour in one State, under the Laws thereof, escaping into another, shall, in Consequence of any Law or Regulation therein, be discharged from such Service or Labour, but shall be delivered up on Claim of the Party to whom such Service or Labour may be due.

SECTION. 3. New States may be admitted by the Congress into this Union; but no new State shall be formed or erected within the Jurisdiction of any other State; nor any State be formed by the Junction of two or more States, or Parts of States, without the Consent of the Legislatures of the States concerned as well as of the Congress.

The Congress shall have Power to dispose of and make all needful Rules and Regulations respecting the Territory or other Property belonging to the United States; and nothing in this Constitution shall be so construed as to Prejudice any Claims of the United States, or of any particular State.

SECTION. 4. The United States shall guarantee to every State in this Union a Republican Form of Government, and shall protect each of them against Invasion; and on Application of the Legislature, or of the Executive (when the Legislature cannot be convened) against domestic Violence.

ARTICLE V.

The Congress, whenever two thirds of both Houses shall deem it necessary, shall propose Amendments to this Constitution, or, on the Application of the Legislatures of two thirds of the several States, shall call a Convention for proposing Amendments, which, in either Case, shall be valid to all Intents and Purposes, as Part of this Constitution, when ratified by the legislatures of three fourths of the several States, or by Conventions in three fourths thereof, as the one or the other Mode of Ratification may be proposed by the Congress; Provided that no Amendment which may be made prior to the Year One thousand eight hundred and eight shall in any Manner affect the first and fourth Clauses in the Ninth Section of the first Article; and that no State, without its Consent, shall be deprived of it's equal Suffrage in the Senate.

ARTICLE VI.

All Debts contracted and Engagements entered into, before the Adoption of this Constitution, shall be as valid against the United States under this Constitution, as under the Confederation.

This Constitution, and the Laws of the United States which shall be made in Pursuance thereof; and all Treaties made, or which shall be made, under the Authority of the United States, shall be the supreme Law of the Land; and the Judges in every State shall be bound thereby, any Thing in the Constitution or Laws of any State to the Contrary notwithstanding.

The Senators and Representatives before mentioned, and the Members of the several State Legislatures, and all executive and judicial Officers, both of the United States and of the several States, shall be bound by Oath or Affirmation, to support this Constitution; but no religious Test shall ever be required as a Qualification to any Office or public Trust under the United States.

ARTICLE VII.

The Ratification of the Conventions of nine States, shall be sufficient for the Establishment of this Constitution between the States so ratifying the Same.

The Word "the", being interlined between the seventh and eighth Lines of the first Page, the Word "Thirty" being partly written on an Erazure in the fiftienth Line of the first Page, The Words "is tried" being interlined between the thirty second and thirty third Lines of the first Page and the Word "the" being interlined between the forty third and forty fourth Lines of the second Page.

Attest William Jackson Secretary

DONE in Convention by the Unanimous Consent of the States present the Seventeenth Day of September in the Year of our Lord one thousand seven hundred and Eighty seven and of the Independance of the United States of America the Twelfth. IN WITNESS whereof We have hereunto subscribed our Names.

G° WASHINGTON
Presid^t and deputy from Virginia

DELAWARE
- GEO: READ
- GUNNING BEDFORD jun
- JOHN DICKINSON
- RICHARD BASSETT
- JACO: BROOM

MARYLAND
- JAMES MCHENRY
- DAN OF ST. THOS. JENIFER
- DANL. CARROLL

VIRGINIA
- JOHN BLAIR—
- JAMES MADISON JR.

NORTH CAROLINA
- WM. BLOUNT
- RICHD. DOBBS SPAIGHT
- HU WILLIAMSON

SOUTH CAROLINA
- J. RUTLEDGE
- CHARLES COTESWORTH PINCKNEY
- CHARLES PINCKNEY
- PIERCE BUTLER

GEORGIA
- WILLIAM FEW
- ABR BALDWIN

NEW HAMPSHIRE
- JOHN LANGDON
- NICHOLAS GILMAN

MASSACHUSETTS
- NATHANIEL GORHAM
- RUFUS KING

CONNECTICUT
- WM. SAML. JOHNSON
- ROGER SHERMAN

NEW YORK
- ALEXANDER HAMILTON

NEW JERSEY
- WIL: LIVINGSTON
- DAVID BREARLEY
- WM. PATERSON
- JONA: DAYTON

PENNSYLVANIA
- B. FRANKLIN
- THOMAS MIFFLIN
- ROBT. MORRIS
- GEO. CLYMER
- THOS. FITZSIMONS
- JARED INGERSOLL
- JAMES WILSON
- GOUV MORRIS

Proposed Amendments
to the Constitution, 1789

CONGRESS OF THE UNITED STATES;

Begun and held at the City of New York, on Wednesday, the 4th of March, 1789.

The conventions of a number of the states having, at the time of their adopting the Constitution, expressed a desire, in order to prevent misconstruction or abuse of its powers, that further declaratory and restrictive clauses should be added; and as extending the ground of public confidence in the government will best insure the beneficent ends of its institution;—

Resolved, by the Senate and House of Representatives of the United States of America, in Congress assembled, two thirds of both houses concurring, that the following articles be proposed to the legislatures of the several states, as amendments to the Constitution of the United States, all or any of which articles, when ratified by three fourths of the said legislatures, to be valid, to all intents and purposes, as part of the said Constitution, namely,—

Articles in Addition to, and Amendment of, the Constitution of the United States of America, proposed by Congress, and ratified by the Legislatures of the several States, pursuant to the Fifth Article of the original Constitution.

ART. I. After the first enumeration required by the first article of the Constitution, there shall be one representative for every thirty thousand, until the number shall amount to one hundred, after which the proportion shall be so regulated by Congress, that there shall not be less than one hundred representatives, nor less than one representative for every forty thousand persons, until the number of representatives shall amount to two hundred, after which the proportion shall be so regulated by Congress, that there shall not be less than two hundred representatives, nor more than one representative for every fifty thousand.

ART. II. No law varying the compensation for services of the senators and representatives shall take effect, until an election of representatives shall have intervened.

ART. III. Congress shall make no law respecting an establishment of religion, or prohibiting the free exercise thereof, or abridging the freedom of speech, or of the press, or the right of the people peaceably to assemble, and to petition the government for a redress of grievances.

ART. IV. A well-regulated militia being necessary to the security of a free state, the right of the people to keep and bear arms shall not be infringed.

ART. V. No soldier shall, in time of peace, be quartered in any house without the consent of the owner, nor in time of war, but in a manner prescribed by law.

ART. VI. The right of the people to be secure in their persons, houses, papers, effects, against unreasonable searches and seizures, shall not be violated; and no warrants shall issue, but upon principal cause, supported by oath or affirmation, and particularly describing the place to be searched, and the persons or things to be seized.

ART. VII. No person shall be held to answer for a capital or otherwise infamous crime, unless on a presentment or indictment of a grand jury, except in cases arising in the land or naval forces, or in the militia when in actual service, in time of war or public danger; nor shall any person be subject, for the same offence, to be twice put in jeopardy of life or limb; nor shall be compelled, in any criminal case, to be a witness against himself; nor be deprived of life, liberty, or property, without due process of law; nor shall private property be taken for public use without just compensation.

ART. VIII. In all criminal prosecutions, the accused shall enjoy the right of a speedy and public trial, by an impartial jury of the state and district wherein the crime shall have been committed, which district shall have been previously ascertained by law; and to be informed of the nature and cause of the accusation; to be confronted with the witnesses against him; to have compulsory process for obtaining witnesses in his favor; and to have the assistance of counsel for his defence.

ART. IX. In suits at common law, where the value in controversy shall exceed twenty dollars, the right of trial by jury shall be preserved, and no fact tried by a jury shall be otherwise reëxamined, in any court of the United States, than according to the rules in common law.

ART. X. Excessive bail shall not be required, nor excessive fines imposed, nor cruel and unusual punishments inflicted.

ART. XI. The enumeration, in the Constitution, of certain rights, shall not be construed to deny or disparage others retained by the people.

ART. XII. The powers not delegated to the United States by the Constitution, nor prohibited by it to the states, are reserved to the states, respectively, or to the people.

FREDERICK AUGUSTUS MUHLENBERG, *Speaker of the House of Representatives.*
JOHN ADAMS, *Vice-President of the United States, and President of the Senate.*

Attest. JOHN BECKLEY, *Clerk of the House of Representatives.*
SAMUEL A. OTIS, *Secretary of the Senate.*

Virginia Resolutions

24 December 1798

Resolved, That the General Assembly of Virginia doth unequivocally express a firm resolution to maintain and defend the Constitution of the United States, and the Constitution of this state, against every aggression either foreign or domestic; and that they will support the Government of the United States in all measures warranted by the former.

That this Assembly most solemnly declares a warm attachment to the union of the states, to maintain which it pledges all its powers; and that, for this end, it is their duty to watch over and oppose every infraction of those principles which constitute the only basis of that Union, because a faithful observance of them can alone secure its existence and the public happiness.

That this Assembly doth explicitly and peremptorily declare that it views the powers of the Federal Government as resulting from the compact to which the states are parties, as limited by the plain sense and intention of the instrument constituting that compact; as no further valid than they are authorized by the grants enumerated in that compact; and that, in case of a deliberate, palpable, and dangerous exercise of other powers not granted by the said compact, the states, who are parties thereto, have the right and are in duty bound to interpose for arresting the progress of the evil, and for maintaining within their respective limits the authorities, rights, and liberties appertaining to them.

That the General Assembly doth also express its deep regret, that a spirit has in sundry instances been manifested by the Federal Government to enlarge its powers by forced constructions of the constitutional charter which defines them; and that indications have appeared of a design to expound certain general phrases (which, having been copied from the very limited grant of powers in the former Articles of Confederation, were the less liable to be misconstrued) so as to destroy the meaning and effect of the particular enumeration which necessarily explains and limits the general phrases; and so as to consolidate the states, by degrees, into one sovereignty, the obvious tendency and inevitable consequence of which would be to transform the present republican system of the United States into an absolute, or, at best, a mixed monarchy.

That the General Assembly doth particularly PROTEST against the palpable and alarming infractions of the Constitution in the two late cases of the "Alien and Sedition Acts," passed at the last session of Congress: the first of which exercises a power nowhere delegated to the Federal Government, and which, by uniting legislative and judicial powers to those of executive, subverts the general principles of free government, as well as the particular organization and positive provisions of the Federal Constitution: and the other of which acts exercises, in like manner, a power not delegated by the Constitution, but, on the contrary, expressly and positively forbidden by one of the amendments thereto,—a power which, more than any other, ought to produce universal alarm, because it is levelled against the right of freely examining public characters and measures, and of free communication among the people thereon, which has ever been justly deemed the only effectual guardian of every other right.

That this state having, by its Convention which ratified the Federal Constitution, expressly declared that, among other essential rights, "the liberty of conscience and of the press cannot be cancelled, abridged, restrained or modified by any authority of the United States," and from its extreme anxiety to guard these rights from every possible attack of sophistry or ambition, having, with other states, recommended an amendment for that purpose, which amendment was in due time annexed to the Constitution,—it would mark a reproachful inconsistency and criminal degeneracy, if an indifference were now shown to the palpable violation of one of the rights thus declared and secured, and to the establishment of a precedent which may be fatal to the other.

That the good people of this commonwealth, having ever felt and continuing to feel the most sincere affection for their brethren of the other states, the truest anxiety for establishing and perpetuating the union of all and the most scrupulous fidelity to that Constitution, which is the pledge of mutual friendship, and the instrument of mutual happiness, the General Assembly doth solemnly appeal to the like dispositions of the other states, in confidence that they will concur with this Commonwealth in declaring, as it does hereby declare, that the acts aforesaid are unconstitutional; and that the necessary and proper measures will be taken by each for co-operating with this state, in maintaining unimpaired the authorities, rights, and liberties reserved to the states respectively, or to the people. . . .

Chronology

Date	Madison's Life	America	The World
1751	Birth of James Madison, Port Conway, Virginia, 16 March		
1755		French and Indian War begins	
1760			George III becomes king of Great Britain (reigns until 1820)
1762	Attends Donald Robertson's school, Virginia		
1763		French and Indian War ends	
1765		Stamp Act	
1767	Tutorial studies at home with Rev. Thomas Martin		
1768	Birth of Dolley Payne, 20 May, Guilford County, North Carolina		
1769	Enters College of New Jersey, Princeton		
1770		Boston Massacre	
1772	Graduates from College of New Jersey		
1773	Ponders legal career, but studies prove discouraging	Boston Tea Party; Virginia House of Burgesses appoints committee of correspondence	
1774		First Continental Congress meets at Philadelphia	
1775		Battles of Lexington and Concord; Second Continental Congress meets at Philadelphia; George Washington made commander of colonial forces; battle of Bunker Hill	
1776	Delegate to Virginia Convention, Williamsburg	Virginia Convention declares Virginia independence; Declaration of Independence	
1777	Defeated for seat in Virginia House of Delegates; appointed to Council of State	Articles of Confederation adopted	
1778			France enters alliance with United States
1779			Spain enters the war against Great Britain
1780	Elected to Continental Congress		

Date	Madison's Life	America	The World
1781		Cornwallis surrenders at Yorktown; Articles of Confederation ratified	
1783	Engaged to Kitty Floyd; engagement broken off; term in Continental Congress expires	Treaty of Paris with Great Britain ends Revolutionary War	
1784	Elected to Virginia House of Delegates; travels in New York State with Marquis de Lafayette		
1785	Elected to American Philosophical Society; writes (anonymously) Memorial and Remonstrance		
1786	Attends Annapolis Convention	Shays's Rebellion in Massachusetts; Enactment of Virginia Statute for Religious Freedom; Annapolis Convention	
1787	Elected again to Continental Congress; elected to Federal Convention; prepares Virginia Plan; with Hamilton and Jay, writes essays supporting ratification of the Constitution *(The Federalist)*	Federal Convention produces Constitution of the United States	
1788	Serves at Virginia ratifying convention, Richmond	Constitution ratified	
1789	Elected to House of Representatives; sponsors Bill of Rights; assists President Washington in preparing state papers	First Federal Congress convenes in New York; George Washington becomes first president	Beginning of French Revolution
1790	Leads House of Representatives in major legislation	Hamilton's Report on the Public Credit; third session of the First Federal Congress meets in Philadelphia	
1791	Birth of John Payne Todd, son of Dolley Payne Todd	Second Congress convenes	
1792	Active in congressional opposition to Hamilton's program		War of the First Coalition against France; abolition of the French monarchy
1793	Writes Helvidius essays	Washington begins second term as president; Third Congress convenes	Execution of Louis XVI; beginning of war between France and Great Britain
1794	Marries Dolley Payne Todd, 15 September	Jay's Treaty with Great Britain	Toussaint-Louverture leads movement for independence of Haiti from France
1795	Leads opposition to Jay's Treaty	Beginning of Yazoo lands fraud; Fourth Congress convenes	
1796			End of the War of the First Coalition against France
1797	Declines mission to France; retires to Montpelier	John Adams becomes second president; Fifth Congress convenes; Alien and Sedition Acts passed	XYZ affair
1798	Assists Jefferson in preparing Virginia and Kentucky Resolutions		Quasi-War with France; beginning of War of the Second Coalition against France
1799	Elected to Virginia House of Delegates; writes Virginia Report of 1800	Sixth Congress convenes; death of Washington	Napoleon Bonaparte seizes power in France
1800	Defends broad interpretation of freedom of the press	Federal government moves to Washington, D.C.	Treaty of San Ildefonso transfers Louisiana from Spain to France

DATE	MADISON'S LIFE	AMERICA	THE WORLD
1801	Appointed secretary of state	Thomas Jefferson becomes third president; Seventh Congress convenes	Tripolitan War (1801–1805); Great Britain and Ireland joined into the United Kingdom; end of the War of the Second Coalition against France; Alexander I becomes emperor of Russia
			Treaty of Amiens restores peace between France and the United Kingdom
1803	Leads shaping of foreign policy in Jefferson's cabinet	Eighth Congress convenes; Louisiana Purchase; *Marbury* v. *Madison*	War between France and Great Britain renewed
1804		Lewis and Clark expedition; Aaron Burr kills Alexander Hamilton in duel	Napoleon becomes emperor of the French
1805		Jefferson begins second term as president; Ninth Congress convenes	War of the Third Coalition against France
1806		Monroe-Pinkney Treaty	Napoleon issues Berlin Decree closing Continental ports to the British; beginning of war between France and Prussia and Russia
1807		Tenth Congress convenes; Embargo Act passes; *Chesapeake-Leopard* affair	Spencer Perceval serves as prime minister of the United Kingdom (May–June); replaced by earl of Liverpool; peace between France and Prussia and Russia; British orders in council
1808	Elected fourth president of the United States		
1809	Becomes fourth president, with George Clinton as vice president	Eleventh Congress convenes; repeal of Embargo; Nonintercourse Act	
1810	Seeks concessions from European belligerents	Annexation of West Florida; trade with France resumes; *Fletcher* v. *Peck*; Macon's Bills No. 1 and No. 2	Beginning of Hildalgo revolt in New Spain (Mexico)
1811		Twelfth Congress convenes; Battle of Tippecanoe; Congress refuses to recharter Bank of the United States	Beginning of independence movements in Great Colombia (Colombia, Ecuador, and Venezuela)
1812	Urges Britain to repeal orders in council of 1807; rebuffed, sends war message to Congress; elected to second term as president	Declaration of war against Great Britain; surrender of Detroit; USS *Constitution* defeats HMS *Guerrière*	Napoleon invades Russia
1813	Begins second term as president, with Elbridge Gerry as vice president	Thirteenth Congress convenes; Battles of River Raisin, Fort Meigs, Lake Erie, the Thames, Lake Champlain, Chrysler's Farm; destruction of Buffalo; British blockade of American ports	Beginning of wars of liberation against Napoleon
1814	Reorganizes Cabinet; flees Washington before the British army	End of embargo; Hartford Convention; Americans capture Fort Erie; battle of Lundy's Lane; British burn public buildings at Washington; British bombard Fort McHenry; Treaty of Ghent negotiated	Napoleon abdicates, goes into exile at Elba
1815	Popularity rises with peace	Battle of New Orleans; Fourteenth Congress convenes; ratification of Treaty of Ghent	Napoleon defeated at Waterloo, exiled to Saint Helena
1817	Retires from presidency; becomes founder of American Colonization Society and Agricultural Society of Albemarle; retires to Montpelier	James Monroe becomes fifth president; founding of University of Virginia	

DATE	MADISON'S LIFE	AMERICA	THE WORLD
1819	Decries sectional tensions over slavery	Panic of 1819	Treaty with Spain
1820		Missouri Compromise	
1821	Refuses to publish notes of the Federal Convention		Mexico proclaims its independence from Spain
1822			Liberia founded under sponsorship of American Colonization Society
1825	Marquis de Lafayette visits Madison at Montpelier	University of Virginia opens	
1826	Named rector of University of Virginia	Deaths of John Adams and Thomas Jefferson	
1827		John Quincy Adams becomes sixth president	
1829	Attends Virginia Constitutional Convention		
1831		Andrew Jackson becomes seventh president; death of James Monroe	
1834	Writes "Advice to My Country"		
1835	Harriet Martineau visits Madison at Montpelier		
1836	James Madison dies, 28 June, Montpelier	Independence of Texas	
1849	Dolley Madison dies, 12 June, Washington, D.C.		

Synoptic Outline of Contents

The synoptic outline provides a general overview of the conceptual scheme of the encyclopedia, listing the entry term of each article.

The outline is divided into six parts:

James Madison
James Madison's Thought
James Madison's America
American Politics in the Age of Madison
Foreign Affairs
James Madison's Contemporaries

Each of these parts is divided into several sections. Because the section headings are not mutually exclusive, certain entries in the encyclopedia are listed in more than one section.

JAMES MADISON

JAMES MADISON'S LIFE AND CAREER

Madison, James
    Birth and Childhood
    Education
    American Revolution
    Continental Congress
    Secretary of State
    Presidency
    Retirement
Princeton University

JAMES MADISON'S INTERPRETERS

Adams, Henry
Biographies of James Madison
Martineau, Harriet
Rives, William Cabell
Smith, Margaret Bayard
Trist, Nicholas P.

JAMES MADISON'S THOUGHT

WRITINGS

Federalist, The
Helvidius
Memorial and Remonstrance
Virginia Report of 1799–1800

INFLUENCES ON MADISON

Hume, David
Locke, John
Montesquieu
Smith, Adam

POLITICAL PHILOSOPHY

Mercantilism
Nullification Doctrine
Political Economy
Republicanism
Sectionalism
Slavery
States' Rights

RELIGION

Anglican Church
Baptists
Religion, Establishments of
Virginia Statute for Religious Freedom

JAMES MADISON'S AMERICA

Agriculture
American Colonization Society
Mercantilism
Public Lands
Slavery

JAMES MADISON'S VIRGINIA

Albemarle County, Virginia
Madison, James
    Childhood
    Education
    Retirement
Memorial and Remonstrance
Montpelier
Orange County
Privy Council of Virginia
Virginia Report of 1799–1800

Index